Fodor's

CITYGUIDE
BOSTON

FODOR'S TRAVEL PUBLICATIONS, INC.

NEW YORK • TORONTO • LONDON • SYDNEY • AUCKLAND

WWW.FODORS.COM/

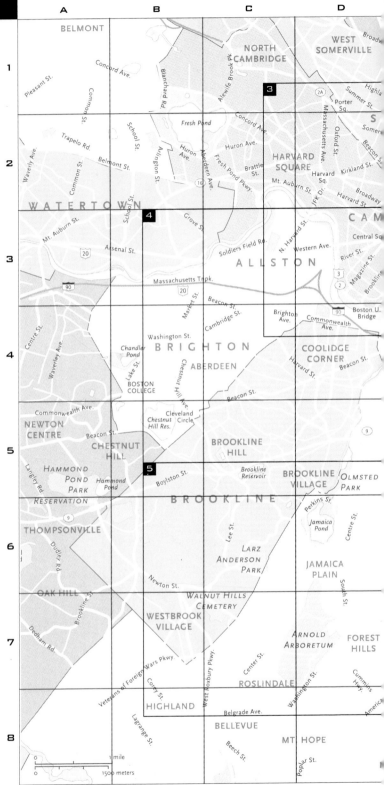

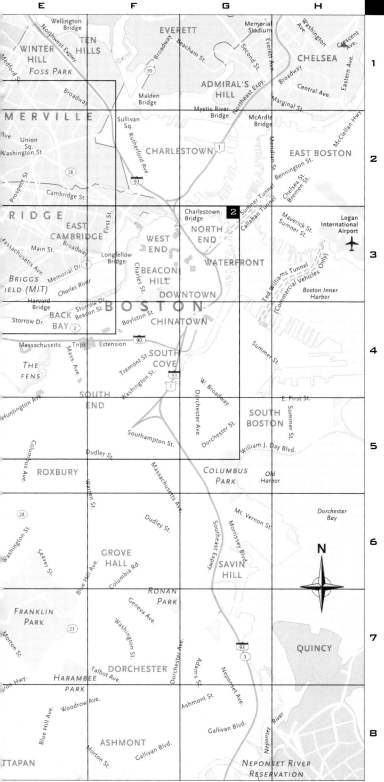

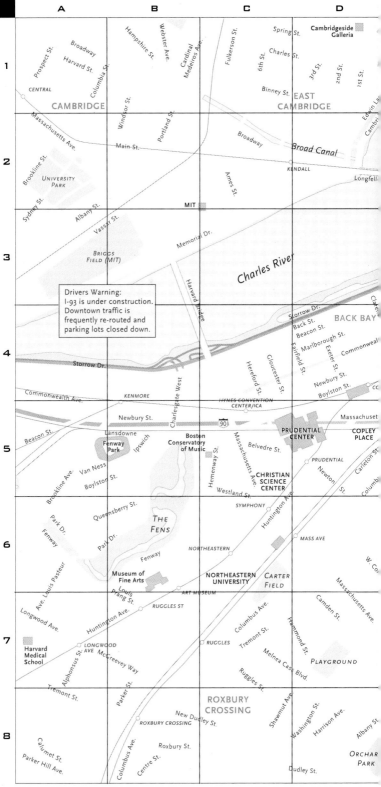

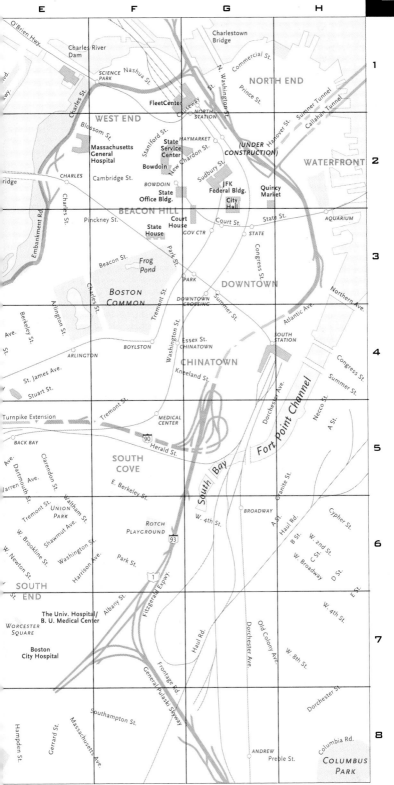

E   F   G   H

O'Brien Hwy.

Charlestown
Bridge

Charles River Dam

1

SCIENCE PARK
Nashua St.
N. Washington St.
Commercial St.

Charles St.

FleetCenter

NORTH STATION

NORTH END

Prince St.

Hanover St.

Summer Tunnel

Callahan Tunnel

WEST END

Blossom St.

Stanford St.

Causeway

HAYMARKET

State Service Center

New Chardon St.

Sudbury St.

(UNDER CONSTRUCTION)

WATERFRONT

2

Massachusetts General Hospital

Bowdoin

BOWDOIN

JFK Federal Bldg.

Quincy Market

CHARLES

Cambridge St.

State Office Bldg.

City Hall

BEACON HILL

Pinckney St.

Court House

State House

Court St.

GOV CTR

State St.

STATE

AQUARIUM

3

Embankment Rd.

Charles St.

Beacon St.

Frog Pond

Park St.

Congress St.

DOWNTOWN

Northern Ave.

Charles St.

BOSTON COMMON

Tremont St.

PARK

DOWNTOWN CROSSING

Summer St.

Atlantic Ave.

Alington St.

Berkeley St.

St.

Washington St.

Essex St.

CHINATOWN

SOUTH STATION

Congress St.

4

ARLINGTON

BOYLSTON

CHINATOWN

Kneeland St.

Dorchester Ave.

Summer St.

St. James Ave.

Stuart St.

Turnpike Extension

Tremont St.

MEDICAL CENTER

90

Herald St.

Fort Point Channel

Necco St.

A St.

BACK BAY

Ave.

Clarendon St.

Dartmouth St.

Warren St.

SOUTH COVE

E. Berkeley St.

South Bay

5

Tremont St.

Union Park

Waltham St.

Shawmut Ave.

Washington St.

ROTCH PLAYGROUND

93

W. 4th St.

BROADWAY

Granite St.

A St.

Haul Rd.

Cypher St.

W. 2nd St.

B St.

C St.

W. Broadway

D St.

6

W. Brookline St.

W. Newton St.

Harrison Ave.

Park St.

1

E St.

SOUTH END

WORCESTER SQUARE

The Univ. Hospital/ B. U. Medical Center

Albany St.

Fitzgerald Expwy.

Haul Rd.

Dorchester Ave.

Old Colony Ave.

W. 4th St.

W. 8th St.

7

Boston City Hospital

Hampden St.

Gerrard St.

Massachusetts Ave.

Southampton St.

General Pulaski Skyway

Frontage Rd.

ANDREW

Preble St.

Dorchester St.

Columbia Rd.

COLUMBUS PARK

8

DOWNTOWN, BEACON HILL, BACK BAY, SOUTH END, THE FENWAY

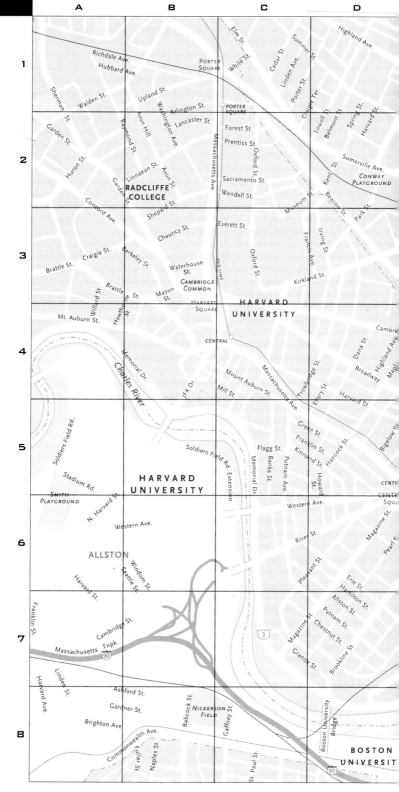

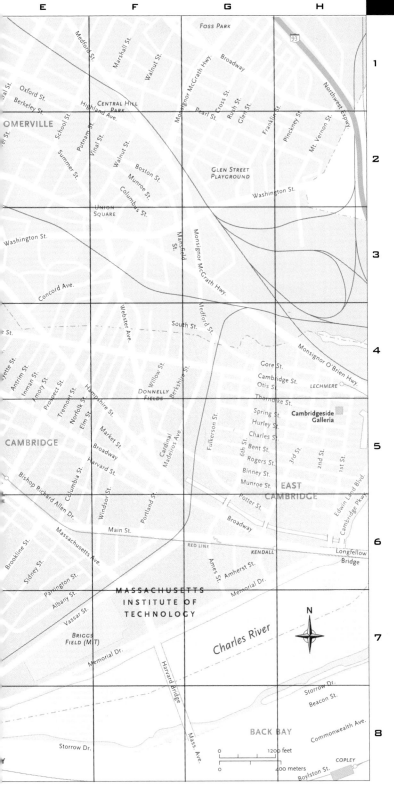

E   F   G   H

1

FOSS PARK

Medford St.

Marshall St.

Walnut St.

Monsignor McGrath Hwy.

Broadway

Northwest Expwy.

Oxford St.

Berkeley St.

CENTRAL HILL PARK

Highland Ave.

Cross St.

Ruth St.

Glen St.

Pearl St.

Franklin St.

Pinckney St.

Mt. Vernon St.

2

SOMERVILLE

School St.

Putnam St.

Vinal St.

Walnut St.

Boston St.

Munroe St.

Columbus St.

GLEN STREET PLAYGROUND

Washington St.

Summer St.

UNION SQUARE

Mansfield St.

Monsignor McGrath Hwy.

3

Washington St.

Concord Ave.

Webster Ave.

South St.

Medford St.

4

Monsignor O'Brien Hwy.

Lafayette St.

Antrim St.

Inman St.

Emory St.

Prospect St.

Tremont St.

Norfolk St.

Hampshire St.

Elm St.

Willow St.

Berkshire St.

DONNELLY FIELDS

Gore St.

Cambridge St.

Otis St.

Thorndike St.

LECHMERE

CAMBRIDGE

Market St.

Broadway

Harvard St.

Columbia St.

Windsor St.

Portland St.

Cardinal Medeiros Ave.

Fulkerson St.

Spring St.

Hurley St.

Charles St.

6th St.

Bent St.

Rogers St.

Binney St.

Munroe St.

Cambridgeside Galleria

3rd St.

2nd St.

1st St.

EAST CAMBRIDGE

5

Bishop Richard Allen Dr.

Massachusetts Ave.

Main St.

Potter St.

Broadway

RED LINE

KENDALL

Edwin Land Blvd.

Cambridge Pkwy.

Longfellow Bridge

6

Brookline St.

Sidney St.

Parrington St.

Albany St.

Vassar St.

MASSACHUSETTS INSTITUTE OF TECHNOLOGY

BRIGGS FIELD (MIT)

Memorial Dr.

Ames St.

Amherst St.

Memorial Dr.

N

7

Charles River

Harvard Bridge

Storrow Dr.

Beacon St.

8

Storrow Dr.

Mass. Ave.

BACK BAY

Commonwealth Ave.

0   1200 feet

0   400 meters

COPLEY

Boylston St.

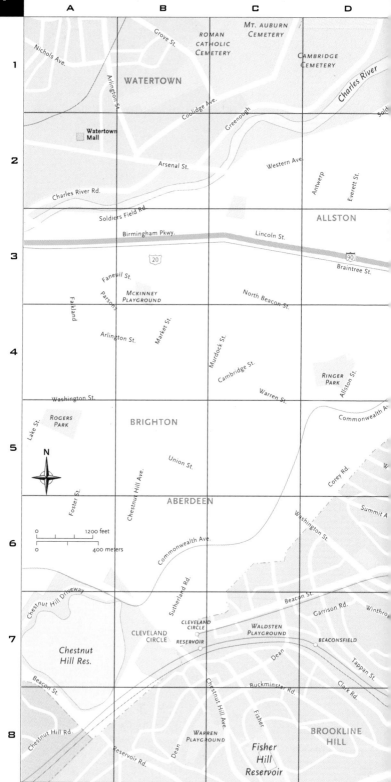

ALLSTON, BRIGHTON, BROOKLINE (NORTH)

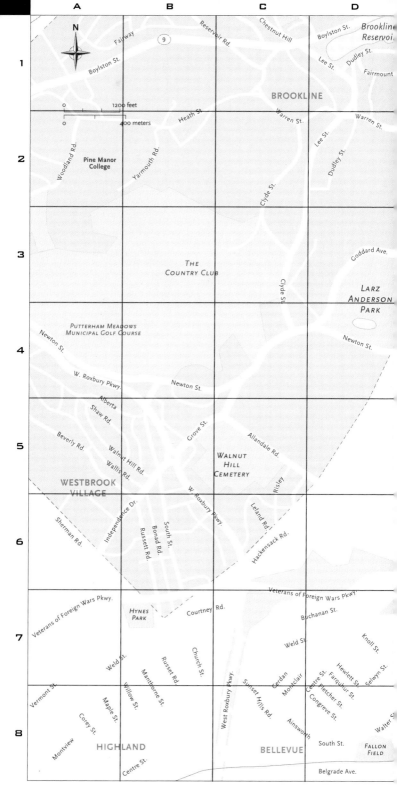

A   **B**   **C**   **D**

N

Fairway

Reservoir Rd.

Chestnut Hill

Boylston St.

Brookline Reservoir

Boylston St.

Lee St.

Dudley St.

1

Fairmount

1200 feet

400 meters

BROOKLINE

Heath St.

Warren St.

Warren St.

Lee St.

Woodland Rd.

2

Pine Manor College

Yarmouth Rd.

Clyde St.

Dudley St.

3

THE COUNTRY CLUB

Clyde St.

Goddard Ave.

LARZ ANDERSON PARK

PUTTERHAM MEADOWS MUNICIPAL GOLF COURSE

Newton St.

4

W. Roxbury Pkwy.

Newton St.

Newton St.

Alberta

Shaw Rd.

Beverly Rd.

Walnut Hill Rd.

Grove St.

Allandale Rd.

5

Wallis Rd.

WALNUT HILL CEMETERY

Risley

WESTBROOK VILLAGE

W. Roxbury Pkwy.

Sherman Rd.

Independence Dr.

South St.

Bonad Rd.

Russett Rd.

Leland Rd.

Hackensack Rd.

6

Veterans of Foreign Wars Pkwy.

HYNES PARK

Courtney Rd.

Veterans of Foreign Wars Pkwy.

Buchanan St.

7

Weld St.

Knoll St.

Veterans of Foreign Wars Pkwy.

Weld St.

Russet Rd.

Church St.

Manthorne St.

Gerdan

Montclair

Hewlett St.

Farquhar St.

Selwyn St.

Centre St.

Pletcher St.

Vermont St.

Maple St.

Willow St.

West Roxbury Pkwy.

Sunset Hills Rd.

Congreve St.

Walter St.

8

Corey St.

Ainsworth

Montview

HIGHLAND

Centre St.

BELLEVUE

South St.

FALLON FIELD

Belgrade Ave.

STREETFINDER

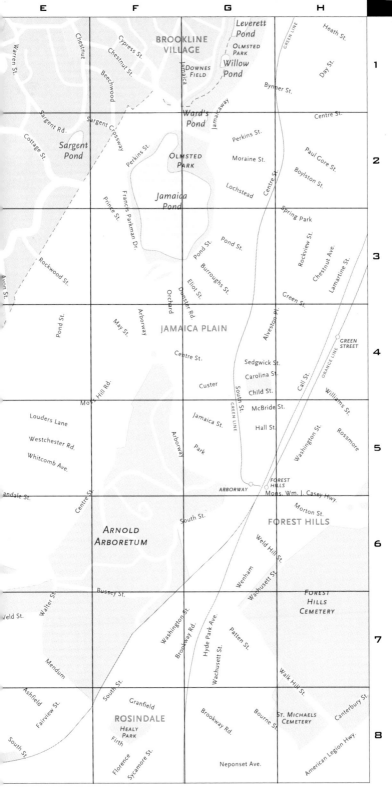

E   F   G   H

Warren St.

Chestnut

Cypress St.

Chestnut St.

BROOKLINE VILLAGE

Leverett Pond

Heath St.

Beechwood

Jamaica

DOWNES FIELD

OLMSTED PARK

Willow Pond

Day St.

1

Bynner St.

Sargent Rd.

Sargent Crossway

Ward's Pond

Centre St.

2

Cottage St.

Sargent Pond

Perkins St.

Perkins St.

Moraine St.

Paul Gore St.

Boylston St.

Francis Parkman Dr.

Prince St.

OLMSTED PARK

Jamaica-way

Jamaica Pond

Lochstead

Centre St.

Rockwood St.

Avon St.

Spring Park

3

Pond St.

Pond St.

Rockview St.

Chestnut Ave.

Lamartine St.

Burroughs St.

Eliot St.

Green St.

Pond St.

Arborway

May St.

Orchard

Dunster Rd.

JAMAICA PLAIN

Alveston Pl.

GREEN STREET

4

Centre St.

Sedgwick St.

Carolina St.

Call St.

ORANGE LINE

Williams St.

Custer

Child St.

South St.

McBride St.

Washington St.

Rossmore

Louders Lane

Mo's Hill Rd.

Jamaica St.

GREEN LINE

Hall St.

5

Westchester Rd.

Whitcomb Ave.

Arborway

Park

andale St.

Centre St.

ARBORWAY

FOREST HILLS

Mons. Wm. J. Casey Hwy.

Morton St.

FOREST HILLS

ARNOLD ARBORETUM

South St.

Weld Hill St.

6

Weld St.

Walter St.

Bussey St.

Wenham

Wachusett St.

FOREST HILLS CEMETERY

Washington St.

Brookway Rd.

Hyde Park Ave.

Patten St.

7

Mendum

Wachusett St.

Walk Hill St.

Ashfield

Fairview St.

South St.

Granfield

ROSINDALE

HEALY PARK

Firth

Brookway Rd.

Bourne St.

ST. MICHAELS CEMETERY

Canterbury St.

8

South St.

Florence

Sycamore St.

Neponset Ave.

American Legion Hwy.

JAMAICA PLAIN, ROSLINDALE, BROOKLINE (SOUTH)

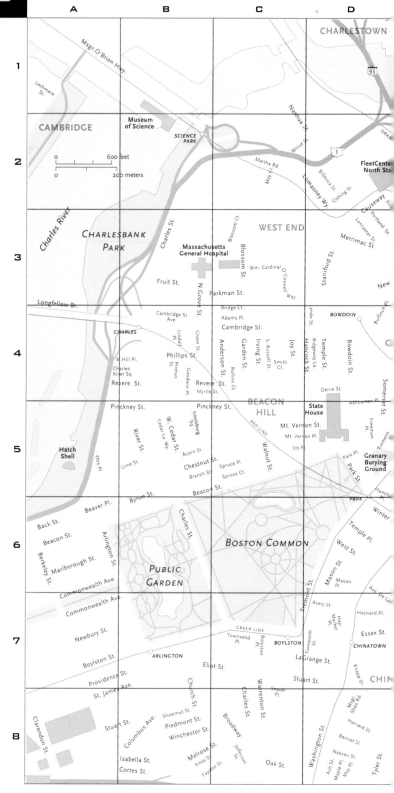

6

CHARLESTOWN

1

93

Lechmere St.

Msgr. O'Brien Hwy.

CAMBRIDGE

Museum of Science

SCIENCE PARK

Nashua St.

ORA

2

600 feet

200 meters

Martha Rd.

May St.

Lomasney Wy.

Minor St.

Billerica St.

Cotting St.

1

FleetCente North Sta

Causeway

Fa

Portland St.

Lancaster St.

Charles River

CHARLESBANK PARK

Charles St.

Blossom Ct.

WEST END

Merrimac St.

3

Massachusetts General Hospital

Blossom St.

Wm. Cardinal O'Connell Way

Staniford St.

New

Fruit St.

N. Grove St.

Parkman St.

Longfellow Br.

Cambridge St. Ave.

Bridge Ct.

Adams Pl.

Cambridge St.

BOWDOIN

Bulfinch

Bowdoin St.

G

CHARLES

Lindall Pl.

Grove St.

Anderson St.

Garden St.

Irving St.

S. Russell St.

Joy St.

Smith Ct.

Temple St.

Ridgeway Ln.

Hancock St.

yrde St.

Bowdoin St.

Somerset St.

4

W. Hill Pl.

Phillips St.

Primus

Rollins Ct.

Charles River Sq.

Revere St.

Goodwin Pl.

Myrtle St.

Derne St.

Ashburton Pl.

Pinckney St.

Pinckney St.

BEACON HILL

State House

Freeman Pl.

5

River St.

W. Cedar St.

Cedar La. Wy.

Louisburg Sq.

Acorn St.

RED LINE

Mt. Vernon St.

Mt. Vernon Pl.

Joy Pl.

Park St.

Hatch Shell

Otis Pl.

Lime St.

Chestnut St.

Branch St.

Spruce Pl.

Spruce Ct.

Walnut St.

Granary Burying Ground

Hamilt

PARK

Winter

Back St.

Beaver Pl.

Byron St.

Beacon St.

Charles St.

Temple Pl.

6

Beacon St.

Berkeley St.

Marlborough St.

Arlington St.

BOSTON COMMON

West St.

Mason St.

Mason Pl.

Commonwealth Ave.

PUBLIC GARDEN

Ave. De Lal

Commonwealth Ave.

Tremont St.

Avery St.

Hayward Pl.

Newbury St.

GREEN LINE

Townsend Pl.

Boylston Pl.

BOYLSTON

Tamworth St.

Hay Market Pl.

Essex St.

CHINATOWN

7

Boylston St.

ARLINGTON

Eliot St.

LaGrange St.

Knapp St.

CHIN

Providence St.

St. James Ave.

Church St.

Warrenton St.

Stuart St.

Magi Shea Rd.

Clarendon St.

Stuart St.

Columbus Ave.

Shawmut St.

Piedmont St.

Winchester St.

Charles St.

Broadway

Seaver Pl.

Washington St.

Harvard St.

Bennet St.

8

Isabella St.

Cortes St.

Melrose St.

Knox St.

Fayette

Jefferson

Oak St.

Nassau St.

Ash St.

Maple Pl.

May Pl.

Tyler St.

STREETFINDER

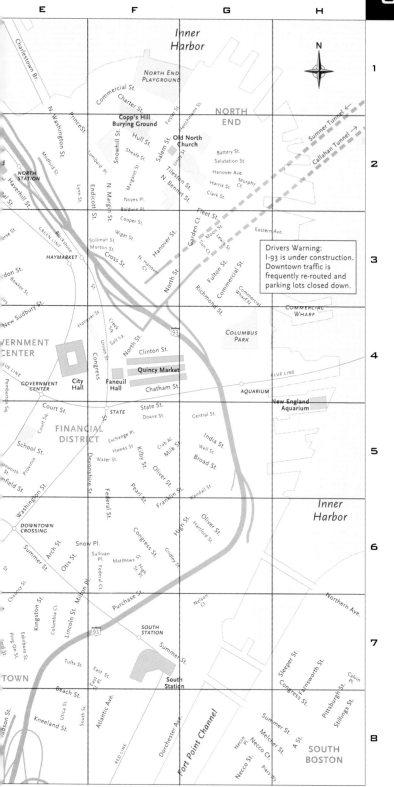

Inner
Harbor

N

NORTH END
PLAYGROUND

Commercial St.
Charter St.
Copp's Hill
Burying Ground
Old North
Church

NORTH
END

Summer Tunnel
Callahan Tunnel

Battery St.
Salutation St.
Hanover Ave.
Murphy
Ct.
Harris St.
Clark St.

N. Washington St.
PrinceSt.
Medford St.
NORTH
STATION
Haverhill St.
Lynn St.
Endicott St.
N. Margin St.
Snowhill St.
Hull St.
Sheafe St.
Margaret St.
Salem St.
Lombard Pl.
Tileston St.
N. Bennet St.
Noyes Pl.
Baldwin Pl.
Cooper St.
Wiget St.
Hanover St.
Union St.
Ferenchmen St.
Foster St.

Fleet St.

Eastern Ave.

GREEN LINE
Buckstone
HAYMARKET
Stillman St.
Morton St.
Cross St.
N. Hanover
Ct.
North St.
Garden Ct.
Moon St.
Sun Ct.
Lewis St.
Fulton St.
Richmond St.
Commercial St.
Commercial
Wharf N.

Drivers Warning:
I-93 is under construction.
Downtown traffic is
frequently re-routed and
parking lots closed down.

don St.
Bowker St.
New Sudbury St.
COMMERCIAL
WHARF

VERNMENT
CENTER
BLUE LINE
Hanover St.
Creek
Sq.
Salt La.
Union St.
North St.
Clinton St.
Quincy Market
COLUMBUS
PARK

GOVERNMENT
CENTER
Pemberton Sq.
City
Hall
Congress
Faneuil
Hall
Chatham St.
BLUE LINE
AQUARIUM
New England
Aquarium

Court St.
Court Sq.
STATE
State St.
Doane St.
Central St.

FINANCIAL
DISTRICT

School St.
osworth
Province
nfield St.
Washington St.
Devonshire St.
Federal St.
Exchange Pl.
Hawes St.
Water St.
Kilby St.
Crab Al.
Oliver St.
Milk St.
Well St.
India St.
Broad St.

Pearl St.
Franklin St.
Wendell St.

Inner
Harbor

DOWNTOWN
CROSSING
Summer St.
Arch St.
Snow Pl.
Otis St.
Sullivan
Pl.
Matthews St.
Federal Ct.
High
St. Pl.
Congress St.
Gridley St.
High St.
Oliver St.
Hartford St.

St.
Chancy St.
Kingston St.
Columbia Ct.
Lincoln St.
Milton Pl.
Purchase St.
Nelson
Ct.
Northern Ave.

Edinboro St.
ping On St.
SOUTH
STATION
Summer St.
Sleeper St.
Congress St.
Farnsworth St.
Pittsburgh St.
Calvin
Pl.
Stillings St.

TOWN
Tufts St.
East St.
East
Pl.
SOUTH
Station

Beach St.
dson St.
Utica St.
South St.
Kneeland St.
Atlantic Ave.
Dorchester Ave.
RED LINE
Fort Point Channel
Summer St.
A St.
Necco
Pl.
Necco St.
Melcher St.
Necco Ct.
Piers Wy.
SOUTH
BOSTON

E   F   G   H

1

2

3

4

5

6

7

8

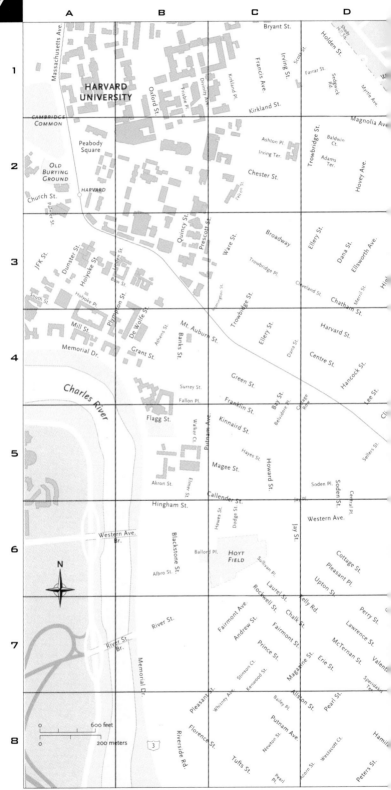

A   **B**   **C**   **D**

1

Bryant St.

HARVARD
UNIVERSITY

Massachusetts Ave.

Oxford St.

Frisbie Pl.

Divinity Ave.

Kirkland Pl.

Francis Ave.

Irving St.

Scott St.

Holden St.

Shady Hill Sq.

Farrar St.

Sedgwick Rd.

Myrtle Ave.

Kirkland St.

CAMBRIDGE
COMMON

Magnolia Ave.

2

Peabody
Square

OLD
BURYING
GROUND

HARVARD

Church St.

Palmer St.

Ashton Pl.

Irving Ter.

Chester St.

Felton St.

Trowbridge St.

Baldwin
Ct.

Adams
Ter.

Hovey Ave.

3

JFK St.

Dunster St.

Holyoke St.

Linden St.

Bow St.

Holyoke Pl.

South St.

Plympton St.

De Wolfe St.

Quincy St.

Prescott St.

Ware St.

Broadway

Trowbridge Pl.

Remington St.

Ellery St.

Dana St.

Ellsworth Ave.

Cleveland St.

Merill St.

Chatham St.

4

Mill St.

Memorial Dr.

Grant St.

Athens St.

Banks St.

Mt. Auburn St.

Trowbridge St.

Ellery St.

Dana St.

Harvard St.

Centre St.

Hancock St.

Lee St.

5

Charles River

Surrey St.

Fallon Pl.

Flagg St.

Walker Ct.

Putnam Ave.

Kinnaird St.

Hayes St.

Magee St.

Akron St.

Elmer St.

Green St.

Franklin St.

Belvidere Pl.

Bay St.

Cogie
Roberts

Howard St.

Sellers St.

Soden Pl.

Soden St.

Central Pl.

Callender St.

Jay Pl.

6

Western Ave.
Br.

N

Hingham St.

Blackstone St.

Ballord Pl.

Albro St.

HOYT
FIELD

Sullivan Pl.

Hewes St.

Dodge St.

Jay St.

Western Ave.

Cottage St.

Pleasant Pl.

Upton St.

Laurel St.

7

River St.

Memorial Ctr.

River St.
Br.

Fairmont Ave.

Andrew St.

Rockwell St.

Chalk St.

Fairmont St.

Prince St.

Stinson Ct.

Kenwood St.

Magazine St.

Erie St.

Kelly Rd.

Lawrence St.

McTernan St.

Perry St.

Valent

Speridakis
Ter.

8

0   600 feet

0   200 meters

3

Pleasant St.

Whitney Ave.

Florence St.

Riverside Rd.

Tufts St.

Bailey Pl.

Newton St.

Putnam Ave.

Alston St.

Acorn St.

Pearl
Pl.

Westacott Ct.

Pearl St.

Peters St.

Hamil

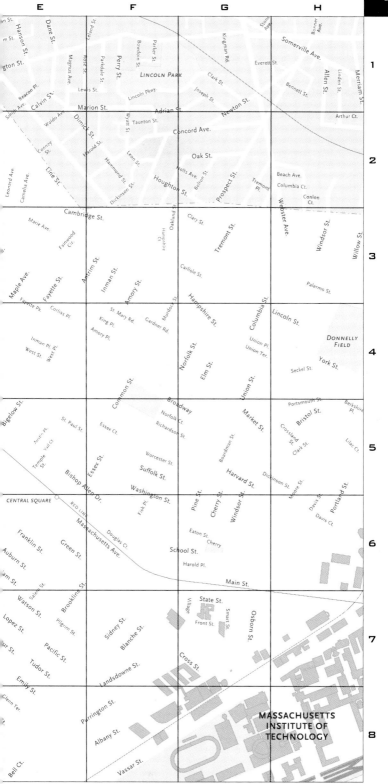

E   F   G   H

an St.   Dane St.   Leland St.   Pine St.   Parker St.   Stone Ave.   Bonner Ave.

Hanson St.   Bowdoin St.   Kingman Rd.   Somerville Ave.

m St.   Magnus Ave.   Rose St.   Parkdale St.   Perry St.   Everett St.   Linden St.   Allen St.   Merriam St.

gton St.   Reacon Pl.   Lewis St.   LINCOLN PARK   Clark St.   Bennett St.

Calvin St.   Lincoln Pkwy   Joseph St.   **1**

Smith Ave.   Marion St.   Adrian St.   Newton St.   Arthur Ct.

Leonard Ave.   Waldo Ave.   Dimick St.   Wyatt St.   Taunton St.   Concord Ave.

Cooney St.   Harold St.   Leon St.   Oak St.   Beach Ave.   **2**

Line St.   Hammond St.   Dickinson St.   Houghton St.   Holts Ave.   Bolton St.   Prospect St.   Tremont Pl.   Columbia Ct.   Conlon Ct.

Camellia Ave.   Cambridge St.   Clary St.   Webster Ave.

Marie Ave.   Farmwood Ctr.   Oakland   Tremont St.   Windsor St.   Willow St.   **3**

Maple Ave.   Antrim St.   Inman St.   Amory St.   Hampshire Ct.   Carlisle St.   Palermo St.

Fayette St.   Hampshire St.

Fayette Pk.   Corliss Pl.   St. Mary Rd.   Murdock St.   Columbia St.   Lincoln St.   DONNELLY FIELD   **4**

Inman Pl. Pl.   King Pl.   Gardner Rd.   Union Pl.   York St.

West St.   West St.   Amory Pl.   Norfolk St.   Union Ter.   Seckel St.

Elm St.   Union St.

Bigelow St.   Common St.   Broadway   Market St.   Portsmouth St.   Berkshire Pl.

St. Paul St.   Essex Ct.   Norfolk Ct.   Crossland St.   Bristol St.   **5**

Austin Pl.   Vail Ct.   Richardson St.   Boardman St.   Clark St.   Lilac Ct.

Temple St.   Essex St.   Worcester St.   Dickinson St.   Moore St.

Bishop Allen Dr.   Suffolk St.   Harvard St.   Davis St.   Portland St.

CENTRAL SQUARE   Washington St.   Pine St.   Cherry St.   Windsor St.   Davis Ct.

RED LINE   Fisk Pl.   **6**

Franklin St.   Green St.   Massachusetts Ave.   Douglas Ct.   Eaton St.   Cherry

Auburn St.   School St.

am St.   Harold Pl.   Main St.

Watson St.   Brookline St.   Salem St.   Pilgrim St.   Village   State St.

Lopez St.   Front St.   Smart St.   Osborn St.   **7**

ur St.   Pacific St.   Sidney St.   Blanche St.

Tudor St.   Landsdowne St.   Cross St.

Emily St.

Glenn Ter.

Purrington St.   MASSACHUSETTS INSTITUTE OF TECHNOLOGY   **8**

Bell Ct.   Albany St.   Vassar St.

CENTRAL CAMBRIDGE

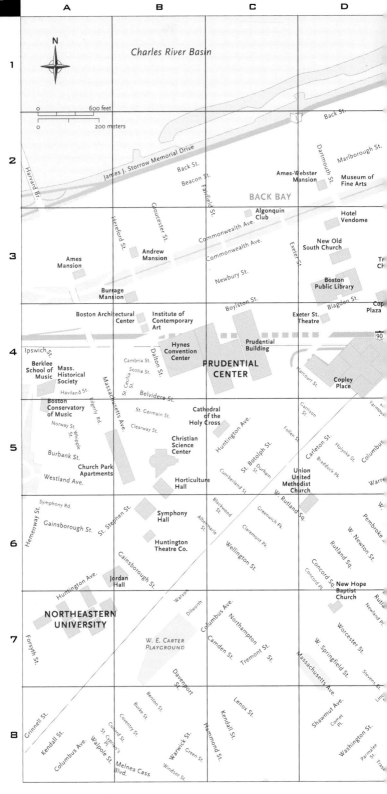

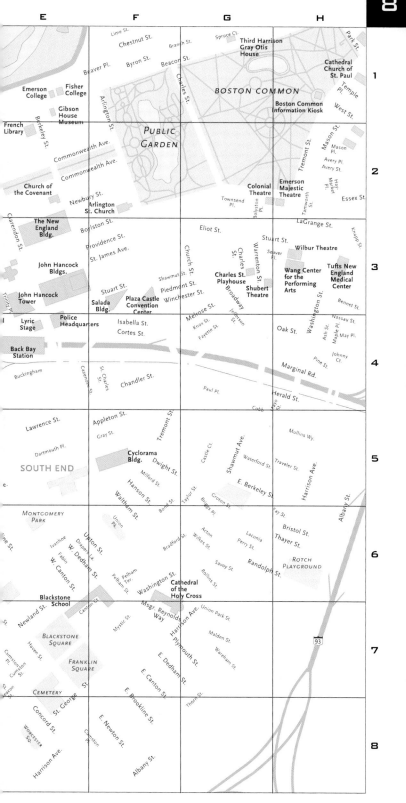

E   F   G   H

Lime St.

Chestnut St.

Branch St.

Spruce Ct.

Park St.

Beaver Pl.

Byron St.

Beacon St.

Third Harrison
Gray Otis
House

Cathedral
Church of
St. Paul

1

Emerson
College

Fisher
College

Charles St.

Temple
Pl.

West St.

Gibson
House
Museum

BOSTON COMMON

Arlington St.

French
Library

Berkeley St.

Mason St.

Mason
Pl.

PUBLIC
GARDEN

Boston Common
Information Kiosk

Avery Pl.

Avery St.

Commonwealth Ave.

Tremont St.

Hay
Market
Pl.

2

Commonwealth Ave.

Church of
the Covenant

Newbury St.

Arlington
St. Church

Townsend
Pl.

Boylston St.

Colonial
Theatre

Emerson
Majestic
Theatre

Tarmorth St.

Essex St.

Clarendon St.

The New
England
Bldg.

Boylston St.

Eliot St.

Stuart St.

LaGrange St.

Knapp St.

Providence St.

Church St.

Warrenton St.

Seaver St.

Wilbur Theatre

3

St. James Ave.

Charles St.

Stuart St.

Wang Center
for the
Performing
Arts

Tufts New
England
Medical
Center

John Hancock
Bldgs.

Shawmut St.

Charles St.
Playhouse

Shubert
Theatre

Piedmont St.

Washington St.

John Hancock
Tower

Trinity Pl.

Stuart St.

Salada
Bldg.

Plaza Castle
Convention
Center

Winchester St.

Broadway

Bennet St.

Lyric
Stage

Police
Headquarters

Isabella St.

Melrose St.

Knox St.

Johnson St.

Oak St.

Ash St.

Nassau St.

Maple Pl.

May Pl.

Cortes St.

Fayette St.

Back Bay
Station

Buckingham

Cazenove St.

St. Charles St.

Chandler St.

Paul Pl.

Marginal Rd.

Pine St.

Johnny
Ct.

4

Herald St.

Cobb St.

Lawrence St.

Appleton St.

Tremont St.

Mullins Wy.

Gray St.

Dartmouth Pl.

Cyclorama
Bldg.

Dwight St.

Castle Ct.

Shawmut Ave.

Waterford St.

Traveler St.

SOUTH END

Milford St.

E. Berkeley St.

Harrison Ave.

5

Hanson St.

Taylor St.

Groton St.

Albany St.

Waltham St.

Bond St.

Briggs Pl.

Fay St.

MONTGOMERY
PARK

Union Pk.

Acton St.

Laconia St.

Bristol St.

Thayer St.

6

Ivanhoe

Draper's La.

W. Dedham St.

Bradford St.

Wilkes St.

Perry St.

Fabin St.

W. Canton St.

Pelham St.

Pelham Ter.

Savoy St.

Randolph St.

ROTCH
PLAYGROUND

Blackstone
School

Canton St.

Washington St.

Cathedral
of the
Holy Cross

Rollins St.

Newland St.

Mystic St.

Msgr. Reynolds
Way

Harrison Ave.

Union Park St.

BLACKSTONE
SQUARE

Haven St.

Malden St.

93

7

Cumston Pl.

Cumston St.

FRANKLIN
SQUARE

E. Berkeley St.

Plymouth St.

Wareham St.

Beacon St.

CEMETERY

St. George St.

E. Canton St.

Concord St.

WORCESTER
SQ.

E. Brookline St.

Thorn St.

8

E. Newton St.

Harrison Ave.

Cumston St.

Albany St.

BACK BAY, SOUTH END

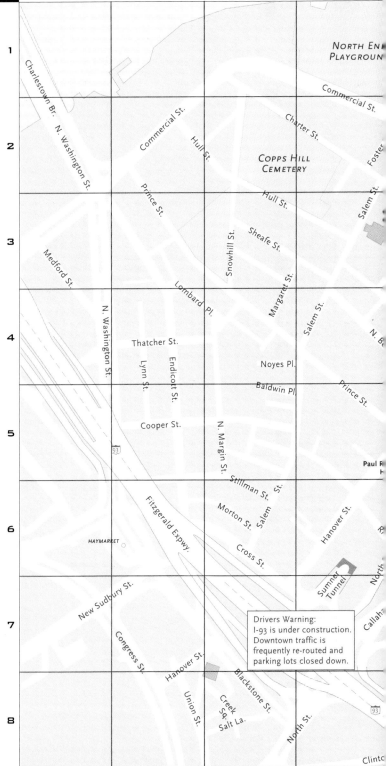

A **B** **C** **D**

1

Charlestown Br.

N. Washington St.

NORTH EN
PLAYGROUN

Commercial St.

2

Commercial St.

Hull St.

Charter St.

COPPS HILL
CEMETERY

Foster

Salem St.

3

Medford St.

Prince St.

Hull St.

Snowhill St.

Sheafe St.

Margaret St.

Salem St.

Lombard Pl.

4

N. Washington St.

Thatcher St.

Lynn St.

Endicott St.

Noyes Pl.

Salem St.

N. Be

Baldwin Pl.

Prince St.

5

Cooper St.

N. Margin St.

93

Paul R
H

6

Fitzgerald Expwy.

HAYMARKET

Stillman St. St.

Morton St. Salem

Cross St.

Hanover St.

R

North

Sumner
Tunnel

7

New Sudbury St.

Congress St.

Hanover St.

Callah

Drivers Warning:
I-93 is under construction.
Downtown traffic is
frequently re-routed and
parking lots closed down.

8

Union St.

Creek
Sq.
Salt La.

Blackstone St.

North St.

93

Clinto

STREETFINDER

E F G H

1

Boston
Inner
Harbor

Constitution
Wharf

2

Henchmann St.

Battery
Wharf

North
ch

Charter St.

3

ity St.

Battery St.

Lincoln
Wharf

Salutation St.

Paul Revere Mall

Hanover Ave.

ston St.

Hanover St.

Harris St.

Murphy Ct.

Union
Wharf

4

St.

St. Stephen's
Church

Clark St.

Commercial St.

Garden Ct.

Fleet St.

North St.

Sargents
Wharf

5

e
e

Moon St.

Lewis St.

Fleet St.

Garden Ct.

Sun Ct.

Lewis St.

Lewis
Wharf

6

nd St.

Fulton St.

Commercial St.

Commercial
Wharf West

nnel

Commercial
Wharf

7

Richmond St.

Atlantic Ave.

WATERFRONT
PARK

8

t.

THE NORTH END

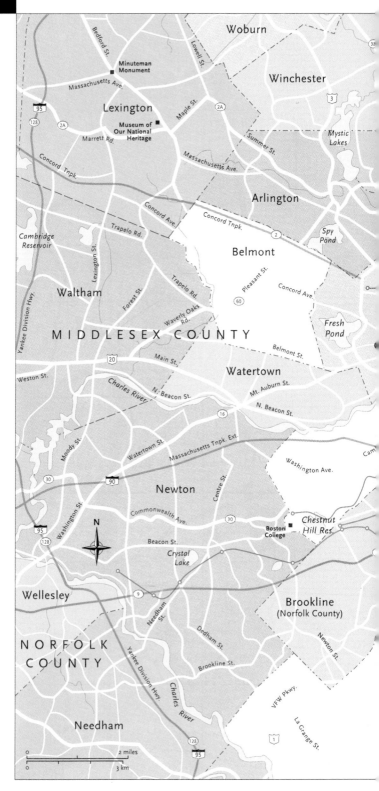

BOSTON AREA

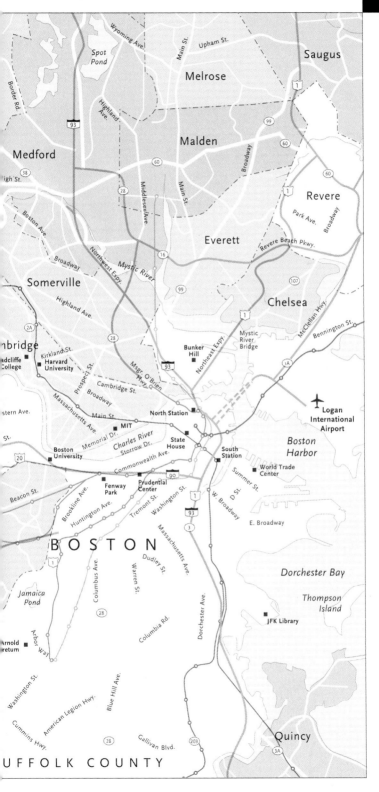

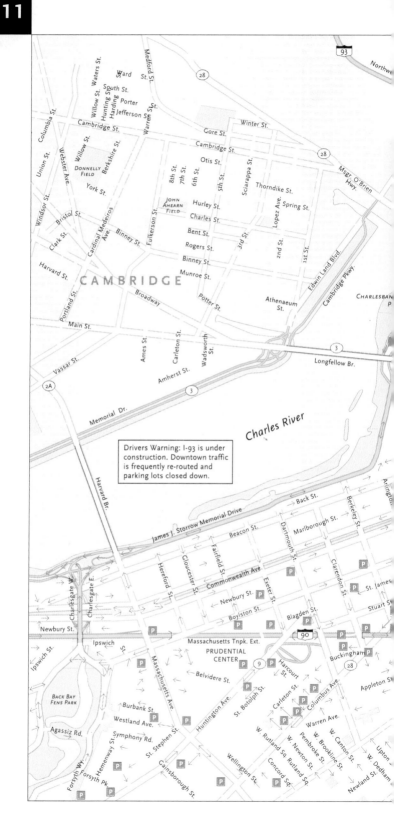

Drivers Warning: I-93 is under construction. Downtown traffic is frequently re-routed and parking lots closed down.

DRIVING AND PARKING

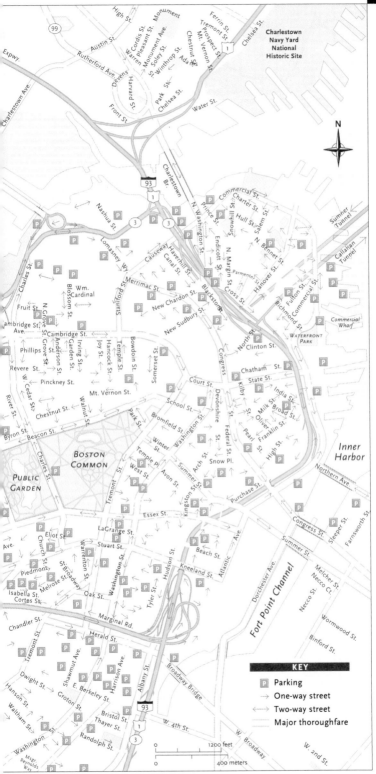

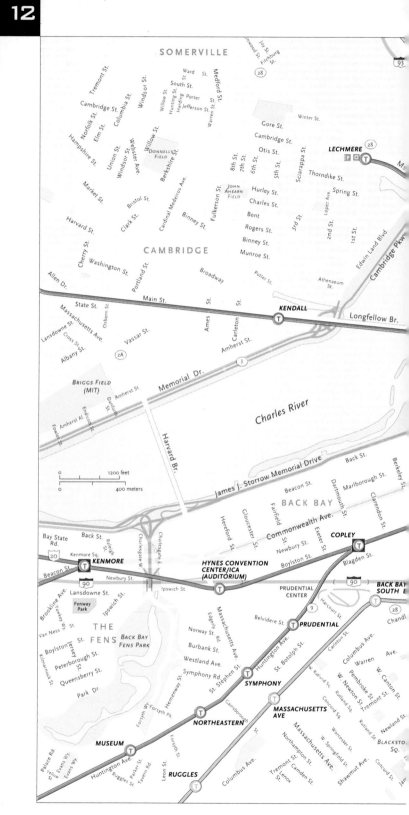

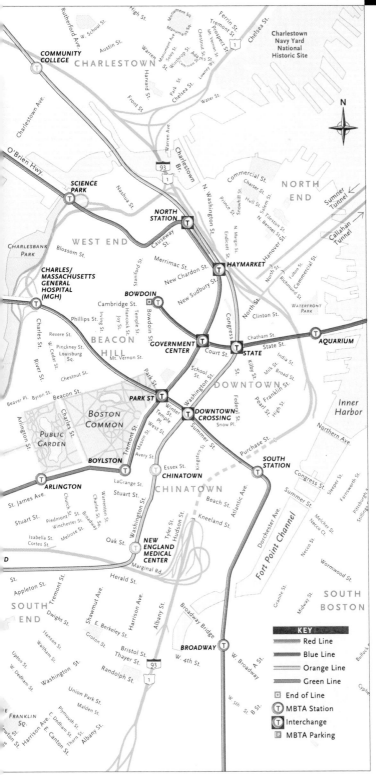

DOWNTOWN BOSTON

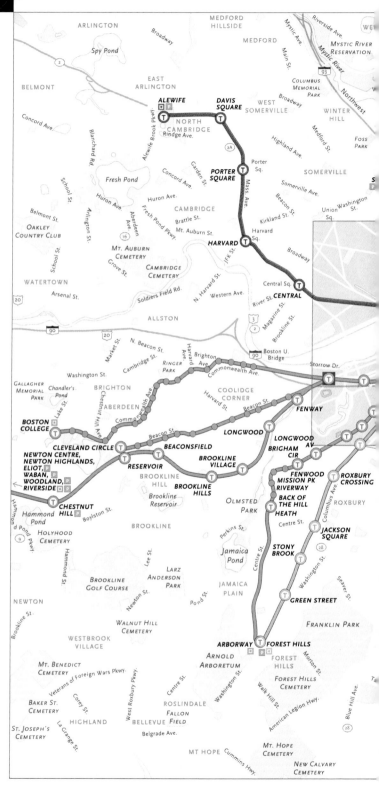

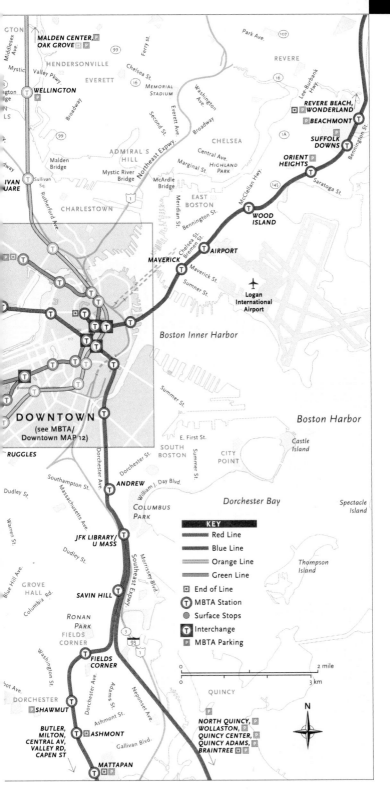

BOSTON AREA

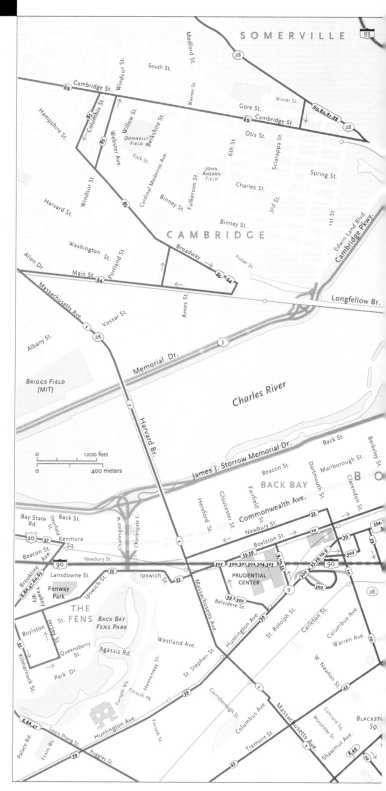

BUSES

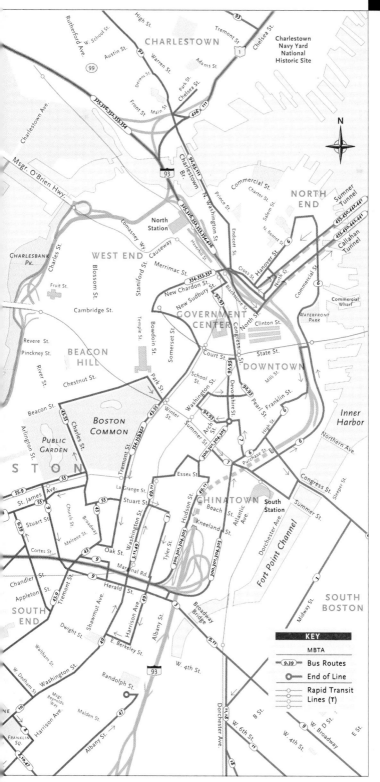

DOWNTOWN BOSTON

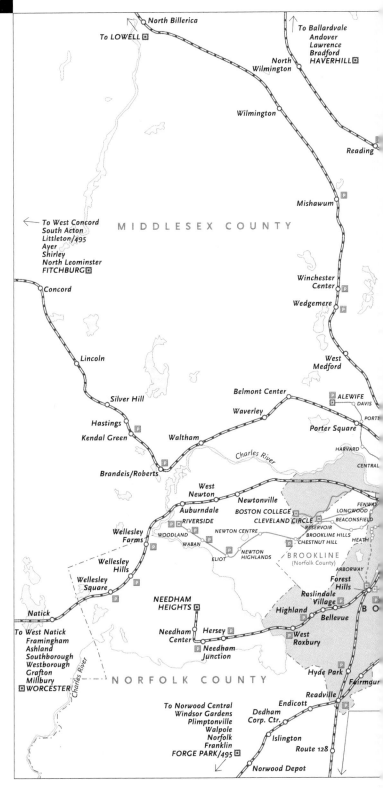

COMMUTER RAIL

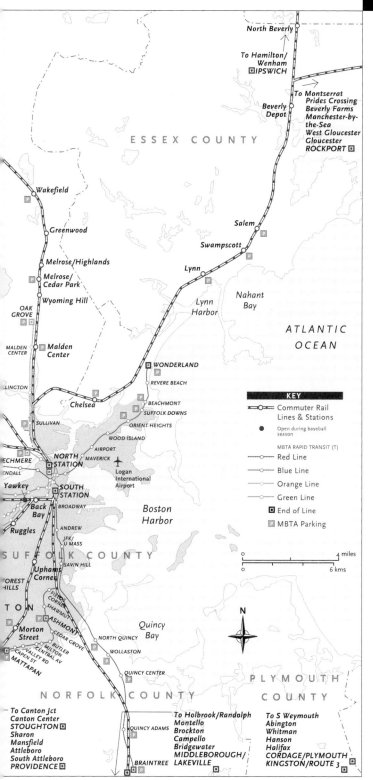

BOSTON AREA

Your Source in the City

MANY MAPS • WHERE & HOW

FIND IT ALL • NIGHT & DAY

ANTIQUES TO ZIPPERS

BARGAINS • BAUBLES • KITES

ELEGANT EDIBLES • ETHNIC EATS

STEAK HOUSES • FISH HOUSES

BISTROS • TRATTORIAS

CLASSICAL • JAZZ • CABARET

COMEDY • THEATER • DANCE

BARS • CLUBS • BLUES

COOL TOURS

HOUSECLEANING • CATERING

LOST & FOUND • THE CABLE GUY

GET A LAWYER • GET A DENTIST

GET A NEW PET • GET A VET

MUSEUMS • GALLERIES

PARKS • GARDENS • RINKS

AQUARIUMS TO ZOOS

BASEBALL TO ROCK CLIMBING

FESTIVALS • EVENTS

DAY SPAS • DAY TRIPS

HOTELS • HOT LINES

PASSPORT PIX • TRAVEL INFO

HELICOPTER TOURS

DINERS • DELIS • PIZZERIAS

BRASSERIES • CAFÉS

BOOTS • BOOKS • BUTTONS

BICYCLES • SKATES

SUITS • SHOES • HATS

RENT A TUX • RENT A COSTUME

BAKERIES • SPICE SHOPS

SOUP TO NUTS

Fodor's

CITYGUIDE
BOSTON

FODOR'S TRAVEL PUBLICATIONS, INC.

NEW YORK • TORONTO • LONDON • SYDNEY • AUCKLAND

WWW.FODORS.COM/

FODOR'S CITYGUIDE BOSTON

EDITOR
Robert I. C. Fisher

EDITORIAL CONTRIBUTORS
Lisa Amand, Fawn Fitter, Stephanie Schorow

EDITORIAL PRODUCTION
Linda K. Schmidt

MAPS
David Lindroth Inc., *cartographer*; Bob Blake, *map editor*

DESIGN
Fabrizio La Rocca, *creative director*; Allison Saltzman, *text design*;
Tigist Getachew, *cover design*; Jolie Novak, *photo editor*

PRODUCTION/MANUFACTURING
Robert B. Shields

COVER PHOTOGRAPH
James Lemass

Series created by Marilyn Appleberg

COPYRIGHT

SPECIAL SALES

CONTENTS

METROPOLITAN LIFE

On a bad day in a big city, the little things that go with living shoulder-to-shoulder with a few million people wear us all down. But the special pleasures of urban life have a way of keeping us out of the suburbs—and thankful, even, for every second of stress. The field of daffodils in the park on a fine spring day. The perfect little black dress that you find for half price. The markets—so fabulously well stocked that you can cook any recipe without resorting to mail-order catalogs. The way you can sometimes turn a corner and discover a whole new world, so foreign you can hardly believe you're less than a mile from home. The never-ending wealth of possibilities and opportunities.

If you know where to find it all, the city cannot defeat you. With knowledge comes power. That's why Fodor's has prepared this book. It will put phone numbers at your fingertips. It'll take you to new places and remind you of those you've forgotten. It's the ultimate urban companion—and, we hope, your **new best friend in the city.**

It's the **citywise shopaholic,** who always knows where to find something, no matter how obscure. We've made a concerted effort to bring hundreds of great shops to your attention, so that you'll never be at a loss, whether you need a special birthday present for a great friend or some obscure craft items to make Halloween costumes for your kids.

It's the **restaurant know-it-all,** who's full of ideas for every occasion—you know, the one who would never send you to Café de la Snub, because he knows it's always overbooked, the food is boring, and the staff is rude. In this book we'll steer you around the corner, to a perfect little place with five tables, a fireplace, and a chef on her way up.

It's a **hip barfly buddy,** who can give you advice when you need a charming nook, not too noisy, to take a friend after work. Among the dozens of bars and nightspots in this book, you're bound to find something that fits your mood.

It's the **sagest arts maven you know,** the one who always has the scoop on what's on that's worthwhile on any given night. In these pages, you'll find dozens of concert venues and arts organizations.

It's also the **city whiz,** who knows how to get you where you're going, wherever you are.

It's the **best map guide** on the shelves, and it puts **all the city in your briefcase** or on your bookshelf.

Stick with us. We lay out all the options for your leisure time—and gently nudge you away from the duds—so that you can truly enjoy metropolitan living.

YOUR GUIDES

No one person can know it all. To help get you on track around the city, we've hand-picked a stellar group of local experts to share their wisdom.

Lisa Amand, our dining critic, is occasionally tempted to take out a personal ad that goes like this: Married female looking for steady relationship with comfortable, casual, inexpensive, and somewhat provocative restaurant. She's found several places that fit the bill, but, working as a restaurant reviewer for *Boston* magazine, she's had to put up with a lot of one-night stands. Still, she prizes her neighborhood favorites, where, as she puts it, "everyone knows your (middle) name." Lisa moved to Boston from Sonoma, California, four years ago but still suffers from Seasonal Affective Disorder—not so much because of the cold weather but because she can't dine alfresco every day. She has also written for the *San Francisco Examiner, San Francisco Chronicle, Wall Street Journal,* and *Boston Herald.* She now divides her time between New York and Boston and knows well the cuisine on Amtrak's Northeast Direct.

Although her conspicuous lack of a Boston accent gives her away as a transplant, **Fawn Fitter** nevertheless manages to pass for a native, thanks to her fearsome eye for a Filene's Basement bargain. Like many people who come to Boston to attend college, she fell in love with the city and decided to stay. In the 13 years since then, she's become a freelance writer whose work has appeared in publications ranging from the *Boston Herald* to *Cosmopolitan*; she also edits, teaches writing, and cohosts a discussion group for freelance writers on the Well on-line service. For this guide she researched five chapters: Basics; Arts, Entertainment, & Nightlife; Parks, Gardens, & Sports; Hotels; and Help!. Her favorite Beantown basics: the Louis Comfort Tiffany windows at Arlington Street Church, in-line skating on the Esplanade, cannoli and cappuccino in the North End, and Free Friday Flicks at the Hatch Shell.

Stephanie Schorow has yet to drop her r's, despite seven happy years residing in the Boston area. A former newswoman for the Associated Press, and editor for the TAB Newspapers, she now claims the title of assistant lifestyles editor for the *Boston Herald.* She put herself on speed dial in order to cover the myriad shops and sights in our Shopping and Places to Explore chapters, and compiled our Parks and Gardens section. Her favorite haunts in Boston are the bookstores around Harvard Square, Chinatown bakeries, and the jogging path around Castle Island. A former Cantabrigian, she refuses to divulge her secret for finding parking in Harvard Square. Normally a mild-mannered reporter, she has adopted some ferocious driving habits by cruising Boston streets "but only out of self-preservation."

Marilyn Appleberg, who conceived this series, is a city-lover through and through. She plots her urban forays from an archetypal Greenwich Village brownstone with two fireplaces.

It goes without saying that our contributors have chosen all establishments strictly on their own merits—no establishment has paid to be included in this book.

HOW TO USE THIS BOOK

The first thing you need to know is that everything in this book is **arranged by category and by alphabetical order** within category.

Now, before you go any farther, check out the **city maps** at the front of the book. Each has a number, in a black box at the top of the page, and grid coordinates along the top and side margins. On the text pages, every listing in the book is keyed to one of these maps. Look for the map number in a small black box preceding each establishment name. The grid code follows in italics. For establishments with more than one location, additional map numbers and grid codes appear at the end of the listing. To locate a museum that's identified in the text as **7** *e-6*, turn to Map 7 and locate the address within the e-6 square. To locate restaurants that are nearby, simply skim the text in the restaurant chapter for listings identified as being on Map 7.

Where appropriate throughout the guide, we name the neighborhood in which each sight, restaurant, shop, or other destination is located. We also give you the nearest T-stop, plus complete opening hours and admission fees for sights; closing information for shops; and credit-card, price, reservation, and closing information for restaurants.

At the end of the book, in addition to an **alphabetical index,** you'll find **directories of shops and restaurants by neighborhood.**

Chapter 1, Basics, lists essential information, such as entertainment hot lines (for those times you can't lay your hands on a newspaper). **Chapter 8, Help!,** covers resources for residents—everything from vet and lawyer referral services to caterers worth calling.

We've worked hard to make sure that all of the information we give you is accurate at press time. Still, time brings changes, so always confirm information when it matters—especially if you're making a detour.

Feel free to drop us a line. Were the restaurants we recommended as described? Did you find a wonderful shop you'd like to share? If you have complaints, we'll look into them and revise our entries in the next edition when the facts warrant. So send us your feedback. Either e-mail us at editors@fodors.com (specifying *Fodor's CITYGUIDE Boston* on the subject line), or write to the *Fodor's CITYGUIDE Boston* editor at 201 East 50th Street, New York, New York 10022. We look forward to hearing from you.

Karen Cure
Editorial Director

chapter 1

BASICS

essential information

To help make your time spent in Boston more efficient and pleasant, many of the most important practical details on its whys and wherefores have been gathered together in this introductory chapter to facilitate ready reference. Beyond the essential facts and organizations listed below, you have only to stop the nearest Bostonian in the street to ask for directions or information to discover that courtesy to visitors is a Boston tradition. Keep in mind, however, that even though the city may be best known for the long-running television sitcom Cheers—the name of a convivial bar where everyone knows your name—don't expect to be patted on the back and be called by your first name during the first five minutes of an introductory chat. New Englanders to the core, Bostonians have an initial reserve. Some call it primness; others mark it up to just capital-C-courtesy. If between your visits to Beacon Hill and Fenway Park you catch a glimpse of the Boston character, you'll no doubt realize that you're in one of the most civilized cities in the United States.

ATLAS

The many layers of Boston's historic past translate easily into a simple lesson in urban geography: the city can be seen as a series of concentric circles, with the oldest and most famous attractions clustered within easy walking distance of the Boston Common and State House. Many leading attractions are on the well-marked Freedom Trail; none is far off the track. You might draw an arbitrary line across the peninsula, stretching from, say, the Arthur Fiedler Footbridge (at the Charles River near Beacon and Arlington streets) to South Station, explore everything north of it—with a side trip into the Back Bay—and truthfully say that you had seen Boston. In fact, that is all many visitors ever see. This remarkable compactness is a boon to the pedestrian explorer (in central Boston there should be no other kind!), and it assures a virtually complete edu-

cation in the earliest history of the town. But just as Boston outgrew its cramped peninsular quarters, so too must the serious traveler's curiosity extend beyond that random demarcation. We begin our gazetteer of Boston near the heart of things, in the Back Bay, and follow the circles outward to Charlestown, the "Streetcar Suburbs," and beyond.

The numbered codes at the beginning of the entries refer to the map section at the back of the book. Note that neighborhoods may also be detailed on other maps in the section. To place the hundreds of stores, historic sites, restaurants, hotels, museums, and other wonders listed throughout the chapters of this guide, just consult the quadrant coordinates found in these map codes.

8

THE BACK BAY

With hundreds of stylish Victorian residences—French-influenced, Italianate, Neo-Gothic, etc.—the streets of Boston's fabled Back Bay are a virtual 19th-century museum unto themselves. Extending along the Charles opposite Cambridge as far as Kenmore Square, south and west of Beacon Hill, the gracious rhythm of the Back Bay—the main east-west streets, including Beacon, Marlborough, and Boylston streets and Commonwealth Avenue are bisected by eight streets named in alphabetical order from Arlington to Hereford—recalls that the district was modeled after Baron Haussman's recent replanning of Paris. The Back Bay once was a bay, and the district was actually a colossal mid-19th-century landfill project; when it was complete, it was *the* place for well-to-do Bostonians to build the elegant brownstone row houses that would later supply condominiums for generations yet unborn. Fortunately, the facades haven't changed, and a walk down **Commonwealth Avenue** is still an architectural delight. Shop-till-you-droppers head here for **Newbury Street,** Boston's eight-block-long version of New York City's Fifth Avenue. Leading historic points of interest include the two masterpieces of **Copley Square,** H. H. Richardson's Neo-Romanesque **Trinity Church,** with its interior decorations by John La Farge and Edward Burne-Jones, and McKim, Mead, and White's **Boston Public Library,** a magnificent Renaissance-style palazzo. But the Back Bay is also home to Boston at its most modern—thanks to the **Prudential Center,** the **Hancock Tower,** and the **Copley Place** shopping complex. Also here is **Symphony Hall,** the **Christian Science Church Center,** and one of the city's most beautiful parks, the **Public Garden.**

6

BEACON HILL

Say the name of Boston, and many people will picture a row of Charles Bulfinch townhouses on Beacon Hill—a neighborhood which still conjures up images of opulence, wealth, and proper Boston Brahmins. Another living museum of the best of American city planning in the 19th century, Beacon Hill is a time-machine district that was once address to Henry James, Oliver Wendell Holmes, and Admiral Samuel Eliot Morrison. Named for the tallow pot that was set on the summit of the steep and craggy hill that was once here, Beacon's hill was leveled off in the 18th century so that Bulfinch's magnificent "new" **State House**—precursor to Washington, D.C.'s Capitol and arguably the most architecturally distinguished of all American seats of state government—could be built. Today, the Hill beckons with other stately sights, including fabled **Park Street Church** (the hymn "America" was first sung here), the **Old Granary Burying Ground,** the grand **Harrison Gray Otis House,** and the splendid **Boston Athenaeum.** In addition, four of Boston's most enchanting urban stage sets are here posing for your Nikon: **Louisburg Square**—once home to the Alcotts and William Dean Howells—**Chestnut Street, Mount Vernon Street,** and **Acorn Street** (the latter Ye Olde Colonial Boston at its best). On the north side of the hill, the **Black Heritage Trail** traces Boston's impressive African-American roots. Stop in at the **Bull & Finch Pub,** the watering hole ("...where everybody knows your name") that inspired the sitcom *Cheers,* for a festive Paul Revere over ice. At the foot of the hill, stroll along Charles Street where you can be distracted by fine antique stores as well as the latest flavors of gelato.

1

CHARLESTOWN

Across from the North End and the Mystic River (which Master Revere, Gentleman, crossed that night in a rowboat with muffled oars) is Charlestown, where the USS *Constitution*—the legendary

"Old Ironsides"—is docked at the **Charlestown Navy Yard** National Historic Site, a decommissoned shipyard reborn as a complex of msueums, restaurants, and apartments (you come upon the Yard almost immmediately after alighting from the Charlestown Bridge). Nearby is the **Bunker Hill Monument,** a handsome and climbable granite obelisk located on Breed's Hill where the 1775 battle was actually fought. Today, Charlestown is a neighborhood in flux, with elegantly restored Federal townhouses on Winthrop Square cheek by jowl with working-class quarters. City Square is Charlestown's main commerical district and home to several of the district's eateries, now developing devoted followers among the "Townies" (as old-time Charlestown residents are called).

6

CHINATOWN

Bordered by the old "Leather District" business area, the Combat Zone, the buildings of the Tufts New England Medical Center, Chinatown may have borders that are constrained, yet it remains one of the larger concentrations of Chinese-Americans in the United States. Of course, the concentration of restaurants is the main lure, now interspersed with fabulous Thai and Vietnamese eateries—a reflection of the latest wave of immigration into Boston. Most restaurants and business are located along Beach and Tyler streets and Harrison Avenue. The area around the interesection of Kneeland Street and Harrison Avenue is the center of Boston's textile and garment industry. The area is centered around the **Asian-American Civic Center,** housed in the former Quincy School at 90 Tyler Street, built in 1848 to teach arriving Irish and Italian immigrants. To find this landmark, just look for the welcoming statue of Confucius. Chinatown remains isolated from the South End by the Massachusetts Turnpike and its junction with the Southeast Expressway in much the same way the Fitzgerald Expressway isolates the North End from downtown.

6

DOWNTOWN BOSTON: FINANCIAL DISTRICT, DOWNTOWN CROSSING, THEATER DISTRICT, WATERFRONT

Today, modern Boston's zero center of gravity is its Downtown—but no

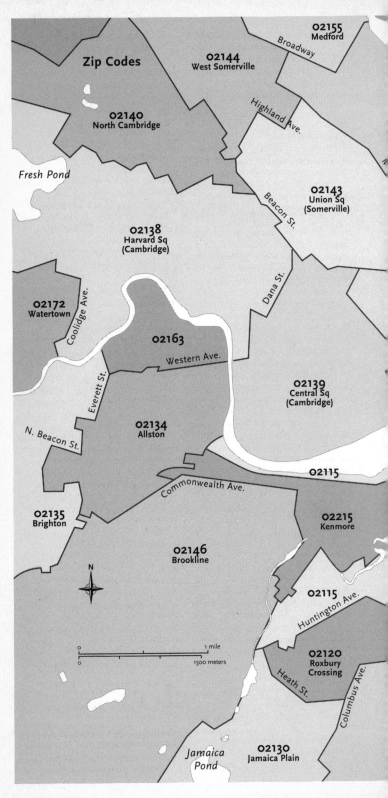

Zip Codes

O2155 Medford

Broadway

O2144 West Somerville

Highland Ave.

O2140 North Cambridge

Fresh Pond

O2143 Union Sq (Somerville)

Beacon St.

O2138 Harvard Sq (Cambridge)

O2172 Watertown

Coolidge Ave.

Dana St.

O2163

Western Ave.

O2139 Central Sq (Cambridge)

Everett St.

O2134 Allston

N. Beacon St.

Commonwealth Ave.

O2115

O2135 Brighton

O2215 Kenmore

N

O2146 Brookline

O2115

Huntington Ave.

0 1 mile
0 1500 meters

O2120 Roxbury Crossing

Heath St.

Columbus Ave.

Jamaica Pond

O2130 Jamaica Plain

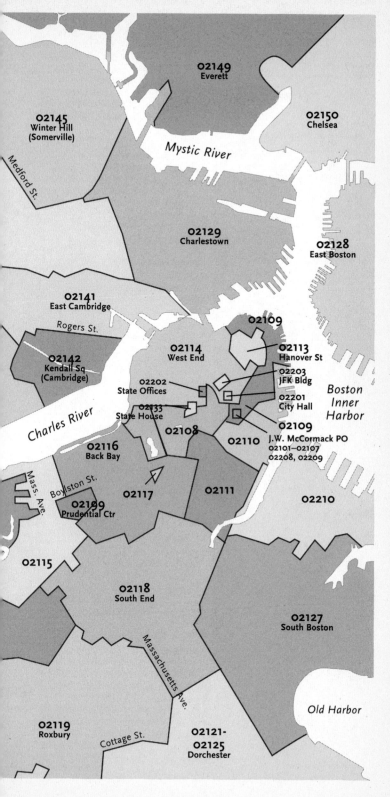

02149
Everett

02145
Winter Hill
(Somerville)

02150
Chelsea

Mystic River

Medford St.

02129
Charlestown

02128
East Boston

02141
East Cambridge

Rogers St.

02109

02142
Kendall Sq
(Cambridge)

02114
West End

02113
Hanover St

02203
JFK Bldg

02202
State Offices

02201
City Hall

02133
State House

Charles River

Boston
Inner
Harbor

02116
Back Bay

02108

02109
J.W. McCormack PO
02101–02107
02208, 02209

02110

Mass. Ave.

Boylston St.

02169
Prudential Ctr

02117

02111

02210

02115

02118
South End

02127
South Boston

Massachusetts Ave.

02119
Roxbury

Cottage St.

02121–
02125
Dorchester

Old Harbor

5

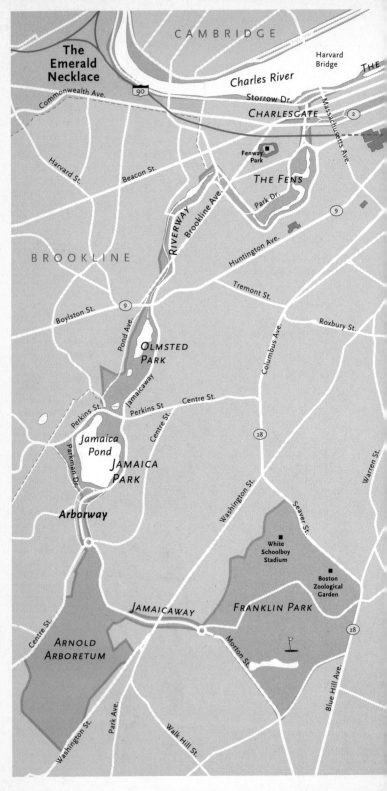

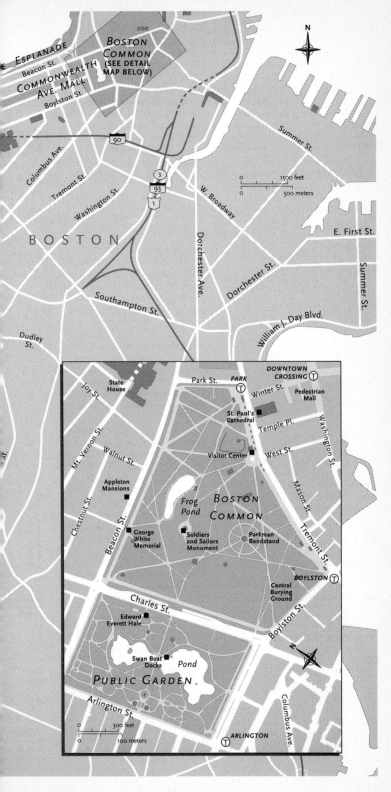

N

ESPLANADE
Beacon St.
COMMONWEALTH
AVE. MALL
Boylston St.

BOSTON COMMON
(SEE DETAIL MAP BELOW)

90

Columbus Ave.
Tremont St.
Washington St.

3
93
1

Summer St.

W. Broadway

0   1500 feet
0   500 meters

BOSTON

Dorchester Ave.

Dorchester St.

E. First St.

Summer St.

Southampton St.

William J. Day Blvd.

Dudley St.

State House
Joy St.
Park St.
PARK
Winter St.
DOWNTOWN CROSSING T
Pedestrian Mall

St. Paul's Cathedral
Temple Pl.
Washington St.

Mt. Vernon St.
Walnut St.
Visitor Center
West St.
Mason St.

Appleton Mansions
BOSTON COMMON

Chestnut St.
Beacon St.
Frog Pond

George White Memorial
Soldiers and Sailors Monument
Parkman Bandstand
Tremont St.

BOYLSTON T

Central Burying Ground
Boylston St.

Charles St.

Edward Everett Hale
N

Swan Boat Docks
Pond

PUBLIC GARDEN

Arlington St.
Columbus Ave.

0   300 feet
0   100 meters

ARLINGTON T

7

Bostonian ever uses that term pure and simple. The city center is bordered by Faneuil Hall and Quincy Market on the north, Chinatown and South Station on the south, Tremont Street and the Common on the west, the harbor to the east, and is actually home to several of Boston's most distinctive neighborhoods, including Chinatown (*see above*), the Financial District, Downtown Crossing, the Theater District, and the Waterfront. Whew! You can see why even natives sometimes can't even give directions with any great certainty. To make matters worse, this is where the city's high-rise "Manhattanization" has proceeded most intensively. What this means is that the streets are now not only narrow at the bottom but at the top. Still, there are some landmark streets and buildings that—along with a map—can help you keep your bearings. The nicely restored **Old State House,** with its 18th-century lion and unicorn, still stands at the head of State Street. Nearby are the dramatic **King's Chapel,** the charming **Old Corner Bookstore Site,** and the legendary **Old South Meeting House** and **Boston Tea Party Ship and Museum**—all remain among the nation's most important historic sites. Boston's city center shopping area is called **Downtown Crossing**—the main commercial thoroughfare is Washington Street, home to those monuments to the mercantile mentality, **Filene's** (and its famed Basement) and **Macy's,** the erstwhile Jordan Marsh. Over by the harbor you'll find the **New England Aquarium** and **Rowes Wharf,** Boston's most glamorous waterfront development.

1

EAST BOSTON
With the airport, it's across the inner harbor to the north and east. Once a uniformly Italian neighborhood, East Boston is now alos home to a thriving Latino population. Santarpio's Pizza is famous here, and sports a line stretching down Chelsea Street every night.

2

THE FENS
Marking the beginnning of Boston's Emerald Necklace—to use the term that describes the string of sylvan parks that thread its western end—the Fenway remains the most scintillating pendant, a verdant 19th-century masterpiece designed by the noted landscape architect Frederick Law Olmsted. Wide meadows, trees, and tranquil gardens await, but here, too, are some of the city's most dazzling attractions—the immense, important **Museum of Fine Arts** and the idiosyncratic and incredibly lovely **Isabella Stewart Gardner Museum** (home to America's greatest Titian), while nearby, fabulous **Fenway Park**—built in 1912 and still boasting a field that's real turf—is still a place where hope for another World Series pennant springs eternal. **Kenmore Square,** a favorite haunt for Boston University and Northeastern University students, adds a bit of neon flavor to the mix.

6

GOVERNMENT CENTER
Government Center marks one corner of what Bostonians usually have in mind when they refer to their downtown district—but they rarely refer to this section anyway. Not only does Government Center house that which they can't fight—**City Hall**—it also features some of the bleakest architecture in the city, thanks to barren plazas, an unsightly upside-down ziggurat (housing City Hall), and the icily modern skyscrapers of the **John F. Kennedy Federal Office Building.** Just behind City Hall, however, are two of Boston's most popular sights—Charles Bulfinch's elegant **Faneuil Hall** and the three long, granite warehouse structures that make up **Quincy Market (also known as Faneuil Hall Marketplace).** Faneuil Hall is renowned as the "Cradle of Liberty," while Quincy Market was Boston's leading 19th-century provisions area. Twenty years ago, the complex was outfitted as a retail urban centerpiece in a pioneering effort at urban recycling. Today, huge crowds still flock here for a dazzling selection of boutiques and food-stalls, eager to contemplate the Doric facade of Quincy Market—an exquisite Alexander Parris 1826 design—while chowing down on lobster rolls. At the waterfront end of Quincy Market is **Marketplace Center,** another shopping complex. Also here is one of Boston's most colorful setpieces, the open-air food stalls of the **Haymarket** and the **Union Oyster House,** the city's oldest restaurant. Separating Government Center from the North End is the **Fitzgerald Expressway,** due to be replaced by a Central Artery underground highway early in the next century.

9
THE NORTH END

In Paul Revere's day, this was the heart—in fact, very nearly the entirety—of Boston. The North End occupies the northernmost tip of the city's main peninsula, cut off from Boston's other neighborhoods by the Central Artery and Government Center, but lying just on the other side of the Faneuil Hall Marketplace. Not surprisingly, you'll find some of the most famous shrines of Revolutionary Boston here, including the **Paul Revere House**—the oldest house in Boston (with its diamond-paned windows and second-floor overhang, it looks like a holdover from the Middle Ages, and it almost is)—and the **Old North Church,** of "One if by land, two if by sea" fame, the **Copp's Hill Burying Ground,** and the **Pierce-Hichborn House.** In the 19th century, the North End became an immigrant quarter—Irish, Jews, and finally Italians. The Italians stayed and today, despite creeping gentrification, the district is still home to a voluble, zesty Italian population and the businesses that serve the neighborhood: delightful groceries, bakeries, churches, social clubs, cafés, and tempting *trattorias.*

6
THE OLD WEST END

Just a few brick tenements are all that remain of this area north of Beacon Hill across Cambridge Street and west of the Central Artery. Landmarks include the **Charles River Park apartment and retail development** and **Mass General,** as the local public hospital is known. However, you're more likely to find yourself in the area to visit the **Museum of Science** or to watch the Celtics play basketball at the new **FleetCenter.**

1
SOUTH BOSTON

This area juts due east toward the outer harbor and its cluster of islands; it is not to be confused with the South End. Another landfill project of the mid-1880s, it came into its own around 1900 with the influx of Irish immigration, and the Irish are still an important presence. It's the site of the **Boston Children's Museum** and the world's only **Computer Museum.** Hundreds of artists have descended on A Street, once a stretch of abandoned warehouses next to the post office, now transformed into posh lofts and galleries.

8
THE SOUTH END

Not to be confused with South Boston, this area hugging the Huntington Avenue flank of the Back Bay, southeast of the Back Bay and due south of Chinatown, is another 19th-century development. But with its park-centered squares and blocks of extravagantly embellished bowfront Victorian houses, it's less Parisian in style than English. To see elegant house restorations, head for **Rutland Square** or **Union Park.** Today the South End is one of Boston's liveliest neighborhoods—gentrification is transforming this black/gay/hispanic/asian multiethnic and polyglot enclave. Some of the city's hippest eateries have opened up side-by-side with Spanish bodegas, Thai restaurants, and Middle Eastern groceries. South End landmarks include the **Boston Center for the Arts, Bay Village** (birthplace of Edgar Allan Poe), and the **Cathedral of the Holy Cross.**

7
CAMBRIDGE

A city of over 100,000 residents on the opposite bank of the Charles, Cambridge is often considered to be synonymous with a particular institution it happens to have played host to since 1636—**Harvard University,** centered around the square of the same name. Many residents quite naturally resent this attitude, since a good part of the city comes and goes without much involvement in the life of the Ivy League giant. The high-tech crowd might also point out that **Massachusetts Institute of Technology,** or **MIT,** down at the river end of Massachusetts Avenue, now looms larger than ever, thanks to its role in mapping out future technologies. Still, Harvard remains the main lure for visitors, thanks to its Georgian-style architecture and its superlative museums, such as the **Fogg Art Museum, the Peabody Museum of Archeology and Ethnology,** and the **Arthur M. Sackler Museum.** Despite being home to vast numbers of writers, radicals, and free thinkers of all kinds, Cambridge also has concentrated ethnic and working-class neighborhoods in East Cambridge and Cambridgeport, seemingly light years from the Colonial-era mansions, such as the **Longfellow National Historic Site** and the **Dexter Pratt House,** on tony **Brattle Street ("Tory Row")** near Harvard Square. The latter brings in the crowds drawn to theaters, booksellers, and coffeehouses, but **Central Square** remains the workaday downtown of Cambridge.

1

SUBURBAN AREAS

South of the Back Bay Fens is **Roxbury,** a largely black neighborhood that merges along its eastern border with biracial but poorly integrated **Dorchester,** and **Jamaica Plain**—a kind of mini-Cambridge—one of the first of the "streetcar suburbs" brought into existence by turn-of-the-century trolley lines. West of Kenmore Square is the separate municipality of **Brookline,** which almost completely cuts off **Allston** and **Brighton,** two residential and industrial Boston neighborhoods, from the rest of the city. Brookline, long home to many of the Boston area's Jewish families, now shares with Allston and Brighton an increasing number of Asian residents.

Farther south still are **West Roxbury, Roslindale, Hyde Park, and Mattapan,** virtual suburbs within the city. People here are more likely to identify themselves as coming from these neighborhoods than as hailing from Boston itself. After all, parts of them are farther from Beacon Hill than Cambridge, Medford, or Winthrop.

BANKS

As the financial center of New England, Boston has no shortage of banks. The name you're most likely to notice is BankBoston (617/434–2200), the giant offspring of the recent merger between BayBank and Bank of Boston. BankBoston's ubiquitous offices and ATMs are easily spotted by their green/blue/white signs. Other common names around the city are Fleet Bank (617/346–4000), Citizens Bank (617/725–5500), and US Trust (617/726–7000). There's no need to avoid the smaller neighborhood banks in your quest for cash, though; almost any ATM you see is affiliated with one of the national banking networks and will accept your bank card. Be aware, though, that some banks impose a service charge of $1 to $3 on non-account holders. Cash machines in grocery stores also charge an extra fee of as much as $2.50.

CURRENCY EXCHANGE

Most large bank offices, particularly in the Back Bay and the Financial District, have currency exchange desks. You can also exchange foreign currency in Terminals C and E at Logan International Airport.

6 *f-6*

THOMAS COOK CURRENCY SERVICES

A service of the Thomas Cook travel agency, this office offers 120 currencies. *160 Franklin St., 617/426–0016; 399 Boylston St., 617/267–5506.*

ENTERTAINMENT INFORMATION

BOSTIX

Bostix is Boston's official entertainment information center and the largest ticket agency in the city, with two main offices—Faneuil Hall Marketplace and Copley Square. A full-price Ticketmaster outlet, Bostix also offers half-price tickets for the same day's performances, beginning at 11 AM; just consult the "menu board" in front of the booths for the available events, but note that people start queuing up well before the ticket windows open. *Faneuil Hall Marketplace, Government Center, 617/723–5181 (recorded message). Tues.–Sat. 10–6, Sun. 11–4. Copley Sq., near Boylston and Dartmouth Sts. Mon.–Sat. 10–6, Sun. 11–4.*

TICKETMASTER

Ticketmaster allows phone charges to major credit cards, weekdays 9 AM–10 PM, weekends, 9–8. It also has outlets in local stores; call for addresses. *617/931–2000, 617/931–2787.*

For a complete rundown of Boston's entertainment scene, *see* Chapter 5.

GAS STATIONS

Note that in Boston, as with many modern city centers, gas stations are far and few between. Most stations are located on the city outskirts and on main highway routes.

4 *e-5*

ANTHONY'S SHELL

4455 Harvard St., Brookline, 617/566–9358.

2 *a-5*

FENWAY TEXACO SERVICE

1241 Boylston St., The Fens, 617/247–7905.

7 *a-5*

MEMORIAL DRIVE SUNOCO
810 Memorial Dr., Cambridge, 617/864–2200.

8 *c-7*

SOUTHGATE MOBIL
841 Massachusetts Ave., South End, 617/427–4464.

HOLIDAYS

Boston's banks, post offices, schools, offices, and most businesses close on these days. *See* Events *in* Chapter 2 for holiday festivities.

New Year's Day (January 1)

Martin Luther King's Day (3rd Monday in January)

Presidents' Day (3rd Monday in Febuary)

Memorial Day (last Monday in May)

Independence Day (July 4th)

Labor Day (1st Monday in September)

Columbus Day (2nd Monday in October)

Election Day (1st Tuesday in November)

Veterans' Day (November 11th)

Thanksgiving (4th Thursday in November)

Christmas (December 25th)

LIQUOR LAWS

The legal drinking age in Massachusetts is 21. Residents will need a Massachusetts driver's license (or, for nondrivers, a Massachusetts identification card) as proof of age. Nonresidents from elsewhere in the U.S. can show their driver's licenses or a military ID; otherwise, a passport will do, although some bars ask out-of-staters for two forms of ID. During the week, most bars and restaurants serve alcohol from 8 AM until 1 AM, a few until 2. On Sunday, alcohol is served beginning at 11 AM in Boston and noon in Cambridge. Some restaurants may have only a beer and wine license; others have no license but allow you to bring your own alcohol. Check the restaurant listings for details.

NO SMOKING

In Boston and Cambridge, smoking is prohibited in public buildings and some restaurants, and many other spaces restrict smoking to designated areas. The town of Brookline prohibits smoking in all restaurants. If you don't know whether you can light up, ask—it's always best to err on the side of courtesy.

PARKING

Parking spaces in Boston are hard to find—and even when you do find one, you may not be able to park there! Many city streets are designated for resident-parking only; others are subject to a variety of restrictions (always posted). Be sure to read the signs carefully; if you park illegally, your car may be ticketed or towed away. Metered parking varies in cost and time, from 25 cents for an hour to 25 cents for 10 minutes, and meter readers are merciless. Repeat offenders face heavy fines and the prospect of getting "the boot," a steel clamp that immobilizes the front wheel of a scofflaw's car. In other words, don't leave town without paying your parking tickets, or you risk being "booted" upon your return!

If you don't have the option of being car-free, leave it in a parking lot. Although lots are expensive—from $3/hour to $25/day, depending on the lot and the time of day—they're a bargain compared to parking tickets that start at $20 and escalate steadily from there. You'll find major parking garages at Government Center and Quincy Market, under Boston Common (entrance on Charles Street), beneath Post Office Square, at Copley Place and the Prudential Center, and behind the John Hancock Tower. Smaller lots are tucked in corners and between buildings throughout the city. Look for a blue sign with a white P and an arrow pointing toward the garage or lot entrance. Here's a list of some large, centrally located parking facilities; all are open 24 hours a day, 7 days a week:

8 *c-4*

AUDITORIUM GARAGE
Adjacent to the Hilton and directly across the street from the Sheraton Hotel and Towers, which connects to

both the Hynes Convention Center and the Prudential Center shopping mall. *50 Dalton St., 617/247–8006.*

6 *b-6*

BOSTON COMMON GARAGE

Between the Public Garden and Boston Common, steps to Beacon Hill, and newly renovated. *Zero Charles St., 617/954–2096.*

8 *d-4*

COPLEY PLACE GARAGE

Beneath the Copley Place shopping center, convenient to both the Back Bay and the South End. *110 Huntington Ave., 617/375–4488.*

6 *f-4*

GARAGE AT POST OFFICE SQUARE

In the center of the Financial District and just two blocks from Faneuil Hall. *Zero Post Office Sq., 617/423–1430.*

8 *e-3*

JOHN HANCOCK GARAGE

Behind the Back Bay's tallest building, a short walk from "restaurant row" in the South End. *100 Clarendon St., 617/421–5050.*

8 *c-4*

PRUDENTIAL CENTER GARAGE

In the heart of the Back Bay, with entrances on all four sides of the Prudential Center. *617/267–2965.*

PARKS INFORMATION

Boston is not only home to the oldest public park in the United States—the Boston Common—the city also features other verdant jewels, such as the Boston Public Garden, the Fens—designed by no less than Frederick Law Olmsted—and Boston's Emerald Necklace, a chain of parks that extends along the Fenway, Riverway, and Jamaica Way to Jamaica Pond, the Arnold Arboretum, and Franklin Park. For information about Boston's "lungs," contact:

DEPARTMENT OF PARKS & RECREATION

1010 Massachusetts Ave., 617/635–4505.

PERSONAL SECURITY

While Boston's crime rate is at an all-time low, that's no excuse for abandoning common sense. If you venture far from the well-known paths, be sure to do it in daylight or with a friend. At the very least, know how you're going to get back to your hotel.

More importantly for your day-to-day safety, everything you've heard about Boston drivers is true. They can and do run red lights, drive in the breakdown lane, pull a luxury sedan abruptly into an opening scarcely large enough for a motorcycle, and look straight through you while cutting you off! You're more likely to be in a mutual fender-bender than hit while on foot, but nonetheless, it's best to stay alert while crossing streets—even when with the light. Using footpower, Bostonians can be as genteel as can be, but once they get behind a wheel, watch out. Be careful out there!

PUBLICATIONS

BOSTON GLOBE

The *Globe* is the daily newspaper of record in Boston and the home paper of Pulitzer-winning columnist Ellen Goodman. Check Thursday's Calendar section before making weekend plans. Available at any newsstand.

BOSTON HERALD

This tabloid daily, while not as widely read as the *Globe*, has stellar sports coverage and features some of the liveliest reportage in town. Thursday's Scene section is another good guide to the week's events. Available at any newsstand.

BOSTON MAGAZINE

If you want to know what's hot with the locals, pick up this slick and colorful monthly magazine's annual "Best of Boston" issue, which hits the newsstands in August. The rest of the year, the focus is on those—travelers, you're in luck!—who visit the city solely to dine, shop, and attend cultural events. Available at any newsstand.

BOSTON PHOENIX

The local "alternative" weekly paper, which comes out on Thursdays, is the definitive authority on local controversies, nightlife, and lifestyles. For those planning to move to Boston, it's also the single largest source of roommate-wanted ads. Available at most news-stands; the Styles section is distributed free in corner newsboxes.

IMPROPER BOSTONIAN

This glossy bimonthly tabloid, available free at corner newsboxes, caters to the city's affluent, young (under 35) social scenesters. Check here for details about wine tastings, hip fund-raisers, and other events at which to see and be seen.

THE TAB

This chain of 17 community papers, focusing on local news and arts, is dis-tributed free in different editions for Boston, Brookline, and several suburban communities (there's also an Allston-Brighton edition that isn't free). It's also *the* place to advertise for child care.

RADIO STATIONS

You can tune in any listening preference once you're in the Boston area: jazz, classical, talk, folk, alternative rock, Spanish, top 40—even a smattering of country. In addition to dozens of com-mercial stations and a plethora of tiny, eclectic college stations with ranges of no more than a mile or two, Boston also boasts two of the nation's preeminent public radio stations (WBUR and WGBH). Here's a taste of what's popu-lar and available:

AM

850	WEEI	Sports
950	WROL	Religious
1030	WBZ	News, talk, Bruins hockey
1330	WRCA	Hispanic music/talk

FM

88.1	WMBR	Local and folk music
89.1	WBUR	National Public Radio
89.7	WGBH	National Public Radio
92.9	WBOS	Oldies
94.5	WJMN	"Jam'n"—dance music
97.7	WCAV	Country
98.5	WBMX	"Mix 98.5"—adult contemporary
99.5	WOAZ	"Oasis"—smooth jazz
100.7	WZLX	Clas...
101.7	WFNX	Alter... prog...
104.1	WBCN	Album-oriented rock
106.7	WMJX	"Magic"—soft adult contemporary
107.9	WXKS	"Kiss 108"—top 40 hits

For a complete listing of local AM and FM stations, check the back of the *Globe*'s "TV Week," which comes in Sunday's paper.

SIGHTSEEING INFORMATION

6 *d-6*

BEANTOWN TROLLEYS

These red trolleys depart from the Com-mon every 15 minutes from 9 AM–4 PM, offering a narrated tour of the city's most popular attractions for $16. You can get on and off the trolley at any stop, as often as you'd like. If you opt not to get off and explore, the entire tour will take you about 1 ½ hours. *14 Park Plaza, Transportation Bldg., 617/ 236–2148. T stop: Arlington.*

6 *d-6*

BOSTON COMMON VISITOR INFORMATION CENTER

Located on the Common, this kiosk marks the beginning of the Freedom Trail and is one of the best places to get maps, brochures about historic attrac-tions, and information about the city and current events. It's run by the Greater Boston Convention & Visitors Bureau (*see below*) and staffed by many helpful, patient, and multilingual employees. Also available: a complete listing of sightseeing tours, many of which depart from here. *147 Tremont St., between West St. and Temple Pl., Beacon Hill/Downtown Crossing, no phone. Mon.–Sat. 8:30–5. T stop: Park St.*

6 *d-6*

BOSTON TROLLEY

Another of the ubiquitous trolley tours, this one operates blue vehicles and makes its rounds every 20 minutes from 9 AM–3 PM; tours cost $16, starting on the Common and stopping at all the expected attractions. *345 D St., South Boston, 617/876–5539.*

CAMBRIDGE DISCOVERY

The Cambridge Discovery kiosk at the main entrance to the Harvard Square T station offers books, maps, and brochures to help you find food, lodging, entertainment, shopping, and other Cambridge attractions. Guided tours of Old Cambridge, Harvard Yard, and Harvard Square also leave from this point. *Harvard Sq., Cambridge, 617/497–1630. Mon.–Sat. 9–5, Sun. 1–5. T stop: Harvard.*

GREATER BOSTON CONVENTION & VISITORS BUREAU

This information center in the Prudential Tower offers maps and brochures in many foreign languages as well as the most current list of the city's hotel rates and attractions. The popular "Duck Boat" tours leave from here; they squire visitors through Boston (quacking at attractions) by both land and water on amphibious vehicles originally designed for the military. *800 Boylston St., Prudential Plaza, Back Bay, 617/536–4100. Weekdays 8:30–6, weekends 10–6. T stop: Hynes Convention Center/ICA.*

MASSACHUSETTS OFFICE OF TRAVEL & TOURISM

If you want to take a day trip beyond Boston, begin your planning in this state office, which provides information on destinations and events all over Massachusetts. Staffers will happily point you to other sources of information, from the National Park Service to local Chambers of Commerce. Call the toll-free number at any time for a recording of events, "Great Dates in the Bay State." *100 Cambridge St., Saltonstall Bldg., 13th floor, Government Center, 800/227–MASS or 617/727–3201. Weekdays 9–5. T stop: Bowdoin.*

NATIONAL PARK SERVICE VISITOR CENTER

This information center is right on the Freedom Trail, just across from the Old State House. Watch an eight-minute film on Boston history for the background you'll need to appreciate the Freedom Trail, visit the art exhibits, then ask the superbly friendly and well-informed Park Service rangers for maps, advice, and directions. You'll also find a gift shop, a wheelchair ramp, public rest rooms, and information about other national parks in Massachusetts and elsewhere in the country. *15 State St., Beacon Hill, 617/242–5642. Weekdays 8–5, weekends 9–5. T stop: State St.*

OLD TOWN TROLLEY

Yet another trolley tour, in vehicles that are colored eye-popping orange and green. Boston trolleys start on the Common and run every 10 minutes from 9 AM–4:30 PM for $16; in the summer, Old Town Trolley also offers an hour-long $12 tour of Cambridge, which starts in Harvard Square. *329 W. 2nd St., South Boston, 617/269–7010.*

TAXES & GRATUITIES

In Massachusetts, a sales tax of 5% is levied on all purchases except clothing under $175, food bought in stores (but not restaurant meals), and services. Price tags do not reflect the sales tax, which is added to your total at the cash register. An occupancy tax of 9.7% is added to the price of your hotel room when you pay the bill.

In restaurants, tip 15% for good service, 20% for excellent service. For taxis, the standard tip for trips under $1 is 25 cents; for anything more, it's 15–20% of the total.

At your hotel, give your bellhop 50 cents per bag ($1 for particularly heavy bags). For the maid, $5 per week, per person, is standard; for less than a week, $1 a day is the norm. The doorman should get 50 cents for hailing a taxi and $1 if he has helped with the bags. For room service, give 10–15% of the bill; for laundry or valet, 15%.

Inadequate or unpleasant service does not require, or deserve, a tip. For extraordinary service, be generous with both your tip and your praise.

TELEVISION

The main local channels and their network affiliates are as follows:

2	WGBH-TV (PBS)
4	WBZ-TV (CBS)
5	WCVB-TV (ABC)
7	WHDH-TV (NBC)

25   WFXT-TV (Fox)

38   WSBK-TV (UPN)

56   WLVI-TV (WB)

68   WABU-TV (Independent)

Cable service in the metropolitan area varies by town; Beacon Hill has no cable service. To find your favorite show, check the local TV listings.

TRANSPORTATION

With a city that also boasts many other "oldest's," it's only fitting that Boston has America's oldest subway system, better known as the "T." Most Bostonians ride the T for the same reasons you should: it's safe, efficient, fast, and—except at the start and end of the business day—comfortable. If the subway can't get you there, a city bus can. Pick up a surface transit map and bus schedules at the Park Street T station. Taxis can be expensive and often get bogged down in traffic, but they're a treat when your feet hurt.

The Massachusetts Bay Transportation Authority (MBTA) operates the subway, local buses, and commuter train service. For travel information and directions to anywhere via public transportation, call the **MBTA Customer Service line** at 617/222–3200 or 800/392–6100, weekdays 6:30 AM–11 PM and weekends 7:30–6. For **senior citizen and special-needs access passes,** call 617/222–5438.

For general information about traffic, delays, and other how-to-get-around issues, call **Smart Traveler,** 617/374–1234.

Of course, if you're a visitor to Boston and out for the best camcorder-perfect views of Boston, both old and new, *walk* whenever possible. Be sure to wear comfortable shoes—the brick sidewalks and granite cobblestones common in the older parts of the city are not kind to the less practically shod!

bus

MBTA buses provide crosstown, express, and local service in the city and far into the suburbs. The basic fare on local buses is 60 cents; children ages 5 to 11 pay 30 cents. Seniors and special-needs riders pay 15 cents at all times. Express buses are $1.50 or $2.00 depending on the destination. Seniors pay half-fare on other than local buses. Since schedules

vary greatly, obtain a timetable for each line you intend to use.

Note: There is no free transfer between bus lines or between the bus and the subway.

subway

The four subway lines—Red, Blue, Orange, and Green—all intersect in a square of stations in the center of the city. The **Red Line** starts at Braintree and Mattapan in the south; the routes join near South Boston and continue north to the suburb of Arlington. The **Blue Line** starts in Revere, north of Boston, and runs to Bowdoin station on weekdays and to Government Center weeknights and weekends. The **Orange Line** begins in suburban Malden and ends at Forest Hills. The **Green Line,** the oldest line, uses trolleys that run underground downtown and rise to street level further out. It begins at Lechmere in Cambridge and divides into four routes: the B line, which runs along Commonwealth Avenue and ends at Boston College; the C line, which runs along Beacon Street and ends at Cleveland Circle, the D line, which ends far into the suburbs at Riverside in Newton, and the E line, which travels along Huntington Avenue and ends at Heath Street. Buses continue along the E line's former route to Arborway.

To find a T station, look for the sign with a "T" in a circle. To figure out which train will take you in the direction you want to go, determine whether you're heading inbound or outbound. *Inbound* refers to trains going toward downtown (the square formed by Park, Washington, State, and Government Center); *outbound* refers to those heading away from downtown.

The T operates Monday–Saturday 5 AM–12:30 AM and Sunday 6 AM–12:30 AM. Smoking is prohibited in T stations and on trains. Animals are also prohibited unless they're traveling in carrying cases; Seeing Eye dogs are the only exception.

The basic fare is 85 cents; for children ages 5 to 11 the fare is 40 cents; children 4 and under ride free. Senior citizens and special-needs riders pay 30 cents at all times with special access passes. You must use tokens, which are sold at all stations; some stations will also allow you to use exact change. There are additional fare charges to and from certain points on several of the lines. Above-ground Green line trains heading outbound—stops after Kenmore on the B, C, and D lines, and stops after Prudential on the E line—are free.

Transfers from one subway line to another are free *as long as you don't exit the subway system*. If you do exit the system, you will have to pay again to get back in. One station where you need to be particularly careful is Copley, on the Green line, where there's no free transfer from inbound to outbound trains. If you discover at Copley that you're headed in the wrong direction, ride to the next stop to change trains.

Instead of waiting in long lines for tokens every time you enter the subway system, do what the locals do: buy multiple tokens to save time. If you're staying for a few days, buy a **Boston Passport Tourist Pass.** These multi-ride passes for tourists allow unlimited travel on all MBTA subways and local buses, as well as $50 worth of discounts in restaurants, museums, and entertainments in Boston. A three-day pass costs $9, a seven-day pass costs $18. If you're staying for more than a week and think you'll be spending a lot of time on the T, consider investing in a monthly T pass. It's convenient and economical, and monthly passholders can bring one guest with them free on Sundays. For **pass information and sales locations,** call 617/222–5218.

taxi

You'll find taxi stands in front of all major hotels and tourist attractions. You can also hail a cab on the street, New York City–style, by walking to the curb and extending your arm (available taxis will have a lit sign on top), although this doesn't always work on rainy days and during rush hours. The best way to guarantee service is to go to a hotel cab stand or, better yet, call for a pick-up. All cab companies listed here operate 24 hours a day, 7 days a week.

Bay State Taxi Service: 617/566–5000

Cambridge Taxi: 617/547–3000

Checker Taxi: 617/536–7000

Independent Taxi Operators Association: 617/426–8700

Red Cab: 617/734–5000

Red & White Cab: 617/242–8000

Town Taxi: 617/536–5000

It's usually no problem to get a cab from Logan International Airport, although you may be asked at busy times to share a ride with other people going to the same area. If you share, ask the driver in advance what your fare will be. Remember to take traffic into consideration in calculating both the length and cost of the ride.

commuter rail

The MBTA Commuter Rail (occasionally called the "Purple Line") serves the suburbs from North Station and South Station. For information about routes and schedules, call 617/222–3200 or 800/392–6100.

getting to the airport

Boston's legendary traffic can make Logan International Airport seem much farther away than it is. The "Big Dig"—construction to expand and move underground the highway that runs through the heart of Boston—promises to relieve downtown congestion by the end of the decade. Until then, allow ample travel time by taxi, or use public transportation whenever possible to avoid the city's notorious 10-hour "rush hour." For detailed information on getting to and from the airport, call the 24-hour **Ground Transportation Service** line at 800/23–LOGAN.

BY SUBWAY

The subway can get you from downtown to your plane in half an hour or less. Take the Blue Line to the Airport T station, then the free Massport Shuttle Bus to your terminal. One shuttle serves Terminals A and B, and one serves Terminals C, D, and E—check the sign in front of the station to determine where you want to go. *Blue Line runs Mon.–Sat. 5:30 AM–12:48 AM, Sun. 6 AM–12:48 AM.*

BY U.S. SHUTTLE

Door-to-door minibus service is available between home, office, or hotel and Logan Airport, 24 hours a day, 7 days a week. Fare and pick-up times vary by distance; advance reservations are required. Call for details. 617/894–3100.

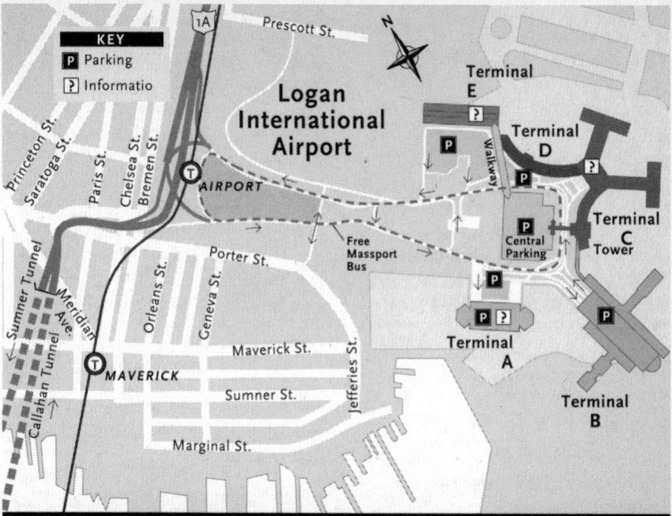

Logan International Airport map showing terminals A, B, C, D, E, Central Parking, Free Massport Bus, and surrounding streets (Prescott St., Princeton St., Saratoga St., Paris St., Chelsea St., Bremen St., Porter St., Orleans St., Geneva St., Maverick St., Sumner St., Jefferies St., Marginal St., Meridian Ave.). KEY: P Parking, ? Information. Sumner Tunnel, Callahan Tunnel, AIRPORT and MAVERICK T stations.

Airline — Terminal	A	B	C	D	E
Aer Lingus ☎ 800/223-6537					●
Air Alliance ☎ 800/776-3000					●
Air Atlantic/Canadian Airlines ☎ 800/426-7000					●
Alitalia ☎ 800/223-5730 (Departures Only)				●	
(Int'l Arrivals Only)					●
American ☎ 800/433-7300				●	
(Int'l Arrivals Only)					●
American Eagle ☎ 800/433-7300		●			
America West ☎ 800/235-9292		●			
ATA ☎ 800/225-2995					●
British Airways ☎ 800/247-9297					●
Business Express/Delta Connection ☎ 800/345-3400			●		
Cape Air ☎ 800/352-0714	●				
Canadian Airlines ☎ 800/426-7000					●
Charter Flights (most)				●	
Colgan Air ☎ 800/272-5488	●				
Comair ☎ 800/354-9822			●		
Continental ☎ 800/525-0280	●				
Delta Airlines/Delta Express ☎ 800/221-1212			●		
Delta Shuttle ☎ 800/221-1212 (LaGuardia only)		●			
Eastwind Airlines ☎ 800/644-3592	●				
Icelandair ☎ 800/223-5500					●
KLM ☎ 800/374-7747					●
Korean Air ☎ 800/438-5000					●
Lufthansa ☎ 800/645-3880					●
Midway Airlines ☎ 800/446-4392		●			
Midwest Express ☎ 800/452-2022	●				
Northwest Airlines ☎ 800/225-2525					●
Olympic ☎ 800/223-1226					●
Qantas ☎ 800/227-4500		●			
Sabena ☎ 800/955-2000 (Departures Only)			●		
(Int'l Arrivals Only)					●
Spirit Airlines ☎ 800/772-7117	●				
Swissair ☎ 800/221-4750					●
TAP Air Portugal ☎ 800/221-7370					●
TWA/TW Express ☎ 800/221-2000			●		
United/United Express ☎ 800/241-6522			●		
US Airways/US Airways Express ☎ 800/428-4322		●			
(Int'l Arrivals Only)					●
US Airways Shuttle ☎ 800/428-4322 (LaGuardia Only)	●				
Virgin Atlantic ☎ 800/862-8621 (Int'l Arrivals Only)					●
(Departures Only)		●			

17

BY WATER SHUTTLE

Zip across Boston Harbor between Logan Airport and Rowes Wharf in the Financial District in just seven minutes, year-round. At Logan, catch the Massport Shuttle Bus to your airline terminal. One-way fare $8; seniors $4; children under age 12 free. Round-trip fare is $14. *Waterfront, 617/330–8680. Weekdays every 15 min 6 AM–8 PM plus Fri. every 30 min 8 PM–11 PM; Sat. every 30 min 10 AM–11 PM; Sun. to Logan every 30 min noon–8 PM, from Logan every 30 min 12:15 PM–8:15 PM.*

WEATHER

Like much of the Northeast, Boston can grind to a standstill under layers of snow and ice in winter, or swelter and stick in summer. But the city has its charms in every season. In winter, red-brick buildings behind streetlights twinkling through falling snow turn ordinary streets into picture postcards. In spring, the days are clear, the Public Garden is in bloom, and the sailboats return to the Charles River. In summer, harbor cruises, sidewalk cafés, outdoor concerts, and oceanside parks offer a cooling respite from the heat and humidity. And autumn, when university life takes over the city once more, is crisp and clear as only a New England fall can be.

For free local weather reports, updated several times a day, call *617/936–1234.*

For the current temperature, call **Time and Temperature,** *617/NERVOUS or 617/637–1234.*

If you're planning a day on the water, check the **Marine Weather Forecast,** *617/569–3700.*

chapter 2

PLACES TO EXPLORE

galleries, gargoyles, museums, and more

Come back, America, Your Mother is Calling You." Boston's 1976 Bicentennial slogan inspired millions of people to visit the birthplace of America's mighty struggle toward a national identity and independence. Today, as then, visitors and natives alike love to explore Boston's celebrated Freedom Trail—an odyssey of 16 historic sites that allows you to touch the very wellsprings of American civilization. But Boston is so much more than just Faneuil Hall, Paul Revere's House, and the Bunker Hill Monument. No matter what age, civilization, or subject you're interested in, Boston is sure to come up with just the ticket.

Let's start with Boston's celebrated museums. When you consider such marvels as forty-three Monets, the greatest Titian in America, John F. Kennedy's rocking chair, John Singleton Copley's spectacular Watson and the Shark, and Paul Revere's lantern, it's little wonder museum-going is what a trip to Boston is often all about. Who wouldn't be dazzled by the sumptuousness of Boston's Museum of Fine Arts or the technical wizardry at the Museum of Science. And while such world-class institutions merit an afternoon or more, Boston offers a variety of smaller, but no less fascinating, museums—some ensconced in the city's most historic areas, others a bit off the beaten track.

Talking in art terms, venerable old Boston used to be like one gigantic Old Master painting. In days gone by, oh-so-proper collectors turned up their Brahmin noses at nudes and similar "distasteful" works. Today, of course, the MFA's newest West Wing, a site for changing exhibits, is making a bold foray into the avant-garde—and those who come to view its permanent collection seem not put off a bit. Across town at the small but often sizzling Institute of Contemporary Art, visitors witnessing the latest in visual exploration may find themselves uttering the famous tag line, "But is it art?" Those who journey to the List Visual Arts Center at MIT will find some more cutting-edge—some might even say over-the-edge—art.

A sometimes overlooked gem is the Fogg Art Museum in Cambridge—Harvard's treasure house is also famous as a training ground for many of America's leading art curators, while the nearby Sackler Museum has galleries gleaming with ancient Chinese jades and Japanese gilded Buddhas. Those technically inclined will want to consider a trek into Cambridge to visit MIT's museum (where science is presented with a sense of humor), as well as a pilgrimage to the city's Computer Museum.

In addition to the city's many museums, the chapter below details hundreds of other sights—Revolutionary-era buildings, Gilded-Age monuments, elegant 19th-century town houses and cobblestoned streets, the latest in modern architecture, and the city's best scenic viewpoints. Whether explored by foot, by bus, or by duck (duck? read on), visitors to Boston will happily find the city compact and accessible, with sites almost on top of each other. Only the brave, however, will attempt to explore by car. (If the traffic and one-way streets don't get them, the meter maids will!) Our advice is to come into Boston by the MBTA subway (the "T") or park in one of the various garages.

One can also opt for one of the many tour buses and trolleys weaving through the city (including the popular Duck Tours, conducted in amphibious vehicles) or sign up with the various walking tours, of which many are tailored for specific tastes. Or visitors can go it by foot since many of the popular sights are within walking distance of each other: They simply pick a neighborhood and head off on their own.

With kids in tow, a good central place to start is the Public Garden with its swan boats and kid-friendly statue of Mother Mallard and her ducklings. Another *family summer adventure might be one of the various whale-watching cruises.*

Two among the city's most noted attractions are the Freedom Trail and the Black Heritage Trail. For a general overview of each, see Historic Buildings & Areas, below. Sights on both these trails are also discussed under each individual site name—for those who want to make their own fabulous Boston itinerary.

where to go

ART MUSEUMS

In addition to their permanent treasures, many of Boston's museums host an overstuffed calendar of temporary museum exhibitions—truly, a moveable feast. Even New Yorkers have turned pea-green with envy at the number of blockbuster art shows that have skipped the Big Apple in favor of a Boston venue: the recent Renoir, Leonardo da Vinci, and Early Picasso retrospectives are just a few examples. Many of these spectaculars sell out well in advance— so visitors should call ahead to reserve tickets. Many of the museums are closed Mondays but have extended hours on other days, plus times for reduced admissions. To avoid museum feet and gallery gout, remember to take time-outs: opt for lunch at the Gardner, or lingering over the harbor view from the John F. Kennedy Museum.

7 b-2
BUSCH-REISINGER MUSEUM

In this museum-within-a-museum, you'll find some of the finest examples of Bauhaus works outside of Germany. Founded in 1902 as a "Germanic Museum," the Busch-Reisinger—which is housed in Werner Otto Hall inside the Fogg Art Museum—became the only museum in the United States specializing in Central and Northern European art. The collection encompasses a wide range, including medieval, Renaissance, and Baroque sculpture, and porcelain of the 18th century, but the museum is most famed for its collection of German Expressionism (the style once derided as "degenerate" by the Nazis). Highlights include works by Max Beckmann

(his evocative 1927 *Self-Portrait in a Tuxedo*) Franz Marc, Paul Klee, Edvard Munch, and Kandinsky. Tours: weekdays 2 PM, Sept.–mid-June; Wed. 2 PM, mid-June–Sept. To arrange group tours, call 617/496–8576. Note: One ticket admits visitors to all three Harvard University art museums. *Harvard University, 32 Quincy St., Cambridge, 617/495–9400. $5 adults, $4 senior citizens, $3 students, 18 and under free, free to all Sat. 10–noon. Mon.–Sat., 10–5, Sun. 1–5. T stop: Harvard Sq.*

3 f-6
MARGARET COMPTON GALLERY

This Massachusetts Institute of Technology gallery features changing exhibits of art, photography, and memorabilia. *77 Massachusetts Ave., Bldg. 10, Cambridge, 617/253–4444. Free. Weekdays 10–5. T stop: Kendall Sq.*

7 b-2
FOGG ART MUSEUM

A gem of an art museum, the Fogg has a permanent collection that spans European and North American art from the Middle Ages to the present in all media (sculpture, paintings, prints, drawings, and photography), all housed in an elegant building done in the 16th-century Italian Renaissance manner. Founded in 1891, opened in 1895, the museum was envisioned as a kind of sublime "laboratory" for art and art history studies. The collection is most noted for its Old Master drawings, which contain works by such masters as Renoir, Van Gogh, Monet, Fra Angelico, Rubens, Botticelli, Michelangelo, Manet, Lautrec, and Leonardo. Holdings include some of the best medieval sculpture, early Renaissance paintings, and 19th- and 20th-century French, English, and American paintings found anywhere, including an extensive selection of Whistler, Picasso, and Ingres. An ongoing exhibit, "Investigating the Renaissance," firmly places glorious works of the past in their historical context, a boon for both art students and art lovers. Another ongoing exhibit, on African sculpture, examines the visual power of African art. The museum also has a stimulating collection of Harvard-related artifacts, including the university's "ceremonial silver" and 16th-century "President's Chair," the regal (though uncomfortable) seat for every Harvard president at commencement. No parking. Tours: weekdays 11 AM, Sept.–mid-June; Wed. 11 AM, mid-June–Sept. To arrange group tours, call 617/496–8576. Note: One ticket admits visitors to all three Harvard University art museums. *Harvard University, 32 Quincy St., Cambridge, 617/495–9400. $5 adults, $4 senior citizens, $3 students, 18 and under free, free to all Sat. 10–noon. Mon.–Sat. 10–5, Sun. 1–5. T stop: Harvard Sq.*

7 *b-1*

HARVARD UNIVERSITY MUSEUMS

In reality there are four separate museums under one roof. *See* Botanical Museum; Mineralogical and Geological Museums; Museum of Comparative Zoology; *and* Peabody Museum of Archaeology and Ethnology, *below and under* Science Museums. *24 Oxford St., Cambridge, 617/495–1910. T stop: Harvard Sq.*

8 *b-4*

INSTITUTE OF CONTEMPORARY ART (ICA)

A visit to the ICA will help you forget all those "Banned-in-Boston" saws characterizing the city as a stuffy, conservative holdout. The ICA showcases contemporary art by local, national, and international artists of painting, sculpture, multi-media, video, and work that defies classification. Located in a recycled Richardsonian-style police station, it has no permanent collection. There are also evening lectures featuring prominent critics, artists, and scholars. *955 Boylston St., Back Bay, 617/266–5152. $5.25 adults, free Thurs. 5–9. Wed.–Sun. noon–5, Thurs. noon–9. Tours weekends at 1 and 3. T stop: Hynes Convention Center/ICA.*

CALLING ON MRS. JACK

One of the wonders of the Isabella Stewart Gardner Museum is the feeling that Mrs. Jack—as Mrs. Gardner was affectionately known—might once again magically stroll into her grand salons at any moment. More a house than a museum, the Gardner keeps its Gilded Age interiors evergreen through special events during the year.

Christmas Cheer
   Mrs. Gardner's holiday table is recreated every December, down to her china, silverware, glassware, candelabra, and—oh, yes—placecards for her favored guests. Among the floral displays, note the place settings for John Singer Sargent, Sarah Bernhardt, Nellie Melba, and other to-die-for guests.

Eastertime Elegance
   Inspired by the Ca d'Oro and other Venetian palaces, Mrs. Gardner annually festooned the "Romeo, Romeo, Wherefore Art Thou Romeo" balconies of her courtyard with spectacular trailing sprays of nasturtiums. Today, the staff lovingly continues to do so. Ten to 15 feet long, the sprays enchant from March to April—although you can only catch the bright orange blossoms for a two-week period.

Happy Birthday!
   Every April in honor of Mrs. Gardner's birthday the museum offers a memorial service to her in the beautiful Chapel of the Long Gallery. Just this past year, the chapel's radiant stained-glass window, originally from Soissons Cathedral, was cleaned. Mrs. Jack must be beaming, too.

Taking a Shine to the Gardner
   Like many museums, the Gardner has an ongoing restoration program for its many treasured Old Master paintings. Recently, Rembrandt's Self Portrait, one of the jewels of the collection, was restored to all its chromatic splendor. Glowing as if painted yesterday, it now possesses a bit more chiaro and a bit less scuro.

Viva Vivaldi
   Come September, the annual concert season at the Gardner gets underway. Chamber music groups—the Orion String Quartet and the Chamber Music Society of Lincoln Center are among the favorites—and soloists offer concerts most Saturdays and Sundays in the regal Tapestry room. Happily, tickets can often be bought at the door. Concerts are offered through early May.

2 b-6

ISABELLA STEWART GARDNER MUSEUM

A Venetian Gothic palazzo rose in Boston, bringing one woman's fantasy to life. The elegant home of socialite art collector Isabella Stewart Gardner was built to showcase her collection of what she humbly referred to in her bequest to the city as "an aggregation of pictures, statuary, works of art, bric-a-brac, furniture, books, and papers." Those "pictures" include some of the most beautiful Old Master paintings in America, with nonpareil works by Piero della Francesca, Titian, and Botticelli on view, collected for Mrs. Gardner by Bernard Berenson, the famed Harvard scholar of Renaissance art. She called the house Fenway Court, and when it opened in opened in 1903, it quickly became known as an institution with as idiosyncratic a history as any in Boston (or America, for that matter).

One of the terms of her will allowed that not one objet d'art or canvas could be moved—today, Mrs. Jack would have no difficulty recognizing her bibelot-filled salons. Except, that is, for 13 little cards stuck to the walls, indicating the paintings stolen on March 19, 1990, which included a priceless Vermeer and a stunning Rembrandt. No matter, the Gardner collection is so rich, one barely notices. Here is Titian's *Rape of Europa*—many consider this the greatest Renaissance painting in the United States—Giorgione's *Christ Carrying the Cross*, and John Singer Sargent's extraordinary *El Jaleo* (housed in its own Moorish-Spanish room). Sculptures, stained glass, textiles, furniture, books from all over the world are also on view—all in all, a monument to one woman's taste. Nonetheless, a first-floor gallery has revolving small exhibits—one was recently devoted to Boston's Botticellis—often curated by the Gardner director, Hilliard Goldfarb. The courtyard particularly reveals Mrs. Gardner's love for the city of Venice—it is all done in 15th-century Venetian Gothic, with the balconies, window frames, paintings, and sculpture coming directly from that city. Covered by a skylight, it is always filled with flowers from the museum's own greenhouses. From September to May concerts are held in the elegant Tapestry Room at 1:30 PM Saturday and Sunday. You can also have lunch in a small café until 4 PM. In all, an easy and charming trip out of this time and place. Park at the nearby Museum of Fine Arts garage. *280 The Fenway, 617/566–1401 (also for recorded concert information), 617/566–1088 for café. $9 adults, $7 senior citizens, $5 students, $3 ages 12–17, under 12 free. Tickets for concerts and galleries $15 adults, $11 senior citizens, $9 students, $7 ages 12–17; $4 ages 5–11; free admission to café and gift shop only. Museum Tues.–Sun. 11–5, some Mon. holidays. T stop: Museum.*

3 g-6

LIST VISUAL ARTS CENTER

Founded by Albert and Vera List, pioneer collectors of modern art, this exhibition space at the Massachusetts Institute of Technology has three galleries showcasing exhibitions of cutting-edge art and mixed media that often challenge conventional ideas about art. *Weisner Bldg., 20 Ames St., 617/253–4680. Free. Weekdays noon–6, weekends 1–5. Closed July and Aug. T stop: Kendall Sq.*

2 b-6

MUSEUM OF FINE ARTS (MFA)

Copley's *Watson and the Shark*, Gauguin's *Where Have We Been? Where Are We Going?*, Donatello's *Madonna of the Clouds* . . . you get the picture. This museum ranks as one of the best museums in America (many put it in the top five) and it remains the museum jewel in Boston's crown. A shorter description of the museum's holdings might be possible if we were to list the areas in which its collections are *not* strong, rather than those in which they are. The most famous part of the collection focuses on the French Impressionists—there are hundreds of canvases, including 43 by Monet. In addition, there is a wide survey of European paintings from the 11th to the early 20th centuries. Equally outstanding are the American decorative arts and sculpture from the colonial period to the present, with emphasis on the pre-Civil War culture of New England—featured are silver by Paul Revere and John Coney, period rooms, and the Karolik Collection of 18th-century furniture. Also superb are the Asiatic collections, which form the most extensive assemblage under one roof; a significant classical collection,

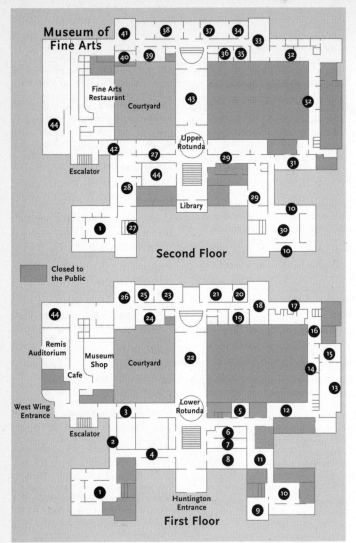

Museum of Fine Arts

Second Floor

Fine Arts Restaurant

Courtyard

Upper Rotunda

Escalator

Library

Closed to the Public

First Floor

Remis Auditorium

Museum Shop

Cafe

Courtyard

Lower Rotunda

West Wing Entrance

Escalator

Huntington Entrance

1	Japanese Art	**16**	19th-C American	**31**	Medieval Art
2	Islamic Art	**17**	American Federal	**32**	European Decorative Arts
3	Brown Gallery	**18**	Copley & Contemp		
4	Indian Art	**19**	American Neo-Classic & Romantic	**33**	Impressionism
5	Egyptian Mummies			**34**	19th-C French & English
6	Graphics	**20**	Amer Folk Painting	**35**	Post-Impressionism
7	Musical Instruments	**21**	19th-C Landscape	**36**	Coolidge Collection
		22	American Modern	**37**	18th-C Italian
8	Nubian Art	**23**	American Masters	**38**	Dutch & Flemish Art
9	Etruscan Art	**24**	Early 20th-C		
10	Greek Art	**25**	Am. Impressionism	**39**	Renaissance
11	Near-Eastern Art	**26**	20th-C American & European	**40**	Spanish Chapel
12	18th-C Amer Furn			**41**	Baroque Art
13	18th-C French Art	**27**	Chinese Art	**42**	Himalayan Art
14	18th-C Boston	**28**	Bernat Galleries	**43**	Tapestries
15	English Silver	**29**	Egyptian Art	**44**	Special Exhibitions
		30	Roman Art		

representing the 6th, 5th, and 4th centuries BC, as well as the early Roman Imperial period; collections covering the entire range of Egyptian art; plus an important permanent collection of paintings and sculpture by artists who have emerged since the early 1900s. Fifteen galleries contain the MFA's recently rehung and reorganized European painting and sculpture collection, dating from the 11th to the 20th centuries.

In addition, there is a trove of prints dating from the 15th century—particularly those by Dürer and Goya—that is considered one of the largest and finest in the world. The museum contains an excellent textile and costume department, reflecting Eastern and Western cultures, plus a priceless collection of historical musical instruments. And if that weren't enough, the West Wing, a modern addition designed by I. M. Pei, features changing exhibitions and blockbusters such as "Picasso: the Early Years," on view in early 1998. Just outside the museum is the Tenshin-En, or Japanese Garden, the "garden of the heart of heaven," which allows visitors to experience landscape as a work of art. In short, there's more here than you could hope to take in in a month, let alone a day—and that's not even counting the well-stocked gift shop. Fortunately, you'll also find a good restaurant, a cafeteria, and a gallery café serving light snacks. In Fraser Court—a charming oasis of green trees and statuary—beverages are served on the terrace from April to October. From October to April, a "Ladies Tea" is served from 2:30 to 4:30 inside near the main entrance. One-hour tours are offered Monday to Friday. Memberships are available. The museum also offers art classes and special art activities for children. "The Children's Room" is a drop-in workshop for kids age 6 to 12; it is held year-round, call for schedule. A parking garage is on Museum Road across from the West Wing entrance. *465 Huntington Ave., 617/267–9300. $10 adults, $8 senior citizens, 17 and under free; admission reduced by $2 Thurs. and Fri. after 4, voluntary admission Wed. 4–9:45. No admission fee for those visiting only museum shop, restaurants, or auditorium. Entire museum Mon.–Sun. 10–5, Wed. 10–10; West Wing also Thurs. and Fri. 10–10 with admission reduced by $2. 1-hr tours weekdays. T stop: Museum.*

7 *b-1*

PEABODY MUSEUM OF ARCHAEOLOGY & ETHNOLOGY

Pre-Columbian, American Indian, and Central and South American artifacts are arranged in ways that will delight and educate young minds. Plus there's an interesting museum shop. *11 Divinity Ave., Cambridge, 617/495–2248. $5 adults, $4 senior citizens, students, $3 children 3–13. Free Sat. 9–noon. Group rates available for tours, call in advance. Admission also covers Botanical Museum, Mineralogical and Geological Museum, and Museum of Comparative Zoology. Mon.–Sat. 9–5, Sun. 1–5. T stop: Harvard Sq.*

7 *b-2*

ARTHUR M. SACKLER MUSEUM

Founded in 1985, the Sackler is the newest of Harvard's art museums. The building itself is controversial (*see* Modern Architecture, *below*) but not so the excellent collections. The top three floors house the permanent collections of ancient, Asian, and Islamic works, installed on a rotating basis to allow for more displays of art. The outstanding holdings include one of the world's finest collections of ancient Chinese jades and Chinese cave reliefs, fine collections of Chinese bronzes, Greek vases and Roman sculpture, a large group of Japanese woodblock prints, and a small but exemplary group of Persian miniature paintings and calligraphy. A ground-floor space has changing exhibits. Tours are offered Monday to Friday at noon, from September to mid-June; and on Wednesdays at noon, from mid-June to September. To arrange group tours, call 617/496–8576. Note: One ticket admits visitors to all three Harvard University art museums. *Harvard University, 485 Broadway, Cambridge, 617/495–9400. $5 adults, $4 senior citizens, $3 students, 18 and under free, free to all Sat. 10–noon. Mon.–Sat. 10–5, Sun. 1–5. T stop: Harvard Sq.*

8 *d-3*

WIGGIN GALLERY

Part of the Boston Public Library, the Wiggin Gallery offers changing exhibitions from the very extensive library collections of 19th- and 20th-century American, French, and English prints, drawings, and watercolors, and from a century's worth of international photography. Just off the gallery are a series of dioramas showing artists at work through the ages. *Boston Public Library, Copley Sq., 3rd floor, 617/536–5400. T stop: Copley.*

BRIDGES

6 *e-1*

CHARLESTOWN BRIDGE

This bridge takes North Washington Street across the Charles River just where the river meets the harbor. *N. Washington St.*

6 *a-6*

ARTHUR FIEDLER BRIDGE

This bridge connects Beacon Street with the park at the Charles River where Hatch Memorial Shell is situated, and is named for the beloved late conductor of the Boston Pops concerts. A layered aluminum bust of Fielder by Ralph Helmick, installed in 1984, overlooks the Esplanade near the foot of the bridge. *Across Storrow Dr.*

3 *f-8*

HARVARD BRIDGE

Contrary to its name, this bridge will lead you directly to . . . MIT. Notice the designation of "Smoots," a reference to a long-lived college prank (in which students reportedly used a classmate, named Smoot, to measure the bridge by turning him, end over end, across the bridge!). *Massachusetts Ave. at Charles River.*

6 *a-4*

LONGFELLOW BRIDGE

(Edward March Wheelwright, 1900–07.) Dubbed the "Salt and Pepper Bridge" because of the shape of the pillars, this bridge connects Boston peninsula to the mainland. When built, it was dubbed the "New Cambridge Bridge." In 1927, however, the official name became Longfellow Bridge, to honor the poet whose poem, "The Bridge," describes this point. The figures on the pillars commemorate an alleged Viking landing on the banks of the Charles. *Across Charles from western end of Cambridge St. to Cambridge.*

3 *b-5*

WEEKS MEMORIAL BRIDGE

A graceful footbridge that was built to join the Cambridge Harvard campus to the new Graduate School of Business Administration on the Boston side of the Charles. This is a good spot to watch the Harvard crew team practice on the river. *DeWolfe St., Cambridge.*

CHURCHES & HOUSES OF WORSHIP

6 *c-4*

AFRICAN MEETINGHOUSE

Built in 1806 by black laborers to house the First African Baptist Congregation, this is the oldest African-American church building still standing in the country. It was a school for black children until 1834 and a place of worship until 1904 (see Abiel Smith School *in* Historic Buildings & Areas, *below*), and, most importantly, a meeting place for political and antislavery activists. It was often called the "Black Faneuil Hall" or the "Abolition Church." William Lloyd Garrison's New England Anti-Slavery Society was founded here January 6, 1832. When the city's black community began its migration to South Boston and Roxbury, the building became a synagogue. It is now under the auspices of the Museum of Afro-American History and has been restored to its mid-1850s appearance. A major renovation is in the wind, however: a 19th-century school room is now being recreated and exhibits added with the aim of showcasing the quest for equal education in Boston. These additions and restorations will mean the meetinghouse will be closed to the public until at least 1999. On the Black Heritage Trail. *8 Smith Ct., at Joy St., Beacon Hill. Closed for renovation until 1999. T stop: Charles/MGH, Bowdoin.*

B *7-2*

ARLINGTON STREET CHURCH (UNITARIAN UNIVERSALIST)

(Arthur Gilman, 1861.) Tiffany stained-glass memorial windows enhance the impressive edifice, whose exterior was inspired by London's St. Martin-in-the-Fields. The Georgian brownstone church was the first built in the Back Bay, with its congregation established in 1729. It's a bit of an engineering marvel, as it is supported by 999 wooden piles driven into the landfill. *355 Boylston St., at Arlington St., Back Bay, 617/536–7050. Weekdays 10–5. Sun. service at 11. T stop: Arlington.*

B f-6

CATHEDRAL OF
THE HOLY CROSS

(Patrick Keely, 1873.) This enormous Gothic cathedral dominates the corner of Washington Street and Monsignor Reynolds Way. It is the premier church of the Archdiocese of Boston, New England's largest Catholic church edifice, and the episcopal seat of Bernard Cardinal Law. *Washington St., South End, 617/542–5682. Mass weekdays at 9 AM, Sun. at 8 AM and 9:30 AM; in Spanish Sun. at 11 AM and Tues.–Thurs. at 7 AM. T stop: Chinatown; then Bus 49 to Cathedral.*

6 b-5

CHARLES STREET
MEETINGHOUSE

(Asher Benjamin, 1807.) This brick, Federal-style church was built for a white Baptist congregation and, like most New England churches, was segregated during its earliest period. Its original location beside the Charles River allowed for immersion baptism, but in 1920 the widening of Charles Street (to accommodate the new automobiles) necessitated moving the entire church building back 10 feet. In 1876 the church was bought by the African Methodist Episcopal Church, which remained here until 1939. It was the last black institution to leave Beacon Hill (the north slope of which was originally a black neighborhood). After years of use for community activities, it was bought by an architect for use as an office and retail space. On the Black Heritage Trail. *Mount Vernon and Charles Sts., Beacon Hill. T stop: Charles/MGH.*

3 b-3

CHRIST CHURCH
(EPISCOPAL)

(Peter Harrison, 1761. Restoration: Isaiah Rogers, 1825.) By the architect of King's Chapel, this is Cambridge's oldest church and one of the three remaining Anglican churches in Boston. After its fearful (justifiably) Loyalist congregation fled in 1774, the church was used as a barracks. George and Martha Washington worshipped here New Year's Eve 1775, in the midst of what was then a shambles. Today it has been beautifully and faithfully restored. *Zero Garden St., Cambridge, 617/876–0200. Weekdays 7:30–6. Services July–Aug., Sun. at 8 and 10; Sept.–June, Sun. at 8, 10, and 12:30; Year-round, Wed. at 12:10. T stop: Harvard Sq.*

B e-2

CHURCH OF THE COVENANT
(PRESBYTERIAN/
CONGREGATIONAL)

(Richard M. Upjohn, 1866.) Originally the Central Congregational Church, this Gothic Revival structure was designed by the son of the architect of New York's famed Trinity Church. Its exquisite Tiffany stained-glass windows (added 1893 to 1914) are complemented by its nearly 240-foot-tall steeple. Since 1977 the church chapel has also housed the Gallery NAGA, which shows painting, sculpture, and photography. (*See* Galleries, *below.*) *67 Newbury St. at Berkeley St., Back Bay, 617/266–7480. Tues.–Fri. 9 AM–noon. Sun. service at 10. T stop: Arlington.*

6 d-4

CHURCH OF ST. JOHN THE
EVANGELIST (EPISCOPAL)

(Attributed to Solomon Willard, 1831.) A rough-stone Gothic church, it is thought to have been designed by the man who embellished the work of Bulfinch and Parris. The church was built by the congregation of the Rev. Lyman Beecher, father of Harriet Beecher Stowe. Stained-glass windows in the new vestibule are by Gyorgy Kepes. *33 Bowdoin St., West End, 617/227–5242. Sun. service at 10:30. T stop: Bowdoin.*

B f-2

EMMANUEL CHURCH OF
BOSTON (EPISCOPAL)

(A. R. Estey, 1861.) Since the 1970s, this Back Bay brownstone Gothic church has focused on "a special ministry through art," featuring festivals, concerts, jazz events, and the Ninots Puppet Theater. The church is also home of the Emmanuel Movement, a pioneer in holistic health. Every Sunday from September to May, a Bach cantata is included as part of the liturgy. Within the church is the Leslie Lindsey Chapel—a Gothic-style memorial created in 1924 in memory of a young bride who perished with her husband on the *Lusitania*. It was said that the young girl's body washed ashore in Ireland, still bedecked with her family's wedding gift of rubies and diamonds, then sold by the parents to fund this chapel. *15 Newbury St., Back Bay, 617/536–3355. Mon.–Thurs. 9–5 by appointment only. Sun. service at 11. T stop: Arlington.*

8 *e-2*

FIRST BAPTIST CHURCH (AMERICAN BAPTIST)

(H. H. Richardson, 1871.) This congregation commissioned Richardson's first Boston church, to be followed by his masterpiece, Trinity. The tower's frieze and angels are rich embellishments befitting a Victorian-era ecclesiastical edifice. They are by Frédéric-Auguste Bartholdi (who would later create the *Statue of Liberty*). At the corners, the trumpeting angels have led people to irreverently dub this the Church of the Holy Beanblowers. Free guided tours available. *110 Commonwealth Ave. and Clarendon St., Back Bay, 617/267–3148. Weekdays 10–4. Sun. service at 11. T stop: Copley.*

8 *b-5*

FIRST CHURCH OF CHRIST, SCIENTIST

(Franklin I. Welch, 1894. Extension: Charles E. Brigham and Solon Beman, 1904.) The first permanent Christian Science church, this massive edifice was built by founder Mary Baker Eddy, who called the original rough-granite Romanesque edifice "our prayer in stone." In the Byzantine extension the central dome's cupola soars 224 feet above the plaza. It contains one of the largest organs in the world—13,389 pipes. *Massachusetts and Huntington Aves., 617/450–2000. Mother church, Mon.–Sat. 10–4, Sun. 11:15–2; free 30-min tour. On Mon. original edifice only open for tours. T stop: Hynes Convention Center/ICA.*

8 *e-2*

FIRST LUTHERAN CHURCH

(Pietro Belluschi, 1957.) This contemporary redbrick church in the Back Bay takes its inspiration from the past seriously but has a charming lightness of spirit, which is keynoted by a pretty courtyard. *299 Berkeley St., Back Bay, 617/536–8851. Weekdays 9:30–3:30. Sun. services at 8:30 and 11, additional 10 AM service in summer. T stop: Arlington.*

7 *a-2*

FIRST PARISH CHURCH (UNITARIAN UNIVERSALIST)

(Isaiah Rogers, 1833.) This wooden Gothic Revival church was built with funds partially contributed by Harvard College (to ensure pews would be available for students' use). The Old Burying Ground is next door (*see* Graveyards,

below). Today, the church provides space to the Nameless Coffeehouse, one of New England's oldest, donation-run, coffeehouses. *3 Church St., at Massachusetts Ave., Harvard Sq., Cambridge, 617/876–7772. Weekdays 8–4. Sun. service at 10:30. T stop: Harvard Sq.*

8 *e-2*

FIRST & SECOND CHURCH OF BOSTON (UNITARIAN)

(Ware and Van Brunt, 1867. Replacement: Paul Rudolph, 1968.) The actual edifice is new, but this church's historic origins are very old, as this was the fifth meetinghouse of Boston's first Puritan congregation, incorporated in 1630. When its 1867 English Gothic edifice was ravaged by fire in 1968, all that remained was the spire and the frame of a rose window—both were incorporated into the imaginative modern design of the new church built on the site. The auditorium, where musical and theatrical performances as well as art exhibits take place from time to time, is shared with Emerson College. *66 Marlborough at Berkeley Sts., Back Bay, 617/267–6730. Summer, weekdays 10–3; winter, weekdays 9–5. Sun. service at 11. T stops: Copley, Arlington.*

6 *e-5*

KING'S CHAPEL

(Peter Harrison, 1749–54.) This prerevolutionary church was the first Anglican church in Boston and the official seat of the Church of England, much favored by the Crown. It was established, therefore, much against the wishes of the Puritans, who had left England to escape the Church of England's influence. Indeed, the first wooden chapel was located on a corner of the adjacent burying ground, as no Puritan would sell land to the Anglicans. The current structure was created by applying rough-dressed granite around the original, so as not to interrupt services. Unfortunately, a stone spire was never built—but a grace note was provided by the addition of a portico with magisterial Ionic columns, designed by Bulfinch. The whitewashed interior is a masterpiece of Georgian calm and elegance: note the high-backed box pews (No. 102 belonged to Oliver Wendell Holmes), while the raised pulpit is the oldest one in use on the same site in this country. As a royalist church, King's Chapel received gifts—the silver communion plate as well as the ceremonial vestments—from no less than King George III and Queen Anne. Offering a not-so-subtle counterpoint, the largest bell of the church was fashioned by one of Boston's leading antiroyalists, the noted silversmith and patriot Paul Revere ("the sweetest bell we ever made," he claimed). In 1787, King's Chapel became America's first Unitarian Church. There is a noon musical recital year-round every Tuesday from 12:15 to 1 PM and a poetry reading in "the King's English" every Thursday. Now a National Historic Landmark. (See Graveyards, below.) On the Freedom Trail. *58 Tremont St., at School St. 617/227–2155 or 617/523–1749. Donations appreciated. June–Labor Day, Fri.–Sat. and Mon. 9:30–4, Tues.–Wed. 9:30–11 AM, Sun. 1–3; Labor Day–mid-Nov., Fri.–Sat. and Mon. 10–2; mid-Nov.–mid-Apr., Sat. 10–2; mid-Apr.–May, Fri.–Sat. and Mon., 10–2. Sun. service year-round 11; Wed. service year-round 12:15. T stop: Park St.*

8 *d-3*

NEW OLD SOUTH CHURCH (UNITED CHURCH OF CHRIST)

(Cummings and Sears, 1874.) Only in Boston could something termed new have been built in 1874! The original Congregational church was founded in 1669, and included parishioners Benjamin Franklin, Samuel Adams, and William Dawes. This is its third home, the second having been the famed Old South Meetinghouse in the North End (*see below*). The church became part of the United Church of Christ denomination about 20 years ago. *645 Boylston St., at Dartmouth St., 617/536–1970. Weekdays 8:30–6, Sat. 9–4. Sun. service at 11. T stop: Copley.*

9 *d-3*

OLD NORTH CHURCH (CHRIST CHURCH) (EPISCOPAL)

(Attributed to William Price, 1723.) On the night of April 8, 1775, this church entered the annals of American folklore when sexton Robert Newman used lanterns from its steeple to signal to Paul Revere that the British were about to attack Boston. "One if by land, and two if by sea; And I on the opposite shore will be; Ready to ride and spread the alarm through every Middlesex village and farm"—thanks to these words from Henry Wadsworth Longfellow's poem, "Paul Revere's Ride," the noted patriot became a hero to countless school chil-

dren. Today, Revere's legend endures, and every April 18, descendants of the patriots raise lanterns in the church belfry in a traditional reenactment. The Wren-inspired edifice housed the city's second Anglican congregation. Formally known as Christ Church, it's the oldest church standing in the city of Boston. The original steeple, added in 1740, was lost during a hurricane in 1804; its replacement suffered a similar fate in 1954. The present one is topped, however, with the original 1740 weather vane.

The interior is graced with two brass English chandeliers, first lit Christmas Day 1724. The high box pews still have brass plates indicating the names of the original owners, and the Johnson organ, dating from 1759, still functions. Beneath the church are crypts holding the remains of 1,100 members of the original congregation. Restored to its original character and rededicated December 29, 1912, the church is now a National Historic Landmark. There is a small gift shop and museum with revolutionary artifacts and modern reproductions for sale. Behind the church is the quaint Washington Memorial Garden, its walls studded with several unusual commemorative plaques—including one for the Rev. George Burrough, who was hanged in the Salem Witch Trials in 1692. Robert Newman, who carried the famous pair of lanterns to the steeple, was his great-grandson. Tours (groups by appointment) last about 20 minutes and include a short history of the church. On the Freedom Trail. *193 Salem St., between Charter and Hull Sts., 617/523–6676. Daily 9–5. Sun. services at 9, 11, and 4. Free (donations appreciated). T stops: Haymarket and North Station.*

6 *e-5*

OLD SOUTH MEETINGHOUSE

(Robert Twelve, 1729.) After a lengthy renovation—its first in 100 years—the Old South Meetinghouse reopened in fall of 1997. Old South has long been Boston's premier symbol of both spiritual quest and spirited debate. One of Boston's three remaining 18th-century Anglican houses of worship, it was erected to replace an earlier cedar meetinghouse that was built in 1699 and housed the Third Church of Boston. Reminiscent of Christopher Wren's London churches, the structure also served as a meetinghouse where issues of the day were discussed. Grand in size, it could hold more people than Faneuil Hall. More than 5,000 people, in fact, jammed into Old South on December 16, 1773, for that famed meeting held to protest the tea tax that became the overture to the notorious Boston Tea Party. It was from Old South that the colonial "Indians" set out for Griffin's Wharf via Milk Street. In 1775, in punishment no doubt, General Burgoyne turned the interior of Old South into a riding academy for British cavalry and the pews and pulpit into kindling. It was lovingly restored as a place of worship after the Revolution. Exhibitions depict colonial and revolutionary Boston. Today the meetinghouse has permanent and revolving exhibitions, concerts, and lectures, and tours are held by special arrangement. Now a National Historic Landmark, Old South is part of the Boston National Historic Park. On-site is a small gift shop. *310 Washington, Downtown, 617/482–6439. $3 adults, $2.50 senior citizens, students, $1 children. Daily 9:30–5. T stop: State St. or Downtown Crossing.*

6 *d-4*

OLD WEST CHURCH (UNITED METHODIST)

(Asher Benjamin, 1806.) This imposing structure harks back to the days when the West End was a fashionable Boston address. It was built on the site of a meetinghouse/church building constructed in 1737. In 1776 the British tore down its steeple to prevent it from being used as a signal tower (à la Old North), and the interior was converted to a barracks. The present impressive Federal-style building lost its congregation when, at the end of the 19th century, this was no longer considered a desirable residential area. From 1894 to 1958 it was the West End Branch of the Public Library, which was used as a polling place on election day—John F. Kennedy voted here in 1960. Since 1964 it is once again a place of worship. Concerts are occasionally offered, utilizing the church's fine Charles Fisk organ. *131 Cambridge St., at Stanford St., 617/227–5088. Usually open weekdays 9–5 but call*

DECONSTRUCTING HENRY

Henry Hobson Richardson was Boston's most soigné, amazing, and prestigious architect of the Gilded Age period. His spectacular Neo-Romanesque structures mixed together the look of "muscular Christianity" (from England), the style of the Romanesque Auvergne (from France), cruciform floor plans and folkloric trim (from Byzantium), and the self-righteousness of the very, very best Brahmins (from Boston). Take a tour of his finest Boston buildings and discover five jewels in Boston's architectural crown.

Trinity Church (Copley Square)
The architectural showpiece of Boston, this is a breathtaking extravaganza of Richardsonian Romanesque—Byzantine gold, red sandstone, and La Farge's stained glass all contribute to the riveting interior, shaped almost like a railroad station (and Richardson designed those, too), but custom-tailored for the original rector, Reverend Phillips Brooks, that ultimate Boston Brahmin and author of "O Little Town of Bethlelem."

Trinity Church Rectory (233 Clarendon St.)
Several blocks from its parent Trinity Church, this has a show-stopping Romanesque arch entryway. Here Richardson's vigorous use of ornament and terra-cotta trim is magnificently apparent.

Sever Hall (Harvard Yard)
Sunlight plays over the rough-hewn surfaces and sculpted volumes of this building's impressive facade. Clearly, one of the greatest buildings of America's Romanesque Revival.

Stone Bridge (Boylston St. Entrance)
A delightful ornament to the Back Bay Fens, this is a brutish yet romantically evocative bridge—a perfect complement to the F. L. Olmsted–designed park.

First Baptist Church (110 Commonwealth Ave.)
Known as the "Church of the Holy Bean Blowers"—look up at the figures on the soaring campanile—this was Richardson's first essay in Romanesque Revival. Those "bean blowers" were actually sculpted by Bartholdi, who also did the Statue of Liberty.

to confirm. Sun. service at 11. T stops: Bowdoin, Charles/MGH.

6 d-5

PARK STREET CHURCH

(Peter Banner, 1809.) Henry James called this early 19th-century church "the most impressive mass of brick and mortar in America." The church is also a fairly historic mass, too—William Lloyd Garrison delivered his first antislavery speech here on July 4, 1829, and on July 4, 1831, the stirring anthem "America" ("My Country Tis of Thee") was first performed in public. Built on the site of the town granary, the brick church is a highly elegant illustration of Federal-era church architecture. The square brick tower is crowned by a four-stage wooden tower and its spire—clearly, one of the most beautiful in all New England—rises to a breathtaking 217 feet. Whether the site where Park Street Church was dubbed "Brimstone Corner" because brimstone (used to make gunpowder during the War of 1812) was stored in the church's basement or because the sermons preached here were of a particularly fiery nature, it's still a colorful nickname for so stately a church. Group tours by appointment. On the Freedom Trail. 1 Park St., at Tremont St., 617/523–3383. Late June–Aug., Tues.–Sat. 9:30–3:30; rest of year by appointment only. Sun. services at 9 AM, 10:45 AM, and 6:30 PM. Free (donations appreciated). T stop: Park St.

6 d-5

ST. PAUL'S CATHEDRAL (EPISCOPAL)

(Alexander Parris and Solomon Willard, 1820.) When built, this church was something new for Boston—a post-Revolution Episcopal church in a Greek-style temple edifice. The fine granite Greek Revival church with sandstone columns has an interior that is more welcoming than the rather stark exterior (left unadorned due to lack of funds). Both Daniel Webster and Dr. John C. Warren, pioneer in the use of ether, were parishioners. When built, this was an uptown church in a neighborhood of fine homes—now it's a downtown church amid businesses and shopping establishments. 138 Tremont St., across from Boston Common, 617/482–5800. Weekdays noon–6. Sun. services at 8 and 11; daily services at 12:10

and 5:15; Holy Eucharist in Chinese at 12:30. Luncheon concerts Thurs. at 12:45. T stop: Haymarket.

9 f-4

ST. STEPHEN'S ROMAN CATHOLIC CHURCH

(Charles Bulfinch, 1804. Restoration: Chester Wright, 1965.) This is the only Charles Bulfinch–designed church that survives in Boston. Centuries old, the church still thrives in its currently Italian enclave. Rose Kennedy, matriarch of the Kennedy clan, was christened here; 104 years later, it held mourners at her funeral. St. Stephen's was originally built for a congregation founded in 1714 by a group of artisans who had been worshiping in an old brick meetinghouse. Their new church was surmounted by an impressive clocktower and a belfry that housed a bell from Paul Revere's foundry. Unitarian from 1813 to 1849, the church became Roman Catholic in 1862 when its original congregation began moving to more fashionable outposts in the city, abandoning the North Side to incoming Irish. In 1965 the church was restored under the aegis of the late Richard Cardinal Cushing. On the Freedom Trail. 401 Hanover St., at Charles St., 617/523–1230. Daily 8:30–5. Sun. services at 8:30 and 11. T stops: Haymarket, Aquarium.

8 e-3

TRINITY CHURCH (EPISCOPAL)

(Henry Hobson Richardson, 1877. Porch: Shepley, Rutan, and Coolidge, 1897.) Romanesque triumphant, this famous house of worship is considered the best work by Richardson, the architect who uniquely transformed the Romanesque style into an American idiom, becoming, in the process, one of America's most famous architects. Notice the richly carved exterior and lavishly decorated interior with paintings by John La Farge. The stained-glass windows are gems, designed no less by La Farge, William Morris, and Sir Edward Burne-Jones. In the cloister, there is a window of carved stone from St. Botolph's Church, Lincolnshire, England. As the Back Bay is composed completely of landfill, the church is also triumphant from a technological standpoint—more than 4,500 wooden piles support the foundations. There are free tours by appointment, as well as free

organ recitals Friday at 12:15 PM. *206
Clarendon St., Copley Sq., Back Bay, 617/
536–0944. Mon.–Sat. 8–6, Sun. 8–7:30.
Sun. services at 8, 9, 11, and 6. Donations
accepted. T stop: Copley.*

8 *e-3*

TRINITY CHURCH RECTORY

(H. H. Richardson, 1879.) Although
characteristic of his massive style, this
ivy-covered building by Richardson was
considerably altered (a third floor was
added) after his death in 1893. On the
National Register of Historic Places.
(*See* Trinity Church, *above.*) *223 Clarendon St., at Newbury St. T stop: Copley.*

8 *d-5*

UNION UNITED
METHODIST CHURCH

(A. R. Estey, 1877.) A lovely country-style
parish church in the South End, the
Union United Methodist Church was
designed by the same architect who did
Emmanuel Episcopal Church. The congregation was established in 1818. In
1950 the NAACP held their convention
here—the last to be held in a church
building. *485 Columbus Ave., South End,
617/536–0872. Weekdays 9:30–4:30. Sun.
service at 10:45. T stop: Prudential on
Green Line (Arborway).*

6 *c-4*

VILNA SHUL

Completed in 1920 by Jews from Vilna
(in what is now Lithuania), the two-story
Vilna Shul is a historical gem now
undergoing the intriguing, often-frus-
trating process of restoration. Sadly, of
the more than 50 synagogues that once
dotted Beacon Hill, it's the last intact
example. The distinctive, L-shaped second floor sanctuary has separate seating
for men and women, in keeping with
Orthodox tradition. Skylights flood the
space with natural light, while Stars of
David are seen in the upstairs window
and worked into the iron grillwork of the
fence. The building, abandoned in 1985,
was bought by the Vilna Center for Jewish Heritage in 1995. Restorers are now
puzzling over the unusual designs on
the wall and peeling through the layers
of paint and history, to determine the
delicate path of conservation. *14–18
Phillips St., Beacon Hill, 617/523–2324.
Apr.–Nov., Sun. 1–5. Donations welcome.
T stop: Charles/MGH.*

GALLERIES

Boston's reputation as an educational
center also extends to the visual arts, a
fact that helps to account for a healthy
local output of paintings, sculpture,
photography, and crafts. Numerous galleries display and sell the work of
Boston-area, as well as national-level,
artists. You can find the latest multi-
media piece or purchase a 19th-century
Tarbell oil—such venerable treasures
often surface from private collections in
estate sales—and there is no shortage
of them in a town famous for old
money. The main concentration of galleries in Boston is found on Newbury
Street. There has also been a recent pro-
liferation of alternate-space galleries,
akin to the type often found in New
York's SoHo, in East Cambridge, the
South End, and the Fort Point Channel
Area. Note: The "art scene" slows down
considerably during the summer; gallery
hours and weeks may be shorter. In general, call for summer hours.

fine art

8 *e-3*

ALPHA GALLERY

Specializing in 20th-century American
and European painting, sculpture, and
works on paper, Alpha also stocks master prints from the late 19th century to
the present. *121 Newbury St., Back Bay,
617/536–4465. T stop: Copley.*

8 *d-3*

ARDEN GALLERY

Featuring a group of nationally exhibited
and collected national and area artists,
Arden concentrates on abstractionists,
pattern painters, and contemporary real-
ists. *129 Newbury St., 617/247–0610. T
stop: Copley.*

8 *f-7*

BROMFIELD GALLERY

This artist-run gallery shows contemporary art in all media by New England
artists, with shows changing monthly.
*560 Harrison Ave., South End, 617/451–
3605. Closed Sun. and Mon. T stop: N.E.
Medical Center.*

8 *d-3*

CHASE GALLERY

Contemporary representational artists
from New England and New York are

the forte here, with original paintings, sculpture, and studio furniture regularly exhibited. *129 Newbury St., 617/ 859–7222. Closed Sun. and Mon. T stop: Copley.*

8 *d-3*

CHILDS GALLERY

Whistler, Benson, and Woodbury are some of the name spotlighted here. The extensive stocks encompasses sixteenth- to early 20th-century American and European prints, paintings, drawings, watercolors, and sculpture. *169 Newbury St., 617/266–1108. Closed Sun. T stop: Copley.*

8 *d-3*

COPLEY SOCIETY OF BOSTON

Founded in 1879, this is the oldest art association in America. The nonprofit membership organization seeks to make the arts more visible, accessible, and understandable. Exhibitions are devoted to noted artists as well as aspiring talent, mainly from the New England area. *158 Newbury St., Back Bay, 617/536–5049. Closed Sun. and Mon. T stop: Copley.*

6 *f-7*

MARIO DIACONO GALLERY

Contemporary painting with a strong conceptual bent is the lure here. *207 South St., 617/350–3054. Closed Sun. and Mon. T stop: Downtown Crossing.*

6 *e-8*

DYANSEN GALLERY

Paintings, drawings, and original lithographs are shown, with frequent exhibits by celebrity painters. You can expect a hard sell. *132A Newbury St., Back Bay, 617/262–4800, 800/936–6901. Closed Mon. T stop: Copley.*

6 *f-7*

FEDERAL RESERVE BANK OF BOSTON

This features exhibitions every two months of works by New England artists, including paintings, prints, sculpture, photography, and crafts. There is also a selection of fine art dispersed throughout the building. *600 Atlantic Ave., 617/973–3453. Closed weekends. Tour Fri. 10:30.*

8 *f-3*

FIRST EXPRESSIONS

This nonprofit gallery features the work of art students who make up with enthusiasm and unencumbered creativity for what they lack in sophistication and technique. A place to catch *really* emerging talent. *81 Arlington St., Back Bay, 617/695–2808. Closed Sun. and Mon. T stop: Arlington.*

8 *c-7*

GALLERY AT THE PIANO FACTORY

Multi-media exhibitions in a small, lower-level gallery space, of the work of the artist-residents of this converted commercial building (*see* Piano Craft Guild *in* Historic Buildings & Areas, *below*). Mainly paintings and sculpture; some graphics, photography, and crafts. Call for current show; each artist is responsible for setting her/his gallery schedule. *791 Tremont St., South End, 617/437–9365. Hours vary.*

7 *e-5*

GALLERY 57, CAMBRIDGE ARTS COUNCIL

Contemporary paintings, prints, collages, and sculptures draw Cantabrigians. *City Hall Annex, 57 Inman St., Cambridge, 617/349–4380. Closed weekends. T stop: Central Sq.*

8 *e-2*

GALLERY NAGA

Boston-area artists are done proud at this gallery, which features regional painting, sculpture, prints, and artist's furniture. *67 Newbury St., Back Bay, 617/ 267–9060. T stop: Arlington.*

8 *h-6*

GENOVESE/SULLIVAN GALLERY

With a range of contemporary sculpture, paintings, and prints, this place also has an emphasis on installations. *47 Thayer St., Downtown, 617/426–9738. Closed Sun. T stop: N.E. Medical Center.*

8 *d-3*

GUILD OF BOSTON ARTISTS

Regionally focused, the Guild is a nonprofit gallery for representational watercolors, oils, graphics, and sculptures done by guild members. *162 Newbury*

St., Back Bay, 617/536–7660. Closed Sun.
and Mon.

8 *d-3*

HALEY & STEELE

This remains a leading resource for fine
19th-century British historical, sporting,
marine, architectural, and botanical
prints. 91 Newbury St., Back Bay, 617/
536–6339. Closed Sun. and Mon. T stop:
Arlington.

6 *c-8*

HARCUS GALLERY

Harcus has a regional spotlight, often
beamed on modern and contemporary
painting, sculpture, and graphics by
Boston-area artists. In addition, stock
also includes work by major artists. 6
Melrose St., 617/451-3221. Closed Sun. and
Mon. T stop: Boylston.

7 *c-4*

HURST GALLERY

The range is wide here—from African,
Asian, and Native American art and arti-
facts, both ancient and modern, through
pre-Colombian arts. 53 Mount Auburn
St., Cambridge, 617/491–6888. Closed
Sun. and Mon. T stop: Harvard Sq.

8 *b-4*

KAJI ASO STUDIO, GALLERY NATURE & TEMPTATION

Ten exhibits a year range from multi-
media groups to one-person shows and
usually feature work by students and
members of the Studio and cross-cul-
tural exchange artists from Japan. 40 St.
Stephen St., Back Bay, 617/247–1719.
Closed Sun. and Mon. T stop: Arlington.

6 *e-7*

KINGSTON GALLERY

Alternative art space open to all contemporary art forms takes top billing here,
with avant-garde paintings, drawings,
sculpture. 129 Kingston St., Downtown,
617/423–4113. Closed Sun.–Tues. T stop:
Downtown Crossing.

8 *f-2*

BARBARA KRAKOW GALLERY

One of Boston's most respected contemporary galleries, Krakow is noted for
its American and European paintings,
sculpture, drawings, and prints by
emerging and established artists. 10

Newbury St., Back Bay, 617/262–4490.
Closed Sun. and Mon. T stop: Arlington.

3 *a-4*

LOWELL GALLERY, CAMBRIDGE ART ASSOCIATION

This gallery shows works in all media by
members, with a full schedule of temporary shows. 25R Lowell St., 617/876–
0246. Closed Sun., Mon., and Aug. University Pl. Gallery, 124 Mt. Auburn St.,
Cambridge, 617/876–0246. Closed Sun. T
stop: Harvard Sq.

8 *f-2*

ANDREA MARQUIT FINE ARTS

This gallery specializes in contemporary
masters and emerging artists, and offers
consulting services to collectors and
corporations. Photography is offered in
addition to sculpture and painting. 38
Newbury St., 4th floor, Back Bay, 617/
859–0190. Closed Sun.–Tues. T stop:
Arlington.

8 *f-2*

MERCURY GALLERY

Here you'll find American paintings
from the 1930s to the present. 8 Newbury St., Back Bay, 617/859–0054. Closed
Sun. T stop: Arlington.

8 *f-5*

MILLS GALLERY

As part of the Boston Center for the
Arts, this gallery features contemporary
work, often in very mixed media, of
emerging and established artists. 549
Tremont St., South End, 617/426–8835.
Closed Mon. and Tues. T stop: NE Medical
Center.

8 *f-2*

NEWBURY FINE ARTS

Contemporary painting and prints are
on the menu here, with special emphasis on Pop Art. 29 Newbury St., Back
Bay, 617/536–0210. T stop: Arlington.

8 *d-3*

NIELSEN GALLERY

This 30-year-old gallery features contemporary paintings, drawings, and sculpture. 179 Newbury St., Back Bay, 617/
266–4835. Closed Sun. and Mon. T stop:
Copley.

8 *e-2*

PEPPER GALLERY

Established and emerging artists are showcased here, with offerings of contemporary representational paintings, prints, drawings, and photographs. *38 Newbury St., Back Bay, 617/236–4497. T stop: Arlington.*

8 *d-3*

PUCKER GALLERY

Contemporary American and European graphics, paintings, sculptures, and ceramics, along with Inuit and West and Southern African works, draw collectors here. *171 Newbury St., Back Bay, 617/ 267–9473. Closed Sun. T stop: Copley.*

8 *f-2*

RICHARDSON-CLARKE

Featuring some noted names, this gallery offers drawings and paintings from the 16th to the 20th centuries, both American and European. *38 Newbury St., 617/266– 3321. Closed Sun.–Tues. T stop: Arlington.*

8 *d-3*

ROLLY-MICHAUX

For the blue-chip collector, a leading resource for 20th-century paintings, silk screens, sculpture, and graphics by Moore, Calder, Picasso, Chagall, Miró, and Matisse. The gallery also offers 18th-century French antiques. *290 Dartmouth St., Back Bay, 617/536–9898. Closed Sun. and Mon. T stop: Copley.*

8 *d-3*

JUDI ROTENBURG GALLERY

Boston collectors come here for twentieth-century American painting and sculpture by Zygmund Jankowski, Oliver Balf, Roz Farbush, and Harold and Judi Rotenburg, among others. *130 Newbury St., Back Bay, 617/437–1518. Closed Sun. and Mon. T stop: Copley.*

9 *g-6*

JOHN STOBART GALLERY

This maritime-themed gallery offers paintings and original prints. *113 Lewis Wharf, 617/227–6868. Closed Sun. and Mon. T stop: Haymarket.*

8 *b-7*

HARRIET TUBMAN HOUSE, UNITED SOUTH END SETTLEMENTS

Year-round exhibits of local and Massachusetts artists are held here, with a concentration on the works of women and artists of color. There are also occasional shows of children's work. *566 Columbus Ave., 617/375–8132. Closed Sun.*

8 *c-3*

VOSE GALLERIES

Established in 1841, this is the oldest art gallery in America. It specializes in 19th- and 20th-century American art, including works from the Hudson River School and Boston School, and American Impressionists, such as Frank W. Benson, John Henry Twachtman, Theodore Robinson, and Childe Hassam. *238 Newbury St., Back Bay, 617/ 536–6176. Closed Sun. T stop: Copley.*

8 *f-2*

HOWARD YEZERSKI GALLERY

Cutting-edge exhibitions, including videos and installations, by some of the country's best-known contemporary and experimental painters, sculptors, and photographers draw the critics here. *11 Newbury St., Back Bay, 617/262–0550. Closed Sun. and Mon. T stop: Arlington.*

prints & photographs

8 *b-3*

JOHN CALLAHAN GALLERY

Along with prints, lithographs, silk screens, and etchings by international and regional contemporary artists, this place also provides framing services. *285 Newbury St., Back Bay, 617/859– 2825. Closed Sun. and Mon. T stop: Hynes Convention Center/ICA.*

8 *e-2*

ROBERT KLEIN GALLERY

If you want to add an Ansel Adams, Diane Arbus, Man Ray, Edward Weston, Paul Outerbridge, and Irving Penn to your collection, drop by. *38 Newbury St., Back Bay, 617/267–7997. T stop: Arlington.*

2 *a-4*

PHOTOGRAPHIC RESOURCE CENTER

This nonprofit photographic center has rotating exhibits every six to seven weeks; national, international, and regional in scope. The center offers a library of photography books and other information. *602 Commonwealth Ave., downstairs, enter on Blanford St., 617/*

353–0700. T stop: Blanford. $3 adults, $2 senior citizens, students; free Thurs.

crafts/art works

 8 *d-3*

ALIANZA

Stunning contemporary glassware, ceramics, jewelry, and woodworking objects in a storefront that begs you to browse. Annual shows include "Tea and Fantasy," with whimsical teapots, and "Clockworks," showcasing sculptural clocks. *154 Newbury St., Back Bay, 617/ 262–2385. T stop: Copley.*

8 *d-4*

ARTFUL HAND GALLERY

Featuring the work of American artisans, the gallery has decorative pottery, gold and silver jewelry, mixed media, and metalwork. Insured shipping is offered and the prices are on the high side. There's fine work mixed in with the trendy knickknacks, but the gallery does have frequent artist demonstrations and receptions. *Copley Pl., 100 Huntington Ave., Back Bay, 617/262–9601. T stop: Copley.*

7 *a-2*

CAMBRIDGE ARTISTS COOPERATIVE

This artist-owned and operated cooperative gallery has a wide mix of fine crafts and artwork by more than 200 artists. Especially noteworthy are the works in glass, the decorative pottery, and handmade silver jewelry. You'll also find silk scarves, other kinds of "wearable art," fiber art and ceramics. *59-A Church St., Harvard Sq., Cambridge, 617/868–4434. T stop: Harvard Sq.*

3 *f-5*

CLAYGROUND

Located between Kendall and Central squares, this two-decades-old shop, in a funky storefront Victorian, offers functional handmade pottery by local artists. *91 Hampshire St., Cambridge, 617/661– 7376. Nearest T stop: Central Sq.*

3 *a-2*

FRESH POND CLAY WORKS

This long-time studio features functional high-fire porcelain pottery—much of it made by the studio owners right in the back of the shop. Pretty work and very affordable. *368 Huron Ave., Cambridge, 617/492–1907. T stop: Porter Sq.*

3 *a-2*

MOBILIA

Contemporary American and European art and crafts in a variety of media: textiles, ceramics, wood and leather, and furniture with an emphasis on the avant-garde. There's art to wear and unique studio art jewelry. Exhibitions change monthly. *358 Huron Ave., Cambridge, 617/876–2109. Closed Sun. T stop: Porter Sq.*

6 *f-4*

SIGNATURE & GROHE GALLERY

American crafts gallery specializing in top-of-the-line ceramics, metal work, and jewelry, by such craftspeople as Josh Simpson (glass) and Judy Motzkin (ceramics). The Grohe Glass Gallery, in the back of the store, features the work of glass artists, focusing on one artist at a time. *24 North St., across from Faneuil Hall, 617/227–4885. T stop: Haymarket, Government Center.*

8 *d-3*

SOCIETY OF ARTS & CRAFTS

The country's oldest nonprofit crafts organization (established in 1897), represents more than 350 artists working in all media, experimental as well as tradiional. Its two well-stocked galleries include both retail and exhibition space, with about six curated shows presented annually. Items for sale include works in glass, fiber, and metal, plus furniture. *175 Newbury St., 1st and 2nd floors, Back Bay, 617/266–1810. T stop: Copley.*

6 *e-6*

SOCIETY OF ARTS & CRAFTS

This is another branch of the crafts organization. *101 Arch St. Downtown crossing, 617/345–0033. Closed weekends. T stop: Downtown Crossing.*

GRAVEYARDS

6 *d-6*

CENTRAL BURYING GROUND

Two acres purchased in 1756 became an addition to the Common and the burial place of, among many others, the great portrait painter Gilbert Stuart. Stones date back to 1755 and identify many Tea Party participants, Revolutionary War patriots, and members of old Boston families. Also buried here in unmarked graves are British soldiers killed in the Battle of Bunker Hill. *The Common, near Railroad Mall. T stop: Boylston.*

9 *C-2*

COPP'S HILL BURIAL GROUND

In 1659, when King's Chapel Burying Ground became too crowded, this cemetery was first established as the North Burying Ground. Many of Boston's Founding Fathers are buried here. Note the early fieldstone and slate markers, which vividly depict the Puritans' view of death via the symbols they used: hourglass, skull, cherubs. They make for an interesting if none-too-cheerful reverie. During the Revolution, the British cannonry fired on Bunker Hill from here and some tombstones sport pockmarks—the result of British target practice (see Daniel Malcolm's stone). The Snowhill side of the cemetery contains the remains of more than 1,000 slaves and freedmen including Prince Hall, founder of the Masonic African Lodge. Also interred here are Robert Newman, the sexton who hung the lanterns in the steeple of Old North; Increase, Cotton, and Samuel Mather, those noted fire-and-brimstone ministers; and Edmund Hartt, builder of the USS *Constitution*. On the Freedom Trail. *Bounded by Charter, Hull, and Snowhill Sts., North End. Daily sunrise–sunset. Free. T stop: North Station.*

6 *e-5*

KING'S CHAPEL BURYING GROUND

Some of Boston's most fabled figures are buried in this most historic of resting places, including John Winthrop and his family; William Dawes, Paul Revere's relatively unsung compatriot on the famous ride; and Elizabeth Pain, who bore a minister's child and is thought to be the inspiration for Hester Prynne in Hawthorne's *The Scarlet Letter*. Puritan Isaac Johnson was the first to be buried here in 1630, in what was his garden. Soon, records show, Brother Johnson's plot became "a poor place for vegetables"—people in Boston loved Brother Johnson so much they wanted to be buried near him. Consequently, it

became an official burial ground, now the oldest in Boston. *See also* King's Chapel *in* Churches & Houses of Worship, *above. Next to King's Chapel, Tremont, and School Sts. Daily sunrise–sunset. T stop: Park Street, Government Center.*

1 *C-2*

MOUNT AUBURN CEMETERY

Henry Wadsworth Longfellow, Winslow Homer, Mary Baker Eddy, Amy Lowell, Dorothea Dix, Charles Bulfinch, and Buckminster Fuller are among the dead buried here, along with 70,000 of the not so famous dead. The Massachusetts Horticultural Society created this cemetery-cum-garden in 1832. Tombstones exhibit a wide variety of styles, including elaborate Victorian-era monuments that are very un-New England. Self-guided tours may be taken by following the maps available at the office, including one of the horticulture and another of famous grave sites. Best seasons to take a stroll here are early spring and fall. *580 Mount Auburn St., Cambridge, 617/547–7105. Summer, daily 8–7; winter, daily 8–5. T stop: Harvard Sq.; then Watertown or Waverly Bus to cemetery.*

7 *a-2*

OLD BURYING GROUND

Located between First Parish Church and Christ Church, set aside circa 1631, this was also known as God's Acre. Interred here are early Cambridge settlers; Revolutionary War veterans, including black soldiers Cato Stedman and Neptune Frost; as well as the first eight of Harvard's presidents. Also note the mileage marker, dated 1794, on the Garden Street fence. The burying ground is locked; to gain access you must speak to the sexton of Christ Church. *Massachusetts Ave. and Garden St., Cambridge. T stop: Harvard Sq.*

6 *d-5*

OLD GRANARY BURYING GROUND

(Entrance gates: Solomon Willard, 1830.) This cemetery, opened in 1660, is named for its location near the granary, which stored grain for use in times of shortage. The most distinctive monument marks the graves of Benjamin Franklin's parents, Josiah and Abiah (seek out the inscription). Here patriots James Otis, Paul Revere, Samuel

Adams, John Hancock, and Robert Treat Paine, as well as the victims of the Boston Massacre, also found peace. In addition, the graves of Peter Faneuil and "Mother Goose" Elizabeth Foster Goose, are here. The early Puritan markers are stark, later ones less so. No stone rubbing, *please!* On the Freedom Trail. *83–115 Tremont St., adjacent to Park Street Church. Beacon Hill. Daily sunrise–sunset. T stop: Park St.*

HISTORIC BUILDINGS & AREAS

Boston is a cornucopia of architecturally significant buildings, although, alas, many of the city's neighborhoods have been seriously diminished, if not totally destroyed by the modern forces of "progress" and "urban renewal." Take the time, when walking around areas such as the Financial District, to notice the architectural details on many buildings now overshadowed by skyscrapers. This alphabetical listing covers Boston's most historic buildings, monuments, and houses, as well as notable structures and districts, including outstanding structures and institutions located in nearby Cambridge. If hours are not given, the site is not open to the public.

6 *b-5*

ACORN STREET

Boston at its Time-Machine best, this lovely little cobblestoned Beacon Hill address is the most photographed street in the city. Its toylike row houses, designed by Cornelius Coolidge, were once home to Beacon Hill's servant population, coachmen, and tradesmen—they moved out long ago, replaced by high rollers who could afford what has become some of the city's priciest real estate. Snap the street from the top of the hill—the beautiful trees are from the gardens on Mount Vernon Street—but also zoom in on the Georgian details of the buildings, including the ornamental acorns adorning Nos. 1, 3, and 5. Don't use your car on Acorn—it's paved with the rough cobblestones that were once common on Beacon Hill and they're murder on tires. Anyway, this is a street you have to get to know on foot in order to be properly introduced. *Between Willow and West Cedar Sts. T stop: Charles/MGH.*

8 *c-3*

ALGONQUIN CLUB

(McKim, Mead, and White, 1887) A large and elaborate Renaissance-Revival building, this was designed by New York City's most famous turn-of-the-century architects. *217 Commonwealth Ave., Back Bay, 617/266–2400. T stop: Copley.*

6 *e-4*

AMES BUILDING

(Shepley, Rutan, and Coolidge, 1889.) Dominating the downtown skyline until 1914, this solid-looking 13-story edifice was once the tallest office building on the entire Eastern seaboard. Predating the steel frame by a few years, its outer walls are 9 feet thick at its base, making it the second-tallest wall-bearing structure in the world (the first is the Monadnock Building in Chicago). The Romanesque style of the building's ornament bears eloquent tribute to Henry Hobson Richardson, Boston's architectural genius and mentor to the firm of Shepley, Rutan, and Coolidge. *1 Court St., Government Center. T stop: Government Center.*

8 *d-3*

AMES-WEBSTER HOUSE

(Peabody and Stearns, 1872. Altered: John Sturgis, 1882.) Inspired by the 17th-century chateau of Anêt, this enormous Back Bay mansion once featured some of the swellest reception rooms in Boston (adorned with stained-glass windows by eminent artist John La Farge), all centered around a three-story, very grand staircase. Commissioned by Frederick L. Ames, a fabulously wealthy railroad tycoon, the house has the only known murals in the United States by French Academician Benjamin Constant. Unfortunately, this "Back Bay Queen Anne palace" now houses offices not open to the public. Its exterior—a wedding-cake affair with Fontainbleau chimney and porte cochere—is impressive enough. *306 Dartmouth St., at Commonwealth Ave., Back Bay. T stop: Copley.*

6 *d-5*

AMORY-TICKNOR HOUSE

(Charles Bulfinch, 1804.) Designed for Thomas Amory, a wealthy merchant, this brick mansion was dubbed Amory's Folly because of its oversized proportions. It is the only Federal town house surviving (albeit much altered) from the original Bulfinch-designed development on Park Street. Legend has it that Amory was holding his housewarming party when word came of bankruptcy-level losses at sea. The house was subsequently divided and in 1806 it became a quite fashionable boardinghouse. General Lafayette boarded here during a visit in 1824. Another distinguished resident was famed literary figure George Ticknor, whose second-floor library constituted one of the country's greatest private collections. He later gave his collection to the Boston Public Library, which he helped found. *Park and Beacon Sts., Beacon Hill. T stop: Park St.*

6 *f-5*
SAMUEL APPLETON BUILDING

(Coolidge and Shattuck, 1924. Renovation: Irving Salsberg, 1981.) A wonderful Classical Revival, round building that bears a second look—preferably from afar. But don't miss having a close-up look at the lobby with its gilded ceiling. The structure was named after wealthy businessman Samuel Appleton, brother to pioneering local textile financier Nathan Appleton. *110 Milk St., Downtown. T stop: Aquarium.*

6 *c-5*
APPLETON-PARKER HOUSES

(Alexander Parris, 1819.) Now National Historic Landmarks, these lovely early Greek Revival town houses were built for two wealthy Boston merchants as mirror images of each other. They each boast fine examples of Beacon Hill's noted purple windowpanes (produced when glass imported from England, circa 1820, contained too much manganese). In 1843, Fanny Appleton was married to Henry Wadsworth Longfellow at No. 39. The Women's City Club of Boston obtained No. 40 in 1913 and No. 39 in 1940, which they subsequently sold to a private developer. The mansions are not open to the public although at times, they are opened for special charity tours. *39–40 Beacon St., Beacon Hill, 617/227–3550. T stop: Park St.*

7 *b-3*
APTHORP HOUSE

Part of Harvard University's Adams House, this was built in 1760 as a residence for the rector of Christ Church. Apthorp House's lavishness led Cam-

bridge Puritans to dub it the Bishop's Palace (causing East Apthorp, the rector, to hightail it back to England). During the Revolution, British General Burgoyne was detained here. Since 1916 it has housed the Adams House dorm's master. For a view of Harvard and the Charles at its prettiest, head several blocks south of Adams House along De Wolfe Street to the Weeks Memorial footbridge over the river. Memorial Drive along here offers enchanting vistas, made all the more enjoyable by being vehicle-free during spring and summer Sundays. *Harvard University, Cambridge. T stop: Harvard Sq.*

8
BACK BAY

Today, the Back Bay is one of Boston's most distinctive neighborhoods. Before 1921, however, it was *literally* a bay. A dam was built across the wide yet shallow body of water in hopes of creating a low-cost source of electric power. Alas, what was created was a sewage trap, odorous and insect ridden. Landfill began in order to avoid a health hazard, and what resulted in the late 19th century was a homogeneous residential area, designed along the lines of Baron Haussman's Paris. Covering 580 acres, it was laid out on broad, straight avenues, the most noteworthy of which is still Commonwealth Avenue. (*See also* Atlas *in* Chapter 1.) *T stops: Arlington, Copley, Hynes Convention Center/ICA, Prudential.*

6 *g-5*
BATTERYMARCH BUILDING

(Henry Kellogg, 1928) This handsome, richly hued Art Deco building is a welcome sight among its undistinguished modern neighbors. To create the illusion of sunlight, the color of the bricks shifts from dark brown to beige as the building rises, an effect worth noting. *60 Batterymarch St., at Franklin St., Downtown. T stop: South Station.*

8 *g-4*
BAY VILLAGE

This oasis of 19th-century architecture is close to the theater district and Chinatown and well worth a look. The houses were developed concurrently with Beacon Hill; Edgar Allan Poe once lived here. Although the neighborhood fell on hard times during the first part of this century, historic restoration began taking place in the 1950s. The brick sidewalks and gas lamps are more recent restorations. *Piedmont, Church, Melrose, and Fayette Sts., South End. T stop: N.E. Medical Center.*

6

BEACON HILL

Want to feel truly transported back to 19th-century Boston? Just explore this gaslit, cobblestoned, quaint original neighborhood of the Boston Brahmins, famed throughout America for the charm of Chestnut and Acorn streets and the Henry Jamesian grace of Louisburg Square. Bordered on the south by the Boston Common and encircled by Charles, Cambridge, and Bowdoin streets, Beacon Hill originally comprised three separate hills, in a region known to the Indians back in 1620 as Shawmut. Early settlers dubbed these three hills "Trimountain" and stuck a warning beacon atop the highest of the three, hence the name Beacon Hill. A desire for space and profit (not necessarily in that order) led to the considerable leveling of Trimountain, and an elegant residential area was born, developed by, among others, architect Charles Bulfinch and attorney Harrison Gray Otis. It grew up around Bulfinch's magisterial State House, which was erected on the Hill's highest point in 1795. As globe-circling Yankee traders continued to establish their fortunes, a syndicate of local entrepreneurs began the development of Beacon Hill's slopes. Most of the brick residences that we see on the Hill today are the product of that period. The "best" families moved into grand houses on Chestnut, Beacon, and Mount Vernon streets here, along with such nationally known figures as Henry James and Harriet Beecher Stowe. Today, some "Boston Brahmins" still call Beacon Hill home. The area remains beautifully preserved—a walk along its cobblestoned and brick-paved streets, many of them still steep, will transport you back in time. (*See also* Acorn Street, *above, and* Beacon Street, Charles Street, Chestnut Street, Louisburg Square, Mount Vernon Street, Harrison Gray Otis House [First and Second], *and* Pinckney Street, *below.*) *T stops: Park St., Charles/MGH.*

6 *c-5*

BEACON STREET

The quintessential Beacon Hill address, Beacon Street still features some fine houses by Charles Bulfinch, Boston's first professional home-grown architect. Oliver Wendell Holmes called Beacon Street "the sunny street that holds the sifted few," and for some stretches of this thoroughfare, it seems little has changed in the 20th century. (*See* Appleton-Parker Houses, William Hickling Prescott House, *70–75 Beacon Street, and* Somerset Club, *above and below.*) *Between Park and Charles Sts. T stop: Park St.*

6 *f-6*

ALEXANDER GRAHAM BELL'S GARRET

Reconstructed in the lobby of the Bell Atlantic building is the actual workshop in which Alexander Graham Bell invented the telephone. It used to be located at 109 Court Street in Scollay Square (and was almost destroyed in the square's redevelopment). Also on display is the world's first working switchboard, operated by E. T. Holmes at 342 Washington Street in May 1877, along with replicas of the first model telephones. Look out of the window and you'll see a diorama of Boston as it was when Bell himself looked out on the square. A taped message gives you the history of the telephone, as well as the mural. The building itself, designed by architects Cram and Ferguson in the late 1940s (remodeled in 1992), is a good example of Boston's fleeting fascination with the Art Deco style. *New England Telephone Headquarters Bldg., 185 Franklin St., main lobby, 617/743–4747. Weekdays 8:30–5. Free. T stop: South Station.*

8 *e-3*

BERKELEY BUILDING

(Codman and Despredelle, 1905.) A beautifully decorated Beaux Arts–style building, the Berkeley is a triumph of enameled terra-cotta, copper, and glass, all used with high style and a sense of lightness. Look at the details up close, then cross Boylston Street to get a wide-angle view. *420 Boylston St., at Berkeley St., Back Bay. T stop: Arlington.*

BLACK HERITAGE TRAIL

This is a do-it-yourself walking tour that explores the history of Boston's black community during the 19th century. The community was centered in the West End, between Pinckney and Cambridge, Joy and Charles streets—what is now the north slope of Beacon Hill. The trail includes homes, monuments, schools, even what might have been a notorious gaming house. The 14 sites on the trail reveal a rich, fascinating story that is continuing to unfold today. Obtain a pamphlet from the National Park Service Visitors Center, 15 State Street or at the Museum of Afro-American History, 46 Joy Street. You can also tour the trail under the auspices of a National Park Service ranger (*see* Specialized Tours, *below*). *617/742–1854 or 617/742–5415.*

6 *f-4*

BLACKSTONE BLOCK

Named for Boston's first settler, William Blaxton, this is Boston's oldest commercial district, and, in fact, one of the oldest neighborhoods of the New World. It was here that Boston butchers plied their trade for more than 100 years—today, most people still venture here with food in mind, to dine at the historic Union Oyster House. The area retains its original winding street plan, which dates back to the 17th century, although most original buildings are gone. Still, there are several structures remaining from the 18th century, along with a picturesque group of buildings that extend down through the present day. This is where Haymarket, the famed colorful cacophonous outdoor produce market, takes place early in the morning every Friday and Saturday. *Hanover St., Government Center. T stop: Haymarket.*

6 *d-5*

BOSTON ATHENAEUM

(Edward C. Cabot, 1847-49. Enlarged: Henry Forbes Bigelow, 1913.) This five-story building, a National Historic Landmark, is a repository of all things civilized: books, art, serenity. Founded in 1807, it is one of the oldest libraries in the country. From 1872 to 1876 it functioned as an art gallery, exhibiting American and European painting and sculpture—much of which would later reside in the Museum of Fine Arts. Some remain in the second-floor gallery and other parts of the building. In addition to material from the Athenaeum's own fine collections of photography, prints, and American art before 1950, there are periodic exhibitions of the work of local artists and artisans. The library contains more than 700,000 titles, including some of the world's most prized collections: the King's Chapel Library, sent in 1698 by England's William III; tracts from the John Quincy Adams Library;

and part of George Washington's personal library. The public can visit the first two floors, which include the gallery, and may call 24 hours ahead for an appointment for a free guided tour of the rest of the building, 3 PM on Tuesdays and Thursdays. (*See also* Libraries, *below*.) *10½ Beacon St., Beacon Hill, 617/227– 0270. Weekdays 9–5:30; Sept.–May also Sat. 9–4. T stop: Park St.*

8 *f-2*

BOSTON CENTER FOR ADULT EDUCATION OR BAYLIES MANSION

Founded in 1933, this is the oldest institution of continuing adult education in Boston. It is housed in a commanding Back Bay residential mansion built in 1904 by Walter C. Baylies. *5 Commonwealth Ave., 617/267–4430. Building open to public. T stop: Arlington.*

6 *c-6*

BOSTON COMMON

See Chapter 6.

6 *d-5*

BOSTON MASSACRE SITE

Blood and tears once cemented this spot, where former slave Crispus Attucks and four other were killed by British soldiers on March 5, 1770, (the incident was immortalized in an engraving by Paul Revere—a potent image that helped fuel the Revolution). It's easy to miss this star set in a circle of cobblestones in front of the Old State House—it's located in a traffic island. On the Freedom Trail. *In front of Old State House, 206 Washington St., at State St. T stop: Government Center.*

6 *f-4*

BOSTON STONE

In centuries gone by, this stone was used as the starting marker in measuring distances from Boston. Embedded in the rear of the corner house here, it had been brought from England by a painter in 1700 and had been originally used to grind pigment and linseed. *Marshall and Hanover Sts. near Government Center. T stop: Government Center, Haymarket.*

3 *b-4*

BRATTLE HOUSE

(William Brattle, circa 1727.) Listed in the National Register of Historic Places, this 18th-century, gambrel-roof, colonial clapboard house belonged to Loyalist William Brattle, who wisely fled Boston in 1774. Between 1840 and 1842 it was the residence of Margaret Fuller, noted early feminist and editor of *The Dial*. It now houses the Cambridge Center for Adult Education. Feel free to wander in; you'll probably be tempted to sign up for a class. *42 Brattle St., Cambridge, 617/547–6789. T stop: Harvard Sq.*

3 *b-4*

BRATTLE STREET

One of Boston's most beautiful and historic addresses, this Cambridge street was named for William Brattle, who lived at No. 42 (built circa 1727; *see above*). The street was nicknamed Tory Row in the late 18th century in light of the sympathies of those who resided here. It now has some of Cambridge's oldest homes and some of its most sumptuous mansions. The most famous of these is the Longfellow National Historic Site (105 Brattle St.; 617/876–4491); other mansions open for tours by the public include the Dexter Pratt House—immortalized in Longfellow's "The Village Blacksmith," it's also known as the Blacksmith House—(56 Brattle St.; 617/547–6789) and the Hooper-Lee-Nichols House (159 Brattle St.; 617/547–4252). *Near Harvard Sq., Cambridge. T stop: Harvard Sq.*

6 *f-5*

BRAZER BUILDING

(Cass Gilbert, 1896.) On the site of Boston's first meetinghouse (1632), this is a very early steel-frame building, with an unusual shape that is interesting at both top and bottom. *27 State St., at Devonshire St., Downtown. T stop: State St.*

6 *c-3*

BULFINCH PAVILION (ETHER DOME) OF MASSACHUSETTS GENERAL HOSPITAL

(Charles Bulfinch, 1818–23.) Another of Charles Bulfinch's outstanding public buildings in Boston, this distinctive building—adorned with a black and green marble cupola and ivy-color Ionic columns, houses the famed Ether Dome, the amphitheater where the first use of ether for major surgery was demonstrated. The Ether Dome was the hospital's operating room from 1821 to 1867; it's now a National Historic Landmark. Pick up a pamphlet in the hospital's volunteer department for a self-guided tour. *Massachusetts General Hospital, Fruit St., West End. Weekdays 9–4. T stop: Haynes Convention Center/ICA.*

8 *f-1*

BULL & FINCH PUB

Historic sight? Well, not quite, but you'd be surprised how many visitors make this TV shrine their first Boston sight-seeing stop. Like them you might find yourself humming the words, ". . . where everybody knows your name" as you walk by this Beacon Hill water-hole. Yes, this is the bar that inspired the long-running NBC sitcom *Cheers,* as evidenced by the yellow *Cheers* flag and the tourists clustered outside. The interior has merely a passing resemblance to its TV counterpart, but the bar has, generated a mini-industry of *Cheers* T-shirts and other goods. The Hampshire House restaurant sits above the Bull and Finch. *84 Beacon St., 617/227–9605. T stop: Arlington.*

 g-2

BUNKER HILL MONUMENT

(Solomon Willard, 1825.) The first major encounter of the Revolutionary War, the Battle of Bunker Hill occurred June 17, 1775 (it actually took place on Breed's Hill, but never mind). The colonists' resolve and bravery have become legend with the (reported) words of Col. William Prescott: "Don't fire till you see the whites of their eyes!" Although they suffered huge losses, the British captured the hill, and, in fact, the colonists' cannon taken from here now resides in the Tower of London. The monument was conceived in anticipation of the 50th anniversary of the battle. Quincy granite was moved to Boston via Massachusetts's first railway, constructed for the very task. The cornerstone was laid by General Lafayette on June 17, 1825, during an impressive ceremony at which Daniel Webster spoke. Work continued in fits and starts, due to lack of steady funds, until June 17, 1843, when the monument was finally dedicated. In the lodge at the base, dioramas tell the story of the battle. Ranger programs are conducted hourly. Run by the National Park Service, the monument is part of the Boston National Historic Park and is on the Freedom Trail. *Monument Sq., Charlestown, 617/242–5641. Lodge daily 9–5, Monument daily 9–4:30. Free. T stop: Community College.*

To bring Bunker Hill alive, take in the multimedia show in the round: "The Whites of Their Eyes"—14 screens, 1,000 color slides, 22 life-size costumed figures, seven channels of sound bring to life the Battle of Bunker Hill and describe the events leading up to this first important battle of the American Revolution. There is a large gift shop and also free parking. *55 Constitution Rd, adjacent to USS Constitution, Charlestown Navy Yard, Charlestown, 617/241–7575. Continuous showings every 30 min Sept.–Nov., daily 9:30–4, and June–Aug., daily 9:30–5; closed Dec.–Apr. 1. $3 adults, $1.50 children, $8 parents and 2 children. T stop: Haymarket; then MBTA Bus No. 92 or 93 to City Square.*

CAMBRIDGE

Take a trip north across the Charles River (there are 10 bridges to choose from) to visit Cambridge—home to Harvard and MIT, and to experience the buzz of student life, the trendy restaurants, the shops, the amazing bookstores, the film festivals (the first Humphrey Bogart fest was held here), the dance, the theater, the academic heritage, and the university-town feel. Cambridge, initially called New Towne, was chosen in 1636 as the site for a college. The town's name was changed to Cambridge after the university in England; the college was named for John Harvard, the Charlestown man who left his fortune and his books to the newborn institution. Harvard Square is just an eight-minute T ride away from Boston, but remember there's more to Cambridge than Harvard (though its treasures, such as the Fogg Art Museum and Widener Library, are hard to beat). There are working-class neighborhoods and an ethnic mix of peoples, including Portuguese and Greek. In addition, there are historic mansions galore (*see* Brattle House, Brattle Street, Harvard Yard, Longfellow National Historic Site, *and* Pratt House, *above and below*). *T stops: Harvard Sq., Porter Sq., Central Sq., Kendall Sq.*

6 f-4
CAPEN HOUSE (YE OLDE UNION OYSTER HOUSE)

Ye Olde Union Oyster House, Boston's landmark dining house, was initially the residence and dry goods shop of Hopestill Capen, built circa 1714. On the premises over the shop between 1771 and 1775, Isaiah Thomas published the inflammatory *Massachusetts Spy*. Later

the Duc d'Orléans lived and taught French here—he would thereafter return to France as King Louis Philippe. Since 1826 the house has been occupied without interruption by the Union Oyster House, Boston's oldest restaurant. (*See* Chapter 3). *41 Union St., near Government Center, 617/227–2750. T stop: Government Center.*

6 g-5
CENTRAL WHARF

(Attributed to Charles Bulfinch, 1816.) Central Wharf is the remains of what was once a row of 54 four-story brick and granite buildings, designed to receive cargo from unloading ships (they were then waterside). Part of what remains of the wharf is now occupied by the New England Aquarium. *Milk St. between India St. and Fitzgerald Expressway. T stop: Aquarium.*

6 b-5
CHARLES STREET

Beacon Hill's only true commercial street, it has a profusion of boutiques and restaurants. Along with lower Chestnut Street, this forms Beacon Hill's "antiques row." *From Cambridge St. to Beacon St. T stop: Charles/MGH.*

1 f-2
CHARLESTOWN

This community, across the Charlestown Bridge, was where Boston began. It has been a flourishing seaport since its founding in 1629, and became historically significant as the site of the Battle of Bunker Hill. From 1800 it has also been home to the Charlestown Navy Yard and has remained one of Boston's most insular and private neighborhoods. Winthrop Square and Monument Square boast fine 18th- and 19th-century architecture. (*See* Bunker Hill Monument, City Square, *and* USS Constitution, *above and below*.) *T stop: Community College.*

6 b-5
CHESTNUT STREET

This archetypal Beacon Hill thoroughfare offers a near-textbook overview of Federal-style residential architecture. Promenade down the street, note the gas lamps, cast-iron fences, boot scrapes, and chimney pots, and let the centuries roll back. If you walk no other street on Beacon Hill, walk this one—its loveliness will reward you handsomely.

Between Brimmer and Cedar Sts., Beacon Hill. T stops: Charles/MGH, Park St.

6 d-7
CHINATOWN

Boston's close-knit Chinese-American community (America's third largest) is highly concentrated in a colorful area adjacent to the theater district. The Chinese Gate, pagoda telephone kiosks, and Chinese street signs mark the spot—as if they were needed. (*See also* Atlas *in* Chapter 1; for selected restaurants in the area, *see* Chapter 3.) *Between Beach, Harrison, Tyler, and Hudson Sts. T stop: Chinatown.*

2 4-b
CITGO SIGN

This splash of red, white, and blue, which overlooks Kenmore Square, has been part of the Boston skyline for oh-so-many years. The 60-foot-square neon Citgo display was turned off as a sign of the times—energy conservation—in 1979, and was in danger of demise. Mainly due to the efforts of the Society for Commercial Archaeology, Oklahoma-based Citgo has pledged to keep it lit and maintained as it is the last of six similar signs that once dotted the United States. *Kenmore Sq. T stop: Kenmore Sq.*

1 f-2
CITY SQUARE

Originally known as Market Square, City Square was the center of life in colonial Charlestown and became renowned as the starting point for Paul Revere's famous ride. *T stop: Community College.*

6 d-5
CLAFIN BUILDING

(William G. Preston, 1884.) Named after the wealthy family that gave the state a pile of educational money and a governor, William Clafin, in the years 1869-71, this building was originally built for Boston University. Its rugged face of dark stone is one that Bostonians have come to love. *20 Beacon St., Beacon Hill. T stop: Park St.*

9 e-3
CLOUGH HOUSE

Built in 1715, this was the home of Ebenezer Clough, a Son of Liberty and one of the Boston Tea Party "Indians." Restored in 1968, it is now used by

Christ Church. *21 Unity St., near Paul Revere Mall. Not open to public. T stop: Haymarket.*

6 c-7
COLONIAL THEATRE

(Clarence H. Blackall, 1899–1900.) In the theater district, this elegant theater building is sumptuously decorated on the inside; it was considered one of America's most elegant when it opened. No less personages than George M. Cohan, Vivien Leigh, Noël Coward, and Fred Astaire have graced the stage, which continues to be well used. *106 Boylston St., Back Bay, 617/426–9366. T stop: Boylston.*

6 h-3
COMMERCIAL WHARF

(Attributed to Isaiah Rogers, circa 1833. Renovation: Halasz and Halasz, 1968.) East of Atlantic Avenue, this large, single granite building was originally part of Granite Wharf, then was severed from it in 1868 for the creation of Atlantic Avenue. The remaining section was renovated between 1954 and 1968, and it now houses upscale apartments, as well as offices, fronting the harbor filled with pleasure boats. *T stop: Aquarium.*

8
COMMONWEALTH AVENUE

Beginning at the Public Garden at Arlington Street, this wonderful, Parisian-like, broad (240 feet wide at either side), residential boulevard features a 100-foot-wide, tree-shaded central mall. Pronounced by Winston Churchill to be one of the world's most beautiful thoroughfares, he is said to have walked its length in the 1930s. A sign of the times: What were once private aristocratic Back Bay residences are increasingly being occupied by institutions and businesses. "Com Ave," as it's generally referred to by natives, continues through Kendall Square into Brookline. *T stop: Arlington, Copley.*

3 b-2
COOPER-FROST-AUSTIN-HITCHINGS HOUSE

Built circa 1691, this saltbox house is the oldest complete 17th-century structure still standing in Cambridge. *21 Linnean St., Cambridge. T stop: Harvard Sq.*

B d-4

COPLEY PLAZA HOTEL

(Clarence H. Blackall and Henry Hardenbergh, 1912.) The fine exterior of this elegant hotel competes with its classic and classy Copley Square neighbors—Trinity Church and the Boston Public Library. Built on the site of the original Museum of Fine Arts, the grande dame of Boston hotels has catered to presidents, princes, and the premier social events of many an era. *St. James Ave. between Trinity Pl. and Dartmouth St. T stop: Copley.*

B d-3

COPLEY SQUARE

Named for John Singleton Copley, Boston's most celebrated 18th-century portrait painter, this urban focal point, rich in architecture and culture, is secured by the presence of H. H. Richardson's Trinity Church and McKim, Mead and White's Boston Public Library. A gracious note is also set by Henry Hardenbergh's Copley Plaza Hotel, while the striking exclamation point soaring over all is the John Hancock Tower (I. M. Pei, 1975), the tallest building in New England. The square itself, redone in 1989, is a pleasant spot to relax in warm weather, particularly near the fountain where Nancy Schon's sculpture *The Tortoise and the Hare* attracts youngsters. Warning: this is a popular spot for skateboarders, too! *T stop: Copley.*

6 f-4

CUNARD BUILDING

(Peabody and Stearns, 1902.) Built for the Cunard Steamship Line, nautical embellishments understandably abound, giving a jaunty air to the structure. It's also adorned by the stone lions of the British Empire (the former colonials don't bear a grudge). *126 State St., Downtown. T stop: State St.*

B c-2

CUSHING-ENDICOTT HOUSE

(Snell and Gregerson, 1871.) In its day, this was one of Back Bay's handsomest and most elegant houses. Built for Thomas Forbes Cushing in the French Academic style, it was later home to William C. Endicott, secretary of war under President Cleveland and descendant of Governor John Endicott. The house was occupied by an Endicott until 1958 and later served as a residence for women. It now houses offices. *163 Marlborough St., Back Bay. T stop: Copley.*

6 g-5

CUSTOM HOUSE

(Ammi B. Young, 1847.) This magnificent granite Greek Revival structure was built on pilings at harbor's edge; it's no longer waterside because of landfill of the area between Long and Central wharfs. It was enlarged in 1915 (Peabody and Stearns) by the addition of a 30-story clock tower, becoming Boston's first, and, for a long while, its only, skyscraper. Trivia: Each of the building's 32 Doric columns weighs 42 tons. After standing empty for years, it was purchased for $6 million by the Marriott Corp., which has turned it into luxury time-share units after $30 million in renovations. The move disturbed some historical purists, but the units have been selling briskly. Purchase prices range from $15,000 to $20,000 a week depending on the season. Also, a street-level museum is planned. The clock, which long was stopped, was finally reactivated in 1997. *State and India Sts., 617/790–1400. T stop: Aquarium.*

6 6-4

CUSTOM HOUSE BLOCK

(Isaiah Rogers, 1849. Restoration: Anderson, Notter, and Feingold, 1973.) Remaining from Boston's busy seaport past, this huge granite building was a storehouse for goods awaiting duty imposition. Nathaniel Hawthorne toiled here as a customs inspector. (*See* Long Wharf, *below.*) A National Historic Landmark, it now houses apartments, offices, and shops. *Long Wharf at end of State St. T stop: Aquarium.*

B f-5

CYCLORAMA

(William Blackall, 1884.) One of the most spectacular spaces in Boston, the Cyclorama was famed for its huge glass dome, the second largest in the United States (only the Capitol is larger), built to house the 400-by-50-foot painting *Battle of Gettysburg* by Paul Philippoteaux (1884, and now removed). Subsequently, Alfred Champion purchased the vast space for use as a commercial garage—it was here that the spark plug was invented. Now appropriately recycled as an exhibition and event space for the Boston Center for the Arts, the Cyclorama hosts numerous events, including a popular antiques show every year. The BCA has also added three small theaters, the Mills Gallery, and artist studio space. *Boston Center for the Arts, 539 Tremont St., South End, 617/ 426–5000. Weekdays 9–5. Free. T stop: N.E. Medical Center, Prudential.*

9 *d-3*

DODD HOUSE

Built in 1805 on part of the first provincial governor's estate, Dodd House was the residence of an old North End family. *190 Salem St., North End. T stop: Haymarket.*

1 *e-5*

DOUGLASS SQUARE

Famed Abolitionist Frederick Douglass once spoke here and James Michael Curley vowed that when he became mayor he would rename the square after Douglass, and he did. *Tremont and Cabot Sts.*

6 *b-6*

81 BEACON STREET

In 1952, former ambassador Joseph P. Kennedy occupied an apartment here in order to "keep an eye on" an important political contest: the U.S. Senate race that pitted his son John F. Kennedy against the incumbent, Henry Cabot Lodge. In case you don't remember, JFK won. *T stop: Park St.*

8 *c-3*

EXETER THEATER

(Henry Walker Hartwell and William Cummings Richardson, 1885.) Renovated in 1975, this granite and brownstone building is one of the Back Bay's Victorian gems. The building now houses Waterstone's Booksellers. Previously, this was Boston's oldest continuously operating movie theater until it was closed and replaced by Conran's, the home furnishings emporium. Initially it was the First Spiritual Temple built for the Working Union of Progressive Spiritualists. Today, a glass extension houses Friday's restaurant downstairs. *26 Exeter St., at Newbury St., Back Bay. T stop: Copley.*

6 *f-4*

FANEUIL HALL

(John Smibert, 1742. Enlarged: Charles Bulfinch, 1805.) A main monument of the Freedom Trail, Boston's most historic marketplace/meeting place was justifiably dubbed the "Cradle of Liberty," for it was here in the upstairs meetinghall from 1760 to 1775 that leaders James Otis and Samuel Adams, among others, oversaw the birth of the American revolutionary spirit—long before a single shot was fired. Built by wealthy French Huguenot merchant Peter Faneuil (pronounced by most Bostonians as "Fan'l"), Faneuil Hall is the only Colonial period public building still standing—besides the Old State House—although enlargement by Bulfinch in 1805 greatly altered its original dimensions. Atop the building's exterior is Shem Drowne's famed gilded copper weather vane in the shape of a grasshopper—crafted in 1742, it symbolizes prosperity and the port of Boston (stolen in 1974, it was later recovered, having never left the premises).

Celebrating the hall's unique double function as food market and oratorical venting place, a plaque is set in its east wall, bearing the words of Francis W. Hatch: "Here orators in ages past, / Have mounted their attack, / Undaunted by proximity of sausage on the rack." Today the tradition continues, as the hall is often the setting for political debates or presidential addresses, while the food shops of the Fanueil Hall Marketplace (*see below*) help tourists fuel up for the Freedom Trail. On the third floor is the Ancient and Honorable Artillery Company Museum, added in 1898 (617/227–1638). Happily both the marketplace *and* meeting place still flourish. Part of the Boston National Historic Park, the hall is often closed for events (a closed-circuit TV set-up then offers a glimpse of the famous podium). Tours by advance reservation only. On the Freedom Trail. *Faneuil Hall Sq., Boston National Historic Park, 617/242– 5642. Daily 9–5. Free. T stop: Haymarket, Government Center.*

6 *f-4*

FANEUIL HALL MARKETPLACE

This historic and commercial area near the once-thriving waterfront had fallen on hard times until an imaginative revitalization process was put into effect. The results are a Cinderella story if there ever was one. The historic buildings became part of a lively urban agora, where shops, restaurants, food vendors, pushcarts, outdoor entertainment, and happenings draw Bostonians and tourists daily. The people are part of the scene and they come in droves—reportedly more than visit Disneyland. Daytime and evening it hums. The area is also called Quincy Market, after the central market building that contains the popular food outlets. (For individual restaurants, *see* Chapter 3; for individual shops, *see* Chapter 4.) *Fanueil Hall Marketplace. T stop: Government Center.*

2 *b-5*

FENWAY

What was a murky, unsightly, unsanitary stretch of mudflats became, in the 19th century, a serene area of parkland called the Back Bay Fens. Marking the beginning of Boston's "emerald necklace," the Fenway was landscaped by none other than Frederick Law Olmsted. Set among the irregular reedbound pools, broad meadows, and flower gardens are some of Boston's most famous educational, medical, and cultural institutions, including the Museum of Fine Arts and the Isabella Stewart Gardner Museum (*see* Art Museums, *above*), as well as the New England Conservatory of Music, Northeastern University, and the Harvard Medical School. *T stop: Kenmore Sq.*

6 *e-5*

FIRST PUBLIC SCHOOL SITE

A plaque indicates the site of the Boston Latin School, America's first public school building, which was erected in 1645. Among the pupils were Ben Franklin, John Hancock, and Samuel Adams. The school was demolished to build King's Chapel. Ben Franklin's statue stands on the spot. On the Freedom Trail. *School St. at Old City Hall, Downtown Crossing. T stop: State St.*

8 *e-1*

FISHER JUNIOR COLLEGE

(Henry Brown, 1903.) A Victorian mansion built for the King family (Mrs. King née Spalding of rubber ball fame), it has housed Fisher since 1939. Features include a reception hall, an atriumlike stairway covered with an opaque glass dome, and a marble hanging stairway with a 24-karat gold-plate balustrade. The dining room (president's office) is paneled with Circassian walnut and has a European marble fireplace; the rug (custom made in Burma) carries the same pattern as the ceiling. The library has hand-carved rosewood doors with sterling silver knobs. On the third floor is a balcony with a view of the Charles River. Group tours are Monday to Friday by appointment. *118 Beacon St., Back Bay, 617/536–4647. June–Aug., weekdays 8:30–4:30; Sept.–May, Sat. only 9–3. Free. T stop: Arlington.*

6 *c-6*

FLAGSTAFF HILL

On this high point on the Boston Common, the early town's gunpowder was stored. It's now the last remaining hill left within the Common. It was a recruitment area for the Civil War. *Boston Common. T stop: Park St.*

6 *g-5*

FLOUR & GRAIN EXCHANGE BUILDING

(Shepley, Rutan, and Coolidge, 1890-92.) Here's a little bit of Disney in downtown Boston with a fabulous facade worthy of the Loire Valley (if not Camelot). Set on a pleasant triangular plaza, the building was originally constructed for the Chamber of Commerce out of pinkish gray granite from Milford. *177 Milk St., at India St., Downtown. T stop: Aquarium.*

9 *c-3*

44 HULL STREET

This 200-year-old North End house is Boston's narrowest—only 9 feet 6 inches wide. *Across from Copp's Hill Burying Ground, North End. T stop: Haymarket.*

FORT WARREN

Built originally to protect the harbor from attack, it was used as a place of imprisonment for Confederate soldiers in 1864. *Georges Island, Boston Harbor.*

6 *f-5*

BENJAMIN FRANKLIN'S BIRTHPLACE SITE

A bronze bust is nestled in the cast-iron facade and a brass plaque marks the place where, in 1706, Benjamin Franklin was born to Josiah and Abiah Franklin. The 15th of 17 children, he was christened at Old South Church; later, he was apprenticed to a half-brother as a printer, had a tiff and took off for Philadelphia. The rest is history. *Boston Post Bldg., 17 Milk St., Downtown Crossing. T stop: Downtown Crossing.*

6

THE FREEDOM TRAIL

A unique attraction in Boston, the Freedom Trail traces the birth and early turbulent history of our nation in 2½ miles and 16 historic sights. Indicated by a red-painted (albeit fading) or redbrick line, the trail threads the arena across which our nation strode to national identity and independence. Few other tours bring the traveler so frequently eye-to-eye with our country's modest, heroic beginnings. The trail was actually the brainchild of Boston journalist William Greenough Schofield who, in 1951, sugggested the city's wealth of historic sites be linked in a self-guided walking sequence. In a city where the foot can be as swift as any set of wheels, it's only natural that the Freedom Trail has become a popular choice for an eager army of bipeds. Many participants start at the Boston Common Visitor Information Center or National Park Service Visitors Center at 15 State Street and pick up an easy-to-follow map of the trail. You can also tour the trail under the guidance of a National Park Service guide (see Walking Tours, below). Try to allow a full day to complete the entire route comfortably, although some have been known to cram it into a few aerobic-paced hours.

Suggested Itinerary: Get your bearings at the the very hub of the Hub, the **Boston Common,** and the Visitors Infor-

A TINY HISTORY OF BOSTON

1624
William Blackstone arrives (four years after the Pilgrims on the Mayflower) and settles Shawmut Peninsula—the original name for Boston.

1632
After John Winthrop arrives with his Puritans, Boston becomes the capital of the Massachusetts Bay Colony.

1636
Harvard is founded—the only college in the New World until 1693.

1719
Mother Goose is published by Thomas Fleet.

1742
The "Cradle of Liberty," Faneuil Hall, is constructed.

1773
The Boston Tea Party takes place—the Sons of Liberty dump 343 chests of tea from England into Boston Harbor to protest England's tea taxes.

1775
Paul Revere rides out on April 18 to warn the Minutemen the British are coming—the American Revolution explodes.

1798
Charles Bulfinch's magisterial State House on Beacon Hill is inaugurated.

1826
Quincy Market, another Bulfinch design, opens as the city's commercial centerpiece.

1876
Alexander Graham Bell demonstrates the first telephone from his Boston atelier.

1900
The Boston Symphony Orchestra sets up shop in the new Symphony Hall.

1903
The first World Series is held—between the Boston Pilgrims (later to become the Red Sox) and the Pittsburgh Pirates.

1928
The first computer is designed at the Massachusetts Institute of Technology.

1959
John F. Kennedy declares his candidacy for the presidency of the United States.

1996
The 100th running of the Boston Marathon takes place.

mation Center on Tremont Street and then head for the **State House,** Boston's finest piece of Federalist architecture. Several blocks away is the **Park Street Church,** whose steeple is considered by many to be the most beautiful in all of New England; here, the anthem "America" was first sung. Reposing in the church's shadows is the **Old Granary Burying Ground,** final resting place of Samuel Adams, John Hancock, Paul Revere, and "Mother" Goose. A short stroll will bring you to **King's Chapel,** built in 1754. Nearby is the **Old Corner Bookstore,** one-time publisher of Hawthorne, Emerson, and Longfellow and the **Old South Meetinghouse,** where pre-tempest arguments over a tax on tea were heard in 1773. Overlooking the **site of the Boston Massacre** is the earliest known public building in Boston, the **Old State House.**

Fuel up at **Faneuil Hall**—the first floor has numerous eateries—then explore its Assembly Room, the virtual "Cradle of Liberty." Cross the plaza to explore **Quincy Market,** a shopping extravaganza housed in a Greek Revival jewel, then pass under the Expressway to enter the North End. Discvoer **Paul Revere's House** and the "One if by Land, Two if by Sea" church, the **Old North Church.** From **Copp's Hill Burying Ground,** cross the bridge over the Charles, and check out the **USS Constitution.** Climb to the top of the **Bunker Hill Monument** for the incomparable vistas. Finally, head for the nearby Charlestown water shuttle, which returns you directly to the downtown area. Congratulations: your mere three-mile trek has taken you through three centuries of our country's noblest history.

The following are on the Freedom Trail; for details on each, check the section of this book listed in parenthesis:

Boston Common (*see* Chapter 6)

State House and Archives (*see* Historic Buildings & Areas, *below*)

Park Street Church (*see* Churches & Houses of Worship, *above*)

Old Granary Burying Ground (*see* Graveyards & Cemeteries, *above*)

King's Chapel (*see* Churches & Houses of Worship, *above*)

Site of the First Public School (*see* Historic Buildings & Areas, *below*)

The Old Corner Bookstore (*see* Historic Buildings & Areas, *below*)

Old South Meetinghouse (*see* Churches & Houses of Worship, *above*)

Old State House (*see* Historic Buildings & Areas, *below*)

Boston Massacre Site (*see* Historic Buildings & Areas, *above*)

Faneuil Hall (*see* Historic Buildings & Areas, *above*)

Paul Revere House (*see* Historic Buildings & Areas, *below*)

Old North Church (*see* Historic Buildings & Areas, *below*)

Copp's Hill Burial Ground (*see* Graveyards, *above*)

USS *Constitution,* Charlestown Navy Yard (*see* Historic Buildings & Areas, *below*)

Bunker Hill Monument (*see* Historic Buildings & Areas, *above*)

6 *c-6*
FROG POND
West of the Long Path (Oliver Wendell Holmes Walk), this spot on the Boston Common was where cattle drank and generations of Boston youngsters have frolicked. Now, restored to its former glory, it's still a popular place for ice skating (*see* Chapter 6). *T stop: Park St.*

6 *h-4*
GARDNER BUILDING
Set at the end of South Street, this building, erected circa 1763, was one of several simple brick warehouses that originally lined Long Wharf (Boston's oldest). Renovated in 1973, it now houses the Chart House restaurant. *60 Long Wharf. T stop: Aquarium.*

6 *a-6*
GIBSON HOUSE MUSEUM
(Edward C. Cabot, 1859.) Built for the Gibson family, who occupied it from 1859 to 1956, this house's high-ceiling interior is filled with rich, dark, overstuffed furnishings and objects typical of the Victorian age. In fact, this Back Bay residence, which serves as a museum of the period, is one of the few

homes of that era intact and open to the public, thanks to the Victorian Society, which calls it home. You must take a tour—given at 1, 2, and 3 PM—in order to see the house (see Specialized Tours in Guided Tours, below). Groups of 10 or more by appointment only. 137 Beacon St., 617/267–6338. $5. May–Oct, Wed.–Sun.; Nov.–Apr., weekends. T stop: Arlington.

6 b-5
GEORGE GRANT HOUSE
Grant was the first black graduate of Harvard College and an instructor at Harvard Dental School. A noted dentist, he also was the inventor of the wooden golf tee. He lived here from 1890 to 1910. On the Black Heritage Trail, but interior not open to the public. 108 Charles St., Beacon Hill. T stop: Park St.

6 f-5
GREAT FIRE OF 1872 PLAQUE
A conflagration that started at Summer and Kingston streets ended here after leveling 65 acres of the city. Milk and Devonshire Sts., at Post Office.

8 e-2
HADDON HALL
(J. Pickering Putnam, 1894.) A stately Back Bay building, this 11-story structure, now used for offices, was originally built as a residential hotel. Not open to the public. 29 Commonwealth Ave., at Berkeley St., Back Bay. T stop: Arlington.

6 e-4
EBENEZER HANCOCK HOUSE
On what was once known as Hancock Row, this is Boston's oldest extant brick dwelling, built circa 1760. Although owned by John Hancock, 1764-85, his brother Ebenezer, who was paymaster of the Continental Army, lived in the three-story, redbrick house. Now offices. 10 Marshall St., near Government Center. Not open to public. T stop: Government Center.

9
HANOVER STREET
Part of the Freedom Trail wends its way along this tightly packed thoroughfare to the Old North Church, but many people come to this well-used main street of the North End's Italian community just to visit the street's many aromatic caffès

and ristorantes. Many festas—or saints' days—are held here (see Events, below). Between Cross and Commercial Sts., North End. T stop: Haymarket.

6 d-5
CHESTER HARDING HOUSE (BOSTON BAR ASSOCIATION)
(Thomas Fletcher, 1808.) This was built as a residence and studio of American painter Chester Harding, who lived here from 1827 to 1829. Favored by Boston society and British aristocracy, he also deigned to do Daniel Boone's portrait. An ophthalmologist named Angel bought the home in 1829—his wife was active in the Congregational Church . . . until it erected a mission building right next door, obstructing the couple's view of Beacon Hill. Needless to say, Dr. Angel bequeathed his home to the Unitarian Church. The Boston Bar Association acquired the building in the early 1900s. Restored in 1962-63, it's now a National Historic Landmark. 16 Beacon St., Beacon Hill, 617/742–0615. Not open to public. T stop: Park St.

7 c-4
HARVARD LAMPOON BUILDING
(Edward Martin Wheelwright, 1909.) The Lampoon's editorial offices were built on land donated by its business manager at the time—namely, William Randolph Hearst. The bitingly satirical Harvard undergraduate humor magazine was founded in 1876. The odd shape of the building does give you pause. 57 Mount Auburn St., Cambridge, 617/495–7801. Not open to public.

7 a-2
HARVARD SQUARE
This is the old town center of Cambridge—and present-day hubbub of activity, diversity, and what must be Guinness Book of World Records material for the number of bookstores it sustains per square foot. Although there are still faint signs of a youthful 1960s counter-culture, the Square has taken a giant homogenizing leap into the present.

7 a-1
HARVARD UNIVERSITY
On the campus of Harvard University—the main campus is between Massachusetts Avenue and Cambridge Street—you'll find some of the oldest,

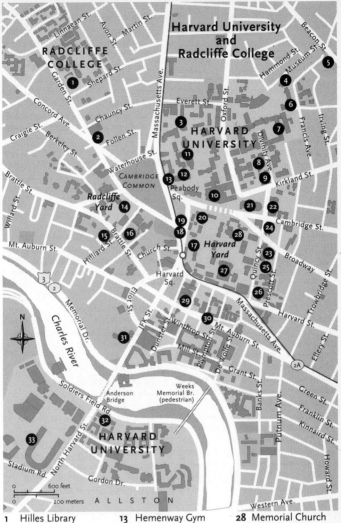

Harvard University
and
Radcliffe College

1	Hilles Library	13	Hemenway Gym	28	Memorial Church
2	Longy School of Music	14	Byerly Hall	29	Holyoke Center
3	Harkness Commons & The Graduate Ctr	15	Loeb Drama Center	30	Harvard Lampoon Castle
		16	Gutman Library	31	Kennedy School of Government
4	Rockefeller Hall	17	Massachusetts Hall		
5	American Academy of Arts & Sciences	18	Harvard Hall	32	Harvard Business School
		19	Holden Chapel	33	Soldiers Field
6	Divinity School	20	Stoughton Hall		
7	Harvard Biological Laboratories	21	Memorial Hall/ Sanders Theater		
8	Sherman Fairchild Biochemistry Lab	22	George Gund Hall		
		23	Fogg Museum		
9	Adolphus Busch Hall	24	Arthur M. Sackler Museum		
10	Science Center	25	Carpenter Center for the Visual Arts		
11	Law School	26	Harvard Union		
12	Austin Hall	27	Widener Library		

most beautiful academic buildings in the country, belonging, of course, to the oldest and most prestigious university in America. Every summer (June to August) there are free one-hour historic tours of Harvard Yard, the center of it all. The cows are gone but the grassy yard remains. Enter through Johnson Gate (or one of the seven other gates); originally called College Yard, it was enclosed as the campus grew. Around it are some of the country's most historic academic buildings, offering a pageant of architectural history from the early 18th century onward, including buildings by Charles Bulfinch and Henry Hobson Richardson. Note particularly the Holden Chapel (1742)—a high-style Georgian affair once called "a solitary English daisy in a field of Yankee dandelions." For more on Harvard, *see* Art Museums, *above; see* Colleges and Universities *in* Chapter 8 for a description of the school's fame; directly below is a list of the campus's more notable buildings. *1350 Massachusetts Ave., 617/495–1573. Tour June–Aug., Mon.–Sat. at 10, 11:15, 2, and 3:15, plus Sun. at 1:30 and 3; Sept.– May, weekdays at 10 and 2, plus Sat. at 2. Rest of year tour is conducted for incoming students and is not as historically oriented; call first. Reserve for groups of 25 or more. T stop: Harvard Sq.*

HARVARD HALL

Designed by Sir Francis Bernard, royal governor from 1761 to 1769, Harvard Hall was built in 1764. The handsome redbrick edifice is topped by a lovely bell tower and originally housed the first classroom of the "colledge."

HOLDEN CHAPEL

This impressive Georgian monument was built in 1742 with an endowment from the widow of Samuel Holden, once director of the Bank of England. Uses have included lumber room, medical hall, and carpentry shop; today, it's home base for the Harvard and Radcliffe choral societies.

HOLLIS HALL

A grand Dormitory building designed by Thomas Dawes, Hollis Hall was built in 1762.

HOLWORTHY HALL

This imposing edifice was built in 1812 with the proceeds of a state lottery.

MASSACHUSETTS HALL

Built in 1718, it's Harvard's oldest standing building and the quintessential ivy-covered hall of academia. Holds freshmen as well as the president's offices.

MEMORIAL CHURCH

(Coolidge, Shepley, Bullfinch, and Abbott, 1932.) Dedicated on Armistice Day in 1932, the church memorializes on its walls the names of Harvard's fatalities from the two World Wars and the Korean and Vietnam conflicts. Home to the University choir, it is topped by a 197-foot spire.

SEVER HALL

(H. H. Richardson, 1880.) This famed architect not only created this Cambridge landmark of Richardsonian Romanesque, he also left his mark on nearby Austin Hall.

STOUGHTON HALL

(Charles Bulfinch, 1804.) This dormitory that has housed the likes of Emerson, Thoreau, and Edward Everett Hale.

UNIVERSITY HALL

(Charles Bulfinch, 1813.) A vision in White Chelmsford granite afloat in a sea of red brick, University Hall was built originally to house a "Common Hall" for dining as well as classrooms and a two-story chapel. Since 1849 it is used more for administrative offices. There were outdoor privies along here, known as University Minor, until indoor plumbing was installed in the late 1870s.

WIDENER MEMORIAL LIBRARY

See Libraries, *below.*

6 *a-5*

HATCH MEMORIAL SHELL

The scene of the immensely popular Boston Pops Esplanade concerts (*see* Events, *below*), as well as ballet, dance, films, and musical concerts, this shell replaced an earlier one in 1940. *Charles River Esplanade at Arlington St. T stop: Charles/MGH.*

6 *b-4*

LEWIS HAYDEN HOUSE

Lewis Hayden was a slave who escaped from Kentucky via the Underground Railroad later to become leader of Boston's abolitionist movement. This house, built in 1833, became a station on the Railroad to Canada. It is said that Lewis and his wife, Harriet, kept kegs of gunpowder under the front stoop to light in the event their recapture were ever to become a real possibility—happily, it did not. Harriet Beecher Stowe visited the house in 1853, where she saw 13 newly escaped slaves. In 1873, Hayden was one of two black representatives elected to the Massachusetts legislature. On the Black Heritage Trail. *66 Phillips St., Beacon Hill. Not open to public. T stop: Charles/MGH.*

6 *f-3*
HAYMARKET
A riot of color and activity, this famed open-air pushcart produce market is set on the edge of Boston's famous Italian North End. *Blackstone between North and Hanover Sts., near Government Center. Fri. and Sat. sunrise–sunset. T stop: Haymarket.*

3 *b-4*
JOHN HICKS HOUSE
Built in 1760, this is a gambrel-roofed wooden residence typical of its time. Owner Hicks was a Son of Liberty, a participant in the Boston Tea Party, and one of the three Cambridge patriots shot by the British returning from Lexington and Concord. The house is now home to Harvard's Kirkland House library. *64 John F. Kennedy St. and South St., Cambridge. Not open to public. T stop: Harvard Sq.*

8 *b-5*
HORTICULTURAL HALL
(Wheelwright and Haven, 1901.) This brick Beaux-Arts headquarters of the Massachusetts Horticultural Society (MHS) (founded in 1829) contains the country's oldest and best-known horticultural library. Ask about the New England Spring Flower Show at the Bayside Expo Center, staged by the MHS since 1871—it's how Boston knows spring has arrived (*see* Events, *below*). The building also contains the offices of *Boston Magazine. 300 Massachusetts Ave., at Huntington Ave., Back Bay, 617/536–9280. Weekdays 8:30–4:30. T stop: Symphony.*

8 *a-3*
HOTEL CHARLESGATE
(J. Pickering Putnam, 1891.) A once-fashionable apartment building, this structure suffers no lack of architectural embellishment. *535 Beacon St., at Charlesgate East, Back Bay. T stop: Hynes Convention Center/ICA, or Kenmore.*

8 *d-3*
HOTEL VENDOME
(William G. Preston, 1875. Additions: J. F. Ober, 1881. Renovation: Stahl-Bennett, 1975.) This glorious French Second Empire–style building was, in the 1800s, Boston's most fashionable hotel. President Grant, Samuel Clemens (Mark Twain), Sarah Bernhardt, P. T. Barnum, and Oscar Wilde were all guests. Much more importantly, it was here in October 1879 that Thomas Edison demonstrated his incandescent lamp for the first time. It then became the first public building to have electric lighting—in the form of 50 massive chandeliers. Tragically, it was also the site of one of the worst disasters in Boston firefighting history, when nine men died putting out a fire here in 1972. In 1975, it was renovated to become offices and retail space. *Dartmouth St. and Commonwealth Ave., Back Bay. T stop: Copley.*

6 *c-4*
JOY STREET
An important center on the Black Heritage Trail, this north slope of a Beacon Hill street was not named for the pursuit of, but for Dr. John Joy, a Boston apothecary. *Between Beacon and Cambridge Sts., Beacon Hill. T stops: Charles/MGH, Bowdoin.*

2 *b-4*
KENMORE SQUARE
Student headquarters for nearby Boston University, this square, located near Fenway Park, sustains a great many late-night clubs and eateries. *Between Back Bay and Charles River. T stop: Kenmore Sq.*

4 *f-5*
JOHN F. KENNEDY NATIONAL HISTORIC SITE
Suburban birthplace of John F. Kennedy, 35th President of the United States, this house has been restored to its 1917 appearance. Joseph and Rose Kennedy lived here from 1914 to 1921 and it is furnished with property of the Kennedy family, including personal mementos, such as JFK's crib, the bed he was born in, and his books and toys. Two of the three floors are open to the public. National Park Service personnel give

tours and answer questions. *83 Beals St., Brookline, 617/566–7937. Mid-Mar.–Nov., Wed.–Sun. 10–4:30; tour every hr. $2. T stop: Coolidge Corner, walk north on Harvard St. 4 blocks.*

9 *6-e*

ROSE FITZGERALD KENNEDY BIRTHPLACE

The North End birthplace, in 1890, of the daughter of John "Honey Fitz" Fitzgerald (Boston politician extraordinaire, congressman, and mayor) and the mother of JFK, RFK, and Teddy. *4 Garden Ct., North End. Not open to public. T stop: Haymarket.*

6 *h-3*

LEWIS WHARF

(Attributed to Richard Bond, 1836. Renovation: Carl Koch and Associates, 1965-71.) In the 1850s this wharf was home port to the clipper ships that transported speculators to the California gold rush, with its buildings serving as warehouses for foreign merchants. Long neglected, the granite buildings were, in the 1960s, renovated into condos, leaving commercial space on the ground level, plus a lovely little garden. There's also a croquet court, well used by the Boston Croquet Club. *East of Atlantic Ave. near Commercial St., North End. T stop: Haymarket.*

3 *a-3*

LONGFELLOW NATIONAL HISTORIC SITE

Built in 1759 by John Vassall, a Loyalist who chose to flee on the eve of the Revolution, this august abode became General Washington's headquarters during the siege of Boston—in fact, he and his wife, Martha, celebrated their 17th wedding anniversary here in January 1776. In 1791 it was owned by a wealthy doctor, Andrew Craigie, who added rooms for lavish entertaining. The house came to be known as Craigie Castle, but he died leaving debts, and his wife was forced to accept lodgers; in 1837, Henry Wadsworth Longfellow was one of them. In 1843, Longfellow married Fanny Appleton, and her wealthy father bought the house for them as a wedding present. It became, quite naturally, a home of love and letters, where Longfellow lived until his death in 1882. His oldest daughter preserved the first floor and all is almost as he left it—books, furnishings, pictures. On view is the chair given to him by the children of Cambridge on

his 72nd birthday. It was made from the wood of the "spreading chestnut tree," cut down when a road was widened, but immortalized thanks to the poet's lyrics. This National Historic Site offers concerts during the summer. *105 Brattle St., Cambridge, 617/876–4491. $2. Mid-May–Oct., Wed.–Sun. 10–4:30; Nov.–mid-Dec., Wed.–Sun. noon–4:30. Guided tour only; last tour departs at 4. Hrs may vary in fall and winter; call ahead. T stop: Harvard Sq.*

6 *4-h*

LONG WHARF

Built circa 1710 and originally known as Boston Pier, this is the oldest existing wharf in Boston. Although its halcyon days of serving the clipper ships as they arrived in the busy port are over, it thrives once again. Several retail shops occupy the granite building and harbor tours and Provincetown excursions leave from here (*see Boat Tours in Guided Tours, below*). The addition of Marriott's Long Wharf Hotel has also been a boost to the area. *East of Atlantic Ave., Downtown. T Stop: Aquarium.*

8 *e-3*

LOUIS, BOSTON

(W. G. Preston, 1862.) This three-story, redbrick, French Academy–style building originally housed the collections of the Boston Society of Natural History. The celebrated store of Bonwit Teller was the sole occupant from 1947 to 1989, when Louis, Boston—the city's homegrown, prestigious men's clothiers—moved in. The store preserves the building under terms of the lease. *234 Berkeley St., Back Bay, 617/262–6100. T stop: Arlington.*

6 *b-5*

LOUISBURG SQUARE

One of Boston's urban showpieces, this genteel square (it's pronounced Louisburg, not Louie-burg) beguiles with old-world charm and is the essence of Beacon Hill tradition, character, and gracious lifestyle. Originally planned in 1826 by S. P. Feller but not finished until 1834, the enclave, with its private park, is pleasing to the eye, even though the houses are not particularly distinguished in design. Former residents include Louisa May Alcott (No. 10) and *Atlantic Monthly* editor William Dean Howells (No. 4), while famed "Swedish Nightingale" Jennie Lind was married at No. 20 in 1852. The square is also home to Massachusetts Senator John Kerry and heiress wife Teresa Heinz; there was a huge local fuss when the couple had a fire hydrant moved from in front of their house around the corner. Christmas Eve is a very special traditional time here: windows are candlelit, caroling fills the air. *Between Mount Vernon and Pinckney Sts., Beacon Hill. T stop: Charles/MGH.*

7 *a-3*

LOWELL HOUSE

(Charles A. Coolidge, 1930.) One of the more patrician addresses of Harvard, this handsome building is marked by two large interior courts and an entrance tower with a blue dome, which contains, of all things, bells from a Russian monastery. Harvard undergraduates living here, however, bemoan the fact that there are no Charles River views. You can get into the courtyard, but the building is usually locked during the summer, unless summer school is in session. *Winthrop and Mount Auburn Sts., Cambridge, 617/495–2283. T stop: Harvard Sq.*

8 *b-5*

MAPPARIUM

Step "inside" the world and stand on a glass bridge within this huge, colorful stained-glass globe, 30 feet in diameter. See land surfaces, meridians, the International Date Line, and ocean depths. It was built panel by panel (there are 608) in a bronze frame and is the only one of its kind in the world. A brief talk by a guide is available throughout the day. *Christian Science Center, Massachusetts and Huntington Aves., 617/450–3790. Mon.–Sat. 9:30–4. Free. T stop: Hynes Convention Center/ICA.*

7 *h-7*

MASSACHUSETTS INSTITUTE OF TECHNOLOGY (MIT)

In 1865, this noted institution opened (as Boston Tech in the city's rented Mercantile Hall) as a school for "practical science." Today, more than a century later, it's a breeding ground for budding Einsteins and one of the most prestigious engineering and science colleges in the world. At this location since 1916, it extends along the Charles River on 128 acres, with more than 9,000 students attending the schools of Architecture and Planning, Engineering, Humanities, Management, and Social Science. Don't go looking for Harvard's ivied Georgian elegance—much of the campus has a cool, businesslike ambience. Still, major modern masters, such as Alvar Aalto and I. M. Pei, have created signature buildings here. *East Campus:* Rogers Building, Hart Nautical Galleries, Hayden Memorial Library. *West Campus:* Tech Coop, MIT Chapel, Kresge Auditorium, Baker House (*see Modern Architecture, below*). *77 Massachusetts Ave., Cambridge, 617/ 253–1000. T stop: Kendall Sq.*

9 *f-7*

MCLAUTHLIN BUILDING

Listed on the National Register of Historic Places, this is one of the few surviving cast-iron buildings in Boston. Built sometime during the mid-19th century, it has a lovely cast-iron facade, whose delicate windowpanes give the structure an almost lacy effect. It was updated in 1979 for condo dwellers and retailers. *120 Fulton St., North End. T stop: Haymarket.*

7 *b-2*

MEMORIAL HALL

(Henry Van Brunt and William Ware, 1878) Originally constructed as a Victorian-era tribute to the Civil War dead, this noted building has served many other purposes and has been the setting for large-scale social events, including Harvard's legendary freshman mixers. On the National Register of Historic Places, the distinctive Gothic structure, replete with architectural flourishes and Tiffany stained-glass windows, also contains the Sanders Theater, a 1,200-seat venue for concerts, music groups, and the popular Christmas Revels. For information for the theater call 617/495–2420. *Harvard University, Cambridge and Quincy Sts., Cambridge. Weekdays 10–6. Free. T stop: Harvard Sq.*

9 *f-8*

MERCANTILE WHARF BUILDING

(Gridley J. F. Bryant, 1857. Reconstruction: John Sharatt and Associates, 1976.) This well-preserved Italianate granite edifice was originally built to house riggers and sailmakers who serviced the then-busy harbor port. As part of the Waterfront Urban Renewal Project, 100 mixed-income apartments were created, beginning around 1975. The interior is a six-story skylit atrium with ground-level shops. The glass-enclosed elevator and tree- and plant-filled mall add interest. *75–117 Commercial St. (also fronts on Atlantic Ave., between Cross and Richmond Sts.), North End. T stop: Haymarket.*

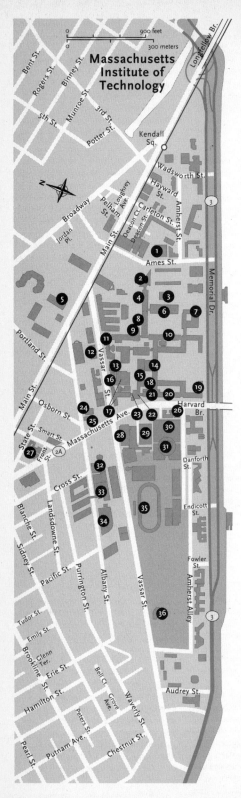

Massachusetts Institute of Technology

1   List Visual Arts Centre
2   Ralph Landau Building
3   Green Building
4   Whitaker Building
5   Laboratory for Computer Science
6   Dreyfus Building
7   Hayden Memorial Library
8   Dorrance Building
9   Compton Labs
10 Eastman Labs
11 Fairchild Building
12 Cyclotron
13 Brown Building
14 Maclaurin Bldgs
15 Bush Building
16 McNair Building
17 Sloan Laboratories
18 Homberg Building
19 Pierce Laboratory
20 Pratt School
21 Rogers Bldg/Hart Nautical Gallery
22 Center for Advanced Engineering Study
23 Guggenheim Lab
24 Superconducting Generator Test Facility
25 High Voltage Research Lab
26 Center for Advanced Visual Studies
27 MIT Museum
28 du Pont Athletic Center
29 Stratton Building Student Center
30 MIT Chapel
31 Kresge Auditorium
32 Nuclear Reactor Laboratory
33 F Bitter National Magnet Laboratory
34 Nabisco Lab
35 Steinbrenner Stadium
36 MIT Solar Demo Building

6 *c-5*

GEORGE MIDDLETON HOUSE

Built in 1797, this small wooden house on Beacon Hill is one of Boston's oldest—possibly *the* oldest on the Hill. Its original owners were black: George Middleton, a jockey and horsebreaker; and Lewis Glapion, a barber. Middleton, a colonel during the American Revolution, led the "Bucks of America," an all-black company. On the Black Heritage Trail. *5–7 Pinckney St., Beacon Hill. Not open to public. T stop: Charles/MGH, Bowdoin.*

6 *f-5*

MILK STREET

This is the path the "Indians" (a.k.a. John Hancock and his tribe) took from the Old South Meetinghouse on their way to that famous tempest in a tea pot. Turn right onto Congress Street and you'll see the site where they were headed, now occupied by the Boston Tea Party Ship and Museum. *Between Washington St. and Atlantic Ave. T stop: Downtown Crossing.*

6 *c-5*

MOUNT VERNON STREET

One of Beacon Hill's most famous addresses, this street boasts several noted sites (*see below*). On the south side of the street a proviso limited the height of these buildings to one story, while most row houses were set back approximately 30 elegant feet from the sidewalk. Note the iron handrails attached to some building fronts—they were provided to prevent Beacon Hill grande dames from slipping in the snow. *Between Louisburg Sq. and Walnut St., Beacon Hill. T stop: Charles/MGH.*

32 MOUNT VERNON STREET

This home once belonged to Julia Ward Howe, noted suffragette and composer of the "Battle Hymn of the Republic," and her husband, Dr. Samuel Gridley Howe, founder of the Perkins Institute for the Blind. *T stop: Charles/MGH.*

51–55 MOUNT VERNON STREET

(Charles Bulfinch, 1803-04.) An example of the socially progressive custom of "daughter" houses, this was built for unmarried girls, usually close to the parents' house (*see Nichols House Museum, below*). *T stop: Charles/MGH.*

57 MOUNT VERNON STREET

(Charles Bulfinch, 1804.) Like the Nichols House at No. 55, this row house mansion was built for an early Beacon Hill developer, Jonathan Mason, and was originally occupied by his daughter, who later became Mrs. Samuel Parkman. It was sold in 1838 to Cornelius Coolidge, who added the Greek Revival front entrance. Daniel Webster lived here (1817–19), as did Charles Francis Adams, son of President John Quincy Adams. *T stop: Charles/MGH.*

59 MOUNT VERNON STREET

(Edward Shaw, 1837.) Stately and serene, this is an exemplary Beacon Hill Greek Revival residence. *T stop: Charles/MGH.*

6 *b-5*

83 MOUNT VERNON STREET

This residence belonged to Unitarian leader William Ellery Channing. Charles Dickens and his wife, Catherine, dined here February 2, 1842. *T stop: Charles/MGH.*

85 MOUNT VERNON STREET

See Harrison Gray Otis House (Second), below.

87 MOUNT VERNON STREET

(Charles Bulfinch, 1805.) On a lot next door to the second house he designed for Harrison Gray Otis, this freestanding Beacon Hill edifice was built by Bulfinch for Bulfinch. Alas, financial setbacks forced him to sell to prominent merchant Stephen Higginson before ever occupying it. Among later residents was Charles Jackson Paine, a Civil War general, railroad tycoon, and yachtsman. It now houses the Colonial Society of Massachusetts. *Not open to public. T stop: Charles/MGH.*

131 MOUNT VERNON STREET

Henry and William James lived here in the 1860s. *T stop: Charles/MGH.*

6 *h-7*

MUSEUM WHARF

(M. D. Stafford, 1889. Renovation: Cambridge Seven and Dyer Brown Associates, 1975.) An old woolens warehouse at the edge of Fort Point Channel is now home to the wonderful Boston Children's Museum (*see* Art Museums, *above*) as well as the Computer Museum. The focus on the parklike wharf is the building's exterior elevator shaft and the Hood milk bottle snack kiosk. *Congress St. Bridge, Fort Point Channel. T stop: Aquarium.*

---

8 *c-3*

NEWBURY STREET

This major Boston street begins at Arlington Street at Boston Public Garden. Once an elegant Back Bay residential address, it is now home to a high concentration of chic boutiques and boîtes, art galleries, and hair and facial salons, all located in former town houses. Outdoor cafés add to the charm. Newbury Street has the some of the highest commercial rents in the nation, ranked right up there with Rodeo Drive in Beverly Hills and Wentworth Avenue in Palm Beach.It becomes a bit more casual (almost funky) as you move west, away from the Garden. *T stops: Arlington, Copley, Hynes Convention Center/ICA.*

---

8 *b-6*

NEW ENGLAND CONSERVATORY OF MUSIC

Located in the Fenway, founded in 1867, this is the oldest music conservatory in America. *290 Huntington Ave., Back Bay, 617/262–1120. T stop: Symphony.*

---

8 *d-3*

NEW ENGLAND HISTORIC GENEALOGICAL SOCIETY

The society, founded in 1845 (originally located at Ashburton Place), contains a comprehensive collection, including 17th-century wills, deeds, diaries, and journals, as well as a research library emphasizing local and family histories. Since renovations completed in 1996, the collections on the 5th and 6th floor are now wheelchair-accessible. There is a $15 fee to use facilities. *101 Newbury St., Back Bay, 617/536–5740. Tues., Fri., and Sat. 9–5; Wed. and Thurs. 9–9; closed Sat. before Mon. holidays. T stop: Copley.*

---

8 *e-3*

NEW ENGLAND MUTUAL LIFE INSURANCE COMPANY

(Cram and Ferguson, 1941.) This 10-story Back Bay building houses what was the first chartered mutual life insurance company in the country. Inside the Newbury Street entrance are four dioramas depicting the development of Back Bay. In the front lobby, note the eight historic murals by Charles Hoffbauer done in 1943. *501 Boylston St., Back Bay, 617/266–3700. Lobby open weekdays 8–4. T stops: Arlington, Copley.*

---

6 *c-5*

NICHOLS HOUSE MUSEUM

(Attributed to Charles Bulfinch, 1804.) A Federal row house built by Jonathan Mason, one of the original Beacon Hill developers, it was the home, for some 80 years, of Rose Standish Nichols, world traveler, landscape architect, and author of *English Pleasure Gardens*. The house, containing an eclectic array of 15th- to 20th-century furnishings, is the only private home on Beacon Hill open to the public. Guided tours only. *55 Mount Vernon St., 617/227–6993. $5. May–Oct., Tues.–Sat. noon–5; Nov., Dec., and Feb.–Apr., Mon., Wed., and Sat. noon–5. T stop: Park St.*

---

2 *c-6*

NORTHEASTERN UNIVERSITY

Founded in 1898 and located in the Fenway, this is the largest private university in the country. Most students are commuters; many specialize in applied studies, such as engineering, nursing, law, and business administration. *360 Huntington Ave., 617/373–2000. T stop: Northeastern.*

9

NORTH END

This is the oldest residential section of the city center of Boston, having been developed by the early settlers in the 17th and 18th centuries. It later became a port-of-entry neighborhood absorbing successive waves of immigrants. First came the Irish, then the East European Jews, and, finally, since the late 19th century, it has been a solidly Italian area (although it is now being heavily colonized by an influx of latter-day, yuppified urban professionals). Go not only for the Freedom Trail's historic sites (Paul Revere House, Old North Church, Copp's Hill Burying Ground, Pierce-Hichborn House), but also for a lovely feeling of a quaint world apart—narrow winding streets, old women dressed in black leaning out of their windows, clusters of men conversing in Italian, aromatic *caffés*, tempting *pasticcerias*. All in all, the North

End still offers up a charming old-world flavor. At Hanover and Salem streets there is an open market daily, and in the summer there are lively street *festas* (*see* Events, *below*). The neighborhood is accessible via the pedestrian tunnel under the Central Artery, at Hanover Street. *T stop: Haymarket.*

9 *e-6*

NORTH SQUARE

Most sightseers go to visit North Square because at No. 19 you'll find the oldest abode in Boston—Paul Revere House (*see below*); just next door is the Pierce-Hichborn residence (*see below*). Across the way is the Rachel Revere Park. Paved with cobblestones, this North End square was the site of a colonial-era marketplace. *T stop: Haymarket.*

8 *d-3*

OLD BOSTON ART CLUB

(William Ralph Emerson, 1881.) Wonderfully elaborate Queen Anne Revival edifice that once housed the Boston Art Club (until 1948), since 1970, it has been the Copley High School. *152 Newbury St., at Dartmouth St., Back Bay. Not open to public. T stop: Copley.*

6 *e-5*

OLD CITY HALL

(Gridley J. F. Bryant and Arthur Gilman, 1865. Renovation: Anderson, Notter Associates, 1969.) French Second Empire (architecturally second to few in the city) in style and happily recycled for use as office space when the municipal government moved to the new City Hall in the 1960s (things change, even in Boston). Fittingly, there's also a fine French restaurant here, Maison Robert, which spills into the courtyard in mild weather (*see* French *in* Chapter 3). Adjacent to King's Chapel, the Old City Hall is now a National Historic Landmark. *School St., Downtown. T stop: Downtown Crossing.*

6 *e-5*

OLD CORNER BOOKSTORE BUILDING

As the offices for the legendary publishing firm of Ticknor and Fields, this quaint building was the Boston literary salon for the likes of Longfellow, Emerson, Holmes, Whittier, Hawthorne, Julia Ward Howe, and Harriet Beecher Stowe in 1812. Built in 1712 on the site of the home of Anne Hutchinson—a woman banished from Boston in 1638 for her unorthodox religious beliefs—the two-story brick building was originally constructed for apothecary Thomas Crease. Restored in 1964 to its 1828 character, it was then occupied by the *Boston Globe*'s downtown offices. Begininng in 1982, it housed the Historic Boston offices and the Globe Corner Bookstore, plus retail space; in 1997, the space was turned over to the *Boston Globe* for travel books, maps, T-shirts, bags, and other items, many touting the Globe's Web site at www.Boston.com. On the Freedom Trail. *Washington St. and School St., 617/367–4004. Mon.–Sat. 9–6, Sun. noon–5; hours vary. T stop: State St., Downtown Crossing.*

6 *e-5*

OLD STATE HOUSE

The center of Colonial government built in 1713 at what was the very crossroads of Boston, this is the city's oldest surviving public building, albeit much altered. Before the Revolution it was called the Town House (the original was built here in 1658, burned 1711). Outside, on March 5, 1770, the Boston Massacre took place. The spot is marked by a circle of stones (*see* Boston Massacre Site, *above*).

Referred to as the Temple of Liberty, the Old State House is where all business of government took place until 1798 (the first floor was used as a Merchants' Exchange, the upper floors contained the Courts of Suffolk County, Council Chamber of the Royal Governors, General Assembly of the Province). In 1766 the first public viewing gallery was opened, and from the east end balcony the newly written Declaration of Independence was first read to the populace, July 18, 1776. (The tradition continues to this day; *see* Events, *below*). The brick facade is adorned with a unicorn and a lion, symbols of British royalty. These are copies; the originals were burned by the fervent patriots upon British evacuation. When the new State House was built (1798), this building was subsequently used as a firehouse, rental space for merchants and tradesmen, a newspaper office, and Boston City Hall (1830–41). After coming dangerously close to demolition, it was restored in 1882 to house the Bostonian Society, which still maintains a museum of local history (*see* History Museums, *below*). *206 Washington St., 617/720–3290. $3* *adults, $2 senior citizens, students, $1 ages 6–18. Daily 9:30–5. T stop: State, Government Center.*

6 *d-5*

OMNI PARKER HOUSE HOTEL

(Desmond and Lord, 1927.) The original Parker House began as a tavern on this site in 1855. Famed as the hostelry that created the roll bearing its name, it's still going strong (the rolls and the hotel). *60 School St., at Tremont St., Downtown, 617/227–8600. T stop: Downtown Crossing.*

6 *c-4*

HARRISON GRAY OTIS HOUSE (FIRST)

(Charles Bulfinch, 1796.) Lucky man, this Otis. Speculator, lawyer, congressman, and Boston mayor, he had three local houses designed for him by his friend, the famed architect Charles Bulfinch. This was the first—a beautifully proportioned, delicately detailed Federal house, the interior of which has been lovingly and painstakingly restored to reflect as closely as possible the decor and furnishings (some belonged to the Otis family) of 1790-1820. Today, many visitors are astonished by the brilliant colors and lavish furnishings that research showed were the hallmarks of that era. Overcoming a checkered past, including its use as a women's Turkish bath, Chinese laundry, and rooming house, the house is now home base for the Society for the Preservation of New England Antiquities, the largest regional preservation organization in the country. It houses a wonderful library of architectural and photographic archives (open by appointment only), and hosts a variety of lectures and special hands-on programs for kids as well. (*See* Specialized Tours *in* Guided Tours, *below*). *141 Cambridge St., 617/227–3956. Wed.–Sun. 11–5. $4 adults, $3.50 senior citizens, $2 students and children under 12. Guided tour only, on hr, last tour at 4. Groups by reservation only. T stops: Charles St., Bowdoin, Government Center.*

6 *b-5*

HARRISON GRAY OTIS HOUSE (SECOND)

(Charles Bulfinch, 1802. Remodeled: Peabody and Stearns, 1882.) This fine freestanding, stately Beacon Hill mansion set on a hill is the second one built by Bulfinch for his friend Otis, third

mayor of Boston. Used as the setting for that stylish, now-classic Steve McQueen film *The Thomas Crown Affair*. *85 Mount Vernon St., Beacon Hill. Not open to public. T stop: Charles/MGH.*

6 *c-5*

HARRISON GRAY OTIS HOUSE (THIRD)

(Charles Bulfinch, 1806.) The third of Otis's Bulfinch-designed residences boasts a lovely entryway. It is now owned by the American Meteorological Society. *45 Beacon St., Beacon Hill. Not open to public. T stop: Park St.*

6 *c-5*

PARKMAN HOUSE

(Cornelius Coolidge, 1825.) From 1853 to 1908, this was the home of the unfortunate Parkman family. In 1849, the father, Dr. George Parkman, was bludgeoned to death by John White Webster, a debt-ridden professor at the Harvard Medical School (the impecunious Webster owed money to Parkman, for which the latter was insisting on repayment). Today, the house is used by the mayor to receive distinguished visitors. *33 Beacon St., Beacon Hill. Not open to public. T stop: Park St.*

6 *d-5*

PARK STREET

Along the Common, Park Street was laid out in 1804 by Charles Bulfinch. Facing the Common were houses designed by Bulfinch—an imposing row once known as Bulfinch Row. The only town house remaining is on Park and Beacon streets (*see* Amory-Ticknor House, *above*). *T stop: Park St.*

6 *d-5*

PARK STREET "T" STATION

(Wheelwright and Haven, 1897. Renovation: Arrowstreet, 1978.) The central transfer point of the four MBTA lines, this was America's first subway station, beginning operation September 1, 1897. The two copper-roof, granite-face entry kiosks are now National Historic Landmarks. *Tremont St. T stop: Park St.*

6 *c-4*

PHILLIPS SCHOOL

Although built in 1824 near Beacon Hill's black section (outer north slope), this school was not open to black children until 1855, at which time it became one of Boston's first interracial schools. On the Black Heritage Trail. *Anderson and Pinckney Sts. Not open to public. T stop: Charles/MGH.*

 c-7

PIANO CRAFT GUILD

Built circa 1853, this South End industrial building was initially the Chickering Piano Factory and claimed to be the second-largest building in the world. Saved from the wrecker's ball, it was converted to artists' studio space and residences in 1972; all in all, creative South End recycling. Gallery hours vary, call for current show. *791 Tremont St., 617/437–9365. T stops: Back Bay, Prudential.*

9 *e-6*

PIERCE-HICHBORN HOUSE

This lovely three-story house was built around 1711 by Moses Pierce, a glazier and one of the founders of New North Church. The dwelling was bought in 1781 by Nathaniel Hichborn, boat builder and cousin of Paul Revere, and is now owned by the Paul Revere Memorial Association. Its architectural style contains elements from both the 17th and 18th centuries; inside are rooms with period furnishings. *29 North Sq., 617/523–1676. $2.50, $4 combined admission for Paul Revere and Pierce-Hichborn houses. Guided tour daily at 12:30 and 2:30; call to confirm. T stop: Haymarket.*

6 *b-5*

PINCKNEY STREET

Essentially the dividing line between the north and south slopes of Beacon Hill, Pinckney Street's architectural styles are as varied as its residents. Upper Pinckney once attracted those with a literary bent and is still a relatively Bohemian stretch where many writers and students hang their hats. From Anderson and Pinckney, there's a *spectacular* view of the Charles River with MIT directly across the water (*see 74½ Pinckney Street and John J. Smith House, below*). *T stop: Charles/MGH.*

3 *b-4*

PRATT HOUSE

Immortalized in Longfellow's "The Village Blacksmith"—a granite marker commemorates the site of the "spreading chestnut tree," long gone—this is the house where Dexter Pratt once lived and plied his trade. The 1808 clapboard

house now houses courses for the Cambridge Center for Adult Education as well as a popular bakery and eatery. (*See Longfellow National Historic Site, above.*) *56 Brattle St., Cambridge, 617/547–6789. Mon.–Sat. 9–6. T stop: Harvard Sq.*

6 *c-5*

WILLIAM HICKLING PRESCOTT HOUSE

(Asher Benjamin, 1808.) Built for merchant James Smith Colburn and later lived in by William Hickling Prescott, famed historian, this Federal-style house has been turned into a museum featuring antique furniture, a collection of Chinese export trade porcelain, and a restored "best bedchamber." There is also a fine costume collection. The house serves as headquarters of the Massachusetts Society of Colonial Dames and is open for guided tours. *55 Beacon St., 617/742–3190. $4. Tues., Wed., and Sat. noon–4. T stop: Harvard Sq.*

6 *f-4*

QUINCY MARKET

(Alexander Parris, 1824-26. Restoration and conversion: F. A. Stahl and Associates and Benjamin Thomas Associates, 1976.) Originally an 1826 design of Alexander Parris, built at the urging of then-mayor Josiah Quincy as a revenue-producing scheme, Quincy Market was planned to expand the cramped market facilities then centered in the ground floor of Faneuil Hall. For the past almost-thirty years, both complexes have been joined as part of a project that has become the model for all big-city building recycling schemes. Today, the central of three 535-foot-long Greek Revival commercial buildings (the others are called South Market and North Market) flourishes once more as part of the clamorous, glamorous Quincy Market/Faneuil Hall Marketplace, both of which house dozens and dozens of restaurants, and knickknack, gift, and book purveyors. Along the sides, the Bull Market (named for the Bull weather vane atop the copper-dome roof) is where vendors sell a wide variety of gifts and crafts. Outside, entertainment and special events (street performers, marching bands, music, etc.) bring in even more crowds. Note: No pets allowed in buildings. *Quincy Market/Faneuil Hall Marketplace, 617/338–2323. Mon.–Sat. 10–9, Sun. noon–6; food stalls open for breakfast as early as 7. T stops: Haymarket, Government Center, State St., Aquarium.*

3 c-4
RADCLIFFE COLLEGE

Bounded by Garden, Mason, Brattle streets, and Appean Way, Radcliffe was established in 1879 to provide women with an education comparable to that available to men at Harvard. In 1894, Radcliffe became, in effect, Harvard's sister school, and in 1965 the two institutions merged administrations and became coeducational, blurring all but the historic differences between them. In the Schlesinger Library at the Radcliffe Institute, America's most extensive library pertaining to women's studies includes major collections of the work of Susan B. Anthony, Julia Ward Howe, and Harriet Beecher Stowe. *Radcliffe Yard, Cambridge, 617/495–8000. T stop: Harvard Sq.*

9 e-5
PAUL REVERE HOUSE

Built circa 1676, this two-story clapboard house with leaded windows, sloping roof, and second-story overhang is the oldest surviving dwelling in Boston. Typical of early settlers' homes, this was where patriot Paul Revere resided from 1770 to 1800 with his mother, five children from his first wife, and 11 from his second (you will no doubt wonder where they put them all). Exhibits include his tools, saddlebags, pistols, and colonial furnishings. Restored to its original appearance in 1908 by Joseph Chandler, it is now a National Historic Landmark. Special events are scheduled throughout the year, many designed to delight children—silhouette-makers ply their skills, the staff dresses up in period costumes and serves apple pandowdy, a dulcimer player entertains, or the 10th Regiment Afoot—in full antique British regalia—may muster on the premises; call for the monthly calendar. On the Freedom Trail. *19 North Sq., North End, 617/523–1676. $2.50. Nov.–Apr. 14, daily 9:30–4:15; Apr. 15–Oct., daily 9:30–5:15. Closed Mon. Jan.–Mar. T stop: Haymarket.*

8 f-2
RITZ-CARLTON HOTEL

(Strickland, Blodgett, and Law, 1927. Addition: Skidmore, Owings, and Merrill, 1981.) In the Back Bay, the Ritz-Carlton is Boston's last bastion of an opulent era long gone. The original part was joined by a 16-story addition in 1981. From the serene dining room there is a grand view of the Public Garden and the Swan Boats (*see* Chapters 3 and 7). *Arlington St. and Commonwealth Ave. T stop: Arlington.*

6 c-4
ROLLINS PLACE

A private court built in 1843 by John W. Rollins, this was meant as housing for Beacon Hill tradesmen and artisans. Note the trompe l'oeil Greek-Revival villa at the end—only the portico is real. Similar cul de sacs are nearby: Bellingham Place, Goodwin Place, and Sentry Hill Place. *Revere St., Beacon Hill. T stop: Charles/MGH.*

8 d-6
RUTLAND SQUARE

A lovely spot in the South End, Rutland Square features Italianate bowfront houses built between 1865 and 1875, all surrounding a fenced-in ellipse-shape garden. *Between Tremont St. and Columbus Ave., South End. T stop: Chinatown, Back Bay.*

9 c-6
SALEM STREET

In the 19th century, when Jews were settling the area, this was the millinery and garment industry area. It is now solidly Italian and lined with meat and provisions shops. Little wonder this narrow and colorful street has an authentic old-world feel to it. *Between Cross and Charter Sts., North End. T stop: Haymarket.*

6 e-4
SEARS BLOCK

(Built circa 1845. Remodeled: Stahl and Bennett, 1969.) This tapering granite skeleton building seems destined to ride on the fame of the giant steaming teakettle hanging over the entranceway of the unassuming coffee shop that presently occupies it (*see* Steaming Kettle, *below*). *City Hall Plaza at Court St. T stop: Government Center.*

6 e-4
SEARS CRESCENT

(Built in 1816, with Sears Block added in 1848; restored by Don Stull Associates, 1969.) This redbrick block was once the hub of Boston's publishing world—

noted men of letters, such as Emerson and Hawthorne, were frequent visitors. *City Hall Plaza, Government Center. T stop: Government Center.*

6 *c-5*

17 CHESTNUT STREET

(Charles Bulfinch, 1808.) Built for Mrs. Swan, early Beacon Hill developer (the only woman among them), it later became the home of Julia Ward Howe, author of the "Battle Hymn of the Republic." *17 Chestnut St., Beacon Hill. T stop: Park St.*

6 *b-6*

70–75 BEACON STREET

(Asher Benjamin, 1828.) These three-story Greek Revival residences facing the Public Garden are among the handsomest structures in Boston. Number 71 was given by Mayor Harrison Gray Otis to his son as a wedding present. Today, thankfully, they are as well-preserved as family jewels. *70–75 Beacon St., Beacon Hill. Not open to public. T stop: Park St.*

6 *c-5*

74½ PINCKNEY STREET

"The hidden house of Beacon Hill," this is a charming, and *very* private, private residence. To take a quick peak, access is gained via the No. 74 front entry. *74½ Pinckney St., Beacon Hill. T stop: Charles/MGH, Park St.*

6 *c-4*

SMITH COURT RESIDENCES

Throughout the 19th century, this "slope" of Beacon Hill was a noted black neighborhood. Smith Court retains five wooden residential structures typical of the housing that black tradesmen and servants occupied. William C. Nell, America's first published black historian and early leader in the battle to desegregate Boston's public schools, lived at No. 3 from 1851 to 1856. On the Black Heritage Trail. *2–6 Smith Ct., west off Joy St. Not open to public. T stop: Bowdoin, Charles/MGH.*

6 *c-4*

ABIEL SMITH SCHOOL

Thanks to a legacy left to the city by white merchant Abiel Smith for the education of black children, this schoolhouse was built in 1834 to house what became Boston's first black school (replacing the African Meetinghouse). It closed in 1855 when segregation in Massachusetts public schools was outlawed, and black children were permitted to attend the public school closest to their homes. Now, it is a fitting home to the Museum of Afro-American History (*see* History Museums, *below*). On the Black Heritage Trail. *46 Joy St., at Smith Ct. T stop: Bowdoin, Charles/MGH.*

6 *c-5*

JOHN J. SMITH HOUSE

Smith was an active abolitionist elected to the Massachusetts House of Representatives in 1868 and 1872; he was also the first black man appointed to the Boston Common Council. He resided in this house from 1878 to 1893. On the Black Heritage Trail. *86 Pinckney St., Beacon Hill. Not open to public. T stop: Bowdoin.*

6 *c-5*

SOMERSET CLUB

(Alexander Parris, 1819.) Originally the David Sears mansion, this massive granite Greek Revival building was famed architect Alexander Parris's first in Boston. With decorative work done by Solomon Willard, lion's-head door knockers, and a stylish bowfront, this was considered a somewhat ostentatious residence by demure Beacon Hill residents. Today, it remains one of the most handsome houses on the hill and is home to the Somerset Club, a prestigious men's club founded in 1851. *42 Beacon St., Beacon Hill. Not open to public. T stop: Park St.*

1 *g-5*

SOUTH BOSTON

Sometimes called America's Dublin, but more familiarly known as Southie, South Boston was founded as part of Dorchester in 1630. Annexed to Boston in 1804, the building of a bridge in 1805 brought development. In the 19th century it became an industrial and shipping area, attracting a large, predominantly Irish, immigrant population. Leading sights include Frederick Law Olmsted's Pleasure Bay, the star-shape Fort Independence, and Marine Park (lovely views of the harbor islands); leading day is, of course, St. Patrick's, with a major parade and sundry festivities. *T stop: Broadway.*

B

SOUTH END

Created by landfill, this part of Boston was, in the middle of the 19th century, a fast-growing residential area of elegant brick and brownstone town houses. Replaced by the Back Bay as Boston's "most fashionable" neighborhood, the South End fell on hard times and only recently have rediscovery and reclamation made their mark. Ethnic diversity (black, Hispanic, Lebanese, among *many* others) is a key characteristic of this section. Also, some of the city's most beautiful Victorian town houses are located around Rutland Square. The main thoroughfares are Harrison, Washington, Shawmut, and Tremont. In particular, Tremont has come alive with the growth of restaurants, stores, and coffee shops. Gentrification also has meant the growth of an active and vibrant gay community here. *Between Columbus and Harrison Aves. T stops: N.E. Medical Center, Prudential.*

6 *f-7*

SOUTH STATION

(Shepley, Rutan, and Coolidge, 1898.) The part of the station that survives is a fitting tribute to the heyday of American railroads. When completed, South Station was the world's railway terminus and was soon to become the nation's busiest. In the 1960s, when train travel seemed an anachronism, most of the station was demolished; thankfully, the headhouse was saved from demolition by inclusion in the National Register of Historic Places in 1975. Today, restoration along with a resurgence of train travel on the northeast corridor has given the whole complex a new life and it is now part of a revamped Downtown Boston Transportation Center. South Station's refurbished lobby is filled with shops, eateries, and newsstands to help you while the time waiting for a train. A new eight-story bus station—official title: Intermodal Transportation Center—is under construction and already in use with access at nearby South Station on Atlantic Avenue. A central skylit rotunda forms the heart of the new bus terminal. *Summer St. and Atlantic Ave. T stop: South Station.*

6 *d-5*

STATE HOUSE

(Charles Bulfinch, 1795-98. Northern Extension: Charles E. Brigham, 1889-95.

Wings: Clipston Sturgis, 1914-17.) Built on a cow pasture that belonged to the John Hancock family, this magnificent Federal building was said to have impressed President Monroe to such an extent that he immediately chose Bulfinch (Boston's leading architect) to design the reconstruction of the U.S. Capitol. Originally the dome was shingled and whitewashed, then it was covered with copper (by Paul Revere and Sons in 1802) and then, until 1872, painted gray when it was covered with 23-karat gold leaf (it was temporarily repainted gray during World War II to avoid attack), making it a gleaming landmark. The dome is topped by a pine cone, symbolizing a valued industry of the state in that era—lumber. The second-floor Hall of Flags features battle flags from the Civil War through World War II. In the House Chamber see the renowned "Sacred Cod," ode to another once-major industry; elsewhere, in the Great Hall, is the giant, modernistic clock designed by New York artist R. M. Fischer—this caused an uproar when it was installed in 1986 due to its cost of $100,000. The public is allowed to sit in on House or Senate sessions (year-round, usually Mon.–Thurs. at 1 PM; call for complete schedule). On the Freedom Trail. *Beacon St. between Hancock and Bowdoin Sts., 617/727–3676. Tours weekdays 10–4, last tour at 3:30. Research library: 617/727–2590. Weekdays 11–5. Free. T stop: Park St.*

6 *g-5*

STATE STREET BLOCK

(Gridley J. F. Bryant, 1858.) Remnant of a once-flourishing sea trade in Boston by the same architect of Old City Hall, these large granite warehouses were originally much larger (and, in fact, used to extend to the water). The mansard roofs were later additions. *1 McKinley Sq., State to Central Sts. T stop: State St.*

6 *e-4*

STEAMING KETTLE

Way back in 1873, coppersmiths Hicks and Badger fashioned this oversize kettle made to hold 227 gallons, 2 quarts, 1 pint, and 3 gills (a competition to guess exactly how much liquid the kettle could hold riveted the city in 1875); back then, the kettle even "steamed," making it one of Boston's quaintest landmarks. It weighs 200 pounds and marks the spot where Boston's largest tea emporium was once located. Now it marks the location—no surprises here—of a Starbucks. *Sears Block, 65 Court St. T stop: Government Center.*

6 b-6

SWAN BOATS

Take a ride on one of the pedal-powered Swan Boats—a traditional, warm-weather Boston treat. These boats have been plying the lagoon at the Boston Public Garden since 1877. This simple, inexpensive, and charming Boston tradition is a treat for the young and young-at-heart—and if your children have read the classic *Make Way for Ducklings*, it will be even more meaningful for them. For more on the Boston Public Garden, *see* Chapter 6. *Boston Lagoon, 617/522-1966. $1.75 adults, 95¢ children. Mid-Apr.–June 20 and day after Labor Day–mid-Sept., daily 10–4; June 21–Labor Day, daily 10–5. T stop: Arlington.*

8 b-6

SYMPHONY HALL

(McKim, Mead, and White, 1900.) Legendary home of the Boston Symphony Orchestra (BSO), this huge redbrick Renaissance Revival concert hall was built after an intense study of acoustics by the architects, probably the earliest known study of its kind. It paid off—this is one of the best in the world, called a "Stradivarius among halls." The BSO, now under the baton of Seiji Ozawa, celebrated its 100th anniversary here in 1981. The orchestra's season usually runs from October to April. Symphony Hall has also been home since 1885 to the beloved Boston Pops—their season runs May to mid-July. *301 Massachusetts Ave., at Huntington Ave., 617/266–1492. T stop: Symphony.*

6 c-5

34 BEACON STREET

(Cornelius Coolidge, 1825.) Once the residence of the Cabots, since 1909 home to the Little, Brown and Company publishing house. *34 Beacon St. Not open to public. T stop: Park St.*

6 c-5

THE TUDOR

(S. J. F. Thayer, 1885–87) This nine-story Beacon Hill building is an incongruity because of its height, the abundance of detail, and the variety of forms. *34½ Beacon St. at Joy St. Not open to public. T stop: Park St.*

6 c-5

29A CHESTNUT STREET

(Charles Bulfinch, 1802.) A noted occupant of this Federal-period mansion was actor Edwin Booth, a favorite on the Boston theatrical circuit. He was playing here the night his brother John Wilkes Booth shot President Lincoln in Washington. *29A Chestnut St., Beacon Hill. T stop: Park St.*

6 a-5

UNION BOAT CLUB BOATHOUSE

On the Esplanade, behind Hatch Memorial Shell, this is America's oldest rowing club, in operation since 1851. The boathouse itself was built at the turn of the century. *75 Embankment Rd., 617/523–9718. Not open to public. T stop: Charles/MGH.*

8 f-6

UNION PARK SQUARE

A wonderful South End square harking back to the 1850s when this was *the* fashionable section. Town houses surrounding a fenced-in area replete with fountains and flowers. Today, Union Park Square remains a jewel in a transitional setting. *Between Tremont St. and Shawmut Ave., South End. T stop: Prudential.*

6 h-2

UNION WHARF

Originally built circa 1846 (renovated in 1979 by Moritz Bergmeyer), this wharf conversion consists of office and residential town house condominiums. *North of Atlantic Ave. and Commercial St. T stop: Haymarket.*

1 g-2

USS CONSTITUTION & USS CONSTITUTION MUSEUM

She was dubbed "Old Ironsides" because cannonballs reportedly "bounced off" her durable oak sides. The world's oldest warship, the USS *Constitution* is still under U.S. Naval commission. She is 175 feet long, was built in Boston with copper and brass-work crafted by *the* Paul Revere, and launched in 1797. Tour two of her three decks; sailors, in period uniforms, will answer questions. One of her 44 guns is shot off at 8 AM and at sunset. Every July 4, she is towed out into the harbor where a 21-gun salute is rendered; when she redocks, she is turned so her hull weathers evenly. Personnel at the nearby museum will answer all the questions you might have after visiting the ship; the museum also has some kid-friendly interactive exhibits that will make the War of 1812 come alive. On the Freedom Trail. (*See* Events *and* History Museums, *below.*) *Charlestown Navy Yard, Charlestown, 617/242–5670. Daily 9:30–sunset, lower deck closes at 3:50. Free. T stop: Haymarket, then MBTA bus No. 92 or No. 93 to Navy Yard.*

7 *a-3*

WADSWORTH HOUSE

Built circa 1726, this lovely yellow-clapboard colonial house was, until 1849, the official residence of the president of Harvard University. Albeit more famous as having served as Gen. George Washington's first headquarters in July 1775, it is now the office of the Harvard Alumni Association. *1341 Massachusetts Ave., Cambridge. Not open to public. T stop: Harvard Sq.*

8 *h-3*

WANG CENTER FOR THE PERFORMING ARTS

(Clarence M. Blackall, 1925.) Built in 1925 as the Metropolitan Theatre, this former movie palace is one of the world's largest, seating 4,200. The stage, also one of the largest, is 60 feet wide, 30 feet high, and 60 feet deep. Recently renovated (and renamed) for use as a performance space for dance, opera, and theater events, it was expanded in 1982 and again in 1990 and then renamed for benefactor An Wang of the Wang computer company in 1983. *270 Tremont St., 617/482–9393. Open, other than for performances, by appointment only. T stop: Boylston and N.E. Medical Center.*

6 *e-6*

WASHINGTON STREET

Back in the 17th and 18th centuries, this was the only road that ran the length of Boston (then still a peninsula). It begins at Dock Square, and the part of it that is Downtown Crossing—the heart of Boston's downtown shopping district—is closed to traffic and is an attractive pedestrian mall. Here you will find two department store giants—Macy's and Filene's (with its famed bargain basement)—and a host of chains and other specialty shops. *T stop: Downtown Crossing.*

6

WATERFRONT

Along Atlantic Avenue, Boston's waterfront is no longer the bustling port of clipper ship days, but it is a vital area of renovation, redevelopment, and reclamation. A satisfying merging of past and present, it now bustles with people residing, shopping, and dining, all at water's edge in the former 19th-century granite warehouses on Commercial, Long, and Lewis wharfs. For one of the more striking waterfront Boston vistas, take in the view from under the arch of the Rowes Wharf redbrick complex. *T stop: Aquarium.*

6 *e-5*

WINTHROP BUILDING

(Clarence H. Blackall, 1893.) The great-granddaddy of the Pru and the Hancock skyscrapers, this nine-story gracefully slender edifice was the first building in Boston to use a steel skeleton as opposed to thick load-bearing masonry walls. With its elegant overhanging cornice and on the National Register of Historic Places, it's rightly considered a gem. *276 Washington St., Downtown. T Stop: Downtown Crossing.*

7 *a-3*

WINTHROP SQUARE

Surrounded both by aging and modern buildings, this was the original market square of Cambridge in the 17th and 18th centuries. On the west side of Winthrop Street is the old Training Field School, built in 1827. *Mount Auburn St., Cambridge. T stop: Harvard Sq.*

8 *f-3*

WOMEN'S EDUCATIONAL & INDUSTRIAL UNION

(Parker, Thomas, and Rice, 1906. Restoration: Shepley, Bulfinch, and Abbot, 1973.) This Boston institution is landmarked by its swan insignia (though new, it's descended from the original logo of the union), which pays homage to the fact that the Industrial Union and the Swan Boats arrived on the Boston scene in the same year—1877. The Union was founded to foster educational and employment opportunities for women; today, it continues to aid the poor and elderly. The retail shop has handmade items and crafts, including jewelry, pottery, housewares, and rugs. *356 Boylston St., Back Bay, 617/536–5651. T stop: Arlington.*

HISTORY MUSEUMS

6 g-7

BOSTON TEA PARTY SHIP & MUSEUM

A full-size working replica of the brig *Beaver II*, one of the ships raided by the Sons of Liberty who, disguised as Indians, had a party systematically dumping a British cargo of tea to protest the import tax levied by the Crown. Retaliation resulted in the closing of Boston Harbor—drawing the rebellious colonies closer to revolt. The *Beaver II* is located where the original Tea Party took place; it was then called Griffin's Wharf. You are encouraged to throw a bale of tea overboard (this time they are attached to ropes for easy retrieval) and are then rewarded with a complimentary cup of tea (iced in summer). Costumed guides in the museum, exhibits, documents, and audiovisual presentations. Full reenactment annually on December 16 (*see* Events, *below*) and for large groups by reservations. *Congress St. Bridge, 617/338–1773. $7. Memorial Day–Labor Day, daily 9–6; Labor Day–Dec. 1 and Mar.–Memorial Day, daily 9–5. T stop: South Station.*

8 c-3

FIRST CORPS OF CADETS MUSEUM

Established in 1876, this is a museum of weapons, some of which date back to King George II, plus weapons, uniforms, flags, equipment, and paintings used by the American military starting from 1726 through the end of World War II. Tours last about two hours. *227 Commonwealth Ave., 617/267–1726. Free. Open by appointment only. T stop: Copley.*

7 h-8

HART NAUTICAL GALLERIES

MIT's nautical history museum focuses on the techniques of nautical exploration and engineering with ship models illustrating the evolution of ship design and construction, including models from Viking ships to the *Mayflower*, the USS *Constitution* to the present. Historic photographs and artifacts explore merchant and naval shipbuilding programs of World War II, including the contribution of women to their success. *77 Massachusetts Ave., Bldg. 5, Cambridge, 617/253–4444. Free. Daily 9–8. T stop: Kendall Sq.*

7 b-1

HARVARD SEMITIC MUSEUM

Mixing anthropology and education, this small but packed museum houses art and artifacts from the ancient Middle East pertaining to the history of Semitic peoples. An upstairs area holds a fine collection of Egyptian mummy cases—and also serves as a classroom for the Department of Near Eastern Languages and Civilization. Rotating exhibits explore varied subjects, such as the history of writing. *6 Divinity Ave., Cambridge, 617/495–3123. Free. Weekdays 10–4, Sun. 1–4. T stop: Harvard Sq.*

1 h-6

JOHN F. KENNEDY LIBRARY & MUSEUM

In a spectacular waterfront building designed by I. M. Pei, the legacy of the JFK presidency is kept alive through library archives, a 20-minute film, and Camelot-era memorabilia and photos from the Kennedy family history. While archives are reserved for accredited scholars, visitors may wander through historically fascinating exhibits that delve into the Kennedy family's triumphs and tragedies. During the summer, the president's 26-foot sloop, the *Victura,* kept in shipshape condition, rests outside the building. Inside, White House memorabilia includes the president's desk just as it was when he left for Dallas, plus a stunning variety of gifts to the Kennedy presidency, including a walrus-bone model of an American whaler from Nikita Khrushchev. The 1960 presidential campaign has been re-created through banners, posters, buttons, even the television studio in which Kennedy debated Richard M. Nixon. One of the newer exhibits focuses on the late Jackie Kennedy Onassis, including samples of her distinctive wardrobe and film clips of her White House tour. In a darkened hall, continuous videos of the first news bulletin of the President's assassination and his funeral introduce a somber note in an otherwise upbeat museum. On site are a small café and gift shop. Free parking. *Columbia Point, 617/929–4523. $6 adults, $4 senior citizens and students, $2 ages 6–15, under 6 free. Group rates available. Daily 9–5. T stop: JFK/Mass. University Station on Red Line (Ashmont), then free MBTA shuttle-bus from station (every 20 mins daily 9–5).*

6 *c-4*

MUSEUM OF AFRO-AMERICAN HISTORY

On Beacon Hill, this museum is located in two of the most important sights on Boston's Black Heritage Trail—the historic Abiel Smith School and the African Meetinghouse. The museum was established in 1964 to promote the history, particularly in New England, of black Americans. Headquarters occupy the Abiel Smith School, the first public school for black children in Boston. The upstairs serves as offices for the Park Service; pick up brochures and maps for the Black Heritage Trail there. A gift shop downstairs features T-shirts and books about black history. The museum's changing exhibits and activities are held next door in the African Meetinghouse (*see* Churches, *above*), the oldest extant African-American church building in the United States, and once nicknamed the Black Faneuil Hall. The museum hosts a variety of activities during February, Black History Month, and in May stages a reenactment of the assembly of the Civil War's black 54th regiment. *Museum headquarters, 46 Joy St., 617/742–1854. $3 suggested donation. Weekdays 10–4. African Meetinghouse, 8 Smith Ct. (off Joy St.). $3 suggested donation. Memorial Day–Labor Day, daily 10–4. T stop: Park St.*

6 *f-4*

MUSEUM OF THE ANCIENT & HONORABLE ARTILLERY COMPANY OF MASSACHUSETTS

The company—the oldest military organization in the Western Hemisphere—was chartered in 1638 by John Winthrop, the state's first governor, to protect the early settlers of Massachusetts. The military museum and library, located on the third floor of historic Faneuil Hall, contain firearms, artifacts, flags, militia material, cannon, and uniforms—everything relative to the organization. *Faneuil Hall, Dock Sq., 3rd floor, 617/227–1638. Free. Weekdays 10–4. T stop: Haymarket, Government Center.*

MUSEUM OF OUR NATIONAL HERITAGE

This small but dynamic institution displays items and artifacts from all facets of American life, with the museum's focus on everyday life as well as on the famous Americans who shaped our history. An ongoing exhibit, "Lexington Alar-m'd," shows what Revolutionary-era life was like through ordinary objects used in the home from the kitchen to the bedroom. Another ongoing exhibit highlights the country's fraternal organizations. The museum also hosts lectures, family programs, and films; there's a well-stocked gift shop. *33 Marrett Rd., Lexington, 617/861–6559. $1 suggested donation. Mon.–Sat. 10–5, Sun. noon–5.*

6 *e-5*

OLD SOUTH MEETINGHOUSE

Not only is this the second-oldest church building in Boston, but it has been witness to pivotal events in the American Revolution, such as the raucous gathering of December 16, 1773, at which Samuel Adams denounced the British ships, laden with taxable tea, moored in Boston Harbor. Reminiscent of Christopher Wren's London churches, it's a beauty. Today, it's one of Boston's three remaining 18th-century Anglican churches. When built it not only served as a house of God but as a meetinghouse where issues of the day were discussed—grand in size, it could hold more people than Faneuil Hall. The meeting on December 16, 1773, to protest the tea tax became the overture to the famed Boston Tea Party. It was from here that the colonial "Indians" set out for Griffin's Wharf via Milk Street.

In 1775, in punishment no doubt, General Burgoyne turned the interior of Old South into a riding academy for British cavalry and the pews and pulpit became kindling. After the Revolution, however, it was lovingly restored as a place of worship; Then, in 1876, it was nearly demolished when the congregation moved to a new church in Copley Square. Recent renovations have provided a new light and sound system, an underground educational facility, new exhibits, air-conditioning, and structural modifications that make the 650-seat facility wheelchair-accessible. Temporary exhibitions are held; one recent show, "Voices of Protest," traced free speech at the Old South from the times of Sam Adams to the more recent days of David Duke and Jocelyn Elders. The meetinghouse also offers a 3-hour historical tour program on Wednesdays, July through August, at 9:45 AM (*see* Walking Tours *in* Guided Tours, *below*). Old South is now a National Historic Landmark and part of the Boston National Historic Park (*see also* Historic Buildings & Areas, *above*). *310 Washington St., 617/482–6439. $3 adults, $2.50 senior citizens, students, $1 children 6–18, under 6 free. Daily 9:30–5. T stop: State St. or Downtown Crossing.*

6 *e-5*

OLD STATE HOUSE MUSEUM

Here you'll find one of Boston's holiest spots—the balcony where, on July 18, 1776, the Declaration of Independence was first read to the public (*see* Events, *below*). The Old State House was built in 1713 over the ruins of the first Town House, undergoing many transformations and barely saved from destruction in 1880. Its upper floors housed the official chambers of the British colonial government; here, too, American patriots voiced their arguments for autonomy. When the state government moved to Beacon Hill in 1798, the building was rented out to tradesmen until it became Boston's City Hall in 1830. After the city government moved, the building lapsed into decline but was saved by a determined citizenry in 1880. Substantial renovations were made in 1991. The first floor's permanent exhibit focuses on Boston's revolutionary history, with such artifacts as a musket found after the Boston Massacre (you can see the site where it took place from a window), a three-corner hat, John Hancock's inaugural clothing, and a vial of tea from the Boston Tea Party. There are also video, audio, and other interactive exhibits. A spiral staircase leads to the halls where government and judicial business was transacted; now the space houses exhibits on Boston history that change every six months. The museum is maintained by the Bostonian Society. Immediately outside the Old State House is a visitor's center at 15 State Street run by the National Park Service, open daily 9–5 and 9–6 from June to August. *206 Washington St., 617/720–3290. $3 adults, $2 senior citizens and students, $1 ages 6–18. Daily 9:30–5. T stop: State St.*

1 *g-2*

USS CONSTITUTION & USS CONSTITUTION MUSEUM

Better known as "Old Ironsides," the USS *Constitution* remains at the ready, anchored at the Charlestown Navy Yard—a fascinating study in keeping history alive, and afloat. Just 200 yards away is the USS *Constitution* Museum, located in an 1832 granite building designed by Alexander Parris that was originally used to house pumping machinery for the drydock. This museum contains artifacts and hands-on exhibits pertaining to the ship—firearms, logs, and navigational instruments. Upstairs, a series of photographs and artifacts explains the *Constitution*'s most recent renovation. Other exhibits take you step by step through the *Constitution*'s most important battles and even on an 1844 exploration and discovery journey. Old meets new with an awesome video battle "fought" at the helm of a ship's wheel. A 10-minute film narrates the history of the ships, and shows the lower decks which are off-limit to visitors. (*See* Historic Buildings & Areas, *above*.) *Constitution Wharf, Charlestown Navy Yard, Charlestown, ship 617/242–5670, museum 617/426–1812. Constitution free; museum $4 adults, $3 senior citizens, $2 ages 6–16, under 6 free; ages 16 and under free weekends. Ship daily 9:30–sunset, 20-min tours, last tour at 3:50. Museum Mar.–May and Sept.–Nov., daily 10–5; June–Labor Day, daily 9–6; Dec.–Feb., daily 10–4. T stop: Haymarket, then MBTA Bus 93 to Charlestown City Sq. or MBTA water shuttle from Long Wharf.*

LIBRARIES

6 *d-5*

BOSTON ATHENAEUM

Founded in 1807, the Athenaeum is not only one of the country's oldest libraries, but a distinctly Boston institution that recalls the era of Brahmin splendor. The library, which grew out of the local Anthology Club, moved in 1849 to its present quarters, magnificently modeled after Palladio's Palazzo da Porta Festa in Vicenza, Italy, by architect Edward Clark Cabot. In 1873-74, two of the building's four galleries were occupied by the newly incorporated Museum of Fine Arts. In 1876, artwork from the Athenaeum went to the new Copley Square location to form the nucleus of the Fine Arts museum's collections. Remaining at the Athenaeum are paintings by Stuart, Harding, and Allson; sculpture by Greenough, Houdon, William Wetmore Story, plus major collections of historical prints as well as photographs, including daguerreotypes and ambrotypes, that document the history of photography in New England. The book collection ranges from volumes of George Washington's private library to one of the finest collections of detective fiction; there are numerous special holdings, from Gypsy literature to pamphlets of the Confederacy. The stacks are only open to members (a mere 1,049 ownership shares exist—highly prized and usually passed down from generation to generation), although accredited researchers may apply for an annual membership. Nonmembers can, however, visit the beautifully appointed first and second floors, and view the lofty, magisterial Reading Room by tour—in days gone by, grand dames, with pet Pekingese in tow, would do their research here on pre-Revolutionary Boston over tea and sweet biscuits (it's the only way, really).Visitors are also welcome in the second-floor gallery that has revolving shows of art and sculpture, usually with a literary bent. *10½ Beacon St., 617/227–0270. Free. Weekdays 9–5:30; Sept.–May, also Sat. 9–4; tour Tues. and Thurs. at 3 with 24-hr advance reservation. T stop: Park St.*

8 *d-3*

BOSTON PUBLIC LIBRARY

(McKim, Mead, and White, 1888-95.) A keystone of Copley Square, this library contains some of the world's most rare and valued collections—but the building's extraordinary art and architecture make it an amazing spot for visitors, even for those without a library card! This was the first (1852) large-scale free public library in the United States. ("Free to All" is carved in stone above the entrance.) Constructed of granite, the Italian Renaissance-style edifice is based on the Bibliothèque St. Geneviève in Paris; the interior is graced with the art of Edwin Austin Abbey, John Singer Sargent, Augustus Saint-Gaudens, and Pierre Puvis de Chavannes. As you enter, be sure to touch for good luck one of the sienna-marble lions on the magnificent stairway leading to the second level; you will see where the rough stone has been smoothed by such entreaties. The entrance doors are by Daniel Chester French; the seated figures representing *Art* and *Science* are by Bela Pratt. *Don't miss* the lovely central courtyard on the main floor. The library has undergone a multi-million dollar renovation: the Puvis paintings, depicting the elements of sci-

ence, have been restored, as has the exquisite Bates Reading Room. The striking though darkened Sargent murals—depicting Christianity and Judaism—are now scheduled for restoration. Adjacent is the modern addition by Philip Johnson, built in 1972, which contains the circulating collection. Members of the staff give marvelous (and succinct) art and architecture tours. The library also has free year-round events for kids, including films, story-telling, and music programs. There are also special events for young adults as well as numerous author lectures, often in the Rabb Lecture Hall. Call for information. *666 Boylston St., Copley Sq., 617/536–5400. Mon.–Thurs. 9–9, Fri.–Sat. 9–5, Sun. (Oct.–May only) 1–5. T stop: Copley.*

6 *5-c*

CLUB OF ODD VOLUMES

One of the houses built by the Mount Vernon Association developers, this early-19th-century residence now houses a literary dining club (incidentally, the name refers to incomplete sets of books). Founded in 1887, it's the second-oldest book collectors' club in America. Not open to the public, unless a special exhibit is taking place. *77 Mount Vernon St., Beacon Hill, 617/227– 7003. T stop: Park St.*

1 *h-6*

JOHN F. KENNEDY LIBRARY & MUSEUM

See History Museums, *above.*

7 *a-1*

WIDENER MEMORIAL LIBRARY

The largest university library in the world and the third-largest in the United States, the Widener's 10 floors hold the equivalent of 50 miles of books. Harry Elkins Widener was a book collector who perished on the *Titanic* in 1912— rumor had it that he went back to his stateroom at the last minute to salvage a first edition of Bacon's *Works*. His collection formed the library's nucleus. The library, built thanks to the Widener family's millions, also contains panoramic models of Cambridge and Harvard dating from 1667, 1775, and 1936. The lobby and Memorial Room (containing Widener's personal collection) are the only parts open to the public. *Harvard Yard, Cambridge, 617/495–2413. During academic year, weekdays 9 AM–10 PM, Sat.*

9–5, Sun. noon–5; hrs vary during school breaks, particularly on evenings and weekends. Closed weekends in summer. Tour Thurs. at 3. Stacks open only to those with Harvard ID. T stop: Harvard Sq.

MODERN ARCHITECTURE

Towering hotels and commercial buildings, huge, mixed-use projects, and enclosed urban malls are changing the face of Boston dramatically. Master architects from Alvar Aalto to Le Corbusier to James Sterling all have left their calling cards on the Boston landscape. In addition to such award-winning buildings, however, there are also those modernist buildings that Bostonians love to hate.

3 f-7
BAKER HOUSE

(Alvar Aalto, 1947.) This undulating, rugged redbrick MIT dormitory building was designed to provide as many rooms as possible with a view of the Charles River. The structure is well respected for its consideration of the student's lifestyle rhythms and needs. *362 Memorial Dr., 617/253–3161. T stop: Kendall Sq.*

8 b-4
BOSTON ARCHITECTURAL CENTER

(Ashley, Myer, and Associates, 1967.) The center, one of the few American schools of architecture not affiliated with a university, held a competition to choose a designer. The result is an attractive, very "glassy" building. A Richard Haas trompe l'oeil mural has been painted on the blank wall (seen by looking east at the building from Newbury Street). A gallery features architecture- and design-related exhibits. *320 Newbury St., at Hereford St., Back Bay, 617/536–3170. Free. Mon.–Thurs. 9 AM–10 PM, Fri. 9–8, Sat. 9–5, Sun. noon–5. T stop: Hynes Convention Center/ICA.*

6 e-5
BOSTON COMPANY BUILDING

(Pietro Belluschi, Emery Roth, and Sons, 1970.) This 41-story red-granite building employs that old modernist trick of revealing many of its structural elements. The structure is at one of those addresses that tells you nothing about where it is actually located. Would that be too practical? *1 Boston Pl., Court and Washington Sts., Downtown Crossing. T stop: Downtown Crossing.*

6 e-5
BOSTON FIVE CENTS SAVINGS BANK BUILDING

(Parker, Thomas, and Rice, 1926. Addition: Kallman, McKinnell, and Wood, 1972.) An eye-catcher, this edifice contrasts a new all-glass, curtain-walled structure with the curving beams and columns of the solid Renaissance original wing. The addition now houses Borders Books (where poetry readings are now held right outside the former bank vaults). *24–30 School St., Downtown Crossing. T stop: Downtown Crossing.*

8 d-3
BOSTON PUBLIC LIBRARY ADDITION

(Philip Johnson, 1972.) This gigantic modern addition, presumably designed to complement the older Renaissance building of the library, echoes the original in materials, size, and shape, if not scale. Inside, there's a typical Johnson note—a skylit center bay. Tours for groups by reservation. *666 Boylston St., at Exeter St., 617/536–5400. Mon.–Thurs. 9–9, Fri. and Sat. 9–5; Oct.–May, also Sun. 1–5. T stop: Copley.*

7 b-3
CARPENTER CENTER FOR THE VISUAL ARTS

(Le Corbusier, 1963.) Next door to the Fogg Art Museum, this is America's only Le Corbusier, still controversial among more staid Bostonians, but much loved by architecture buffs. It currently houses Harvard's Visual and Environmental Studies school; an interior passageway facilitates viewing without disturbing classes in progress. On the ground floor is an exhibition space where resident artists display their works (modern art predominates), and there's a popular film series hosted by the Harvard Film Archive. *Quincy St., Cambridge, 617/495–3251, for film schedule 617/495–4700. Free. T stop: Harvard Sq.*

6 e-4
CENTER PLAZA BUILDING

(Welton Becket and Associates, 1966-69.) Once described as a skyscraper "lying on its side," this precast concrete-and-brick office building faces City Hall

Plaza. It echoes the curving Sears Crescent Building nearby. Because its curves and structure hug the ground, it's considered one of the more human buildings of the 1960s urban renewal era. There's a pleasant two-story shopping arcade inside. *1 Center Plaza, at Government Center. T stop: Government Center.*

8 *b-5*

CHRISTIAN SCIENCE CHURCH CENTER

(I. M. Pei and Partners with Cosutta and Ponte, 1975.) Set on 14 acres, this is the worldwide religious and administrative headquarters of the Church, and one of I. M. Pei's most impressive designs. The complex consists of a 28-story administration building, a Sunday school, and a five-story Colonnade Building with offices and service facilities, set elegantly around a spectacular 670-foot-long reflecting pool (actually part of the cooling system) and fountain. Beneath is a 550-car garage. The Visitors Tour Center is in the building that publishes the *Christian Science Monitor*, founded in 1908 and purportedly read daily from "Boston to Bombay." Tours of the various buildings are available from 9:30 to 4. Tours of the Mapparium are every 15 minutes. (*See* First Church of Christ, Scientist *in* Churches, *above.*) *Massachusetts and Huntington Aves., Back Bay, 617/450–2000. Free. T stop: Prudential.*

6 *e-4*

CITY HALL & PLAZA

(Kallman, McKinnell, and Knowles with Campbell, Aldrich, and Nulty, and Le Messurier Associates, 1969.) Overlooking Fanueil Hall, Boston's City Hall remains the focal point of the Government Center complex. The interior space is meant to symbolize an open, accessible city government, although many in Boston might take issue with the execution of that lofty aim—the whole complex has been roundly criticized for its brutalist, cold, mechanical air. The skylit lobby is actually the third floor, with two floors of offices below. The 9-acre concrete plaza was intended to achieve harmony between the Old and New Boston; many Bostonians— mourning the raffish, but all-too humanely scaled Scollay Square that it replaced—say it has failed. However, the space is well used in summer months for rallies, rock 'n' roll shows, fairs, and other events. *1 City Hall Sq., Government*

Center. *617/725–3285. Free. T stop: Government Center.*

8 *c-5*

COLONNADE HOTEL

(Irving Salsberg and Associates, 1971.) The concrete columns (from which the hotel got its name? or vice versa?) make this a stylistic cousin to Pei's Christian Science Church Center across the street. *120 Huntington Ave., at Newton St. T stop: Prudential.*

8 *d-4*

COPLEY PLACE

(Neiman-Marcus, the shopping galleries, the offices, the Westin Hotel: The Architect's Collaborative, 1984; Boston Marriott Copley Place: The Stubbins Associates, 1984; residences: Vitols Associates, 1984.) Bordered by Dartmouth Street, Huntington Avenue, Harcourt Street, and the Southwest Corridor, Copley Place is set between the Back Bay and the South End, straddling an interchange of the Massachusetts Turnpike and tracks of the rapid transit lines. As Boston's largest mixed-use development, it uses up 3.7 million square feet on 9½ acres. This is a world apart, and if you don't believe this, just try to find a way to get into the complex without running your hands along the outside of the building. (Tip: Enter through the Westin Hotel.) Ironically, once inside you'll never know you're in Boston. Copley Place's components include two convention-oriented skyscraper hotels (the 36-story Westin and the 39-story Marriott); a 385,000-square-foot retail complex that boasts a two-level gallery of upscale shops and restaurants, and a 12-screen cinema; and, as anchor, a three-level Neiman-Marcus, the first in New England. In addition, four seven-story office buildings are grouped around the nine-story central atrium, the centerpiece of which is a 60-foot-high waterfall sculpture. There are also 1,000 residential units and parking for more than 1,400 cars. A glass-enclosed pedestrian walkway connects it all to the Prudential Center. (*See also* Chapter 4.) *100 Huntington Ave., Copley Sq., 617/369–5000 or 617/262– 6600, Ext. 293. T stop: Copley.*

8 *d-3*

COPLEY SQUARE PLAZA

(Sasaki, Dawson, and Demay, 1968.) A pedestrian plaza ringed by trees, this popular piazza is cooled by a fountain and used by passers-through, footsore tourists, and ray-hungry sunbathers—not to mention people-watchers of all persuasions. *Boylston and Dartmouth Sts. and St. James Ave., Back Bay. T stop: Copley.*

 f-5

EXCHANGE PLACE

(WZMH Group, 1984) The original 1891 Stock Exchange building by Peabody and Stearns was meant to be supplanted by a gleaming, black high-rise tower, but after an outcry, the rear of the old Exchange was lopped off and a new 40-story skyscraper of mirrored glass was allowed to rise behind it—another graphic example of how old meets new in Boston. *53 State St., near Congress St., Downtown. T stop: Government Center.*

8 *e-3*

500 BOYLSTON

(John Burgee and Philip Johnson, 1988) An oft-ridiculed, sleek structure, with overblown arches and other kitschy elements, this structure houses offices and stores at the ground level and is an awkward Post-Modernist standout on the street. The architects also designed International Place, the city's largest office complex. *500 Boylston St., Back Bay. T stop: Arlington, Copley.*

 f-7

FEDERAL RESERVE BANK OF BOSTON

(Hugh Stubbins and Associates, 1977.) Designed with downdrafts and wind pressures in mind, this building has a outline that brings to mind nothing so much as an old-fashioned washboard. Free operations tours are available for groups approximately once a month (write three or four weeks in advance). There is a ground-floor art gallery for New England-based artists and a performance series is held in an adjacent auditorium. *600 Atlantic Ave., at Summer St., 617/973–3451 or 617/973–3453. T stop: South Station.*

6 *e-4*

GOVERNMENT CENTER

(I. M. Pei, 1964.) Built on the site of the old, cluttered, hurly-burly area known as Scollay Square, this 60-acre complex houses the administrative center of local and state government. Pei had overall charge of the scale and character of the individual new buildings and how they related to one another and the surrounding historic area. (*See Center Plaza Building, City Hall and Plaza, and John F. Kennedy Federal Office Building, above and below.*) *T stop: Government Center.*

8 *e-3*

(OLD) JOHN HANCOCK BUILDING

(Cram and Ferguson, 1947.) This was actually the second Hancock Building (the first is at 200 Clarendon Street; Parker, Thomas, and Rice, 1922.) Topped by a metallic, stepped pyramid crowned by a spire, it was the tallest building in the city for 20 years until the Prudential went up in 1965. Looking down St. James Avenue, and seeing the Pei tower behind it, it's difficult to believe that only 28 years separate the two. The building's top spire is particularly important as a Boston weather landmark: if the tower's light is a steady blue, clear skies are ahead, flashing blue means clouds, steady red means rain ahead, while flashing red means snow. (*See Hancock Tower, below.*) *200 Berkeley St., Back Bay. T stop: Copley.*

8 *e-3*

HANCOCK TOWER

(I. M. Pei and Partners, 1975.) This 60-story building has been controversial from the time it was on the drawing boards—considering its neighborhood placement, its gigantic scale, and towering height. Following completion, the glass tower popped its windows during episodes of high winds and temperature extremes—*that* did little to enhance Boston's admiration of this tower (all 10,344 windows were ultimately replaced). The fact that the tower's highly reflective mirrored glass and its modern design are side-by-jowl to the venerable Trinity Church imparts a surrealistic note to its form (Trinity's architect, H. H. Richardson, could never have imagined the new dimension that was added to his Trinity Church by the creation of its melted-edge reflection in the Hancock Tower's side). The view of Boston from the top of the glass structure *is* spectacular. *Hancock Pl. and Copley Sq., Back Bay. 617/572–6429. T stop: Copley.*

6 *h-5*

HARBOR TOWERS

(I. M. Pei and Partners, 1971.) Twin 40-story residential towers, these were built on the site of an old wharf designed by Charles Bulfinch in 1805 (nary a fragment retained). Complete with a seven-story parking facility. *India Wharf. T stop: Aquarium.*

6 *d-3*

HEALTH, WELFARE, & EDUCATION SERVICE CENTER/COMMONWEALTH OF MASSACHUSETTS

(Paul Randolph, coordinating architect. Shepley, Bulfinch, Richardson, and Abbot with Desmond Lord, 1970.) This hammered-concrete structure is quite a production—not surprising, considering how many "producers" there were. Another example of imposing but ultimately people-unfriendly urban renewal. *Stanford, Merrimac, New Chardon, and Cambridge Sts., West End. T stop: Bowdoin.*

7 *a-3*

HOLYOKE CENTER

(José Luis Sert, 1961-65.) This popular addition to the Harvard Square area houses shops as well as the Harvard Information Center and Health Services. Maps of Harvard and historic Cambridge are available. *1350 Massachusetts Ave., Cambridge, 617/495–1573. Mon.– Sat. 9–4:45. T stop: Harvard Sq.*

8 *b-4*

JOHN B. HYNES CONVENTION CENTER

(Kallmann, McKinnell, and Wood, 1988.) The major convention site within Boston proper, the Hynes hosts everything from *Star Trek* confabs to sports equipment shows. Designed by the architects of Boston's City Hall, it can hold 22,000 conventioneers. *900 Boylston St., Back Bay, 617/954–2000 or 617/424–8585. T stop: Hynes Convention Center.*

6 *g-5*

INTERNATIONAL PLACE

(John Burgee Architects with Philip Johnson, 1987-91) Boston's largest office building (1.8 million square feet of space) was controversial when developed by flamboyant developer Donald Chiofaro. Even designer Philip Johnson once called it "2 million goddamm square feet that do not belong in this part of Boston." However, the complex has become a glistening landmark on the Boston skyline, with one 46-story tower (covered with a grid of Palladian windows, no less) and a newer 35-story mate (complete with a conical crown). There's also a ground-level atrium. *1 International Pl., between High and Purchase Sts., Downtown. T stop: South Station.*

6 *e-4*

JOHN F. KENNEDY FEDERAL BUILDING

(The Architects Collaborative with Samuel Glaser Associates, 1966.) Facing City Hall, this is a concrete-and-glass federal office building, definitely on the utilitarian-looking side. Guess that's how the General Services Administration wanted it. It does contain a Robert Motherwell mural, *New England Elegy*, painted in 1966. *Cambridge and Sudbury Sts. T stop: Government Center.*

6 *g-4*

MARRIOTT LONG WHARF HOTEL

(Arnaldo Cossuta, 1981.) In scale and materials, the redbrick building is an echo of the warehouse structures that were a common sight on the wharfs in Boston's clipper ship days—so much so that some observers think it's a recycling job rather than a from-scratch modern construction. *296 State St., North End, 617/227–0800 or 800/228–9290. T stop: Haymarket.*

6 *f-5*

JOHN W. MCCORMACK POST OFFICE & COURT HOUSE

(Cram and Ferguson, 1931) A striking, Art-Deco style building with elaborate ornamentation, this was built by the architects of the nearby New England Telephone building. *Congress St. at Post Office Sq., Downtown. T stop: South Station.*

6 *h-8*

MIT CHAPEL

(Eero Saarinen, 1956.) A major modernist statement, this Saarinen masterwork stirred up Boston's conservative critics when unveiled. The architect created a cylindrical brick chapel—illuminated by light entering from above (how appropriate)—dramatically topped with a Theodore Roszak aluminum sculpture. Water in an exterior moat reflects interestingly on the interior walls. *Massachusetts Ave., across from main building, 617/258–8422. T stop: Kendall Sq./MIT.*

2 *b-6*
MUSEUM OF FINE ARTS, WEST WING
(I. M. Pei and Partners, 1981.) Built with granite from the same quarry as the original MFA, this $22-million, three-story wing added 80,000 square feet of dramatic interior space to the venerable original. Created to host temporary exhibitions, it is an elegant building with a spectacular 225-foot-long galleria, topped by a soaring 57-foot-high glass barrel vault that permits daylight to enter. With striking élan, it manages to merge beautifully with the classic old Beaux-Arts structure. For details on collections, *see* Art Museums, *above. 465 Huntington Ave., Fenway, 617/267–9300. T stop: Museum.*

6 *h-5*
NEW ENGLAND AQUARIUM
(Cambridge Seven, 1969, 1973, 1979.) Located on Central Wharf (which dates back to 1816), the Aquarium has recently been undergoing dramatic reconstruction. Inside, the aquarium's focal point is a three-story, 40-foot-diameter tank encircled by a ramp that ascends through a four-story central space. Scheduled for completion in early 1998 is a new West Wing, a 16,500-square-foot area for changing exhibitions (Schwartz and Silver Architects)—its angled forms will echo natural landscapes and its exterior will be covered with interlocking stainless-steel panels, creating a suitable and shimmering "fish scale" effect. An expanded outside seal exhibit is planned using a raised tank, so viewers can watch animals both above and below the surface. A new Education Center, with a working marine hospital for viewing, was completed in July of 1995. (*See also* Chapter 6.) *Central Wharf at Milk St., 617/973–5200. T stop: Aquarium.*

9 *d-5*
NORTH END BRANCH, BOSTON PUBLIC LIBRARY
(Carl Koch and Associates, 1965.) This Italian villa-style library with open-to-the-sky atrium contains a 14-foot-long model of Venice's Doge's Palace. All in

all, a proud addition to the North End Italian community, which is taking its past into a hopeful future. *25 Parmenter St., between Hanover and Salem Sts., North End, 617/227–8135. Closed weekends. T stop: Haymarket.*

6 *f-4*
1 WASHINGTON MALL
(Eduardo Catalano, 1972.) Made of concrete and highly reflective glass, this building complements its structural neighbors well. *Between State St. and City Hall Plaza, Government Center. T stop: Government Center.*

6 *f-6*
100 FEDERAL STREET
(Campbell, Aldrich, and Nulty, 1971) Once home to the First National Bank and now housing Bank/Boston, this 37-story red Carnelian–granite structure has been frivolously described as "pregnant" due to the outward thrust of its cantilevered middle stories. *100 Federal St., Downtown, 617/434–2200. T stop: South Station.*

8 *c-4*
PRUDENTIAL COMPLEX
(Charles Luckman and Associates, 1960-70.) The beginning of the "New Boston," the Prudential Complex is, in retrospect, 1960s urban renewal at its worst. This 27-acre complex, set between the Back Bay and the South End, was built primarily over the old Boston and Albany rail yards (that was the good part), contains uninspired flat-roofed apartment and office towers, a hotel, specialty shops, as well as the Lord & Taylor and Saks Fifth Avenue department stores. Central to all is the 52-story Prudential tower, the second tallest in New England. Thankfully, 15 acres—devoted to landscaping and windswept plazas—help soften the blow. After a major face-lift in the mid-1990s, a host of shops, a food court, and other amenities were added to create another climate-controlled shopping area (connected via a series of walkways to Copley Place). The ambience is pure American mall, but the shops are cheerful and there's a few interesting nooks amid the corporate crannies. (*See also* Prudential Tower, *below.*) *Bounded by Boylston and Exeter Sts. and Huntington and Massachusetts Aves., Back Bay, 800/ SHOP–PRU. T stop: Prudential.*

8 *c-4*

PRUDENTIAL TOWER

(Charles Luckman and Associates, 1959-65.) This 52-story, 750-foot tower was a lone, inelegant, monolith when built as the first phase of the much-disdained Prudential Complex. It was the tallest building in New England until the sleek Hancock Tower took up the challenge and surpassed it. Views as far as the Cape, Vermont, and New Hampshire may be had on a clear day from the 50th-floor observation deck. (*See* Viewpoints, *below.*) *800 Boylston St., Back Bay, skywalk 617/236–3318. T stop: Prudential on Green Line (Arborway).*

6 *g-5*

ROWES WHARF

(Skidmore, Owings, and Merrill, 1988.) Known for its dramatic arch (some call it pompous, others just adore it), Rowes Wharf was built on the site of the original 19th-century structure, torn down in 1960. The 15-story complex houses the Boston Harbor Hotel, luxury condos, restaurants, bars, shops, a marina, and offices. From the marina, you can catch a shuttle to Logan Airport or take a cruise in Boston Harbor. Few other places in Boston offer such a wonderful, cool spot for a seaside view. *Atlantic Ave., between Fosters and India Wharf, Downtown. T stop: Aquarium, South Station.*

7 *b-2*

ARTHUR M. SACKLER MUSEUM

(James Stirling, 1985.) One of Boston's most important statements in modern architecture, Harvard's newest art museum is striking, to say the least. The brick Post-Modernist exterior design has drawn criticism for its theatricality—its entry, flanked by two giant cement columns, has been likened to a coffin. But the controversy is offset by the fact that much of this stellar collection (devoted to Asian cultures) is finally being seen for the first time. This is the prestigious Scottish architect's first American building; he did the expansion of the Tate Gallery in London. (*See* Art Museums, *above.*) *85 Broadway, Cambridge, 617/495–9400. T stop: Harvard Sq.*

6 *5-f*

75 STATE STREET

(Graham Gund Associates with Skidmore, Owings, and Merrill, 1989.) Adding new interest to the skyline and a successful modern addendum to the Financial District, this 31-story beige-and-red granite tower features eye-catching diagonals and gold-leaf ornamentation at its crown. In the lobby, a lush skylit arcade is lined with mahogany shopfronts and worth a look. The name etched into the granite says "Fleet Center," but don't confuse it with the huge new sports arena. *75 State St., Downtown. T stop: State St.*

6 *5-f*

60 STATE STREET

(Skidmore, Owings, and Merrill, 1977.) This slim, 38-story ribbed-granite tower has the Bay Tower Room at the top—a fine place for food with a view (*see* Chapter 3). *Congress St., Downtown. T stop: Government Center.*

8 *c-2*

330 BEACON STREET

(Hugh Stubbins and Associates, 1959.) A 17-story apartment building, this structure has an undulating facade in keeping with the pattern—if not the scale—made by the rows of neighboring brownstones. *330 Beacon St., Back Bay. T stop: Hynes Convention Center/ICA.*

OUTDOOR ART

6 *f-3*

ASAROTAN

(Mags Harries, 1976.) This landmark artwork has been temporarily removed for the duration of the massive Central Artery project (to be completed early in the next century)—even so, such is the fascination of its design, the work remains much on the city's mind. The artwork's name, Greek for unswept floors, is fitting, for here—where the produce-filled Haymarket takes place—the artist has embedded in the street paving an array of bronze castings of discarded fruit, fish, vegetables, a pizza slice, even pages of the *Boston Globe*. You can see samples of similar art by Harries at the Porter Square T station, in which she plays on the theme of lost gloves. *Blackstone and Hanover Sts. T stop: Haymarket.*

3 g-6

THE BIG SAIL

(Alexander Calder, 1965.) MIT has a profusion of outdoor artwork; this 40-foot steel "stabile" by Calder (known for his mobiles) is one of the more memorable. The piece also acts as a wind baffle so that the revolving doors in I. M. Pei's adjacent Green Building would function despite unplanned-for wind resistance. The MIT campus also has outdoor works by Louise Nevelson, Henry Moore, and Dimitri Hadzi. *McDermott Ct. in front of Green Bldg., MIT campus, Cambridge. T stop: Kendall Sq.*

1 g-6

GAS TANK RAINBOW

(Corita Kent, 1971.) When Sister Corita, a nun and printmaker who designed the "Love Stamp," first created the 150-foot-high rainbow splashes on one of the gigantic Boston Gas storage tanks, furious critics claimed a profile of Ho Chi Minh could be seen in the design (this was at the height of the Vietnam conflict—although Sister Corita herself reasonably explained that it was a fluke of the splattered design). Proving that over time, the controversial becomes the commonplace, Boston Gas reproduced her art exactly when the gas tank was replaced about 20 years later! It is now, on the new tank, said to be the largest copyrighted work of art in the world. *Victory Rd., visible from Southeast Expressway.*

6 f-4

GRASSHOPPER WEATHER VANE

(Shem Drowne, 1742.) One might say that the grasshopper—a traditional good-luck symbol—is one of Boston's true survivors. This is the original cast by master tinsmith Drowne, and it has weathered many a storm. *Faneuil Hall, roof. T stop: Government Center.*

6 h-7

H. P. HOOD MILK BOTTLE

This vintage-1930s highway lunch stand is 40 feet high—clearly, one of Boston's more unusual landmarks. Bought for use as a refreshment stand for museum-goers, this delightful oddity had to be cut in half, floated down the Charles, and then reassembled. For those who care, the bottle's theoretical capacity is 200,000 quarts. *Museum Wharf, 300 Congress St. T stop: Aquarium.*

6 g-5

INDIA WHARF PROJECT

(David von Schlegell, 1972.) Two pairs of two bent, stainless-steel planes face each other—set at harbor's edge, this sculpture is stark, albeit sun-drenched. *Harbor Towers. T stop: Aquarium.*

6 b-6

MAKE WAY FOR DUCKLINGS

(Nancy Schon, 1987.) A bronze mother duck and her ducklings, inspired by the classic children's book by Robert McCloskey, are a magnet for children who love to touch and "ride" the quackers. Despite clamors for reproductions, Schon consented only once to duplicate her work, at the request of the Soviet Union's First Lady Raisa Gorbachev; in 1991 a duck duplicate was installed in Moscow's Gorky Park. Schon also did a popular kid-friendly *Tortoise and the Hare* sculpture in Copley Square, the site of the finish of the Boston Marathon. *Public Gardens, Back Bay, near Charles and Beacon Sts. T stop: Arlington.*

8 d-3

NEWBURY STREET MURAL

(Joshua Winer, 1991.) A trompe l'oeil mural, five stories high, this artwork features more than 50 characters from Boston's history, from Gilded-Age art collector Isabella Stewart Gardner to computer mogul An Wang. *Newbury and Dartmouth Sts. T stop: Copley.*

8 d-4

PAINT & HENRY

(Deborah Butterfield, 1987.) Popular rendition in welded sheet copper of horses based on the artist's own herd at her Montana ranch. *Copley Pl. T stop: Copley.*

6 b-6

THE PARTISANS

(Arcangelo Cascieri, 1958–60.) Although technically on loan, this haunting, enigmatic piece, which pays tribute to beaten but not defeated guerrilla freedom-fighters, has become one of the most asked about works in the city. *Tremont St. side of Boston Common. T stop: Arlington.*

8 e-3

TEDDY BEAR
(Robert Shure, 1991.) Okay, so this 12-foot-high bronze bear—complete with alphabet blocks spelling out FAO (for the FAO Schwarz toy store)—may not qualify as High Art. But no one can deny it's one of the most photographed spots in the city for camera-happy parents and kids. Another popular site in this vein is the *Bugs Bunny* and *Daffy Duck* bronzes outside the Warner Bros. store in Fanueil Hall Marketplace. *Boylston and Berkeley Sts., Back Bay. T stop: Arlington.*

6 e-4

THERMOPYLAE
(Dimitri Hadzi, 1966.) The plaza facing City Hall, in front of the office building named for the late president, is an appropriate place for a piece of sculpture inspired by Kennedy's book, *Profiles in Courage. John F. Kennedy Federal Bldg. T stop: Government Center.*

SCIENCE MUSEUMS

2 a-4

BOSTON UNIVERSITY OBSERVATORY
This place is mostly for star-struck kids, but good for all ages. Wednesday nights April to September from 8:30 to 9:30 and October to March from 7:30 to 8:30 are "open telescope" nights. Weather permitting, of course, you can try to pick out your favorite planets and stars. Knowledgeable staff members give a short introduction and are on hand to answer any question. *725 Commonwealth Ave., 617/353–2625 or 617/353–2630. Free. T Stop: Boston University (Green, B line).*

7 b-1

BOTANICAL MUSEUM
One of the four museums within the Harvard Museums of Cultural and Natural History, the Botanical Museum houses the world-famous Ware collection, known as the "Glass Flowers." Created in Dresden between 1887 and 1936 by two German artists—Leopold Blaschka and his son, Rudolph—as a tool for the teaching of botany, the "garden" of life-size models and enlarged flowers and anatomical sections represents more than 800 species. *24 Oxford St., Cambridge, 617/495–3045. $5 adults,*

$4 senior citizens and students, $3 ages 3–13, free Sat. 9–noon. Admission also covers Mineralogical and Geological Museums, Museum of Comparative Zoology, and Peabody Museum of Archaeology and Ethnology. Call ahead for group-tour rates. Mon.–Sat. 9–5, Sun. 1–5. T stop: Harvard Sq.

6 h-5

CHILDREN'S MUSEUM
Follow the Museum Wharf signs displaying a milk bottle (you'll see why when you get there) to get to the kind of hands-on museum kids love. Participation leads to learning as well as fun. Exhibits include a two-story Climbing Sculpture, a Science Playground, and a Hall of Toys. A walk over the Kid's Bridge leads to a multicultural exhibit of interactive videos and sound booths, created to support children and their families in a world becoming increasingly diverse. One exhibit is "Teen Tokyo," highlighting Japanese youth culture today, including a Japanese subway car, a karaoke booth, and an animation computer. Throughout the year there are all-day festivals, many of which are joint efforts with a particular ethnic community to promote multicultural awareness in Boston. There's a terrific museum shop with a great selection of kids' books, as well as a Resource Center for educational use, and Recycle, where craftsworthy industrial raw materials are sold in bulk. *300 Congress St., 617/426–6500 or 617/426–8855. $7 adults, $6 senior citizens and ages 2–15, $2 age 1 and under, $1 Fri. 5–9 for all. Fall–spring, Tues.–Thurs., Sat.–Sun. 10–5, Fri. 10–9; summer, Mon.–Thurs., Sat.–Sun. 10–6, Fri. 10–9. T stop: South Station.*

6 h-5

COMPUTER MUSEUM
This might well be a museum where your children will teach you a thing or too. Learn the secrets of the machines that rule our lives at more than 170 interactive exhibits, ranging from a 15-gear Virtual Reality bike to buying and selling shares of stock in a simulated global market. Check out the Walk-Through Computer 2000, where you can really "get inside" technology. And you might spend some time in the Best Software for Kids Gallery, where you can try out more than 50 top software choices that you may consider buying later. The museum also has an impres-

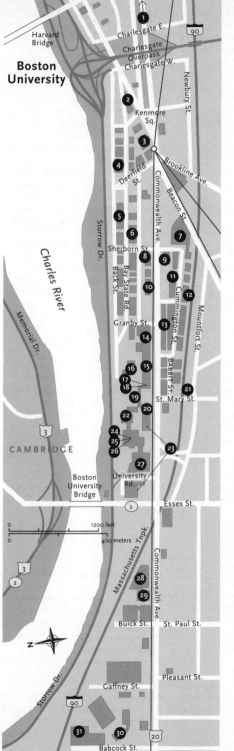

Boston University

1 BU Theatre
2 Myles Standish Residential Area
3 Barnes & Noble at BU
4 Shelton Residential Area
5 Admissions Reception Center
6 The Towers Residential Area
7 Metcalf Science Center
8 School of Education
9 School of Management
10 Sargent College of Allied Health Professions
11 College of Communication
12 College of Engineering
13 Warren Towers
14 Tsai Performance Center
15 Graduate School of Arts & Sciences
16 Sch of Social Work
17 College of Liberal Arts
18 Judson Boardman Coit Observatory
19 Marsh Chapel
20 School of Theology
21 South Campus Residential Area
22 School of Law
23 Metropolitan College
24 University Information Center
25 Mugar Memorial Library
26 Special Collections
27 Sherman Union
28 School for the Arts/ Art Gallery/ Concert Hall
29 College of General Studies
30 West Campus Residential Area
31 Case Physical Education Center

sive area devoted to computing history, such as an authentic "hackers garage" where the personal computer revolution began. With Celebrity-Robot-in-residence R2-D2 from the *Star Wars* movies, this place is anything but user-unfriendly. The museum can be "visited" online via an interactive site on the World Wide Web at http://www.tcm.org. *300 Congress St., 617/426–2800 or 617/423–6758. $7 adults, $5 senior citizens and children, under 2 free, ½ price Sun. 3–5. Summer, daily 10–6; winter, Tues.–Sun. 10–5. T stop: South Station.*

7 *b-1*

HARVARD UNIVERSITY MUSEUMS

In reality there are four separate museums under one roof. *See* Botanical Museum; Mineralogical and Geological Museums; Museum of Comparative Zoology; *and* Peabody Museum of Archaeology and Ethnology, *above and below. 24 Oxford St., Cambridge, 617/495–1910.*

6 *b-1*

CHARLES HAYDEN PLANETARIUM

For an earthbound visit to the final frontier, check out the sophisticated planetarium shows (which change regularly) projected by a multi-image system featuring a $2-million Zeiss planetarium projector. One show may take you on a visit to Mars, another may explain the stars you see above you on earth. Shows are held throughout the day, usually on the hour 10:30–4:30, with occasional evening performances; advance reservations by phone are suggested as performances often sell out (there's a $1.50 handling fee for phone orders). The museum also conducts laser shows Thursday through Sunday to the music of such space rockers as Pink Floyd and the Grateful Dead. *Science Park at Charles River Dam, 617/523–6664. Planetarium and laser shows $7.50 adults, $5.50 senior citizens and children. T stop: Science Park.*

7 *g-7*

MIT MUSEUM

An engaging mix of technology, artistry, and hijinks marks this lively institution. Ongoing exhibitions include samples of hologram art, such as a holographic rain forest. There's also the "Hall of Hacks," which celebrates the often-complex

tricks MIT students have staged on the campus and revolving exhibitions, some focusing on art, some on science. *265 Massachusetts Ave., Cambridge, 617/253–4444. $3 adults; $1 senior citizens, students, and children. Tues.–Fri. 10–5, weekends noon–5. T stop: Central Sq.*

7 *b-1*

MINERALOGICAL & GEOLOGICAL MUSEUMS

This is the place to come for exhibitions of minerals, gemstones, meteorites, and materials of geological interest *and* sparkling aesthetic splendor. *24 Oxford St., Cambridge, 617/495–3045. $5 adults, $4 senior citizens and students, $3 ages 3–13, free Sat. 9–noon. Call ahead for group-tour rates. Admission also covers Botanical Museum, Museum of Comparative Zoology, and Peabody Museum of Archaeology and Ethnology. Mon.–Sat. 9–5, Sun. 1–5. T stop: Harvard Sq.*

7 *b-1*

MUSEUM OF COMPARATIVE ZOOLOGY

Also known as the "Agassiz Museum," here's where you (and your children) can marvel at the creatures of the world, from African warthogs, to a live ant farm, to the world's largest turtle shell and George Washington's pheasants. Dinosaur-inclined minds will love the 42-foot-long skeleton of the ancient underwater *Kronosaurus*. *24 Oxford St., Cambridge, 617/495–3045. $5 adults, $4 senior citizens and students, $3 ages 3–13, free Sat. 9–noon. Call ahead for group-tour rates. Admission also covers Botanical Museum, Mineralogical and Geological Museum, and Peabody Museum of Archaeology and Ethnology. Mon.–Sat. 9–5, Sun. 1–5. T stop: Harvard Sq.*

6 *b-1*

MUSEUM OF SCIENCE

The spark for this institution can be traced to the Boston Society of Natural History, founded in 1830. Now more than 450 exhibits—many of them interactive—cover astronomy (*see* Charles Hayden Planetarium, *above*), astrophysics, anthropology, progress in medicine, computers, the organic and inorganic earth sciences. Play virtual volleyball, stomp on the Musical Steps, and see new life emerging in a chicken hatchery as well as 50 other species of animals. The Transparent Woman, a Plexiglas model of a human female, "discusses" her anatomy, parts of which light up. Also, live demonstrations of high-voltage electricity feature the world's largest air-insulated Van de Graaff generator, which produces 15-foot bolts of lightning. A wide variety of courses, programs, and events are available throughout the year, including blockbuster exhibitions such as a recent show focusing on the technological discoveries of Leonardo da Vinci. Check out the Galaxy Café with its great view of the river, and a shop that sells science-related and hobby items. *Science Park at Charles River Dam, 617/723–2500 or 617/523–6664. $8. Daily 9–5, Fri. 9–9 (extended hrs July 5–Sept. 5). T stop: Science Park.*

The Museum of Science also contains the **Mugar Omni Theater,** which has state-of-the-art film projection and sound systems. The 76-foot-high, four-story domed screen wraps around and over you, and 27,000 watts of power drive the 84 loudspeakers. Films deal with such fascinating topics as the Titanic and Yellowstone Park. *617/523–6664. $7.50 adults. Advance purchase of tickets advised 3 or 4 days ahead for weekends and holidays (V and MC accepted for phone orders with $1 handling fee). Reduced-price combination tickets available for museum, planetarium, and Omni Theater. Shows from* 11 AM.

 7 *b-1*

PEABODY MUSEUM OF ARCHAEOLOGY & ETHNOLOGY

Pre-Columbian, American Indian, Central and South American artifacts are arranged in ways that will delight and educate young minds. Plus there's an interesting museum shop. *11 Divinity Ave., Cambridge, 617/495–2248. $5 adults, $4 senior citizens and students, $3 ages 3–13. free Sat. 9–noon. Call ahead for group-tour rates. Admission also covers Botanical Museum, Mineralogical and Geological Museum, and Museum of Comparative Zoology. Mon.–Sat. 9–5, Sun. 1–5. T stop: Harvard Sq.*

STATUES & MONUMENTS

Like most cities, Boston has seen its share of controversies over public art—one immediately thinks of the uproar during the Vietnam era over an alleged profile of Ho Chi Minh "visible" in the Gas Tank Rainbow. And yet that, like so many other public works, won acceptance, and ultimately great affection from a public that views such attractions on a daily basis. Other than such modern monuments, Boston also is rich in memorials and monuments to the great and noted.

6 *f-4*

SAMUEL ADAMS

(Anne Whitney, 1880.) Sculpted in bronze, this statue is a portrait of the American patriot and Boston's "man of the town meeting." Sharp-eyed art lovers may notice hatched lines and etched images of fish, seaweed, and other ocean life in the pavement surrounding the statue. It's part of a 1995 public art installation by Ross Miller to dramatize the city's original shoreline. *Dock Sq. in front of Faneuil Hall. T stop: Government Center.*

6 *f-4*

ARNOLD "RED" AUERBACH

(Lloyd Lillie, 1985.) In this life-size bronze tribute to the cigar-stomping Celtics basketball legend, he looks as he did courtside in the old Boston Gardens. Lillie's statue of another Boston legend, Mayor Curley, is nearby. *South Market, Faneuil Hall Marketplace. T stop: Government Center.*

6 *d-5*

BEACON HILL MONUMENT

This memorial pillar is a restoration of the 1790 original done by Charles Bulfinch to commemorate events leading up to the American Revolution—the first such monument. *Massachusetts State House legislators' parking lot. T stop: Park St.*

B *e-3*

PHILLIPS BROOKS STATUE

(Augustus Saint-Gaudens, 1907.) In a work finished by Saint-Gaudens's students during the master's final illness, Brooks, Trinity's pastor, is depicted—somewhat startlingly—with Christ touching his shoulder. Brooks, whose efforts led to the construction of Trinity Church, was the most fashionable rector of his time. A mainstay of the Harvard community, he was renowned for his sermons in his day, but is now remembered mainly for penning the hymn "O! Little Town of Bethlehem." *Trinity*

Church, Copley Sq., northeast corner. T
stop: Copley.

6 e-6

ROBERT BURNS

(Henry Hudson Kitson, 1917.) The
famed Scottish poet is depicted with his
pet collie. First intended for the Public
Garden, the statue was relocated downtown in 1975. *Winthrop Sq., Otis and
Devonshire Sts. T stop: State St.*

8 d-3

PATRICK ANDREW
COLLINS MEMORIAL

(Henry Hudson Kitson and Theo Alice
Ruggles Kitson, 1908.) On the Commonwealth Avenue Mall, this is a stone
obelisk topped by a bust of the former
Boston mayor (1902-05). The Mall is
dotted with statues, some of folks who
were important to Boston, others of
more obscure origin. *Commonwealth
Ave. Mall between Clarendon and Dartmouth Sts. T stop: Copley.*

6 f-4

JAMES MICHAEL
CURLEY MEMORIAL

(Lloyd Lillie, 1980.) For many Bostonians it is not surprising that two statues
were required to depict their larger-than-
life, legendary former mayor. Standing is
Curley the consummate politician;
seated is Curley the compassionate
human being. Like the man it honors,
the memorial makes a mark on the
Boston landscape, in part by removing a
legend from his pedestal—literally—and
putting him at street level. *Curley Memorial Park, Congress and North Sts. T stop:
Haymarket.*

6 d-4

CARDINAL CUSHING
MEMORIAL

(James Rosati, 1981.) The son of Irish
immigrants, Cushing was born and
raised in South Boston and became a
celebrated leader of the Catholic
church. *Cardinal Cushing Memorial Park,
Cambridge and New Chardon Sts. T stop:
Bowdoin.*

BULFINCH'S BOSTON: THE NEOCLASSICAL EYE

*Beginning in the late 18th century, Charles Bulfinch brought the look of Georgian Lon-
don to an expanding Boston. Everywhere this most stylish of architects brought the elegance of Robert Adam to Boston's city scene. Here's a Whitman's Sampler of some of his
best buildings.*

State House (Beacon St.)
*One of the greatest works—perhaps the greatest—of classical architecture in Amer-
ica and arguably our most distinguished seat of state government. Poised between
the Georgian and Federal periods, the buildings has exquisite Corinthian columns
and a dome once sheathed in copper by one Paul Revere.*

First Harrison Gray Otis House (141 Cambridge St.)
*The first of three houses Boston's mayor built for himself and his family, this is less
sumptuous than the others but is the only one open to the public. The dining room
is set up as though Master Otis were about to come in and pour a glass of Madeira.*

Third Harrison Gray Otis House (45 Beacon St.)
*The best of Boston society gathered in the regal salons of this house—consuming
10 gallons of rum-spiked punch from a crystal punch bowl set upon the staircase
landing.*

Bulfinch Pavilion (Massachusetts General Hospital)
*This domed, granite pavilion, designed in 1818, is a Greek Revival masterpiece, more
probably executed by Bulfinch's assistant, Alexander Parris (architect of Quincy
Market). It was here in the Ether Dome that ether was first used in a surgical operation.*

Faneuil Hall (Faneuil Hall Square)
*As the "Cradle of Liberty" became a pilgrimage shrine to the Revolution, the original
hall couldn't contain the crowds—so Bulfinch stepped in and enlarged the complex,
adding a spectacular second-floor assembly room.*

Stoughton Hall (Harvard Yard)
Designed in 1805, this is Bulfinch's calling card to Harvard.

6 d-5

MARY DYER STATUE

(Sylvia Shaw Judson, 1959.) Dyer was a Quaker who fought for religious freedom, challenging the Puritans' anti-Quaker law. She was jailed three times, being reprieved once at the gallows, but was finally hanged in 1660 on the nearby Boston Common. *State House, front of East Wing. T stop: Park St.*

6 g-3

EMANCIPATION GROUP STATUE

(Thomas Ball, 1875.) Lincoln the Emancipator is depicted with an about-to-be-freed slave at his feet. It's a duplicate casting of the one Ball did for placement in the nation's capital. The statue's paternalistic posturing seems, at worst, offensive and, at best, out-of-touch with today's standards on racial equality. *Park Sq. at Charles Eliot St. and Columbus Ave. T stop: Arlington.*

8 f-2

ETHER MONUMENT

(John Quincy Adams Ward, 1867.) Ornate granite and red marble Victorian tribute to the discovery of ether as a painkiller at the Massachusetts General Hospital. At the top is a figure of a Good Samaritan comforting a youth in pain. *Public Garden near Commonwealth Ave. entrance. T stop: Arlington.*

8 g-1

FOUNDERS MEMORIAL

(Artist: John F. Paramino. Architect: Charles A. Coolidge, 1930.) The monument, created to commemorate the 300th anniversary of the founding of Boston, was placed near the site of an ancient spring. The relief depicts Shawmut's (Boston's Indian name) first white settler, William Blackstone (the recluse spelled it Blaxton), welcoming John Winthrop and his followers, including Ann Pollard, the first white woman to reach Boston. *Boston Common at Beacon and Spruce Sts. T stop: Arlington.*

6 e-5

BENJAMIN FRANKLIN

(Richard S. Greenough, 1856.) Boston's first portrait sculpture was this 8-foot-high bronze tribute to Franklin. One might say it is two-faced, as each profile was given a different expression. The bronze relief tablets at the base (two of them by Thomas Ball) illustrate highlights of the patriot's careers as printer, scientist, and signer of the Declaration of Independence and the Peace Treaty with France. *Old City Hall at School St. T stop: Downtown Crossing.*

8 d-3

WILLIAM LLOYD GARRISON

(Olin L. Warner, 1885.) This work depicts the famed abolitionist and editor in a restful pose, although his inscribed words are fightin'. Reportedly, the Garrison family hated this likeness. *Commonwealth Ave. Mall between Dartmouth and Exeter Sts. T stop: Copley.*

8 g-2

EDWARD EVERETT HALE

(Bela Pratt, 1912.) Humble and genteel, this is a portrait of the clergyman and writer. *Public Garden near Charles St. crossing to Common. T stop: Arlington.*

7 a-1

JOHN HARVARD

(Daniel Chester French, 1885.) The inscription bears three mistakes—he was not the founder, merely a contributor, the year was 1636, not 1638, and, as if to add insult to injury, a student was used as a model since no one knew what Harvard looked like! This explains why it's known locally as the Statue of Three Lies. *University Hall, Harvard Yard. T stop: Harvard Sq.*

6 d-5

ANNE HUTCHINSON STATUE

(Cyrus E. Dallin, 1922.) Anne Hutchison (1591–1643) was banished from Boston for her religious beliefs, including her conviction that women's souls had an equal footing with men's. Dallin also did the North End's *Paul Revere* statue and the *Appeal to the Great Spirit* that sits in front of the Museum of Fine Arts. *State House, South Lawn, near west wing. T stop: Park St.*

7 a-2

IRISH FAMINE MEMORIAL

This haunting figure of a mother cradling a dead child while sending off another child to America was installed in 1997 to mark the anniversary of "Black '47," the worst of Ireland's tragic potato famine years. Created by sculptor Maurice Herron of Derry, Ireland, the bronze statue was intended to honor the one million people who died in the famine and the legions of those who sought a new life in the United States. *Cambridge Common, Cambridge. T stop: Harvard Sq.*

2 b-6

JAPANESE TEMPLE BELL

This bell, contributed as scrap to the Japanese war effort, was found by sailors of the USS *Boston* in Yokosuku, Japan, and brought back to the United States. They presented it to the city of Boston in 1945. Following the war the Japanese "officially" presented the bell to Boston as a symbol of world peace. *Fenway across from Museum of Fine Arts. T stop: Museum.*

6 d-5

JOHN F. KENNEDY

(Isabel McIlvain, 1988.) A tribute to the late president, whose clan continues to make political, social, and cultural history. *State House, Beacon Hill, South Lawn. T stop: Park St.*

8 f-2

THADDEUS KOŚCIUSZKO

(Theo Alice Ruggles Kitson, 1927.) Kościuszko was the famed Polish general who became a member of Gen. George Washington's Continental Army. The sculptor was the first woman to be honored by the Paris Salon. *Public Garden near Boylston St. T stop: Arlington.*

6 f-4

NEW ENGLAND HOLOCAUST MEMORIAL

(1995, Stanley Saitowitz.) The glass-and-steel towers of the Holocaust Memorial, which commemorates Jewish victims of the Nazi horror, rise against a backdrop of 19th-century buildings. Recollections by Holocaust survivors are set into the glass and granite walls; the upper levels of the towers are etched with 6 million numbers in random sequence. Grates set into the granite base cover pits of fiery, steam-shrouded electronic embers symbolizing the "Final Solution." *Blackstone Sq., near Faneuil Hall. T stop: Haymarket.*

6 e-5

JOSIAH QUINCY

(Thomas Ball, 1879.) This bronze statue depicts the father of Boston's municipal government—in fact, the first of three Quincy family mayors (1823-29). Ball, who designed numerous sculptures in Boston, including one of George Washington in the Public Garden, lived his last 30 years in Florence. *Old City Hall at School St. T stop: Downtown Crossing.*

8 c-3

SAMUEL ELIOT MORISON

(Penelope Jencks, 1982.) The country's foremost maritime historian and two-time Pulitzer Prize winner is pictured in rugged garb perched atop a rock. *Commonwealth Mall, Back Bay, between Exeter and Fairfield Sts. T stop: Copley.*

9 e-4

PAUL REVERE

(Cyrus Dallin, 1940.) Boston's great patriot is honored with this equestrian statue, which oversees his namesake North End Park. In the distance, the steeple of Old North forms a suitably stirring background. Also note the bronze plaques on the adjacent walls of the park, which bear stories of famous North Enders of old. *Paul Revere Mall between Old North and St. Stephen's Churches. T stop: Haymarket.*

8 b-3

DOMINGO FAUSTINO SARMIENTO

(Ivette Compagnion, 1973.) South American statesman, writer, and educator, Sarmiento was Argentina's minister to the United States in the 1860s. *Commonwealth Ave. between Hereford and Gloucester Sts. T stop: Copley.*

6 d-5

ROBERT GOULD SHAW & 54TH MASSACHUSETTS REGIMENT MEMORIAL

(Sculptor: Augustus Saint-Gaudens. Architects: McKim, Mead, and White, 1897.) When the Lincoln administration relented in 1863 and allowed blacks into the Union Army, the first black regiment was recruited in Massachusetts (the focus of the movie *Glory*). Shaw, a young, white officer, volunteered to lead them. He fell, along with many of his men, in July 1863 at Fort Wagner, North Carolina. The fund for the memorial was begun by Joshua B. Smith, a runaway slave and former employee of the Shaw family household (who later became a state representative). Booker T. Washington attended the statue's dedication, as did surviving members of the 54th. On the Black Heritage Trail. *Boston Common, northeast corner. T stop: Park St.*

6 *c-6*

SOLDIERS & SAILORS MONUMENT

(Martin Milmore, 1877.) This monument was dedicated on September 17, 1877, with more than 25,000 Civil War veterans participating in the ceremonies. The four figures at the base represent *History, Peace, The Sailor,* and *The Soldier*.; atop is the *Genius of America*. The bas reliefs on the granite base depict *Departure for the War, The Sanitary Commission, The Navy,* and *Return from the War. Boston Common, Flagstaff Hill. T stop: Park St.*

1 *h-5*

SOUTH BOSTON VIETNAM MEMORIAL

(Harry Carroll, 1981.) A memorial to those who didn't come home as well as those who did. On one side of the highly polished black granite monument appears the names of the 25 young men from Southie who lost their lives in Vietnam; on the other side are the words "Welcome Home to all the men and women who served during the Vietnam War, 1961–1975." Dedicated September 13, 1981. *Independence Sq., East Broadway between N and M Sts. South Boston. T stop: Broadway.*

6 -

STATLER FOUNTAIN

(Ulysses Ricci, 1930.) Lovely, graceful Art Deco–inspired bronze fountain presented to the city by the Statler Hotels Corporation. *Park Sq. opposite Boston Park Plaza Hotel. T stop: Arlington.*

8 *d-2*

VENDOME MONUMENT

(Ted Clausen and Peter White, 1997.) On June 17, 1972, weary firefighters had just brought a fire at the Hotel Vendome under control when part of the building collapsed, killing nine of them. Twenty-five years later to the day, a monument was erected in their memory—and that of firefighters everywhere—just yards from the hotel. Cambridge sculptor Ted Claudsen won a competition with his design for a waist-high curved black granite block, 29 feet long, etched with the names of the dead. A bronze cast of a fireman's coat and hat are draped over the granite, as if to say, "The fire is out,

we can rest now." The tactile surfaces of the bronze and granite pull viewers into the story; the emotional intimacy is enhanced with the hotel itself looming in the background. *Commonwealth Ave. Mall near Dartmouth St. T stop: Copley.*

8 *g-3*

GEORGE WASHINGTON

(Thomas Ball, 1869.) This 38-foot-tall bronze monument was Boston's first equestrian statue, and it's a fine one. Look closely: a fiberglass sword has replaced the original vandal-damaged bronze one. *Public Garden at Commonwealth Ave. T stop: Arlington.*

8 *f-1*

GEORGE ROBERT WHITE MEMORIAL

(Daniel Chester French, 1924.) White, an art patron and philanthropist, bequeathed the money for this tribute to himself. French's original title for the monument was a bit more circumspect—"The Art of Giving." Note the elegant Beaux Arts styling by one of its foremost practitioners. *Public Garden at Arlington and Beacon Sts. T stop: Arlington.*

VIEWPOINTS

These are some of the best Boston-filled views. The ones from the Pru and the Hancock serve as good points for orientation; the others afford pretty pieces of the whole that is Boston.

1 *g-2*

BUNKER HILL MONUMENT

Walk the 294 steps (there is no elevator) to the top of the 221-foot-high monument for views of Charlestown, Boston, the harbor, and the Charles and Mystic rivers. *Monument Sq., Charlestown, 617/242–5641. Free. Daily 9–5 (must start climb by 4:30). T stop: Community College.*

9 *c-1*

COPP'S HILL TERRACE

Copp's Hill is the highest point of Boston's North End. After you've visited the historic Copp's Hill Burial Ground, take in the view of the Charlestown Navy Yard and the harbor. *Free. T stop: Haymarket.*

3 f-8

HARVARD BRIDGE

Walk the bridge at sunset and view the Esplanade and the sailing basin, and be dazzled by the sight of Beacon Hill with the gold dome of the State House aglow. Ahead are the buildings of MIT. *Massachusetts Ave. at the Charles River.*

8 e-3

JOHN HANCOCK OBSERVATORY

Start your tour of Boston on the 60th floor (740 feet up) of New England's tallest building, where you are treated to a magnificent view: on a clear day it extends 100 miles. Not only can you see the gold-domed State House and the redbrick town houses of Beacon Hill, but also the White Mountains of southern New Hampshire. All the neighborhoods of Boston can be seen from here, and "Funscopes"—high-powered telescopes—zoom in on famous landmarks, affording a closer look (although, annoyingly, these telescopic views are not free). A multimedia show on the American Revolution is set around a miniature version of Old Boston. Over the windows, photos and captions illustrate the city's history. Several interactive machines let you test your knowledge of Boston trivia (sample: How many windows in the John Hancock? Answer: 10,344), and another machine lets you target the horizon for specific buildings. But the real show is the view itself. *John Hancock Tower, Hancock Pl. at Copley Sq., ticket office Trinity Pl. and St. James Ave., 617/572–6429. $4.25 adults, $3.25 senior citizens and ages 5–17. Mon.–Sat. 9 AM–11 PM; May–Oct., also Sun. 10 AM–11 PM Nov.–Apr., also Sun. noon–11. Last ticket sold at 10. T stops: Copley, Back Bay.*

1 h-6

KENNEDY LIBRARY & MUSEUM

Built on a natural promontory in Dorchester Bay, the library affords visitors an unimpeded view of Boston's skyscrapers as well as fine scenic vistas of the Harbor Islands and the open sea beyond. *Columbia Point, Dorchester.*

6 a-4

LONGFELLOW BRIDGE

A nice place to get views of the Boston skyline over the Charles, this is also a prime spot for catching the Fourth of July fireworks on the Esplanade. *T stop: Charles/MGH.*

6 h-7

MUSEUM WHARF

Outside the Computer Museum (and riding up its glass elevator), there's a good view of the city. *Computer Museum, 300 Congress St., 617/426–2800. T stop: Aquarium.*

6 h-5

NEW ENGLAND AQUARIUM

In addition to viewing the wonderful creatures of the sea within this building, you can also view Boston's historic waterfront from the Harbor View Room on the aquarium's third level. (*See Historic Buildings & Areas, above, and Chapter 6.*) *Central Wharf off Atlantic Ave., 617/973–5200. T stop: Aquarium.*

6 c-5

PINCKNEY & ANDERSON STREETS

From where these two Beacon Hill streets meet you are treated to a wonderful view of the Charles River, dotted with white sails in season.

8 c-4

PRUDENTIAL SKYWALK

The Skywalk Observation Deck on the 50th floor of this 52-story edifice affords a panoramic 360° view—a *great* orientation spot. If you go at sunset, it's downright dramatic! From here you can see sailboats sweeping over the Charles River and the abstract geometry of the nearby Christian Science Church's reflecting pool and plaza. There are chairs for sitting and noisy interactive exhibits on Boston's history. *Prudential Tower, 800 Boylston St., Back Bay, 617/859–0648. $4 adults, $3 senior citizens and ages 2–10, group rates available. Daily 10–10. Last ticket sold at 9:45. T stop: Prudential.*

6 g-4

WATERFRONT PARK

Located on Atlantic Avenue between Mercantile Street and Long Wharf, this park offers great unimpeded views of the harbor, stretching clear across to Logan Airport. On a summer night, it's a fine place to see the harbor lights and catch a cool breeze. *T stop: Aquarium.*

guided tours

Particularly during the summer, Boston is awash with tours—on buses, on trolleys, and by foot. A variety of folks offer a variety of specialized tours (with various degrees of quality) covering aspects of Boston life from its art and architecture to its beer pubs. Many tours are mom-and-pop-type operations; others have been around for decades. For up-to-date information on tours, particularly newer, more specialized tours, call the Greater Boston Convention and Visitor Center, 617/867–8220, or check its Web site at www.bostonusa.com.

A wide variety of coach tours are available. They range from the completely escorted to shuttles that allow you a free schedule between stops. A good planning tip: If you choose the fully escorted, go early in the day so you have some time later to backtrack if you see something or someplace of particular interest to you. If your schedule and stamina permit, this is one city that lends itself to walking, whether on a marked trail, on your own, or on one of the interesting walking tours covered in this section.

BOAT TOURS

You'll get a feel for Boston's seafaring past with a visit to the waterfront and the historic wharfs. Why not extend the experience with a sightseeing cruise out into the harbor. It's a special treat for the footsore and city-bound, not to mention a wonderful way to cool off on a hot summer's day. Special treats among those listed are the musical cruises.

A. C. CRUISE LINE
This firm specializes in excursions to Gloucester, 10–5:30. Boats leave from Northern Avenue and give you time to walk around in Gloucester. There is also a "Country Western" cruise every Thursday, July 1–Labor Day. Discounts for groups of 20 or more. *290 Northern Ave., Boston, 02210, 617/261–6633. $18 adults, $13 senior citizens, $12 under 12. Mid-May–June and Labor Day–Oct., weekends; July–Labor Day, Tues.–Sun.*

BAY STATE CRUISE COMPANY
See Cape Cod without having to fight traffic with a cruise on the *Provincetown*

II to Provincetown, leaving daily 9 AM from the Commonwealth Pier near the World Trade Center. Arrive in Provincetown at noon, then leave for the return trip by 3:30 PM. On Friday and Saturday nights music cruises leave at 8:30 PM, call for reservations. *Bay State Cruise Co., 184 High St., Suite 501, Boston 02110, 617/457–1428, private parties 617/723–8012. Round-trip $30 adults, $23 senior citizens, $21 under 12.*

BOSTON HARBOR CRUISES
This company offers five cruises departing from Long Wharf, including four listed below—Constitution Cruise; George's Island Cruise; Historic Sightseeing Cruise; Sunset Cruise—plus a whale-watching cruise. *1 Long Wharf, 617/227–4321. T stop: Aquarium.*

CONSTITUTION CRUISE
A 45-minute cruise of Boston's inner harbor, this trip offers views of Bunker Hill, Copp's Terrace, and the Old North Church. Passengers may disembark at the Charlestown Navy Yard for a close-up of "Old Ironsides." *1 Long Wharf, 617/227–4321. $6 adults, $5 senior citizens, $4 under 12. Departs Long Wharf June–Sept., daily 10:30–4:30 hourly; call for spring and fall schedule. T stop: Aquarium.*

GEORGE'S ISLAND
A 45-minute tour, this takes in several outer-harbor islands. *1 Long Wharf, 617/227–4321. $7.50 adults, $6.50 senior citizens, $5.50 under 12. Departs Long Wharf June–Sept., daily 10–5 hourly; call for spring and fall schedule. T stop: Aquarium.*

HISTORIC SIGHTSEEING CRUISES
A 90-minute cruise of Boston Harbor with narration by the captain of historical sites in Dorchester Heights, Fort Independence, and the outer harbor. *1 Long Wharf, 617/227–4321. $10 adults, $8 senior citizens, $6 under 12. Departs June–Sept., daily at 11, 1, and 3; call for spring and fall schedule. T stop: Aquarium.*

LIBERTY SCHOONER
Sail Boston Harbor on the *Liberty*, an 80-foot replica of a mid-1800s coastal schooner. *Schooner Liberty Inc., 67 Long Wharf, Suite 1/North, Boston 02110. $25 adults, $12.50 under 12. Daily 2-hr sail from Long Wharf at noon, 3, and 6. T stop: Aquarium.*

MASSACHUSETTS BAY LINES

The company offers a variety of tours from May to October, including a Sunset Cruise, a Harbor Cruise (including the USS *Constitution*), a Blues Cruise (Wednesday night only), and Rock Cruise (Thursday night only). All depart from Rowes Wharf. *60 Rowes Wharf, Boston 02110, 617/542–8000. Sunset Cruise $12 adults, $8 senior citizens and children; Harbor Cruise $8 adults, $5 senior citizens and children. Blues/Rock Cruise $12 adults. Sunset Cruise daily 7–8:30 PM, Harbor Cruise daily on the hr 10–6 PM. T stop: Aquarium.*

THE ODYSSEY

Dining, from brunch to exclusive dinners are available on this cruise ship, with three climate-controlled decks. Options include a Sunday jazz brunch, luncheon daily, dinners served Friday through Sunday, and a moonlight cruise. Costs range from $35 to $75. Clearly, a lovely way to experience Boston Harbor. Leaves from Rowes Wharf. *88 Broad St., 5th floor, Boston, 02110, 617/654–9700. T stop: Aquarium.*

RIVERBOAT CRUISES ON THE CHARLES

The Charles River offers fantastic views of Boston and Cambridge, and you can enjoy it on a 55-minute riverboat cruise that takes in the Esplanade, Beacon Hill, and the State House. *100 Cambridge Pl., Suite 320, Cambridge, 02141, 617/621–3001. $8 adults, $6 senior citizens, $5 children. Departs from Cambridgeside Galleria Mall daily noon–5 on the hr. T stop: Kendall Sq.*

SPIRIT OF BOSTON

Have lunch or dinner and be entertained while cruising Boston Harbor on this ultra-modern 200-foot liner with three decks. The Lunch Cruise offers a New England Lobster Clambake. There's also a year-round brunch cruise. For dinner, there's a Lobster Cruise, offered June–September, and year-round there's a Starlight Dinner Cruise. Board ½ hour prior to cruise time at the World Trade Center, Commonwealth Pier. *Bay State Cruise Co., 184 High St., Suite 501, Boston 02110, 617/457–1450. Lunch Cruise, $32.95, June–Sept., Mon. and Wed.–Sat. 11:30–2; Lobster Cruise, $42.40, June–Sept., Fri, Sat. 7–10; Starlight Dinner Cruise, $55–$65, year-round Sun. 6–9, and Mon., Wed., and Thurs. 7–10.*

SUNSET CRUISE

Watch the sun go down over the harbor and catch the USS *Constitution*'s cannon sound off at the close of day. *1 Long Wharf, 617/227–4321. $10 adults, $8 senior citizens, $6 under 12. Departs Long Wharf June–Sept. daily at 7 PM; call for spring and fall schedule. T stop: Aquarium.*

BUS & TROLLEY TOURS

BEANTOWN TROLLEYS FREEDOM TRAIL SHUTTLE

Seated on red trolleys, you can have a two-hour narrated tour or you can get off and on at 20 different stops with unlimited use. Stops include Faneuil Hall, USS *Constitution*, Beacon Hill, New England Aquarium, and the North End. Board at the Gray Line Ticket Office, Transportation Building in Park Square, 14 S. Charles Street, next to Bennigan's Restaurant. *Brush Hill Tours, Gray Line, 435 High St., Randolph, 02368, 617/236–2148, groups 617/986–6100. $18 adults, $14 senior citizens, $5 children. Jan.–Mar., daily 9–4:30; later hours in summer.*

BOSTON DUCK TOURS

The "ducks" in this tour are the renovated World War II amphibious landing vehicles, which—after an 80-minute tour of the city—leave land and plunge right into the Charles River for a waterside view of Boston! The tour covers Trinity Church, Back Bay, the Old State House, Fanueil Hall, the Public Gardens, the "Cheers" bar, Charlestown, and the State House. Board at the Prudential Center on the Huntington Avenue side. Tickets sold inside the Pru; Group rates are available. *790 Boylston St., Plaza Level, Boston, MA 02199, 617/723–DUCK. $19 adults, $16 senior citizens and students, $10 under 12, 25¢ under 3. Apr.–Nov., daily 9–sunset; tours every ½ hr.*

BOSTON SIGHTSEEING TOURS

This outfit offers tours, with full commentary, of Boston and Cambridge in 19-passenger, air-conditioned coaches. Departures are from hotels in Braintree, Burlington, Dedham, Framingham, Lexington, Natick, Needham, Newton, Randolph, Southborough, Waltham, Westborough, and Woburn. Tour includes USS *Constitution*, Bunker Hill, Freedom Trail sites, and Harvard Square, plus a 1½-hour lunch break in Quincy

Market. Tours last about 6 hours. Reservations are required (call daily noon–9:30). *89 Arcadia Ave., Waltham, 02154, 617/899–1454, in MA 800/237–8687. $36 adults, $9 ages 10–16, 9 and under free.*

GRAY LINE/BRUSH HILL TRANSPORTATION COMPANY

This company offers a variety of tours including the Bean Town Trolley Freedom Trail Shuttle (*see above*). The Cambridge Trolley Tour, a 3-hour Cambridge trip includes the Harvard museums, historical homes on Brattle Street, and the MIT Campus. The company also offers a 3-plus-hour Cambridge, Lexington, and Concord tour; a 7-hour Boston, Cambridge, Lexington, and Concord grand tour, and also tours to Plymouth, Salem, Cape Cod, and the Foxwoods Casino. Many of the tours offer free pickup and return service at major Boston and Cambridge hotels. *435 High St., Randolph, 02368, 617/236–2148, groups 617/986–6100. Cambridge Trolley Tour Apr.–mid-Nov., daily at 9:30. $21 adults, $11 children. Cambridge, Lexington, and Concord Tour late Mar.–mid-Nov., daily at 9:30. $25 adults, $13 children. Boston, Cambridge, Lexington, and Concord Tour late Mar.–mid-Nov., daily at 9:30. $35 adults, $18 children.*

MINUTEMAN TOURS

Eighty-minute tours in open-air blue trolleys cover the North End, Back Bay, Beacon Hill, USS *Constitution*, Faneuil Hall, the Theater District, and other stops. Visitors can also opt for a stop and admission to the Boston Tea Party Ship and Museum. *Old Town Trolleys, 617/876–5539. $15 adults, $6 ages 13 and under; with museum, $18 adults, $8 children. Tour leaves every ½ hr from New England Aquarium.*

OLD TOWN TROLLEY

This old-fashioned, open-air, trackless, motorized orange and green trolley offers a fun alternative to an air-conditioned tour bus. Choose from several tour options, but the most popular is the Boston Tour, a 100-minute narrated tour that covers Back Bay, Beacon Hill, Downtown, the waterfront, Quincy Market, the USS *Constitution*—you will cover 90% of the Freedom Trail. You can get off and on at 19 stops. There is also the Cambridge Tour, a 75-minute tour of Cambridge, which covers Harvard Square, Longfellow House, and Brattle Street. The company also offers a JFK's

Boston Tour that covers the late president's birthplace, his neighborhood, and the JFK Library. Another popular new tour is the Boston and Cambridge BrewPub Tour. *329 W. 2nd St., South Boston, 01227, 617/269–7010, group 617/ 269–7150. Boston Tour $18 adults, $14 senior citizens, $7 ages 5–12. Boston Tour tickets can be purchased at most hotel lobbies and Old Town Trolley Ticket booths at Boston Common, Faneuil Hall, and other sites throughout city. Cambridge Tour $14 adults, $12 senior citizens, $7 ages 5–12. Cambridge Tour tickets can be purchased at all of the above as well as Harvard Square. Boston Tour daily every 15 mins 9–4, with pickups at most major hotels. Cambridge Tour daily nearly every hour 9– 4, Apr.–Oct. only.*

SPECIALIZED TOURS

BAY COLONY HISTORICAL TOURS

English- and foreign language–speaking guides for narrated motorcoach tours of historic areas of Boston and eastern Massachusetts. Special custom-designed packages for special interests include "Boston for Students"—a distinctive educational walking and boating tour of the Freedom Trail, Cambridge, and other sites geared to students. Also of interest, a "nostalgic" tour of Boston for alumni groups of area colleges. Special tours available for senior citizens. A new tour, "Art, Gardens, Music and History: The Best of New England," will cover landmarks and current exhibits and/or concerts. Private tours, corporate, and spouse programs available. Note: Hourly, not per person charge, with minimum; 24-hour answering service. *John F. Kennedy Station, Box 9186, 02114, 617/523–7303.*

BEN FRANKLIN'S BOSTON: A WALKING TOUR & LUNCH

A three-hour tour for those with a serious interest in historical Boston, sponsored by the Old South Meetinghouse. At the helm is Emmy-award winning actor Bill Meikle, who, as Benjamin Franklin, leads the way on a guided Freedom Trail walk. The tour also includes lunch at the French restaurant Maison Robert, where "Dr. Franklin" answers questions. *617/482–6439, group tours 617/648–0628. $32 includes tour, lunch, tax. Tour departs Old South Meetinghouse*

July and Aug., Wed. at 9:45; group tours available by prior arrangement.

BLACK HERITAGE TRAIL

The National Park Service has regular tours of the Black Heritage trail, starting at Shaw Memorial across from the State House on Beacon Street. The tour includes 14 sites and covers the schools, homes, and churches that made up Boston's 19th-century black community. Highlights include the Charles Street Meetinghouse, Smith Court, and the Abiel Smith School. Participants learn about the city's organized resistance to slavery and racism. The tour, which covers over 1½ miles, finishes at the African Meetinghouse. You can also do a self-guided tour, thanks to brochures available at the Park Service office or the Museum of Afro-American History. *617/742–5415. Tour Memorial Day–Labor Day, daily at 10, noon, and 2; tour by appointment only; large groups should call ahead.*

BOSTON PUBLIC LIBRARY

An excellent art and architecture tour of the original library building by McKim, Mead, and White, and its modern addition by Philip Johnson. No reservation necessary, meets in the lobby of the general library building, Boylston Street entrance. *Copley Sq., 617/536–5400, Ext. 216. Free. Mon. at 2:30, Tues. and Thurs. at 6, Fri. and Sat. at 11.*

COOPERS OF BOSTON LIMOUSINE SERVICE

Those who like to be extravagant can try these custom-tailored guided tours in chauffeured sedans, limousines, custom vans, or deluxe motor coaches. Tours of Boston include the Freedom Trail, museums, and the neighborhoods. Also Cambridge, Lexington and Concord, North Shore, Cape Cod, and other areas of New England. For the pampered individual or groups up to 45. Fee does not include site admissions, tolls, parking, mileage, or gratuities. Advance reservations are required. *171 Milk St., 4th floor, 02109, 617/482–1000 or 800/343–2123.*

MAGNIFICENT & MODEST: BEACON HILL WALKING TOUR

After a slide show and tour of the first Harrison Gray Otis House (141 Cambridge St.), well-informed guides walk you through nearby Beacon Hill for a stroll past some of Otis's less-wealthy neighbors. The trip includes the Smith Court Houses, in what was once a thriving black community and to Otis's two other homes—each one more magnificent than the last. *141 Cambridge St, 617/227–3956. $10. May–Oct., Sat. at 3.*

NORTH END MARKET TOUR

Learn the secrets of Italian food with this four-hour tour of the North End's *salumerias* (delis), *pasticcerias* (pastry shops), and wine shops with culinary expert Michele Topor, who has been doing this for 10 years. You'll find out how to pick a good olive oil and see how mozzarella and ricotta are made in a local cheese shop, and finish up with a lunch at a North End eatery. Reservations are absolutely required. *6 Charter St., Boston, 02113, 617/523–3062. $35 without lunch. Wed. and Sat. 10–2.*

VICTORIAN SOCIETY OF AMERICA

These Sunday afternoon walking tours of Victorian Boston are held in the spring and fall; call for exact schedules and prices. The Victorian Society, New England Chapter, devotes itself to the Victorian period with an emphasis on architecture, landscaping, and women's achievements. Tours concentrate on the socioeconomic history and architecture of the time. *Gibson House Museum, 137 Beacon St., Back Bay, 02116, 617/267–6338 or 617/789–3927.*

WOMEN'S HERITAGE TRAIL

This is a walk-it-yourself series of trails covering nearly four centuries of women's history in Boston. The four walks cover downtown, the North End, South/Cove Chinatown, and Beacon Hill, and take in such sites as the Anne Hutchison Statue at the State House, the Nichols House Museum, Louisa May Alcott's home at 20 Pinckney St., and Mother Goose's alleged burial site. The trail began as a project of the Boston Public Schools. *22 Holbrook St., Jamaica Plain 02130.*

WALKING TOURS

BOSTON ADVENTURES

Choose from three 90-minute walking tours: Tour 1, Paul Revere's House and Freedom Trail; Tour 2, the John Hancock Observatory and Freedom Trail; Tour 3, the Mini-Harbor Cruise, Back Bay, Beacon Hill, Freedom Trail, USS *Constitution*, and the Water Taxi cruise on

Boston Harbor. All tours leave from Copley Square, Bostix Ticket Booth at Dartmouth and Boylston streets. Tours end at Faneuil Hall. *617/748–9569. $20 adults, $15 senior citizens, $10 children. Tour 1 daily at 10, Tour 2 daily at 2, Tour 3 daily at noon and 5.*

BOSTON BY FOOT

Since 1976 this nonprofit educational group has been offering walking tours of Boston, guided by trained docents with a special love for their city. Tours concentrate on historic and architectural aspects of Boston. Heart of the Freedom Trail Tour, which lasts 90 minutes, meets at the statue of Samuel Adams, Congress Street near Faneuil Hall. The Copley Square Tour, also 90 minutes, meets at Trinity Church facing Copley Square. The Beacon Hill Tour, 90 minutes, meets at the State House steps, Beacon Street. The North End Tour, 90 minutes, meets at the statue of Samuel Adams, Congress Street near Faneuil Hall. The Waterfront Tour, 90 minutes, explores Boston's revitalized wharfs and warehouses, meets at Samuel Adams statue, Faneuil Hall. The Boston Underground Tour covers Boston's subway system, 18th-century crypts, and the "Big Dig," the Central Artery project now in progress. For younger minds, there's the Boston by Little Feet Tour: A Children's Tour, a 60-minute tour, meets at the statue of Samuel Adams, Congress Street near Faneuil Hall. *77 North Washington St., 02114, 617/367–2345. All tours $7 adults, $5 ages 6–12; purchase tickets from guide. Freedom Trail Tour Tues.–Sat. at 10, Sun. at 2. T stop: State St. or Government Center. Copley Square Tour Fri. at 10, Sat. at noon. T stop: Copley. Beacon Hill Tour weekdays at 5:30, Sat. at 10, Sun. at 2. T stop: Park St. North End Tour Sat. at 2. T stop: State St. or Government Center. Waterfront Tour Fri. at 5:30, Sun. at 10. T Stop: State St. or Government Center. Boston Underground Tour Sun. at 2. Children's Tour Mon. and Sat. at 10, Sun. at 2. T stop: State St. or Government Center.*

BOSTON PARK RANGERS

Boston park rangers give free tours of the Freedom Trail every Saturday and Sunday in July and August starting at the Boston Common Information Booth. *617/635–4505.*

FREEDOM TRAIL

The National Park Service runs regularly scheduled walking tours beginning at the park's service office near the Old State House from spring through fall. The 90-minute tours cover about six sites of the Freedom Trail. Special tours for special needs, and group tours, must be arranged in advance. Off-season tours may be arranged for groups. The park service also gives historical talks at Faneuil Hall every half hour, daily 9–5, except when the hall is closed for city-sponsored events. You may also explore the trail as a do-it-yourself tour; just use the handy brochure to be found at the National Park Service offices; for a list of the various sites on the trail, *see* Historic Buildings and Areas, *above.* The Freedom Trail Foundation has a weekly Freedom Trail events hot line (617/242–5695). *National Park Service, 15 State St., 02109, 617/242–5642. Office fall–spring, daily 9–5; summer, daily 9–6; tours mid-June–Aug., daily 10–3 on the hr; sunset tour Tues. and Thurs. at 6; Apr.–June, weekdays at 2, weekends at 11, 2, and 3; Aug.–Thanksgiving, weekends at 11, 2, 3.*

HISTORIC NEIGHBORHOODS FOUNDATION

This nonprofit educational group gives walkers a sense of the best of the past. Well-trained guides conduct friendly and informal walking tours designed to uncover the character, history, and excitement of Boston neighborhoods. There are regularly scheduled tours each week that explore the North End, Chinatown, the waterfront, and Beacon Hill. Thursdays, at 5:30 PM, there is a Sunset Stroll through Beacon Hill, one of the prettiest times to view the 19th-century enclave. For children age 5 and up, there's a "Make Way for Ducklings Tour," and one of the North End. *99 Bedford St., Boston 02111, 617/426–1885. $5–$15, depending on tour and age. Tour Apr. 15–Aug.; group tours year-round (call ahead).*

WHALE-WATCH CRUISES

A. C. CRUISE LINE

Whale-watching excursions are offered 10–4:30. *290 Northern Ave., Boston, 02210, 617/261–6633. $19 adults, $14 senior citizens, $12 children. Mid-May–June and Labor Day–Oct., weekends; July 10–Labor Day, Tues.–Sun.*

BOSTON HARBOR CRUISES

A five-hour cruise to seek the whales is just one of several cruise itineraries offered by this outfit. *1 Long Wharf, Boston, 02110, 617/227–4321. $22 adults, $19 senior citizens, $16.50 under 12. June–Sept., daily at 10 or 11, depending on weather; call for spring and fall schedule. T stop: Aquarium.*

BOSTON HARBOR WHALE-WATCH

A four-plus-hour cruise, this whale-watch expedition departs from Rowes Wharf aboard the 100-foot *Majestic*. *60 Rowes Wharf, Boston, 02110, 617/345–9866. $20 adults, $18 under 12; group rates available. June–Sept., weekdays at 10, weekends at 9 and 2.*

MASSACHUSETTS BAY LINES

One of the four major cruises this company offers is a whale-watching expedition that explores the Stellwagen Bank, a wildlife sanctuary and prime whale-watching territory. Reservations are advised. *60 Rowes Wharf, Boston 02110, 617/542–8000. $20 adults, $18 senior citizens and children. Late June–Oct., daily 10:30–3:30. T stop: Aquarium.*

NEW ENGLAND AQUARIUM

The Aquarium offers whale-watching adventures from May through October; cruise hours vary throughout the season with most cruises scheduled May to July and September to October with daily morning cruises and a second afternoon cruise on weekends. From July to September, a morning and a 4 PM sunset cruise are offered daily. Reservations are recommended. *New England Aquarium, Long Wharf, 617/973–5281. T stop: Aquarium.*

events

Boston loves a festival and will create one for almost any reason. If these standbys don't satisfy your appetite for seasonal events, call "Great Dates in the Bay State," a hot line run by the Massachusetts Office of Travel and Tourism, at 800/227–6277. It lists six current and upcoming events and is updated every other week.

JANUARY

1 *g-6*

BUDWEISER WORLD OF WHEELS

The Bayside Expo Center in Dorchester starts the year off with New England's largest automotive event, including a showcase of hundreds of customized cars, monster-truck rallies, and other special attractions. *617/265–5800.*

6 *d-7*

CHINESE NEW YEAR

For one day in January or February (depending on the Chinese calendar, date usually falls between January 21 and February 19), every street in Chinatown explodes with firecrackers as residents celebrate the Chinese New Year. Crowds form early to see the lion and dragon dance for good luck. Some of the neighborhood restaurants feature special menus; others set up booths along the streets. *617/542–2574.*

6 *h-7*

JAPANESE NEW YEAR FESTIVAL

This colorful special exhibit at the Children's Museum is designed to show kids how their Japanese peers celebrate the New Year. The lion dance, origami (the art of paper folding), games, and other activities are all colorful—and free with museum admission. *617/426–8855.*

1 *g-6*

NEW ENGLAND CAMPING & RV SHOW

Held at the Bayside Expo Center in mid-January, this is a giant exhibition of everything having to do with camping, from the tiniest of pup tents to trailers that look like hotel rooms on wheels. *617/474–6000.*

1 *g-5*

NEW YEAR'S DAY SWIM

Members of the L Street Brownies, a loosely organized swim club in South Boston, defy the winter each January 1 with an icy swim at Carson Beach. Some of the swimmers, in their eighties and nineties, have been taking this frigid dip for more than 40 years!

FEBRUARY

BLACK HISTORY MONTH
The entire month of February is devoted to a celebration of black history and culture, cosponsored by the Museum of Afro-American History and the African American Meetinghouse. For a complete schedule of events, call 617/742–1854.

BOSTON WINE EXPO
Early February brings this gustatory revel, which includes a rare-wine auction and the Anthony Spinazzola Gala, a banquet considered New England's preeminent culinary event. Call for schedule and locations. 800/544-1660.

6 d-6
DISNEY ON ICE
Mickey, Minnie, and the stars of the current Disney movie present this skating extravaganza at the FleetCenter each year in mid-February. Every tot in town wants to go, so buy tickets early. 617/624–1000.

2 b-8
FREDERICK DOUGLASS DAY
Frederick Douglass spoke in the square at the intersection of Tremont and Cabot streets when he was a mainstay of the Abolitionist movement. Now the square is named after him, and he's honored each February 14 at 11 AM with speeches, a wreath-laying, and the naming of Roxbury's most outstanding citizen. 617/782–7911.

6 a-1
INVENTOR'S WEEKEND
The Museum of Science celebrates imagination and invention on the second or third weekend in February with lectures, special programs, and demonstrations of inventions both cutting-edge and silly by inventors of all ages. It's free with museum admission. 617/523–6664.

5 f-6
MASSACHUSETTS CAMELLIA SHOW
for more than 150 years, this free two-day show at the arnold arboretum has celebrated the delicate, fragrant camellia blossom. 617/738–4300.

1 g-6
NEW ENGLAND BOAT SHOW
Boat lovers dream of summer water sports at this annual exhibition held in mid-February at the Bayside Expo Center. Come to price the new models or just to dream of lazy days cruising the Harbor. Hundreds of exhibits all relate to boating and marine sports; this is a great opportunity for beginning boaters to conduct research before buying. 617/242–6092.

1 g-6
NORTH AMERICAN HOME SHOW
From window frames to wood floors, this event at the Bayside Expo Center covers just about everything having to do with building, renovating, expanding, and upgrading homes of all styles and sizes. 617/474–6000.

8 f-2
THADDEUS KOŚCIUSZKO DAY
This annual ceremony, put on by the Polish-American Congress in honor of a Polish-American hero of the Revolutionary War, takes place at his statue in the Public Garden near Boylston Street at noon on the first Sunday in February. A wreath-laying is followed by commemorative speeches by politicians and members of Polish organizations. 617/859–9910.

MARCH

6 e-5
BOSTON MASSACRE CEREMONY
On March 5, 1770, former slave Crispus Attucks and four other Bostonians were killed by British troops in what came to be known as the Boston Massacre. Now Boston commemorates the event each year on March 5 from noon to 12:30 PM with speeches and music. 617/635–3911.

EVACUATION DAY
On March 17, Boston honors not only St. Patrick, but the day in 1776 on which General Washington expelled British troops from South Boston. Naturally, this provides a fine excuse to take the day off and watch the St. Patrick's Day parade (*see below*)!

1 g-6

NEW ENGLAND FLOWER SHOW

The Massachusetts Horticultural Society sponsors the country's oldest flower and garden exhibition, which has been bringing an early taste of spring to the city every March for more than 125 years. This nine-day production is designed and staged in conjunction with professional and amateur horticulturists. Thousands come to the Bayside Expo Center to revel in acres of landscapes and gardens in peak bloom. Hint: go on a weekday evening to avoid the crush. *617/536–9280*.

1 h-5

ST. PATRICK'S DAY PARADE

South Boston is the heart of Irish Boston so, naturally, the whole city flocks there to fete St. Paddy in grand style. Southie's immense parade, second only to New York's, is held each year on the Sunday before St. Patrick's Day (March 17). It begins at 1 PM, but general festivities tend to start much earlier in the day. Show up in the morning to stake out a spot on the curb. *617/268–8525*.

WOMEN'S HISTORY MONTH

The entire month of March is devoted to a celebration of women's history and achievements. The *Boston Globe* and *Boston Phoenix* feature listings of events held around the area.

APRIL

6 h-7

BIG APPLE CIRCUS

The Boston Children's Museum brings the littlest big top to Boston for four weeks of close-up thrills and clown spills. There's no better way to get a good look at the circus. *617/426–6500*.

8 d-3

BOSTON MARATHON

Held each year on the third Monday in April, this is the oldest and most celebrated marathon in America (*see* Chapter 6), drawing world-class runners as well as amateurs all vying for the most coveted victory outside of the Olympics. The race begins at noon (11:45 AM for wheelchair racers) far out in the suburban town of Hopkinton and wends its

way through Ashland, Framingham, Natick, Wellesley Center, Wellesley Hills, Newton (site of the infamous "Heartbreak Hill"), Brookline, then down Beacon Street to Kenmore Square and on to the finish at the Boston Public Library. The front-runners finish at approximately 2 PM and receive their awards at 6 PM, but determined amateurs continue to straggle in for hours afterward.

More than 1.5 million spectators show up to cheer the runners on, so get up early on Marathon Monday to stake your claim to a good spot along the route—Beacon Street between Cleveland Circle and Coolidge Corner is close enough to the finish to give you an idea of how the race is going, but far enough out that the sidewalks aren't 20 deep with onlookers. Or, for an unusual perspective, watch the finish line (in front of the Boston Public Library) from the top of the Hancock Tower or the Prudential Center. Important: No cars are allowed in Hopkinton after 8 AM or in Copley Square after 9 AM, and the Copley T stop is closed all day. *617/236–1652*.

The following is a listing of some of the things that happen in conjunction with the marathon:

BOSTON MARATHON ROUTE SIGHTSEEING BUS

The weekend before Marathon Monday, Marathon Tours & Travel, Inc., lets you see from a seat—on a motorcoach—what the runners will see on their feet. Two narrated tours of the marathon route depart on Saturday afternoon and Sunday morning. Reserve tickets in advance for this popular tour. *617/242–7845*.

BOSTON MARATHON SPORTS & FITNESS EXPO

Conventures, a specialty firm, hosts a special sports and runners' exposition, with exhibits, demonstrations, and events, at the Hynes Convention Center from 10 AM to 6 PM Saturday and Sunday of Marathon Weekend. *617/236–1652*.

NIGHT-BEFORE SPAGHETTI DINNER

In a tradition as venerable as the Marathon itself, the Boston Athletic Association invites all qualifying runners to carbo-load at a free, all-you-can-eat spaghetti dinner the night before the race from 4 to 9 PM. Call for information and location. *617/236–1652*.

1 g-6

BOSTON'S BIGGEST BABY FAIRE

If you have a baby, are planning to have one, or know someone who does, don't miss this giant trade show held the first weekend in April at the Bayside Expo Center. *617/474–6000.*

2 b-5

RED SOX OPENING DAY

Hope springs eternal as the Boston Red Sox play their first home game of the baseball season at Fenway Park. *617/267–8661.*

PATRIOTS' DAY

Although it's usually overshadowed by the Marathon, the first Monday in April is also a state holiday commemorating the events that marked the beginning of the American Revolution and which led to the birth of the nation:

9 d-3

LANTERN HANGING REENACTMENT

The night before Patriots' Day, at 8 PM, two lanterns are hung in the steeple at Old North Church in the North End, just as they were on the night of April 8, 1775, when they signaled to the patriots in Charlestown that the British were coming—by water, not land. *617/523–6676.*

OLD NORTH BRIDGE REENACTMENT

Get up before dawn and head to Minuteman National Historic Park, half an hour west of Boston between Concord and Lexington on Route 2A, where beginning at 6 AM you'll see a reenactment of the Battle of Lexington at the very spot where the farmers of Concord fired "the shot heard 'round the world." *508/369-6993.*

6 e-4

FLAG-RAISING & PARADE

After a 9 AM flag-raising at City Hall Plaza, the parade heads to the grave of Paul Revere in the Old Granary Burying Ground, and thence to William Dawes's in King's Chapel Burying Ground, for wreath-laying ceremonies. Veterans' and civic organizations participate, including the Ancient and Honorable Artillery Company, founded in 1638. *617/635–3911.*

9 e-4

PAUL REVERE'S RIDE

At approximately 10 AM, a costumed rider leaves Paul Revere Mall in the North End to ride to Lexington, as Paul Revere did the night of April 8, 1775, to warn the colonists that the British were coming. People line his route to cheer him on. *617/536–4100.*

2 b-8

WILLIAM DAWES'S RIDE

At about 10:30 AM, another costumed rider departs—this time from John Eliot Square at the intersection of Roxbury, Centre, and Dudley streets in Roxbury—to retrace the ride of William Dawes, a less-celebrated but equally heroic patriot who took another route to Lexington that night, warning still more colonists.

8 g-1

SWAN BOATS

The return of these foot-pedaled boats—a Boston tradition since 1877—to the Public Garden's pond is a sure sign that winter is over at last. They usually come out of winter storage the last week of April. *617/635–4505.*

MAY

6 b-5

BEACON HILL HIDDEN GARDEN TOUR

Members of the Beacon Hill Garden Club open their gates and courtyards to the public but once a year: on the day of this tour. Whether you're a budding horticulturalist or simply curious, this one-day mid-May event is an opportunity to see the hidden delights of Boston's most charming neighborhood. For information, send a stamped, self-addressed envelope to Box 302, Charles Street Station, Boston, MA 02114. *617/227–4392.*

1 e-7

GREATER BOSTON KITE FESTIVAL

Go fly a kite! At Franklin Park, for one day in mid-May, the sky fills up with a mind-boggling array of kites in all sizes, shapes, and colors. Bring your own, or just come to watch the professionals give demonstrations. Keep an eye out for skydivers, too! *617/635–4505.*

3 *b-4*

HARVARD SQUARE MAY FAIR

On the first Sunday in May, Harvard Square is closed to cars, and the streets fill with crafts booths, fragrant food carts, and several stages of live music. Rain date is the following Sunday. *617/491–3434.*

5 *f-6*

LILAC SUNDAY

The Arnold Arboretum grows several hundred varieties of lilacs; when they're at their lush, fragrant peak, the Arboretum holds a festival in their honor on a Sunday in mid-May. It's the only day of the year that picnics are allowed on the Arboretum grounds. A treat for the eye and nose, not to mention the spirit. *617/524–1718.*

6 *b-6*

"MAKE WAY FOR DUCKLINGS" PARADE

On Mother's Day, a parade of ducks waddles over Beacon Hill to the Public Garden lagoon, just as Robert McCloskey immortalized them in his classic children's book. They're attended by hundreds of children, many dressed in duckling costumes and clutching stuffed ducks. Too cute to miss, even if you don't have kids. *617/635–7383.*

MEMORIAL DAY

Commemorative activities sponsored by local veterans' organizations—wreath-layings, speakers, firing squads, the playing of "Taps"—go on in area cemeteries throughout the long weekend. Of particular note: the ceremony placing flags on veterans' graves in Mattapan's Mount Hope Cemetery beginning at 10 AM on the Sunday before Memorial Day. There's also a small, solemn parade in Dorchester, which begins at 9 AM Monday at the Cemetery at Cedar Grove, located at Adams and Milton streets off Galvin Boulevard. Check the *Globe*'s "Calendar" section for a detailed listing of events. *617/725–3911.*

JUNE

6 *f-4*

ANCIENT & HONORABLE ARTILLERY COMPANY PARADE

On the first Monday in June, the third-oldest standing military organization in the country has its drumhead election. It starts at 12:30 PM with a colorful parade from Faneuil Hall to the State House, followed by a memorial service at the Cathedral of St. Paul, then heads on to the Common for the election, which begins at 3 PM. Each time an official is elected, drums are sounded. At the end of the election—around 4 PM—the National Guard fires cannons. The company then parades around the Common once more before heading off to an invitation-only reception. *617/227–1638.*

8 *g-3*

BAY VILLAGE STREET FAIR

This quintessential street fair, now a quarter-century old, crams more than 100 booths of antiques, collectibles, crafts, and food into the tiny neighborhood of Bay Village. Also present are clowns and mimes, live music, a white elephant sale, and a giant raffle with lots of valuable prizes. Follow the crowds to Church Street between Stuart and Tremont streets. *617/482–6173.*

4 *h-4*

BLOOMSDAY CONCERT

Boston University presents an annual performance of dramatic readings, music, and poetry based on the works of James Joyce. Get tickets in advance for this once-a-year event. *617/353–3831.*

6 *c-7*

BOSTON AIDS WALK

Thousands of people fill the streets for the country's oldest and largest AIDS pledge walk, sponsored by the AIDS Action Committee to benefit local organizations. The walk starts with a mass aerobic workout on the Common near the Boylston T stop. Live bands and art exhibits dot the route, which extends out Commonwealth Avenue to Kenmore Square, down Beacon Street to Harvard Street, back to Commonwealth Avenue, and on to the Esplanade. The festivities continue at the Hatch Shell finish line, where there's usually more live music and a congratulatory vibe. *617/437–6200.*

6 *c-6*

BOSTON COMMON DAIRY FESTIVAL

A Boston law held on the books since colonial times stipulates that cattle have to appear on the Common at least once a year. Since June is Dairy Month, what better time to observe the law? More than 100 head of cattle are corralled on the Common for a week in an annual outdoor exhibit featuring milking contests, butter-churning demonstrations, and the "Scooper Bowl," an ice cream tent offering all-you-can-eat scoops from a dozen manufacturers, all for one small entry fee. 617/734–6750.

BOSTON EARLY MUSIC FESTIVAL

To honor Boston's important role in the revival and popularity of early music, this festival of Medieval, Renaissance, and Baroque music includes demonstrations and performances throughout the city by musicians and instrument makers from all over the world. The Boston Museum of Fine Arts occasionally ties in several special programs, and ensembles throughout the city give special concerts. The festival usually culminates in a rare performance of fully staged Baroque opera. Tickets go fast for all events! The festival is only held in Boston in odd-numbered years—it moves to Berkeley, California, in alternate years. 617/661–1812.

BOSTON GLOBE JAZZ & BLUES FESTIVAL

Top jazz and blues musicians, both local and world-renowned, perform in various indoor and outdoor venues around the city for almost two weeks. The kick-off concert at the Hatch Shell, and many other performances, are free. 617/267–4301.

1 f-2
BUNKER HILL DAY

The Sunday before June 17 at 12:30 PM, a parade begins from Hayes Square in Charlestown and proceeds to the Training Field on Winthrop Street to commemorate the Battle of Bunker Hill (June 17, 1775). There are bands, a drum and bugle corps, floats, a road race, and military organizations, not to mention politicians out to shake hands and kiss babies. Earlier in the day, at 10 AM, there's a special children's parade on the Training Field with decorated doll carriages, wagons, and bikes. 617/241–9511.

8 d-3
CLASSICAL AT COPLEY SERIES

Sponsored by radio station WCRB, these free classical music concerts happen in

Copley Square at noon every Thursday in June (and every Friday in September). Performers include the Boston Pops, the Greater Boston Youth Symphony Orchestra, and the Boston Ballet Orchestra. 617/635–4505.

1 f-7
DORCHESTER DAY

This event, held the first Sunday in June, commemorates the founding in 1630 of Boston and Dorchester. It begins with a big parade at 1:30 PM in which high school bands, military bands, fife and drum corps, militia, floats, mounted patrols, and clowns, all march up Dorchester Avenue ("Dot Ave.") from Dorchester to South Boston. Afterward, there's a memorial Mass. 617/265–2228.

3 g-7
DRAGON BOAT FESTIVAL

The pounding of drums fills the Charles River for one June Sunday as dozens of 39-foot-long handcarved teak dragon boats, rowed by 18-person crews, race from Harvard Bridge to the Hatch Shell. Meanwhile, the Cambridge riverside hosts a Chinese arts festival with martial arts demonstrations, Chinese arts and crafts, Chinese folk and jazz dances, poetry readings, and games. 426–6500 ext. 778.

2 e-4
GAY PRIDE PARADE

The second Saturday of June is Pride Day, when the Back Bay and South End explode with sequins, rainbow flags, loud music, and friendly faces of all sexual preferences lining the sidewalks to watch the city's huge Pride Parade. Pride Day kicks off a month of readings, concerts, marches, and other events commemorating the Stonewall riots in New York, which launched the contemporary gay rights movement. 617/262–3149.

1 g-7
LANDING DAY

On the Saturday before the first Sunday in June at 10 AM (depending on the tide), Dorchester commemorates the landing of Pilgrims on Savin Hill Beach. 617/265–2228 or 617/282–2800.

6 f-2
NORTH END FEASTS

In Boston's Little Italy, almost every Sunday from early June to late August is a *festa* or day in honor of a saint. The season starts the first weekend in June with the feast of Santa Maria DiAnzano and progresses through St. Anthony, St. Jude, the Madonna del Grazie, St. Rocco, St. Joseph, and on and on. North End feasts always include a Sunday procession down Hanover, Endicott, or North streets, with members of feast organizations proudly carrying a statue of the honored saint through the narrow streets while onlookers press close to touch, kiss, or pin money to the statue. Most feasts also include weekend-long street fairs including food booths, rides, entertainment, and raffles. Follow the crowds. You'll find pizza, zeppola, calzone, sausage heros, pastries, and much more—so go with an empty stomach! *617/523–2110.*

8 c-5
ST. BOTOLPH STREET FAIR
One of the largest neighborhood fairs in Boston is held in late June in the South End on St. Botolph Street, between Durham and Albemarle streets. It features live entertainment, a bake sale, and a raw bar, as well as a variety of other foods, beer, and wine. Service booths feature local carpenters, decorators, and health clubs. A large area is set aside for an antiques and collectibles flea market; kids will find face painting, clowns, and balloons. *617/536–3310.*

JULY

8 e-2
BASTILLE DAY
The French had a revolution, too, so every July 14, the French Library at 53 Marlborough Street (between Berkeley and Clarendon) celebrates Bastille Day with a fund-raising block party oozing with ooh-la-la. A champagne reception begins at 5:30 PM under trees festooned with red, white, and blue ribbons. A lavish buffet supper follows at 6:30, and live music has everyone dancing in the streets starting at 8. At the close, everyone sings "La Marseillaise." Reservations are a must for dinner, but the street party is free. *617/266–4351.*

6 a-5
BOSTON POPS ESPLANADE CONCERTS
Following its season of performances at Symphony Hall, the Pops treats Boston to these free outdoor concerts, which usually last two hours. Bring a blanket and a picnic to the Hatch Shell. The concerts usually take place in mid-July and always begin at 8 PM. *617/266–2378.*

6 e-4
DOROTHY CURRAN NOSTALGIA NIGHTS CONCERT SERIES
This free concert series has brought swing (and occasional doo-wop) to City Hall Plaza for almost a quarter-century. Put on your dancing shoes each Wednesday night at 7 PM in July and August. *617/635–3911.*

HARBORFEST
This five-day series of events, held all over downtown the first week of July, includes walking tours of the Charlestown Navy Yard, concerts, a July 3rd fireworks display over the Harbor, kids' activities on City Hall Plaza, and military reenactments. It also features the wildly popular Chowderfest, in which top seafood restaurants compete to see whose creamy clam chowder the public will declare Boston's best. Pay a small admission fee, get a spoon, chow down, and cast your vote as you leave. *617/227–1528*

INDEPENDENCE DAY
Boston is awash with celebrating on the weekend that marks the nation's birth. Fourth of July festivities in Boston begin long before the sun goes down and the fireworks flare up. They begin at 9 AM with a flag raising at City Hall Plaza, followed by a short parade to the Granary Burying Ground for wreath-laying ceremonies at the graves of patriots Paul Revere, James Otis, John Hancock, and Samuel Adams. Here's what else happens that day:

6 f-5
INDEPENDENCE DAY ORATION & PARADE
On July 18, 1776, the newly written Declaration of Independence was read to the Boston populace for the first time from the balcony of the Old State House, then the seat of government. The event is reenacted each July 4th, beginning at 10 AM when the Declaration of Independence is read from the balcony of the Old State House. The celebration then moves on to Fanueil Hall for speeches and patriotic music from 11 AM to noon.

2 *g-1*

USS CONSTITUTION TURNAROUND

Also on July 4, the *Constitution*—"Old Ironsides" to those who love her—is towed from her berth in the Charlestown Navy Yard out into the harbor at 10:30 AM. There, the world's oldest warship (built in 1797) fires a salute with all her 21 cannons. When returned to berth at 2 PM, she is turned so that her hull will weather evenly. There is also an antique boat regatta and parade of boats. The best vantage points: the Navy Yard itself, the Charlestown Bridge linking the North End to Charlestown, or the North End Playground (off Commercial Street). *617/242–5670.*

6 *a-5*

BOSTON POPS ANNUAL FOURTH OF JULY CONCERT

Thousands of Bostonians and visitors forego all other Independence Day events in order to stake out a prime spot on the Esplanade for the Boston Pops' annual July 4th concert at the Hatch Shell—a show which has made the city famous throughout the world as *the* place to spend America's birthday. During the day, musical performances by local and national performers keep the crowd happy while they wait on their outspread blankets (some folks camp out from daybreak to be assured of a good seat). The Pops go on for two hours starting at 8 PM, always concluding with Tchaikovsky's *1812 Overture*, complete with cannons—and then the fireworks begin. *617/266–1492.*

6 *e-4*

PUERTO RICAN DAY FESTIVAL

The first day of this late-July festival includes a banquet with speakers and awards and the crowning of the festival's queen. There is also a mini-marathon from Government Center to Clemente Park—the 8½-mile route wends its way through several Hispanic neighborhoods—as well as a parade and a carnival with food, drink, music, rides, and games. *617/725–3485.*

1 *b-5*

U.S. PRO TENNIS CHAMPIONSHIPS AT LONGWOOD

The oldest and best-known professional tennis championships in the country take over the Longwood Cricket Club in suburban Chestnut Hill for one week in late July or early August, and tennis fans from around the world show up to watch. Get tickets in advance—if you can! *617/731–4500.*

9 *g-8*

WATERFRONT JAZZ SERIES

Spend a sultry summer evening where the ocean breezes are cool, baby, cool. On Fridays at 7 PM in July and August, Christopher Columbus Waterfront Park swings with free jazz concerts. *617/635–3911.*

AUGUST

6 *d-7*

AUGUST MOON FESTIVAL

Chinatown celebrates the largest Chinese festival of the year, held on the day of August's full moon to celebrate health, happiness, an abundant harvest, and the coming of autumn. Festivities include food booths, martial arts and tai chi demonstrations, live music, Asian arts and crafts, and a dragon dance. *617/542–2574.*

8 *f-3*

BLACK & BLUE BALL

The Muscular Dystrophy Association's annual fund-raising dinner dance, held at the Park Plaza Hotel, features live blues, a copious buffet of international foods, and auctions of items such as whitewater rafting trips and romantic getaway weekends. *617/575–1881.*

6 *c-6*

BOSTON PARK ARTS FESTIVAL

Visit the newly renovated Parkman Bandstand on Boston Common to catch performances from local theater, dance, and music groups—ranging from Shakespeare and ballet to Irish step dancing and a Gilbert and Sullivan marathon—almost every day from mid-August to mid-September. All performances are free. *617/635–4505.*

 e-7

CARIBBEAN CARNIVAL

This event, held in Franklin Park, has been bringing tropical revelry to town for 24 years. It starts with a parade with masquerade bands in breathtakingly ornate costumes, then continues with food, music, and the crowning of a King and Queen of Carnival. Don't miss this chance to spend a sultry late August day swaying to the rhythm of a steel drum band and imagining yourself in the islands. 617/635–3911.

6 *f-4*

FANEUIL HALL MARKETPLACE BIRTHDAY CELEBRATION

Great, gray Quincy Market, built in 1826, reopened on August 26, 1976, as part of the restored Marketplace. The South Market Building reopened August 26, 1977, and the North Market Building on the same date in 1978. Now very much a hub of the Hub, the Marketplace celebrates its birthday each year with continuous entertainment and a birthday cake large enough for everyone to have a taste. 617/523–1300.

 h-5

JANTZEN SWIM FOR BOSTON HARBOR & BEACH PARTY

This annual 1-mile swimming race and beach party celebrating a cleaner Boston Harbor is hosted by Save the Harbor/Save the Bay with cosponsor Jantzen, the swimwear manufacturer. The beach party at South Boston's M Street Beach is free to all; the race requires an entry fee. 617/451–2860.

 g-6

MACWORLD

Thousands of Macintosh computer enthusiasts and professionals come from around the world to check out new software and hardware at this annual event held in early August at the Bayside Expo Center. 617/474–6000.

SEPTEMBER

4 *b-5*

ALLSTON/BRIGHTON PARADE

Boston's most ethnically diverse neighborhoods celebrate their melting-pot nature in mid-September with a giant, colorful, proudly polyglot parade down Washington Street. 617/635–3911.

8 *f-3*

BODY & SOUL

This annual conference, sponsored by *Interface* and *New Age Journal*, is held at the Park Plaza Hotel in mid-September and features workshops and lectures on health, personal growth, alternative medicine, spirituality, and creativity. It draws a vibrant crowd as well as many of the big names in holistic education. 617/964–9360.

7 *h-5*

BOSTON FILM FESTIVAL

Now in its 13th year, this two-week festival lacks the glamour of Cannes, but nonetheless attracts stars like Kevin Bacon and Helena Bonham-Carter with its roster of new and re-released independent films shown at the Sony Copley Place and the Kendall Square Theater (*see* Chapter 5). 617/925–1373.

3 *g-7*

CAMBRIDGE RIVER FESTIVAL

For one Saturday in mid-September, the Cambridge side of the riverbank overflows with live music, foods from many nations, participatory public art, an international crafts bazaar, and children's activities. The Cambridge Arts Council has been sponsoring this celebration of the arts for 20 years. 617/349–4380.

6 *c-6*

INTERNATIONAL HARVEST FAIR

This benefit for Oxfam America, the famine-relief organization, takes place on Boston Common the second weekend in September. It features multicultural arts, music, dance, and a crafts fair as well as a "kids' corner," where children can learn about other cultures. 617/482–1211.

3 *b-3*

SEPTEMBERFEST

The Longy School of Music in Cambridge hosts this series of concerts in all genres, from classical to jazz to world music, by faculty and guest artists. Most events are free. 617/876–0956.

4 *f-2*

WGBH ICE CREAM FESTIVAL

One of the nation's preeminent public TV stations hosts a festival of frozen treats, children's activities, and live music in its parking lot the first weekend of September. 617/492–7777.

OCTOBER

6 *d-6*

BOSTON BRUINS/
BOSTON CELTICS

Boston's immensely popular hockey and basketball teams both start their seasons in October at the FleetCenter (*see* Chapter 6). *617/624–1000.*

6 *g-4*

COLUMBUS DAY PARADE

Marching bands, veterans' organizations, the Ancient and Honorable Artillery Company, high school bands, floats, clowns, and more, fill the streets from East Boston to the North End on the Sunday falling closest to October 12. The parade begins at 1 PM and usually lasts 2 hours. *617/635–3911.*

2 *c-4*

HEAD OF
THE CHARLES REGATTA

More than 3,000 collegiate rowers from all over the world—England, Belgium, France, Canada, Mexico, and the United States—bring more than 1,000 shells to the Charles River to compete in the largest single-day regatta in the world. It's exciting even if you don't understand rowing. Just ask any of the thousands of spectators to explain what yoů're watching. Keep an eye out for the 1972 U.S. Olympic rowing team; they've vowed to race every year until they come in last! *617/864–8415.*

6 *d-6*

RINGLING BROS. BARNUM
& BAILEY CIRCUS

The Greatest Show on Earth comes to the FleetCenter each year for the last two weeks of October. The world-renowned three-ring circus starts with the Circus Walk, when the special 30-car train arrives at 11 AM and elephants, horses, dogs, camels, clowns, and other members of the circus make their traditional walk to the arena. *617/624–1000.*

6 *c-6*

TUFTS HEALTH PLAN 10K
FOR WOMEN

Second only to the Boston Marathon in popularity, this race, with more than 4,000 women participating, is one of New England's largest women's road races. All ages and abilities are welcomed. The race, which starts and finishes on Boston Common, is held each year on the Monday closest to Columbus Day (October 12). *617/439–7700.*

NOVEMBER

6 *c-6*

BOSTON COMMON
HOLIDAY LIGHTS

From the Sunday after Thanksgiving through the first week in January, from dusk to midnight, the trees on Boston Common are draped with more than 25,000 multicolored lights. The effect is enchanting—especially in falling snow. *617/725–4505.*

3 *b-4*

CAMBRIDGE CENTER
ANNUAL FOLK FESTIVAL

The Cambridge Center for Adult Education hosts this weekend of local and national folk artists in early November. The low-ticket (usually $10 or less) performances are held in the Center's small acoustic auditorium. Some performers also lead songwriting workshops during the weekend. *617/547–6789.*

1 *h-4*

HOME FOR
THE HOLIDAYS SHOW

The World Trade Center gets into the spirit of the coming season with a weekend festival celebrating three centuries of New England holiday traditions. In addition to entertainment and food, the show includes everything anyone could possibly need for gracious holiday entertaining: antiques, crafts, ornaments, candles, seasonal decorations, and tableware. *617/439–5600.*

8 *h-3*

THE NUTCRACKER

Starting on Thanksgiving Day and ending after the New Year, the Boston Ballet presents its extravagant version of the holiday season's official ballet at the Wang Center for the Performing Arts. A newly redesigned set and magnificent costumes make this a must-see. *617/695–6950.*

8 *b-3*

VETERANS DAY PARADE

Veterans' organizations, the Ancient and Honorable Artillery Company, marching and high school bands, and others, wend their way through the Back Bay and South End, starting at about 11 AM on Commonwealth Avenue at Hereford Street and ending at Columbus Avenue and Arlington Street. *617/635–3911.*

DECEMBER

6 *g-7*
BOSTON TEA PARTY REENACTMENT

The Boston Tea Party Ship and Museum are free all day on December 16 for this reenactment of the world's most famous tea party. The event actually begins at 5 PM at the Old South Meetinghouse with a re-creation of the meeting where the famed event was launched, then moves to the ship, where costumed participants toss tea chests overboard in a moment of history brought to life. *617/338–1773.*

7 *b-2*
CHRISTMAS REVELS

This series of performances at Sanders Theater in Cambridge includes dance, song, skits, and drama reflecting folk and ethnic traditions and rituals. This celebration of the winter solstice—the longest night of the year, after which the days begin to get longer again—is guaranteed lighthearted fun. *617/621–0505.*

8 *c-4*
CHRISTMAS TREE LIGHTING

Each year, the Province of Nova Scotia gifts the people and city of Boston with a 50-foot Christmas tree, which is placed in front of Prudential Center. On the first Saturday in December, the tree lights up with 17,000 multicolored lights as choirs from Massachusetts schools lead the crowd in a traditional carol sing. Santa Claus, the Boston Ballet *Nutcracker* troupe, and a guest conductor round out the party. *617/236–3302.*

FIRST NIGHT CELEBRATION

"First Night" is actually the last night of the year, the day and evening of December 31. Boston started the First Night tradition of mass family entertainment, and it still puts on one of the best New Year's Eve parties anywhere. Up to half a million people come out to play for this full day and night of outdoor and indoor festivities held all over downtown and the Back Bay: a children's festival at 1 PM kicks off the revels, followed by dance, theater, and multi-media performances, face painting, puppet shows, ice sculp-

tures, interactive art exhibits, concerts, and a spectacular Grand Procession at 5:30 PM which everyone can join. Finally, a laser display counts down the last minutes to midnight on the face of the Custom House Tower, culminating at the stroke of 12 with a dazzling fireworks display over the Harbor. A First Night button (available all over the city at a minimal cost in the weeks before the big night) serves as admission to indoor events all over the Back Bay, Beacon Hill, the waterfront, and the South End. Outdoor events are free. A comprehensive listing of the day's events, hour by hour, appears in the *Boston Globe*'s "Calendar" section on the Thursday before First Night. Use it to plot your merrymaking schedule. Also worth noting: many downtown hotels offer special First Night packages with reduced room rates. *617/542–1399.*

8 *b-6*
HANDEL & HAYDN SOCIETY'S MESSIAH

America's preeminent chorus and period instrument orchestra, under the direction of Christopher Hogwood, presents Handel's *Messiah* in a Boston tradition that makes listeners exclaim "Hallelujah!" Performances are at Symphony Hall during the first two weeks in December; five performances are given, usually scheduled for the hours of 3 and 7:30 PM. *617/266–3605.*

3 *b-4*
HOLLY FAIR

The Cambridge Center for Adult Education hosts an annual Christmas fair in its historic Brattle House. Held the second weekend in December, the fair features jugglers, mimes, musicians, and other entertainment as well as arts and crafts and a rummage sale. In a twist on the traditional pony rides, there are llamas to ride and pet. *617/547–6789.*

6 *b-5*
A LOUISBURG SQUARE CHRISTMAS

Beacon Hill's most elegant and prestigious address hosts a lovely Christmas Eve concert and carol sing. The square between Mount Vernon and Pinckney streets is even lovelier than usual with wreaths on every door and candles glowing in windows. This informal free event, which seems less organized than spontaneous, is the traditional prelude to midnight services at Church of the Advent.

ART EVENTS

april

ANNUAL ARTISTS' BALL

The annual costume ball at the Boston Center for the Arts Cyclorama is big, bold, brash, and a little over-the-top—a sure bet for an evening of fun. A panel of celebrity judges awards prizes for the most outrageous, the most authentic, and the best couple or group costumes. Appropriately, the ball takes place on the Saturday closest to April 1, 8 PM–1 AM. It benefits the South End Open Studios. 617/426–5000.

may

8 *d-3*

ART NEWBURY STREET

For one Sunday afternoon in mid-May (and one in September), the dozens of art galleries along Newbury Street throw open their doors and host a seven-block-long street party complete with artists at work on the corners and sidewalk performances of classical music on almost every block. 617/267–7961.

august

4 *f-6*

COOLIDGE CORNER ARTS-&-CRAFTS FAIR

Brookline artists are showcased in this outdoor arts-and-crafts fair, which takes over the intersection of Harvard and Beacon streets in Brookline for one day in August. A heavenly afternoon for those who like to start holiday shopping early! 617/232–0821.

september

8 *d-3*

ART NEWBURY STREET

For the second time in a year, Art Newbury Street turns the city's poshest row into a street party celebration of art. Some 25 galleries take part in this event, which closes Newbury Street to traffic for one September Sunday afternoon. In coming years, this will expand into a planned Boston Art Festival, with arts-related events all over the Back Bay. 617/267–9473.

8 *f-5*

SOUTH END ARTISTS OPEN STUDIOS

More than 100 artists who live and work in the South End throw open their studios on the last weekend of September. Take a free guided shuttle-bus or a self-guided walking tour, stop by the Boston Center for the Arts for food and performances (also free), and keep your eyes open for a special piece of work worth taking home. 617/424–5000.

october

8 *f-5*

ELLIS MEMORIAL ANTIQUES SHOW

For more than 20 years, antiques dealers from across the country have been coming to the Cyclorama at the Boston Center for the Arts to show and sell their wares. A local museum or private collector often hosts an exhibit, too. Best of all, there's an appraisal day, when you can bring your family heirlooms and find out what they're *really* worth. 617/426–5000.

november

1 *h-4*

NEW ENGLAND CRAFTS FESTIVAL

Artisans from New England and beyond gather at the World Trade Center for three days in early November to demonstrate fine crafts such as glass-blowing, weaving, and carving. You'll find both traditional and contemporary work—and it's all for sale. 617/439–5600.

december

1 *g-6*

CHRISTMAS ARTS-&-CRAFTS SHOW

This early December show at the Bayside Expo Center features more than 200 exhibits created by artisans from across the nation. Naturally, there's a special section for wreaths, trimmings, and other holiday paraphernalia. It's a great source for last-minute gift ideas! 508/359–6545.

day trips
out of town

escorted

BRUSH HILL TOURS/ GRAY LINE

Tours depart from the major Boston hotels, and all tours have historical commentary. For tours to Lexington and

---

Concord, see Bus & Trolley Tours, above. 435 High St., Randolph, 02368, 617/236–2148, groups 617/986–6100.

Plymouth: The Pilgrim's Path by Land and Sea: Weekends 9:30 AM May–early June, daily 9:30 AM June–Oct. $32 adults, $16 children. Includes boatride. Plimouth Plantation: Sat. and Sun. 9:30 AM May–early June; daily 9:30 AM June–Oct. Includes Plymouth and admission to plantation. $20 adults, $11 child 6–12, under 6 free.

Salem, the Witch City: Includes Marblehead, Salem Witch Museum, House of 7 Gables, Peabody Essex Museum, Pickering Wharf. Sat., Sun. 9:30 AM May–early June; daily 9:30 AM June–Oct.

Cape Cod and Provincetown Tour: Harbor cruise, Kenney Memorial, art colony. Sat., Sun. 9:30 AM late May–mid-June; daily 9:30 AM June–Aug. $37 adults, $19 children.

Autumn on Old Cape Cod: Daily 9:30 AM Sept.–Oct. $37 adults, $19 children. Also Fall Foliage Spectacular: Walden Pond, Fitzwilliam Inn, apple orchards, daily 9:30 AM late Sept.–Oct. $37 adults, $19 children. Lunch is additional.

PETER PAN BUS LINES

The bus company offers buses to Foxboro, Sturbridge Village, Provincetown, Worcester Common Fashion Outlet, Basketball Hall of Fame, Springfield, and Mystic Seaport, Conn. Tourco, 52 Elliot St., Boston, 02116, 800/237–8747; Peter Pan Bus Lines, 1776 Main St., Springfield, 01103.

on your own

For information and directions call the Massachusetts Office of Travel and Tourism, 617/727–3201, or write them at 100 Cambridge St., Boston, 02202.

GLOUCESTER

Thirty-seven miles from Boston, and accessible via trains from North Station, Gloucester is the quintessential salty seaport. America's oldest, it's harbor to rugged boats and fishermen—most of Portuguese and Italian heritage. Go to the harbor at 3 PM and watch the boats return with the day's catch. It's colorful—not to mention aromatic! The Cape Ann Historical Society and the medieval Hammond Castle Museum are both worth a visit. Last weekend in June is the Blessing of the Fleet. There's a lovely public beach and, of course, great seafood restaurants. A. C. Cruise Line has excursions to Gloucester (see Boat Tours, above). *Cape Anne Historical Society, 27 Pleasant St. Mar.–Jan., Tues.–Sat. 10–5. Hammond Castle Museum, 80 Hesperus Ave. June–Memorial Day, daily 9–6; Memorial Day–Oct. 12, Wed.–Sun. 10–4; Nov.–June 1, weekends 10–5.*

LEXINGTON & CONCORD

Twelve and 18 miles from Boston are two dandy sites that will make history-lovers out of most travelers. Lexington—accessible via MBTA bus Monday to Saturday—was Paul Revere's destination the night of his famed ride. Today, pay homage at Lexington Green to the first Minutemen who attempted to stop the British march to Concord on April 19, 1775. Beneath the monument are buried seven of the Minutemen who died that day. Guided tours are given of Buckman Tavern, where the colonists gathered and where the wounded were brought afterward, as well as of the Hancock-Clarke House, where Samuel Adams and John Hancock were warned by Revere to flee (April 18, 1775). Munroe Tavern was headquarters to the British. *Buckman Tavern, 1 Bedford St., 617/862–5598; Hancock-Clarke House, 36 Hancock St., 617/861–0928; Munroe Tavern, 1332 Massachusetts Ave., 617/674–9238. All open Mon.–Sat. 10–5; mid-Apr.–Oct., also Sun. 1–5.*

On your way to Concord via Route 2A—you can also get there by B and M train from North Station to Concord Center—you pass through the 800-acre Minuteman National Historical Park (sections of which are actually located in both towns). At the Battle Road Visitors Center—also called the Minute Man National Historical Park Visitor Center—you'll find film, maps, and other historical exhibits. The park also contains the Old North Bridge (a replica), which marks the spot where the farmers of Concord fired "the shot heard 'round the world." You can also check out the Wayside Inn, residence of Concord's Muster Master 1775 and where Nathaniel Hawthorne later lived. Guided tours are available. In Concord, stop in at the North Bridge Visitors Center for information on Concord's rich literary heritage. Among the historic and fascinating sites are: Orchard House, where Louisa May Alcott wrote *Little Women* (1868) and where her

father, Bronson, operated the School of Philosophy—today, the house is a study center of 19th-century philosophy; The Ralph Waldo Emerson House, where the famed writer lived 1835–82; Sleepy Hollow Cemetery, which holds, on Author's Ridge, the grave sites of the Alcott family, Thoreau, Nathaniel Hawthorne, Margaret Sydney, and Ralph Waldo Emerson; and 1½ miles south of Concord you'll find Thoreau's Walden Pond along Route 126, now a state beach, where you may picnic or ponder. *Battle Rd Visitors Center. Mid-Apr.–Oct., daily 9–5. North Bridge Visitors Center, 174 Liberty St., 508/369–6993. Summer, daily 9–5; winter, daily 9–4. Orchard House, 399 Lexington Rd., 508/369–4118. Emerson House, 28 Cambridge Turnpike, Rte. 2A, 508/369–2236. Sleepy Hollow Cemetery, Bedford St., 508/371–6299. Walden Pond, 508/369–3254.*

NEW BEDFORD

Fifty-four miles from Boston, New Bedford is the well-known 19th-century whaling port whose fame was spread by Herman Melville's writings. For a visitor there are glimpses of the whaling-era past, a seagoing atmosphere, and wonderful scenic vistas. Of interest, the New Bedford Whaling Museum, established in 1902, is the largest American museum devoted to the age of whaling, an era that lasted some 200 years in New Bedford. The Seamen's Bethel has a pulpit in the shape of a whaler's hull. The New Bedford Area Office of Tourism has free information packets with suggested walking tours. August is a special time for the Blessing of the Fleet and a Seafood Festival. *New Bedford Whaling Museum, 18 Johnny Cake Hill, 508/997–0046. $4.50 adults. Mon.–Sun. 10–5. New Bedford Area Office of Tourism, Wharfinger Bldg., Waterfront Visitors Center, Pier No. 3, 508/979–1745 or 800/508–5353.*

NEWBURYPORT

Thirty-eight miles north of Boston, Newburyport is an historic shipbuilding port with lovely Federal-style mansions and a restored Market Square District. Note the Custom House designed by Robert Mills, architect of D.C.'s Washington Monument. Walk High Street for its lovely 19th-century architecture; visit Cushing House, at No. 98, built in 1808 for the first American ambassador to

China. Three miles from Newburyport, Plum Island-Parker River National Wildlife Refuge, open dawn to dusk, offers wonderful bird-watching opportunities, especially during spring and fall migrations, as well as panoramic views from the observation towers (no camping or pets). *Greater Newburyport Chamber of Commerce, 29 State St., 508/462–6680.*

OLD STURBRIDGE VILLAGE

Approximately 56 miles west of Boston, Old Sturbridge Village is a spectacular re-creation of a typical rural New England community at the beginning of the 19th century. Covering 200 acres, the "living" museum includes 40 buildings where costumed guides farm, cook, and make candles, pottery, and brooms. The buildings, furnishings, dress, and tasks are authentic to the tiniest detail. Special times to visit: during maple sugaring and sheep shearing! Restaurants and places to shop are plentiful. Peter Pan Bus Lines provides service to the complex. *Rte. 20 W, 508/347–3362. $15 adults, $7.50 ages 6–15, under 6 free. Late Apr.–early Nov., daily 9–5; late Nov.–early Apr., Tues.–Sun. 10–4.*

PLYMOUTH

Thirty-four miles south of Boston, Plymouth is where—as we all learned in third grade—the *Mayflower*'s Pilgrims landed in 1620 and set up the first permanent settlement in the New World. First stop: needless to say, is Plymouth Rock, traditional stepping-stone to the Pilgrims' new home. Other sights include the *Mayflower II*, a full-scale replica of the original (this one crossed the Atlantic in 1957 in 53 days); Cole's Hill Burying Ground, where the Pilgrims who died that first winter were buried. Most fascinating is Plimoth Plantation, a living museum of that era and re-creation of an early Pilgrim village faithful to old records and written eyewitness accounts. The thatched-roof cottages are furnished true to the period, and the "inhabitants" in period dress go about their daily tasks. Nearby is an accurate reconstruction of a 17th-century Indian village staffed by Native Americans. Without a car, you can get to Plymouth through P and B bus service. *508/746–1622. $18.50 adults, $11 ages 5–12 (including entry to Mayflower II); plantation only, $15 adults, $9 ages 5–12. Apr.–Nov., daily 9–5.*

QUINCY

This industrial South Shore suburb located eight miles south of Boston is noted as the birthplace of America's second and sixth presidents, John Adams and John Quincy Adams. In addition to the saltbox birthplaces of each, you can tour the Adams National Historic Site, bought by John and Abigail Adams, where four generations of Adamses have lived. United First Parish Church is where John Adams and John Quincy Adams and their wives are buried. Quincy is accessible via the Red Line to Quincy Center, then transfer to Randolph Southshore Plaza bus No. 238. *Adams National Historic Site, 135 Adams St. United First Parish Church, 1306 Hancock St. South Shore Chamber of Commerce, 617/479–1111.*

ROCKPORT

Forty-one miles from Boston, Rockport—like Gloucester—is part of Cape Ann and is famed not only as a fishing port but also as an artists' colony, which developed in the 1920s. Galleries and shops line Main Street. The rocky shores (granite was quarried here in the 19th century) and a picturesque village provide a charming setting for a day of salty breezes and charming vistas. Walk to the end of Bearskin Neck for an impressive view of the open Atlantic and also the old weather-beaten lobster shack—called "Motif No. 1" because of its popularity as a subject for amateur painters. Note: Rockport is *very* popular with tourists in season and is accessible via trains from North Station. *Rockport Chamber of Commerce, 508/546–6575.*

SALEM

Only 16 miles from Boston, Salem, founded in 1626, is rich in history. While it is inexorably linked with the witch-hunt trials of the 1690s, Salem also has a proud maritime tradition. The Peabody Essex Museum is America's oldest continuously operating museum (1799), where you'll find art and artifacts brought back from sea voyages to Asia and the exotic Pacific Islands. Nearby, the Essex Institute contains rooms from several period houses, carefully restored to reveal everyday life in the 18th and early 19th centuries. Everyone will want to tour the House of Seven Gables, immortalized by Nathaniel Hawthorne's novel of the same name, to see the secret staircase;

nearby is the Custom House where Hawthorne once toiled. Tour the old wharfs now part of the Salem Maritime National Historic Site. Other sights include the Witch House, Judge Corwin's home and site of the preliminary hearings, and the Witch Dungeon, for a live presentation of the trials. Pioneer Village re-creates the life of early settlers circa 1630. Finish up at Pickering Wharf, reborn as a shopping/eating complex à la Faneuil Hall. Salem is accessible via train from North Station.

Peabody Essex Museum, East India Sq., 161 Essex St., 508/745–1876. May–Oct., Mon.–Sat. 10–5, Sun. noon–5; Nov.–Apr., Tues., Wed., Thurs., and Sat. 10–5, Fri. 10–8, Sun. noon–5. House of the Seven Gables, 54 Turner St., 508/744–0991. July–Labor Day, daily 9:30–6; Labor Day–June, daily 10–4:30. Pioneer Village, Rtes. 1A and 129, 508/745–0525. Mid-May–Oct., Mon.–Sat. 10–5, Sun. noon–5. Salem Chamber of Commerce, Town Hall, Beach Rd., 508/465–3581.

chapter 3

RESTAURANTS

Doesn't anybody eat home anymore? When you're on vacation you don't have much choice, but these days even Bostonians are going out to restaurants in record numbers. And the city has risen to the occasion in grand style. Beantown may have taken a long time to develop a reputation as a great restaurant town, but now that it has arrived, it seems there's a new place opening every week. Not only that, the city—which is as close as one can get to where America's food customs began—is alive today with many of the country's most cutting-edge chefs. Boston's fall from the grace of Puritan austerity is amply revealed by some of their headline-making creations. New England "chowdah" has given way to cappuccino chanterelle soup, baked beans have been traded in for black-truffle flan, steam-table turkey is now Vermont quail stuffed with Hawaiian macadamia nuts and basted with maple syrup, while apple pandowdy has been replaced by passionfruit crumble. Yes, there are still great places where you can feast on the bean and the cod, as they say, but there is so much more to enjoy today.

While it's difficult keeping up with all the new restaurants, it's even harder categorizing them. Where does one draw the line when a restaurant bills itself as Mediterranean one day, tilts more to France the next, and then heads to Italy or Spain the day after? The terms pan-Asian and Fusion have been so much bandied about that their meanings have become diluted; and Eclectic (or Global) hasn't fared much better. However, Boston's dining scene proves there are times no other adjectives will suffice. How else to describe "tamarind-glazed halibut and steamed littlenecks with a fried jasmine rice cake, sesame spinach, crunchy Napa carrot slaw, and a cashew dipping sauce." And, after all,

didn't Boston's ice-cream parlors come up with the concept of the "mix-in" many decades ago?

Along with the rest of the country, Boston is becoming chef-obsessed. Cult followings and fans lining up for autographs (cookbooks in hand) or photo-ops are not unheard of. Boston has always had its food superstars—Julia Child, who lives in Cambridge and is still going strong at 85, is often seen dining around town. More recently, the eminent Jasper White has been at the helm of the Legal Seafood empire, while other chefs have settled into their own glorious eateries, like Todd English (Olives and Figs), Gordon Hamersley (the consistently excellent Hamersley's Bistro), Lydia Shire and Susan Regis (sophisticated Biba and Pignoli), Chris Schlesinger (the fiery East Coast Grill), and Stan Frankenthaler (Salamander and Red Herring). Once these stars were line cooks. It's fascinating to watch the evolution of gifted chefs—moving from sous chef, then to chef, and on up to the newest pinnacle, executive chef. Many of the successful ones develop loyal fans, so when they leave to feather their own nests, the diners, knowing a good thing when they taste it, follow. All eyes were on Andy Husbands (formerly of East Coast Grill) as he constructed and opened the stylish Tremont 647; ditto for Barbara Lynch, who left Galleria Italiana with plans to open a new place downtown.

Trends? Boston's got 'em. On one hand, people are eating steak, downing martinis, and smoking cigars. On the other are those whose attempts to eat healthy are pushing chefs to new creative heights with vegetable-centered choices (no one thinks twice these days when diners quiz the wait staff on ingredients). Late dining has also arrived. Boston used to turn into a ghost town once the clock struck 10 or 11 PM, but no longer—neighborhood bars, supper clubs, and rock 'n' roll sushi are now going strong through the wee hours of the morning. Dining at the bar is also more popular than ever, and it's a good *thing because sometimes it's the only practical way to experience hot restaurants-of-the-moment. Maybe you get a sudden urge, or maybe you just like your perch for viewing the action, chatting up the bartender, or peering into the kitchen—whatever, it certainly takes the sting out of not getting a reservation.*

While plenty of dishy gossip makes the rounds, Boston's restaurant community is a tight-knit one with an unfailing spirit of camaraderie. New openings are always crowded with former colleagues of the owner and staff—curious, hungry, and supportive. Divining the secrets of Boston's ever-mercurial restaurant world is a constant challenge—a week seldom passes without an opening or closing, a glamorous revamping, or a change of ownership or cast or menu— so there will certainly be changes this guide doesn't reflect. Pick up your newspaper or chat up your friends and relatives to find the latest news—there's so much happening, you may even need hourly updates.

general information

NO SMOKING

More and more restaurants are hanging up the "No Smoking" sign. Many, of course, still have "Smoking" sections, but be sure to inquire when making reservations if you feel you're going to have to lite up after dining.

RESERVATIONS

Telephone ahead for reservations since they will determine that the particular restaurant is still in business and that a table will be available. If reservations are not accepted, you can at least find out whether to expect a long wait before being seated. As for dress, most diners know that the priciest place still sometimes require tie and jacket—check when booking.

TIPPING

The rule of thumb is approximately 15% of the total. Don't forget that, here as elsewhere, the quality of service is the final determinant of the tip—adjust up or down accordingly. Boston restaurants do not as a rule add a service charge to the bill. Some do only with parties of six or more. There is a 5% tax on all meals.

KEY

Boston has an abundance of restaurants offering a variety of food in every price range. The following represents a good cross section of what is available. The price of dinner at these restaurants has been classified on the basis of a complete dinner for one, excluding wine, tip, and tax, as follows:

Very Expensive ($$$$)	over $40
Expensive ($$$)	$25–$40
Moderate ($$)	$15–$25
Inexpensive ($)	under $15

Assume that in all locations the prices for lunch will be somewhat lower. The following abbreviations are used for credit cards: AE, American Express; D, Discover; DC, Diners Club; MC, MasterCard; V, Visa.

restaurants by cuisine

In addition to the usual ethnic categories, which are arranged alphabetically, we have included the following special listings (also in alphabetical order) for your convenience and pleasure: Breakfast/Brunch; Cafés and Pubs; Museum Munches; Rooms with a View; and Wine and Tapas Bars.

For Boston's most talked about restaurants, *see* the Contemporary category.

AMERICAN

The following selection is traditional in focus; for "new" American or "regional" American cooking, *see* Contemporary *and* Soul/Southern.

8 *b-4*

BOODLE'S OF BOSTON

If you think this place has a silly name, you're wrong—it's actually named after one of the historic private clubs of London, a fabled hangout of dukes and earls. Clubby, in fact, is the design note here, which sets a sedate British tone. The food, however, is American, and the reliable specialty of the kitchen is grilling—large servings of meats, as well as fish, are cooked over mesquite, hickory and sassafras wood, and accompanied by a variety of condiments. Options include filet mignon, swordfish, or shrimp and tenderloin brochette, and grilled oysters with brie. Boodles also has an expansive beer selection. *Back Bay Hilton, 40 Dalton St., Back Bay, 617/266–3537. AE, DC, MC, V. T stop: Hynes Convention Center/ICA. $$$*

6 *f-4*

DURGIN-PARK MARKET DINING ROOM

Here before you were, and certainly here before the Marketplace became a festive tourist destination; here since 1827, to be precise. The world around may be changing fast, but not at Durgin-Park. Like an old-fashioned heirloom jewel in a new setting, this place seems unfazed by it all. The wait is still long, the tables are communal, the atmosphere is harried, the wait staff hasn't gone to finishing school, but this Yankee eatery has a niche. Perhaps it's the rare prime rib (22-ounce portions), the charcoal-broiled steaks and chops, the fresh seafood, the tasty corn bread, the hearty clam chowder, and the nothing less than fabulous Indian pudding and warm apple pandowdy—in one waitress's words, "Everything we've always had." The crowd (take that word literally!—they only take reservations for parties of 15 or more) is a mix of tourists, natives, politicos, and matrons. *340 Faneuil Hall Marketplace, North Market Bldg., upstairs, Government Center, 617/227–2038. AE, D, DC, MC, V. T stop: Government Center. $$*

3 *f-3*

EAT

There are no upper-case letters, no pretensions at this down-home restaurant located in Somerville's up-and-coming Union Square. Plates of roasted chicken or bass with potato-leek hash are uncomplicated and bountiful, while salads remind you what's ripening on the vine. The comfy decor feels like your grandmother's parlor, but without the matching china, linens, or lamps, and everyone seems to enjoy the moderate prices. An intimate bar in the back of the dining room makes you wish you could dine there. You can. Cast your vote: Is this the best Somerville restaurant? *253 Washington St., Somerville, 617/776–2889. Reservations not accepted. D, DC, MC, V. No lunch. $$*

8 *e-4*

THE HARD ROCK CAFE

Outside, the stone facade bears the inscription "Massachusetts Institute of Rock;" Inside, Madonna's bustier, Keith Richards's jacket, and the Aerosmithsonian—a whole wall devoted to the Boston band—beckon to those who like their burgers hearty and their noise deafening. The Boston link in this international rock museum-cum-restaurant chain is a clone of the others: rock 'n' roll memorabilia, good barbecue, and the ubiquitous logo sweatshirt and other Hard Rock merchandise in the adjacent shop. Tourists and prepubescent teens predominate. *131 Clarendon St., Back Bay, 617/424–7625. Reservations for 15 or more. AE, MC, DC, V. T stop: Back Bay. $$*

3 *b-4*

HENRIETTA'S TABLE

Named after a famed 700-pound pig that lives on Martha's Vineyard, this restaurant seems to be New England captured within four walls. The decor announces the theme: the clapboard ceiling is painted a clean vanilla, while blue hutches scattered around the room are filled with collectibles, while the menu continues it with fine selections of maple-glazed pork roast and smoked salmon. Not only do regional vegetables feature prominently at table, there is a veritable farm stand on-site where you can purchase beans, jams, and flower seeds. The crowd is a mix of hotel guests, visiting academics, and locals who appreciate the down-home farmhouse feel. The Sunday brunch is popular. *The Charles Hotel, One Bennett St., Harvard Sq., Cambridge, 617/864–1200. AE, DC, MC, V. T stop: Harvard Sq. $$*

6 *d-6*

LOCKE-OBER

A virtual taste of the Victorian age, Locke-Ober was built in 1875 and has been a longtime bastion of the Boston Brahmin. The decor is an orgyization of hand-carved mahogany, gilded flocked wallpaper, rich leather seats—the sort of men's-club ambience that Oliver Wendell Holmes would have loved. Indeed, women were barred from the hallowed Men's Bar on the first floor until 1970 (note: the nude mural over the bar is draped in black when Harvard loses to Yale). It's an interesting spot for lunch, which can be a tad more casual. Upstairs, in the gilded Ober Room, the ambience is like an elegant private club. The Victorian decor is only one part of the attraction. The other is the attentive European-style service and food. The continental menu is extensive; specialties include the famed lobster Savannah, roast duckling, and steak tartare. Save room for Indian pudding or baked Alaska. Jackets are required; no jeans or running shoes, please. *3 Winter Pl., Downtown Crossing, 617/542–1340. AE, D, DC, MC. V. T stop: Downtown Crossing. $$$$*

7 *g-3*

MAGNOLIA'S SOUTHERN CUISINE

This very popular Inman Square spot serves authentic Southern cooking in a fun setting, painted in primary colors. Summertime means Maryland crab cakes and blackened fish in season, with very good fried green tomatoes. The menu also includes jambalaya and shrimp étouffée. Take the T to Central Square, then there's a 10-minute walk. *1193 Cambridge St., Cambridge, 617/576–1971. Reservations essential. AE, D, MC, V. Closed Sun., Mon. No lunch. T stop: Central Sq. $$*

9 *b-4*

OASIS CAFE

American food in an Italian neighborhood? How else to explain why and how they named this restaurant? Oasis prides itself on large portions of downhome dishes like roast of the day, meat loaf, cajun catfish, lots of barbecue, fritters, burgers, corn bread, pies and cakes. *Everything* is homemade. The decor is Art Deco–inspired pink and black, and bric-a-bracked with old radios, flapper statues, and moderne masks. Taped jazz from the 1930s and 1940s also helps let the years roll back. Beer, wine and cordials are all on tap. *176 Endicott St., North End, 617/523–9274. Reservations not accepted. AE, DC,*

MC, V. Weekend brunch. T stop: Haymarket. $$

8 *f-2*

THE RITZ CAFÉ

Much Boston business (not to mention politics) is conducted at this café over very good omelets and eggs Benedict. It's Brahmin busy and popular and the see-and-be-seen quotient is high. Open from 6:30 AM to midnight, one can have all three meals here, without getting bored. Choose from the smoked duck pizza, rabbit fricassee, or grilled portobello sandwich. Voted Best Hamburger by *Boston* magazine, this pricey version ($11) is praised for the savory condiments, crispy shoestring fries, and, of course, this luxurious setting. Harp music is played in the evenings from 6:30 to 10. Please, no jeans, shorts, or athletic clothing/shoes. *The Ritz-Carlton Hotel, 15 Arlington St., Back Bay, 617/536–5700. AE, MC, V. Weekend brunch. T stop: Arlington. $$$$*

1 *d-1*

THE ROSEBUD DINER

Who says you can't go back in time? Step into this adorable 1941 diner and you'll feel like you're in a Frank Capra film. Original wood paneling, windows, high wooden booths, and cobalt blue tiles lend authenticity to the cozy confines. Come for above-average Reuben burgers, affordable specials of swordfish kebabs, or blackened Cajun sirloin, served with all the trimmings. The staff makes you feel at home, especially if you hunker down at the counter for a quick dinner or a beer. Rosebud is located in an out-of-city area with lots to offer in terms of music, movies, bars, and other casual restaurants. *38 Summer St., Somerville, 617/666–6015. T stop: Davis Sq. $*

1 *g-5*

224 BOSTON

A real find in an area devoid of great restaurants, not only because the neighborhood is residential, but because the food is top-notch and reasonably priced. A very mixed, very relaxed crowd of businesspeople, gay couples, creative types, and extended families gather here for generous offerings of butternut-squash soup, charbroiled chicken, halibut braised in cider, and fried oysters, all prepared in the open kitchen. Teapots arranged on a wooden hutch make you feel at home, as does the friendly wait staff. Stop for a drink on one of the old-fashioned red vinyl stools in the artful ocher-wall barroom. *224 Boston St., Dorchester, 617/265–1217. AE, MC, V. T stop: Andrews Sq. $$*

AMERICAN CASUAL

2 *b-5*

ATLAS BAR AND GRILL

You'll feel in a playful mood if you dine here. Yes, the decor is colorful and swanky—cone-shape blue and red stools, shiny wooden tables, enormous curved booths. But the next room actually has virtual reality games such as Mind Shaft, Interface, and Time Portal; upstairs, there's even a pool table. Food ranges from portobello burgers to penne primavera to rump steak. The young crowd spills over from the many Lansdowne Street clubs. Kitchen open until 1 AM. *145 Ipswich St., Kenmore Sq.,*

617/437-0300. AE, MC, V. No lunch week-days. T stop: Kenmore Sq. $$

2 *a-5*

AUDUBON CIRCLE

Clean, spare lines, African wood, high ceilings, and barely a bottle is in sight at this upscale bar that attracts both students from nearby Boston University and well-dressed professionals. Besides exceptional sandwiches and hamburgers, there are clever appetizers (Asian potstickers served in white take-out containers) and a few serious entrées. The dense chocolate cake with espresso and cinnamon cream comes with a warning. *838 Beacon St., Kenmore Sq., 617/421–1910. Reservations not accepted. AE, DC, MC, V. T stop: Kenmore Sq. $$*

7 *a-3*

BARTLEY'S BURGER COTTAGE

Harvard—located just across the street—is one respected institution: Bart-

---

BOSTON UNCORKED

Serious gourmands know a great meal needs a great bottle of wine. Just drink a fabulous Clos Pegase and see what it can do to your lobster pizza at Biba! Boston is a wine-friendly town like few others, as its annual Boston Wine Festival proves every year. Held between January and April, the festival is a 13-week-long extravaganza, featuring theme dinners, lectures by famed vintners, and special courses, most held at the Rowes Wharf Hotel and its glittering array of restaurants. Wine lovers flock to the festival. After all, where else can you learn how to saber the head from a Nebuchadnezzar of Moët? Here's a small sampling of events held during the 1998 event. For information, call 617/330–9355 or 617/439–7000.

Battle of the Cabernets
Eight champions from around the world are pitted against each other in a grand world series "taste-off."

Cognac & Cigars
Finesse the choice of the finest cigars with your favorite cognac tastes.

Rare Fine Wine Auction
This is the time to snag that elusive '67 Yquem, '21 Latour, or '45 Croft. Complete with a wine and hors d'oeuvres reception.

Champagne Tête de Cuvée Dinner
One heck of a grande bouffe, accompanied by legendary champagnes, such as La Grand Dame, Cristal, and Krug.

Grand Swiss Dinner
Swiss delicacies are served up along with great bottles of Valsangiacomo, Badoux, and other vivacious vintages.

Dominus Vertical
Imagine tasting one of California's greatest wines in a series of sips going back to its fabled beginnings.

Serena Sutcliffe Dinner
One event of the "Masters" series, sponsored by the Institute of Masters of Wine, this is hosted by Sotheby's famed authority.

ley's may be another. Students, hippies, and those who want to discuss love and death and Keanu Reeves sit at long undivided tables, amid 1960s posters and pictures of pies and frappés. This is definitely not a bar, but it is a great destination for a burger (the selection numbers 40). Some say they are the best in town—others say they are the greasiest. Don't forget the onion rings, salads, and sandwiches as well. Wash them down with a raspberry lime rickey. *1246 Massachusetts Ave., Cambridge, 617/354-6559. No alcohol. Reservations not accepted. No credit cards. Closed Sun. T stop: Harvard Sq. $*

6 *f-4*

BELL IN HAND TAVERN

This is the oldest tavern in the U.S., although it wasn't always on this site—indeed, Benjamin Franklin's very own childhood home was torn down to make way for this place. The Bell in Hand was named by its original proprietor, Jim Wilson, who was Boston's town crier until 1794. Today, you can enjoy a fine burger, sandwich, and draft beer here while drinking in the time-stained ambience. *45 Union St., Government Center, 617/227-2098. AE, D, MC, V. T stop: Government Center, Haymarket. $*

2 *a-5*

CASK 'N FLAGON

Good luck getting through the crowd before or after a baseball game at Fenway Park. But it's a good-natured bunch who gather at this perfectly located watering hole for generous salads, reliable half-pound burgers, sandwiches, and ribs. *62 Brookline Ave., Kenmore Sq., 617/536-4840. AE, DC, MC, V. T stop: Kenmore Sq. $$*

8 *b-3*

CHARLEY'S EATING & DRINKING SALOON

Sidewalk seating for the parade on Newbury Street doesn't get any better. Victoriana in Back Bay, Charley's comes complete with dark wood and black-upholstered booths and serves up chain-operation ribs, New York sirloin, London broil, burgers, and overstuffed chicken sandwiches. Long-established (but in new, larger quarters on Newbury), this is a lively favorite drawing single Bostonians to its bar, and tourists and suburbanites to its restaurant. Weekend brunch is served. *284 Newbury St., Back Bay, 617/266-3000. AE, DC, MC, V. T stop: Hynes Convention Center/ICA. $$*

1 *b-5*

The Mall at Chestnut Hill, Brookline, 617/964-1200.

6 *f-4*

CLARKE'S

After work, patrons are packed like sardines into this wood and brick-lined saloon in Quincy Market, most out for a good burger in a neighborhood tavern environment. Pictures of star athletes and teams (his passion is baseball) reflect the owner's love of sports, and, in fact, Clarke's offers a shuttle bus to Bruins and Celtics home games. Live music is offered Thursday through Sunday. A separate dining area is available for those who want to forget this is basically a bar. There's a weekend brunch. *21 Merchants Row, Faneuil Hall, 617/227-7800. AE, DC, MC, V. Sat. and Sun. brunch. $*

8 *a-3*

CROSSROADS ALE HOUSE

The quintessential dark and smoky neighborhood restaurant/bar, Crossroads offers an American menu, featuring pizza, burgers, and daily specials. More than 30 kinds of beer are available; pizza is $1 on Mondays, and on Wednesdays, it's *free* with a pitcher of beer (needless to say students love this place). Sunday brunch buffet, plus jukebox, games, darts. *495 Beacon St., Back Bay, 617/262-7371. AE, MC, V. T stop: Hynes Convention Center/ICA. $*

8 *e-4*

THE DELUX CAFE & LOUNGE

This cozy pine-paneled restaurant and bar has a loyal following who would prefer to keep the place a secret. No such luck when the good food is so inexpensive and the atmosphere so hip. It can get really packed and noisy at night but waiting for a table feels more like a good party than an inconvenience. A chicken sandwich comes with homemade chutney and tangy Asian slaw, while salmon in parchment, potato-crust cod, or daily risotto is complicated enough for any foodie. The menu changes every six weeks. *100 Chandler St., South End, 617/338-5258. Reservations not accepted. No credit cards. No lunch. T stop: Back Bay. $*

8 *b-4*

DIVISION SIXTEEN

Ensconced in a former police station, this lively singles' bar and bi-level restaurant has an Art Deco look with pinkish walls and a glamorous mural of 1940s-jazz musicians and singers. It is most popular with people who don't mind smoke and loud music. A dozen different varieties of extra-large (10-ounce) burgers are cooked to order with a variety of toppings and served with fries. There are also nachos, buffalo chicken wings, big salads, and pricier entrees of chicken, ribs, or steak. It's an extremely popular place with a crowd. The brick-lined courtyard patio is open summers. *955 Boylston St., Back Bay, 617/353–0870. Reservations for 5 or more. AE, D, DC, MC, V. No lunch. T stop: Hynes Convention Center/ICA. $$*

6 *g-4*

DOCKSIDE

When you're ready to trade a bleacher seat for a bar stool, bucket of fries, and seven TVs and two large-screens permanently tuned to football, basketball, etc., this is the place (located between the JFK Expressway and McKinley Square). Immortals such as Larry Bird have hung out here, so pack your autograph book. Too bad you missed the night Jack Nicholson tended bar. *183 State St., Downtown, 617/723–7050. AE, DC, MC, V. T stop: Aquarium. $*

5 *h-5*

DOYLE'S

The sign on the door says LICENSED VICTUALLER and this genuine 1882 landmark follows through with its old-fashioned decor of high wooden booths and transoms over a long bar—signs and prices posted on the wall are pure World War II. The extensive, inexpensive menu ranges has some excellent fare. *Boston* magazine claims their strawberry pancakes are the "Best of Boston." The clientele is a real mix and everyone is welcome. *3484 Washington St., Jamaica Plain, 617/524–2345. Reservations not accepted. No credit cards. T stop: Forest Hills. $*

 h-5

FARRAGUT HOUSE

You can dine at the bar or stretch out in a booth at this traditional spot where the lampshades look like Tiffany and the dark wood-and-brick decor and working fireplace are homey. Upstairs is a more formal dining area. The food is straight-ahead fish-and-chips, surf and turf, meat loaf, and prime rib. The atmosphere is relaxed and so typical of this section of the city. *149 P St., South Boston, 617/268–1212. AE, DC, MC, V. T stop: Broadway. $*

8 *d-3*

FRIDAY'S

Tiffany lamps and antique appointments, an eclectic and extensive menu with Italian and Mexican overtones, new wave individual pizzas, as well as pita bread and croissant sandwiches is what you get at this predictable chain. Free hors d'oeuvre buffet weekday evenings. More than 350 bar drinks are served, including a rainbow of fruity, fizzy daiquiris. There's also a kids' menu. Glass-enclosed dining area for Newbury Street watching. Weekend brunch is offered. *26 Exeter St., Back Bay, 617/266–9040. Reservations not accepted. AE, DC, MC, V. T stop: Copley Sq. $*

6 *e-6*

THE GOOD LIFE

It's the "Days of Wine and Roses" in this retro hangout where quilted red-vinyl and plywood paneling give you a thirst for monster-size martinis. It's definitely trendy, some might call it contrived, but the more you hear Frank Sinatra crooning, the more you just want to kick back and enjoy it. At lunch it's business suits; at night it's blue jeans and bowling shirts. Everyone seems to like the steamed mussels, steak and pasta specials, burgers and hand-cut chips. Open and going strong 'til 2 AM, with live lounge music downstairs Friday nights. *28 Kingston St., Downtown, 617/451–2622. Reservations not accepted. AE, MC, V. T stop: Downtown Crossing. $*

6 *f-5*

HOULIHAN'S

This casual restaurant/bar in the State Street Building near the Marketplace is usually filled with singles looking for fun. The food offered at this link in a nationwide chain is as eclectic as the decor: fajitas, burgers, onion soup, salads, seafood. Outdoor patio in fine weather. Dancing in the lounge every night. *60 State St., Faneuil Hall, 617/367–6377. AE, DC, MC, V. No breakfast. T stop: Government Center. $*

8 *f-3*
PARISH CAFE

This is a big, sleek bar known for ingenious, gourmet sandwiches created by famous—at least they are to the locals—area chefs. *Boston* magazine claims they are the city's "Best Sandwiches." One top pick is the Schlesinger, a warm banana bread topped with Jack cheese, ham, and mango chutney, courtesy of Chris Schlesinger of the East Coast Grill. The staff takes care with the food and is courteous to both big spenders and those who nurse a coffee and talk. Food is served late and the sidewalk patio is a big draw when weather permits. *361 Boylston St., Back Bay, 617/247–4777. Reservations not accepted. AE, DC, MC, V. T stop: Arlington. $*

8 *d-3*
SMALL PLANET BAR AND GRILL

Call it global or just spicy, the menu really does cover the world with burgers (including turkey and veggie versions), nachos, steamed mussels, paella, and lasagna. The smaller, but substantial, late-night selection brings together hungry college students, tourists, and anyone in the neighborhood. Owner Frank Bell contributes a percentage of his profits to charity. The outdoor tables at the Boylston Street location are always in demand. The branch in Cambridge has live music. Sunday brunch is offered. *565 Boylston St., Back Bay, 617/536–4477. Reservations not accepted. AE, D, DC, MC, V. No lunch Mon. and Tues. T stop: Copley Sq. $*

4 *e-4*
SUNSET GRILL AND TAP

A good spot to study collegiate drinking habits, this is a boisterous place with an international collection of 500 microbrews (110 on tap). The menu of simple appetizers, burgers, and ribs is surprisingly good. You can count on this neighborhood for a high concentration of students and affordable, lively restaurants. *130 Brighton Ave., Brighton, 617/254–1331. Reservations not accepted. AE, D, MC, V. T stop: Harvard Ave. $*

4 *E-4*
WONDER BAR

One visit reveals why this is such a draw for hungry music-lovers and neighborhood folks too tired to cook: this place

pleases the senses. The tin ceilings are 18 feet, the tables are of blond wood, and behind the long bar is a dreamy mural of hearts, stars, and moon. The menu tends to small dishes—spicy, garlicky shrimp or sausages and melted mozzarella, all served on mellow terracotta plates. When the candles are lit at 9:30 PM, the live jazz begins. *186 Harvard Ave., Allston, 617/351–COOL. Reservations not accepted. AE, D, MC, V. T stop: Harvard Ave. $*

2 *c-5*
WOODY'S GRILL & TAP

Calling its 8-ounce ground sirloin "the Back Bay Burger" is an illusion of grandeur at this Fenway renovation within walking distance from the fancier neighborhood. The thin-crust pizza is tasty, as are generous dishes of pasta, pork chops, and rotisserie chicken. Many entrees are served with a mountain of garlic-mashed potatoes, and garnished with arugula and Parmesan. Although you can eat at the bar, the young and vocal crowd—a youth hostel is down the street—is far more interested in a liquid diet. *58 Hemenway St., Fenway, 617/375–WOOD. AE, DC, MC, V. T stop: Symphony. $$*

BREAKFAST/ BRUNCH

6 *f-6*
CAFÉ FLEURI

Only when you are flush and starving should you come to the sumptuous nine-station prix-fixe buffet Sunday brunch proffered here. The airy courtyard atrium overlooking the Park at Post Office Square is a popular downtown spot for power breakfasters, or lunch or dinner any day. But it is their "chocolate bar" buffet of cakes, tortes, mousses, fondues, and brownies—served on Saturday for unabashed chocoholics—that sets this spot apart. *Hotel Meridien, 250 Franklin St., Downtown, 617/451–1900. Reservations essential. AE, DC, MC, V. T stop: Downtown Crossing. Chocolate bar $$, brunch $$$$*

8 *f-3*
CAFÉ ROUGE

Guests who don't want to venture out of this noted hotel stop at this informal dining room for the buffet breakfast of muffins, eggs, juice, and coffee, all prix fixe. Lunch is also available. *Boston Park Plaza Hotel, 50 Park Plaza, Back Bay, 617/426–2000. AE, DC, MC, V. T stop: Arlington. $$*

5 *g-3*

CENTRE STREET CAFÉ

It's no surprise there's a line at this little storefront place that serves heaping plates of vegetarian omelettes and Huevoos Rancheros. The staff is cool, the setting relaxed—by the end of the meal, you wish you could stay all day. With only 19 seats and enormous popularity, that's not going to be on the agenda. Instead, book a return trip for dinner when the food still tastes farm fresh and the mood is romantic in an alternative kind of way. Every night the chef does a different pasta and quesadilla dish, besides catches of the day like sautéed salmon topped with olive-caper sauce or blue fish on rice with Asian vegetables and Indonesian soy sauce. If you're truly lucky, the half chicken with lime chipotle molasses–barbecue sauce will be on the carte. *597 Centre St., Jamaica Plain, 617/524–9217. Reservations not accepted. No credit cards. Weekend brunch. T stop: Green St. $$*

8 *d-5*

CHARLIE'S SANDWICH SHOPPE

In the 1940s, top black musicians, such as Duke Ellington, ate here when they came to town, having been barred by Boston's "refined" dining establishments. Duke knew a good thing when he spotted it, for this longtime (since 1927) South End luncheonette serves up fine daily specials and Southern-style corn bread and sweet-potato pie. But it's best known for its breakfast egg platters like Cajun omelet with spicy sausage, and pancakes filled with cranberries, bananas, or blueberries. No wonder the biggest complaint here is that they are not open for dinner. *429 Columbus Ave., South End, 617/536–7669. Reservations not accepted. No credit cards. Closed Sun. T stop: Back Bay. $*

7 *a-3*

HOUSE OF BLUES CAMBRIDGE

One of the world-famous clubs owned by Dan Aykroyd and the late John Belushi's wife, Judy, where you can eat a Southern-style dinner downstairs and watch the music on closed-circuit television. Every night is a live performance of blues, some given by famous musicians. The Gospel brunch has become so popular there are two seatings—the spread includes cornbread, grits, fried catfish, and French toast. *96 Winthrop St., Harvard Sq., 617/491–2583. Reservations essential for brunch. AE, D, MC, V. T stop: Harvard Sq. $$*

6 *e-5*

HUNGRY TRAVELER

The name says it all—this is a popular place for people-on-the-run, located just behind Old City Hall and on Pi Alley, and offering up square-deal bacon and eggs, sandwiches, soups, and specials. The crowds start to pile in at 6:00 AM and continue through late afternoon, often lured by the daily specials, Shepherd's Pie to Ziti Primavera to Philadelphia Cheese Steaks. *29 Court St., Downtown, 617/742–5989. No credit cards. No dinner. T stop: Government Center. $*

8 *e-2*

ROMANO'S BAKERY AND SANDWICH SHOP

Energy flows with the coffee in the AM and continues all day long, thanks to those tempting homemade pastries. This aromatic Back Bay bakeshop has tables handy to enjoy croissants, bagels, blueberry muffins, and the cheesiest cheese Danish. Quiches, soups, sandwiches, too. Opt for espresso, cappuccino, brewed decaf, or regular. *33 Newbury St., Back Bay, 617/266–0770. Reservations not accepted. No credit cards. No dinner. T stop: Arlington. $*

1 *f-2*

TRIDENT BOOKSELLERS AND CAFE

Ah, the café/bookstore! This is one of those idyllic place to dawdle over a cappuccino, peruse a slick European magazine, play chess, or write in your journal. The perpetual breakfast ranges from eggs Benedict to granola with yogurt to Belgian waffles. The staff is helpful on all fronts, whether you are searching for a specific book or choosing a drink with medicinal qualities, like the Yin Yang Milkshake, the Nerve Soother, or the Backache. Open daily from 9 AM to midnight. *338 Newbury St., Back Bay, 617/267–8688. Reservations not accepted. AE,*

D, DC, MC, V. Wine and beer. T stop:
Hynes Convention Center/ICA. $

CAFÉS AND PUBS

1 f-2
ARTISAN CAFÉ
Located in an innocuous shopping center, this subdued coffee shop is full of
art and goodies. Owner Henry Patterson
sells his own brand of teas, chai (the fragrant brew from India), fancy coffee
drinks, sandwiches, and decadent
desserts. Paintings, lamps, even the
chairs you are sitting on, are made by
local artists and are for sale. Bunker Hill
Mall, Charlestown, 617/242–6819. Reservations not accepted. AE, DC, MC, V. T
stop: Community College. $

6 b-6
BULL & FINCH PUB
Yes, this is the place "where everybody
knows your name." Beloved shrine to
fans of the sitcom Cheers, this spot can
pack a wallop when thronged with loud
and friendly crowds. Karaoke and live
bands take over, to boot, Thursday
through Saturday evenings. But if you
venture in on a quiet fall afternoon you
can enjoy a fine brew and great burger.
84 Beacon St., at Hampshire House, Beacon Hill, 617/227–9605. AE, D, DC, MC,
V. T stop: Arlington. $

9 d-6
CAFFÉ PARADISO
One of the best ways to travel to Europe
without a passport, this café is a good
choice in the North End for old-world
ambience. Mornings feel especially Italian as you sit at one of the tables facing
the sidewalk enjoying your caffe con latte
and pastry. Late at night, it's also a spirited place, when it's time for more coffee and perhaps a cannoli or some
homemade gelato. An entirely different
scene pervades the Cambridge spot,
where college kids and starving artists
congregate to discuss the latest Jane
Campion flick, eat a substantial, inexpensive lunch of soup, salad, and sandwiches, and plan a late night out. 255
Hanover St., North End, 617/742–1768.
AE, MC, V. T stop: Haymarket. $

3 c-4
1 Eliot Pl., Cambridge, 617/868–3240. T
stop: Harvard Sq.

8 d-3
REBECCA'S
This small New England chain of restaurants is functional looking and self-serve,
but offers excellent baked-on-premises
pastries, particularly the brownies and
apple pie. Excellent and economical
lunch choices are featured, such as
soups, salads, and generous sandwiches
on thick, hand-cut bread. 112 Newbury
St., Back Bay, 617/267–1122. AE, DC, MC,
V. No dinner. T stop: Copley Sq. $

6 f-5
75 State St., Government Center, 617/
261–0022. T stop: State St.

2 c-2
290 Main St., Cambridge, 617/494–6688.
T stop: Kendall Sq.

8 c-4
800 Boylston St., Back Bay, 617/266–
3355. T stop: Prudential Center.

6 b-5
THE SEVENS
Ask the staff here what's the best dish
on the menu and the answer will probably be..."the waitress." Prim-and-
proper Beacon Hill-ers let down their
reserve here—the place is like a
friendly home-away-from-home, with
good cheer, conversation, and a fine
pub lunch usually on tap. Get those
mugs of draft beer right up to 1 AM. 77
Charles St., Beacon Hill, 617/523–9074.
T stop: Charles/MGH. $

8 b-4
SONSIE
So much more than a café, this jewel
box of a restaurant draws a steady pool
of admirers. The scene is at its best in
the mornings, when the marble-topped
tables and rattan chairs facing the street
offer a perfect place from which to
watch the day unfold. Over-size cups of
coffee paired with a muffin or scone
encourage another visit for lunch or dinner. 327 Newbury St., Back Bay, 617/351–
2500. AE, MC, V. T stop: Hynes Convention Center/ICA. $

6 b-4
STARBUCKS
That jolt of java is a bit pricey here—but
you get to sit on comfy seats, be com-
forted by Swedish woods, and chill out
with a chatty crowd. 97 Charles St., 617/
227–3812.

6 *b-5*

1 Charles St., 617/742–2664.

7 *a-3*

36 JFK St., 617/492–4881.

CARIBBEAN

7 *e-6*

GREEN STREET GRILL

Tongue-searing, eye-watering dishes draw the crowds here to this low-ceilinged, brightly painted boîte, located upstairs from the convivial Charley's Bar jazz club. The laid-back clientele digs the decor and the inventive cooking, which features such feats as peppered tenderloin of beef stuffed with brie and a four-alarmer Scotch Bonnet sausage, spiced with rosemary, garlic, and banana. Monday night specials are a great deal. After dinner, stick around for live music or a magic show. *280 Green St., Cambridge, 617/876–1655. AE, MC, V. No lunch. T stop: Central Sq. $$$*

7 *f-6*

RHYTHM & SPICE

Pan-Caribbean is served up here—conch fritters, jerk chicken, curried goat, and oxtails with pepper sauce and mango chutney let you island-hop the night away. This festive place is located near MIT and around 10 PM on weekends, the tables are cleared and everyone is up and dancing to the reggae, soca, or calypso bands. With or without the music, an international crowd comes to sip rum drinks and kick back at the bar. *315 Massachusetts Ave., Cambridge, 617/ 497–0977. T stop: Central Sq. $$*

CHINESE

6 *e-8*

CARL'S PAGODA

Gutsy diners used to ask Carl to concoct his specialties just for them, but since he retired a loyal following still tracks here for Hong Kong–style Chinese food—noodle soups, barbecue chicken or pork, and other straight-ahead dishes. Understand this upstairs restaurant is small and not much to look at. *23 Tyler St., Chinatown, 617/357–9837. No credit cards. T stop: Chinatown. $*

6 *e-7*

CHAU CHOW

Aficionados of simple Chinese fare come to this hole-in-the-wall establishment to savor the seafood specialties. Salt-baked jumbo shrimp in the shell is always a good choice, also the steamed sea bass, the fried noodles with seafood, the fried squid, and any of the soups. Some people swear Chau Chow's special house ginger sauce could resurrect the dead. *52 Beach St., Chinatown, 617/426–6266. Reservations not accepted. No credit cards. If you want either, go across to the newer, bigger Grand Chau Chow at 45 Beach St. T stop: Chinatown. $*

6 *e-7*

CHAU CHOW CITY

Almost the size of China itself, this is the third in the Chau dynasty, with 1,200-seats, and offering dim sum daily beginning at 8:30 AM and tasty food until 3 AM weekdays and 4 AM weekends! On the third floor you can find a display showing the world's third largest shark fin, along with fish tanks—but who wants to sit facing the poor creatures who will soon expire for your pleasure. Head instead, when it is not filled with a wedding party, to the third floor, where you can dine amid mirrors and gilded dragons. The non-smoking mezzanine feels most Western. *83 Essex St., Chinatown, 617/426–6266. Reservations not accepted. AE, D, MC, V. T stop: Chinatown. $*

6 *e-7*

IMPERIAL TEAHOUSE

Choose from a wide selection of Cantonese and Mandarin dishes at this oft-recommended spot in the heart of Chinatown. Sample the lemon duck or chicken or the baked shrimp with peppers and scallions; vegetarian dishes are special here, along with the dim sum served upstairs—a fun traditional-brunch alternative on Sundays (expect a wait). *70–72 Beach St., Chinatown, 617/426–8439. AE, MC, V. T stop: Chinatown. $*

7 *e-6*

MARY CHUNG

Originally a cult spot for hungry MITers, Mary Chung closed, but nostalgia has brought this unpretentious spot back—once again a favorite for satisfying Chinese and Mandarin specialties and terrific dim sum. The place is noted for its pork-filled dumplings with chili oil, fried chicken fingers, and bean curd with hot sauce. *447 Massachusetts Ave., Cambridge, 617/864–1991. Reservations not accepted. No credit cards. Wine and beer. No smoking. Closed Tues. Weekend dim sum. T stop: Central Sq. $*

CONTEMPORARY

8 *g-2*

AUJOURD'HUI

The food stays in step with the times here (the name means "today") but the decor conjures up all the elegances of a gentler age—sumptuous oak paneling, tables laid with antique china, and, of course, potted palms, to echo the verdant views of the stately Public Garden across the way. The menu is rich in possibilities, including rack of lamb, medallions of veal, and carpaccio of sirloin, and there's a popular Alternative Cuisine option for the health conscious. A five-course tasting menu might showcase miso-crust salmon, camelized sea scallops, roast venison, cheese, and a warm chocolate cake with espresso ice cream. Diners staying in this elegant hotel will be glad they don't have far to go after their meal. Sunday brunch is popular. *Four Seasons Hotel, 200 Boylston St., Back Bay, 617/451–1392. Reservations essential. AE, DC, MC, V. No lunch Sat. T stop: Arlington. $$$$*

8 *f-2*

BIBA

A Boston landmark, this Lydia Shire restaurant is almost as famous for its decor as for its cuisine. Designed by Adam Tihany, the second-floor dining room—smartly overlooking the Public Garden—has lustrous cherry and oak floors and is topped off by a patchwork of primitive paintings on the ceiling. Shire is often touted as one of America's most innovative chefs, and when you try her extravagant creations—black-pepper and black sesame-seed–crust triangle of tuna adorned with green-pea tendrils drizzled with a purple-rose butter sauce, anyone?—you'll have to agree. The menu always has Shire's signature lobster pizza, and could include citron-marinated lamb sirloin, brochette of Vermont quail, and duckling foie gras, and a wild, technicolorful salad with beef carpaccio on skewers. Needless to say, the trendy bar crowd downstairs is just as technicolor-

ful, as they nibble on tapas while scouting for companionship. Be forewarned, it can, and does, get noisy. Sunday brunch is offered. *272 Boylston St., Back Bay, 617/426–7878. Reservations essential. AE, D, DC, MC, V. No lunch Sat. T stop: Arlington. $$$$*

5 *h-2*

BLACK CROW CAFFÉ

It starts the day as a coffee shop, selling pastries, breads, and rolls with the java. Around lunch time, the Black Crow turns into a jumping sandwich spot. By dinner, it takes on a bistro flair, serving hot Caribbean and Mediterranean dishes and innovative salads from its constantly changing menu. Its progressive, multiracial atmosphere is the very soul of Jamaica Plain. *2 Perkins St., Jamaica Plain, 617/983–9231. AE, MC, V. Closed Mon. $$*

3 *g-6*

BLUE ROOM

Mediterranean with a dash of Latin is the way they describe their menu here, but "interesting" and "provocative" might be better adjectives. They certainly describe the lobster and mussel "chowder," drizzled with coconut milk and cilantro. Or the No. 1 Tuna, a sushi-quality slab bathed in a chard tomato sauce. Or the salad (once featured in *Bon Appetit*), a whole head of romaine stuffed with goodies and sauced with a spicy Roquefort. The grilled fish, chicken, and duck is never predictable and sometimes the sides of beans or cole slaw are even better. At the heart of the place is an open kitchen, complete with wood-burning grill. Elsewhere, the eye takes in silvery zinc tables, rich red-brick walls, and burnt-orange banquettes. The expanded bar area means more opportunities to drink and share appetizers. In warm weather the congenial staff creates a low-price lunch on a grill outside the restaurant and you carry your plate to one of the patio tables. This is one of the area's best places for dining al fresco. Sunday brunch can by yummy. *One Kendall Sq., Cambridge, 617/494–9034. Reservations essential. AE, D, DC, MC, V. T stop: Kendall Sq. $$$*

6 *c-7*

BREW MOON

Handy to the Wang Center and the Theater District, and located within the massive Massachusetts State Transportation Building, this place is an eye-catching place to enjoy herb-crusted sirloin, spiced-bronzed grilled swordfish, and the special beers brewed on site. The beer vats accent the decor, along with a dyed-and-studded-with-leather concrete floor and lighting fixtures that whimsically catch the changing phases of the moon. *115 Stuart St., 617/523–6467. AE, MC, V. T stop: Boylston. $$*

8 *g-2*

BRISTOL LOUNGE

Noted for its afternoon High Tea, the Bristol Lounge also attracts people to the Four Seasons Hotel for its fine lunch and dinner. The menu has dishes of all sizes: a turkey club sandwich, lobster salad, entreés of steak or fish, and a daily special (if it's meat loaf, it's Monday). Yummy tapas are served at all hours and include smoked duck quesadilla, glazed scallops, grilled portobello sandwich, and a crab salad. On Sundays, Bristol goes Belgian with a $32 brunch of Belgian waffles, omelettes, cheese blintzes, or smoked seafood. The Viennese dessert buffet is Friday and Saturday evenings. *200 Boylston St., Back Bay, 617/388–4400. AE, D, DC, MC, V. T stop: Arlington.*

8 *a-4*

CLIO

Located in one of Boston's best boutique hotels, Clio is one of Boston's newest arrivals—a much anticipated and, now, much appreciated restaurant. The room is chic, with chocolate-color walls, lots of white wood, and a wild-leopard pattern on the carpet. The dashing young chef, Ken Oringer, insists his kitchen is a theater—so passersby can study his staff through large windows. Dramatic, too, are the big white plates that frame Oringer's creations: English pea soup, vine-ripened tomato salad, caramelized swordfish, and glazed short ribs. For those who prefer the chef to make the decisions, there are two tasting menus, one vegetarian. Sunday brunch is featured. *Eliot Hotel, 370A Commonwealth Ave., Back Bay, 617/536–7200. AE, D, DC, MC, V. No lunch. T stop: Hynes Convention Center/ICA. $$$$*

7 *g-4*

DADDY-O'S

The cream-and-turquoise interior is homage to the 1956 Chevy that once belonged to the owner's father; the pink is the color of a 1955 Cadillac. And the two life-size soft sculptures of beatniks playing the bongos? Well, it's all intentionally passé in a jazzy way. But the cooking is totally *au courant* at this Cambridge hideaway located halfway between Inman and Kendall squares. Comfort food from the fifties is often served, as well as more exotic fare, such as the mixed grill of chorizo, spicy pork, and chicken with corn fries, banana salsa, and gumbo greens. Herbs are picked from the restaurant's garden, which offers one of the area's most tranquil settings. Sunday brunch is often Latin-inspired. *134 Hampshire St., Cambridge, 617/354–8371. D, MC, V. Beer and wine. Open Mon. summer only. T stop: Kendall Sq. $$*

7 *f-3*

EAST COAST GRILL

They call Chris Schlesinger the "grill guru" and this owner/chef and cookbook author may be among the few today to induce barbecue nirvana. He presides over this deservedly popular Inman Square restaurant, now expanded to provide more elbow room to tackle generous plates of ribs, brisket, chicken, steak, and lots of seafood (with a tropical bent). Fiery specialties include Pasta from Hell, Latin-rubbed grilled mahi-mahi, and a wicked pepper-crust tuna. The decor is both hot and cool—neon flames dance in the window while the room's blue lights conjure up the ocean. Opt for a margarita, served with little plastic monkeys hanging from the glasses. This is definitely a gregarious place: Diners are encouraged to buy a six-pack for the sous-chefs, visible in the open kitchen as they grill the night away. Try the Sunday brunch. *1271 Cambridge St., Cambridge, 617/491–6568. Reservations not accepted weekends. AE, DC, MC, V. No lunch. T stop: Central Sq. $$$*

1 *c-1*

FLORA

Arrive in jeans or a tux here—it's that sort of place. Set within a 1930s bank, Flora is graced with barrel-vault ceilings, burnished copper torcheres, and pretty bouquets—the floral accents pay tribute to the name of the owner's mother and often highlight the orange and blue color accents of the room. Mary Jo and husband/chef Bob Sargent serve up fine seasonal American cuisine, including roasted skate, herb gnocchi, and poached halibut. Many diners come here before taking in the evening show at the Capital, an old (and cheap) movie house across the way. Sunday brunch is offered. *190 Massachusetts Ave., Arlington, 617/641–1664. D, MC, V. Beer and wine. Closed Mon. $$*

9 f-6
FRANKLIN CAFÉ

This busy bar doubles as a destination restaurant and was a hit the moment it opened in Boston's quickly gentrifying, intensely hip South End neighborhood. A small but inventive menu offers tuna carpaccio, chicken meat loaf, grilled veal chop, and cornmeal-crust catfish. Lack of desserts makes lounging undefendable, but just be happy you made the scene—the problem of containing a quart within a pint pot sums up the crowd here. Dinner is served until 1:30 AM. Chef/co-owner Dave DuBois promises weekend brunch soon. *278 Shawmut Ave., South End, 617/350–0010. Reservations not accepted. AE, MC, V. No lunch. T stop: Back Bay. $$*

1 d-1
GARGOYLES ON THE SQUARE

The little stone creatures after which this restaurant is named peer out from wall and shelf, watching as you dine. Choose from a spirited, well-executed dinner menu, or if you eat at the small bar, a less expensive bar menu. The seasonal vegetarian plate is so tasty it might convert you. Jazz Sunday nights adds to the refined, relaxed mood. *215 Summer St., Somerville, 617/776-5300. AE, DC, MC, V. Closed Mon. No lunch. T stop: Davis Sq. $$$*

8 f-4
ICARUS

This is an imaginative New American cuisine beautifully executed by chef/co-owner Chris Douglass in an elegant and romantic two-level dining room. The menu, which changes seasonally, boasts winners like seared duck breast with black mission figs and a Wellfleet little-neck clam roast. Douglass's involvement with local farmers is evident in his cooking. Extensive wine list; diners are welcome in the cozy bar. From September to May, Icarus offers Sunday brunch. Jazz is played every Friday night except in July. *3 Appleton St., South End, 617/ 426–1790. Reservations essential. AE, DC, MC, V. No lunch. T stop: Back Bay. $$$$*

6 f-6
JULIEN

Named in honor of Boston's first French restaurant—which opened in 1794 on this very site—Julien is a favored place for Boston's power brokers. Set within the old Federal Reserve building, it's now the jewel in the crown of an elegant French-owned hotel. Renaissance Revival gilded cornices, Queen Anne wingback chairs, and an N. C. Wyeth mural featuring George Washington make for regal surroundings. The kitchen then kicks in with great French élan—what business deal could not be delivered over such extraordinary dishes as rare duck breast accompanied by a salad garneé with crisp duck skin? The wine list, of course, leans to Europe. The

---

BAR DINING

Eating at the bar is not only more casual, it's the cool thing to do. Not only does it mean the evening can be more spontaneous, it can, sometimes, be the only way to get into those chichi places!

Ambrosia (French)
The most beautiful part of this restaurant is the bar. Opt for chive blinis and caviar.

Audubon Circle (American)
Everything on this small menu is clever and oh-so-tasty.

Chez Henri (French)
The lights are low and the dinner is leisurely—that's only fitting in a place of such Gallic elan.

Clio (Contemporary)
Stop for a cocktail, then stay for a blow-out that would please any gourmand.

Dali (Spanish)
The bar is dripping with atmosphere. How can you not share the tapas with your neighbor?

Eat (American)
At this cozy bar it's all but impossible to get to chat with Adam, the gregarious bartender.

Gargoyles (American)
Yes, the tables are lovely, but for true at-home vibes, check out the bar.

Restaurant Zinc (French)
Even if you can get a reservation, eating at the bar feels so much more cosmopolitan.

downtown location draws a predominately business clientele, especially at lunch. *Hotel Meridien, 250 Franklin St., Downtown, 617/451–1900. Reservations essential. AE, DC, MC, V. T stop: Downtown Crossing. $$$$*

8 *d-3*

THE OAK ROOM

Tapestry-cover chairs, L-shape banquettes, crystal chandeliers, wood paneling, and mahogany-trim mirrors: Quite the place to indulge in appetizers of oysters Rockefeller or lobster bisque, and modern interpretations of classics like thick grilled steaks, veal and lamb chops, and New England seafood. And of course, Chateaubriand, tableside. The adjacent Oak Bar has a rainbow of specialty martinis (Black Forest Chocolate and Georgia Peach), a humidor of cigars, an oyster bar, and live music. Jacket and tie required. *Copley Plaza Hotel, 138 St. James Ave., Back Bay, 617/267–5300. Reservations essential. AE, D, DC, MC, V. No lunch. T stop: Copley Sq. $$$$*

1 *f-2*

OLIVES

Enemies have been known to dine together in order to get a reservation (only available for parties of six or more) at this famous place that draws raves and crowds. Chef/owner Todd English, a glamorous and influential force on the local dining scene, creates rustic specialties in the wood-burning oven. Some say the restaurant is named after English's wife Olivia, others are convinced it is because the cuisine is only from countries where olives are grown. Regardless, most agree that the food is excellent. *10 City Sq., Charlestown, 617/242-1999. AE, DC, MC, V. Closed Sun. and Mon. No lunch. T stop: Community College $$$*

4 *g-6*

PROVIDENCE

Chef Paul O'Connell had to wait out a recession as sous chef for other top restaurants, but now has established his own reputation with dishes like smoked veal brisket with potato dumplings, and crispy cod cheeks and lobster. The ambience is exotic with columns galore, a midnight-blue ceiling, and wrought-iron details. Brunch is served on Sunday. *1223 Beacon St., Brookline, 617/232–0300. AE, DC, MC, V. Closed Mon. No lunch. $$$*

1 *f-2*

R. WESLEY'S BISTRO

R. Wesley, who says that's his legal name, doesn't take himself too seriously. But there is nothing funny about his way with venison and veal, boar and beef, fish and fowl. Plates are both artful (dish edges can be adorned with red peppers and parsley) and abundant. The chef says his cuisine is "a little bit of everything. I guess that's American." Signature dishes include pan-roast sirloin, served in a wine reduction along with roasted clams, onions, and potato pancakes, and the chocolate peanut buttercream torte dessert. Food this good, and a menu that changes every two weeks, justifies frequent visits. The place is stylish without knowing it and so small, you can see when flames leap from the stove top. A bar with four stools and outrageously inexpensive wine by the glass add to the pleasure. Though this place may be off the beaten path of many visitors, it is definitely worth the trip. *31 Cambridge St., Charlestown, 617/242–7202. Reservations not accepted, but if you call ahead they will put your name on waiting list. AE, MC, V. Beer and wine. Closed Mon. No lunch Tues., Wed., or weekends. T stop: Community College. $$*

8 *f-2*

THE RITZ-CARLTON DINING ROOM

The Ritz-Carlton is not just for celebrating your 25th wedding anniversary any longer. Yes, the Venetian crystal chandeliers, the cobalt-blue glassware appointments, and the green of the Public Garden filling the windows help to create the gracious and serene atmosphere with which the Ritz is synonymous, but, today, the kitchen is headed up by a dashing young chef from California, Mark Allen. His specials are impressive—native roast duck in Cassis, lobster with whiskey sauce, and rabbit with Swiss chard and herbed gnocci are just three temptations. Some diners will remain staunchly faithful to the fabled chateaubriand-for-two and the sublime soufflés; healthier sorts will opt for the spa menu. On Sunday there's a lavish buffet brunch. Jacket required after 6 PM, and no jeans, shorts, athletic clothing/shoes. The recently renovated Roof Restaurant is open during the summer for the $75-prix fixe dinner and dancing under the stars, and a Sunday jazz brunch. Of course, reservations always. *Ritz-Carlton Hotel, 15 Arlington*

St., 2nd floor, Back Bay, 617/536–5700. AE, DC, MC, V. No smoking. Sun. brunch. T stop: Arlington. $$$$

3 h-6

SALAMANDER

Stan Frankenthaler, one of Boston's most noted chefs, calls his food "celebratory American," yet spices and influences from all over the world can be tasted in such creations as tandoori swordfish, peanut-crust tuna, or crispy-fried whole bass *garneé* with spicy dipping sauce and cooling pickles. Appetizers are complex and satisfying, often Asian-tinged. How can one ever save room for that skillet-baked deep-dish fruit pie (for two)! The epitome of casual elegance, the restaurant is done up in the colors of "food and earth," with *pinot noir*–russets setting the palette and a wood grill/open kitchen serving as a centerpiece. The sky-lit atrium has a bar and more relaxed seating, and is open for an economical breakfast and lunch. *1 Athenaeum St., Cambridge, 617/225-2121. Reservations essential in dining room. AE, D, DC, MC, V. Closed Sun. T stop: Kendall Sq. $$$*

6 f-4

SEASONS

Some of Boston's most illustrious chefs got their start here. Now, it is Michael Taylor's turn; he promises more variations on Seasons's theme—but that's only natural from a restaurant that completely revamps its menu four times a year. America's bounty is featured in all its glory: chilled potato leek soup, squid salad, marinated duckling in ginger soy with scallions, rack of lamb, seared rabbit. As always, this remains a special treat for the out-of-towner, due to the spectacular setting—a spacious glass-wall dining aerie overlooking Faneuil Marketplace, Quincy Market's gold dome, and the Custom House Tower clock. *Regal Bostonian Hotel, North & Blackstone Sts., Faneuil Hall, 617/523-3600. Reservations essential. AE, DC, MC, V. T stop: Haymarket. $$$$*

8 b-4

SONSIE

This is undeniably one of Boston's most seductive restaurants at night when the mood shifts from cosmopolitan café to bustling brasserie. Deco lamps illuminate terra-cotta walls, and the deep room and bar fills with neigh-borhood yuppies, local news anchors and athletes, tourists and the bridge-and-tunnel crowd. Asian overtones bring a lightness to the menu, which always features a pasta, pizza, and sirloin, along with specials like lobster ravioli or grilled swordfish with tequila-batter shrimp. Desserts are awesome, especially the chocolate bread pudding. *327 Newbury St., Back Bay, 617/351-2500. AE, MC, V. T stop: Hynes Convention Center/ICA. $$$*

8 e-6

TREMONT 647

All eyes were on this stylish restaurant when it opened in 1997. The decor is as smart looking as the clientele who are drawn to chef/owner Andy Husbands' big bold flavors. His "Adventuresome American" covers all the Asian and Latin bases: Sea bass wrapped in banana leaf, barbecue pork with three-onion salsa, and balsamic soaked chicken are some faves. Appetizers include—gasp!—Tibetan mo-mos (a.k.a. Peking ravio-lis—a sort of dough basket) stuffed with spiced pork; for dessert, you can't go wrong with the So Good Pear Tart. If you opt for pizza, try The Works—an over-the-top creation adorned with shrimp, chicken, and andouille sausage. Set within a South End Victorian, Tremont 647's interior is chic yet informal, with wrought-iron sconces and chandeliers and lush purple and red banquettes. The mahogany bar and the tables next it offer more spontaneous dining options. *647 Tremont St., South End, 617/266-4600. AE, DC, MC, V. Nearest T stop: Back Bay. $$$*

8 f-2

29 NEWBURY

After dining on the New American food served here you could have trouble pouring yourself into the designer clothes sold at the surrounding boutiques of Newbury Street. Still, the fast-metabolism crowd here seems none the worse for wear after feasting on coconut-milk mussel soup, black-pepper fet-tucini, and creme brulee. This chic *boite* is on the ritzy end of Newbury so the people-watching better be top-notch. The comfortable dining room has stunning gold and green patterned banquettes and doubles as an art gallery. At the intimate bar, hairdressers rub elbows with stockbrokers. Sunday brunch is served and the Newbury side-

walk dining patio in open in season. *29
Newbury St., Back Bay, 617/536-0290.
AE, DC MC, V. T stop: Arlington. $$$*

CUBAN

8 *a-4*

MUCHO GUSTO CAFE & COLLECTIBLES

Lucy and Desi photos, 1950s cookie jars,
Mr. Machine toys, and Formica tables
make a visit to this place a blast from
the past. As Oz Mondejar, the efferves-
cent owner, explains, it's all to conjure
up 1950s-Cuba (get the Arnaz refer-
ence?) and his family heritage. He's a
genuine host, making sure diners are
content with their bowls of black bean
soup, empanadas, Cuban sandwiches,
"Old Clothes" (shredded beef), or
entreés of shrimp creole or pork chops
marinated in citrus and garlic. Oz's
mother, Aida, not only provided inspira-
tion, she is the cook. A shot of potent
coffee completes the meal. Sunday
brunch is offered. *1124 Boylston St., the
Fens, 617/236–1020. Reservations not
accepted. MC, V. Beer and wine. Closed
Mon. No lunch Tues, no dinner Sun. T
stop: Hynes Convention Center/ICA. $$*

DELICATESSEN

6 *g-5*

BAKEY'S

This must be the Boston Brahmin version of a deli—antique English wooden
booths, a quaint square bar, 19th-cen-
tury lamps, Asian rugs, fresh linen, and
fresh flowers. But the menu delivers—
fresh turkey and Reuben sandwiches are
specialties. A lavish breakfast menu is
also offered. *45 Broad St., Downtown,
617/426–1710. AE, MC, V. Closed Sat.,
Sun. T stop: State St. $*

4 *f-6*

RUBIN'S KOSHER DELICATESSEN & RESTAURANT

This strictly kosher (no dairy products)
restaurant is an authentic deli serving
matzo ball soup, potato pancakes, noodle pudding, stuffed cabbage and, of
course, a high and hot pastrami sandwich. *500 Harvard St,, Brookline, 617/
566–8761. Reservations not accepted. No
credit cards. Closed Sat. T stop: Coolidge
Corner. $*

FISH AND SEAFOOD

Boston's fish and seafood restaurants
are among the best anywhere.

6 *h-7*

ANTHONY'S PIER 4

If it was good enough for Elizabeth Taylor it probably is good enough for out-of-
town guests and birthday celebrations.
Photos of Liz and other celebrities adorn
the "Wall of Respect" at this popular,
long-established, and none-too-serene
two-story waterfront seafood restaurant
that has wonderful harbor views (best in
the PM) from the decks and through a
wall of glass. Imported Dover sole,
broiled scrod, fried oysters, and Maine
lobsters by weight, are the big items
here, along with steaks and lamb for car-
nivores. The extensive wine list is 30
pages. Order your Grand Marnier or
chocolate soufflé along with the entree.
Outdoor dining in fine weather. *140
Northern Ave., Waterfront, 617/423-6363.
Reservations essential. AE, DC, MC, V. T
stop: South Station. $$$*

6 *h-7*

BARKING CRAB

A jumble of buoys, life preservers, and
crab traps hung with Christmas lights;
meals served on paper plates with plas-
tic utensils; a wood stove to keep the
interior cozy year-round—you get the
picture. This urban lobster pound
proves fun, day or night. In warm
weather you can sit at picnic tables
under the red and yellow tent and
admire the skyline rising above the
murky waters of Fort Point Channel. If
you want to get down and dirty, use
stones to smash your crabs and lobsters
or just feast on specials of grilled sword-
fish, salmon, and trout. *88 Sleeper St.,
Waterfront, 617/426–CRAB. Reservations
not accepted. AE, D, DC, MC, V. No
brunch summer. T stop: South Station. $$*

9 *g-7*

BOSTON SAIL LOFT

When you get that urge to sit out and
dine waterside (and we do feel that
call—humans, after all, are 78% percent
water), this is a pleasant spot, hard by
Commercial Wharf, to take in the vista
of Boston Harbor. The sole, scrod, and
lobster standards would please an old
sea salt—and plenty of those other diners who frequently pack this place. *80*

Atlantic Ave., Waterfront, 617/227–7280.
AE, DC, MC, V. T stop: Aquarium. $

9 e-5

DAILY CATCH

Not only do you watch as your meal is prepared on the stove here, you get to eat out of the very same frying pan in which it was cooked. If you go to the branch in the Italian North End, you'll find the original tiny and informal restaurant—just look for the painting of a squid on the storefront window. Actually, just follow your nose—nearly every dish here is topped with garlic! Sicilian-style calamari is the house specialty, served stuffed with linguini or in a wonderful salad. Broiled fish, a good clam chowder, lobster fra diavola, and an oyster bar are other options. The newer locations have similar food and more comfort, but only the North End has that special local color. Wine and beer only. Credit cards and reservations accepted only at the Northern Avenue location. No smoking in Brookline and North End. 323 Hanover St., North End, 617/523–8567. $$

6 g-6

261 Northern Ave., near Fish Pier, Waterfront, 617/338–3093. T stop: South Station.

4 f-6

441A Harvard St., Brookline, 617/734–5696. T stop: Coolidge Corner.

1 g-4

JIMMY'S HARBORSIDE RESTAURANT

For what it's worth, locals have been coming here since 1923 for the requisite clam chowder, finnan haddie, lobster, sea scallops, and other delights from the deep. The three-tier dining room overlooking the harbor has a predictable nautical theme, but the fact that the clientele tends to dress up makes a meal here feel like a special occasion. Free hors d'oeuvres in the lounge. 242 Northern Ave., Waterfront, 617/423–1000. Reservations essential. AE, DC, MC, V. No lunch Sun. T stop: South Station. $$$

3 e-8

JONAH'S SEAFOOD CAFÉ

Come here on a fine spring day and the gardens, trees, and fountains of Jonah's will make you feel as if you're dining alfresco. The restaurant is built on a landscaped terrace jutting from the base of a spectacular 14-story atrium and there is a 100-foot-high "Great Window," which offers a relaxing view of the Charles. A fabulous, albeit pricey, buffet table offers a dazzling array of foods. Fridays are devoted to seafood; on Saturdays, the lure is the lobster. Sunday brunch is featured. Hyatt Regency Cambridge, 575 Memorial Dr., Cambridge, 617/492–1234. AE, DC, MC, V. T stop: Boston University. $$$

8 f-3

LEGAL SEA FOODS

Admirers of this 40-year-old Boston tradition remind you that "If it's not fresh, it's not Legal." And it is true that the fish here is of the highest quality. But a great restaurant has to do more, so the Berkowitz family brought masterful Jasper White aboard as executive chef (he has since gone to consulting) to improve the menu. White helped open Legal-C, a colorful restaurant with a Caribbean atmosphere and a jazzier menu that features Creole-style conch and Jamaican trout. Each of the 10 Legals has a different atmosphere depending on the neighborhood, but they all tend to be large and plain. More than 30 varieties of fish are served daily, most of it simply broiled, baked, fried, or steamed. There's also fish chowder, spicy steamed mussels, baked stuffed shrimp, a good list of California wines, and a fine new children's menu. The point is that if you need a Legal—and many tourists head directly to one from the plane—you can find one. Boston Park Plaza Hotel, 35 Columbus Ave., Back Bay, 617/426–4444. AE, D, DC, MC, V. Reservations not accepted. $$$

6 b-7

Legal-C Bar in the Statler Office Bldg., 27 Columbus Ave., Back Bay, 617/426–5566.

8 d-4

Copley Pl., 100 Huntington St., Back Bay, 617/266–7775.

8 c-4

Prudential Center, 800 Boylston St., Back Bay, 617/266–6800.

2 c-2

5 Cambridge Center, Kendall Sq., Cambridge, 617/864–3400.

1 h-3

Logan Airport, Terminal C, 617/568–2800.

1 g-4

NO-NAME RESTAURANT

A paradox: This place is anonymous yet famous. You can't get fish much fresher or cheaper than this. It can be fun, if you like family-style seating where you can rub elbows with strangers and make new friends. The service is brusque, the decor hole-in-the-wall, yet tourists and locals flock here for seafood chowder, broiled or fried fish. There can be a wait at peak times, but, hey, the more the merrier. Best bet: The window seats in the back room offer wonderful harbor views. Wine and beer only. 15½ Fish Pier off Northern Ave., 617/338–7539. Reservations not accepted. No credit cards. T stop: South Station. $$

6 f-4

THE SALTY DOG SEAFOOD BAR & GRILL

This is an informal bar and restaurant that is crowded and noisy. Tourists and suburban families enjoy the fresh seafood and primo location. In the summer there is a popular outdoor café and raw bar with umbrella-shaded tables. Faneuil Hall Marketplace, Quincy Market, cellar level, 617/742–2094. AE, MC, V. T stop: Government Center. $$

8 e-3

SKIPJACK'S

This is home of Boston's best clam chowder, winner of the 1996 and 1997 Chowderfest. Blue neon waves should make it clear what is on the horizon here. High marks are given to these two fish restaurants, which feature more than 30 types of seafood, including enough of the exotic to keep an appreciative crowd of bankers and tourists coming back for more. Along with the clam chowder, the annual crabfest is also definitely worth checking out. Both locales have an outdoor patio. 199 Clarendon St., Back Bay, 617/536–3500. AE, DC, MC, V. Sun. brunch. T stop: Back Bay. $$

4 g-8

2 Brookline Pl., Brookline, 617/232–8887. T stop: Brookline Village.

8 d-4

TURNER FISHERIES

Pricey but luxurious and quiet, this hotel fish restaurant is proudest of its "Hall of Fame" clam chowder (due to the number of wins in the annual Chowderfest).

But chef David Filippeti doesn't just have to rest on those laurels, as he always takes fresh ingredients, then adds Asian flavors, and comes up with winners like pan-seared scallops in miso broth with wasabi potatoes or halibut on filo leaves with risotto. Better: the "untraditional bouillabaisse" with lobster, shrimp, clams, and a brioche pudding. Of course, there's always tried-and-true broiled scrod. Business people and tourists like to listen to nightly jazz in the bar, while ordering from the adjacent oyster bar. Sunday brunch is offered. Westin Hotel, 10 Huntington Ave., Back Bay, 617/262–9600. AE, D, DC, MC, V. T stop: Copley Sq. $$$

6 f-4

UNION OYSTER HOUSE

Like a Wellsian time-machine, this restaurant lets you revisit Ye Olde New England and have fun doing it. Established in 1826, it's the oldest eatery in Boston and has barely changed since the days when Daniel Webster was a regular—the oysters and brandy kept him coming back. Today, tourists come for the history (easy to find, this place is along the Freedom Trail) and the New England seafood. The original U-shape oyster bar is still in place; low-price luncheon specials include the time-honored New England dish of codfish cakes and Boston baked beans. The upstairs dining room overlooks City Hall Plaza, while the Cafe Union Bar wing on the second floor has three cozy wood-panel dining rooms. There's a handy children's menu. As you leave, check out the first-floor booths—they're the originals and one of them has a plaque honoring the table JFK made his own. Sunday brunch is on tap. 41 Union St., 617/227–2750. Reservations essential. AE, DC, MC, V. T stop: Haymarket. $$

FRENCH

8 c-5

AMBROSIA ON HUNTINGTON

Fans find it dramatic, foes say it is over-the-top, but any restaurant that serves chive-flavor pasta tossed in miso-mushroom broth, garnished with arugula, stewed tomatoes, and duck confit, and topped with melted Brie, is sure to inspire strong reactions. Chef Anthony Ambrose fuses Provincial French to Asian cuisines and the dazzling results are often as ornately decorated as the restaurant's interior—high-ceilinged, anchored by an enormous column, and crowned by a bar (which has its own menu) that is a mirrored extravaganza of hand-blown crystal and fancy ironwork. The food is also worthy of an MGM musical production number—fittingly, it arrives via a staircase from the mezzanine kitchen. Star dishes include scallop sashimi served on a cumin and leek salad, pheasant breast with warm figs, and scallops poached in corn cumin and truffle essence. *116 Huntington Ave., Back Bay, 617/247–2400. Reservations essential. AE, MC, V. No lunch weekends. T stop: Prudential. $$$$*

3 *a-3*

CAFÉ CALEDOR

Diners with discerning taste rave about the talents of chef/owner Patrick Noe. His menu is South of France in orientation, and can include such specials as marinated trout, duck with a cherry glaze, monkfish wrapped in grape leaves, and grilled steak with porcini truffle butter. Emulate the French by including a course of handpicked artisan-made cheeses. Then for dessert, give in to temptations of raspberry soufflé or a decadent chocolate-espresso torte. The wine list features some unusual bottles; the wait staff will help you pair them with that veal ragout. Tucked into an intimate basement, the uncluttered rooms are painted the colors of sunshine and moss, a diner-friendly environment that suggests you're in a friend's home rather than a restaurant. *5 Craigie Circle, Cambridge, 617/661–4073. Reservations essential. AE, D, DC, MC, V. No smoking. Closed Sun. and Mon. No lunch. T stop: Harvard Sq. $$$*

8 *e-3*

CAFÉ LOUIS

Even if they're not shopping for clothing by Prada or Dolce & Gabbana, savvy natives head to Louis, Boston for this stylish café. As with any fashion plate, this eatery is beautifully turned out—mustard walls, parchment-covered lights in the shape of moons, wooden wine cases, and vases of fresh flowers set the stage for the creations of an award-winning chef. Michael Schlow knows that the way to overwhelm Boston diners is to make French/Italian/American food that does the oppo-

site. A signature dinner dish is the confit of pork with baby vegetables, while the salade Niçoise with raw tuna is a superlative lunch. The pastry chef also gets kudos for chocolate confections, fruit soups, creme bruleé, and dreamy apple or banana tarts. Outdoor tables are just the right distance from Newbury Street to feel a part of the action, yet private. Note that the café serves dessert and coffee or tea from 3 to 5 PM—just the boost you need to choose between a Lauren or Leger. *234 Berkeley St., Back Bay, 617/266–4680. AE, MC, V. Closed Sun. T stop: Arlington. $$$*

BOSTONIAN FISH STORY

Strange as it sounds, the best restaurants for seafood are not always seafood restaurants per se. Here are a few places where the fish tastes like it was in the ocean just hours ago.

Barking Crab (Fish & Seafood)
Okay, so there is an exception to the theory. Boston's funkiest, most fun place to eat lobsters, crabs, and catch of the day.

East Coast Grill (American)
Just check the blackboard to see where your fish was caught. The raw bar is great.

Giacomo's (Italian)
Along with your fish, order pasta and the noted signature sauce.

Grill 23 & Bar (Steak)
The one place where both beef eaters and fish fanatics are supremely sated.

Ginza (Japanese)
The sushi is inventive and served almost all night long.

Jae's (Korean)
So many decisions, so little time. Such an extensive and excellent menu, from soups to sushi to swordfish.

La Betola (Italian)
Rave reviews for a gifted newcomer and talented chef Rene Michelena.

Legal-C (Fish & Seafood)
The newest of the Legal Sea Foods, where both chef and cuisine are truly, marvelously Caribbean.

3 b-3
CHEZ HENRI

Dress in crimson and gold to match this atmospheric bistro that is reason enough to cross the Charles River. The intensity of the reds on the dining room's chairs and walls is especially intoxicating, while more subtle and romantic shades will be found in the dark bar room, a congenial setting for an espresso, beer, or three-course prix fixe. The menu is a melange of French and Cuban: Paella, pan-roasted quails, vegetables, and saffron couscous, and glazed pork chops with red beans and fried bananas are some top picks. Chef/owner Paul O'Connell runs between this restaurant and the more formal Providence in Brookline. *One Shepard St., Cambridge, 617/354–8980. AE, MC, V. Closed Mon. No lunch. T stop: Harvard Sq. $$$*

8 d-3
DU BARRY FRENCH RESTAURANT

The staff here not only speaks French, they are attentive in that old-fashioned Gallic way that conjures up the style of a bygone era. Blush-pink walls, 16th-century artwork, red upholstered chairs and booths, and classic French food make for a sedate and tranquil meal. If you've got a craving for classic French food, this is the place: escargot, calf brains, cassoulet, cànard à l'orange, chauteaubriand, and lapin Dijonnaise are featured. The glass-enclosed terrace is open year-round, while the tranquil outdoor garden (somewhat of a secret) is a summer treat. *159 Newbury St., Back Bay, 617/262–2445. AE, D, DC, MC, V. Closed Sun. T stop: Arlington. $$$*

8 f-5
HAMERSLEY'S BISTRO

Gordon Hamersley has long enlivened the Boston dining scene with his American-influenced Country French fare and his chefs' habit of wearing baseball caps—a winning way, it turns out, of making the beautifully appointed dining room less intimidating. The menu changes with the four seasons: lemon-garlic roast chicken, grilled mushroom and garlic sandwich on country bread, bouillabaisse, cassoulet, pan-roast lobster, and grilled T-bone steak with smoked tomatoes are some of his mainstays. If you can't snag a reservation, try the small dining room opposite the bar,

or better yet, eat at the bar. Romantic sidewalk seating in warm weather. *553 Tremont St., South End, 617/423–2700. Reservations essential. AE, D, MC, V. No lunch. T stop: Back Bay. $$$$*

6 f-6
JULIEN

See Contemporary, *above.*

8 b-3
L'ESPALIER

Every so often, Bostonians throw aside their Puritan inclinations and demand to satisfy their *goût de luxe* with a blow-out, exceedingly haute meal. Since 1977, when this place opened (and helped launch Boston's restaurant renaissance), L'Espalier has delivered not only luxury, but *calme* and *volupté*, too. Indeed, the Salon is nicknamed the Courtship Room (have your aperitifs here before the fireplace), while insiders call the Parlor the Seduction Room. Chef Frank McClelland fuses New French and Newer American to come up with some remarkable creations, including cappuccino chanterelle soup, duck and foie gras mousseline, spiced rack of lamb with port currant sauce, pheasant with chanterelles, and the Chocolate Stargazing Observatory (don't expect to find these on the menu, however, as it changes often). Preparations are unfailingly imaginative and flawlessly presented, especially on the *Menu dégustation*, a grand sampler of entreés, cheeses, and desserts. Set within a century-old Victorian Back bay town house, L'Espalier remains one of Boston's luxury front-runners. Jackets and ties preferred. *30 Gloucester St., Back Bay, 617/262–3023. Reservations essential. AE, DC, MC, V. No lunch. T stop: Hynes Convention Center/ICA. $$$$*

6 f-7
LES ZYGOMATES

Call it "Les Zygs"—that's the nickname the young and hip crowd that gravitates to this cosmopolitan wine bar/bistro use (in French, the name means the muscles on the face that make you smile). They're drawn here by the extensive choice of wines by the glass (more than 30), the three-course prix fixe (lunch and dinner), and its newish nighttime neighborhood—the Leather District, home to some active bar scenes. Live jazz (and the $19 prix fixe) Sunday through Thursday. *129 South St., Downtown, 617/542–*

5108. *AE, DC, MC, V. No lunch weekends.
T stop: South Station. $$*

6 e-5
MAISON ROBERT

From the outside, this grand Second
Empire–style landmark structure—once
the Old City Hall—looks like the Château
d'Anet in the Loire Valley. Not surpris-
ingly, it's now home to a French restau-
rant. Actually, two. Upstairs is
Bonhomme Richard, a more formal din-
ing room, while downstairs is the more
relaxed Ben's Cafe (with $18 and $25 prix
fixes), both the creation of noted restau-
rateur Lucien Robert. Among the special-
ties are filet mignon with Bearnaise
sauce, poached salmon, ostrich medal-
lions, and sautéed calf's liver with bacon.
For dessert, there is tarte tatin, crepes
suzettes with Grand Marnier, and an
assortment of soufflés. The terrace tables
are romantic and amazingly peaceful,
considering you're in the heart of the city
(and on the Freedom Trail). Jacket and tie
required upstairs. *45 School St., Down-
town, 617/227–3370. AE, DC, MC, V.
Closed Sun. No lunch weekends. Bon-
homme Richard $$$$. Ben's Cafe $$*

8 e-4
MISTRAL

It seemed like this hot new restaurant
opened with an equally hot crowd
already in place. And why not? The high
arched windows and *objets d'art* from
Paris and Provence look casually chic, as
does the wait staff. The front of the
house includes a long bar, while the
back dining area is quieter and more
suited to the accomplishments of chef
Jamie Mammano. Sautéed foie gras,
steamed mussels, rib-eye steak with
horseradish whipped potatoes, and tenderloin of veal with Gorgonzola polenta
are some winners. Both the bistro and
dinner menus offer thin-crust pizzas,
one topped with ham and quail egg. *221
Columbus Ave., South End, 617/867–
9300. Reservations essential in dining
area. AE, MC, V. No lunch. T stop: Back
Bay. $$$*

8 e-4
RESTAURANT ZINC

Boston is eating up this swanky restau-
rant where chef Nick Tischler has more
than a sure touch with the French-influ-
enced food. After all, *Boston* magazine
crowned him Best New Chef of 1997.
The dining room, full of noise, white

linen, and brown leather banquettes,
can be hard to book, so some people
dine at the imported-from-Paris zinc bar.
Appetizers include littlenecks and cher-
rystones from the raw bar, steak tartare,
vichyssoise, and veal sweetbreads, while
entreés could be pan-seared lobster or
Atlantic salmon, smoked to order. Most
popular dish? The French hangar steak
with *pomme pureé.* Desserts are a must:
opt for profiteroles filled with rich home-
made strawberry ice cream or an unre-
lenting chocolate mousse. *35 Stanhope
St., Back Bay, 617/262–4378. Reservations
essential. AE, D, DC, MC, V. Closed Mon.
No lunch. T stop: Back Bay. $$$*

7 a-3
SANDRINE'S

The Art Nouveau entrance may be reminiscent of a Paris Metro station, but one
taste of the cuisine and you are in
Alsace, the French province that borders
Germany and is known for its hearty
dishes. Chef Raymond Ost wants
Boston to try his crispy frogs' legs, traditional onion soup, cassoulet, *flam-
mekeuche* (a thin dough topped with
onions and bacon) and *coq au riesling*
(chicken cooked in a fine Alsatian wine).
Go Tuesday when the special is a big
beautiful bowl of steamed mussels.
Cream-color walls, yellow, cobalt and
green tiles, and banquettes hued to
match make this one of Harvard
Square's most appealing rooms. Sunday
brunch is offered. *8 Holyoke St., Cambridge, 617/497–5300. AE, D, DC, MC, V.
No smoking. No lunch Mon. T stop: Har-
vard Sq. $$$*

GERMAN

8 h-3
JACOB WIRTH'S

The pigs' knuckles are gone, and so is
the sawdust, but Bostonians and
tourists still gather in this high-ceilinged
watering hole that dates from 1868.
Downtown, close to the theater district,
the restaurant/bar continues to serve
hearty German fare such as knockwurst,
bratwurst, and sauerbraten, along with
its own special dark brew. Just as flavor-
ful is the decor—original down to its
19th-century glass-globe lights, oak pan-
eling, and brass rails. A few sidewalk
tables are set out in warm weather. *31
Stuart St., Downtown, 617/338–8586. AE,
D, DC, MC, V. T stop: Boylston. $$*

GREEK

6 d-4

THE FILL-A-BUSTER

Politicians and journalists have taken to this place—and who can blame them? Hearty-with-a-capital-H lamb kabobs, egg-lemon soup, and spinach-cheese pie are just what the doctor ordered on a blustery, cold, and rainy Boston day. The Mediterranean sun comes up with breakfast here (the homemade muffins are famed), but the day ends early after lunch—no dinner is served. Tables or, for those on a run, takeout. *142 Bowdoin St., Beacon Hill, 617/523–8164. No dinner. T stop: Government Center.* $

HUNGARIAN

8 d-4

CAFÉ BUDAPEST

The music here may be provided by violins, the accompanying lyrics may often be "Will you marry me?" That is, if you could hear them in this festive, noisy landmark meant for romantics at heart. Even if you're not about to propose to your Significant Other, you'll enjoy the Hungarian specialties served up in an ornate, old-world setting. Dishes include cold tart cherry soup, sauerbraten, veal cutlet supreme, chicken paprikas, wiener schnitzel, beef Stroganoff, and the renowned stuffed mushrooms—of course, some dishes are for two. The pastries and crepes are a must, as are the dessert wines and the Viennese coffee. The Budapest Lounge is a Victorian delight, replete with curtained booths for cuddling couples. *Copley Sq. Hotel, 90 Exeter St., Back Bay, 617/266–1979. Reservations essential. Jacket required. AE, DC, MC, V. Closed Mon. T stop: Copley Sq.* $$$$

INDIAN

7 e-6

INDIA PAVILION

In a neighborhood known for its Indian restaurants, this is one of the best. Delicious, wonderfully spicy authentic cuisine is served in pleasant surroundings. There's a good choice of vegetarian dishes, too. The place is known for its good value, especially the luncheon special. Don't miss the tandoori breads and *lassi*, a drink to soothe the tummy. Wine and beer. *17 Central Sq., Cambridge, 617/547–7463. AE, D, DC, MC, V. T stop: Central Sq.* $

8 b-3

KASHMIR

Boston magazine chose this as 1997's best Indian restaurant. Most diners want to take advantage of being on Newbury Street, so the umbrellaed outdoor tables fill first (even when there is a chill in the air). The three downstairs rooms are decorated with photographs of India, traditional and modern Indian art, and fabrics. Start with mulligatawny soup and *samosas* (spicy turnovers), then luxuriate in the tandoori mixed grill of shrimp, chicken, and lamb that has been marinated in yogurt. The lunch buffet is an economical way to taste everything. *279 Newbury St., Back Bay, 617/536–1695. AE, MC, V. T stop: Hynes Convention Center/ICA.* $$

8 a-4

KEBAB-N-KURRY

In this very good Back Bay spot—Boston's oldest Indian restaurant—you can have it mild or you can have it fiery. The basement restaurant is intimate and exotic in a way that appeals to all the foreign students in the neighborhood, as well as tourists and working couples too tired to cook. Tandoori specialties shine, as does the four-alarm lamb vindaloo or the mild saag. Beer and wine only. *30 Massachusetts Ave., Back Bay, 617/536–9835. AE, DC, MC, V.* $$

IRISH

6 g-4

THE BLACK ROSE

Begorrah! This is just the place to chow down on Yankee pot roast, fish-and-chips, and lamb stew before a Celtics game. Gaelic memorabilia, live Irish music, and big-screen sports TV complete the picture. Don't forget to cap off the evening with an Irish coffee. *160 State St., Government Center, 617/742–2286. AE, MC, V. T stop: Government Center.* $

6 f-4

GREEN DRAGON TAVERN

Once known as the "headquarters of the Revolution," this was the erstwhile watering grounds of Samuel Adams, Daniel Webster, and Paul Revere. Today, it still seems ready to welcome the Sons of Liberty (who actually planned the Boston Tea Party here). The decor is lace-curtain colonial, while the menu has gone Irish—beef stew to bangers and mash (plus 12 great brews on tap). *11 Marshall St., Government Center, 617/367–0055. AE, D, MC, V. T stop: Haymarket. $*

5 *f-1*

MATT MURPHY'S

On the surface this handsome Irish pub may seem like a place to stop and down a pint—but it is so much more. The food is most enticing, beginning with heavy dark bread served on a rustic round of wood to start your meal. Sandwiches and salads (with toasted barley) are extraordinary, entreés even better. The fish-and-chips even come wrapped in the *Irish Times*. It is especially popular on Wednesday quiz nights. The fact that diners share big wooden tables makes this a very friendly spot. Sunday brunch is featured. *14 Harvard St., Brookline Village, 617/232–0188. Reservations not accepted. No credit cards. T stop: Brookline Village. $*

ITALIAN

8 *c-3*

ANGELO'S RESTAURANT

It was the killer cioppino—a boullabaisse-type dish of various shellfish cooked in white wine and plum tomato sauce—that put chef/owner Angelo Caruso on the map. Then his homemade pasta received raves. If you come, don't be shy about standing at the open kitchen to see how the pros do it. The dining room is warm and rich, with walls hued in ruby red, mustard, and marble, with curtains and tablecloths in beige. The location across from Copley Square could not be more convenient for shoppers, tourists, and those who don't want to go to the North End. *575 Boylston St., Back Bay, 617/536–4045. AE, DC, MC, V. Beer and wine. T stop: Copley Sq. $$$*

8 *c-3*

ARMANI CAFÉ

Dining in a designer clothing boutique is now as natural as chatting on a cell phone while mulling a plate of pasta. This is one of the prettiest store cafés around, thanks to its mahogany bar, tile floors, and mustard walls. For those who care more about food than fashion, there are ambitious veal, steak, and chicken entreés. Upstairs is a quieter, more serious dining area—but the Newbury Street sidewalk tables, which extend the length of the store, remain especially seductive when summer makes its brief appearance in Boston. *214 Newbury St., Back Bay, 617/437–0909. AE, D, DC, MC, V. T stop: Copley Sq. $$$*

9 *e-5*

ARTÚ

Rosticceria and trattoria in one, Artú is noted for its grilled and roasted meats, such as *agnello arrosto* (roast leg of lamb with marinated eggplant and roasted peppers), but the chef also has a fine way with seafood, as the *quazzetto alla Donato* (seafood stew) reveals. In fact, this is one of the more deliciously serious kitchens in the North End. *6 Prince St., North End, 617/742–4336. AE, MC, V. T stop: Haymarket. $$*

7 *g-6*

BERTUCCI'S PIZZA

These are popular, unpretentious spots that families with children, tourists, college kids, or anyone watching their pennies, have come to rely upon. Wood-fire brick ovens produce delectable thin-crust pizza at this growing chain of restaurants. Have the *quattro stagioni* (mushrooms, peppers, artichokes, and prosciutto); the *sporkie* (sweet sausage and ricotta cheese); or the *melanzana* (eggplant). The Somerville branch even has a Boccie court. *799 Main St., Cambridge, 617/661–8356. Reservations not accepted. AE, D, MC, V. $*

6 *f-4*

22 Merchant's Row, Faneuil Hall, 617/227–7889.

3 *b-4*

21 Brattle St., Cambridge, 617/864–4748.

3 *d-2*

197 Elm St., Somerville, 617/776–9241.

6 *d-5*

BLACK GOOSE

Just across the way from the scholarly ambience of the Boston Atheneum, the Black Goose draws crowds for both lunch and dinner. Corinthian columns adorning the decor and fine *tricolore* salads and pesto pastas accent the menu.

21 Beacon St., 617/720–4500. AE, D, MC, V. T stop: Park St. $$

6 e-5

CAFE MARLIAVE

This downtown old-world Italian-American restaurant has a strong local following. The menu is the usual veal scaloppine, lasagna, manicotti, and swordfish à la Columbo. There is a roof-garden dining room. 10 Bosworth St., Downtown Crossing, 617/423–6340. AE, DC, MC, V. T stop: Downtown Crossing. $$$

8 c-3

DAVIO'S

Popular, brick-walled, and brass-appointed, this Back Bay basement restaurant specializes in modern Northern Italian dining. The emphasis is on fresh seafood, pasta, and veal dishes, and there is a wide choice. Upstairs on the parlor floor is the less expensive café for pasta, pizza, and sandwiches. Luncheon specials are offered daily. In Cambridge, outdoor dining in season overlooks the Charles River, and, in Boston, overlooks Newbury Street. Sunday brunch is offered. 269 Newbury St., Back Bay, 617/262–4810. AE, D, MC, V. T stop: Hynes Convention Center/ICA. $$$, café $$

3 h-5

Royal Sonesta Hotel, Cambridge, 617/661–4810. T stop: Lechmere.

6 b-5

FIGS

Pizza fiends rave about the unusual inventions of Olives's noted chef Todd English. They are thin-crust, Roman-style, and topped with glorious combinations of figs, prosciutto, asparagus, shrimp, leeks, clams, and homemade chicken sausage. Even people who aren't pizza eaters are won over by the crispy concoctions, particularly the Bianco (no tomato sauce). There are always pastas, risottos, and polentas, too. Toss in a Caesar, spinach, or bibb salad, and dessert, and you've got a perfectly satisfying meal. Except during summer months, a Sunday brunch is featured. 42 Charles St., Beacon Hill, 617/742–3447. Reservations not accepted. AE, DC, MC, V. No smoking. No lunch weekdays. T stop: Charles/MGH. $$

1 f-2

67 Main St., Charlestown, 617/242-2229. T stop: Community College.

9 e-6

FIVE NORTH SQUARE

Many find this a romantic setting, and certainly its corner location a few steps from the Paul Revere House enhances the mood. The menu is a combination of updated and old-fashion Italian dishes: cioppino, mussels angelina, and enormous portions of pasta. Desserts of cheesecake, tiramisù, cannoli, and carrot cake are baked on the premises. The waiters wear bow ties and tuxedo vests, but the clientele can dress as they please. 5 North Sq., North End, 617/720–1050. Beer and wine only. Reservations essential. AE, D, DC, MC, V. No smoking. T stop: Haymarket. $$$

6 c-7

GALLERIA ITALIANA

Remember Big Night and you'll feel like powering on to a second course of truffled chicken or skate wing with sausage here. The food is fine and since the owners are from the Abruzzi region of Italy, the dishes often are too. Hand-crafted pasta might be in the shape of ribbons, square spaghetti, "pillows" stuffed with goat cheese and ricotta or "purses" filled with braised duck, while the gourmet antipasto boasts imaginative concoctions, one with rabbit stew and risotto. Small, bustling, and gregarious, this place remains a Boston favorite. 177 Tremont St., Theater District, 617/423–2092. Reservations essential. AE, D, DC, MC, V. Closed Mon. T stop: Boylston St. $$$

9 e-5

GIACOMO'S

Peace or privacy are not part of the picture at this small, crowded hot spot in the North End. But if you are in a festive mood and really hungry, the open kitchen turns out wonderful charcoal-grilled seafood as well as chicken and sausage; the house specialty is frutta di mare (seafood stew). The well-known Giacomo sauce is a tomato-base lobster sauce with Bechamel. The South End location is more refined and there are a few stools at the chef's bar to watch the oven action. The menus differ slightly but share the same high standards. Beer and wine only. 355 Hanover St., North End, 617/523–9026. Reservations not accepted.

No credit cards. No lunch. T stop:
Haymarket. $$$

 e-5

431 Columbus Ave., South End, 617/536–
5723. T stop: Back Bay.

B c-6

LA BETTOLA

Marisa Iocco and Rita D'Angelo, co-
owners of Galleria Italiano, perfectly
timed the opening of their newest
restaurant with the blossoming of a
neighborhood that has become both
charming and trendy. This welcome
addition to the South End is meant to
feel like an alleyway café, with a striking
burnt orange foyer and a general view of
the kitchen. The nightly prix fixe is the
best way to taste the regional Italian
food, which is given a spin with Mediter-
ranean and Asian accents. Start with
potato cannelloni with morel mush-
rooms or seared skate wing with fried
capers. Entreés vary from monkfish
wrapped with pancetta to New Zealand
lamb with carrot dumplings. The side-
walk tables are usually the first to be
filled. Sunday brunch is featured. 480
Columbus Ave., South End, 617/236–5252.
Reservations essential. AE, D, DC, MC, V.
No lunch. T stop: Mass. Ave. $$$

7 g-6

LA GROCERIA

Everything about this place is old-style
except its look, which sparkles after a
recent renovation brought a pink and
green palette to the place. The pasta is
fresh and made in-house, as are the
seafood, chicken, and veal dishes at this
family-owned Northern Italian restaurant. Tiramisù and cakes are homemade. 853 Main St., Cambridge, 617/547–
9258. Reservations not accepted. AE, D,
DC, MC, V. T stop: Central Sq. $$

9 e-6

MAMMA MARIA

A very pretty, romantic destination in
the North End, Mamma Maria is set in a
19th-century town house and offers truly
inventive nuova cucina fare. Risotto-
stuffed quail with pear brandy, duckling
tortellini, beef with Barolo are some of
the delights of chef Raymond Gillespie.
Dining upstairs in the enclosed patio
with a view of the city skyline is special.
Good wine list. 3 North Sq., North End,
617/523–0077. AE, DC, MC, V. No lunch.
T stop: Haymarket. $$$

B d-3

PAPA RAZZI

These are the Boston outposts of a
chain of sleek, Armaniesque restaurants
that really know how to please the customer. Almost anything can be cooked
to order and the dishes are attractively
presented. Every evening there is a different ricotta special. The veal scallopini
is made with gourmet bread crumbs,
vegetarians can opt for angel-hair pasta
sauteéd with basil and tomatoes, and all
should enjoy the wood-fired peaches
with vanilla gelato for dessert. A weekend brunch is offered. 271 Dartmouth
St., Back Bay, 617/536–9200. AE, DC,
MC, V. T stop: Copley Sq. $$

2 d-1

Cambridgeside Galleria, Cambridge, 617/
577–0009. T stop: Lechmere.

B f-3

PIGNOLI

This sister restaurant to Biba, also
owned by famed Lydia Shire, attracts a
spiffy crowd for its fine food and fun
decor. Pig tails—not pignoli (which
means pine nuts)—are the leitmotif
here and adorn everything from the Ter-
razzo marble floors to the wooden
chairs. You will have to see for yourself
what is hanging from the ceiling. Presid-
ing over this whimsy is a granite bust of
Bacchus, while hand-painted silk lights
hang low over the bar, where a sparkly
late-night crowd congregates. The menu
here is less expensive than Biba, more
straightforward, and can only be catego-
rized as rustic contemporary Italian.
One seasonal menu includes dishes
made with venison or sea bass. Home-
made pastas are offered daily. Sidewalk
tables are appreciated in a neighbor-
hood with few alfresco choices. 79 Park
Sq. Plaza, Theater District/Back Bay, 617/
338–7500. Reservations essential. AE, D,
DC, MC, V. No lunch Sun. T stop: Arling-
ton. $$$

9 b-4

PIZZERIA REGINA

There are those who call this "the best
thin-crust pizza north of Ray's" (that's
in New Yawk, ya know). People magazine named the Regina's America's
"second best pizza" (that's right, Ray's
made number one). No one denies it is
oily, but hard-core fans believe that is
part of the appeal. Though there are
branches in Faneuil Hall and Brookline,
try to get to the original source in the

North End. Wine and beer only. 11½ Thatcher St., North End, 617/227–0765. Reservations not accepted. No credit cards. T stop: Haymarket. $

8 d-3

PIZZERIA UNO RESTAURANT & BAR

The pizza here is Chicago-style (thick crust, topped with vegetables, chicken, shrimp, or sausage) and so is the cheesecake. There is also steak, ribs, salads, submarines, pasta, and even wraps. The Kids Kombo is a basket of chicken "thumbs," mozzarella sticks, and fries. These predictable but attractive chain restaurants offer full table service. 731 Boylston St., Back Bay, 617/267–8554. Reservations not accepted. AE, D, DC, MC, V. T stop: Copley Sq. $

8 b-6

280 Huntington Ave., Symphony, 617/424–1697. T stop: Symphony.

7 a-3

22 John F. Kennedy St., Cambridge, 617/497–1530. T stop: Harvard Sq. Other locations in Faneuil Hall, Kenmore Sq., and Porter Sq., Cambridge.

9 e-5

POMODORO

It's noisy, it's crowded, some might even find it claustrophobic. But since it's impossible to fit any more tables into this tiny storefront, you'll have to line up with the rest of the world clamoring for a meal here. The "new" Italian dishes are more generous than gourmet, yet the preparations are consistent winners. One dish everyone adores is the pan-roasted monkfish with clams and saffron risotto. Watching the chefs in the kitchen is the highest form of entertainment. 319 Hanover St., North End, 617/367–4348. Reservations not accepted. No credit cards. No smoking. T stop: Haymarket. $$$

6 b-5

RISTORANTE TOSCANO

Want a Florentine trattoria in Beacon Hill? Head to this Boston favorite for carefully prepared Florentine and Northern Italian specialties served in a refined and sleek setting. The Italian chef, Vinicio Paoli, takes great care with his ingredients and creates a delectable carpaccio, rack of lamb, risotto, or smoked salmon pasta. 41 Charles St., Beacon Hill, 617/723–4090. AE. No lunch Sun. T stop: Charles/MGH. $$$

2 b-5

SORENTO'S

Even if it looks like just another trendy restaurant with sponged yellow walls and an open kitchen, it isn't—there's a very fine hand in the kitchen, with a winning way and a creative touch. Appetizers are standouts, the linguine is homemade (as are the addictive sourdough rolls, served warm), while college students on tight budgets and couples on dates share pizza and salads. The round sidewalk tables are a treat in warm weather because the street is slightly removed from the urban bustle. 86 Peterborough St., Fenway, 617/424–7070. AE, MC, V. No lunch Sat. and Sun. T stop: Kenmore Sq. $

8 d-3

SPASSO

This trattoria located in the historic Vendome (once the city's most fashionable hotel) has a sparkling, fun atmosphere. The Italian food may not be the most authentic, but diners seem pleased with the grilled pizzas, variety of pastas, herb-roasted half chicken, and daily fish specials. The bar is a neighborhood gathering place. The below street-level courtyard dining is lovely in season. A Sunday brunch is offered. 160 Commonwealth Ave., Back Bay, 617/536–8656. AE, D, DC, MC, V. No lunch. T stop: Copley Sq. $$

9 d-6

TRATTORIA A SCALINATELLA

Just upstairs from the wildly popular Caffé Paradiso espresso bar, this is a tiny, Tuscan-style (brick-walled, wood-beamed, fireplace-bedecked) treasure. The kitchen is one of the most serious around; Treat yourself to the fabulous veal chop roasted over apple wood and finished with a chianti classico glaze, or casarecci mara bosco (pasta with porcini mushrooms and clams), or rack of wild boar, and the zillion-calorie Sicilian bomba (sponge cake made with ricotta, rum, and marzipan) for dessert. Accompanying all this is one of Massachusetts's best wine lists ($23 to $20,000). With a place this small and fashionable (you might be dining next to a Kennedy or a Bruin), reservations are essential.

253 Hanover St., North End, 617/742–8240. AE, MC, V. No lunch. T stop: Haymarket. $$$

6 g-5

TRATTORIA IL PANINO

A stylish local chain of restaurants (that includes the quickly multiplying Il Panino Express), these spots offer an accessible array of pasta, veal, and chicken dishes, risottos, and pizza. The mozzarella is fresh, the olive oil is pure virgin, and the surroundings are attractive. At the downtown branch, there's outdoor seating/dancing and a Sunday brunch. 295 Franklin St., Downtown, 617/338–1000. AE, DC, MC, V. T stop: Downtown Crossing. $$

6 f-4

Faneuil Hall, 617/573–9700. T stop: Haymarket.

9 d-5

11 Parmenter St., North End, 617/720–5720. T stop: Haymarket.

7 a-3

UPSTAIRS AT THE PUDDING

Charming, theatrical—after all, it's on the top floor of Harvard's historic Hasty Pudding Club—and purely Cambridgian, this is a bright spot to enjoy fine Italian-style cuisine. The interior decor is colorful—green walls, red linens, theater posters—and the tweedy and preppy crowd want food that is tasty and beautifully presented, and they usually get it. Boston magazine chose the garden terrace here—all flowers and bougainvillea—as the area's best outdoor dining spot several years running. 10 Holyoke St., Cambridge, 617/864–1933. AE, MC, V. Sun. brunch. T stop: Harvard Sq. $$$

JAPANESE

6 e-8

GINZA

Ever have sushi called Fashion Maki, Spider Maki, and B-52 Maki? Well, here's the place to enjoy them, and even if you don't order such crazy sushi, chances are you'll get reliably fresh fixings, as the gokudo maki—yummy mackerel, pickled ginger, scallions, mountain burdock root, and cucumber—attests. You might sit at the sushi bar and watch real masters at work, but the advantage of a table is that you can tackle the Ginza Cruise, a wooden boat loaded with deli-

cacies and worth the $23.95 per person. This place is so popular that it could be open around the clock. Right now it is open until 4 AM Tuesdays through Saturdays and 2 AM Sundays and Mondays. 16 Hudson St., Chinatown, 617/338–2261. AE, D, DC, MC, V. T stop: South Station. $$

4 h-5

1002 Beacon St., Brookline, 617/566–9688. T stop: St. Mary's.

8 c-4

GYUHAMA

After 10:30 PM the strobe lights go on, the volume goes up, and the waitresses don leather jackets—it's time for rock and roll sushi! But come here then for this place's always fresh sushi and sashimi. The sushi chefs at this Back Bay basement may look severe but when you taste their creations, you'll appreciate their concentration. Whether you eat raw fish or teriyaki, save room for the refreshing green tea ice cream. Tatami rooms are great for large parties. 827 Boylston St., Back Bay, 617/437–0188. Reservations not accepted. T stop: Copley Sq. $$

3 c-1

KOTOBUKIYA

One of six Japanese restaurants collectively known as the Common Market, this sushi bar is one of the area's most economical places for hand rolls of salmon or tuna, nigiri or maki. The great thing about this group of restaurants is how they each offer different kinds of food—ramen, tempura, teriyaki, etc.—and how you can order from one and sit at another. Located in the Porter Exchange building. 1815 Massachusetts Ave., Cambridge, 617/492–4655. AE, D, DC, MC, V. T stop: Porter Sq. $

8 b-3

MIYAKO

This two-story restaurant is on one of the busiest corners of Newbury Street, so, naturally, its outdoor tables are in high demand. So is the sushi—judging from the lightning-quick moves of chef/owner Hideo Noguchi. With the colors of the tuna, salmon, and bass deep and rich, you know everything will taste fresh. Those who don't indulge in raw fish can eat rolls made with shiso leaf, avocado, and cucumber, or opt for seaweed salad and quail eggs. Waitresses in kimonos and slippers keep the hot sake coming. 279A Newbury St., Back

Bay, 617/236—0222. AE, D, DC, MC, V. T stop: Hynes Convention Center/ICA. $$

6 *g-5*

NARA

You could easily overlook this little restaurant tucked away on a tiny street, but head for this small sushi bar with wooden booths for the economical lunch special—served in a tray, it comes complete with salad and fruit. As you devour the chef's choice of raw fish and a little covered bowl of rice, you are served endless cups of barley tea. *85 Wendell St., Downtown, 617/338—5935. AE, D, DC, MC, V. Closed weekends. T stop: Downtown Crossing. $*

6 *g-5*

SAKURA-BANA

Based in the Financial District, this good low-frills spot draws a lunch-time crowd eager for a sushi fix. Sit at the sushi bar if you want to learn how to make maki with softshell crab. The menu also offers teriyaki and tempura. Sake, beer, and wine. *57 Broad St., Downtown, 617/542—4311. AE, DC, MC, V. T stop: State St. $$*

6 *f-5*

TATSUKICHI

Near Quincy Marketplace, this is an authentic spot for fresh sushi and sashimi. There is also *kushiage* (lightly batter-fried chicken or veggies on skewers served with two sauces). The food draws a large Japanese clientele. There is entertainment nightly in the Karaoke Bar, where light fare is served. Western or tatami room seating is offered. The sushi bar is the place to sit if you want to watch the chef create. *189 State St., Downtown, 617/720—2468. AE, D, DC, MC, V. T stop: Haymarket. $$*

KOREAN

8 *d-6*

JAE'S CAFE AND GRILL

Jae's restaurants boast extensive menus of Korean, Japanese, and eclectic dishes, all given a Californian spin. If anything, there are too many choices—-noodles, sauces, meat or vegetarian combinations galore. Happily, almost everything is good (especially if you like ginger and garlic!), so it's not surprising each restaurant attracts a happening crowd.

Korean specialties include steam or fried dumplings, vegetable kebab with peanut sauce, great curries and grilled dishes, *yukhai* (marinated raw beef), and kimchi. There is also a Korean and Japanese sushi bar. The Theater District spot has three floors and offers traditional Korean tableside grilling. *520 Columbus Ave., South End, 617/421—9405. AE, DC, MC, V. T stop: Massachusetts. Ave. $$*

7 *g-3*

1281 Cambridge St., Cambridge, 617/497—8380. T stop: Central Sq.

6 *d-7*

112 Stuart St., 617/451—7788, Theater District. T stop: Arlington.

7 *e-5*

KOREANA

The attraction here is the grill built into the table where you cook your own meat, if not your own tongue—watch out: the beef can come out scalding hot! The cooking is fun, and so are the condiments: bean sprouts, kimchi, fried zucchini, and seaweed. If you are lost in the process, a waitress or fellow diner will steer you. There is also a nice sushi bar here where you can experiment with such exotica as a bowl of raw fish and lettuce that comes topped with salmon roe and a quail egg. Along with some Japanese dishes, there is also a selection of Korean sushi. *154 Prospect St., Cambridge, 617/576—8661. AE, D, MC, V. T stop: Central Sq. $$*

MEDITERRANEAN

3 *b-4*

CASABLANCA

This restaurant has a great deal to offer in a bustling area with more stores than great restaurants. Chef Ana Sortun stretches the bounds of creativity with her North African/Mediterranean dishes. The location is idyllic, in the heart of Harvard Square and downstairs from the wonderful art-house cinema, the Brattle. The decor is consistent with the name—rattan chairs, ceiling fans, and murals of Bogie and Bergman. Eat in the active bar/café or the quieter, non-smoking dining room. *40 Brattle St., Cambridge, 617/876—0999. Reservations essential in dining room. AE, MC, V. Weekend brunch. T stop: Harvard Sq. $$$*

8 c-6

CLAREMONT CAFÉ

Clearly a restaurant that tastes as good as it looks! An authentic artiness emanates from this place—and we're talking the crowd as well as the original paintings and photographs hanging on the walls. The food is an interesting mix of Mediterranean and South American influences, with specials like Tunisian lamb chop with potato gratin. If the test of a chef is the simplest of dishes, the roast chicken here gets high marks. At the more complicated end of the spectrum is spinach ravioli stuffed with pumpkin and goat cheese. The sidewalk tables are a big draw, especially for brunch. A little café room next to the restaurant area takes care of the spillover and offers a more casual setting. Weekend brunch is offered. *535 Columbus Ave., South End, 617/247–9001. Reservations not accepted. AE, MC, V. No smoking. Closed Mon. T stop: Massachusetts Ave. $$$*

6 b-5

LALA ROKH

Tucked away on a quaint Beacon Hill street is this little bit of Persia. Azita Bina-Seibel and brother Babak Bina want to introduce diners to traditional food from their homeland, and do so in an old town house, in rooms painted pale yellow and hung with family photographs and maps. The Eastern Mediterranean dishes challenge the diner: While some of the ingredients are tried-and-true (such as garlic, yogurt, eggplant, lamb, and mint), the combinations are novel. The crowning course is a dessert of saffron-and-rosewater scented ice cream sprinkled with pistachios. *97 Mt. Vernon St., Beacon Hill, 617/720–5511. AE, DC, MC, V. No smoking. No lunch. T stop: Charles/MGH. $$*

 b-4

RIALTO

Few Bostonians were surprised when Jody Adams won the 1997 James Beard Award for Best Chef Northeast. She calls her menu Mediterranean, and her strong flavors virtually transport diners to the sun-drenched regions of France, Italy, and Spain. The raw beef salad is drizzled with truffle oil, the halibut is braised in vermouth, and the oxtail-stuffed cabbage is served on polenta. But save room for the spectacular desserts—you can feast on them alone!

Soft lighting, earth colors, and banquette seating add to the romance of an evening at one of Cambridge's most privileged restaurants. *Charles Hotel, One Bennett St., Cambridge, 617/864–1200. Reservations essential. AE, DC, MC, V. No smoking. No lunch. T stop: Harvard Sq. $$$$*

MEXICAN, SOUTHWESTERN, AND TEX-MEX

8 b-4

CACTUS CLUB

Complete with a stuffed buffalo head over the bar and other Southwest touches such as animal skulls, the decor at this overblown Santa Fe spot is a hoot. The large portions of Southwestern dishes such as fajitas, baby back ribs, chicken barbecue, and grilled meats are satisfying, and the humongous drinks encourage finding someone to share them with. The young and the raucous head to the bar, while the spacious dining is more civilized. *939 Boylston St., Back Bay, 617/236–0200. AE, MC, V. Sun. brunch. T stop: Hynes Convention Center/ICA. $$*

7 a-3

CASA MEXICO

Follow your nose to this small, informal Harvard Square basement Mexican restaurant. Brick floors and Mexican tiles set the scene for chili rellenos, enchiladas de camerones, mole poblano (that's garlic, onion, chile, and chocolate), tostados de chorizo. Of course, flan for dessert. *75 Winthrop St., Cambridge, 617/491–4552. AE, CB, DC, MC, V. T stop: Harvard Sq. $$*

8 b-3

CASA ROMERO

This is a sweet place that needs the public's TLC. Low-beam ceilings, colorful ceramic tile tables, wrought iron, leather chairs, plants and flowers convince you that you are in someone's home. You are. Senor Leo Romero, a former teacher who is active in the community, is a real host in his casa. And the Classic Mexican food of salads, ceviche, chicken mole poblano, enchiladas verdes, camerones Veracruz, and avocado or garlic soup, are family recipes. The walled garden patio is a serene escape from the Newbury Street bustle. Did we mention their great sangria and week-day lunch specials? *30 Gloucester St., Back Bay, 617/536–4341. D, DC, MC, V. No Smoking. T stop: Hynes Convention Center/ICA. $$*

8 *e-3*

COTTONWOOD CAFÉ

This is Cordon Bleu Barbecue—a fetching place (located within the Robert A. M. Stern–designed Houghton Mifflin Building) to enjoy Tex-Mex specialties amid the etched-glass lizards and cactus skeletons of two sophisticated rooms. You'll find the standards on the menu, but the chef can get those taste-buds really dancing with such selections as a *barbecola*—chicken in bourbon barbecue sauce—or the *paella paz*, a mouthwatering delight with grilled chicken and shrimp. Wash every-thing down with a fresh-fruit margarita. It's popular, so reserve. *222 Berkeley St., Back Bay, 617/247–2225. AE, D, MC, V. T stop: Arlington. $$*

6 *d-6*

FAJITAS & 'RITAS

You might find a three-piece suiter from the Bank of Boston kicking-back at this fun place, using the crayons provided to doodle up his tablecloth and (yes, it's allowed!) the neighboring walls. Of course, after a hard, stress-filled day, there's nothing like a good chicken bur-rito and a wicked margarita. *25 West St., Downtown, 617/426–1222. Closed Sun. AE, MC, V. T stop: Downtown Crossing. $*

4 *h-5*

SOL AZTECA

Recommended for the consistency of the food and the conviviality of the atmosphere, Sol Azteca is one of Boston's Mexican mainstays. It offers several cheerful dining rooms in which to enjoy mole poblano, puerco en adobo, queso asado, enchiladas verdes, and their delicious tasty sangria and Mexican beer. *914A Beacon St., 617/262–0909. AE, MC, V. No lunch. T stop: St. Mary's. $$*

NIGHT-OWL DINING

No one can accuse Boston of rolling up the sidewalk now. Restaurants are open late in neighborhoods all over the map.

Atlas Bar and Grill (Bars and Burgers)
Fun, high-tech games, and a big menu to boot bring the crowds here.

Chau Chow City (Chinese)
Go on—indulge that 3 AM craving for an egg roll.

Franklin Café (American)
Gen-X young, the crowd here chows down on the fabu food to all hours.

The Good Life (Bars and Burgers)
Frank Sinatra is crooning on the sound system—reason alone for having another martini?

Gyuhama (Japanese)
Incredible raw fish amid a rock 'n' roll atmosphere.

Mistral (French)
Once you take in the scene arena, check out the divine grilled pizza with shaved ham and quail eggs.

Parish Café (Bars and Burgers)
There's nothing simple about these sandwiches—all named after the regional cult-chefs who concocted them.

Trident (Breakfast)
Breakfast, books, chili, and more—served until midnight.

MIDDLE EASTERN

3 *b-4*

ALGIERS

The fact that this is in the same building as the Brattle Theater is more important than the food. A Middle Eastern restaurant on two levels, Algiers is popular with local artists, students, and people who want to talk and take their time. They do so over sandwiches, soups, hummus, stuffed grape leaves, and feta salads. Large selection of coffees and teas. *40 Brattle St., Cambridge, 617/492–1557. T stop: Harvard Sq. $*

8 *b-3*

JAFFA

This simple, brick-lined restaurant is a half-block from scene-heavy Newbury Street, yet worlds away in terms of pre-tensions. Each table is adorned with a single flower, and that is about the extent of the decor—but the lemon- and mint-scented tabouli tastes like it was just made, and the grilled kabob sandwiches are brimming with chicken and lamb. Naturally, there are grape leaves, falafels, hummus, and baba ghanoush. Prices are reasonable, with specials offered at weekday lunch. The small wine list features wines from Italy, Israel, and California. *48 Gloucester St., Back Bay, 617/536–0230. Reservations not accepted. AE, D, MC, V. T stop: Hynes Convention Center/ICA. $*

MUSEUM MUNCHES

2 *a-6*
CAFÉ AT THE GARDNER
During the the Gilded Age, Isabella Stewart Gardner would offer refreshments of champagne and doughnuts to guests at her spectacular art-stuffed Fenway Court. Today, the connoisseurs who throng the Gardner can continue to satisfy more than their aesthetic lives by heading to the Conservatory, where the museum's café is elegantly housed. Smoked-salmon club sandwiches, anyone? In fact, all quiches, sandwiches, and desserts are tastefully proper. In summer weather, you can enjoy dining on the garden terrace. *280 The Fenway, The Fens, 617/566–1088. No dinner. T stop: Museum. $$*

2 *b-6*
FINE ARTS RESTAURANT
This spot offers a feast for the tastebuds after the Museum of Fine Arts' Gauguins, Renoirs, and Copleys have presented a feast for the eyes. You used to think of steam-table cafeteria food when chowing down in a museum—but how about fresh saffron fettucine with Maine lobster and crabmeat and leeks *concassé*? Or braised lamb shank with root vegetables in a Madeira sauce? Jim Dodge, author of three cookbooks, has made this one of the more delicious restaurants in Boston, offering up food that is tied into the seasonal harvests of the Northeast. Better: he often tailors half of his menu to sync with the current in-house art blockbuster. "Picasso: The Early Years" gave you a taste of Pablo's Spain with such delights as sweet clam and *bacalao* fritters with roasted apples and red onions, or a crisp calamari chili *aioli*; The big 1998 Victoria and Albert Museum exhibition showcases delicacies of the Victorian Empire. The room is a quiet, stylish haven that has touches of Jazz-period 1920's elegance and over-

looks the museum's grand three-story Galleria. Lunch is offered Monday through Saturday, dinner Wednesday through Friday, while a brunch is featured on Sunday. *465 Huntington Ave., The Fens, 617/369–3474. AE, MC, V. T stop: Museum. $$*

PORTUGUESE

7 *f-3*
CASA PORTUGAL
A small, informal, and welcoming authentic Portuguese restaurant, Casa Portugal is located near Inman Square, a Portuguese neighborhood. The emphasis is on hearty pork and seafood dishes such as the marinated pork with clams and a mean squid stew. Portuguese wines and homemade pastries are also available. *1200 Cambridge St., Cambridge, 617/491–8880. AE, MC, V. D. No lunch. Nearest T stop: Central Sq. $$*

7 *f-3*
SUNSET CAFÉ
The wine and beer is from Portugal— and so is the clientele. This Inman Square neighborhood eatery serves up spicy and satisfying Portuguese food, in plain but pleasant surroundings. The specialties are octopus soup and *chourico* (Portuguese sausage). Also Portuguese music Friday and Saturday from 8:30 PM to midnight. *857 Cambridge St., Cambridge, 617/547–2938. AE, DC, MC, V. T stop: Central Sq. $$*

ROOMS WITH A VIEW

6 *f-5*
BAY TOWER ROOM
Spectacular is the only way to describe the view of the waterfront and the harbor, and you drink it all in from the 33rd floor here. A private dining club during the day, this place becomes a softly lit romantic restaurant open to the public in the evening. Thanks to the view, the American fare plays only a supporting role here. In the adjacent lounge *great* martinis and dance music Friday and Saturday evenings. Jacket required, no jeans. *60 State St., 33rd floor, Downtown, 617/723–1666. Reservations essential. AE, DC, MC, V. No lunch. Closed Sun. T stop: State St. $$$$*

6 *h-5*

ROWES WHARF RESTAURANT

A major draw in one of Boston's best hotels, this place has wonderful views. Harbor and skyline vistas only enhance the plush upstairs dining room and top regional American cuisine offered here by chef Daniel Bruce (via New York's "21" and Le Cirque). Seafood specialties include crab cakes, Maine lobster sausage over lemon pasta, basil-wrapped halibut, and lemon and sage-roast chicken. Bruce is known to lead his staff on mushroom hunts and you could be tasting those finds in his signature dish, stone-ground polenta. *Boston Harbor Hotel, 70 Rowes Wharf, 2nd floor, Waterfront, 617/439–3995. Reservations essential. AE, DC, MC, V. Sun. brunch. T stop: Aquarium. $$$$*

LET'S DO BRUNCH!

Weekend brunch has become a way of life for natives and visitors alike.

29 Newbury (American)
One of Newbury Street's most sought-after places for people watching.

Bob the Chef's (Soul/Southern)
A mellow place with down-home meals that will satisfy the hungriest diners.

Claremont Café (Mediterranean)
The South End's hippest, most relaxed spot has the fixings for a chic yet informal Sunday.

Daddy-O's (American)
Chef Paul Sussman's dishes boast flavors and ingredients from all over the map.

Flora (American)
A stylish bank in the '30s has now become a memorable restaurant for the '90s.

Matt Murphy's (Irish)
Chef/owner Matt Murphy certainly knows how to start a Sunday.

Mucho Gusto Café (Cuban)
A storefront filled with collectibles and tasty Cuban-American cooking.

Tremont 647 (American)
Come as you are, but bring a sense of humor. The wait staff wears their pajamas on Sunday.

---

3 *e-8*

SPINNAKER ITALIA

Panoramic city and river views from the area's only revolving dining room make this a romantic choice for tourists, parents visiting their college kids, and wide-eyed couples. Come for drinks or Northern Italian dinner. *Hyatt Regency Hotel, 575 Memorial Dr., 16th floor, Cambridge, 617/492–1234. AE, D, DC, MC, V. No lunch. T stop: Boston University. $$$*

8 *c-4*

TOP OF THE HUB

What culinary masterpieces could top the view here from the 52nd floor of New England's second-tallest building. The greatest draw is the scenery, particularly at sunset. Still, the chef tries his best with a six-course tasting menu "in harmony with the sea" for two people, lamb with couscous, or grilled swordfish. Lunch ranges from a pastrami sandwich to rare tuna salad. Music is played nightly in the adjoining lounge for dancing. No jeans or sneakers, please. Sunday brunch is an occasion. *Prudential Center, Back Bay, 617/536–1775. Reservations essential. AE, DC, MC, V. No smoking. T stop: Hynes Convention Center/ICA. $$$*

The following also offer a delicious view with dinner:

Anthony's Pier 4 (Fish and Seafood)

Biba (Contemporary)

The Chart House (Steak)

Jimmy's Harborside Restaurant (Fish and Seafood)

SOUL/SOUTHERN

8 *c-7*

BOB THE CHEF'S RESTAURANT

Photographs of jazz legends and a live quartet help get you in the right frame of mind at this place, located on the South End/Roxbury border. Brick and yellow-sponge walls make a pleasant setting for spareribs, pork chops, or "glorified chicken," all of which come with corn bread and sides of collard greens, candied yams, or black-eyed peas. Down-home desserts are peach cobbler and sweet-potato pie. Sunday brunch is fun. *604 Columbus Ave, South End, 617/536–*

6204. AE, D, MC, V. Wine and beer. Closed Mon. $$

5 *h-5*

JAKES BOSS BARBECUE

The menu says "B-B-B-Bad to the bone" and *Boston* magazine says this place offers the best barbecue in town. Jake, in fact, has a serious reputation to uphold. Before this location across from Doyle's, he was manning the pit at Jake & Earl's, next to the famous East Coast Grill in Cambridge. And the choice of meats? Oink, Moo, or Cluck. The sauces sound just as fun: One Bomb, Two Bomb, or Three Bomb. *342 Washington St., Jamaica Plain, 617/983–3701. Reservations not accepted. D, DC, MC, V. Closed Mon. T stop: Forest Hills. $*

 d-1

REDBONES

Don't wear your best white shirt to this funky, noisy rib joint—the food is finger-licking good and served in heaps. No wonder the locals adore this place. So much so that reservations won't mean you won't have to wait—but you won't regret it. No one leaves hungry after heaping ribs, brisket, fried catfish, wood-grilled chicken, and sausage with succotash, dirty rice (cajun rice with chicken livers, ground pork, and peppers), corn fritters, and hushpuppies. For those who can't decide on a beer, the bar wall has dial-a-brew. All-you-can-eat lunch specials keeps this place hopping all day. Grab a seat at the little counter in the back of the restaurant if you want to watch the real action and the massive number of rib slabs as they are cooked and cut. *55 Chester St., Somerville, 617/628–2200. No credit cards. T stop: Davis Sq. $$*

SPANISH

7 *d-1*

DALI RESTAURANT

As original and whimsical as the painter himself, this restaurant turns a mundane meal into a party. The facade is purple, the interior is red and festooned with dried peppers, cured hams and braids of garlic, and the intoxicating taste of garlic is in almost every dish. An authentic Iberian specialty is the fresh fish baked in salt. Or feast on tapas of sautéed mushrooms or pork sausages

with figs. The marinated olives are practically a holy rite. Pitchers of sangria disappear quickly and there is an extensive Spanish wine selection. *415 Washington St., Somerville, 617/661–3254. AE, MC, V. No lunch. T stop: Harvard Sq. $$*

7 *a-3*

IRUNA

It's no wonder this small old-world Spanish restaurant is a favorite with students. The portions are generous, the prices low. Delicious flan and chocolate mousse for dessert top off a hearty meal, while the patio is tucked away from the bustling Square—a wonderful spot to drink sangria in the summer. *56 John F. Kennedy St., Cambridge, 617/868–5633. Closed Sun. T stop: Harvard Sq. $*

STEAK

8 *b-4*

THE CAPITAL GRILLE

A classic oak-paneled and brass-appointed New York-style steak house, the Capital has garnered a reputation for its bountiful portions of dry-aged (on premises) steaks, and lobsters, lamb, and veal chops; seafood and chicken as well. Amenities include phone service at every table and, for regular patrons, private wine storage bins. Inside the front entrance, you may view the steaks "aging." Valet parking available. *359 Newbury St., Back Bay, 617/262–8900. AE, DC, MC, V. No lunch. T stop: Hynes Convention Center/ICA. $$$$*

 h-4

THE CHART HOUSE

Located in the historic Gardner Building—built circa 1760, it was a storehouse for tea prior to the famous Party—this place is the Boston outpost for a locally popular chain steak house. Three floors of brick walls, exposed beams, and old nautical memorabilia make a handsome setting, especially when combined with the lovely view of Boston Harbor from the upstairs windows. Besides steak, there is seafood and prime rib. Mud pie is a special dessert, as is the homemade cheesecake. *60 Long Wharf, Waterfront, 617/227–1576. AE, DC, MC, V. T stop: Aquarium. $$$*

8 *f-3*

GRILL 23 & BAR

Formerly the grand lobby of the old Salada Tea Building, this prestigious restaurant reeks of brass, wood paneling, marble columns, and, now (in the smoking section), cigar smoke. Gourmands are drawn by the 18-ounce New York sirloin, the aged prime beef, the grilled fish and vegetables, and the great hash browns, not to mention sumptuous desserts like pumpkin cheesecake with white chocolate sauce. The wine list runs the gamut from $20 to $200; sommelier Alicia Towns knows just the Pino Noir to complement that Wild Striped Bass in Fennel Broth. The chef's table offers a tasting menu. Jacket and tie suggested. *161 Berkeley St., Back Bay, 617/542–2255. Reservations essential. Jacket and tie suggested. AE, D, DC, MC, V. No lunch. T stop: Back Bay. $$$$*

8 *d-3*

MORTON'S OF CHICAGO

This Chicago import has Boston steaklovers raving over humongous portions of prime aged beef. The 24-ounce porterhouse is their major claim to fame and the macho setting appeals to businessmen who power-dine on expense accounts. *1 Exeter Pl., Back Bay, 617/266–5858. Jacket and tie required. Reservations essential. AE, DC, MC, V. T stop: Copley Sq. $$$*

8 *d-4*

PALM

When the Boston outpost of this national chain opened last year, the big news was the walls festooned with caricatures of local politicians and sports celebrities like Gov. Weld, Larry Bird, and Bobby Orr. The steady stream of suits and designer jeans seems to indicate this is a place "to see and be seen." Carnivores come for the chance to order over-size aged steaks, and indulge in a cigar and martini as well. *200 Dartmouth St. in the Westin Hotel, Back Bay, 617/867–9292. Reservations essential. AE, D, DC, MC, V. No lunch weekends. T stop: Back Bay. $$$$*

SWISS

6 *d-6*

CAFÉ SUISSE

Swiss continental fare with frequently occurring festivals of regional European cuisine is served in a contemporary set-

ting. There's a buffet breakfast daily. Sundays offers up a jazz brunch. *Swissotel Boston—The Lafayette, One Ave. de Lafayette, Downtown Crossing, 617/451–2600. AE, D, DC, MC, V. T stop: Downtown Crossing. $$$*

TEA

8 *g-2*

BRISTOL LOUNGE

Sumptuously appointed, the Bristol Lounge is one of the attractions of the luxe Four Seasons Hotel. Its rooms offer an unsurpassed view of the Public Garden and the variety of seating arrangements—loveseats to straight-back chairs—brings comfort to weary shoppers, hotel guests, and out-of-towners, who appreciate an elaborate and traditional tea, served daily 3 to 4:30 PM. Full tea ($17.50) includes a scone with real Devonshire cream, delicate pastries, and tea sandwiches. Tea Royal ($24.50) is all of the above, plus a Kir Royale. Dress as you please. *200 Boylston St., Back Bay, 617/388–4400. AE, D, DC, MC, V. T stop: Arlington. $$*

8 *f-2*

THE RITZ-CARLTON

Latter-day heroines out of a Henry James short story, grande dames, and ladies with shopping bags from Chanel enjoy the Ritz-Carlton's dainty teas, served in a second-floor lounge. Soigné waiters make sure their tea cups are never less than half-filled, a harpist soothes the afternoon away with the tinkle of Mozart, and the ambience of mahogany furniture and tea silver-strainers lulls all back to a gentler age. Afternoon tea ($16.50) is served daily 3 to 5:30 PM and includes a three-tier tray of sandwiches, and scones with real Devonshire cream and pastries; light tea ($12.50) is minus the sandwiches. Here is your chance to dress up—no blue jeans or running shoes, please. *15 Arlington St., Back Bay, 617/536-5700. AE, D, DC, MC, V. T stop: Arlington. $*

7 *a-3*

TEALUXE

Ting! That's the sound of the egg timer on your table, signaling that your very special pot of tea has been brewed. That's the way they do things at this quaint place, which is set within Loulou's Lost & Found, an *Elle Decor*–stylish boutique in Harvard Square. Tealuxe doesn't exactly serve afternoon tea. It serves up tea all day long, 140 different kinds of herbal and black, from energy-boosters to aphrodisiacs. If you have difficulty making a decision, just call over the resident expert—"the tea tender." After enjoying tea and the appealing array of baked goods, like lavender-scented shortbread, shop Loulou's for kitschy plates and vintage knickknacks from old European hotels and New York clubs. *Zero Brattle St., Cambridge, 617/441–0077. No reservations. Credit cards for purchases over $10 only. T stop: Harvard Sq.* $

THAI

8 *b-5*
BANGKOK CUISINE

Near Symphony Hall, this narrow storefront—ornately decorated and chandeliered—was Boston's first exposure to the cuisine of Thailand, and many still consider it the best. Those who like it hot won't be disappointed. Coconut soup, *pad thai* (fried sweet noodles), *satay* (chicken or beef skewers served with a peanut sauce), *kai pad bai kra praw* (chicken with basil, garlic, and peppers) are all savory and satisfying. Service is always gracious. *177A Massachusetts Ave., The Fens, 617/262–5377. AE, DC, MC, V. Wine and beer. T stop: Symphony.* $$

8 *d-4*
HOUSE OF SIAM

Pretty in pink, this dressy looking restaurant has much to offer on the surface, and even below. After all, the staff treats you like royalty and dishes can be cooked to order depending on how hot and spicy you like. The shrimp in garlic-chili-tamarind sauce has a real kick. Conveniently located across from the Westin Hotel, this place is a top Thai pick. *21 Huntington Ave., Back Bay, 617/267–1755. AE, DC, MC, V. No lunch Sun. T stop: Back Bay.* $$

6 *b-4*
THE KING & I

Paradise beef is just this side of paradise here, while other specialties are delicate and fine-tuned. This is a friendly place that has become a favorite for people who like their food to be tongue-tinglingly good. *145 Charles St., Beacon Hill, 617/227–3320. D, MC, V. T stop: Charles/MGH.* $$

VEGETARIAN

6 *g-6*
COUNTRY LIFE

No, this is not Boston's only vegetarian restaurant, but it is certainly the finest. The menu has real flair and flavor, as anyone can vouch who has tasted the garbanzo dumplings, black-eyed pea soup, or vegetable potpie. *200 High St., Downtown, 617/951–2534. Closed Sat. T stop: South Station.* $

VIETNAMESE AND SOUTHEAST ASIAN

7 *g-1*
ELEPHANT WALK

The menu here is a fascinating tour of Cambodian/French specialties. This isn't "new" fusion but "old"—Cambodia was run by the French for more than a century and the gallic touch made significant inroads during the 19th century. The menu ranges from coq au vin to Cambodian spring rolls to a challenging shrimp paste. Try the delicate salads or the curries that will make your tastebuds tap-dance—either way, many agree this is a very fine Asian spot. *70 Union Sq., Somerville, 617/623–9939. AE, D, DC, MC, V.* $$$

4 *d-3*
SAIGON

This is an old Boston favorite, a tried and true place in a neighborhood known for its fine Asian restaurants. One taste of the house soup, and you'll feel like you're in Ho Chi Minh City. The food will get that internal heating system going; you've never quite tasted anything like their deliciously bizarre southeast Asian fish sauce—and the place is easy on the wallet. Note that the food's the thing here, not the decor. *431 Cambridge St., Allston, 617/254–3373. No credit cards.* $

WINE AND TAPAS BARS

1 *f-2*
DUCKWORTH LANE

The owner of this small local chain (there are four now including Wellesley and Newtonville) enjoys going to yard sales and wants her restaurants to have an unstudied look. They do. A bistro feeling radiates from these places, thanks to their flea-market treasures and chicly sponged walls. If you don't want to eat and share those little plates called tapas, the dinner fare is quite good and the prices a welcome relief. Sunday brunch is featured. *66 Charles St., Charlestown, 617/242–6009. AE, DC, MC, V. No smoking. No lunch. T stop: Community College. $$*

 6-d

1657 Beacon St., Brookline, 617/730–8040. T stop: Washington Sq.

■ 8 *f3*
RED HERRING

So winning was Salamander, Stan Frankenthaler's first restaurant, that he decided to open another, more casual place. Set within the dramatic 270-degree glass nose span of the flat-iron Statler Building, his new spot delivers in many ways. The food is fun (how about raw tuna in wonton cups?) and the decor is dramatic (why not, since the place is near the theater district?). Dishes are said to be appetizer-size, yet often are just perfect for one person. The intention is to share and taste and it can be a game to crowd onto the tables colorful plates of maki rolls, trout salad, onion tart, fried oyster sandwich, smoked eel over sesame spinach, and spinach salad with duck confit. Most dishes go beyond yum to yum-yum. *One Columbus Ave., Theater District/Back Bay, 617/423–1581. Reservations not accepted. AE, D, DC, MC, V. No smoking. Closed Sun. T stop: Arlington. $$*

chapter 4

SHOPPING

The avid shopper in Boston can make tracks from the chic boutiques on Newbury Street to the pushcarts of Quincy Market and end up with every item on a shopping list checked off, all in a single day. You will run out of money long before you run out of shops. Today, the thrust of Boston's new mercantile image is definitely putting the "up" into upscale: witness the shops in Copley Place and along Newbury Street. But the old Yankee tradition of good value for a dollar persists, especially at that famous local bastion, Filene's Basement—Lord help us, it's as famous as the Freedom Trail!—celebrated for its drastically reduced prices on designer men's and women's clothes. Just remember: The longer the stuff stays on the racks there, the cheaper it gets.

Then again, Boston was never quite the town for tiaras, osprey feathers, and silk roses. As Isabella Stewart Gardner used to point out, "Boston women wrap themselves in their virtue—that is why they are so ill-dressed." Blame it on the purse-proud ostentation of the Brahmins—the Boston sense of style has always been on the subtle side. At times, if you're an Linda Evangelista-lookalike you can still feel like an animated fashion poster among comfortable Bostonians, with their leather-patched elbows and baggy sweaters (city natives love making a sweater say "aunt"). Some natives still think that if you notice a Bostonian is well dressed, he or she is overdressed. Then again, there are plenty of resident fashionistas who can give the Rue de la Paix a good run for its money. Still, when it comes to Boston Chic, the easiest way is look like you work on State Street and summer in Maine—without going broke.

Since so many come to Boston to soak up the literary ambience, here are a few words on books. The range of bookstores is vast—there are more than 30 places alone around Harvard Square. Some book hounds prefer Barnes and Noble or Borders because these giants stock everything, A to Z. Others prefer those little specialty shops where customers have to count on serendipity—even the staff may be hard-pressed to tell what they have and where it is. On a rainy Boston day, you'll find that knowing just a few of these booksellers' addresses will beat having an umbrella!

Note: There is no tax on clothing, but other items are taxed 5%. Many stores, particularly those on Newbury Street and Harvard Square, keep extended shopping hours in the summer and some are open late into the evening year-round, particularly those catering to the younger crowd. Unless noted otherwise, all the listed stores accept credit cards and are open seven days a week; most have limited hours on Sundays and many stay open until 7 or 8 PM on Thursdays.

department stores

6 e-6
FILENE'S
Although famed for its Basement (see Clothing for Women, below), Filene's is a full-service department store: clothing for women, including American designers like Ellen Tracy, Anne Klein, DKNY; a full line of updated and classic men's clothing, including Andrew Fezza, Perry Ellis, and Polo/Ralph Lauren. Jewelry, shoes, cosmetics (including the Lancôme Institute de Beauté), leather goods, housewares, linens, and gifts from Lalique, Lladro, Baccarat, and Waterford. 426 Washington St., Downtown Crossing, 617/357–2100. T stop: Downtown Crossing.

7 a-3
THE HARVARD COOP
"The most famous collegiate store in the world," the Coop is no longer for students only. Founded in 1882 by a handful of Harvard students who sold school supplies and used books out of a grocery store, the Harvard Cooperative

Society sells records, books, art prints, sweatshirts, insignia housewares, stationery, electronics, cameras, appliances, and computer programs. Now one of New England's largest stores (on three floors), it includes one of the most complete bookstores in America, with a stock of more than 100,000 titles. The book department has slightly longer hours than the rest of the store; the Kendall Store, known as the MIT Coop, located near MIT, sells CDs and tapes. (See also Books, below.) *1400 Massachusetts Ave., Harvard Sq., Cambridge, 617/499–2000. T stop: Harvard Sq.*

3 *g-6*

3 Cambridge Center, Kendall Sq., Cambridge, 617/499–3200. T stop: Kendall Sq.

8 *c-4*

LORD & TAYLOR

The well-bred American classics are featured: Anne Klein, St. John, Adele Simpson, Ralph Lauren, as well as clothing for men and children, a crystal and gift department, a beauty salon, and restaurant. *Prudential Center, 617/262–6000. T stop: Prudential.*

6 *e-6*

MACY'S

The New York–based retail giant bought and then renamed Jordan Marsh, New England's largest department store since the mid-19th century. It carries men's and women's clothing, including top designers, as well as housewares, furniture, and cosmetics. Like Filene's, it has direct access to the Downtown Crossing T station, which connects by tunnel to the Park Street station. *450 Washington St., Downtown Crossing, 617/357–3000. T stop: Downtown Crossing.*

8 *d-4*

NEIMAN-MARCUS

The first New England store of the noted Dallas-based high-fashion retailer, this place has three levels stocked with goodies. *5 Copley Pl., 100 Huntington Ave., 617/536–3660. T stop: Copley.*

8 *c-4*

SAKS FIFTH AVENUE

A mecca for stylish and expensive clothes, including the latest from Dior, Anne Klein, Calvin Klein, YSL Rive Gauche; juniors to women, casual to designer wear, plus a fine men's department. *Prudential Center, 617/262–8500, T stop: Prudential.*

malls

3 *h-5*

CAMBRIDGESIDE GALLERIA

Just across from the Royal Sonesta Hotel (near the Museum of Science), this three-level mall boasts branches of Filene's, Lechmere, and Sears, as well as a variety of specialty shops including Abercrombie & Fitch, Ann Taylor, Talbots, Bath & Body Works, J. Crew, and Banana Republic. There's even a Harley-Davidson Motorclothes outlet, further proof that the outlaw look is in. There's a waterfront food court. *100 CambridgeSide Pl., Cambridge, 617/621–8666. Mon.–Sat. 10 AM–9:30 PM; Sun. 11 AM–7 PM. T stop: Kendall, Free daily shuttle runs every 15 mins from Kendall Sq; Lechmere.*

8 *d-4*

COPLEY PLACE

Back Bay's glitzy shopping mall offers upscale shopping with an emphasis on the "up," although the second-level shops are a bit more affordable. Here's where you'll find scores of well-off European and Japanese tourists indulging in the latest in designer duds and accessories. Anchored by the ritzy, Dallas-based retailer Neiman-Marcus, it also boasts the likes of Gucci, Tiffany, and Louis Vuitton. Between-shopping R&R can be enjoyed at a mix of restaurants and cinemas. Copley Place is connected to the **Prudential Center** and its universe of shops via a series of over-street walkways. *1 Copley Pl., 617/369–5000 or 617/262–6600, ext. 293. Most stores open: Mon.–Fri. 10 AM–8 PM (a few have hours until 9 PM weeknights); Sun. noon–6 PM. T stop: Copley, Back Bay.*

6 *e-6*

DOWNTOWN CROSSING

The city's traditional, bustling shopping district is now a pedestrian mall where you will find two retailing giants— Filene's (with its renowned Basement now operating as a separate store) and Macy's, which purchased the venerable but ailing Jordan Marsh chain a few years back. Despite some seedy storefronts and pushcart vendors selling touristy knickknacks, the area exudes energy—with shoppers running the gamut from slouchy-clad teens to suited Financial District professionals. Recent additions of **Loehmann's** and **Marshalls** give Filene's Basement a run for the discount buck. In the spring, summer, and fall a wide range of performers entertain shoppers still on the run as well as those parked on benches provided for the weary and footsore. *T stop: Downtown Crossing.*

 f-4

FANEUIL HALL MARKETPLACE

Sneer, if you must, at its blatant commercialism, but visitors flock to this great urban agora for the multitude of food stalls (mainly in Quincy Market), shops, and restaurants, housed in the historic market buildings. Adjacent to Quincy Market is **Marketplace Center,** a soaring steel, glass, and neon canopy sheltering even more shops and eating stops. During the summer, when musicians and magicians entertain the crowds and locals and out-of-towners mingle in the outdoor bars, it's hard to work up disapproval. *T stop: Government Center, Haymarket.*

THE MALL AT CHESTNUT HILL

Located 5 miles west of Boston, on Route 9 and Hammond Pond Parkway, the Mall is a collection of fine specialty shops, plus Bloomingdale's and Filene's. The Atrium at Chestnut Hill, 300 Boylston Street, Chestnut Hill, also has a full pride of shops.

 c-4

PRUDENTIAL CENTER

Connected both to Copley Place and the Hynes Convention Center, the Prudential Center offers access to Lord & Taylor and Saks Fifth Avenue and to more climate-controlled shopping in a host of apparel, footwear, and specialty shops. Ann Taylor and the Florida-based chain Chicos have outlets here, as do The Body Shop and Talbot's Kids. Snack in the food court, take in the view from the 50th floor skywalk, and pick up travel information from a well-stocked information booth. *800 Boylston, Back Bay, between Gloucester and Exeter Sts. T stop: Prudential*

shopping neighborhoods

6 *c-5*

BEACON HILL

The main shopping street of this charming area is Charles Street, where the city's densest concentration of antiques shops mingle with boutiques and eateries. *T stop: Park St., Charles/MGH.*

8 *c-3*

BOYLSTON STREET

Boylston, running parallel and a block south of Newbury, is home to Prudential Center (Lord & Taylor, Saks Fifth Avenue, and numerous boutiques and specialty shops), plus a cluster of well-known chains and shops at 500 Boylston. *T stop: Boylston.*

3 *b-4*

HARVARD SQUARE

Yet more shops await across the Charles River in Cambridge. The Harvard Square area, with its large concentration of youth-oriented shops as well as the Harvard Coop, draws its share of shoppers and tourists. With more than 30 bookstores dotted in and around the Square, this is hallowed ground for book lovers. There are plenty of places to catch a cup of java; determined people-watchers can hang out near "the pit," a section near the T entrance where cliques of nose-ringed youth mingle with street musicians and end-of-the-world evangelists. Shopaholics bent on specialty items will find a host of even more unusual boutiques, craft shops, and other stores if they make the trek west on Massachusetts Avenue to **Porter Square** or east to **Central Square,** both served by the T. *T stop: Harvard Sq.*

8 *c-3*

NEWBURY STREET

This chic Back Bay thoroughfare, considered Boston's most fashionable street, is where the street meets the elite. Tucked among the art galleries and day spas, are clothing boutiques, many offering the wares of young, cutting-edge designers, and branches of famed New York stores such as Brooks Brothers. There's also an astounding number of hair-styling salons. Walking from the posh Arlington Street intersection to the more gritty and student-filled blocks near Massachusetts Avenue can be an exercise in trend spotting. *T stop: Arlington, Copley, Hynes/ICA.*

specialty shops

ANTIQUES

Good antiques browsing and buying are to be found on Charles Street—the Antiques Row of Beacon Hill—as well as on Newbury Street.

6 *b-4*
ALBERTS-LANGDON, INC.
Fine Asian antiques, primarily from China and Japan, are featured here, along with porcelain, furniture, and paintings. Some contemporary Japanese pottery, too. *126 Charles St., Beacon Hill, 617/523–5954. No credit cards. Closed Sun. T stop: Charles/MGH, Park St.*

6 *b-5*
ANTIQUES AT 80 CHARLES
Antiques, collectibles, and knickknacks in silver, porcelain, china, and other materials, in a packed-to-the-gills shop. *80 Charles St., Beacon Hill, 617/742–8006.*

8 *f-5*
ANTIQUES ON TREMONT
This small, basement shop is shoehorned with china, vases, rugs, and odds and ends displayed in a quaint setting. *550 Tremont St., South End, 617/451–3329. T stop: N.E. Medical Center.*

8 *d-2*
AUTREFOIS ANTIQUES
A fine selection of country French and some Italian 18th- and 19th-century antiques and furniture is the main focus here. Chinese lamps and vases, ivory and silver, are also on tap. *125 Newbury St. Back Bay, 617/424–8823. Closed Sun.*

6 *b-4*
BOSTON ANTIQUE CO-OP I & II
A cooperative effort on the part of a variety of dealers means new stock arrives often. The amount of items, the age of the stock, and the quality will make the heart of an incurable collector (like you) beat faster. There is jewelry, 17th- and 18th-century paintings, picture frames,

Victorian whites, shawls, paisleys, beaded dresses, quilts, rugs, furniture, textiles, and linens—18th to 20th centuries. Browsing is encouraged and there's a wide price range, so every pocket will be tempted. *119 Charles St., Beacon Hill, 617/227–9810 or -9811. T stop: Charles/MGH.*

6 *b-4*
BRADSTREET'S ANTIQUARIANS
The shop offers American furniture and paintings, with some English and Oriental goods. *51 Charles St., Beacon Hill, 617/723–3660. T stop: Charles/MGH.*

8 *d-3*
BRODNEY GALLERY
Richard Brodney, brought up in the antiques business by his father, painter Edward Brodney, buys estates and sells the paintings, bronzes, jewelry, continental porcelain, silver platters, inlaid furniture—many objects run into the four figures. The store itself is stunning. *145 Newbury St., Back Bay, 617/536–0500. T stop: Copley.*

3 *h-4*
CAMBRIDGE ANTIQUE MARKET
More than a bit off the beaten track, the market has four floors and 150 dealers of antiques and collectibles from the 18th through the 20th century, including furniture, silver, quilts, clocks, radios, cameras, vintage clothing, and toys. *201 Msgr. O'Brian Hwy., 617/868–9655. Closed Mon. T stop: Lechmere.*

8 *e-2*
CAMDEN COMPANIES INC.
This large shop nearly overflows with American and European vases, paintings, furniture, and lamps. If you're not up to being Martha Stewart, avail yourself of the shop's many on-site services—from custom slipcovers and pillows, to lamp making and rewiring, to furniture painting. *211 Berkeley St., 617/421–9899. Closed Sun. T stop: Arlington.*

3 *b-1*
CONSIGNMENT GALLERY
A true find for those who love collectibles, reproductions, and most importantly, bargains. Furniture, chests, china, glassware, and silver are sold on consignment (prices drop the longer objects are in the shop), plus a sparkling

collection of marcasite jewelry, antique and reproduction. The downstairs selection is cheesier, but the prices go down, too. A wonderful place to browse and chat with owner Colin Nealon and his wife. *2044 Massachusetts Ave., Cambridge, 617/354–4408. T stop: Porter Sq.*

6 *b-4*

JUDITH DOWLING

High-quality Japanese and Asian art and antiques—scrolls, screens, lacquer, basketry, ceramics, and prints—arranged in a spare, elegant style befitting a Japanese garden. *133 Charles St., Beacon Hill, 617/523-5211. Closed Sun.*

6 *b-4*

EUGENE GALLERIES

This is a wonderful place for art and antiques lovers to browse. Its huge collection of old prints, etchings, early maps, city views, and books cover a range of subjects, from views of Boston to exquisitely rendered flowers. Old postcards, too! *76 Charles St., Beacon Hill, 617/227–3062. T stop: Charles/MGH.*

6 *b-4*

GEORGE GRAVERT

French country furniture, antiques, and decorative accessories are the engraved calling cards here. *122 Charles St., Beacon Hill, 617/227–1593. No credit cards. Closed Sat., Sun.*

6 *b-4*

POLLY LATHAM ANTIQUES

Ceramics from China and Japan take the spotlight here, along with other decorative objects from Asia. *96 Charles St., Beacon Hill, 617/723–7009. Closed most Sun.*

6 *b-4*

MARIKA'S ANTIQUE SHOP

American, European, Japanese, and Chinese antiques—Marika shops the world for jewelry, silver, paintings, and miscellaneous antiques. *130 Charles St. Beacon Hill, 617/523–4520. T stop: Charles/MGH.*

6 *b-4*

STEPHEN SCORE

American country furniture and folk art are found in this charming but easy-to-miss shop (it's one and a half blocks from Charles Street). *73 Chestnut St., Beacon Hill, 617/227–9192. Often closed Sun. T stop: Charles/MGH.*

8 *f-2*

SHREVE, CRUMP & LOW

Knowledgeably managed, this famed jewelry shop has attracted the carriage trade for decades. Now Shreve also features an antiques department, rich in fine 18th- and 19th-century English and American furniture; English, Irish, and American silver; Sheffield porcelains; brass fireplace equipment; prints. One special Beacon Hill fancy is China-trade furniture and export porcelain. *330 Boylston St., Back Bay, 617/267–9100. Closed Sun. T stop: Arlington.*

6 *b-5*

UPSTAIRS DOWNSTAIRS

The store, offering prints, pictures, hand-painted furniture, cabinets, chests, and other furniture, has the atmosphere of an upscale country store. *93 Charles St., Beacon Hill, 617/367–1950. T stop: Charles/MGH.*

auction houses

6 *d-5*

SKINNER'S

When you're in New York City and want to purchase a fine Old Master painting, Victorian vase, or Islamic rug, you head to Sotheby's or Christie's. When you're in Boston, you head here. Currently the fourth largest auction gallery in the nation, Skinner's conducts over 60 auctions annually, both here and at its main office in Bolton, MA. Everyone from Richard Gere to Yo-Yo Ma has bought at Skinner's—although only one lucky buyer was able to snag Fitz Hugh Lane's *View of West Beach* (for a record $3.8 million). *63 Park Plaza, Beacon Hill, 617/350–5400. T stop: Arlington.*

collectibles specialists

8 *a-4*

THE NOSTALGIA FACTORY

At this fun place, the merely ordinary can become the highly collectible overnight. Filled as a "gallery of old advertising," the shop sells paperabilia galore, including movie posters and political advertising, ranging from 1960-era Kennedy posters to Nixon-Agnew buttons. *336 Newbury St., Back Bay, 617/236–8754. T stop: Hynes Convention Center/ICA.*

furniture specialists

6 *b-4*

CHURCHILL GALLERIES

From a late 19th-century French writing table to a Regency console with marble top, this elegant shop is full of the fine period furniture that would have pleased Edith Wharton. *103 Charles St., Beacon Hill, 617/722–9490. T stop: Charles/MGH.*

ART SUPPLIES

7 *e-5*

PEARL

The New York City store put this place on the map in a big way and, today, the Boston store has almost as big a following. *579 Massachusetts Ave., Cambridge, 617/547–6600. T stop: Central Sq.*

BASKETS

3 *b-1*

CHINA FAIR

A quirky little store, China Fair has a great selection of baskets, plus glassware, silverware, paper goods, and kitchen odds and ends. *2100 Massachusetts Ave., Cambridge, 617/864–3050. T stop: Porter Sq.*

A NEWBURY STREET SHOPPING SPREE

Oliver Wendell Holmes once stated that Boston is "the grand emporium of modesty." If Mr. Holmes were to venture down Newbury Street today, however, he would quickly change his tune. The throughfare is lined with luxury stores—it's Fifth Avenue, the Rue de la Paix, and the Via Condotti all wrapped up in one grand package. Here's the crème de la crème—and the berries that go on top, too.

Cartier
Diamonds are a Bostonian girl's second-best friend—she would probably prefer the silver jewelry on sale here. 40 Newbury St., 617/262–3300.

Divino
Que bella! Browse at the Versace boutique at 12 Newbury Street, then head here to actually buy from the house's sportier line. 73 Newbury St., 617/536–8830.

Betsey Johnson
Fuschia petticoats, Lady Hamilton vests, biker robe de galas—this is the place to ensure you Make An Entrance tonight at Man-Ray. 201 Newbury St., 617/236–7072.

Bjoux
One of the most baublecious stores in town, this stocks fine couturier threads. Owner Barbara Jordan became famous after buying several of Princess Di's frocks and auctioning one of them off for charity. 141 Newbury St., 617/424–8877.

Burberrys
"A Boston man is the East Wind made flesh"—so went an old adage. Today, some elegant Burberry raincoats, lined with the famous black-and-gold Burberry tartan, can help tame those blustery Boston days. 2 Newbury St., 617/236–1000.

Chanel
Every fashion maven's Santa Claus list has something Chanel on it. 5 Newbury St., 617/859–0055.

Pierre Deux
To make your rec room look like Marie Antoinette's country-chic Hameau, check out the soigné fabrics and French Provencial furniture on tap here. 111 Newbury St., 617/536–6364.

Avenue Victor Hugo
Need some fashion inspiration from old back issues of Italian Vogue? Head to this chic shop—and stock up on all sorts of other vintage periodicals and books. 339 Newbury St., 617/266–7746.

Laura Ashley
You'll still find those nostalgic velvets and laces adorning the frocks here—but even Laura Ashley is modernizing its Gainsborough looks for the millenium. 83 Newbury St., 617/536–0505.

BEAUTY

A large number of Boston's most chi-chi salons line Newbury Street, with another concentration in Harvard Square and along Massachusetts Avenue in Cambridge.

fragrance & skin products

3 *b-4*

THE BODY SHOP

One of the original "green" businesses, this international chain now has multiple outlets around the country. Its soap, bubble baths, facial creams, shampoos, and other products are made from natural ingredients, many of them from the Third World. *1440 Massachusetts Ave., Harvard Sq., Cambridge, 617/876–6334. T stop: Harvard Sq.*

8 *c-4*

Prudential Center, 800 Boylston St., Back Bay, 617/375–0070. T stop: Prudential.

6 *e-6*

277 Washington St., Downtown, 617/227–8288. T stop: Downtown Crossing.

6 *g-4*

200 State St., Downtown, 617/261–1870. T stop: State St.

8 *d-4*

CASWELL-MASSEY

Boston outpost of the nation's oldest apothecary (in business in New York since 1752), this pretty and fragrant shop has a full range of products from soap to sachets to massage oils. Their cologne was specially blended for the Washingtons—George and Martha—and their cold cream was first made for Sarah Bernhardt! *Copley Pl., 100 Huntington Ave., 617/437-9292. T stop: Copley.*

3 *b-4*

COLONIAL DRUG

Don't expect another trendy soap-and-suds spot—this is the place for the serious nose. The shop's name may seem prosaic but the stock is "scentational": more than 1,000 perfumes, from Chanel to Guerlain to Gucci, plus a selection of men's colognes. Not a spot to pick up a quick guilt-trip present for mom—the pricey perfumes live up to the 50-year-old store's motto: "The people with absolutely no common sense." *49 Brattle St., Harvard Sq., Cambridge, 617/864–2222. No credit cards. Closed Sun. T stop: Harvard Sq.*

6 *f-4*

CRABTREE & EVELYN

Around the world, Crabtree & Evelyn are known for shops and toiletries worthy of a Dickensian heroine. At their Boston address, pick up their well-known English scented soaps and potpourri. Great stocking stuffers: Fine English brushes and those prettily packaged comestibles. *Faneuil Hall Marketplace, South Market Bldg., 617/723–7733. T stop: Government Center, Haymarket.*

8 *d-4*

Copley Pl., 100 Huntington Ave., 617/266–2778. T stop: Copley.

1 *b-5*

Chestnut Hill Mall, 617/244–0476. T stop: Chestnut Hill.

8 *d-2*

FRESH 21 CENTURY

With delightful scents like chocolate milk, cranberry-orange, clove-mint, and hazelnut, you don't know whether to wash with these soaps or nibble on them. Since 1994, the store has produced its own varieties of luxury soaps using exotic scents and generous amounts of "shea butter"—which give the creamy texture *and* the oft-hefty price tag (as much as $6 a bar). There are also other brands of glycerin soaps, soap dishes, candles, and other bath niceties in an elegant setting brimming with goodies. *121 Newbury St., Back Bay, 617/421–1212. T stop: Copley.*

hair

6 *f-2*

AVANTI

This quality hair salon does it all, from haircutting and coloring to perms. *11 Newbury St. Back Bay, 617/267–4027. Closed Sun. T stop: Arlington.*

3 *b-4*

CAROL'S CUTTING CO.

Small, unisex salon for cuts, perms, coloring. Popular with Harvard students—the low prices may be part of the reason. *1678 Massachusetts Ave., Cambridge, 617/547–9436. Closed Mon.–Sun. in summer. T stop: Harvard Sq.*

8 *d-3*

DIEGO AT THE LOFT

The chicest heads in town sport cuts from this salon. Very expensive, especially if Diego himself wields the shears. *143 Newbury St., Back Bay, 617/262–5003. Closed Sun. T stop: Copley.*

3 *b-4*

The Galleria, 57 John F. Kennedy St., Cambridge; 617/661–7660. Closed Sun. T stop: Harvard Sq.

8 *f-2*

ECO CENTRIX

This Newbury Street salon has two floors of cutting and is noted for attention to men's styling. *30 Newbury St., Back Bay, 617/262–2222. T stop: Arlington.*

8 *d-3*

GENESES

Hair styling and coloring, plus full-service health and facial salon are featured here. *170 Newbury St., 617/720–4555. Closed Sun. (all branches). T stop: Copley.*

6 *e-8*

123 South St., Downtown, 617/451–3516. T stop: South Station.

3 *b-1*

JUDY JETSON, INC.

With a name like this, little wonder this salon has a wicked-cool-looking exterior. Owned and operated by women, the shop offers cuts, perms, and corrective coloring for men and women. Owners have also opened Jet Screamer, a shoe, clothing, and jewelry store at 1735 Massachusetts Avenue, where newly coifed customers can get a 10% discount after their cut! *1765 Massachusetts Ave., Cambridge, 617/354–2628. T stop: Porter Sq., Harvard Sq.*

7 *a-3*

LA FLAMME BARBER SHOP

This is the place where Harvard men have gotten cut and trimmed for a century (opened 1898, as a matter of fact). Since 1980, women have had the same opportunity; perms and hennas, too. *21 Dunster St., Cambridge, 617/354–8377. T stop: Harvard Sq.*

7 *a-2*

49 Brattle St., Cambridge, 617/876–7986. No credit cards. Closed Sun. T stop: Harvard Sq.

8 *f-2*

MARIO RUSSO

A salon with some of the best stylists in town, Mario Russo has full-service for women and men; cuts, color, styling, perms, facials, eyebrow and eyelash tinting, waxing, and nail care. *9 Newbury St., Back Bay, 617/424–6676. Closed Sun. T stop: Arlington.*

8 *c-5*

PICCADILLY HAIR DESIGN

Quality hair care is proffered here, from cuts to color, manicures to pedicures. Tanning, too. *150 Huntington Ave., 617/267–6000. T stop: Prudential.*

8 *d-2*

SAL SANNIZZARO

Head to toe—hair styling, facials, manicures, and pedicures. *119 Newbury St., Back Bay, 617/536–1811. Closed Sun., Mon. T stop: Copley, Arlington.*

8 *f-5*

SANTA FE

Funky little shop, with an (always) interesting array of people coming and going, Santa Fe gives good cuts plus excellent coloring. Some customers swear by Roberto. *528 Tremont St., South End, 617/338–8228. T stop: N.E. Medical Center.*

8 *c-4*

SUPERCUTS

If you don't want fancy—you want fast and cheap—then this is the place. Call ahead to ensure a shorter wait. *829 Boylston, Back Bay, 617/236–0310. T Stop: Copley.*

3 *c-1*

2150 Massachusetts Ave., Cambridge, 617/492–0067. T stop: Porter Sq.

skin & makeup services, massages & day spas

8 *e-2*

BON VISAGE

Excellent skin care for men and women by knowledgeable, dedicated, and hardworking expert Maureen Burke is the main feature here. Other draws: Waxing, brow-shaping, makeup, manicures, pedicures, hair cutting and coloring, and reflexology. *69 Newbury St., 2nd floor, Back Bay, 617/536–0800. T stop: Arlington.*

8 *f-2*

ELIZABETH GRADY FACE FIRST

Skin care specialists, the staff here offers deep-pore cleansing facials for men and women, makeup application and instruction—even lash tinting, brow shaping, waxing, paraffin hand treatments, and (deep sigh) back massage. *11 Newbury St., Back Bay, 617/536–4447. T stop: Arlington.*

3 *b-1*

2166 Massachusetts Ave., Cambridge, 617/497–7546. Closed Sun. T stop: Porter Sq.

1 *b-5*

200 Boylston St., Chestnut Hill, 617/964–6470. T stop: Chestnut Hill.

8 *f-2*

EUROPEAN SKIN CARE

With more than 30 years of expert European skin care and treatment, this salon is known for its fine facials, peelings, makeup, acne treatments, hair removal by waxing and electrolysis, body massage, and skin care products. Hair salon, too. *20 Newbury St., 3rd floor, 617/266–2422. Closed Sun., Mon. T stop: Arlington.*

3 *b-4*

LE PLI SALON & DAY SPA

Services include facials, massage, waxing, makeup, hair cutting and coloring, manicures, pedicures, and herbal wraps. *5 Bennett St., Cambridge, 617/547–4081. T stop: Harvard Sq.*

8 *f-2*

THE SPA ON NEWBURY

This day spa has quickly earned a fine reputation for its facials, massages, mud baths, waxing, and aromatherapy. *38 Newbury St., Back Bay, 617/859–7600. T stop: Arlington.*

8 *f-2*

30 NEWBURY DAY SPA

A full-service day spa, 30 Newbury offers facials, pedicures, manicures, paraffin treatments, massages, eyebrow and eyelash tinting. *30 Newbury St., 4th floor, Back Bay, 617/437–7775. T stop: Arlington.*

BOOKS

general

6 *e-6*

BARNES & NOBLE

One of the champion chains of booksellers, Barnes & Noble is noted for its mega-selections, and this branch delivers three full floors stocked with books on every topic under the sun. There's an excellent general range, strong in travel books, fiction, and children's literature, while the magazine selection is hard to beat. A popular draw is the full calendar of author readings. *395 Washington St., Downtown, 617/426–5502. T stop: Downtown Crossing.*

2 *b-4*

BARNES & NOBLE AT BU

This shop—catering to Boston University students—is among New England's largest bookstores with several floors filled with best-sellers, out-of-print collections, magazines, maps, and a café. *660 Beacon St., Kenmore Sq., 617/267–8484. T stop: Kenmore Sq.*

6 *e-6*

BORDERS

Along with Barnes & Noble, Borders is noted for its vast and impressive selection of books, videos, magazines, and CDs. This spacious downtown location (in a grand and historic former bank) features a small café. Numerous authors' readings and other literary events draw the literati. *10–24 School St., Downtown, 617/557–7188. T stop: Downtown Crossing.*

6 *e-5*

BUCK A BOOK

This chain of discount bookstores, with overstocks of fiction, nonfiction, and children's books, plus stationery and gift wrap, continues to grow and grow. Books can run $3 and up, but there are always finds for just a buck. *125 Tremont St., Downtown, 617/357–1919. T stop: Boylston, Park St.*

6 *e-5*

38 Court St., Downtown, 617/367–9419. Closed Sun. T stop: Government Center.

3 *b-4*

30 John F. Kennedy St., Cambridge, 617/492–5500. T stop: Harvard Sq.

3 h-1

274 Elm, Somerville, 617/776–1919. T stop: Davis Sq.

8 e-3

GLOBE CORNER BOOKSTORE

Once headquartered in the historic Old Corner Bookstore Building in Downtown Crossing, this chain has now moved on to two other addresses and both carry a wide selection of new books dealing with all aspects of life and travel in New England and the world. Specialties include maps, guides, history, art, literature. *500 Boylston St. Back Bay, 617/859–8008. T stop: Copley.*

3 b-4

28 Church St., Cambridge, 617/497–6277. T stop: Harvard Sq.

3 b-4

HARVARD BOOKSTORE

Befitting its name, this is a shop well-stocked with scholarly publications, mostly paperback selections. Very strong in fiction, literary criticism, literary journals, psychology, and philosophy, the shop also has hardcover remainders. Special orders are welcomed. *1256 Massachusetts Ave., Cambridge, 617/661–1515 or 661–1616. T stop: Harvard Sq.*

7 a-3

THE HARVARD COOP

If you want to find a bookstore that can deliver *both* the latest Stephen King best-seller and that obscure university-press tome on Charlotte Brontë, this is the place. One of Cambridge's most noted bookstores, the Coop is a Harvard landmark. Bursting with more than 100,000 titles, it also stocks stationery, housewares, and other urban necessities, while its brother store, the MIT Coop, located in Kendall Square, even sells CDs and tapes. Note that the Harvard Square branch bookstore has slightly longer hours than the Kendall branch. *1400 Massachusetts Ave., Harvard Sq., Cambridge, 617/499–2000. T stop: Harvard Sq.*

3 b-4

HARVARD UNIVERSITY PRESS DISPLAY ROOM

A retail outlet of the prestigious university press, this shop features all Harvard University Press books full price, with damaged ones at least 50% off. *Holyoke Center Arcade, 1354 Massachusetts Ave.,*

Cambridge, 617/495–2625. T stop: Harvard Sq.

6 f-6

LAURIAT'S INC.

Serving New England since 1872, Lauriat's features a large selection of hardcover and paperback books, plus cards and gifts. *45 Franklin St., Downtown, 617/482–2850. Closed Sun. T stop: Downtown Crossing.*

8 d-4

Copley Pl., Back Bay, 617/262–8857, 617/262–8858. T stop: Copley.

3 g-6

THE MIT COOP

This is the brother store to the famed Harvard Coop (*see above*).

3 Cambridge Center, Kendall Sq., Cambridge, 617/499–3200. T stop: Kendall Sq.

8 d-4

RIZZOLI BOOKSTORES AND ART BOUTIQUES

Pick up a catalog from the Louvre, listen to the Vivaldi, and buy the latest issue of *British Vogue*—then check out the extensive stock of art books, European travel guides, and other dreamy publications. *Copley Pl., Back Bay, 617/437–0700. T stop: Copley.*

8 a-4

TRIDENT BOOKSELLERS AND CAFÉ

One of Boston's more alternative bookstores, Trident is well stocked with art books, fiction, women's studies, psychology, philosophy, meditation, and children's books, plus an impressive magazine selection. Delightfully, there's more, including great gifts, such as bonsai trees, crystals, incense, and the like. In the café, soup, quiche, hummus, salads, and pastries, cappuccino, and espresso await hungry browsers. P.S.: This is a nifty place to just hang out in. *338 Newbury St., Back Bay, 617/267–8688. T stop: Hynes Convention Center/ICA.*

8 c-3

WATERSTONE'S BOOKSELLERS

On three floors of a beautiful historic building, Waterstone's is the first U.S. outlet of a large U.K.-based bookstore chain. Best-sellers are always discounted, and there are frequent promotional discounts. Particularly impressive is their local interest section. *26 Exeter St., Back Bay, 617/859–7300. T stop: Copley.*

3 *b-4*

WORDSWORTH

A popular source for hardcovers and paperbacks at discount prices, WordsWorth usually offers 15% off on hardcovers and 10% off on paperbacks. Besides fiction, the store is strong on computer science, music, art, architecture, and children's books. Just up Brattle Street at No. 5, is WordsWorth Gifts, a pleasant place for calendars, cards, stationery, jewelry, and other knick-knacks. *30 Brattle St., Cambridge, 617/354–5201. T stop: Harvard Sq.*

antiquarian

8 *f-7*

ARS LIBRI LTD.

Connoisseurs, historians, and book lovers everywhere have made this one of the most respected bookshops in the nation. The specialty is books about the fine arts with the focus on rare and out-of-print scholarly works, and illustrated books dating from the 16th century to the present. As you browse this light and airy shop, be sure to check the display cases for a first edition Henry Matisse edition de luxe ($7,000), artworks by Marcel Duchamp, or other very special items. Ars Libri also offers free catalogs of its stock of antiquarian master drawings. *560 Harrison Ave., South End, 617/357–5212. Closed Sun. T stop: N.E. Medical Center, Massachusetts Ave.*

8 *a-4*

AVENUE VICTOR HUGO

Looking for that old issue of *Life* with Rita Hayworth on the cover? Check this place out for its huge selection of new and used magazines and books. In addition, Hugo has one of the city's largest biography selections. Specialties also include science fiction; music, art, and architecture; photography; literature; mysteries—and a wide range of magazines. The store's time-stained and well-worn storefront was recently featured in *Elle Decor's* shopping piece on Boston. *339 Newbury St., Back Bay, 617/266–7746. T stop: Hynes Convention Center/ICA.*

3 *b-1*

THE BOOKCELLAR

A funky, downstairs hangout for lovers of books and bargains, this place offers a good selection of fiction and nonfiction, plus magazines and other odds and ends. Occasional author readings are held here. *1971 Massachusetts Ave., Cambridge, 617/864–9625. T stop: Porter Sq.*

6 *e-6*

BRATTLE BOOKSHOP

Descendant of America's oldest continuously operating antiquarian bookshop (since 1825), the Brattle has more than 200,000 used and rare books. It's well stocked with magazines, too, including old copies of that 19th-century periodical, *Puck.* Also check out the fine sections on Boston, New England, town histories, and the Civil War. Photo albums, ephemera, documents, and autographs are also offered. *9 West St., Downtown, 617/542–0210. Closed Sun. T stop: Downtown Crossing.*

8 *e-3*

BROMER BOOKSELLERS

For the connoisseur, bromer offers a fascinating selection of fine and rare editions, including illustrated books of all periods, first editions, juveniles, and miniatures. One specialty: miniature books. *607 Boylston St., 2nd floor, 617/247–2818. Closed Sat., Sun. T stop: Arlington, Copley.*

3 *a-3*

BRYN MAWR BOOKSTORE

Stocked with used and, in some cases, hard-to-come-by paperbacks and hardcovers, this shop benefits the noted college's scholarship fund. *373 Huron Ave., Cambridge, 617/661–1770. Closed Sun., Mon. T stop: Porter.*

3 *b-3*

CANTERBURY'S BOOKSHOP

Canterbury's sells antiquarian and new scholarly books, offering a warehoused selection of 200,000 volumes—one of New England's largest stocks. *1675 Massachusetts Ave., Cambridge, 617/864–9396. Closed Sun. T stop: Harvard Sq., Porter Sq.*

3 b-4

STARR BOOKSHOP, INC.

Established in 1930, the Starr is a small shop with a nice selection of used scholarly works, with specialties in literature, philosophy, biography, art, and photography. *29 Plympton St., Cambridge, 617/547–6864. T stop: Harvard Sq.*

special-interest

3 b-4

GROLIER POETRY BOOK SHOP, INC.

This poetry shop has been in Harvard Square since 1927 and stocks the work of more than 10,000 poets—clearly the place to come for small press, little magazines, spoken-word cassettes, and, needless to say, poetry readings. Mail and search orders are welcomed. *6 Plympton St., Cambridge, 617/547–4648. Closed Sun. T stop: Harvard Sq.*

3 b-1

KATE'S MYSTERY BOOKS

A favorite Cambridge haunt, this is one of the Hub's best spots for mystery and horror fiction. Nearly every major mystery writer is represented. There's a special emphasis on local authors—and you'll be surprised at how many of those there are. Check out the full calendar of author events. *2211 Massachusetts Ave., Cambridge, 617/491–2660. T stop: Porter Sq.*

3 b-4

MANDRAKE

The emphasis here is on fine arts, architecture, design, psychiatry, and philosophy. *8 Story St., Cambridge, 617/864–3088. No credit cards. Closed Sat., July–Aug. T stop: Harvard Sq.*

3 b-4

MILLION YEAR PICNIC

The stock of current and back-issue comics here includes the rare and the hard-to-find. *99 Mount Auburn St., downstairs, Cambridge, 617/492–6763. T stop: Harvard Sq.*

3 e-4

NEW WORDS

The place to read up on our brave new world—specialties here include feminist presses, lesbian and gay literature, and international fiction. There's even a non-sexist and PC children's section. *186 Hampshire St., Cambridge, 617/876–5310. T stop: Central Sq.*

3 b-4

PANDEMONIUM BOOKS AND GAMES

Science fiction, fantasy, and horror books fans head here for a large selection of titles, including used books. Everything is discounted 10% off retail. *8 John F. Kennedy St., Cambridge, Harvard Sq., 617/547–3721. T stop: Harvard Sq.*

3 b-1

SASUAGA JAPANESE BOOKSTORE

One of the area's newer stores, this shop specializes in Japanese books, magazines, comics, software, compact discs, plus books about Japan in English. *7 Upland Rd., Cambridge, 617/497–5460. T stop: Porter Sq.*

3 b-4

SCHOENHOF'S FOREIGN BOOKS

Literature in over a dozen languages is served up here—along with (happily) dictionaries galore, grammar books, and reference tools in more than 160 languages, plus a strong selection of language-learning records and cassettes. *76A Mount Auburn St., Cambridge, 617/547–8855. Closed Sun. T stop: Harvard Sq.*

3 b-4

SEVEN STARS

New Agers love the selections here—healing, Christianity, oriental medicine, mythology, Eastern and Western philosophy and metaphysics, astrology, homeopathy, and holistic medicine are just a few of the specialties. *58 John F. Kennedy St., Cambridge, 617/547–1317. T stop: Harvard Sq.*

8 f-5

WE THINK THE WORLD OF YOU

A full-service bookstore for the gay community (and beyond), this popular spot has a selection that is often eclectic—humor to mystery to cooking to erotic to travel—and thorough. The emphasis, of course, is on books with a gay orientation. *540 Tremont St., South End, 617/423–1965. T stop: N.E. Medical Center.*

CLOTHING FOR CHILDREN

3 *b-4*

CALLIOPE

Crammed to the gills, this children's clothing store features some designers and brand names, all in the brightest of colors. They try to keep their stock full of everything but the run-of-the-mill. Look for the imported infants' wear, and their wonderful selection of cuddly stuffed animals (including some that are more costly than the real thing). *33 Brattle St., Cambridge, 617/876–4149. T stop: Harvard Sq.*

8 *f-2*

THE EXCLUSIVE OILILY STORE

The sunflower-yellows, Tahitian-fuchsias, oranges, pinks, and purples can blind the soberly clothed when walking into this children's clothing shop, part of a dazzlingly chic and charming international chain. They're now making some luxe-peasant accessories for adults, too. *31 Newbury St., Back Bay, 617/247–9299. T stop: Arlington.*

8 *d-4*

GAP KIDS

The Gap clothing chain for the younger set, Gap Kids is loaded with the sort of designer duds that make any 3-year-old look 30. *Copley Pl., Back Bay, 617/262–2370. T stop: Copley.*

8 *c-3*

201 Newbury St., Back Bay, 617/424–8778. T stop: Copley.

6 *g-4*

200 State St., Downtown, 617/439–7844. T stop: Aquarium.

3 *b-4*

15 Brattle St., Harvard Sq., Cambridge, 617/864–0719. T stop: Harvard Sq.

3 *h-5*

Cambridgeside Galleria, Cambridge, 617/494–9181. T stop: Kendall.

3 *b-4*

SATURDAY'S CHILD

Clothing from all over the world—Indonesia, France, Japan, and more—is the draw here, plus shoes, accessories, toys, and cards. *1762 Massachusetts Ave., Cambridge, 617/661–6402. T stop: Porter Sq.*

CLOTHING FOR WOMEN/GENERAL

classic

8 *f-2*

ANN TAYLOR

This national chain features high-quality yet comfortably affordable career fashions; linen and gab slacks; silk blouses, suits, and dresses, lovely scarves, hosiery, belts, and bags. Some swear by their own line of stylish shoes. *18 Newbury St., 617/262–0763. T stop: Arlington.*

8 *f-2*

199 Boylston St., Back Bay, 617/244–4848. T stop: Arlington.

6 *f-4*

111 Faneuil Hall Sq., 617/742–0031. T stop: Government Center, Haymarket, State St.

3 *h-5*

Cambridgeside Galleria, 100 Cambridgeside Pl., Cambridge, 617/225–2779.

3 *b-4*

414 Brattle St., Cambridge, 617/864–3720. T stop: Harvard Sq.

3 *b-4*

APRIL CORNELL

Charming floral-printed cottons and linens, many imported from India, are fashioned into loosely flowing dresses, blouses, and skirts. Upstairs, the store has an impressive selection of bedspreads, tablecloths, napkins, place mats, and home furnishing accessories. April Cornell also has an excellent outlet store in Faneuil Hall. *43 Brattle St., Cambridge, 617/661–8910. T stop: Harvard Sq.*

6 *f-4*

Faneuil Hall Marketplace, North Market Bldg., Downtown, 617/248–0280. T stop: Government Center, Haymarket.

8 *e-3*

LAURA ASHLEY

This London-based floral-print chain does up its charming patterns, mainly in cotton and corduroy, as women's skirts, dresses, and accessories. You can also find Laura Ashley home furnishings in the shop at 75 Arlington (*see* Furniture & Furnishings, *below*). *83 Newbury St, Back Bay, 617/536–0505.*

1 b-5

Chestnut Hill Mall, 617/965–7640. T stop: Chestnut Hill.

8 f-2

BURBERRYS

For men and women aspiring to the distinctive English-country-weekend look, including their famed rainwear, plus ties, scarves, and shirts. 2 Newbury St., 617/236–1000. Closed Sun. T stop: Arlington.

3 b-3

LOOKS

A designer boutique whose dresses, skirts, blouses, and sweaters will create that stylishly collegiate appearance. Stuffed with pricey, but well-made, garb, this is one of a number of trendy clothing boutiques along Massachusetts Avenue, between Harvard and Porter Squares. 1607 Massachusetts Ave., Cambridge, 617/491–4251. T stop: Harvard Sq.

3 b-4

PENNSYLVANIA COMPANY

Casual, comfortable, youthful weekend wear is stocked here, mostly in cotton and knits. 28 John F. Kennedy St., Harvard Sq., Cambridge, 617/491–8536. T stop: Harvard Sq.

3 b-4

1024 Commonwealth Ave., Kenmore Sq., 617/731–0980. T stop: Kenmore Sq.

3 b-2

PEPPERWEED

These contemporary fashions are neither trendy nor stuffy, nor will you see them all over the place. American, European, and Japanese designers are featured, plus accessories—belts, hats, stockings, socks. 684 Massachusetts Ave., Cambridge, 617/547–7561. Closed Sun. T stop: Porter Sq.

8 d-4

POLO/RALPH LAUREN

Here's where to buy Lauren's interpretations of the classic American look—from silk rep ties to schoolmarm shirtwaists. The renowned designer's store features classic yet modish apparel for women, men, and boys, plus his signature accessories. Copley Pl., 100 Huntington Ave., 617/266–4121. T stop: Copley.

3 b-4

SETTEBELLO

With an emphasis on quality workmanship and fabric, Settebello features classic—and expensive—Italian imports for women. 52C Brattle St., Cambridge, 617/864–2440. Closed Sun. T stop: Harvard Sq.

3 b-2

SUSANNA

A fabulous place to find moderately priced scarves to spice up any outfit. Plus dresses, hats, and jewelry, with the emphasis on the feminine. All in all, a favorite Cambridge boutique. 1776 Massachusetts Ave., Cambridge, 617/492–0334. T stop: Porter Sq.

6 e-6

TALBOTS

No surprises here. Since 1947, Talbots has been considered the quintessential purveyor of timeless, conservative women's clothing. 25 School St., Downtown, 617/723–0660. T stop: Downtown Crossing.

3 h-5

Cambridgeside Galleria, 100 Cambridgeside Pl., 617/621–1414. T stop: Lechmere.

1 b-5

Chestnut Hill Mall, 617/964–9900. T stop: Chestnut Hill.

contemporary

8 a-4

ALLSTON BEAT

Offbeat street fashions for young 'uns with money to burn, plus a selection of blouses, skirts, pants, hosiery, and other accessories. 348 Newbury St., Back Bay, 617/421–9555. T stop: Hynes Convention Center/ICA.

3 b-4

36 John F. Kennedy St., Harvard Sq., Cambridge, 617/868–0316. T stop: Harvard Sq.

8 c-3

BANANA REPUBLIC

At one time, this chain offered durable, great-looking travel clothes from a catalog (remember?) that was a joy to read. Now, some say the stores seem like just another faceless clothes hanger. Prices at this upscale Gap-y place are moderate to steep. 201 Newbury St., Back Bay, 617/267–3933. T stop: Copley.

6 *f-4*

Marketplace Center, 617/439–0016. T stop: Government Center, Haymarket.

1 *b-5*

Chestnut Hill Mall, 617/332–1992. T stop: Chestnut Hill.

8 *d-4*

BENETTON

Colorful, youthful, casual, and affordable—this mass-merchandiser of stylish Italian-knit sportswear for women, men, and children is particularly strong on sweater dressing. Great scarves and gloves, too! Copley Pl., 100 Huntington Ave., 617/437–7790. T stop: Copley.

8 *g-2*

344–50 Boylston St., 617/267–9669. T stop: Arlington.

1 *b-5*

Chestnut Hill Mall, 617/965–7931. T stop: Chestnut Hill.

8 *c-3*

BETSEY JOHNSON

Colorful body-hugging and eye-popping clothes from one who does this sort of thing well. Wide price range for styles that are relentlessly youthful. Compatible accessories as well. 201 Newbury St., Back Bay, 617/236–7072. T stop: Copley.

8 *d-2*

BJOUX

A glittering bauble of a store for exclusive designer clothing, from the likes of Vera Wang. Owner Barbara A. Jordan, a noted local charity patron, managed to buy three of Princess Diana's ball gowns in Christie's 1997 auction, with the intention of displaying them in her shop. 141 Newbury St., 617/424-8877. Closed Sun. T stop: Copley.

3 *b-4*

CLOTHWARE

Contemporary women's sportswear, this store has a decided emphasis on sleek, natural styles. 52 Brattle St., Cambridge, 617/661–6441. T stop: Harvard Sq.

8 *b-3*

CULTURE SHOCK

Club clothes for the light of limb from designers such as Moschino, BCBG, and Vivienne Westwood. This is the spot to buy that daring little dress your

mother always warned you about. 286 Newbury St., Back Bay, 617/859–7256.

8 *e-3*

DIVINO

Versace-owned, this boutique offers the famed Italian company's line of jeans and other sportswear for men and women. 73 Newbury St., Back Bay, 617/536–8830. Closed Sun. T stop: Arlington.

8 *c-3*

EMPORIO ARMANI

For those who like even their jeans to be sleek, E/A features the noted designer's smartly styled casual clothes and sportswear. 210–214 Newbury St., Back Bay, 617/262-7300. T stop: Copley.

8 *d-4*

THE GAP

Hey, Sharon Stone wore one of their T-shirts to the Oscars. Even so, this ubiquitous clothing chain is managing to dress-down all of America. Its many outlets feature (generally) well-made pants, shirts, skirts, jackets, and accessories for men and women. Copley Pl., 100 Huntington Ave., 617/247–1754. T stop: Copley.

6 *f-4*

Marketplace Center, Downtown, 617/951–9300. T stop: Haymarket, Government Center.

8 *e-3*

101 Newbury St., 617/267–4055. T stop: Arlington.

6 *e-6*

425 Washington St., Downtown Crossing, 617/482–1657. T stop: Downtown Crossing.

3 *h-5*

Porter Sq., Cambridge, 617/864–2255. T stop: Porter Sq.

3 *h-5*

Cambridgeside Galleria, 100 Cambridgeside Pl., Cambridge, 617/494–9386. T stop: Lechmere.

3 *b-4*

15 Brattle St., Cambridge, 617/864–9077. T stop: Harvard Sq.

2 *b-4*

533 Commonwealth Ave., Kenmore Sq., 617/262–9595. T stop: Kenmore Sq.

3 b-4

JASMINE SOLA SOLAMEN

In distinctly youthful style, this three-in-one store offers contemporary silk, rayon, linen, and cotton casual wear, as well as a large stock of dresses. The Cambridge shop also has Sola shoes for men and women. To complete her outfit: hats, belts, bags, hosiery, and jewelry. *37 Brattle St., Cambridge, 617/354–6043. T stop: Harvard Sq.*

8 a-4

329 Newbury St., Back Bay, 617/437–8466. T stop: Hynes Convention Center/ICA.

8 e-2

LOUIS, BOSTON

One of Boston's most celebrated men's stores devotes its top floor to designer women's clothes from Donna Karan, Gucci, and Calvin Klein. Do have a bite in their charming tiny café, open for breakfast, lunch, and afternoon tea. *234 Berkeley St., Back Bay, 617/262–6100. Closed Sun. T stop: Arlington.*

8 c-3

SERENDIPITY

This moderately priced store specializes in natural fiber clothing complimented by a full line of shoes, jewelry, and accessories. *229 Newbury St., Back Bay, 617/437–1850. T stop: Copley.*

3 b-4

1312 Massachusetts Ave., Cambridge, 617/661–7143. T stop: Harvard Sq.

8 a-4

URBAN OUTFITTERS

Generation-Xers love this 21st century version of a general store. Soup to nuts, it's got a little bit of everything—clothing, housewares, novelties, toys; tees, polos, jeans, leggings, sweats, Oxfords, knits, camp shirts, bags, belts, socks, all for men and women. Hot-hot-hot lines include Kikit, Diesal, Girbaud, French Connection, Esprit, E. G. Smith, Generra, and Urban Outfitter's own labels: Rust, Free People, Ecouté. *361 Newbury St., Back Bay, 617/236–0088. T stop: Hynes Convention Center/ICA.*

3 b-4

11 John F. Kennedy St., Cambridge, 617/864–0070. T stop: Harvard Sq.

designer

8 f-2

CHANEL

It took some fancy footwork in construction, but the House of Chanel managed to open this Newbury Street boutique at No. 5, in honor, *bien sûr,* of its famous namesake perfume. Set within the Ritz-Carlton Hotel, this oh-so-chic boutique offers a complete selection of Chanel dresses, separates, bags, shoes, and accessories, plus a perfume and makeup counter. What can we say, but oooh la la. *5 Newbury St., Back Bay, 617/859–0055. T stop: Arlington.*

3 b-2

GYPSY MOON

Worth a peek just for possibly the most ornate dressing room on Massachusetts Avenue. Romantic, cultish, and definitely really-special-occasion dresses, capes, shawls, velvet bodices, and other Goddess-worshipping garb can be found here. Clearly, a place where rocker Stevie Nicks—or vampire writer Ann Rice—would browse. *1780 Massachusetts Ave., Cambridge, 617/876–7095. T stop: Harvard Sq. or Porter Sq.*

8 f-2

GIANNI VERSACE

The late, famed designer's Boston showcase has his glamorous designs upstairs and his home furnishings—including rugs, pillows, and other items—downstairs. Here, you're likely to hear the exceedingly well-clad staff thanking customers in Japanese. *12 Newbury St., Back Bay, 617/536–8300. T stop: Arlington.*

8 f-2

GIORGIO ARMANI

Enduringly sophisticated, Armani is the Italian master of understated tailoring. The first floor is for women, while upstairs, you'll find suits for men, plus accessories. *22 Newbury St., 617/267–3200. Closed Sun. T stop: Arlington.*

8 d-4

GUCCI

The house that pioneered the use of the status-symbol logo is now riding high once again, thanks to designer Tom Ford. His complete Gucci collection is housed here in an elegant space of Italian marble, wood, and brass. Also here are the Gucci basics—women's and men's apparel, plus the famed signature "G"s on accessories, jewelry, and small and large leather goods. *Copley Pl., 100 Huntington Ave., Back Bay, 617/247–3000. T stop: Copley.*

 f-2

HERMÈS

The *très chic* French line of scarves, ties, belts, and other fashion accessories also has the appropriate *mon dieu* prices. *22 Arlington St., Back Bay, 617/482–8707. Closed Sun. T stop: Arlington.*

8 *f-2*

SONIA RYKIEL BOUTIQUE

The famed Parisian designer's lean, easy-to-wear knitted separates are always *très Francaise*. *Heritage on the Garden, 280 Boylston St., 617/426–2033. Closed Sun. T stop: Arlington.*

discount & off-price

6 *e-6*

FILENE'S BASEMENT

The bargain basement store, famous for more than 80 years (albeit now no longer operated by Filene's). This renowned place is full of tourists spending their vacation money, guilt-free, because they know that this is one of Boston's top attractions. The beeline for a bargain may make even the most proper Bostonian not so; sometimes standing back and watching the action is even more fun than being in it. Overstocks, closeouts, clearances (irregulars and samples, too) from some of the best, most prestigious stores in the country—among them Neiman-Marcus, Bergdorf Goodman, Saks Fifth Avenue—find their way to Filene's Basement and so will you. There's clothing for men (including Brooks Brothers) and children; housewares, too. How about a marked-down wedding dress? There's also a fur boutique. The facts: The merchandise is reduced 25% after 14 selling days, 50% after 21, 75% after 28. After 30 days on the selling floor, unsold merchandise is given away to charity. *Downtown Crossing, 426 Washington St., 617/542–2011. T stop: Downtown Crossing.*

6 *e-6*

LOEHMANN'S

The expanding New York-area off-price clothing store opened here in 1996 and has been giving Filene's Basement a run for the money, thanks to the many designer labels significantly marked down. *373–387 Washington St., Downtown Crossing, 617/338–7177. T stop: Downtown Crossing.*

vintage/resale shops

These stores offer an alternative. For those with a good eye and patience, the rewards are fashions in the finest fabrics that are just as stylish now as they were "then." Buy carefully and wisely, as most vintage shops have a final-sale policy.

6 *e-3*

BOOMERANGS

What goes around, comes around to this well-lighted, airy, resale shop operated as a nonprofit business to benefit the local AIDS Action Committee. Lots of donated merchandise from corporations, so there's some new stuff among the more "experienced" clothes, plus housewares, jewelry, knickknacks, and nice selection of vinyl records. *60 Canal St., Downtown, 617/723–BOOM. T stop: Haymarket.*

8 *d-2*

CHIC REPEATS

If you really don't want to pay a lot for that slinky beaded gown, here is where to go. Run by the Junior League of Boston, the store has designer labels and high-end dresses, blouses, and accessories. *117 Newbury St., Back Bay, 617/536–8580. Closed some Sun. T stop: Copley.*

7 *h-5*

THE GARMENT DISTRICT

This large warehouse space has a vast array of men and women's vintage, used, and new clothing, 1920s–1990s. Large selection of rayon print dresses from the 1940s; sweaters, cashmere, and tweed men's overcoats; used jeans. New and used shoes and Western boots; restyled and new hats; jewelry, including some funky 1960s stuff. *200 Broadway, Kendall Sq., Cambridge, 617/876–5230. T stop: Kendall Sq.*

3 *b-4*

OONA'S EXPERIENCED CLOTHING

For the experienced old-clothes "picker," this shop could be a source of treasures—and well-priced ones at that. But it takes patience; the clothes are crammed onto racks leaving little room to spare. There are kimonos; dresses from the 1930s and 1940s, including some Jean Harlowish bias-cut numbers; Hawaiian shirts; 1950s skirts and blouses. For men there's also a wide selection of shirts, leather jackets, used jeans. New and vintage jewelry. *1210 Massachusetts Ave., Cambridge, 617/491–2654. T stop: Harvard Sq.*

8 *d-3*

SECOND TIME AROUND

This good quality consignment shop features a frequent buyer program; The staff is more than willing to bargain, too. Look for dresses, suits, and casual clothes. *167 Newbury St., Back Bay, 617/247–3504. T stop: Copley.*

3 *b-4*

8 Elliot St., Harvard Sq., Cambridge, 617/491–7185. T stop: Harvard Sq.

CLOTHING FOR WOMEN/SPECIALTY

lingerie & nightwear

In addition to the specialty stores listed here, the main department stores have a fine selection of lingerie.

8 *c-4*

CACIQUE PARIS

Quality lingerie and fashion accessories are showcased here in a naughty-but-nice display. *Prudential Center, 800 Boylston St., Back Bay, 617/266–4045. T stop: Prudential.*

8 *d-2*

TOP DRAWER

Top dollar for fine, often handmade, nightgowns, slips, camisoles, and dainty little somethings in shades of pastels. Also specialty clothing for children and accessories for the bedroom and bathroom. *112 Newbury St., Back Bay, 617/267–7001. T stop: Copley.*

8 *d-4*

VICTORIA'S SECRET

A fantasy-lingerie chain—whether male or female fantasies we'll leave to the cultural pundits. The frequently held sales are a *shopper's* fantasy. *Copley Pl., Back Bay, 617/266–7505. T stop: Copley.*

6 *f-4*

Faneuil Hall Market Pl., 617/248–9761. T stop: Government Center.

3 *h-5*

Cambridgeside Galleria, 100 Cambridgeside Pl., Cambridge, 617/252–9028. T stop: Lechmere.

1 *b-5*

The Mall At Chestnut Hill, 300 Boylston St., Newton, 617/964–7177.

maternity

6 *e-5*

MATERNITY WORK

For the mother-to-be, this is a handy outlet store featuring brand-name casual and career clothes. Some marked-down slightly damaged goods. *10 Milk St. Downtown, 617/542–6344. Closed Sun. T stop: Downtown Crossing.*

8 *f-2*

MIMI'S MATERNITY

This national chain features comfortable maternity clothes, both casual and professional. *10 Newbury St., Back Bay, 617/262–8012. T stop: Arlington.*

1 *b-5*

Chestnut Hill Mall, 617/964–5833. T stop: Chestnut Hill.

shoes & boots

For the basic chain shops, head to Winter Street.

8 *f-2*

ARCHE

Yes, Virginia, there might be a shoe that's both stylish and comfortable. It might be Arche, a French import featuring latex soles in sandal, pump, and boot styles. *314 Boylston St., Back Bay, 617/422–0727. Closed Sun.*

8 *d-4*

BALLY OF SWITZERLAND

Super expensive, high-quality footwear for men and women, Bally footwear is always imported from Switzerland, Italy, and France. Fine accessories, too. *Copley Pl., 100 Huntington Ave., level one, 617/437–1910. T stop: Copley.*

1 *b-5*

Chestnut Hill Mall, 617/244–5307. T stop: Chestnut Hill.

6 *f-4*

CUOIO

Cuoio means leather in Italian and this shop features fashionable Italian leather shoes and boots, for women only. Some accessories, including lovely pieces for the hair. *Faneuil Hall Marketplace, South Market Bldg., 617/742–4486. T stop: Haymarket, Government Center.*

8 *d-2*

115 Newbury St., Back Bay, 617/859–0636. T stop: Copley.

8 *d-4*

JOAN & DAVID

Extremely stylish made-in-Italy designs for men and women are the specialties here, plus some sweaters and accessories. *Copley Pl., 616/536–0600. T stop: Copley.*

1 *b-5*

Chestnut Hill Mall, 617/630–9520. T stop: Chestnut Hill.

3 *b-4*

SOLA

The shoe side of Jasmine Sola Solamen, this is a wonderful shoe store featuring a wide variety of styles and prices. Shoes by Kenneth Cole, Via Spiga, Nickels, Espace, La Bastile, Thom Brown, Bellini, plus an excellent selection of boots. *37 Brattle St., Cambridge, 617/354–6043. T stop: Harvard Sq.*

8 *b-4*

329 Newbury St., Back Bay, 617/437–8466. T stop: Hynes Convention Center/ICA.

8 *a-4*

THOM BROWN

Shoes with attitude, Thom Brown's men's and women's designs put the "hip" in hip hop. If you want club footwear you don't want to mess with, head for this cramped but often crowded shop. *331 Newbury St., Back Bay, 617/266–8722. T stop: Hynes Convention Center/ICA.*

3 *b-1*

VINTAGE, ETC.

This funky little shop concentrates on European comfort shoes—the kind favored by the college crowd. You know—German, Danish, Swiss shoes, and, of course, Swedish clogs. Also a selection of hosiery. *1798 Massachusetts Ave., Cambridge, 617/497–1516. T stop: Porter Sq.*

CLOTHING FOR MEN/GENERAL

classic

8 *f-2*

ALAN BILZERIAN

Street-inspired designs aimed for at the youth market means this place is stocked with plenty of European and Japanese designers. The store has accessories as well as clothes, plus vintage shoes downstairs. *34 Newbury St., Back Bay, 617/536–1001. T stop: Arlington.*

3 *b-4*

THE ANDOVER SHOP

Simply put, fashionable, traditional, and expensive. *22 Holyoke St., Cambridge, 617/876-4900. Closed Sun. T stop: Harvard Sq.*

8 *e-3*

234 Clarendon St., Back Bay, 617/247–3300. Closed Sun. T stop: Copley.

8 *d-4*

BEYLERIAN

A favorite shopping spot for many of Boston's professional athletes, Beylerian is a pricey place for men to buy designer sweaters, pants, ties, and other items. *Copley Pl., 100 Huntington Ave., 617/536–6616. T stop: Copley.*

8 *e-2*

BROOKS BROTHERS

Nothing trendy here—even the exterior looks incredibly solid. Even so, shirt colors are getting florid and accessories are positively Ralph Laurenesque. Brooks Brothers is America's oldest, long favored for its fine moderate-to-expensive suits and sportswear, cut traditionally (for women and boys, too). *46 Newbury St., Back Bay, 617/267-2600. T stop: Arlington.*

6 *f-5*

75 State St., Downtown, 617/261-9990. T stop: Government Center.

1 *b-5*

Chestnut Hill Mall, 617/964–3600. T stop: Chestnut Hill.

8 *f-2*

BURBERRYS

For men and women, the place to come for that toney English-country-weekend look. Clothing, scarves, umbrellas, luggage, and, of course, the famed trench-coats, almost all of which feature the distinctive Burberrys check. *2 Newbury St., 617/236–1000. Closed Sun. T stop: Arlington.*

8 *f-3*
JOS. A. BANKS CLOTHIERS
The roots of "the Boston look" were cultivated here long ago; today, fans still come here for direct-from-the-manufacturer, excellent first-quality, this-season's clothing at 30% off. The style is Traditional with a capital T: suits, jackets, coats, and accessories as well as rugged wear for both men and women. *399 Boylston St., Back Bay, 617/536–5050. T stop: Arlington.*

3 *b-4*
J. PRESS
For 81 years, this has been the purveyor of quintessential Ivy League togs—both ready-to-wear and (that ultimate luxury) bespoke. Expensive, but not showily so. *82 Mount Auburn St., Cambridge. 617/547–9886. T stop: Harvard Sq.*

8 *e-2*
LOUIS, BOSTON
Perhaps it's only fitting that the most famous Boston fashion label has turned out to be one in men's clothing. The home of those legendary $2,000 suits and the finest cashmere sweaters, Louis, Boston is the city's most elegant men's shop. It was founded way back in 1924, but the house style is trendy (not gimmicky, thank heavens)—and expensive; prices soar to the ozone level when you go shopping among the wide array of clothing by European artisans. Arranged primarily by style rather than size. There's also women's clothing, and a tiny café open for breakfast, lunch, and afternoon tea. *234 Berkeley St., Back Bay, 617/262–6100. Closed Sun. T stop: Arlington.*

1 *b-5*
MARTINI CARL
Sophisticated European men's clothing is offered here, contemporary yet classic in style, with an emphasis on wonderfully fine fabrics. Suits can be found up to size 52, and there's tailoring on premises for two- or three-hour service. Footwear and accessories, too. *Chestnut Hill Mall, 617/552–5143. T stop: Chestnut Hill.*

8 *d-4*
POLO/RALPH LAUREN
The bluest-chip clothing, the famed designer's lines of sportswear and suits are musts for any Bank of Boston broker. *Copley Pl., 100 Huntington Ave., Back Bay, 617/266–4121. T stop: Copley.*

8 *e-2*
SIMON'S
Established in 1905, Simon's has an extensive selection of fine men's clothing at discount, including private-label suits, slacks, and jackets, plus a full line of 100% cotton shirts. Accessories galore, and alterations, too. *220 Clarendon St., Back Bay, 617/266–2345. T stop: Arlington.*

contemporary

8 *d-3*
BACK BAY HARLEY-DAVIDSON
If you want that outlaw chic look, head here for hats, jackets, and other apparel with the distinct Harley-Davidson logo. For the ultimate accessory, try out one of their custom bikes. *160 Newbury St., Back Bay, 617/236–0840. T stop: Copley.*

8 *e-3*
EDDIE BAUER
Boston, of course, is far from being rain- or snow-proof—so chances are natives *and* Freedom Trail–visiting tourists will want to opt for clothes that are reversible, hooded, woolen lined, and sporty. Eddie Bauer's snow parkas, walking jackets, mountain leggings, and other necessities of life will more than fit the bill. *500 Boylston, Back Bay, 617/262–6700. T stop: Copley.*

8 *c-3*
EMPORIO ARMANI
The great Giorgio started out with men's clothes, so you can be sure his jeans and casual clothes are some of the best around. *210–214 Newbury St., Back Bay, 617/262-7300. T stop: Copley.*

8 *c-3*
NIKETOWN
One of the newer—and more controversial—shops, Niketown opened in the summer of 1997 in a striking new structure (designed by the firms Oregon and Ruhl Walker) whose tall glass windows, round corner tower, and lead-coated copper roof made it an instant street stand-

out. Video monitors show every Nike ad ever made, glass tubes serve as merchandise conduits, and the sound of games reverberates in parts of the store. Oh, yes, they have shoes, too. But the store's opening Boston Marathon display angered many Bostonians since Nike was not a marathon sponsor, as were other shoe companies. *200 Newbury St., Back Bay, 617/267–3400. T stop: Copley.*

8 *a-4*

PATAGONIA

Outdoor clothing with panache and a sense of adventure, Patagonia mostly does you up—no surprise—in earth colors. But even if you're not planning a trek to Tibet, you can wear their stylish gear around town or on a picnic with the kids. For both men and women. *346 Newbury St., Back Bay, 617/424–1776. T stop: Hynes Convention Center/ICA.*

8 *d-2*

RICCARDI

Boston men can now be as cutting-edge as any New Yorker, thanks to the snappy Moschino, Byblos, and Thierry Mugler designs offered here. Accessories, too. *116 Newbury St., Back Bay, 617/266–3158. Closed Sun. T stop: Copley.*

3 *b-4*

SOLAMEN

The men's side of Jasmine Sola Solamen (more noted for her dress shop), including shoes in a variety of styles and designs. *37 Brattle St., Cambridge, 617/354–6043. T stop: Harvard Sq.*

resale/vintage/surplus

8 *a-4*

ARMY BARRACKS, INC.

More counterculture than spit-and-polish, this surplus store has U.S. and European military clothes and equipment—a place to pick up both tie-dye shirts and camouflage pants. There's also a dog-tag-stamping machine. *328 Newbury St., Back Bay, 617/437–1657. T stop: Hynes Convention Center/ICA.*

3 *d-6*

KEEZER'S

Well known as the "poor man's Brooks Brothers," this store has been a Cambridge tradition since 1895 (albeit in a new location) for musty as well as new tuxedos, tweed sportcoats, suits, overcoats, sportswear—mostly used, some new. Low prices, buys, too. *140 River St., Cambridge, 617/547-2455. Closed Sun. T stop: Central Sq.*

8 *b-4*

MASS ARMY NAVY STORE

Good source for Levi's, Lee's, CPO shirts, khakis, peacoats, new and used military surplus. Shoes and boots by Timberland, Converse, and Reebok. Camping items and surplus goodies including Swiss army knives, Eastpak bags, and knapsacks. *895 Boylston St., Back Bay, 617/267–1559. T stop: Copley.*

3 *b-4*

1436 Massachusetts Ave., Cambridge, 617/497–1250. T stop: Harvard Sq.

unusual sizes

8 *f-2*

ROCHESTER BIG & TALL CLOTHING

With fashions for hard-to-fit men, Rochester features suits, sportswear, tuxedos, in sizes 46 regular to 60 extra long. Perry Ellis, Pierre Cardin, Charles Jourdan, and shoes by Cole-Haan, Bally, and Nike, are some of the favored lines. *399 Boylston St., Back Bay, 617/247–2727. T stop: Arlington.*

CLOTHING FOR MEN/SPECIALTY

shoes & boots

8 *d-4*

BALLY OF SWITZERLAND

The finest leathers are used in Bally's high-quality European footwear and accessories. *Copley Pl., 100 Huntington Ave., level one, 617/437–1910. T stop: Copley.*

1 *b-5*

Chestnut Hill Mall, 617/244–5307. T stop: Chestnut Hill.

8 *f-2*

CHURCH'S

Veddy proper English shoes for men are offered here in a quiet, conservative setting. *399 Boylston St., Back Bay, 617/424–1077. T stop: Arlington.*

8 *d-2*

COLE-HAAN

Two floors of classic leather men's and women's shoes beckon here, plus belts, purses, and other accessories. *109 Newbury St., Back Bay, 617/536–7826. T stop: Arlington.*

8 *d-3*

EL PASO

If you're hankering for specialty Western boots—casual to extravagant—check out the Nocona, Larry Mahan, Rios of Mercedes, Texas Boot Company, Lucchese lines here. Custom designed to order, too. Other offerings include Western shirts, outerwear, belts, and Native American jewelry. Prices range from $60 to $900. For men and women. *154 Newbury St., Back Bay, 617/536–2120. T stop: Copley.*

6 *b-4*

HELEN'S LEATHER SHOP

This longtime Beacon Hill boutique specializes in exotic leather boots for men and women: alligator, ostrich, buffalo, shark, python, anteater, frog, lizard. Also stocks Nocona, Lucchese, Dan Post, Tony Lama, Justin, and Frye. Jackets, handbags, briefcases, luggage, and accessories and will ship anywhere. *110 Charles St., 617/742–2077. T stop: Charles/MGH.*

6 *b-5*

NAHAS LEATHER

Handy resource for shoes and boots for both men and women. Bass, Frye, Clarks, Rockport, Timberland, Birkenstock, and 9 West are the most popular lines. *65 Charles St., Beacon Hill, 617/723–6176. T stop: Charles/MGH.*

COINS

6 *e-5*

OLD BOSTON COIN CO., INC.

This is the spot to head for when you're just getting into the field—coin and stamp hobbyists come here on their way to becoming full-fledged collectors. And kiddies (of all ages) flock here for a wide array of historic baseball cards. *44 Bromfield Rd., Downtown, 617/542–7720. Closed Sun. T stop: Park St.*

COMPUTERS & SOFTWARE

COMPUSA

Located in what passes for Boston's Silicon Valley, twenty miles west of Boston's city center, this is a main resource for great computer bargains. Finding the store is a bit difficult, but head off Exit 13 of the Mass Pike and start asking directions. *500 Cochituate Rd., Framingham, 508/875–8300.*

7 *a-2*

CYBERSMITH

This was one of the first (and we mean one of the first three) Cybercafés around—a fab place to try out (and buy) new software and games and cruise the net. *36 Church St., Cambridge, 617/492–5857. T stop: Harvard Sq.*

6 *f-4*

Faneuil Hall, Government Center, 617/367–1777. T stop: Government Center.

6 *f-5*

EGGHEAD SOFTWARE

Everything you need—from basic computer hard/software to graphic design tools to modems to laptops to.... The staff is young and generally helpful. *1 Liberty Sq., Financial District, 617/426–0540. T stop: Government Center.*

4 *f-6*

1327 Beacon St., Brookline, 617/734–6616. T stop: Coolidge Corner.

7 *d-4*

1000 Massachusetts Ave., Cambridge, 617/354–3051. T stop: Harvard Sq.

7 *c-7*

MICROCENTER

This is a vast store with just about everything—soft/hardware, peripherals, both PC and Macs. Fans say this is where to go when you want to be sure they have a product and you don't care about the price. *727 Memorial Dr., Cambridge, 617/234–6400. T stop: Central Sq.*

6 *d-6*

VIRTUALLY WIRED

This is a fine place for public access to computers—surf the net, learn about computers in a user-friendly setting, and sign up for classes and tutorials. There's also a nice stock of video and virtual reality games. *19 Temple Pl., Downtown, 617/542–5555. Closed Sun. T stop: Park St.*

COSTUME RENTAL

6 *d-8*

BOSTON COSTUME CO.

Cavemen to Las Vegas showgirls—all the trappings are here to make any day an early Halloween. This is basically a theatrical costume resource and has been a long-time Boston mainstay. Custom work is also done. *69 Kneeland St., Chinatown, 617/482–1632. Closed Sun. T stop: N.E. Medical Center.*

CRAFTS

See also Galleries *in* Chapter 2.

6 *7-g*

ARTSMART

Whimsical, wacky, and often wild collections of glassware, lamps, home accessories, candles, and other items offer happy hunting grounds for that extra touch for the living room or study. *272 Congress St., 617/695–0151. T stop: South Station.*

3 *b-2*

IRIS GALLERY

An assortment of crafts designed to meet every taste, from American-made jewelry, lamps, desk accessories, scarves, ties, picture frames, clocks, boxes, vases, and more. *1782 Massachusetts Ave., Porter Sq., Cambridge, 617/661–1192. T stop: Porter Sq.*

8 *d-4*

PAVO REAL GALLERY

A fantasy zoo of papier-mâché and metal creatures created by seven artists who share a common theme of animal sculpture. Noteworthy are the ceramic works of Mexican artist Sergio Bustamante; Silver jewelry, mirrors and other crafts are also strong. *Copley Pl., 100 Huntington Ave, 617/437–1280. T stop: Copley, Back Bay.*

6 *f-4*

WHIPPOORWILL CRAFTS

Whimsical and oft-kitchy American-made crafts are the forte here, along with jewelry, ceramics, and glass. *126*

Faneuil Hall Marketplace, 617/523–5149. T stop: Haymarket, Government Center.

8 *c-4*

Prudential Center, 800 Boylston, 800/860–9551. T stop: Hynes Convention Center/ICA.

8 *b-3*

ZOE

This Newbury shop, owned by the people at Artsmart, features an array of art and accessories for the home. *279 Newbury St., Back Bay, 617/375–9135. T stop: Hynes Convention Center/ICA.*

ELECTRONICS & AUDIO

3 *h-5*

CAMBRIDGE SOUNDWORKS

From stereos to the latest in cutting-edge sound, this is a top source for electrical components of all kinds. located in the CambridgeSide Galleria complex. *100 CambridgeSide Pl., Cambridge, 617/225–3900. T stop: Lechmere.*

3 *c-8*

GOODWIN'S AUDIO

High end, high performance audio and video equipment is offered here—stereo components to surround sound. The place to check out if you're shopping for the "Ferrari"s of the field. *870 Commonwealth Ave., The Fens, 617/734–8800. T stop: BU West.*

8 *f-3*

TWEETERS

This is one of Boston's leading resources for TVs, stereos, camcorders, Walkmans, and all sorts of other electronic goodies. No computers, however. *350 Boylston St., Back Bay, 617/262–2299. T stop: Arlington.*

7 *a-3*

104 Mt. Auburn St., Cambridge, 617/492–4411. T stop: Harvard Sq.

ETHNIC ITEMS & CLOTHING

8 *b-3*

MAYAN WEAVERS

Handmade Mayan shirts, jackets, ponchos, scarves, and sweaters, as well as jewelry and native artifacts, provide a bit of lovely Latin sizzle to any wardrobe. *268 Newbury St., Back Bay, 617/262–4352. T stop: Hynes Convention Center/ICA.*

3 *b-2*
NOMAD
Does your Back Bay salon cry out for a Moroccan sheepskin lampshade colored with henna? Then head here for that and other goodies ranging from Afghan rugs to Mexican pottery. Nomad is known for its multicultural clothing, jewelry, textiles, and folk art from around the world. It also features one-of-a-kind tribal pieces. The store's slogan is "where kitsch and couture cohabitate" and the staff's sartorial efforts seem to live up to that. *1741 Massachusetts Ave., Cambridge, 617/497–6677. T stop: Porter Sq.*

8 *d-4*
PAVO REAL
In a shop next to the Pavo Real art boutique, here's a wonderful selection of "export only" quality goods from Mexico and Central and South America, including clothing, hand-knit and machine-knit woolens, and items of very fine Pima cotton. Alpaca sweaters are a specialty in traditional earth tones but also come in terrific shades of blue and green. In addition, you'll find colorful, fashionable accessories, all caringly purveyed. *Copley Pl., 100 Huntington Ave, 617/437–1280. T stop: Copley, Back Bay.*

3 *c-3*
PEABODY MUSEUM GIFT SHOP
Lovely ethnic handicrafts and jewelry from faraway places—Bali, India, Nepal, Peru, Mexico, Japan, and China—are the delights here. *11 Divinity Ave., Cambridge, 617/495–2249. T stop: Harvard Sq.*

8 *d-3*
PEKING ORIENTAL IMPORTS
Colorful and, for the most part, inexpensive imports from the People's Republic of China—baskets, kites, fans, brocade accessories—for sale here will help lend pizzazz to most any room. *159 Newbury St., 617/262–2947. Closed Sun. T stop: Copley.*

3 *c-4*
PREM-LA
A little bit of India in Boston, this shop features handmade jewelry, clothing, art,

and decorative gifts from the land of elephants and emeralds. *1648 Massachusetts Ave., Cambridge, 617/492–7674. T stop: Harvard Sq.*

8 *b-3*
SAFARI EXPRESS
Handmade African and Israeli crafts are the specialty here, including a menagerie of animal forms. *291 Newbury St., Back Bay, 617/437–6666. T stop: Hynes Convention Center/ICA.*

8 *b-3*
SHAMBALA TIBET
If you're into Himalayan chic, then the clothes, jewelry, and artifacts here are just for you. *270 Newbury St., Back Bay, 617/437–0346. T stop: Hynes Convention Center/ICA.*

FABRIC

8 *f-2*
LAURA ASHLEY
To English-country-retreat your home, opt for the popular fabrics that can be purchased by the yard here. *75 Arlington St., Cambridge, 617/357–5151.*

8 *h-4*
NORTH END FABRICS
Located for more than 30 years on the edge of Chinatown, this spot retails high-end textiles including linens, wool suiting, imported lace, silk jacquard, and wool challis. There's even a large inventory of fake "fun" fur. Home-sewers love this place for its drapery and slipcover fabrics. Incidentally, if you have a mind to shop around, there are half a dozen fabric shops all within a few blocks of here. *31 Harrison Ave., 617/542–2763. Closed Sun. T stop: Downtown Crossing, Chinatown.*

8 *e-2*
PIERRE DEUX FRENCH COUNTRY
Thanks to the lovely Souleido fabrics here, you can lend your home the unmistakable charm of French-country-Provence. *111 Newbury, Back Bay, 617/536–6364. T stop: Copley.*

FLOWERS & PLANTS

Most florists have delivery services; inquire if you need door-to-door handling.

3 b-4

BRATTLE SQUARE FLORIST

Look for the large assortment of indoor and outdoor plants, cut flowers, and hanging baskets spilling onto the sidewalk in warm weather here. The busy shop also has a wealth of houseplants from African violets to the more exotic. *31 Brattle St., Harvard Sq., Cambridge, 617/876–9839 and 617/547–7089. T stop: Harvard Sq.*

3 b-4

DUTCH FLOWER GARDEN AT HARVARD SQUARE

The specialty: rare blossoms, such as bulbs imported from Holland. Their dried floral and herb wreaths are fragrant, long-lasting delights. Silk flowers, too. *12 Eliot St., Cambridge, 617/491–0660. T stop: Harvard Sq.*

8 d-3

164 Newbury St., Back Bay, 617/859–0660. T stop: Copley.

6 f-4

FANEUIL HALL FLOWER MARKET

Huge greenhouse market that predates the Marketplace complex, offering exotic fresh flowers, hanging baskets, and seasonal offerings. Open 24 hours a day year-round. *The Marketplace, 7 North St., Government Center, 617/742–3966.*

6 b-5

FRENCH BOUQUET INC.

One of the best Beacon Hill spots for unusual flowers and plants, French Bouquet also offers dried flower arrangements, and a select assortment of vases and pots. *53A Charles St., Beacon Hill, 617/367–6648. T stop: Charles/MGH.*

3 6-c

MAHONEY'S

This extensive garden center—one of several Mahoney's in the Boston area—has plants for the garden and inside the home, plus gardening supplies and gifts. The center is open all year-round. *889 Memorial Dr., Cambridge, 617/354–4145. Nearest T stop: Central Sq.*

8 d-2

WINSTON FLOWERS

Without a doubt, Winston creates some of the most beautiful and eye-catching floral arrangements ever sent to say "Thank you!" or "Thinking of You." The shops also have houseplants, books, pots, and baskets at both of their Back Bay locations. *569 Boylston St., 617/457–4900.*

8 d-3

131 Newbury St., 617/457–1100. T stop: Copley.

1 b-5

Chestnut Hill Mall, 800/457–4901. T stop: Chestnut Hill.

FOOD

baked goods

3 b-4

THE BLACKSMITH HOUSE

Several rapid ownership changes haven't affected the popularity of this spot in Harvard Square, noted for its sweet treats and snacks. Now run by the Hi-Rise Pie Co., which also has a bakery at 208 Concord Ave. (the Hi-Rise Bread Co.) in Cambridge, the eatery—housed in the historic Pratt House—offers buns, brioches, specialty breads, and sandwiches and soups. *56 Brattle St., Harvard Sq., Cambridge, 617/492–3003. T stop: Harvard Sq.*

9 d-4

BOSCHETTO BAKERY

Good North End spot for crusty Italian and French bread, Boschetto is both wholesale and retail. *158 Salem St., North End, 617/523–9350. No credit cards. T stop: Haymarket.*

9 d-4

BOVA'S BAKERY

In the Italian North End, Bova's serves up delicious bread, cookies, and pastries available 24 hours a day, 7 days a week. *134 Salem St., North End, 617/523–5601. No credit cards. T stop: Haymarket.*

6 b-4

PANIFICIO BAKERY

This Beacon Hill hangout has fresh-baked specialty breads and delectable pastries in a quaint, sometimes crowded, setting. *144 Charles St., Beacon Hill, 617/227–4340. T stop: Charles/MGH.*

6 *b-4*

REBECCA'S BAKERY

Savor a pastry or another treat in a historic setting: the ground floor of the Charles Street Meetinghouse, once an antislavery stronghold. *119 Mt. Vernon St., Beacon Hill, 617/742–9542. T stop: Charles/MGH, Park St.*

3 *f-5*

ROSIE'S BAKERY

Beautiful specialty cakes are the special delight here, including some decorated with real flowers. Must-eat: those sinfully delicious brownies worthy of all the accolades they have received. Also check out Chocolate Orgasm, the fabulous chocolate cake. Fresh fruit pies are another best bet. *243 Hampshire St., Cambridge, 617/491–9488. T stop: Central Sq.*

6 *f-7*

2 South Station, Boston, 617/439–4684. T stop: South Station.

1 *b-5*

9 Boylston St., Chestnut Hill, 617/277–5629. T stop: Chestnut Hill.

candy

6 *f-4*

CHOCOLATE DIPPERS

Here's where they take luscious fruits—like strawberries, bananas, and raspberries—and dip them in your choice of dark or milk chocolate. Also a full assortment of truffles, turtles, and other treats. Boxes and baskets available, too. *Marketplace Center, Downtown, 617/439–0190. T stop: Haymarket.*

1 *b-5*

Chestnut Hill Mall, 617/969–7252. T stop: Chestnut Hill.

8 *d-4*

GODIVA CHOCOLATIER

Those who love these justifiably coveted, elaborately boxed sweets know that a Godiva morsel a day keeps the doctor away. *Copley Pl., 100 Huntington Ave., level one, Back Bay, 617/437–8490. T stop: Copley.*

1 *b-5*

The Atrium, 300 Boylston St., Chestnut Hill, 617/969–6992. T stop: Chestnut Hill.

cheese

See Gourmet Goodies, *below.*

3 *a-2*

FORMAGGIO KITCHEN

Their *very* extensive selection of fresh imported cheeses is considered the best by the most. In addition, the store carries baked goods and hot and cold prepared entrées to go. *244 Huron Ave., Cambridge, 617/354–4750. T stop: Harvard Sq.*

fish & seafood

9 *f-3*

BAY STATE LOBSTER CO., INC.

Located at Battery Wharf on the waterfront, this is *the* place for the freshest seafood, including oversize live lobsters. If you're taking one home, this is where to get it. *379–395 Commercial St., North End, 617/523–7960 or 617/523-4588 for wholesale. T stop: Haymarket.*

3 *h-4*

COURT HOUSE SEAFOODS

Cambridge fish market is a main neighborhood resource for taking out and eating in. Fresh food—fish-and-chips, chowder, fried squid rings, broiled seafood, salads—and fast. *484 Cambridge St., Cambridge, 617/876–6716. Closed Sun.*

4 *d-3*

LEGAL SEAFOOD MARKETPLACE

This retail outlet of the renowned seafood restaurant offers some of the freshest fish daily; lobsters can be packed for travel. *33 Everett, Allston, 617/787–2050. Closed Sun.*

gourmet goodies

3 *e-5*

BREAD & CIRCUS

This was one of the first of the natural foods/gourmet grocery stores that have now sprung up coast to coast. Long a Boston-area institution, the stores stock organic and specialty produce (although many consumers may blanch at the prices), fresh herbs, fresh-baked goods, prepared foods such as soups, fish, deli items, and munchies—*healthy* munchies! All in all, the ultimate New Age yuppie hangout. *115 Prospect, Cambridge, 617/492–0070. T stop: Central Sq.*

1 *d-2*

186 Alewife Brook Parkway, Cambridge, 617/491–0040. T stop: Alewife.

1 *c-4*

15 Washington, Brookline, 617/738–8187. T stop: Washington Street (Green, B or Boston College) or Washington Square (Green, C or Cleveland Circle).

3 *b-2*

CAMBRIDGE COUNTRY STORE

The country comes to town in this enticingly aromatic shop where they roast their own coffee beans daily (more than 20 varieties available) and make their own fudge. Grains and a marvelous variety of spices in bulk can be found, plus teas in bulk and coffee by the cup. Candies, party supplies, baskets, etc. Cookware, as well. *1759 Massachusetts Ave., Cambridge, 617/868–6954. T stop: Porter Sq.*

3 *b-4*

CARDULLO'S GOURMET SHOP

This top gourmet shop purveys the usual to the exotic, and everything you can't find elsewhere. Imported specialty foods include truffles and fresh caviar; imported cheeses; large selection of teas. Another draw is the great selection of champagnes, wines, and more than 200 imported beers. *6 Brattle St., Harvard Sq., Cambridge, 617/491–8888. T stop: Harvard Sq.*

6 *b-4*

SAVENOR'S MARKET

Until 1992, this market was located in Cambridge and was known as the place where Julia Child shopped for her meat! Today, it remains a small unit of a large wholesale business that supplies hundreds of restaurants and eateries. The store stocks meats, poultry, seafood, produce, and fancy foods, including some tasty baked goods. *160 Charles St., Beacon Hill, 617/723–MEAT. T stop: Park.*

health food and alternative medicines

3 *c-2*

CAMBRIDGE NATURAL FOODS

Organic produce, home-baked muffins, tempting sandwiches—this grocery store is a cornucopia of healthy things. *1668 Massachusetts Ave., Cambridge, 617/492–4452. T stop: Harvard Sq.*

3 *b-4*

HARNETT'S

Want to stay away from your doctor? Check out this place—a sort of alternative "CVS." *47 Brattle St., Cambridge, 617/491–4747. Closed Sun. T stop: Harvard Sq.*

ice cream

6 *b-8*

BEN & JERRY'S

Stop at the sign of the spotted cow for a delicious Vermont-export: A tantalizing variety of ice-cream and frozen yogurt flavors. A cone of Coffee Heath Toffee Crunch, anyone? *20 Park Plaza, 617/426–0890. T stop: Arlington.*

8 *d-3*

174 Newbury St., Back Bay, 617/536–5456. T stop: Copley.

3 *b-4*

HERRELL'S

This chain was founded by Steve Herrell, the original creator of Steve's Ice Cream, who, after selling his product's name, decided to get back into the ice-cream business. Nondairy ice creams and frozen yogurts augment the extensive variety of regular flavors. *15 Dunster St., Cambridge, 617/497–2179. T stop: Harvard Sq.; 155 Brighton Ave., Allston, 617/782–9599; 350 Longwood Ave., 617/731–9599. T stop: Longwood.*

8 *a-4*

J. P. LICKS HOMEMADE ICE CREAM

Lots of tasty flavors and sorbets for those seeking a light touch are the draws here. *352 Newbury St., Back Bay, 617/236–1666. T stop: Hynes Convention Center/ICA.*

5 *h-4*

674 Centre, Jamaica Plain, 617/524–6740. T stop: Green St.

3 e-6

TOSCANNI ICE CREAM
Creamy, luscious treats—who cares about the calories? This popular local ice-cream shop has now expanded to Harvard Square. *899 Main St., Cambridge, 617/491–5877. T stop: Kendall.*

3 b-4

1320 Massachusetts Ave., Harvard Sq., Cambridge. T stop: Harvard Sq.

FRAMING

8 4-b

THE BACK BAY FRAMERY
Along with custom framing, this place offers photographic services. *303 Newbury St., Back Bay, 617/424–1550. T stop: Hynes Convention Center/ICA.*

3 b-1

FRAMEWORKS
Fine custom framing—even do-it-yourself—is serviced here with the help of the friendly and knowledgeable staff. Also conservation mats and ready-made frames. *2067 Massachusetts Ave., Cambridge, 617/868–6798. T stop: Porter Sq.*

6 b-4

KENNEDY STUDIOS
They claim to have the lowest-priced framing in Boston (based on a written estimate); they're speedy, too. Check out the extensive Boston print and poster collection. *31 Charles St., Beacon Hill, 617/523–9868. T stop: Charles/MGH.*

3 e-5

731 Massachusetts Ave., Central Sq., Cambridge, 617/876–9305. T stop: Central.

6 d-6

140 Tremont, Downtown, 617/338–9483. T stop: Arlington.

6 g-4

200 State St. Downtown. T stop: State.

6 f-5

50 Milk St., Downtown, 617/426–1027. Closed Sun. T stop: Government Center.

GIFTS

6 b-5

BLACKSTONES OF BEACON HILL
Eclectic mix of hand-painted ceramics, lamps, lampshades, ties, table linens,

gardening books, and other knickknacks can all be found here. You pay for the location, but it would be hard not to find something you like here. *46 Charles St., Beacon Hill, 617/227–4646. T stop: Charles/MGH.*

FUN & FUNKY

In the market for a conversation-piece birthday gift? Head to these fab places.

American Animated Classics
A kid's store masquerading as an animated art store for adults, this is the place to pick up original cels from classic cartoons—at, needless to say, the kind of prices you'd pay in a fine arts gallery. 166 Newbury St., Back Bay, 617/424–0640. T stop: Copley.

Condom World
With the breezy slogan "protect and serve," this 6-year-old shop offers an array of condoms and other sex toys—happily, more in a spirit of fun, not sleaze. A few items, however, are definitely X-rated. 332 Newbury St., Back Bay, 617/267–SAFE. T stop: Hynes Convention Center/ICA.

Gargoyles, Grotesques, and Chimeras
The spookiest shopping you'll ever do in Boston! Full-size statues of saints, plus an array of large and small, stone and clay gargoyles and other creatures that go bump in the night. 276 Newbury St., Back Bay, 617/536–0216. T stop: Hynes Convention Center/ICA.

Promised Land
Once upon a time this might have been called a "head shop." Now it's a nonprofit store devoted to the legacy of Jerry Garcia—the Grateful Dead legend—with counterculture clothes, jewelry, products made of (legal) hemp, plus other odds and ends. What a long, strange shopping "trip" it's been, as Jerry might say. The same company also run Cool Beans, also here in the Garage at Harvard Square, which has retro clothing, jewelry, and collectibles. 36 JFK St., Harvard Sq., Cambridge, 617/547–3463 or 617/492–2244. T stop: Harvard Sq.

f-4

BOSTON CITY STORE

Here's where to find that truly memorable Boston souvenir—hardhats to parking meters to vintage street signs. Profits from this city-run store support neighborhood youth programs, to boot. *Faneuil Hall basement, Downtown, 617/ 635–2911. Closed Sun. T stop: Haymarket, Government Center, State St.*

6 *f-4*

CHRISTMAS DOVE

Where Christmas resides year-round—with ornaments, crèches, frosted window scenes, and a general ho-ho-ho atmosphere. *Faneuil Hall Marketplace, 617/523–2173. T stop: Haymarket, Government Center, State St.*

8 *f-5*

F'KIA

Candles, soaps and home accessories, including metal racks and mirrors, are all shown here in a funkily inviting setting. Say hi to Ming, the friendly turtle saved from a soup tureen, then ask owner Ned Hand about the new home furnishings store she's planning for nearby Clarendon Street. *558 Tremont St., South End, 617/357–5553. T stop: N.E. Medical Center.*

3 *b-1*

JOIE DE VIVRE

A Cambridge favorite that lives up to its name with toys, trinkets, and other things that make you smile. Wind-up toys, stamps, strings of chili-pepper lights, old-fashioned kaleidoscopes, cards, crowns, and other delightful little nothings. *1792 Massachusetts Ave., Cambridge, 617/864–8188. T stop: Porter Sq.*

 b-5

J. OLIVER'S

A pleasing place to pick up cards, stationery, colorful wrapping paper, and unusual pens under a ceiling hung with a great selection of charming old-fashioned Christmas ornaments, which are sold all year around. *38 Charles St., Beacon Hill, 617/723–3388. T stop: Charles/MGH.*

 c-3

LONDON LACE

In a delicately scented, airy store, you'll find lace curtains, tablecloths, bedspreads, sheets, pillowcases, napkins, and place mats, many created from century-old patterns. Handmade pillows created from antique pieces of lace, needlepoint, and embroidery draw the eye, while soaps and scents tempt the nose. Be sure to pick up a catalog. *215 Newbury St., Back Bay, 617/267–3506. T stop: Copley.*

3 *b-4*

MDF

This small but distinctive Harvard Square shop features high-end crafts for the home, including glassware, clocks, and teapots. You can't miss the particularly striking black and white pottery by Californian Kathy Ertman. *19 Brattle St., Cambridge, 617/491–2789. T stop: Harvard Sq.*

8 *f-2*

THE WOMEN'S EDUCATIONAL & INDUSTRIAL UNION

A nonprofit social services organization founded in 1877, the Union has several retail outlets. *Gift Shop*—gifts and decorative items. *Collector's Shop*—antiques and collectibles. *Children's Shop*—clothing, newborn–size 4 toddlers, and stuffed animals, too. *Needlework Shop*—hand-painted canvases; Boston scenes make nice souvenirs. Also a *Card & Stationery Shop*. Proceeds go to the Union. *356 Boylston St. Back Bay, 617/536–5651. Closed Sun. T stop: Arlington.*

HOBBIES

ART BEAT

The retail outlet of The Artist in Me—Boston's main craft and hobby resource and learning center—Art Beat has oodles of craft supplies, rubber stamps and bosses, ceramic molds, paper maché kits, doll making supplies, weaving instruments, you name it. The Artist in Me, located in Cambridge (617/491–1661), offers a wide array of craft workshops. To reach this Arlington store, take the No. 77 bus from Harvard Square. *212A Massachusetts Ave., Arlington, 781/646–2200.*

HOBBY CONNECTION

Every day is Christmas morning here—hundreds of Lionel trains and other model train sets, HO scale and up, are for sale. In addition, all sorts of boat, plane, and model kits are available, plus paints, plastics, and, of course, balsa wood. Where else can you find a Titanic model-kit in Boston? *4 Franklin St., Stoneham, 617/438–1697. Closed Sun.*

HOME FURNISHINGS

for the bath

3

BED, BATH & BEYOND
This mega-store has everything you need—and *more*—from Fieldcrest to Ralph Lauren and Martex. *3 Abbot Park, Burlington, 781/272–4588.*

8 *a-4*

BOSTON BED & BATH
Your basic bed linens, plus towels, blankets, comforters, and other such niceties. They often have great sales. *361 Newbury St., Back Bay, 617/491–5431. T stop: Hynes Convention Center/ICA.*

3 *c-1*

1 Porter Sq., Cambridge, 617/491–5431. T stop: Porter Sq.

carpets & rugs

8 *d-3*

DECOR INTERNATIONAL
Dhurries, kilims—including pieces from Poland—and Oriental-style rugs from Iran, Turkey, and 38 other countries are the draws here. Owners Lorraine and Emmanuel Balkin launched their business more than 36 years ago after a vacation trip to Sardinia turned into a textile-buying spree. Ask them about the rugs they sold to Jackie O. *141A Newbury St., Back Bay, 617/262–1529. Closed Sun. T stop: Copley.*

6 *b-5*

MARIO RATZKI ORIENTAL RUGS
A good assortment of antique Persian and Turkish rugs is supplemented here with a nice Whitman's Sampler of Chinese carpets. *40 Charles St., Beacon Hill, 617/742–7850. Closed Sun., Mon. T stop: Charles/MGH.*

china, glassware, porcelain, & pottery

8 *d-3*

BELLEZZA HOME AND GARDEN
Known for its fine Italian bowls, plates, vases, planters, and tiles, Bellezza is also popular for other brightly painted accessories for inside and outside the home. *129 Newbury St., Back Bay, 617/266–1183. T stop: Hynes Convention Center/ICA.*

3 *b-1*

CHINA FAIR
Kitchen utensils and gadgets, baskets, paper products, housewares, and storage items are sold here in a jumbled, bargain-basement setting. *2100 Massachusetts Ave., Cambridge, 617/864–3050. No credit cards. Closed Sun. T stop: Porter Sq.*

3 *b-4*

CRATE & BARREL
Located in a famed Cambridge building—it originally housed the Design Research shop—this chain features distinctive dinner- and glassware, kitchenware, stemware, vases, rugs and kitchen gadgetry. Exclusive imports from around the world, including a large selection of handblown glass, abound. Check out the seasonal inventory, such as patio furniture, and the noted collection of contemporary home furnishings. For the main selection of Crate & Barrel Furniture, head for the shop at 1045 Massachusetts Avenue, in Cambridge. *48 Brattle St., Cambridge, 617/876–6300. T stop: Harvard Sq.; Copley Pl., 617/536–9400. T stop: Copley.*

6 *f-4*

Faneuil Hall Market Pl., 617/742–6025. T stop: Haymarket, Government Center.

1 *b-5*

Mall at Chestnut Hill, Newton, 617/964–1800. T stop: Chestnut Hill.

3 *b-4*

LOULOU'S LOST & FOUND
Elle Decor photographed this place when they did their recent article on shopping in Boston—the Newbury Street storefront is certainly one of Boston's cutest! Inside, pick up tableware, salt and pepper shakers, and other conversation-piece items scavenged from vintage ships and hotels, as well as new items

based on vintage designs. The Cambridge shop, though cramped, has become an exceedingly popular place for tea lovers, thanks to its new "Tealuxe" tea bar, which offers more than 200 varieties for your sipping pleasure (*see* Chapter 3). And yes, one shop is located at Zero Brattle Street. *Zero Brattle St., Harvard Sq., Cambridge, 617/441–0077. T stop: Harvard Sq.*

8 *d-2*
121 Newbury St., 617/859–8593. T stop: Copley.

8 *d-2*
PIERRE DEUX FRENCH COUNTRY
Tres chic et charmant, this is the store that put French Provincial on the map. What is it about French country patterns that seem both eye-catching and sophisticated? Find the answers by perusing Pierre Deux's fabulous Souleido French country patterns for curtains (you can buy fabric by the yard), wallpaper, tablecloths, and scarves. *111 Newbury St., Back Bay, 617/536–6364. T stop: Copley.*

8 *d-2*
POTTERY BARN
A longtime furnishings favorite, Pottery Barn recently got a whole new design makeover and their offerings are snappier than ever. The Newbury shop has a large selection of imported housewares, rugs, tiles, pillows, candles—and yes—pottery. *122 Newbury St., 617/266–6553. T stop: Copley.*

3 *d-5*
1000 Massachusetts Ave., Cambridge. T stop: Central Sq.

8 *d-2*
SIMON PEARCE
The Irish-born, English-trained Simon Pearce has become a favored designer for those who like their glass and pottery bowls, vases, lamps, pitchers, and wine glasses understated, elegant, and simple. Don't look for flash here. *115 Newbury St., Back Bay, 617/450–8388. T stop: Copley.*

furniture & furnishings

3 *b-4*
APRIL CORNELL
The place to buy colorful, imported Indian print fabrics in tablecloths, place mats, napkins, bed linens, pillows, and other accessories. Also pottery and china, plus women's clothes. The store's outlet in Faneuil Hall Market has some real deals. *43 Brattle St., Harvard Sq., Cambridge, 617/661–8910. T stop: Harvard Sq.*

8 *d-4*
BOMBAY COMPANY
The grande dames of old Boston would have loved the English-style items of this store, which is stocked with highly affordable reproduction heirloom-look home furnishings. *Copley Pl., 617/236–5998. T stop: Copley.*

CIRCLE FURNITURE
A wonderful selection of classic cherry, maple, pine, and oak furniture for every room of the house is available here—most items offered finished and unfinished. Prices are very reasonable. Just a few blocks away is a handy outlet store. *199 Alewife Brook Parkway, Cambridge, 617/876–3988. T stop: Alewife.*

3 *c-5*
CRATE & BARREL FURNITURE
Chairs, tables, rugs, lamps, upholstery, kids' furniture, desks—in all, affordable "lifestyle" furniture. *1045 Massachusetts Ave., Cambridge, 617/547–3994. T stop: Central Sq.*

8 *f-2*
DOMAIN
Two floors of high-style couches, loveseats, recliners, end tables, armoires, and home accessories draw the sophisticated shoppers here. *7 Newbury St., Back Bay, 617/266–5252, T stop: Arlington.*

3 *d-5*
THE DOOR STORE
This chain recently went from low-priced, no-frills contemporary furniture models to the sort of elegant-yet-trendy designs—overstuffed sofas, library-ready wingchairs—any yuppie would love. The prices, thankfully, are still on the gentle side. Also, a fine selection of finished and unfinished furniture, and shelf systems. *940 Massachusetts Ave., Cambridge, 617/547–8937. T stop: Central Sq.*

8 *e-3*

DURHAM PINE

Cheerful pine furniture shown by cheerful staff, plus antiques and giftware, are the main offerings in this British-owned shop. *416 Boylston St., Back Bay, 617/437–7660. T stop: Arlington.*

8 *a-4*

HOLD EVERYTHING

This popular space-saving furniture and houseware chain has opened a shop in Boston, featuring many of the items that show how you can stylishly fit a lot into a little. *351 Newbury St., Back Bay, 617/450–9846. T stop: Hynes Convention Center/ICA.*

6 *b-5*

KOO DE KIR

A leopard-print lounge chair in the shape of a huge ladies' pump is typical of the unusual home accessories you'll find here at one of Charles Street's newer shops. Koo carries furniture lines from Mike Moore of San Francisco, plus lamps, candles, and wine racks. *34 Charles St., Beacon Hill, 617/723–8111. T stop: Charles/MGH.*

8 *f-2*

LAURA ASHLEY

The floral designs of the popular English-country fabric designer as applied to home furnishings: fabric, wallpaper, bed linens, and lampshades. You can also buy the fabric for do-it-yourself projects. See the Newbury Street stores for clothing and other accessories. *75 Arlington St., Cambridge, 617/357–5151.*

3 *a-2*

MOHR & MCPHERSON

Here's where to find that unusual Moroccan end table to spice up your living room. The main store has wonderful wrought-iron chandeliers and candlesticks, lamps, and mirrors, plus Lillian August upholstered sofas—but the real showstoppers are the imported Indian, Moroccan, and North African tables, chairs, benches, chests, and cabinets shown in the store's annex across Concord Avenue. Nearly all the imported furniture is handmade, with many pieces brightly painted. *290 Concord Ave., Cambridge, 617/354–6662. T stop: Porter Sq.*

8 *f-2*

PALAZZETTI

High-end stylish and exclusive Bauhaus-style and modern tables, chairs, desks, couches, and home accessories are displayed in a bright, airy showroom. Connoisseurs flock here for those classic-yet-cutting-edge Fornasetti designs. *31 Saint James Ave., South End, 617/482–2950. T stop: Arlington, N.E. Medical Center.*

8 *e-3*

SWEET PEAS HOME

Think Laura Ashley on LSD—colorful handmade tables, desks and chairs, plus one-of-a-kind mirrors, vases, and candleholders, all arranged with panache and generous portions of wit and whimsy. Everything here is handmade, some by local artists, some with a distinct West Coast flare. *216 Clarendon St., Back Bay, 617/247–2828. T stop: Arlington.*

8 *a-4*

URBAN OUTFITTERS

Look here for great choices for the student setting up at home in a dorm or a new apartment, from rugs to glassware to other necessities of urban life—Gothic-style candlesticks, fuchsia pillows, and aubergine-hued desk accessories provide those perfect Generation-X finishing touches. *361 Newbury St., 617/236–0088. T stop: Hynes Convention Center/ICA.*

3 *b-4*

11 John F. Kennedy St., Cambridge, 617/864–0070. T stop: Harvard Sq.

3 *c-5*

WORKBENCH

Well-designed contemporary "lifestyle" furniture is featured here. Easy elegance is displayed in the lamps and wall accessories. Children's furniture, too. *1050 Massachusetts Ave., Cambridge, 617/876–9754. T stop: Central Sq., Harvard Sq.*

8 *f-4*

142 Berkeley St., South End, 617/267–8955. T stop: Arlington.

lamps & lighting

3 *b-1*

CITY LIGHTS

This shop has one of the region's largest selections of restored antique lighting, 1850–1930. *2226 Massachusetts Ave., Cambridge, 617/547–1490. Closed Sun.–Tues. T stop: Porter Sq.*

4 *h-5*

ENLIGHTENMENTS

This spot offers a gracious selection of lighting fixtures, most dating from the 1900s on. *1042 Beacon St., The Fens, 617/277–8666. T stop: St. Mary's.*

3 *3-9*

NEENA'S

This is one of Boston's long-time standards for lighting fixtures. There are also branches in Burlington and Wellesley. *1313 Beacon St., Brookline, 617/232–1900. T stop: Coolidge Corner.*

linens

6 *b-5*

LINENS ON THE HILL

Linens, bath items, soaps, perfume—all delicately scented and colored. Plus tablecloths and dish towels. *52 Charles St., Beacon Hill, 617/227–1255. T stop: Park St.*

8 *d2*

PRATESI LINENS

Elegantissimo! Italian linens for the bed and bath—high quality with equally elevated prices: You can spend hundreds for a sheet. *110 Newbury St. Back Bay, 617/262–5998. T stop: Copley.*

paint & wallpaper

8 *a-2*

JOHNSON PAINT CO.

Winner of a *Boston* magazine "Best of Boston" award, this is a fave for folks who are looking for the latest designer colors and patterns. Anyone for Evening Slipper Silver or Incarnadine? *355 Newbury St., Back Bay, 617/536–4244. T stop: Hynes Convention Center/ICA.*

HOUSEWARES & KITCHEN ESSENTIALS

3 *c-4*

BOWL & BOARD

Hardwood accessories for the home are the focus—salad bowls, cups, plates, chalices, cutting boards, and butcher blocks in a variety of sizes. And great wooden toys! *1063 Massachusetts Ave., Cambridge, 617/661–0350. T stop: Harvard Sq.*

8 *d-3*

KITCHEN ARTS

The place for tools for the creative cook, from the smallest (and most inexpensive) aids to luxury items (Italian ice-cream makers). A specialty: cutlery—repair and sharpening. Calphalon, All-Clads, and Master Chef cookware, Cuisinart food processors and accessories; bakeware, coffee makers, and cookbooks, are all in stock, and they'll ship anywhere via UPS. *161 Newbury St., Back Bay, 617/266–8701. T stop: Copley.*

6 *b-5*

SEASONINGS

This very pleasant and interesting kitchen arts and furnishing shop on Beacon Street, near Charles Street, stocks nifty items—pottery, place mats, utensils, and more. *65 Beacon St., Beacon Hill, 617/227–2810. T stop: Park St.*

6 *e-6*

STODDARD'S

Since 1800, this has been the source for an excellent variety of high-quality cutlery from all over the world—scissors and knives (including Swiss army and J. A. Henckels) by the hundreds, plus fishing rods at downtown store only. *50 Temple Pl.; 617/426–4187. Closed Sun. T stop: Downtown Crossing.*

8 *d-4*

Copley Pl., 100 Huntington Ave., level one, Back Bay, 617/536–8688. T stop: Copley.

1 *b-5*

Chestnut Hill Mall, 617/244–4187. T stop: Chestnut Hill.

8 *d-4*

WILLIAMS-SONOMA

Self-described as the "Tiffany of cookware stores," Williams-Sonoma is the famed San Francisco-based chain known for quality copper, stainless, aluminum, enamel, and iron. Gourmet foods from around the world are now also featured, including packaged spices, herbs, and condiments. All the latest gadgets, plus cookbooks, electrical appliances, porcelain and earthenware, stemware, flatware, and table linens. *Copley Pl., 100 Huntington Ave., level one; 617/262–3080. T stop: Copley.*

6 *f-4*
Marketplace Center, 617/439–7035. T stop: Government Center, Haymarket.

1 *b-5*
The Atrium, 300 Boylston St., Chestnut Hill, 617/969–7090. T stop: Chestnut Hill.

GADGETRY

6 *f-4*
BROOKSTONE
A great shop for fine tools and gadgets, this place has high-tech gizmos for the home and auto. *Marketplace Center, Downtown, 617/439–4460. T stop: Haymarket.*

8 *d-4*
Copley Pl., 617/267–4308. T stop: Copley.

8 *d-4*
THE SHARPER IMAGE
This national chain has all manner of electronic gadgetry—where else can you find a 6-foot-long Star Wars Trooper (only $5,500) and a globe that identifies countries as you touch them? *Copley Pl., 100 Huntington Ave., Back Bay, 617/262–7010. T stop: Copley.*

JEWELRY

For more antique and estate jewelry, *see* Antiques, *above.*

antique & collectibles

8 *d-3*
SMALL PLEASURES
A wonderful selection of antique and estate jewelry, Tiffany glass, and Art Deco objets awaits the collector here. *142 Newbury St., Back Bay, 617/267-7371. Closed Sun. T stop: Copley.*

contemporary

8 *f-2*
CARTIER
The world-famous fine jewelry store now brings a touch of Parisian glamour to the Boston scene. *40 Newbury St., Back Bay, 617/262–3300. T stop: Arlington.*

8 *f-2*
DORFMAN
A suitably elegant backdrop, this store spotlights watches by Cartier, Vaucheron Constantine, Chanel, Patek Philippe, as well as diamond jewelry and Mikimoto pearls. Classical and contemporary jewelry designs; imports, too. *24 Newbury St., Back Bay, 617/536–2022. T stop: Arlington.*

8 *e-2*
JOHN LEWIS, INC.
For more than 30 years, a creator of imaginative jewelry, this boutique specializes in solid precious metals and natural stones, using the finest workmanship. No credit cards. *97 Newbury St., Back Bay, 617/266–6665. Closed Sun., Mon. T stop: Arlington.*

8 *f-2*
SHREVE, CRUMP & LOW
Since 1800, one of Boston's signature sources for jewelry, sterling, pewter, and china. Visiting the bridal registry here was always the Brahmin way to start a proper marriage. Shreve now also features a fine antiques department. *330 Boylston St., Back Bay, 617/267–9100. T stop: Arlington.*

8 *d-4*
TIFFANY & CO.
The prestigious treasure house from New York features bejeweled designs by Jean Schlumberger, Elsa Peretti, and Paloma Picasso. For special gifts and occasions, many corporations swear by the store's offerings in gold, silver, watches, gems, crystal, china, silver, and clocks. *Copley Pl., 100 Huntington Ave., Back Bay, 617/353–0222. T stop: Copley.*

costume jewelry

3 *b-4*
BAAK GALLERY
This small space is filled with silver—earrings, necklaces, pins—ranging from high-end to inexpensive. Head up to the second floor for crafts. *35A Brattle St., Cambridge, 617/354–0407. T stop: Harvard Sq.*

3 *b-4*
BEADWORKS
This flourishing chain is a tribute to a trend that has more staying power than anyone could have predicted: make-

your-own beaded jewelry. You can pick up every imaginable kind of bead, plus take a class in how to put them all together. *15 Church St., Harvard Sq., Cambridge, 617/868–9777. T stop: Harvard Sq.*

8 *a-4*

349 Newbury St., Back Bay, 617/247–7227. T stop: Hynes Convention Center/ICA.

8 *d-3*

MARCOZ

Furniture, decorative objects, plus a nice selection of antique jewelry draw fans here. *177 Newbury St., Back Bay, 617/262–0780. Closed Sun. T stop: Copley.*

8 *b-5*

TWENTIETH CENTURY LTD.

The kind of store that Madonna would have adored during her Material Girl period, Twentieth Century offers up every kind of rhinestone concoction imaginable, plus other jewelry designs—classic to funky, antique to reproduction. *73 Charles St., Beacon Hill, 617/742–1031. T stop: Charles/MGH, Park St.*

KITES

6 *f-4*

KITES OF BOSTON

Let's go fly a kite—but first drop in here to pick out a dazzler, ranging in price from $3 to 1,000. Boomerangs, yo-yos, juggling equipment, Frisbees, and all manner of kinetic equipment are also in stock. They even have the latest in Buggy-kiting—3-wheeled vehicles that are powered by kites! *7 Faneuil Hall, North Market Bldg., Government Center, 617/742–1455. T stop: Aquarium, State St., Government Center.*

LEATHER GOODS

8 *d-4*

COACH

For many women, a Coach handbag is a badge of both style and practicality. Coach has classic purses, wallets, briefcases, and other leather goods, known for their durability and the company's policy of repairing products forever (which accounts for the sticker shock). *Copley Pl., 100 Huntington Ave., Back Bay, 617/262–2782. T stop: Copley.*

8 *e-2*

75 Newbury St., Back Bay, 617/536–2777. T stop: Arlington.

8 *c-3*

IN THE BAG

Shoppers head here for the nice, if small, selection of women's purses, bags, and briefcases. Catch the sales. *217 Newbury St., Back Bay, 617/536–9776. T stop: Copley.*

8 *f-2*

LORENZI OF ITALY

Brilliantly hued wallets, purses, briefcases, and other leather goods in alligator, ostrich, buffalo, lizard, and calfskin are proffered here, all made in Milan, Italy. There's also a small but colorful assortment of Italian scarves. *Heritage on the Green, 310 Boylston St., Back Bay, 617/728–0345. Closed Sun. T stop: Arlington.*

LUGGAGE

8 *d-4*

LOUIS VUITTON

Vuitton's custom services for travelers began more than 131 years ago and, today, remains the ultimate status symbol on bags, luggage, and accessories. There is also a line without the "LV" for those secure—and chic—enough to carry it. *Copley Pl., 100 Huntington Ave., Back Bay, 617/437–6519. T stop: Copley.*

8 *c-4*

TRAVEL 2000 TRAVEL GEAR

A handy outlet for all luggage needs, conveniently located in Prudential Center, Boylston St. side, opposite Legal Sea Foods. *Prudential Center, Back Bay, 617/536–3101. T stop: Copley or Hynes Convention Center/ICA.*

MAPS

6 *d-6*

BOSTON WELCOME CENTER

A popular souvenir and gift store, this center also stocks many maps and guide books to Beantown. *140 Tremont St., Beacon Hill, 617/451–2227. T stop: Park St.*

3 *b-4*

GLOBE CORNER BOOKSTORE

Along with a wide selection of books dealing with all aspects of life and travel in New England, these stores have fine map selections. *28 Church St., Cambridge, 617/497–6277. T stop: Harvard Sq.*

8 *e-3*

500 Boylston St. Back Bay, 617/859–8008. T stop: Copley.

MUSIC & MUSICAL INSTRUMENTS

3 *c-2*

CAMBRIDGE MUSIC CENTER

The staff is super friendly—they like to call themselves the mercantile equivalent of the barbershop quartet—but the store stocks everything new under the sun, from guitars and amps to used instruments, from songbooks to percussion pieces and instructional videos. *1906 Massachusetts Ave., Cambridge, 617/491–5433. T stop: Porter Sq.*

3 *c-2*

CENTRAL SALE MUSIC CO.

The basic stock in trade here is instruments—used and new. Central prides itself on great trade-ins. Along the way, they also service repairs, offer lessons, and sell sheet music. *1702 Massachusetts Ave., Cambridge, 617/876–0687. T stop: Porter Sq.*

NEEDLEWORK

8 *c-3*

THE YARNWINDER

You can buy pricey European sweaters by the drove along Newbury Street or you can come here and get yarns to make your own. Knitting supplies, needlepoint kits, and lush and luscious yarns are in abundance here. *247 Newbury St., Back Bay, 617/262–0028. T stop: Auditorium.*

NEWSPAPERS & MAGAZINES

3 *c-4*

OUT-OF-TOWN NEWS

The place to buy national and international newspapers and magazines, Out-of-Town is one of Harvard Square's mainstays. Open daily 6 AM to midnight. *Zero Harvard Sq., Cambridge, 617/354–7777. T stop: Harvard Sq.*

OFFICE SUPPLIES

6 *f-5*

STAPLES SUPERSTORE

This is the main Boston outpost for the giant nationwide chain. *31 Milk St., Financial District, 617/338–6776. T stop: State St.*

PHOTO EQUIPMENT

6 *e-6*

BROMFIELD CAMERA CO.

A wide array of goods are stocked to meet many of your photo and video needs, with an especially strong selection of Sony video gizmos. Film processing, of course. *10 Bromfield St., Downtown, 617/426–5320. T stop: Downtown Crossing.*

7 *a-3*

SBI

Just about everything from A to Z can be found here, to the delight of budding and professional photographers. *57 JFK St., Cambridge, 617/576–0969. T stop: Harvard Sq.*

RECORDS, TAPES, & CDS

3 *b-4*

BRIGGS & BRIGGS

In addition to a great selection of classical music, mainly on CDs and tapes, there are also in-depth collections of folk, blues, ethnic, Broadway cast albums, and movie sound tracks. Also sheet music. *1270 Massachusetts Ave., Cambridge, 617/547–2007. T stop: Harvard Sq.*

3 *e-5*

CHEAPO RECORDS

Où sont les temps de vinyl? Here, that's where. This Boston favorite stocks used R&B, rock, and jazz; LPs and 45s, along with some new records and CDs. *645 Massachusetts Ave., Cambridge, 617/354–4453. T stop: Central Sq.*

3 *b-4*

HMV

This 23,000-square-foot music emporium, with rock, pop, folk, classical, and New Age offerings, features listening stations and a d.j. spinning music throughout the day. Open until midnight Friday and Saturday in Cambridge. *1 Brattle Sq., Cambridge, 617/868–9696. T stop: Harvard Sq.*

6 *d-6*

24 Winter St., Downtown, 617/357–8444. T stop: Downtown Crossing.

8 *a-4*

LOONEY TUNES

Records, CDs, tapes, and videos are on tap here, along with a large selection of used and out-of-print jazz and rock records. Classical, film, and Broadway sound tracks, comedy, and country are features, plus LPs, 45s, and "Cutouts." *1106 Boylston St., 617/247–2238. T stop: Auditorium.*

3 *b-4*

1001 Massachusetts Ave., Cambridge, 617/ 876–5624. T stop: Harvard Sq., Central Sq.

8 *4-b*

MYSTERY TRAIN II

Used and collectible CDs, tapes, and vinyl draw the youthful fans here. The Newbury Street store enjoys long hours. *306 Newbury St., Back Bay, 617/536– 0216. T stop: Hynes Convention Center/ICA.*

3 *b-4*

1208 Massachusetts Ave., Cambridge, 617/ 497–4024. T stop: Harvard Sq.

8 *f-2*

NEWBURY COMICS

So much more than a comics store: this youth-leaning chain (with more than a dozen outlets in the greater Boston area) specializes in independent and import music as well as current hits, plus T-shirts, Goth-Rock posters, trading cards, lava lamps, and assorted other Gen-X paraphernalia. *332 Newbury St., Back Bay, 617/236–4930. T stop: Hynes Convention Center/ICA.*

6 *f-4*

1 Washington Mall, Faneuil Hall, 617/ 248–9992. Closed Sun. T stop: Government Center.

3 *b-4*

36 JFK St., Harvard Sq., Cambridge, 617/ 491–0337. T stop: Harvard Sq.

3 *g-6*

84 Massachusetts Ave., MIT, Cambridge. T stop: Kendall Sq.

2 *b-4*

NUGGETS

Used and out-of-print jazz, rock, country, and soul records are the special collections here, along with a huge selection of new releases at low prices. New and used cassettes and CDs as well. They trade, and buy as well as sell. *486 Commonwealth Ave., Kenmore Sq., 617/536–0679. T stop: Kenmore Sq.*

4 *g-6*

1354A Beacon St., Brookline, 617/277– 8917. T stop: Coolidge Corner.

3 *e-5*

SKIPPY WHITE'S

New as well as oldies-but-goodies: Rap, R&B, soul, gospel, reggae, and blues, all featured in records, videos, cassettes, and CDs. *538 Massachusetts Ave., Central Sq., Cambridge, 617/491–3345. T stop: Central Sq.*

3 *b-2*

STEREO JACK'S RECORDS

Laid-back and quirky, this institution puts the emphasis on blues and jazz. You can pick up used vinyl as well as CDs and tapes. *1686 Massachusetts Ave., Cambridge, 617/497–9447. T stop: Harvard Sq.*

8 *c-4*

STRAWBERRY'S

This longtime music chain remains popular thanks to its selections of rock, pop, folk, and classical. *761 Boylston St., Back Bay, 617/482–5257. T stop: Copley, Hynes Convention Center/ICA.*

7 *b-7*

750 Memorial Dr., Cambridge, 617/492– 7850. T stop: Central Sq.

8 *4-a*

TOWER RECORDS & VIDEO

One of the ever-growing claimants to the title of "the largest record store in the world," Tower usually moves into major cities with huge multilevel record emporiums, bursting at the seams with bezillions of LPs, 45s, CDs, audio- and videocassettes. Thanks to its heavy student population, Boston can support two of these monsters. Open until midnight most nights. *360 Newbury St., Back Bay, 617/247-5900. T stop: Hynes Convention Center/ICA.*

3 *b-4*
95 Mt. Auburn St., Cambridge, 617/876-3377. T stop: Harvard Sq.

SEWING & NOTIONS

See also Needlework, *above.*

3 *h-4*
DISCOUNT FABRICS
This is a popular neighborhood resource near the Cambridgeside Galleria. *473 Cambridge St., Cambridge, 617/661–8361. T stop: Lechmere.*

6 *d-7*
NORTH END FABRICS
An exceptionally helpful and friendly place, this was voted "Best Fabric Store in Boston" by *Boston* magazine. The stock runs from fashion fabrics to bridal silks to man-made furs to quilting cottons to velvets—-plus a wide selection of notions, trims, and zippers. Not suprisingly, their motto is "Almost Everything." *31 Harrison St., Downtown/Chinatown, 617/542–2763. Closed Sun. T stop: Boylston St., Downtown Crossing.*

SPORTING GOODS & CLOTHING

sports apparel

3 *b-4*
J. AUGUST CO.
Since 1891, this Ivy League shop—across from Harvard Yard—has featured college fashions and athletic sportswear. Everything has Harvard, MIT, and other Ivy League college imprints on it: tees, shorts, sweats, and jackets. Harvard souvenir items, too. *1320 Massachusetts Ave., Cambridge, 617/864–6650. T stop: Harvard Sq.*

3 *b-4*
BRINE'S
Established in 1870 in Harvard Square, this well-stocked shop is a favorite Cam-

bridge spot for sports equipment, including athletic shoes by Adidas, Pony, Nike, Saucony, Brooks, Asics. In addition, Brine's is a favored team outfitter, too. *29 Brattle St., Cambridge, 617/876-4218. T stop: Harvard Sq.*

6 *a-7*
CITY SPORTS
With numerous locations around Boston, many with extended hours, City Sports offers a full range of running shoes, weights, balls and bats, even snorkeling equipment, with special emphasis on the youthful athlete. *480 Boylston St., Back Bay, 617/267–3900. T stop: Arlington.*

6 *e-4*
20–28 Bromfield St., Downtown Crossing, 617/423–2015. T stop: Downtown Crossing.

3 *b-4*
16 Dunster St., Harvard Sq., Cambridge, 617/868-9232. T stop: Harvard Sq.

4 *f-4*
1035 Commonwealth Ave., Allston, 617/782–5212. T stop: Babcock.

3 *b-1*
ROACH'S SPORTING GOODS
For more than 50 years, the store has functioned as hiking, camping, fishing, and hunting specialists. Archery equipment and canoes are also stocked. *1957 Massachusetts Ave., Cambridge, 617/876–5816. Closed Sun. T stop: Porter Sq.*

boating

1 *g-5*
BOXWELL CHANDLERY
A seafaring person's shop for navigation charts, brass fittings, and foul-weather and canvas gear; clothing and footwear, too. *12B St., South Boston (near corner of Dorchester Ave.), 617/241–2800. Closed Sun. T stop: Broadway.*

camping

4 *f-4*
EASTERN MOUNTAIN SPORTS
Their specialty: rugged outdoor equipment and apparel. This place is also popular for its backpacks, tents, sleeping bags, footwear, canoes, and cross-

country skis. Rental of equipment as well. *1041 Commonwealth Ave., Allston, 617/254–4250. T stop: Babcock.*

`6` *e-3*

HILTON'S TENT CITY

A 1947 surplus store, Hilton's Tent City has now grown into an emporium for low-priced hiking, backpacking, tenting, and camping equipment. Footwear includes boots and clothing for both men and women; Cross-country skis; but no running shoes. *272 Friend St., Old West End, 617/227–9242; (800) 362–TENT. T stop: North Station.*

golf

`6` *f-5*

BOSTON LINKS GOLF SHOP

Everything—plus—for the serious and the wanna-be serious golfer can be found here, including clubs, clothes, and accessories. *150 Federal St., Downtown, 617/261–0254. Closed Sun. T stop: State St.*

`8` *d-4*

116 Huntington Ave., Back Bay, 617/859–1800. T stop: Copley.

running

`6` *f-4*

BILL RODGERS RUNNING CENTER

A full line of sports clothing, footwear, and leisure wear with the famed marathoner's logo is sold here, along with Brooks, Reebok, Etonics, Insport, Sporthill, and Nike. *Faneuil Hall Marketplace, North Market Bldg., 617/723–5612. T stop: Haymarket, Government Center.*

`3` *b-3*

MARATHON SPORTS

For distance and track-and-field runners, this is the place to go for personalized service, particularly in trying out running shoes—they don't mind if it takes a while. But don't expect discount prices. Athletic footwear by Adidas, Nike, Brooks, ASCII, and Saucony are offered, along with tennis and volleyball shoes. Warmups, accessories, and books and magazines on running and fitness complete the picture. *1654 Massachusetts Ave., Cambridge, 617/354–4161. T stop: Harvard Sq.*

soccer

`6` *f-4*

THE WORLD SOCCER SHOP

A pushcart business that became a shop, the World Soccer Shop features shirts, hats, mugs, jerseys, jackets, and other items emblazoned with the names and logos of soccer teams from around the world, including the New England Revolution. Run by a couple of guys who live and breathe soccer, the shop testifies to the gradual increase of popularity in the United States of a sport that enthralls the rest of the world. *Faneuil Hall Marketplace, Downtown, 617/248–9696. T stop: Haymarket, Government Center.*

STATIONERY

`8` *c-4*

CRANE & CO.

Cards, letterheads for professional and career use, plus Carte Blanche pens and other accessories, make this an all-in-one resource. *Prudential Center, 800 Boylston St., Back Bay, 617/247–2822. T stop: Prudential.*

`3` *b-2*

PAPER SOURCE

Gild that special gift from their multitude of gorgeous-to-funky wrapping papers (and what looks like tie-dye tissue paper!). Check out their large selection of specialty papers, with names like "Rainbow Marble" or "Speckled Oatmeal." Also decorative stamps, ribbons, and invitation-oriented services. *1810 Massachusetts Ave., Cambridge, 617/497–1077. T stop: Porter Sq.*

`8` *c-4*

PAPYRUS

A wide array of wrapping papers, stationery, and other like accessories are available here. *Prudential Center, 800 Boylston St., Back Bay, 617/262–6449. T stop: Prudential.*

`6` *f-4*

SCRIBE'S DELIGHT

Everything for the writer's cramp: pens, inkwells, calligraphy pens, sets, kits, and books. Also stationery, blank books, gift wraps, seals and sealing wax. *Faneuil Hall Marketplace, 617/523–2572. T stop: Government Center.*

TOBACCONISTS

8 *d-3*

CIGAR MASTERS

Billing itself as Boston's first "cigar café," this Newbury Street frontier is awash with the heady nose of Artier Fuente and other popular brands. Connoisseurs can buy 35-year-old Masahis for about $50 a piece. Not a spot recommended for antismoking types. *176 Newbury St., Back Bay, 617/266–4400. T stop: Copley.*

8 *f-3*

L. J. PERETTI COMPANY

Blenders of tobacco, Peretti will create your own personal blends. *2½ Park Sq., Back Bay, 617/482-0218. Closed Sun. T stop: N.E. Medical Center.*

3 *b-4*

LEAVITT & PEIRCE

A full-service tobacco supply shop, established in 1883, Leavitt & Peirce not only has a wide range of cigars, pipe tobacco, chewing tobacco, and smoking accessories, but chess sets and backgammon games. *1316 Massachusetts Ave., Harvard Sq., Cambridge, 617/547–0576. Closed Sun. T stop: Harvard Sq.*

TOYS & GAMES

3 *b-4*

CURIOUS GEORGE GOES TO WORDSWORTH

Named for the children's series (penned by the late Cambridge author Margaret Rey), this annex of WordsWorth is devoted entirely to children's books, from infants to young adult. There's a 15% discount off hardcovers; 10% off paperbacks. Books can be shipped worldwide. *One JFK St., Harvard Sq., Cambridge. T stop: Harvard Sq.*

6 *f-4*

DISNEY STORE

The next best thing to Disneyland, this vast chain offers up bezillions of Mickeys, Goofys, and Donald Ducks plastered over everything from T-shirts to toys. Look for those great stuffed dolls taken from Disney's fabled cartoon classics (such as *Alice in Wonderland*)! Any tyke will adore the fabulous displays and giant video screens. *Faneuil Hall Market, Downtown, 617/248-3900. T stops: Government Center, Haymarket.*

3 *b-1*

THE ENCHANTED COTTAGE

A Lilliputian-size world of its own, this shop is stocked with dollhouses—already assembled, or do-it-yourself kits—and a wide variety of miniature furnishings, floor coverings, and light fixtures. Architectural plans(!), too. *2512 Massachusetts Ave., Cambridge, 617/491–8818. T stop: Porter Sq.*

6 *e-5*

ERIC FUCHS HOBBIES

Around for nearly 50 years, this is a noted hobby shop with a large selection of model trains, planes, radio-controlled equipment, dollhouses and furnishings kits, military models, plastic models, and so much more. *28 Tremont St., Back Bay, 617/227–7935. T stop: Downtown Crossing.*

8 *f-2*

FAO SCHWARZ

The famed purveyors of fancy fantasies for children, this extravaganza features much that is opulent for the affluent, including life-size stuffed animals and miniaturized powered automobiles. The standards, too—kites, puzzles, dolls, games, and toys, plus a Barbie Boutique in, of course, shades of pink. Although it has stores nationwide, this world-renowned toy emporium has lost none of its exclusivity. A must visit if you have or are a child. Naturally, you'll want a photo op with the huge teddy bear statue in front of the store. *440 Boylston, Back Bay, 617/262–5900. T stop: Arlington.*

3 *b-4*

THE FUNNY FARM

This endearing shop has a huge variety of windup toys, from waddling penguins, swimming ducks, and drumming bears, plus battery-operated toys. Inexpensive, by and large, and the store will ship. *8 Eliot St., Harvard Sq., Cambridge, 617/661–3999. T stop: Harvard Sq.*

3 *a-3*

HENRY BEAR'S PARK

A charming neighborhood children's store, Henry Bear's Park carries a wide selection of books, toys, and games, including such specialty items as Carolle dolls and the Muffy Vander Bear Collection. Also games, dinosaurs, and party favors, but nothing that hints of violence. *361 Huron St., Cambridge, 617/ 547–8424. T stop: Porter Sq.*

3 *b-4*

LEARNINGSMITH

Self-designated as a "general store for the curious mind," Learningsmith has books, software, tapes, home projects, games and other products designed to be both stimulating and fun. Happily, this is the brainchild of WGBH, the PBS Boston affiliate. *25 Brattle St., Cambridge, 617/661–6008. T stop: Harvard Sq.*

6 *h-7*

RECYCLE

A great resource for arts-and-crafts and science projects. Recycle has huge barrels of raw industrial materials such as contact paper, plastic, stickers, buttons, wallpaper, ribbon. Sold in volume by the bag or measure, it's all very cheap—and colorful, popular, and fun. *Boston Children's Museum, 300 Congress St., Downtown, 617/426–8855 (recording) or -6500. Admission to store is free. T stop: Aquarium.*

3 *a-3*

SUSI'S: A GALLERY FOR CHILDREN

Hand-painted furniture, mirrors, wacky animal-motif frames and clocks, puppets, and funkadelic jewelry make a kaleidoscope of colors and forms in this tiny shop. Pricey, but many items are one of a kind. *348 Huron Ave., Cambridge, 617/876–7874. Closed Sun. T stop: Porter Sq.*

8 *c-4*

WARNER BROS. STUDIO STORE

This store is, of course, one big commercial for Warner Bros. cartoons and movies (expect some retail space to be devoted to a current hit, such as the latest *Batman* movie) but a fun place to shop if you don't mind paying top dollar for blatant merchandising. The statue of Bugs Bunny outside the Faneuil Hall store is popular with the kiddies. *800 Boylston St., Prudential Center, Back Bay, 617/859–3770. T stop: Copley.*

6 *f-4*

Faneuil Hall Marketplace, Downtown, 617/227–1101. T stop: Haymarket, Government Center.

VIDEOS

8 *b-6*

BLOCKBUSTER VIDEO

This mega chain of your basic top-40 video stores has several stores in Boston. The South End and Cambridge branches are particularly well stocked. *235 Massachusetts Ave., South End, 617/ 578–9899. T stop: Symphony.*

3 *c-a*

1 Porter Sq., Cambridge, 617/547–6006. T stop: Porter Sq.

8 *c-3*

CITY VIDEO

A more personal place than most, City Video offers particularly in-depth selections of foreign and classic titles—also fun sections of horror and TV golden moldies. *240 Newbury St., Back Bay, 617/ 536–2489. T stop: Hynes Convention Center/ICA, Copley Place.*

3 *a-3*

23 White St., Cambridge, 617/354–7587. T stop: Porter Sq.

7 *e-5*

HOLLYWOOD EXPRESS

The name says it all. Look for their special "By Director" categories. *765 Massachusetts Ave., Cambridge, 617/864–8400. T stop: Central Sq.*

3 *c-2*

1740 Massachusetts Ave., Cambridge, 617/ 497–2001. T stop: Porter Sq.

8 *f-5*

MIKE'S MOVIES

With a more sophisticated selection than most—specialties include foreign, classic, gay/lesbian, and adult—Mike's remains a popular video outpost for the South End and Beacon Hill districts. *557 Tremont St., South End, 617/266–9222. T stop: Copley Place.*

6 *c-4*

250 Cambridge St., Beacon Hill, 617/742– 7771. T stop: Charles/MGH.

VITAMINS

3 *b-3*

HARNETT'S

A favorite of healthy Bostonians, Harnett's is a cornucopia of vitamins, holistic treatises, aromatherapy treatments, and other things good for what ails you. *47 Brattle St., Cambridge, 617/491–4747. T stop: Harvard Sq.*

WATCHES & CLOCKS

8 *b-3*

FINE TIME WATCHES

A leading resource for vintage time-pieces, this store stocks all the main names, including Rolex, Hamilton, Gruen, Tiffany, Patek Philippe, Cartier, Swatch, and—hooray!—also Mickey Mouse. *279 Newbury St., Back Bay, 617/536–5858. T stop: Copley.*

3 *b-4*

SWATCH STORE & MUSEUM

This store-cum-sanctuary is devoted to the history of those popular, waterproof, and colorfully controversial Swiss-made watches. (Recall how they struck a blow for analog against the digital watch craze in the 1980s?) Upstairs is a large selection of watches for sale; downstairs are more than 900 collector's pieces on display, valued from $40 to $25,000. *57 JFK St., Harvard Sq., Cambridge, 617/864–1227. T stop: Harvard Sq.*

WINE & SPIRITS

8 *c-3*

BACK BAY WINES & SPIRITS

One of Boston's most distinguished sources for fine wine, this is known for its Sherry-Lehmanesque stock and quality. If you want a fabulous Lafite-Rothschild, head here. Of course, there are plenty of wonderful, normally priced labels here, too. *704 Boylston St., Back Bay, 617/262–6571. Closed Sun. T stop: Copley Place.*

4 *e-4*

BROOKLINE LIQUOR MART

Ten thousand square feet, more than 3,000 labels of wine, 100 facings of single malts—you get the picture. This is one of Boston biggest liquor stores, located near Boston University. *1354 Commonwealth Ave., Allston, 617/734–7700. Closed Sun. T stop: Allston St.*

6 *f-5*

FEDERAL WINES

This is a fine and distinguished boutique for wines, known for its higher-end offerings. *29 State St., Downtown, 617/367–8605. Closed Sun. T stop: State St.*

4 *h-5*

THE WINE PRESS

Located near Fenway Park, this is a well-known and very popular spot, offering selections from all price categories. *1024 Beacon St., The Fens, 617/277–7020. Closed Sun. T stop: St. Mary's.*

chapter 5

ARTS, ENTERTAINMENT, & NIGHTLIFE

Boston's performing arts scene has always been active, but until recently, it was quite traditional, in both style and outlook. No more! Under the influence of a vibrant hodgepodge of students, immigrants, transplants, and the increasingly visible gay community, the city's social life has expanded to encompass an adventurous array of possibilities. In one week alone, you can see the Boston Symphony Orchestra and local jazz luminaries, sip a Cosmopolitan and puff a stogie in a cigar bar, down a Guinness in an authentically Irish pub, catch cutting-edge theater or a foreign film festival, mosh or merengue on the dance floor, and outfit yourself in either velvet or vinyl. To find out what's going on at any given time, check these sources: the "Calendar" section in the Boston Globe, the "Scene" section of the Boston Herald, and the weekly Boston Phoenix and TAB, all of which come out on Thursday; the Improper Bostonian, which comes out every other week, and the monthly Boston magazine's "Events" feature.

arts

CONCERT HALLS

8 a-4

BERKLEE PERFORMANCE CENTER

Berklee College of Music, which owns this hall, presents more than 300 concerts a year by students, faculty, and internationally acclaimed recording artists. Berklee is internationally known for its jazz programs, but you'll also find folk, rock, and world music here. *136 Massachusetts Ave., 617/266–1400 or 617/266–7455. T stop: Hynes Convention Center/ICA.*

8 a-5

BOSTON CONSERVATORY OF MUSIC

Many of the musical events here are free. The box office is around the corner,

at 8 The Fenway. *31 Hemenway St.; 617/536–6340; box office 617/536–3063, Ext. 42. T stop: Hynes Convention Center/ICA.*

3 b-4

CAMBRIDGE CENTER FOR ADULT EDUCATION (CCAE)

The CCAE's small acoustic auditorium presents local folk, cabaret, and holiday performances which are inexpensive—usually $10 or less—and showcase performers like legendary country bluesman Guy Davis, and classical Indian-influenced jazz group Natraj. *42 Brattle St., Cambridge, 617/547–6789. T stop: Harvard Sq.*

GREAT WOODS CENTER FOR THE PERFORMING ARTS

An outdoor summers-only concert venue that attracts acts ranging from alternative rock festivals to country classics, Great Woods Center is an easy hour's drive from Boston. Get a spot under the canopy, or spread out a picnic blanket in the open seating area on the lawn. *Rte. 140, Mansfield, 508/339–2333, 617/423–NEXT.*

6 h-6

HARBORLIGHTS

This imposing giant white tent pitched on the waterfront serves up top pop, country, jazz, and oldies acts to audiences of all ages. It's a wonderful spot to catch a cool breeze on a sultry summer evening. Rumors have had it moving repeatedly over the last few years, but it hasn't gone anywhere yet. *Fan Pier, Northern Ave., 617/737–6100 or 617/443–0161. T stop: South Station.*

6 a-5

HATCH MEMORIAL SHELL

The Boston Pops perform their famous free summer concerts at this jewel of an acoustic shell set in the loveliest part of the Charles River Esplanade. Local radio stations also put on music festivals here most weekend evenings; watch for major performers and up-and-coming artists alike. Events at the Hatch Shell are free; there's a moderately priced snack bar nearby. The Hatch Shell also has one of the few public rest rooms on the Esplanade. Open mid-April to mid-November. *Charles River Esplanade, off Arlington St., 617/727–9547, ext. 550. T stop: Arlington.*

8 *b-6*

JORDAN HALL

The recently restored home of the Boston Philharmonic is a National Historic Landmark and one of the most acclaimed acoustic spaces in the world. It hosts numerous performances by the Handel and Hayden Society, the Boston Gay Men's Chorus, Boston Baroque, and other local music societies, as well as more than 100 free concerts each year by students and faculty of the New England Conservatory of Music. *New England Conservatory of Music, 290 Huntington Ave, 617/536–02412. T stop: Symphony.*

6 *d-5*

ORPHEUM THEATER

This once-ornate theater is now a popular forum for national and local rock acts intent on avoiding the stadium scene. Cramped, shabby, and occasionally overheated, it's nonetheless an intimate venue well suited to bands and their fervent fans. *1 Hamilton Pl., off Tremont St., 617/482–0650. T stop: Park St.*

3 *b-3*

EDWARD M. PICKMAN CONCERT HALL

This hall at the Longy School of Music hosts chamber music and other forms of classical music. The annual Septemberfest, denoted to a different genre each year, is a monthlong series of lectures and performances. *27 Garden St., Cambridge, 617/876–0956, ext. 120. T stop: Harvard Sq.*

7 *b-2*

SANDERS THEATER

This 1,200-seat theater has been hosting various folk, classical, and literary events for 110 years. It's located inside Memorial Hall, an imposing Gothic building belonging to Harvard University. *Cambridge and Quincy Sts., Cambridge, 617/496–2222. T stop: Harvard Sq.*

1 *d-1*

SOMERVILLE THEATER

This movie house tucks a respectable number of folk, blues, and world music performances into its schedule of art films and second-run movies. Performances take place in the main theater. Don't miss the annual festival of local songwriters, showcase for an astonishing selection of area talent. *55 Davis Sq., Somerville, 617/625–5700. T stop: Davis.*

8 *b-6*

SYMPHONY HALL

One of the world's most acoustically perfect spaces, Symphony Hall is home, from October to April, to Seiji Ozawa and the Boston Symphony Orchestra, and, from May to July, to the Boston Pops under the direction of conductor Keith Lockhart. Visiting orchestras, soloists, and chamber groups also play here throughout the year. On Wednesday evenings, the Symphony holds public rehearsals; proceeds from the (inexpensive) unreserved seating benefit the orchestra's pension fund. *301 Massachusetts Ave., 617/266–1492. Concert information, 617/266–2378. Youth Concerts, 617/638–9375. T stop: Symphony.*

3 *d-8*

TSAI PERFORMANCE CENTER

This Boston University concert hall presents many free concerts by students and faculty, both individually and in ensembles. Worth noting are the BU orchestra, chamber music troupe Alea III, and Boston Musica Viva, a chamber ensemble specializing in contemporary masterpieces and new works. *685 Commonwealth Ave., 617/353–8724. T stop: BU Central (B line).*

8 *h-3*

WANG CENTER FOR THE PERFORMING ARTS

In addition to theater and dance, the gilded 3,700-seat Wang hosts musical events of all types, from rock concerts to chamber music recitals. Renowned orchestras, vocalists, and ensembles all perform here under the auspices of the BankBoston Celebrity Series. *270 Tremont St., 617/482–9393. T stop: Boylston.*

CONCERTS IN CHURCHES

8 *f-2*

EMMANUEL CHURCH

Music lovers of all denominations visit this Episcopal congregation, known as "the Bach church" for its Holy Eucharist services on Sundays at 10 AM. A professional chamber orchestra and chorus plays one Bach cantata each week, performed in chronological order, from mid-September to mid-May. The only cost is what you choose to put in the collection plate. *15 Newbury St., 617/536–3355. T stop: Arlington.*

6 *e-5*
KING'S CHAPEL
local classical performers put on half-hour concerts each tuesday at 12:15 PM in a church with acoustics that are so excellent they need no amplification. The "noon hour recitals" are free, but donations are requested. *58 Tremont st., 617/227–2155. T stops: park st., Government center.*

8 *e-3*
TRINITY CHURCH
Enjoy a free half-hour organ recital in one of Boston's most magnificent churches, the centerpiece of Copley Square. "Fridays at Trinity" concerts take place Fridays at 12:15 PM. *206 Clarendon St., 617/536–0944. T stop: Copley.*

DANCE

ART OF BLACK DANCE AND MUSIC
Performing at venues throughout the city, this company presents the music and dance of Africa, Latin America, and the Caribbean. Call for a current schedule of performances. *617/666–1859.*

8 *b-5*
BALLET THEATRE OF BOSTON
Led by artistic director Jose Mateo, a Cuban-born choreographer, this troupe is bringing bold contemporary ballet to the Boston stage. While this relative newcomer to the local scene hasn't quite reached the popularity of Boston Ballet, it mounts an annual *Nutcracker* that is more intimate than the larger company's lavish production. Performances take place at the Emerson Majestic Theater (*see* Theater, *below*). *186 Massachusetts Ave., 617/262–0961. T stop: Symphony.*

BANKBOSTON CELEBRITY SERIES
Since 1938, this series has been New England's leading presenter of world-class performing arts. The 1998 season will feature dance performances by Tharp!, Alvin Ailey American Dance Theater, the Peking Acrobats, and others, most at the Wang Center for the Performing Arts (*see* Theater, *below*). Call

for a full schedule and locations. *617/482–2595.*

BETH SOLL AND COMPANY
This MIT teacher and choreographer performs at theaters all over Boston; her dances are based on themes from every-

---

SOME ENCHANTED EVENINGS

Looking for a date destination that won't be the same old dinner-and-a-movie? Here are a few suggestions.

Bay Tower Room (Nightlife, Dining & Dancing)
  Swing dancing and stellar views make this the most romantic spot in town.

Boston Ballet (Dance)
  The ballet on Valentine's Day has guaranteed swoon factor.

Boston University Observatory (Free Entertainment)
  If you're feeling starry-eyed, why not show it?

Colonial Theater (Theaters)
  Dress to the nines and take in a show.

Cornwall's (Nightlife, Pubs)
  Beer and backgammon make a perfect low-key evening.

Folk Arts Center of New England (Dance)
  Line, circle, and couple dances are a great way to break the ice.

The French Library (Movie Theaters)
  Read the subtitles together and call each other Gallic endearments.

Free Friday Flicks (Free Entertainment)
  Movies on a blanket beneath the night sky.

Great Woods Center for the Performing Arts (Concert Halls)
  Pack a picnic and sit on the grass.

Joey & Maria's Italian Comedy Wedding (Nightlife, Cabaret)
  After the show, discuss what you don't want your wedding to be like!

Karma Club (Nightlife, Dance Clubs)
  Incense, soft lighting, hypnotic music, and sybaritic couches.

Man-Ray (Nightlife, Dance Clubs)
  This alternative club promises a slightly kinky evening.

---

day life and have been linked to European expressionism. *617/547–8771.*

8 *e-5*
BOSTON BALLET
The city's premier dance company presents four or five classical and modern works each year. It also stages Boston's best-known performance of *The Nutcracker,* which has become even more eye-poppingly extravagant since the sets and costumes were updated in 1996. At press time, the ballet had just decided to move its smaller repertory performances to the lower-capacity Shubert Theater while keeping larger productions at the Wang Center for the Performing Arts (*see* Theater, *below*). *19 Clarendon St., 617/695–6950. T stop: Back Bay.*

DANCE COLLECTIVE
Three Cambridge choreographers have been collaborating since 1974 on dances exploring contemporary life. They hold performances all around town. Call for information. *33 Richdale Ave., Cambridge, 617/576–2737.*

7 *e-6*
DANCE UMBRELLA
This organization devoted to contemporary dance puts together touring companies, brings dancers to the Boston area for performances, and provides services for other dance companies as well. Performances are generally held at the Wang Center for the Performing Arts (*see* Theater, *below*). *380 Green St., Cambridge, 617/492–7578. T stop: Central Sq.*

FOLK ARTS CENTER OF NEW ENGLAND
Learn to do line, circle, and couple dances from around the world by attending the participatory folk dancing events put on by this group at churches, public spaces, and other locations throughout the city and suburbs. You don't need experience or a partner! Dances are inexpensive and occasionally even free. Call for a schedule of dates and locations. *1950 Massachusetts Ave., Cambridge, 617/491–6083.*

FREE ENTERTAINMENT

Many of the listings in Chapter 2, Events, are also one-time free happenings. Keep an eye on the *Boston Globe*'s "Calendar" section and the weekly *Boston Phoenix,* both of which come out on Thursday, for other budget-priced amusements.

1 *g-6*
BOSTON GLOBE TOUR
This one-hour tour of the city's largest newspaper, for ages 12 and up, starts with a slide show, then takes you through the newsroom, composing rooms, printing press room (it's loud!), and more. It's a very detailed tour. Maximum of 30 persons in a group. Tours are by reservation only, so call ahead. *135 Morrissey Blvd., Dorchester, 617/929–2000.*

8 *d-3*
BOSTON PUBLIC LIBRARY CHILDREN'S PROGRAM
Take your kids to the Rabb Lecture Hall for a movie, then on to the Children's Room for story-telling, puppet shows, and crafts demonstrations, and voila! Entertainment for hours. Call for a schedule. *Copley Sq., 617/536–5400. T stop: Copley.*

3 *e-8*
BOSTON UNIVERSITY OBSERVATORY
See stars (and planets, the moon, and other celestial bodies) every Wednesday night, weather permitting. "Open telescope" nights begin at 8:30 PM from April to September, and at 7:30 PM from October to March. Call before you go to make sure the observatory will be open; special events and clouds both can get in the way. Temperatures in the rooftop observatory are often much cooler than those on the street, even in midsummer, so wear warm clothing or take a sweater. *725 Commonwealth Ave., 617/353–2630 (recording). T stop: BU Central (B line).*

6 *h-7*
THE CHILDREN'S MUSEUM
This hands-on heaven, recently described by the *New York Times* as one of the best children's museums in the country, is free to all on Fridays from 6 PM to 9 PM (there's an admission charge the rest of the week). Dress up, pet animals, "visit" Japan, clamber in, around, and through exhibits, and visit the amazing Recycle, where you can pick up leftover craft supplies for next to nothing. You'll almost certainly decide to come back! *300 Congress St., 617/426–*

6500 or 617/426–8855 (recording). T stop: South Station.

6 a-5

FREE FRIDAY FLICKS

This rite of summer takes place at sundown every Friday (weather permitting), late June through August, at the Hatch Shell. Stake out a spot, spread out your blanket, and wait for dusk to fall. Once it's dark, a giant movie screen shows a feature film suitable for all ages. The family-friendly schedule is heavily weighted toward children's fare—expect to see several animated features—but the season traditionally ends with a classic film like *Casablanca* or *The Wizard of Oz*. Your first visit will be the beginning of a beautiful friendship. Note: The Hatch Shell's giant speakers, which can be turned up quite loud, may startle young children or make them uncomfortable, so if your child is sensitive to noise, bring earplugs. *Charles River Esplanade, off Arlington St., 617/727–9547, ext. 550. T stop: Arlington.*

1 h-3

LOGAN INTERNATIONAL AIRPORT

If you wonder how one of the world's busiest airports handles thousands of comings and goings every day, take this 90-minute tour held twice a day, Monday through Friday. You'll see the inside of a jet, customs, a fire control unit, and the weather-reporting bureau. A bus takes you right around the perimeter of the airfield so you get a good idea of the bustle. The tour is by reservation only, and you must apply by mail 3 to 5 weeks in advance. Write to MASSPORT Tour Coordinator, Logan International Airport, Boutwell 1, East Boston, MA 02108. For groups larger than 10, age 9 and older. Special tours for the sight- and hearing-impaired as well as the physically challenged. *Logan International Airport, 617/561-1800. T stop: Airport.*

3 b-4

LONGFELLOW SUMMER FESTIVAL

Take a short walk down elegant Brattle Street from Harvard Square to the home of poet Henry Wadsworth Longfellow, where classical music concerts and poetry readings take place in the garden every Sunday at 4 PM, June–September. Bring a blanket or chair. *Longfellow National Historic Site, 105 Brattle St.,*

Cambridge, 617/876–4491. T stop: Harvard Sq.

2 b-6

MUSEUM OF FINE ARTS BOSTON

In keeping with its mission to make the arts available to all, the main building of the MFA is free every Wednesday from 4 PM to 9:45 PM (voluntary donations are encouraged). This is a good time to wander quickly through, noting what you might want to return to on a later visit, or just to slip in on your way home from work for a midweek meditational visit to your favorite piece of art. Children 17 and under are admitted to the MFA free at all times. *465 Huntington Ave., 617/267–9300. T stop: Museum (E line).*

6 b-1

MUSEUM OF SCIENCE

General admission to this museum is free on Wednesdays after 1 PM (except during summer and school holidays). Take advantage of the opportunity to see the world's largest air-insulated Van de Graaff generator, which produces 15-foot bolts of lightning; the Discovery Room; the live animal demonstrations; and all the other fascinating, fabulous offerings. *Science Park, 617/723–2500. T stop: Science Park.*

MOVIE THEATERS WORTH NOTING

8 d-3

BOSTON PUBLIC LIBRARY

Of course, the BPL isn't a movie theater, but it does offer an excellent film series showing everything from classic science fiction of the 1950s to noteworthy new documentaries. All screenings take place in the huge Rabb Lecture Hall, where there's almost always a good seat to be had. Best of all, the films are free. Many of the branch libraries also have free movies; call for information. *Copley Sq., 617/536–5400. T stop: Copley.*

3 b-4

BRATTLE THEATER

The double features here never fail to fascinate. They change every day, saluting a different theme for each day of the week, e.g., Monday is the famous Film Noir night. Boxy and bare-bones though it may be, the Brattle is run by true cinema connoisseurs who singlehandedly launched the *Casablanca* revival some time ago by creating a cult following among Harvard students. Stop at the concession booth for a scoop of ice cream from Toscanini's, one of the best ice-cream shops in the entire Boston area. *40 Brattle St., Harvard Sq., Cambridge, 876–6837. T stop: Harvard Sq.*

4 *f-6*
COOLIDGE CORNER THEATER
The former balcony was long ago enclosed to provide an extra screen, and the once-large lobby has given ground to a sandwich shop. Still, the Coolidge, with its velvet seats and striking vintage murals, remains one of the few grand movie houses left in the Boston area. Recently purchased by the owners of the Brattle, the Coolidge offers an eclectic and frequently updated bill of art films, foreign films, cult flicks, and classics. Posters and postcards available in the lobby feed a Renovation Fund. The Brookline Booksmith, an independent bookstore across the street, often holds readings here as well. *290 Harvard St., Brookline, 734-2500. T stop: Coolidge Corner (C line).*

8 *e-2*
THE FRENCH LIBRARY
The Ciné Club presents a different French film every week, usually subtitled rather than dubbed into English. Shows are Thursdays at 8 PM and Fridays at 6 PM and 8:30 PM. *53 Marlborough St., 617/266–4351. T stop: Arlington.*

7 *b-3*
HARVARD FILM ARCHIVE
The comfortable downstairs theater at Harvard's Carpenter Center for the Visual Arts screens the work of new and undeservedly overlooked directors. There are usually two programs a day, and sometimes more. Call for a schedule. *24 Quincy St., Cambridge, 617/495–4700. T stop: Harvard Sq.*

7 *h-5*
KENDALL SQUARE THEATER
This sleek Deco/contemporary newcomer to the art-house scene, completed in 1995, has nine screens devoted to the latest out-of-the-mainstream gems of moviemaking. In keeping with the slightly bohemian atmosphere, the snack bar serves espresso along with the usual Raisinets and popcorn. Take

advantage of the free validated parking; the theater is actually at Hampshire and Broadway, quite a long walk from the Kendall Square T. *One Kendall Sq., Cambridge, 617/494–9800. T stop: Kendall.*

2 *b-6*
MUSEUM OF FINE ARTS BOSTON
The MFA shows foreign films in a modern, no-frills theater just inside the main entrance. There are usually two, and sometimes three, films Wednesdays through Sundays. Most films get only one or two showings, so check the schedule regularly. *465 Huntington Ave., 617/267–9300. T stop: Museum (E line).*

7 *a-2*
SONY HARVARD SQUARE
Despite being under chain ownership, this theater retains traces of its past, especially in the main theater where renovations haven't completely erased the telltale signs that this was once an old movie palace. You can still see occasional first-run independent films here; even the studio blockbusters are the thoughtful type rather than shoot-'em-ups. And this is the only place in town to find the participatory cult of the *Rocky Horror Picture Show*, which shows every Friday and Saturday at midnight—so dig out your fishnets and do the Time Warp again. *10 Church St., Cambridge, 617/864–4580. T stop: Harvard Sq.*

1 *d-1*
SOMERVILLE THEATER
If you don't want to pay full price for that movie, come here for second-run movies and current art films. And with a T stop next door and a large city parking lot down the street, it's easy to get to. A recent expansion has added several small screens, but for the full old-time theater experience, albeit with comfy new seats, sit in the balcony of the large original movie house. *55 Davis Sq., Somerville, 617/625-5700. T stop: Davis.*

2 *a-4*
SONY NICKELODEON
Although it was bought by a huge theater chain in the 1980s and occasionally does double duty as a Boston University lecture hall, the boxy, nondescript-looking "Nick" clings to its art-house roots, showing mostly first-run independent films with the occasional blockbuster tucked into the schedule. Though the

cinema's address and sign are on Commonwealth Avenue, the building itself is set far back from the main thoroughfare. Follow the walkway between two BU buildings to the entrance on Cummington Street. *606 Commonwealth Ave., 617/424–1500. T stop: BU East (B line).*

OPERA

6 *f-5*

BOSTON LYRIC OPERA COMPANY

This professional opera company presents three full productions each season, usually including one 20th-century work. In recent years, it has performed classics by Mozart and Strauss, as well as by lesser-knowns. For opera-lovers, the Lyric is the only professional show in town; the bankrupt Opera Company of Boston has temporarily shut down until it finds funding and a new home. *114 State St., 617/248–8660. T stop: State.*

3 *8-C*

BOSTON UNIVERSITY OPERA INSTITUTE

This two-year intensive training course for operatic performers offers several public performances each year, including chamber operas, scenes programs, and two full-scale productions in the Boston University Theater. *855 Commonwealth Ave., 617/353–3350. T stop: BU West (B line).*

8 *b-6*

NEW ENGLAND CONSERVATORY OPERA

The student opera company at the New England Conservatory performs in exquisite Jordan Hall (*see* Concert Halls, *above*). *290 Huntington Ave., 617/536–2412. T stop: Symphony.*

PRISM OPERA

Boston's newest opera company was founded in 1995 and, for its first season, presented two completely sold-out performances of "The Magic Flute," as well as a gala concert of opera arias and ensembles. Performances by this small ensemble-style group are simple rather than ornate, and staged in small-to medium-size venues. Since the fledgling company can't yet afford an orchestra, operas are done to piano accompaniment. *66 Lowell St., Malden, 617/321–7929.*

THEATER

3 *b-4*

AMERICAN REPERTORY THEATER (ART)

The ART, one of the nation's most highly respected professional repertory companies, presents both classic and experimental plays at Harvard's Loeb Drama Center. Recent hits have ranged from the elegiac *King Stag* to the raucous *Ubu Rock,* all starring acclaimed ART actors like Thomas Derrah and Alvin Epstein. In addition to the main stage, the Loeb also has a smaller experimental stage; the ART also hosts new works and visiting artists at the Hasty Pudding Theater and other venues around Boston and Cambridge. ART founder Robert Brustein, who's also the company's artistic director, is himself an attraction; he's among the best-known and most contentious members of Boston's cultural elite. *64 Brattle St., Cambridge, 617/547–8300. T stop: Harvard Sq.*

BANKBOSTON CELEBRITY SERIES

Since 1938, this series has been New England's leading presenter of world-class performing arts. The 1998 season will feature Hal Holbrook in *Mark Twain Tonight!* as well as other theater performances, most at the Wang Center for the Performing Arts (*see below*). Call for a full schedule and locations. *20 Park Plaza, 617/482–2595.*

8 *f-5*

BOSTON CENTER FOR THE ARTS

More than a dozen quirky low-budget troupes share the BCA's four performance areas: a basic 40-seat theater, a 90-seat "black box," a fully equipped 140-seat stage, and the massive Cyclorama, built to hold a 360-degree mural of the Battle of Gettysburg (the painting is now at the battlefield). Performances, which go on year-round, range from Coyote Theater, the in-house Equity troupe, to the contemporary SpeakEasy Stage Company, to innovative, explicit one-person shows. Located in the artsy heart of the eclectic South End, this is one of the best spots in town to check out talented but as-yet unknown locals. *539 Tremont St., 617/426–7700. T stop: Back Bay.*

4 *a-8*

BOSTON CHILDREN'S THEATER

A cast of students from all over the Boston area performs plays based on classical and modern literature, demonstrating to young audiences that there's more to entertainment than Beavis and Butthead. Shows start at 2 PM every Saturday and Sunday, September to April, with weekday shows during school vacations. A traveling troupe takes its show on the road to playgrounds across the city during July and August; those performances are free. *652 Hammond St., Chestnut Hill, 617/277–3277.*

2 *d-1*

CAMBRIDGE MULTICULTURAL ARTS CENTER

more than just a theater, the arts center also hosts musical performances and arts events. Call for a schedule. *41 Second st., Cambridge, 617/577–1400. T stop: Lechmere.*

8 *g-3*

CHARLES PLAYHOUSE

The Charles is home to two of Boston's most popular long-running shows. The Blue Man Group, a loud, messy, exhilarating trio of playful performance artists painted a vivid cobalt, has been appearing on Stage I since 1995. *Shear Madness*, an audience-participation whodunit set in a hair salon, is an 18-year-old institution on Stage II. *74 Warrenton St., 617/426–6219. "Shear Madness," 617/426–5225. T stop: Boylston.*

1 *f-2*

CHARLESTOWN WORKING THEATER

This tiny company in the heart of Charlestown features original works, often by local playwrights. *442 Bunker Hill St., Charlestown, 617/931–2000.*

8 *g-2*

COLONIAL THEATER

The Colonial is a lavish wedding cake of a proscenium theater, preserved (and, where necessary, restored) to reflect the glory of its opening in 1900. Major productions passing through town on their way to or from Broadway often end up here. The rich decor alone is well worth the ticket prices—but make sure you get a seat on the main floor, as the bal-conies are cramped enough to make enjoying the show difficult. *106 Boylston St., 617/426–9366. T stop: Boylston.*

8 *h-2*

EMERSON MAJESTIC THEATER

This 1903 Beaux-Arts beauty recently got a new lease on life with a multimillion-dollar renovation, courtesy of Emerson College (which is devoted to communications and the performing arts). You'll find both student and professional dance, drama, and opera productions here, as well as a reputed ghost who, it is said, haunts the balcony after hours. *219 Tremont St., 617/578–8780. T stop: Boylston.*

8 *g-3*

57 THEATER

Boston's newest live performance space, the 57 presents locally written and produced plays, often one-person shows, which are thought-provoking and occasionally hilarious. It's located in a hotel building in the heart of the theater district. *200 Stuart St., 617/426–4499. T stop: Boylston.*

7 *a-3*

HASTY PUDDING THEATER

Slightly shabby, quite cramped, and not very large, the Pudding is still well worth a visit. Harvard University's Hasty Pudding Theatricals, self-described as "the oldest theatrical organization in the United States," puts on one show a year here, from late February through March, then goes on tour. The Cambridge Theater Company, a professional troupe, uses the space the rest of the year, mounting its own productions and presenting solo performers like Spaulding Gray. The American Repertory Theater occasionally presents shows here, too, as it did with the debut of Steve Martin's *Picasso at the Lapin Agile.* Arrive early to allow time for dinner in Upstairs at the Pudding, the acclaimed restaurant above the theater. *12 Holyoke St., Cambridge, 617/547–8300. T stop: Harvard Sq.*

8 *b-6*

HUNTINGTON THEATER COMPANY

This professional company under the auspices of Boston University is the city's largest professional resident theater company. It produces five plays each season—a mix of new works,

199

established contemporary plays, and classics—with Peter Altman as producing director. *264 Huntington Ave., 617/266–0800. T stop: Symphony.*

8 *e-4*

LYRIC STAGE

The annual presentation of *A Child's Christmas in Wales* is a holiday favorite, but this small theater located on the second floor of the YMCA building also presents new plays, some of them quite experimental. *140 Clarendon St., 617/437–7172. T stop: Arlington.*

1 *a-3*

NEW REPERTORY THEATER

One of the best repertory companies in the area, the suburban New Rep is often the first to present popular off-broadwayish comedies and dramas. It's housed in a huge gothic church one block from the green line trolley stop; you can't miss it. *54 Lincoln St., Newton Highlands, 617/332–1646. T stop: Newton Highlands (D line).*

4 *c-1*

PUBLICK THEATER

This outdoor summer theater presents three or four shows each season on the banks of the Charles. Recent seasons have featured *Guys and Dolls,* Shakespeare's *As You Like It,* and other evergreens. *Christian A. Herter Park, 1175 Soldiers Field Rd., 617/782–5425.*

4 *g-8*

PUPPET SHOWPLACE THEATER

Tucked into a Brookline Village storefront with less than 150 seats, the Puppet Showplace puts on extraordinary shows with marionettes and other puppets. There are also classes, museum-like displays, and special events, and the puppeteers generally talk to the audience after the show. Magic for kids and adults alike. *32 Station St., Brookline, 617/731–6400. T stop: Brookline Village (D line).*

8 *g-3*

SHUBERT THEATRE

The Shubert, a quietly elegant circa-1910 theater with just 1,700 seating capacity, spent much of the last decade dark and empty, but theatergoers lined up for its reopening in early 1997 when it hosted

the touring company of the Broadway blockbuster *Rent.* At press time, the Boston Ballet had just decided to move its repertory performances here from the much larger Wang Center for the Performing Arts (*see below*)—a move that promises to keep the Shubert lit for some time to come. *265 Tremont St., 617/482–9393. T stop: Boylston.*

8 *f-3*

TERRACE ROOM, BOSTON PARK PLAZA

An ornate gilded-lily of a room, the Terrace Room hosts various short-run productions ranging from *Forbidden Broadway* to a troupe of flamenco dancers. Shows generally take place Thursdays through Sundays, but it's best to call for information. *64 Arlington St. at Park Plaza, 617/423–8722. T stop: Arlington.*

8 *f-5*

TRIANGLE THEATER COMPANY

This small troupe stages plays and musicals based on gay and lesbian themes in a small South End theater. *58 Berkeley St., 617/426–3550. T stop: Arlington or Back Bay.*

8 *h-3*

WANG CENTER FOR THE PERFORMING ARTS

With 3,700 seats, the Wang is the preferred venue for large-scale productions like the Boston Ballet or Broadway extravaganzas—well over a million ticketholders passed through its glass doors last year. Ask about guided tours; the breathtaking building, built as a movie house in 1925, was renovated to full gilded glory in the 1980s. *270 Tremont St., 617/482–9393. T stop: Boylston.*

8 *h-3*

WILBUR THEATER

The smallest of the traditional theater houses in the Theater District, the Wilbur has been in and out of foreclosure in recent years, but now seems to be making a comeback with off-Broadway hits like *Stomp* and *Defending the Caveman. 246 Tremont St., 617/423–4008. T stop: Boylston.*

TICKETS

6 f-4

BOSTIX

With kiosks at Faneuil Hall and Copley Square, BosTix is Boston's official entertainment center, a full-price Ticketmaster outlet, and the largest full-service ticket agency in the city. It's also the place to snap up half-price tickets for same-day performances. Starting at 11 AM, a "menu board" at each kiosk announces what's available for that evening. Show up early; locals in the know start lining up well before opening time to ensure the best pickings. *Faneuil Hall Marketplace, 617/723–5181. Cash and traveler's checks only for same-day tickets; no refunds or exchanges. Tues.–Sat. 10 AM–6 PM, Sun. 11 AM–4 PM.*

8 d-3

Copley Sq., corner of Boylston and Dartmouth Sts. Mon.–Sat. 10 AM–6 PM, Sun.

11 AM–4 PM. Both locations closed on major holidays.

6 d-5

NEXT TICKETING

This agency offers a convenient way to charge tickets to events at Great Woods, Harborlights, the Orpheum Theater, Paradise Rock Club, and other selected venues. Order by phone or visit the ticket window at the Orpheum. *1 Hamilton Pl., off Tremont St., 617/423–NEXT (617/423–6398). 24 hours a day. No refunds or exchanges.*

7 a-2

OUT OF TOWN TICKETS AND SPORTS CHARGE

Charge tickets to all major credit cards at this window on the mezzanine level of the main entrance to the Harvard Square T station. *617/497-1118. Mon.–Fri. 9 AM–6 PM, Sat. 9 AM–1 PM. No refunds or exchanges. T stop: Harvard Sq.*

SOMETHING FOR THE YOUNG AT ARTS

It's easy to introduce kids to culture when the attractions are this alluring.

Boston Symphony Orchestra Youth Concerts (Concert Halls)
Conductor-narrated programs, started by Leonard Bernstein, introduce young audiences to orchestral music. Ticket price includes a tour of Symphony Hall.

Boston Children's Theatre (Theaters)
Plays based on classical and modern literature, presented by and for kids.

Boston Globe Tour (Free Entertainment)
Kids 12 and up will thrill to the roar of the printing presses and the bustle of the newsroom.

Boston Public Library (Free Entertainment)
Children's movies, storytellers, puppet shows, and crafts demonstrations, all free.

Boston University Observatory (Free Entertainment)
Take the family on a guided tour of the universe.

Charles Playhouse (Theaters)
The Blue Man Group spews marshmallows, drums up a storm, and makes a wildly irresistable mess in this hit show.

The Children's Museum (Free Entertainment)
Hands-on exhibits tickle every part of a child's imagination.

Free Friday Flicks (Free Entertainment)
Family-oriented movies beneath the stars at the Hatch Shell on warm summer nights.

Longfellow Summer Festival (Free Entertainment)
"Family Days" at the home of beloved poet Henry Wadsworth Longfellow include special tours, games, painting, dancing, and more.

***The Nutcracker* (Dance)**
The classic holiday ballet—fairies, dancing mice, magical trees, and all.

Puppet Showplace Theatre (Theaters)
A genuinely unique place to see fine puppeteering and learn how it's done.

TICKETMASTER

Charge tickets by phone to most major events and many shows in smaller venues, or visit outlets in local stores (call for the nearest one). 617/931–2000 or 617/931–2787. Mon.–Fri. 9 AM–10 PM, Sat.-Sun. 9 AM–8 PM. No refunds or exchanges.

nightlife

BARS

C c-7

ALLEY CAT LOUNGE

Part of an alley of nightclubs in the Theater District, the Alley Cat offers up drinks and contemporary rock. In the early evening, pub grub here is decent. 1 Boylston Pl., 617/351–2510. T stop: Boylston.

6 f-4

ATRIUM LOUNGE

An elegant room overlooking Faneuil Hall Marketplace, the Atrium features a pianist nightly 6:30 to 10:30, sometimes joined by a cabaret artist Saturday night at 9. Regal Bostonian Hotel, North and Blackstone Sts., 617/523–3600. T stop: Government Center.

2 a-5

BOSTON BEER WORKS

A "naked brewery," this place has the works exposed—the tanks, pipes, and gleaming stainless steel and copper kettles used in producing beer. Seasonal brews, in addition to a regular selection, are the draw here for students, young adults, and fans from nearby Fenway Park. The menu has pastas and pub fare. 61 Brookline Ave., 617/536–2337. T stop: Kenmore.

6 b-6

THE BULL & FINCH

Yes, this Beacon Hill bar is best known as the model for Cheers, and tourists line up outside, but inside it looks nothing like the TV bar. Look past the Cheers memorabilia to see a cozy pub, full of brass and stained glass, which was built in England but disassembled and shipped to Boston years ago. The Bloody Marys are stupendous, and the burgers are big and juicy. A DJ spins cur-

rent hits and oldies on weekend nights; there's no cover or minimum. 84 Beacon St., 617/227–9605. T stop: Park St. or Arlington.

2 c-2

CAMBRIDGE BREWING COMPANY

A microbrewery where beer lovers can order a hamburger and wash it down with a beer sampler, a pint of Cambridge Amber, or one of the other standards, this place is a favorite with the twentysomething crowd. The dark Charles River porter is one of which they're especially proud. Open Sunday through Tuesday till 11:30; Wednesday through Saturday till 1. 1 Kendall Sq., Bldg. 100, where Hampshire meets Broadway, 617/494–1994. T stop: Kendall Sq.

8 e-3

COPLEY'S

A small high-ceilinged room with marble-topped tables, caricatures on the wall, and globular chandeliers on each side of the bar—obviously, Henry James would feel right at home here at Copley's. An older business crowd gathers nightly till 11. Copley Plaza Hotel, 138 St. James Ave., 617/267–5300. T stop: Copley.

8 c-3

DAISY BUCHANAN'S

This is a favorite hangout of Boston athletes and young professionals. The jukebox is loud in the simply adorned room at basement level, with pinball and video games in the rear. Free hot dogs are served weekends, which helps explain the overflowing crowd. 240a Newbury St., 617/247–8516. T stop: Copley.

7 a-3

JOHN HARVARD'S BREW HOUSE

Step up to this long, dark bar for a range of ales, lagers, pilsners, and stouts. The Brew House, frequented by a crowd in its twenties, smells like a real English pub; the food is so-so but plentiful. Stained-glass windows of modern figures add to the mock-antique air. 33 Dunster St., 617/868–3585. T stop: Harvard Sq.

6 c-7

MERCURY BAR

Popular among well-heeled young professionals and theatergoers, Mercury has a sleek 100-foot bar facing a row of raised, semicircular booths and a more private dining room off to the side. Bar patrons may order from the extensive tapas menu: anything from mixed olives to grilled Portuguese sardines—food salty enough to encourage imbibing. *116 Boylston St., 617/482–7799. T stop: Boylston.*

8 *e-5*

TIM'S TAVERN

Tim's is a working-class pub that pours its liquor from gallon jugs and offers arguably the best burgers in town—both at very low prices. Other fare, chicken and fish, is similarly reliable and simply served. Open Monday through Saturday 11 to 10:55. *329 Columbus Ave., 617/247–7894. T stop: Back Bay.*

8 *c-4*

TOP OF THE HUB

This has a wonderful view over the entire city; that and the sounds of hip jazz make the pricey drinks worth it. The 52nd-floor lounge, renovated in 1995, is open weeknights till 12:45 and weekends till 1:30 AM. *Prudential Center, 617/536–1775. T stop: Prudential.*

BLUES

3 *b-4*

HOUSE OF BLUES

This was the first House of Blues, and many say it's the best. Yes, there's a Blues Brothers connection: it's co-owned by Dan Aykroyd and the late John Belushi's wife, Judy, as well as other celebrity investors. But the real draws here are the live music and the blues memorabilia. Check out the strangely compelling folk art covering every available wall, the store, and the tiny museum carved out of the restaurant's space—and make sure you try the Sunday Gospel Brunch, a mouthwatering casserole of down-home cooking and uplifting music. *96 Winthrop St., Cambridge, 617/491–2583. T stop: Harvard Sq.*

6 *f-4*

MARKETPLACE CAFÉ

This Quincy Market nightspot and restaurant offers nonstop blues and jazz with no cover charge. The music starts every night at 9 PM in the North Market building adjacent to Faneuil Hall itself. *300 Faneuil Hall, 617/227–9660. T stop: Government Center or Haymarket.*

8 *c-6*

WALLY'S

This tiny blues and jazz club at almost the precise point where the South End meets Roxbury draws an unusually (for Boston) ethnically diverse crowd of music-lovers who pack the joint nightly. There's no cover charge, no dress code, and hardly any room to move—but you won't be able to stop yourself. Rumor has it Wally's is planning to ease the crush by expanding into a neighboring space in 1998. *427 Massachusetts Ave., 617/424–1408. T stop: Massachusetts Ave.*

CABARET

8 *h-6*

MEDIEVAL MANOR

With long tables, flute music, "serving wenches," no silverware, and court jesters dictating when you can visit the rest room, this silly-but-fun 12th-century banquet is worth visiting once just for amusement value. The extravaganza—vaudeville show, strolling minstrels, meal and all—lasts about 3 hours. While the six-course fixed-price meal isn't gourmet, it's plentiful, and if you make reservations 48 hours in advance, you can even arrange for vegetarian options. It's a long walk to the T through an occasionally dicey neighborhood, so take a cab to be safe. *246 E. Berkeley St., 617/423–4900. T stop: N.E. Medical Center.*

8 *h-3*

JOEY & MARIA'S ITALIAN COMEDY WEDDING

You're a guest at a rambunctious Italian wedding—dancing the tarantella, eating the buffet dinner (provided by a well-known North End restaurant), and getting drawn into the action as Joey, Maria, and their respective off-the-wall families are overwhelmed by the emotion of this special day. Will you catch the bouquet? Will someone catch a punch in the nose? You won't know until you attend this interactive comedy cabaret. *New Tremont Playhouse, Tremont House Hotel, 275 Tremont St., 800/733–5639. Closed Sun.–Wed. T stop: Boylston.*

6 *g-7*

BOSTON'S ORIGINAL MYSTERY CAFÉ

Solve a murder over your meal at this long-running mystery dinner theater held at Three Cheers, a restaurant/bar on the waterfront. There's lots of audience participation, so don't be shy! The current show is called "We the Jury." Free parking and group rates make this a great way to entertain guests. *290 Congress St., 617/423–6166. Closed Mon.–Wed. T stop: South Station.*

COMEDY

6 *f-4*
COMEDY CONNECTION
Located under the vast dome of Quincy Market itself, this club yuks it up with national and local comics seven nights a week. Frank Santos, the "R-rated hypnotist," holds court every Thursday evening. *Faneuil Hall Marketplace, 617/248–9700. T stop: Haymarket, Government Center, State St.*

7 *b-3*
THE COMEDY STUDIO
Located at the Hong Kong, a large, bright red Chinese restaurant just outside of Harvard Square, the Comedy Studio presents shows at 8 PM every Saturday and Sunday evening. *1236 Massachusetts Ave., Cambridge, 617/661–6507. T stop: Harvard Sq.*

8 *g-2*
DICK DOHERTY'S COMEDY ESCAPE
Dick Doherty, a local stand-up comic, appears every Wednesday night in the Boston location of his chain of comedy clubs. Headliners change nightly, and Sundays are always open-mike nights. Unlike most other area clubs, Doherty's in Boston is smoke-free. *Remington's, 124 Boylston St., 617/729–2565. Closed Mon., Tues. T stop: Boylston.*

8 *g-3*
NICK'S COMEDY STOP
Nick's attracts local comics and the occasional national name—even Steve Allen makes an appearance now and then. Boston favorite Vinnie Favorito hosts an open-mike night here every Wednesday. Make reservations for weekend nights; Nick's is in the heart of the theater and bar district and can get crowded early. *100 Warrenton St., 617/423–2900. T stop: Boylston.*

DANCE CLUBS

8 *g-2*
AVENUE C
The first club on a pedestrians-only block of clubs called "the Alley," Avenue C plays "alternative" hits old and new and attracts a crowd wearing everything from jeans to little black dresses. Squeeze onto the overcrowded dance floor to dance to late-1980s hits from the likes of the Cure, Depeche Mode, and the Smiths, or slip off to the slightly quieter side room to chat up the attractive stranger who stepped on your foot while trying to maneuver over to the bar. *5 Boylston Pl., 617/423–3832. T stop: Boylston.*

2 *b-5*
AXIS
Though clubs are scattered throughout the city, Lansdowne Street, which runs along one side of Fenway Park, is Party Central. One of the largest and most popular clubs on this block of nightspots, Axis features a dance floor that can accommodate more than 1,000 people sweating and writhing to house, alternative, and industrial dance music. Friday is "X Night," featuring DJs from alternative radio station WFNX. At Sunday's "Gay Night," Axis and neighboring mega-club Avalon combine and let dancers circulate between the two for one cover charge. Some nights are 18-plus; others are over-21 only. Cover varies. *13 Lansdowne St., 617/262–2437. Closed Mon. T stop: Kenmore.*

6 *d-7*
BUZZ
Just where the South End gives way to the Theater District, you'll find one of the city's trendiest gay clubs. Bump and grind with the wall-to-wall hardbodies on the dance floor, or simply savor the sights from the bar. Saturday nights are the week's peak. *67 Stuart St., 617/267–8969. T stop: Arlington.*

6 *d-6*
JOY
Hyper-chic international students throng to this Downtown Crossing club with its mix of techno and acid jazz beats. As with other clubs catering to this acutely trend-conscious crowd, you'll need to be tanned, toned, and Armani'd to the hilt, or you'll be left standing on the sidewalk (pressing a discreet fifty into the doorman's palm

may or may not get you in the door). *533 Washington St., 617/338–6999. T stop: Boylston or Park St.*

2 *a-5*

KARMA CLUB

The newest addition to Boston's club scene is an exotic fantasyland, complete with incense, carved temple doors from the Far East, and an immense stone Buddha who watches the proceedings with a beatific smile. Karma was supposedly intended for a crowd slightly older than the one that frequents Axis and Avalon, but young club-hoppers land here as often as anywhere else. The squishy couches and hypnotic music in back lend themselves well to seduction. *9 Lansdowne St., 617/421–9595. Closed Mon. T stop: Kenmore.*

4 *f-4*

M-80

This dance club next door to the Paradise Rock Club (*see* Pop/Rock, *below*) caters to the whims of Boston's rich young international crowd; it may be the only dance club in town where people order Dom Perignon by the bottle. The patrons are gorgeous and well-dressed, the "Eurohaus" music one loud nonstop beat, and the doormen excruciatingly selective—if you aren't a regular, you might not make it in. *969 Commonwealth Ave., 617/562–8800. Closed Sun.–Tues., Thurs. T stop: Babcock St. (B line).*

7 *f-6*

MAN-RAY

The home of Boston's underground scene and some of the city's best people-watching, Man-Ray pulls in the Gothic, glam, and alternatively lifestyled for long nights of industrial, house, techno, disco, and trance music. Friday night is "Fetish Night," where patrons take their piercings, crushed velvet, and vinyl bustiers very seriously indeed. No, you aren't required to participate in the staged spankings—just don't stare too obviously. "Creative attire" is the general rule; when in doubt, wear black. *21 Brookline St., Cambridge, 617/864–0400. Closed Mon., Tues. T stop: Central Sq.*

8 *h-3*

THE ROXY

Boston's largest dance club, this former big-band ballroom in the Tremont House Hotel attracts a different crowd

for every night of the week. Thursday nights draw in the upscale and attractive young African Americans that make up Boston's Buppie scene. Fridays are Euro night, with international students showing up in their finest and most outrageous clubwear. And on Saturdays, the VIP room fills up with local celebs and sports stars while their entourages take over the rest of the house. *279 Tremont St., 617/338–7699. T stop: Boylston.*

2 *b-5*

THE SPOT

This four-story club features different music on each floor, topped with a roof deck where patrons dance beneath the stars to house music and other high-energy beats. In its previous incarnation as Quest, it was best known as a gay club. Now the crowd is predominantly straight on Thursdays, Saturdays, and Sundays, although Mondays are still popular with gay men, and Fridays draw both gays and lesbians. The spot is a mere block from Lansdowne Street, and usually not as crowded as that particular clubland. *1270 Boylston St., 617/424–7747. Closed Tues. T stop: Kenmore.*

7 *b-6*

WESTERN FRONT

This two-floor reggae, funk, and ska club lies in the heart of the diverse neighborhood of Cambridgeport, about a 15-minute walk from Central Square. The crowd is largely Caribbean, but everyone's welcome. On Friday and Saturday from 7:30 PM to closing, there's Jamaican food to go with the reggae beat. *343 Western Ave., Cambridge, 617/492–7772. Closed Sun., Mon. T stop: Central Sq.*

8 *g-2*

ZANZIBAR

The tropical atmosphere in this two-story club—with 25-foot-tall palm trees and a swing—attracts young professionals who come to flirt, dance, drink at the Tropical Oasis Bar, and shoot billiards upstairs. Zanzibar attracts a slightly older crowd than the other clubs on this pedestrian block called "The Alley." Don't be surprised if you see men actually wearing jackets and ties. *1 Boylston Pl., 617/451–1955. Closed Sun.–Tues. T stop: Boylston.*

DINING & DANCING

6 f-5
BAY TOWER ROOM

During the day, this is a private dining room for corporate functions; it is set high atop a landmark skyscraper in the Financial District. But come evening, it opens to the public just in time to watch the sun set through windows two stories high while sipping a cocktail or, on Fridays and Saturdays, swing dancing to a live quartet. Dress to enchant—nothing else suits the romantic, sophisticated ambience. *60 State St., 617/723-1666. Closed Sun. T stop: State St. or Government Center.*

6 h-4
COOL JAZZ DINNER CRUISE

Cruise the inner harbor on the good ship *Bay State* as you dance to jazz artists sponsored by a local radio station and the renowned Scullers Jazz Club. Dinner is a buffet catered by Joe's American Bar & Grille. The boat departs from and returns to a dock next to the Marriot Long Wharf hotel. *Long Wharf, 617/320-0040. Fri. only. T stop: Aquarium.*

6 e-5
THE LAST HURRAH

Now that retro has returned, this space in the venerable Parker House Hotel with its turn-of-the-century decor is infinitely hip for being safely traditional. Live jazz and swing bands bring in patrons of all ages, from twenty-somethings to those well past retirement. Dinner is served from 5 to 11 PM, and snacks until midnight. *60 School St., 617/227-8600. Closed Sun. T stop: Park St.*

JAZZ

7 e-6
1359 JAZZ CLUB

Walk down a side street in Cambridge's Central Square, enter the run-down Cambridge VFW hall, and head for the back room. Believe it or not, you'll find amazing local jazz here for next to nothing. Tuesday nights are Big Band Nights, often with free swing dancing lessons; Saturday nights are a mix of modern and traditional jazz. This room is one of Boston's best-kept secrets—sshh! *288B Green St., Cambridge, 617/787-1359. T stop: Central Sq.*

8 c-7
BOB THE CHEF'S

This South End restaurant, long beloved by soul food fans, started featuring hot live jazz not long ago. In addition to groups and solo performers, Bob's has regular "Berklee Nights" showcasing students from nearby Berklee College of Music, which is renowned for its jazz programs. Shows start at 7:30 PM. *604 Columbus Ave., 617/536-6204. T stop: Massachusetts Ave.*

8 b-4
INSTITUTE FOR CONTEMPORARY ART (ICA)

The Institute for Contemporary Art has started to open its tiny theater occasionally to cutting-edge jazz performers like John Zorn's Masada and Myra Melford. For those who want to see the future of jazz before it arrives, this is the place to go. Call to find out the current schedule. *955 Boylston St., 617/266-5152. T stop: Hynes Convention Center/ICA.*

7 a-3
REGATTABAR

Jazz lovers adore this club, set in a fine Harvard Square hotel, for the top-notch performers—like Betty Carter, Ahmad Jamal, and Herbie Mann—it often attracts. The room is spacious, yet its low ceilings make it seem cozy and intimate. Casual dress is okay, but why not make an extra effort in honor of the world-class talent? *Charles Hotel, Bennett & Eliot Sts., Cambridge, 617/876-7777. Closed Sun.–Mon. T stop: Harvard Sq.*

7 f-3
RYLES

It's worth the walk from Harvard to Inman Square to visit this two-level Inman Square club done up with mirrors, soft lighting, and jazz posters. Some of the best musicians in the country play here; it's also a great place to check out new local talent. *212 Hampshire St., Cambridge, 617/876-9330. T stop: Central Sq.*

3 c-6
SCULLERS

Another well-known haven for local jazz aficionados, this dimly lit club has hosted the likes of the Count Basie Orchestra. Some parts of the room have a less than optimal view of the stage, unfortunately, but a lovely view of the Charles makes up for it. *Doubletree Guest Suites Hotel, 400 Soldiers Field Rd., 617/783–7290. Closed Sun. T stop: Central Sq.*

8 *c-4*

TOP OF THE HUB

Perched atop the Prudential Building, 52 floors above the Back Bay, the lounge of this recently renovated restaurant has a breathtaking view of the city. Excellent live modern jazz is worth the cost of the somewhat overpriced drinks. *Prudential Center, 617/536–1775. T stops: Prudential, Hynes Convention Center/ICA.*

4 *e-4*

WONDER BAR

The Wonder Bar is a sleek, serene oasis in Allston, a neighborhood bustling with recent immigrants and starving students. Its glass front, wood paneling, exposed brick, and live jazz have all but erased the memory of the previous tenant, a grungy rock club. *186 Harvard Ave., 617/351–2665. T stop: Harvard Ave.*

NIGHTCLUBS

6 *f-6*

JULIEN BAR

Before the historic old Federal Reserve Bank became the Hotel Le Meridien, this ornate and high-ceilinged lounge was the reception room for the bank's governors. Now a pianist plays Gershwin and Porter while you sip a cocktail under the watchful eye of George Washington, who peers down from a vast mural by N. C. Wyeth. *Hotel Le Meridien, 250 Franklin St., 617/451–1900. Closed Sun. T stops: State St., South Station, or Aquarium.*

8 *d-4*

PLAZA BAR

Swank yet not at all stuffy, this is the place to settle down into one of the plush, intimate settees, listen to contemporary jazz, and drink one of the best martinis in Boston. The dress code here is "proper," as befits a place that serves its martinis in an iced mini-carafe. *Copley Plaza Hotel, 138 St. James Ave., 617/267–5300. Closed Sun. T stop: Copley.*

8 *b-4*

PUNCH BAR

This ever-so-British lounge on the second floor of the Sheraton Hotel & Towers has private humidors for regular patrons' personal smokes, as well as a selection of cigars available for visitors. It also boasts Scotch (of course) and imported beers, a circular bar, overstuffed chairs and couches, and an air of retro manliness that isn't even remotely diminished by the giant statues of Punch and Judy flanking the entrance. *39 Dalton St., 617/236–2000. T stop: Hynes Convention Center/ICA.*

7 *h-5*

SAZARAC GROVE

A former warehouse transformed into a modern bar, this hip yet low-key spot in Kendall Square is full of sharp angles and a youngish crowd that wanders over before or after art flicks at the Kendall Square Theater. It's a long walk from the T, so take your car, park at the lot next to the theater, and stroll over for a martini. *One Kendall Sq., Cambridge, 617/577–7850. T stop: Kendall Sq.*

9 *e-5*

STANZA DEI SIGARI

With fringed lamps, red and green leather club chairs, and a wall of local celebs photographed with stogies, this "cigar parlor" in the North End looks like a cross between a stereotypical bordello and a 1950s men's club. You half expect Dean Martin to stroll in and order a Cosmopolitan on the rocks. Speaking of which, the drink selection is staggering—chocolate martini, anyone? *292 Hanover St., 617/227–0295. T stop: Haymarket.*

6 *h-4*

TIA'S

This constantly crowded waterfront watering-hole with loud jukebox music (but no dancing) is one of the hottest pickup joints around for the young singles who live and work downtown. It's literally wall-to-wall on weekends, especially in the summer, when the throng spills onto the patio to catch an ocean breeze. *Marriott Long Wharf, 200 Atlantic Ave., 617/227–0828. T stop: Aquarium.*

PIANO BARS

2 *a-5*
JAKE IVORY'S

Jake's is great fun—loud, brash, and more than a little raucous, especially when the "dueling pianos" are going at it. Requests are not only accepted, but encouraged. *1 Lansdowne St., 617/247–1222. Closed Sun.–Wed. T stop: Kenmore.*

6 *b-8*
NAPOLEON CLUB

One of the city's oldest gay clubs, this intimate former speakeasy in the tiny neighborhood of Bay Village has three separate sections, each with its own piano. The crowd tends to be well-dressed, over 30, and uninhibited about crooning both show tunes and ballads. Liza Minelli has actually been here. The top floor is Josephine's, a dance club open only on weekends. *52 Piedmont St., 617/338–7547. T stop: Arlington.*

POP/ROCK

2 *a-5*
BILL'S BAR

Small and dim, with a standard-issue bar and a few booths along one wall, Bill's seems unremarkable at first glance—but it attracts up-and-coming bands who love the room for its friendly size and decent acoustics. On Tuesdays and Thursdays, Bill's opens the doors connecting it to neighboring dance club Venus de Milo; Sunday is reggae night. *7 Lansdowne St., 617/421–9678. T stop: Kenmore.*

7 *e-5*
CANTAB LOUNGE

Local bands perform rock, blues, blue-grass, and jazz every night from 9 PM to closing at this informal, friendly place in Central Square. Mondays are open-mike nights. On Wednesdays, head downstairs for the Poetry Slam, where poets compete in giving dramatic readings of their own works—most are quite good, some are superb, and the audience is often asked to judge. Please note that the Cantab doesn't take credit cards. *738 Massachusetts Ave., Cambridge, 617/354–2685. T stop: Central Sq.*

6 *e-2*
THE CAUSEWAY

You may walk past the entrance to this tiny second-floor room several times without seeing it, but it's not to be missed—especially after big concerts at the FleetCenter, when the stars have been known to cross the street to jam or hang out. Look for a doorman (the multiple piercings will give him away) to usher you into one of the city's grittiest and most authentic rock clubs. *65 Causeway St., 617/367–4958. T stop: North Station.*

7 *a-2*
CLUB PASSIM

In the 1960s, this basement club was *the* place for folk music, and regulars included Tom Rush and Bonnie Raitt. It has survived, albeit under new ownership and with a new name (it used to be just "Passim"), and is one of the country's few remaining showcase clubs for live folk. A compact kitchen serves up light meals. There's also a small but impressive selection of folk CDs for sale. *47 Palmer St., Cambridge, 617/492–7679. T stop: Harvard Sq.*

1 *d-1*
JOHNNY D'S

An eclectic blend of dance and concert performers come from around the world to play in this restaurant-cum-music hall with a small stage but not a bad seat in the room. Sunday afternoon is a blues jam; Monday night is swing dancing (with lessons before the show); Tuesday is acoustic music night. Come early for dinner and stay for the performance. *17 Holland St., Davis Sq., Somerville, 617/776–2004. T stop: Davis Sq.*

7 *h-5*
KENDALL CAFE

Singer-songwriters ranging from Grammy nominee Tracy Bonham to young sensation Jewel have worked out new material and honed their craft in the small, live music room here, a few steps up from the publike bar. The staff is affable, the atmosphere comfortable, and the location (in the newly hip One Kendall Square complex) includes a conveniently inexpensive parking lot. *One Kendall Sq., Cambridge, 617/661–0993. T stop: Kendall Sq.*

7 *f-6*
THE MIDDLE EAST

One of Boston's best and most eclectic clubs since 1992, the Middle East serves up a tasty stew of jazz, rock, world beat, folk music, performance art, and belly-dancing. The decor is dorm-room basic, but with three different stages—two upstairs and one down—who cares what it looks like? There's also a restaurant serving Middle Eastern food at prices designed to appeal to hungry clubgoers. *472 Massachusetts Ave., Cambridge, 617/354–8238. T stop: Central Sq.*

4 *f-4*

PARADISE ROCK CLUB
National and local rock, jazz, folk, blues, alternative, and country acts all take their turn in this small but incredibly popular club that has drawn big-name talent like Matthew Sweet, Soul Coughing, and the Finn Brothers. U2 made its first Boston appearance here years ago, opening for some other since-forgotten band. Inside, the Paradise resembles a cross between an Islamic temple and a medieval palace, with two tiers of booths and four bars (two on the floor, two in the balcony). Arrive a little early to stake out the best spots along the edge of the floor. *967 Commonwealth Ave., 617/254–2939. T stop: Babcock St. (B line).*

2 *b-4*

THE RAT (THE RATHSKELLER)
The city's original alternative rock club launched the Cars and showcased classic New Wavers like the Police, Talking Heads, and the Go-Go's on their first trips to Boston. Cheap drinks, pinball, video, and an unbelievably loud (earplugs strongly recommended) sound system still draw an eclectic crowd to surf the mosh pit and down pitchers of beer. Black is *de rigeur* here, and scuffed leather jackets and Doc Marten's boots are practically a uniform. Incongruously, the Rat also serves up some of Boston's best ribs upstairs at the Hoodoo Barbecue. *528 Commonwealth Ave., 617/536–2750. Closed Mon., Tues. T stop: Kenmore.*

7 *f-6*

T. T. THE BEAR'S PLACE
Right around the corner from the Middle East (*see above*), T. T.'s is a venue for local rock bands just starting out and honing their chops. Most nights feature three bands, with the music starting at 9 PM. On Monday nights, Stone Soup Poets hosts a reading with featured poets as well as an open mike for all comers. All shows are 18-plus, so the crowd tends to be young. *10 Brookline St., Cambridge, 617/492–0082. T stop: Central Sq.*

3 *b-1*

TOAD
This oddly named room wedged into a long, narrow space in Porter Square attracts quirky local talents who don't quite fall into any particular category. The crowd is a melange of Tufts and Harvard students, young professionals, former hippies, and longtime members of the Cambridge music scene. *1912 Massachusetts Ave., Cambridge, 617/497–4950. T stop: Porter Sq.*

PUBS

6 *f-5*

BLACK ROSE
Walking into this Irish bar is like walking into a pub in Dublin, decorated with family crests, pictures of Ireland, and portraits of the likes of Samuel Beckett, Lady Gregory, James Joyce, and others. The entertainment ranges from traditional *seisiuns* (open-mike sessions) to adventurous interpretations of Celtic themes, but is always, of course, Irish. Dress tends to be on the more formal side of casual. *160 State St., 617/742–2286. T stops: Government Center, Haymarket, or State St.*

2 *b-4*

CORNWALL'S
The wall of board games at the entrance of this low-key, friendly English (not Irish!) pub in Kenmore Square isn't just for show: if you leave your ID as collateral, you can spend hours playing Pictionary, checkers, backgammon, or Trivial Pursuit at no charge. An impressive list of imported English beers and ciders (served by the pint, naturally) complements the bar-food menu, and the servers can and will tell you which beer goes best with the night's dessert specials. Be sure to read some of the plaques hanging over the bar; they honor beloved regulars past and present. *510 Commonwealth Ave., 617/262–3749. T stop: Kenmore.*

5 *h-4*

DOYLE'S
This Jamaica Plain institution is nothing flashy—it's simply the genuine article, a neighborhood pub where the real busi-

ness of a tight-knit community is transacted. Mayors come to press the flesh,
locals suck down pints of beer, and gossip gets confirmed or denied. You're as
likely to run into local politicians here as
you are in City Hall. The food is good,
too: the pancakes have won "Best of
Boston." *3484 Washington St., Jamaica
Plain, 617/524–2345. T stop: Green St.*

7 *d-5*
THE PLOUGH & STARS
A large and faithful local crowd frequents this rowdy and noisy neighborhood pub midway between Central and
Harvard squares. Seven nights a week,
the bartenders serve up Guinness, Bass,
and Harp on tap to patrons squeezed in
to hear live blues, R&B, Irish, and country music. It's also a good place to catch
up on international soccer. The aston-

ishingly large Sunday brunch specials
are worth a daytime visit. *912 Massachusetts Ave., Cambridge, 617/492–9653. T
stops: Central Sq., Harvard Sq.*

3 *f-3*
TÍR NA NÓG
Tiny but not cramped, this cozy newcomer in Somerville's Union Square is
worth the long walk from the T—it was
dubbed one of *Boston Magazine*'s 1997
"Best of Boston" winners for its tasty
food, copious beer, easy parking, and
authentic atmosphere. A house band
livens things up on weekends, and the
traditional Sunday *seisiun* draws old men
with genuine brogues as well as young
women with fiddles. The name, by the
way, means "Land of Eternal Youth."
*366A Somerville Ave., Somerville, 617/
628–4300. T stops: Central Sq., Harvard Sq.*

chapter 6

PARKS, GARDENS, & SPORTS

parks

If you're more in the mood for verdure than bricks and mortar, you're in luck in Boston. Look on any city map and you will see demarcated green areas leading clear from the Common in downtown to Franklin Park in Roxbury. For the most part, what you are looking at was created for the city of Boston in the 19th century by Frederick Law Olmsted, the farsighted landscape architect. The system of public parks, tree-shaded malls, and parkway which Olmsted deemed a necessary respite from the urban environment, and its attendant pressures, is called the Emerald Necklace. The necklace runs from Kenmore Square to Charlesgate to the Back Bay Fens; then to Riverway, the Jamaicaway, on to the wonderful Arnold Arboretum; and over to Franklin Park. Today, the Boston Parks and Recreation Department maintains more than 3,000 acres of parkland in the Boston area, including 50 parks, 90 playgrounds, and 82 squares and malls. For information on any Boston City park, call the Department of Parks & Recreation at 617/635–4505. For information on parks and islands under the jurisdiction of the Metropolitan District Commission, call 617/727–5114, Ext. 530.

Also, in June of 1997, the Boston Harbor Islands National Recreation Area was inaugurated as part of the U.S. Park System. The 1,200-acre park covers 31 islands, to be administered under an unusual public/private partnership. Islands included in the new national park are Castle Island, Long Island, Deer Island, Georges Island, and Sheep Island.

2 *b-6*

THE BACK BAY FENS

The Fens extend from Charlesgate to the Riverway, between Park Drive and Fenway Street. Part of Olmsted's Emerald Necklace, these former mudflats were transformed by him at the turn of the century into a lovely oasis of water, tall grasses, and trees. There are fragrant formal rose gardens as well as some former Victory gardens still tended by private citizens for everyone's pleasure. A lovely H. H. Richardson bridge stands at Boylston Street.

6 *c-6*

BOSTON COMMON

The Common, once used for the grazing of cattle and public executions, is where history lives and present-day Boston plays and picnics. It is the oldest public park in the United States, located on 48 acres originally owned by William Blaxton, the first English inhabitant of the Shawmut Peninsula. In 1634 he sold them to the townspeople, his new neighbors, for £30 ($150), and then he cleared out. Not always a serene spot, it was used as a hanging ground until the 1800s; there were also stocks, a pillory, and a whipping post. Troops camped here before marching off to a multitude of battles; and until 1830 cows were brought here to graze (see the June Boston Common Dairy Festival *in* Events, Chapter 2). It has been a meeting place and, in the Great Fire of 1872, a refuge—and to a certain extent it continues to be both even today. In fine weather there are free concerts, and in winter there is ice skating on Frog Pond. On Boston's First Night, the park is ablaze with Christmas lights and ice sculptures. It's a city oasis for all seasons but, alas, not for all hours. Increasing criminal activity has led to a curfew on the Common and the adjacent Public Garden; both are closed from 10 PM to dawn. Note: There is an information booth on the Tremont Street side of the Common that dispenses advice and brochures. *Bounded by Boylston, Charles, Beacon, Park and Tremont Sts.; on Freedom Trail. T stop: Park St.*

1 *h-5*

CASTLE ISLAND PARK

This spectacular waterfront park is connected to South Boston at City Point. Originally a lookout point in 1634, it's now grown to comprise a city swath of nature set on 40 acres. Located here is Fort Independence, whose stone walls date from the early 19th century and is the oldest fortified military post in the country—Edgar Allan Poe served there in the army in 1827. There is a playground, swimming in Pleasure Bay (aptly named), and saltwater fishing (no license required) from a 250-foot pier. Castle Island Park is also a great spot for walkers and joggers. *T stop: Broadway, then City Point bus.*

6 *a-3*

CHARLESBANK PARK AND THE ESPLANADE

Many a weary jogger has drawn inspiration from the lovely views along the Charles River Esplanade, which continues along the entire length of the Back Bay. In 1931, Mrs. James Storrow donated funds to expand the 2-mile concrete walk along the river's edge into a park. Now there are trees, shrubbery, a band shell—the Hatch Memorial Shell, site of the Boston Pops concerts in summer—bicycle paths, playgrounds, picnic facilities, and lawns for sunbathing. Adjacent to Longfellow Bridge is Community Boating (*see* Sailing, *below*). This park is also a popular in-line skating spot. *T stop: Charles St.*

1 *e-7*

FRANKLIN PARK

The last and largest link in Olmsted's Emerald Necklace is south of Seaver Street between Walnut and Blue Hill avenues. It's one of the prettiest parks in the city, with rolling hills and broad meadows; a music court and a promenade; children's play area and zoo; the William Devine Golf Course; and, most notably, the Franklin Park Zoo—located near the Seaver Street–Blue Hill Avenue corner of the park, this zoo is famed for its walk-through aviary. For visitors, though, the park's main problems are its four-mile distance from downtown and indirect access by public transportation. Note that some of the surrounding communities have had past problems with crime. *Bounded by Seaver St., Walnut, and Blue Hill Aves.*

5 *f-2*

JAMAICAWAY

Another of the links in Olmsted's Emerald Necklace located between Riverway and Arborway, this park is enhanced by Jamaica Pond. Along with a sailing basin, there is a city-owned boathouse for sail and rowboat rentals (permit required). The park also has running paths.

3 *b-4*

JOHN F. KENNEDY PARK

Officially dedicated in May of 1987, this 5-acre park is a memorial to the 35th president of the United States. A monument to the late president utilizes materials indigenous to New England, such as the granite of the foundation, while a variety of trees native to the region are planted about. The entrance pillars are inscribed with quotes from the late president's speeches—truly, a place to rest and reflect. *John F. Kennedy St. and Memorial Dr., Cambridge. T stop: Harvard Sq.*

6 *g-8*

MUSEUM WHARF

There's no shortage of salty breezes here, and there are plenty of benches to enjoy them by. The wharf is one of the more popular places in Boston, thanks to the Boston Children's Museum and the Computer Museum, both located here. The Milk Bottle—a huge vintage 1930s highway lunchstand—was reconstructed here by the Children's Museum and makes a delightful snack bar. *Congress St. Bridge, Fort Point Channel. T stop: South Station.*

6 *f-5*

POST OFFICE SQUARE PARK

In the heart of the financial district, this gem of a park stands out like a green dot in a sea of gray. Finished in 1991, the 1.7-acre urban oasis has more than 100 species of plants and trees, plus two fountains, and ample places to sit. The cheerful Milk Street Cafe is open year-round (closed on Sundays). In the summer, there are scheduled musical performances, and a Park Ranger is often available to answer questions. Built by Friends of Post Office Square, the park is actually an elegant camouflage for a 24-hour subterranean garage facility for 1,400 cars. *Zero Post Office Sq., bounded by Milk, Pearl, Franklin, and Congress Sts., Financial District. T stop: South Station.*

9 *e-4*

PAUL REVERE MALL (THE PRADO)

Originally (and inexplicably) called the Prado, this city-planned, brick-paved area was created in 1933. With its shade trees, benches, and chess tables, it has become a North End neighborhood gathering place where the sound of animated conversation—often in Italian—mixes with the laughter of children at

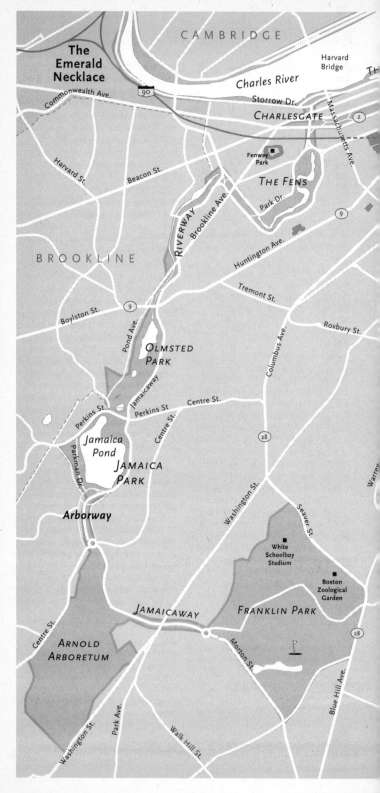

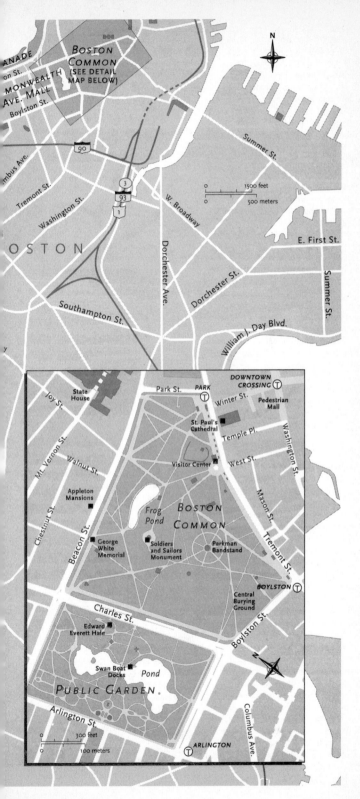

play. A charming spot to rest while touring the historic North End, the mall is designed around Cyrus E. Dallin's equestrian statue of Paul Revere; surrounding brick walls incorporate 13 tablets that record the history of this area from 1630 to 1918. *Between St. Stephen's and Old North (Christ) Churches, North End. T stop: Haymarket.*

2 *c-7*

SOUTHWEST CORRIDOR PARK

What was a wasteland resulting from an abandoned highway project is a new strand in the Emerald Necklace and a proud piece of urban design. This 55-acre linear park, opened in 1987, stretches 4.7 miles across several Boston neighborhoods—from the Back Bay, to the South End, through Roxbury and Jamaica Plain. There are supervised playgrounds, youth activities in summer, interpretive walks, community gardens, as well as tennis, cross-country skiing, baseball fields, and picnic facilities. At the Mission Hill and Boylston Street decks, there are cultural and entertainment events. Beneath the park runs about 25% of the relocated Orange line. *T stops: Back Bay, Massachusetts Ave., Ruggles, Roxbury Crossing, Jackson Sq., Stonybrook; Green St. or Forest Hills on Orange Line.*

9 *f-8*

WATERFRONT PARK

A linchpin of Boston's "New Waterfront," this park, finished in 1976, provides lovely, unimpeded views of the harbor. The bollards and anchor chain along the seawall add an authentic nautical touch, and a graceful 340-foot trellis archway, covered with vines, provides shade in summer. The sea, helpfully, provides the breezes. Children and dogs are welcome: for the former there is a tot lot and ship-shaped timber forms for climbing; for the latter, a doggie convenience station—fire hydrants in three colors. For people there are benches in the shade or sun and plenty of grass on which to sunbathe, picnic, watch the boats coming and going, or see the plane activity at Logan across the harbor. It's an interesting mix of people—North End kids, office workers, guests from the Marriott Long Wharf Hotel, tourists resting their feet. It's also a good spot to keep in mind when you've bought some food in the Quincy Market and can't find a place to sit and eat it—Waterfront Park is just a short walk away

from the madding crowd. *Atlantic Ave. between Mercantile St. and Long Wharf. T stop: Aquarium.*

BEACHES

Most of the Boston beaches are under the supervision of the Metropolitan District Commission (MDC). They are open from the end of June to the beginning of September when lifeguards are on duty daily 10 AM–6 PM. For more information, call 617/727–5114.

In June of 1997, the Boston Harbor Islands National Recreation Area was inaugurated as part of the U.S. Park System. Comprising 31 islands (Castle, Long, Deer, Georges, and Sheep Islands, among them), the 1,200-acre park was developed under a public/private partnership.

1 *g-5*

CARSON BEACH

Day Boulevard, South Boston. *T stop: UMASS.JFK, then 4-min walk.* Note: Carson, Castle Island, L Street, and Pleasure Bay Beach are all part of one, long waterfront.

1 *h-5*

CASTLE ISLAND BEACH

Day Boulevard, South Boston. No bathhouse, but there is the old Fort Independence, a newly refurbished tot lot, picnic area, and rest rooms. *T stop: Broadway on Red Line, then City Point bus to end of line.*

1 *g-5*

L STREET BEACH

Day Boulevard, South Boston. This small beach has a handball court. *T stop: Broadway on Red Line, then City Point bus to end of line.*

1 *g-7*

MALIBU BEACH AND SAVIN HILL BEACH

Morrissey Boulevard, Dorchester. This recreation area features a bathhouse, ball field, playground, park, and tot lot, plus areas for picnicking. *T stop: Savin Hill on Red Line, then 2-min walk.*

1 *h-5*

PLEASURE BAY BEACH

Day Boulevard, South Boston. Another very popular spot—perhaps it's the name! The crowds head for the tot lot, playground, and park. *T stop: Broadway on Red Line, then City Point bus to end of line.*

1 *g-7*

TENEAN BEACH

Morrissey Boulevard, Dorchester. The bathhouse is a plus. *T stop: Fields Corner on Red Line, then Neponset bus to Pope's Hill St.*

beaches north of boston

The following beaches are also under MDC jurisdiction and are within 10 miles of downtown Boston.

CONSTITUTION BEACH

Orient Heights, East Boston. This noisy and crowded beach offers a bathhouse, playground, and handball courts. *T stop: Orient Heights on Blue Line.*

KING'S BEACH

Lynn Shore Drive, Lynn. No facilities.

LYNN BEACH

Lynn Shore Drive, Lynn. Two bathhouses.

NAHANT BEACH

Nahant Road, Nahant. Pluses include a bathhouse, playground, handball courts, barbecue pits, and tot lot. There's a parking fee.

JOHN A. W. PIERCE LAKE

Breakheart Reservation, Lynn Fells Parkway, Saugus. Facilities include picnic areas, hiking trails, and softball diamonds.

REVERE BEACH

Revere Beach Parkway, Revere. This 3-mile beach has three bathhouses. *T stop: Wonderland, Revere Beach on Blue Line.*

SANDY BEACH

Upper Mystic Lake, Winchester. A freshwater beach, with bathhouse and tot lot.

SHORT BEACH

Winthrop Parkway, Winthrop. No facilities.

WINTHROP BEACH

Winthrop Shore Drive, Winthrop. A bathhouse is provided.

beaches south of boston

GREEN HARBOR BEACH

Marshfield. A bathhouse and snack bar are featured here. Parking fee. Not under MDC jurisdiction.

HOUGHTON'S POND

Blue Hills Reservation, Milton. Freshwater beach. Snack bar and bathhouse are the two facilities.

NANTASKET BEACH

Route 22, Hull. Accessible via boat from Rowe's Wharf. A 2-mile beach, with bathhouse, playground, promenade, and a carousel. Parking fee.

WHITE HORSE BEACH

Plymouth. Bathhouse. Parking fee. Not under MDC jurisdiction.

WOLLASTON BEACH

Quincy Shore Drive, Quincy. This popular beach has a bathhouse and tot lot.

BOTANICAL GARDENS

5 *f-6*

ARNOLD ARBORETUM

A visit to the Arnold Arboretum is a botanical tour of the entire North American Temperate Zone—6,000 species, established over a span of more than 115 years (not counting natives here before the garden was established), thrive under the care of Harvard University. Now a National Historic Landmark, this breathtakingly beautiful 265-acre botanical garden was originally opened as a tree farm in 1872. Harvard runs it as a research-education facility in conjunction with the Boston Department of Parks. All 6,000 varieties of ornamental trees, flowers, and shrubs are labeled for your edification. A visit in May is a treat for the senses, with azaleas, dogwoods, flowering cherries, and rhododendrons in riotous bloom. And best of all are the arboretum's famous lilacs—more than 400 varieties, honored on their very own Lilac Sunday, held every May (*see* Events *in* Chapter 2). In 1996, a 40-to-1 scale model of the arboretum (with 4,000 tiny trees) was installed in a revamped visitor center; the model anchors a kind of "green history" exhibit called "Science in the Pleasure Ground." Stop in to pick up a map and a brochure of the extensive programs and tours offered by the arboretum. There is free parking as well as a limited number of permits that enable the physically challenged to drive through the facility. *Rtes. 1 and 203, Arborway, Jamaica Plain, 517/524–1718. Free. Grounds daily sunrise–sunset; visitor center weekdays 9–4, weekends noon–4. T stop: Forest Hills or Arborway. Or Bus 39 from Copley Sq. to Centre St. Walk 4 blocks south.*

6 *b-6*

THE PUBLIC GARDEN

Established in 1859, this lovely 24-acre oasis, once swampy Back Bay marshland, was America's first botanical garden. Today, it features some of the finest formal plantings to be seen in central Boston. Amid the roses and tulips, there are numerous statues—including that of George Washington and "Man Without a Country" author Edward Everett Hale—and a 4-acre, man-made lake, traversed by a graceful stone and iron bridge (inspired, it is said, by New York's Brooklyn Bridge). The lake has long been a haven for ducks, and another sort of "fowl"—Boston's famed Swan Boats, one of the city's most popular summer attractions (*see* Historic Buildings & Areas *in* Chapter 2), which have been in operation since 1877. For the price of a few boat rides and a stale loaf of bread, you can amuse children here for a good hour or more. The formal flower gardens are a blaze of color in season, and the tulips in early spring are very special. These were, in fact, America's first tulip beds, planted with bulbs from Holland. Trees are identified, and bird-watchers are well rewarded. *Bounded by Charles, Beacon, Arlington, and Boylston Sts. Daily sunrise– 10 PM. T stop: Arlington.*

zoos & animal preserves

BLUE HILLS RESERVATION AND BLUE HILLS TRAILSIDE MUSEUM

A 3,600-acre reservation administered by the MDC has miles and miles of hiking trails for those seeking adventure within sight of Boston. Maps of the area, with trails color-coded for easy reading, can be purchased for $1 at the Blue Hills Trailside Museum, located at the western edge of the reservation at the foot of Great Blue Hill. The museum features live animals native to the area and hosts a variety of interpretive programs on the flora and fauna of the Blue Hills. Private programs are available by advance arrangements. There are no guided hikes. *1904 Canton Ave., Milton, 617/333–0690, trail information 617/698– 1802. $3 adults, $1.50 children, $2 senior citizens. Tues.–Sun. 10–5. T stop: Mattapan on Red Line, then Hudson bus.*

1 *e-7*

FRANKLIN PARK ZOO

Things are on the up and up for this venerable Boston attraction. In 1997, the zoo opened a new lion house with the first big cats to be found in any Boston-area zoo in 30 years—complete with a (lion-proof) Land Rover built into viewing areas to allow kids to (safely) get near the King of Beasts. That's just one of the new attractions that continue to improve this 72-acre zoo, which has weathered numerous financial woes and suffers from its location near one of Boston's more financially depressed areas. Director Brian Rutledge, who lives on the grounds and often tours it by horseback, is overseeing a $129-million expansion program, which will upgrade and add to existing exhibitions. The tentlike African Tropical Forest features often lively gorillas and a host of tropical birds, plants, reptiles, and animals in an approximation of their natural habitat. "Bongo Congo," a temporary four-acre enclosure for zebras, ostriches, bongos, and other African grassland animals has been created in the once-empty field called the Promenade. The small children's zoo, which opened in 1984, has animals for petting for children ages 2– 9, plus there's a fabulous snow leopard—strictly for viewing! *Blue Hill Ave., 617/442–2002 or 617/442–4896. $6 adults, $5 senior citizens, $3 ages 2–15. Summer, weekdays 10–4, weekends 10–5; winter, daily 10–4. T stop: Egleston, then Franklin Park bus.*

6 *h-4*

NEW ENGLAND AQUARIUM

This popular attraction often seems to be overflowing with visitors thrilled by the glory of life under (and around) the sea. Inside you'll find penguins, jellyfish, a variety of sharks, and other exotic sea creatures—more than 12,000 specimens of about 650 species of fishes, mammals, birds, reptiles, and amphibians. The star attraction is a re-creation of a coral reef in a four-story, 187,000-gallon circular glass tank that showcases sea turtles, moray eels, sharks, and tropical fish—a tidal wave of kids descends on the tank five times a day as divers descend into its depths to feed its inhabitants. Children will enjoy a hands-on tidal pool exhibit that re-creates the world where the shore meets the sea. Sea lion shows—thankfully, with an emphasis on environmental issues as well as tricks—take place aboard the *Discovery*, a floating pavilion adjacent to the building. Scheduled for completion in early 1998 is a new West Wing, a 16,500-square-foot area for changing exhibitions that will serve as a new "front door." An expanded outside harbor seal exhibit is planned (free to all) with a raised tank so viewers can watch animals from above and below the surface. A new Education Center, with a working marine hospital for viewing, was completed in July of 1995. Whale-watching cruises leave from the wharf from April to October. And for one of the most fabulous views of Boston Harbor, head for the third-level Harbor View Room. Children, needless to say, head first for the snack bar and gift shop. *Central Wharf (between Central and Milk Sts.), 617/973–5200, whale-watching information 617/973–5277. $10.50 adults, $9.50 senior citizens, $5 ages 3–11, under 3 free. Summer, Wed. and Thurs. $1 off 4–7:30. July–Labor Day, Mon., Tues., and Fri. 9–6, Wed. and Thurs. 9–8, weekends 9–6; winter, weekdays 9–5. T stop: Aquarium.*

sports & outdoor activities

Everything you've heard about Boston sports fans is true. With five professional teams (baseball, football, basketball, hockey, and soccer) and dozens of college teams, this is a sports-crazed town where rivalries run hot. If you're from New York, leave your local paraphernalia behind or risk being told, "Yankee (fans), go home!" But if you want to endear yourself to the locals, wear a Bruins jersey, a Celtics T-shirt, or a Red Sox cap. Go to a sports bar during the Beanpot tourney and cheer on one of the four teams battling for Boston's

college hockey crown. Or hang around in the bleachers at Fenway Park with a Fenway Frank and a hopeful grin, talking to strangers about how maybe, just maybe, this is the year.

Weekend warriors and amateurs of all ages will also find ample opportunities to play their own games. Most public recreational facilities are operated by the **Metropolitan District Commission,** 617/727–5114, ext. 555, or by the city's **Parks and Recreation Department,** 617/727–9547.

With four distinct seasons, nearby mountains and oceans, and a plethora of parks, Boston has no shortage of outdoor activities from sedate to extreme. Enjoy!

BASEBALL & SOFTBALL

where to watch

2 *a-5*

BOSTON RED SOX
Baseball is practically a religion in Boston—although the Sox haven't won the World Series since 1918, they did win American League pennants in 1967, 1975, and 1986, and fans' hopes each year are as green as the real grass in the outfield of Fenway Park. Some time in the next few decades, the Sox hope either to renovate or replace their 85-year-old ballpark off Kenmore Square—the oldest park in the major leagues and the smallest (capacity 34,000)—but so far, it's just talk. All the same, now is the time to visit Fenway to admire its old-timey perfection while watching visitors battle the Green Monster, the looming 37-foot left-field wall that stymies all but the most powerful home-run hitters. Baseball season starts in April and ends the first weekend in October; afternoon games generally start at 1:05 PM and evening games at 7:05 PM. *4 Yawkey Way, box office 617/267–1700, recorded information 617/267–8661. T stop: Kenmore.*

where to play

The city Parks and Recreation Department maintains 38 baseball diamonds and 36 Little League diamonds within the city of Boston. Call for details, 617/725–4006.

The Metropolitan District Commission maintains 12 baseball diamonds around the metropolitan area. Call for information, 617/727–7090.

LITTLE LEAGUE

Although it's more popular in the suburbs than in the city, Little League is still the best way to introduce kids to baseball. Call the main Boston office for information about local teams. *800 Boylston St., 617/236–5251.*

BASKETBALL

where to watch

6 *d-2*

BOSTON CELTICS

The famed but aging Boston Garden, where Larry Bird worked magic with a basketball, is vacant and soon to be demolished. It's been replaced by the immense FleetCenter, a 755,000-square-foot sports complex where the Boston Celtics hold court under new coach Rick Pitino, hoping for their first NBA championship since 1986 (they've won 16 since 1957). While the FleetCenter doesn't have the history of its creaky, leaky neighbor, it retains the Garden's famous parquet floor, moved over piece by piece, and all the championship banners waving from the rafters. Unlike the Garden, it also has air-conditioning, many more seats, better food, a 1,200-car parking garage, almost twice as many rest rooms, and—yahoo!—views unobstructed by beams or pillars. *FleetCenter, Causeway St. Celtics information, 617/523–6050. T stop: North Station.*

where to play

BOSTON NEIGHBORHOOD BASKETBALL LEAGUE

This special summer program held across the city for kids under age 18 is extremely popular; call early for locations and times, 617/725–4920.

THE CORPORATE LEAGUE

The largest adult basketball leagues in the area offers year-round competition at all levels of play for both men and women. Most of the 100-plus teams are corporate-sponsored, but noncorporate teams are also welcome. The league also helps connect individual players with existing teams. *Box 1755, Brookline, 617/566–7808.*

PARKS & RECREATION DEPARTMENT

The city maintains 103 basketball courts which may also be used for tennis or street hockey. *617/725–4006.*

BICYCLING

Biking is surprisingly popular despite Boston's aggressive drivers and narrow, winding streets. Many people in the city and inner suburbs commute to work by bicycle instead of by car; some Cambridge streets around Harvard Square actually have bike lanes.

biking resources

3 *g-6*

BICYCLE COALITION OF MASSACHUSETTS

An organization devoted to promoting bicycling in Boston and New England, the Bicycle Coalition helps riders find organized rides, sells a bike map of the area, and puts out a newsletter. Call for details on how to get a permit to bring a bike on the T. *214A Broadway, Cambridge, 617/491–7433. Fax 617/491–8333. T stop: Kendall Sq.*

3 *c-1*

BICYCLE EXCHANGE AT PORTER SQUARE

Located only a few blocks from the Minuteman Bicycle Trail, this shop rents adult-size city bikes for $20 per 24-hour period. *2067 Massachusetts Ave., Cambridge, 617/864–1300. T stop: Porter Sq.*

8 *f-5*

COMMUNITY BICYCLE SUPPLY

Rent an adult-size city bike—a mountain bike/ten-speed hybrid—by the hour ($5/hour, 2-hour minimum), day ($20), or week ($75) at this South End shop serving the city's cyclists for more than 20 years. *490 Tremont St., 617/542–6177. T stop: Back Bay.*

biking trails

2 *e-2*

DR. PAUL DUDLEY WHITE CHARLES RIVER BIKE PATH

Many people don't realize that the Esplanade is merely one segment of an MDC-maintained 17.7-mile loop which runs from the Museum of Science to Watertown Square on both sides of the

Charles River. Watch out for the joggers and in-line skaters, please!

1 *d-1*

MINUTEMAN BICYCLE TRAIL

Built on an old railbed, this trail begins in a small park behind the Davis Square T station in Somerville and runs approximately 15 miles through Cambridge, Arlington, Lexington, and Bedford. It has recently been extended a mile or so in the opposite direction into the center of Somerville so locals can bike to the T for their morning commute.

BILLIARDS

1 *f-2*

GOOD TIME BILLIARDS

Huge and utterly unpretentious, this multi-room amusement emporium in a busy strip mall offers cheap beer and inexpensive billiards as well as batting cages, video games, and plenty of free parking. *30 Sturtevant, Somerville, 617/628-5559. T stop: Sullivan Sq.*

2 *a-5*

JILLIAN'S

This former roller rink at the end of Lansdowne Street is a wildly popular billiards club with 56 pool tables and a refined atmosphere. It also has three bars, a café, darts, shuffleboard, and an arcade with more than 200 sophisticated video games and virtual reality simulators. Professional pool and billiards lessons are available. *145 Ipswich St., 617/437-0300. T stop: Kenmore.*

6 *f-4*

THE RACK

Recently opened adjacent to Quincy Market, this pool hall draws a hip crowd of young professionals from downtown and the North End to shoot 8-ball on 22 new tables with spotless beige felt. *20 Clinton St., 617/725-1051. T stop: Haymarket.*

BOATING

All types of pleasure boats are allowed on the Charles River, the inner Harbor to North Washington Street, Dorchester inner and outer bays, and the Neponset River stretch from the Granite Avenue bridge to Dorchester Bay. Jet skis and inflatables are prohibited.

You can access Boston Harbor from public landings at **Waterfront Park** on Commercial Street in the North End and **Kelly's Landing** on Day Boulevard in South Boston. Public launching areas along the Charles River are located at **Clarendon Street** in the Back Bay, behind the **Hatch Shell,** and at **Brooks Street** (off Nonantum Road) and **the Richard T. Artesani Playground** on Soldiers Field Road, both in Brighton. For information, call the MDC's Harbormaster at 617/727-0537.

To launch trailered boats into the Charles River at the **Monsignor William J. Daly Playground** in Brighton, make advance arrangements by calling 617/727-4708.

1 *a-3*

CHARLES RIVER CANOE & KAYAK CENTER

From April through October, rent canoes, sculls, and kayaks by the hour or day and paddle along the Charles. Lessons are available, as are guided tours of the Charles, other area rivers, and the Massachusetts coast. *2401 Commonwealth Ave., Newton, 617/965-5110.*

5 *g-2*

JAMAICA POND BOATHOUSE

Rent a rowboat by the hour from June through September and explore the 68 acres of Jamaica Pond. You must be age 16 or older and have a swimming certificate. *507 Jamaicaway, Jamaica Plain, 617/635-4505. T stop: Green St. or Bus 39 from Copley.*

BOCCE

Although there's no truly organized league, you can always find older Italian men (and a few younger ones) playing bocce in the North End's **Waterfront Park.** Just ask around.

BOWLING

Candlepin bowling, which uses small, slender pins and a smaller ball, is a New England sport still clinging tenaciously to popularity in the face of the more well-known game of ten-pins. Try them both.

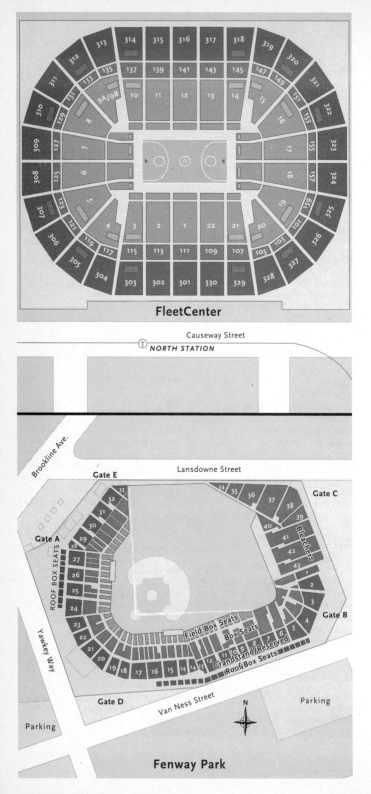

FleetCenter

Causeway Street

Ⓣ *NORTH STATION*

Brookline Ave.

Lansdowne Street

Gate E

Gate C

Gate A

ROOF BOX SEATS

Bleachers

Yawkey Way

Field Box Seats

Box Seats

Grandstand/Reserved

Roof Box Seats

Gate B

Gate D

Van Ness Street

N

Parking

Parking

Fenway Park

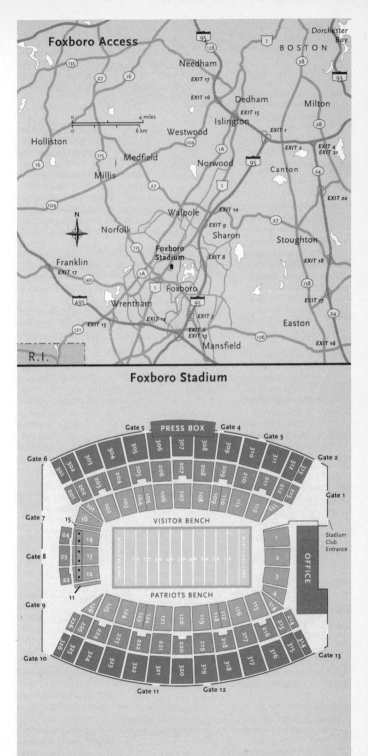

Foxboro Access

Foxboro Stadium

1 *g-7*

BOSTON BOWL FAMILY FUN CENTER

Open 24 hours, this insomniac's dream of a bowling alley has 30 ten-pin lanes, 14 candlepin lanes, a game room with 12 pool tables, an indoor playground, and free parking. *820 Morrissey Blvd., Dorchester, 617/825–3800.*

3 *b-1*

LANES & GAMES

With 34 candlepin lanes and 20 ten-pin lanes, a game room, pool tables, and a sports restaurant and lounge with three big-screen televisions, there's more than enough to do here. League bowling takes precedence, so call ahead for open bowl times. There's free parking, too. *Rte. 2, Cambridge, 617/876–5533. T stop: Alewife.*

2 *a-5*

RYAN FAMILY AMUSEMENT CENTER

Located right across the street from Fenway Park, this is a popular local hangout and a fine place for candlepins, billiards, and video games. *64 Brookline Ave., 617/267–8495. T stop: Kenmore.*

BOXING

8 *b-6*

GREATER BOSTON YMCA

Adults and children 12 and over can learn boxing, from basic technique to conditioning, in courses that usually last 8 weeks. Call for details. *316 Huntington Ave., 617/536–7800. T stop: Northeastern on E line.*

FENCING

1 *a-2*

BOSTON FENCING CLUB

The only fencing school in New England offers group lessons and private instructions in the foil, épée, and saber on weekday evenings and weekend days. *125 Walnut St., Watertown, 617/926–3450.*

FISHING

Freshwater fishing in Boston requires a fishing license, available to those 15 or over; nonresidents can get a special seven-day license. Saltwater fishing needs no license. For information on licenses, regulations, and public fishing areas, call the state **Division of Fisheries & Wildlife** fishing hot line at 800/ASK–FISH.

BLUE HILLS RESERVATION

Operated by the MDC, this wildlife haven in the south suburbs has three different fishing areas: Houghton Trout Pond (trout), Blue Hill Reservoir (sunfish and perch), and Ponkapoag Pond (bass, sunfish, and pickerel). *695 Hillside St., Milton, 617/698–1802.*

1 *h-5*

CASTLE ISLAND

Anyone can toss in a line from this ocean pier which stretches about 250 feet out into the Atlantic. *Day Blvd., South Boston.*

5 *f-2*

JAMAICA POND

This 77-acre freshwater pond within Boston city limits is stocked with trout and bass. Rent a rowboat (*see* Boating, above) or just cast your line from shore! *Jamaicaway, Jamaica Plain.*

FLYING

EAST COAST AERO CLUB

Located at a former air force base just off I-95, half an hour outside of the city, this flying club offers beginning and advanced flight training classes as well as sightseeing tours for those who don't want to take the stick. *Civilian Air Terminal, Hanscom Field, Bedford, 617/274–6322.*

FOOTBALL

where to watch

1 *b-4*

BOSTON COLLEGE EAGLES

Football is practically a religion at BC; be prepared for large, loud crowds. Take the T if you can, as space in the parking lot is limited and town-gown rivalries mean streets in the neighborhood around the stadium are restricted to residents. *Boston College Alumni Stadium, Chestnut Hill, 617/552–2000. T stop: Boston College on B line.*

4 *f-4*

BOSTON UNIVERSITY TERRIERS

The Terriers play on what was once Braves Field, back in the days before the Boston Braves moved to Brooklyn. It's conveniently located only a block from the T. *Nickerson Field, off Commonwealth Avenue between Gaffney and Babcock Sts., 617/353–3838. T stop: Babcock St. on B line.*

4 *f-2*

HARVARD UNIVERSITY CRIMSON

This ivy-covered coliseum is located across the river from Cambridge and across the street from the Harvard Business School. While Harvard isn't exactly known for its athletics, the Harvard/Yale

---

SMALL-SCALE SPORTS

In a town as sports-obsessed as Boston, it's no surprise that kids have their own leagues and special programs for everything from hoops to sloops:

Boston Neighborhood Basketball League (Basketball)
Popular and well-organized coaching program for kids under 18.

Community Boating (Boating)
Kids aged 10–17 who can pass a swimming test can learn to sail for just a dollar!

Jae H. Kim Tae Kwon Do Institute (Martial Arts)
Lessons are available for kids aged 5 and up.

Little League (Baseball & Softball)
It wouldn't be summer without this classic organization.

Massachusetts Youth Soccer Association (Soccer)
Organized soccer leagues for kids up to age 19.

The No Frills Aerobics Factory (Health Clubs)
Special funk and hip-hop classes for kids and teens.

Pop Warner Football (Football)
The pigskin equivalent to Little League, it's launched many a future college player.

Sportsmen's Tennis Club (Tennis)
Summer tennis camp for kids under 18.

---

game is a Boston tradition. Walk from Harvard Square; parking is next to impossible. *Harvard University Stadium, N. Harvard St. and Soldiers Field Rd., Allston, 617/495–2212. T stop: Harvard Sq.*

NEW ENGLAND PATRIOTS

After going all the way to Super Bowl XXXI in 1997, only to be defeated by New Orleans, the Pats are stirring up fans' fervent hopes for their first NFL championship since 1985. Meanwhile, their owner has been making subtle but unmistakable noises about being dissatisfied with Foxboro Stadium, an immense open-air stadium in the suburbs, so who knows where they might end up? For now, though, the team remains in a spot not easily accessible by public transportation. Foxboro is about a 45-minute drive from Boston, but traffic is heavy on game days, so plan your trip in advance and allow plenty of time to get there. *Rte. 1, Foxboro, 800/543–1776.*

where to play

The MDC maintains several football fields in Boston and neighboring communities. For information, call 617/727–7090.

POP WARNER FOOTBALL

New England's pigskin equivalent to Little League has teams in almost every town. Call local parks departments for information. *Boston Parks and Recreation, Sports Department, 617/635–3239.*

GOLF

MASSACHUSETTS GOLF ASSOCIATION

Representing more than 270 golf clubs in the state, this organization looks after the interests of amateur golfers. Ask for a listing of public and private courses in your area. They also provide information on equipment rentals. The office is open weekdays, 9 AM–4:30 PM. *175 Highland Ave., Needham, 617/449–3000.*

courses

Although golf is a popular pastime in Boston, most courses in and around the city are private and restricted to members only. That being said, the city itself runs a lovely and challenging course in Dorchester's Franklin Park:

1 *e-7*

WILLIAM DEVINE GOLF COURSE

Created in the early 1900s by Donald Ross, this 6,100-yard, par-70 course fell into disrepair over the years but was restored (to the tune of $1.3 million) in 1989. Now beautifully maintained, it's easily accessible by public transportation. It's also astonishingly inexpensive: greens fees for Boston residents are just $10 for 9 holes and $17 for 18 holes on weekdays, and $11 and $20 respectively on weekends (nonresidents pay a few dollars more). Open year-round from dawn to dusk, weather permitting. Be careful of your drives; locals also picnic and jog on the grounds. *Franklin Park, Dorchester, 617/265–4084. T stop: Green St.*

lessons

4 *g-4*

WAYLAND GOLF SHOPS

The Boston location of this local golf shop offers lessons as well as a line of equipment. They'll also refer you to local pros upon request. *890 Commonwealth Ave., 617/277–3999. T stop: Babcock St.*

HANDBALL

6 *e-7*

BOSTON ATHLETIC CLUB

This extremely popular health and fitness center downtown offers handball clinics and private lessons to nonmembers as well as members. Courts are kept in top condition and should be reserved in advance. *653 Summer St., 617/269–4300. T stop: South Station.*

HOCKEY

where to watch

6 *d-2*

THE BEANPOT TOURNAMENT

Held on two consecutive Monday nights in February, "the Beanpot" is an annual four-way battle royale for bragging rights as the city's best college hockey team. The four competitors for the coveted silver pot: Northeastern, Harvard, and arch-rivals Boston University and Boston College. BU holds the record for Beanpot championships, with 20 wins in the 45 years of this classic rivalry—

and Terriers fans loudly remind the rest that they're the team to beat. For information, call the FleetCenter at 617/624–1000, or contact the colleges' ticket offices directly: Boston College 617/552–3000, Boston University 617/353–3838, Harvard 495–2211, Northeastern 617/373–4700.

6 *d-2*

BOSTON BRUINS

When the basketball season is over, the Celtics' parquet flooring goes into storage to reveal the ice on which the Boston Bruins put on a hard-charging, head-banging display. Though the last of their five Stanley Cup wins was in 1972, the Bruins fill the FleetCenter night after night, year after year. Games are held from October through April, usually on Thursday and Sunday nights. *FleetCenter, 617/624–1000. T stop: North Station.*

where to play

PARKS AND RECREATION DEPARTMENT

The city's 103 basketball courts can also be used for street hockey. Call for locations, 617/725–4006.

6 *b-6*

If you aren't in the suburbs or on a high school or college team, you may have a hard time finding a rink on which to slap the puck around. If you like skating on natural ice, though, you're in luck— there's almost always a pick-up hockey game going on at the lagoon in the **Boston Public Garden** once it freezes solid.

HORSEBACK RIDING

BOSTON EQUESTRIAN CENTER

This riding academy offers trail rides, an outdoor arena, an indoor ring, and a five-week "learn to ride" class for just $100. Located in suburban Malden, it's just a 15-minute drive from downtown. *Rte. 1 N, Malden, 617/338–8400.*

HORSE RACING

SUFFOLK DOWNS

Boston's only live thoroughbred track, with saddle and harness races throughout the day during the racing season, attracts everyone from curious yuppies to diehard *Racing Form* readers. Suffolk Downs has betting windows, simulcasting from other tracks across the country—even a glassed-in restaurant overlooking the finish line where you can place your bets while eating surf 'n' turf (or hot dogs). The Blue Line stops at the parking lot entrance, just six T stops from downtown. *111 Waldemar Ave., East Boston, 617/567–3900. T stop: Suffolk Downs.*

ICE SKATING

6 *b-6*

BOSTON PUBLIC GARDEN

Once the water in the lagoon is solidly frozen and posted safe for skating, locals head onto the natural ice for bumpy fun. Figure skaters have half the lagoon to themselves—but don't go under the bridge to the other half, or you may stumble into the middle of a fierce hockey game! Bring your own skates or rent at **Beacon Hill Skate Shop,** 617/482–7400, which despite its name is not on Beacon Hill, but at the corner of Charles and Tremont streets near the New England Medical Center T stop.

6 *c-6*

FROG POND

A massive construction project completed in 1996 turned this formerly bare concrete pond on Boston Common into an outdoor skating rink, complete with concession pavilion and incredibly cheap skate rentals. What could be more quintessentially Bostonian than gliding along with a view of Beacon Hill and the Back Bay, then stopping for a sip of hot chocolate? The rink opens after the year's first cold spell, usually right after Thanksgiving, and is free to those with their own skates. *617/635–4505.*

MDC SKATING RINKS

From mid-November to mid-March, the MDC operates 19 rinks in Boston, Brighton, Cambridge, Dorchester, East Boston, Charlestown, Everett, Hyde Park, Lynn, Medford, Milton, Quincy, Revere, Somerville, South Boston, Waltham, West Roxbury, and Weymouth. Listed are the rinks most easily accessible by public transportation. For hours and a complete list of locations, call 617/727–9547.

4 *b-7*

REILLY RINK

Cleveland Circle, Brighton, 617/727–6034. Indoor. Rentals, lessons, sharpening, concessions. T stop: Cleveland Circle.

3 *g-5*

SIMONI RINK

Gore and 6th Sts., Cambridge, 617/782–4708. Indoor. Concessions. T stop: Lechmere.

9 *d-1*

STERITI RINK

Commercial St., North End, 617/782–4708. Indoor. T stop: North Station.

VETERANS MEMORIAL RINK

Somerville Ave., Somerville, 617/623-3523. Indoor. T stop: Sullivan Sq. or Lechmere.

IN-LINE SKATING

8 *e-3*

CITY SPORTS

This outfit rents in-line skates and safety equipment for $20 per day and will apply your rental fees toward the cost of a new pair of skates. You'll need a credit card for a deposit, which is returned to you when you return your rentals. There are six City Sports stores in the area; these two are closest to the great skating spots below. *480 Boylston St., 617/267–3900. T stop; Arlington.*

7 *a-3*

16 Dunster St., Cambridge, 617/868–9232. T stop: Harvard Sq.

8 *e-1*

CHARLES RIVER ESPLANADE

The Dudley Bike Path (*see Bicycling, above*) has been freshly paved from the Museum of Science to the BU Bridge for extravagantly smooth skating. A series of cones often set up on the street side of the **Hatch Shell** is a great spot to practice turns and to pick up tips from more experienced skaters. The best ways to reach the Esplanade: via the Charles Street footbridge or the Arthur Fiedler footbridge, both ramps, or a footbridge with stairs behind Boston University's chapel (go down stairs backwards, and *always* hold on to the railing!).

1 d-1

MINUTEMAN BICYCLE TRAIL

This 15-mile trail (see Bicycling, above) through Cambridge, Arlington, Lexington, and Bedford is as popular with bladers as it is with bikers. It's not ideal for novice skaters, though—it crosses busy streets now and then, and intersections are marked with strips of brick. Attempt this path only after you're confident in your ability both to stop and start without falling and to navigate occasionally rough pavement.

3 c-5

RIVERBEND PARK

Bladers throng to the Cambridge side of the Charles on Sundays from May through October, when Memorial Drive is closed to car traffic from the Western Avenue Bridge (at Central Square) to the Eliot Bridge (just beyond Harvard Square). All four lanes of pavement are car-free from 11 AM to 7 PM. If you're inspired on the spot, there's often a skate rental booth set up on the side of the road near Western Avenue.

MARTIAL ARTS

2 b-4

JAE H. KIM
TAE KWON DO INSTITUTE

This 23-year-old martial arts school is open seven days a week, with more than fifty day, evening, and weekend classes each week for men, women, and children. The health club-like facilities also include exercise machines. The owner, an internationally certified grand master, still teaches some classes. New members can take a free introductory private lesson. 102 Brookline Ave., 617/266–5050. T stop: Kenmore.

3 c-1

2000 Massachusetts Ave., Cambridge, 617/492–5070. T stop: Porter Sq.

RACQUETBALL/ SQUASH

1 g-4

BOSTON ATHLETIC CLUB

Members and nonmembers alike can take lessons in racquetball, handball, and squash at this huge and comprehensive health club (see Health Clubs, below) hidden among the lofts and industry of South Boston's waterfront. A van shuttles members to and from South Station so they don't have to make the rather long walk from the T. 653 Summer St., 617/269–4300 or 888/278–4312. T stop: South Station.

6 f-5

BOSTON RACQUET CLUB

This full-service health club in the center of the Financial District has eight air-conditioned courts for squash and racquetball. Professional lessons are available. Membership is required. 10 Post Office Sq., 617/482–8881. T stop: State St. or Downtown Crossing.

WOBURN RACQUET CLUB

Eight racquetball courts are available to the public for same-day bookings, no membership required. It's a 10-minute drive north of downtown, not far from I-93. 9 Webster St., Woburn, 617/933–8850.

RUNNING & JOGGING

BOSTON MARATHON

What guide to Boston would be complete without mention of The Marathon? This 26.2-mile race, run since 1896, draws world-class runners as well as amateurs, all vying for the most coveted victory outside of the Olympics and, since 1986, prize money. (Women have been welcome since 1972.) The course is run each year on the third Monday in April and wends its way through Hopkinton, Ashland, Framingham, Natick, Wellesley Center, Wellesley Hills, Newton (site of "Heartbreak Hill"), Brookline, then down Beacon Street to Kenmore Square and on to the finish at the Boston Public Library (see Events in Chapter 2 for more information). The front-runners finish at approximately 2 PM and receive their awards at 6 PM, but determined amateurs continue to straggle in for hours afterward. Registered runners can carbo-load at a free, all-you-can-eat spaghetti dinner the night before the race, then run to place or simply finish. Everyone else can stake out spots along the route and cheer themselves hoarse. The deadline for the runners to enter the 1998 race is March 1, 1998, (most years have their deadline around this time). To find out how to become part of this running legend, call the sponsor, the Boston Athletic Association, 617/236–1652.

The bike paths along the **Charles River Esplanade** and **Memorial Drive** are as popular with joggers as they are with bikers and bladers. Ask the front desk at your hotel for information about other routes; many hotels provide guests with jogging maps.

SAILING

6 *h-3*

BOSTON SAILING CENTER

One of the best sailing schools in New England, with a fifty-boat fleet, the Boston Sailing Center guarantees you'll be able to sail in a week. Classes include beginning sailing, advanced sailing, racing, cruising, and both celestial and coastal navigation. *54 Lewis Wharf, 617/ 227–4198. T stop: Aquarium.*

6 *a-5*

COMMUNITY BOATING

America's oldest public boating program offers sailboat rentals and lessons from April through October. Those qualified to sail solo can buy a two-day membership, with unlimited boat use, for $50. Monthlong memberships, during which you can learn to sail solo, are $65. And if you truly love the water, a 75-day membership costs just $160. Adult memberships finance a unique children's program in which kids ages 10 to 17 can sail all season for just one dollar. Community Boating is located on the Charles River Esplanade near the Charles Street footbridge, behind the Hatch Shell. *21 Embankment Rd., 617/ 523–1038. T stop: Charles/MGH.*

SCUBA DIVING

4 *f-8*

EAST COAST DIVERS

New England's number-one diver training center offers year-round lessons, PADI certification, sales, rental, and repairs. They'll even help you plan and book diving trips. *213 Boylston St., Brookline, 617/277–2216. T stop: Brookline Village.*

SKIING

After a full-scale New England snowstorm, it's not uncommon for true enthusiasts to cross-country ski down the sidewalk on their way to work—or toss their downhill skis in the back seat of the car and call in sick!

BLUE HILLS SKI AREA

If you want downhill skiing without a long drive to New Hampshire or Vermont, visit this MDC-run ski area about 30 minutes south of the city. Ideal for beginning and intermediate skiers, it has three slopes (floodlit for night skiing), a 1,200-foot double chairlift, snowmaking, and a ski school. Take Route 128 south to exit 2B and follow the signs. *4001 Washington St., Canton, 617/ 828–5090 or 617/828–5070.*

MIDDLESEX FELLS CROSS-COUNTRY SKI TRAIL

Many parks, hiking trails, and golf courses—and all MDC reservations— open their terrain to cross-country skiers in the winter. This particular park just north of the city offers two loops covering six miles of ungroomed trails over varied terrain. It's open dawn to dusk. *Middlesex Fells, Stoneham, 617/322–2851.*

SOCCER

where to watch

NEW ENGLAND REVOLUTION

Boston's newest professional team takes over Foxboro Stadium in the summer, when the New England Patriots aren't around. After a slow start, major league soccer and popular player Alexi Lalas are picking up fans—this Revolution *will* be televised before too long. *Rte. 1, Foxboro, 800/543–1776.*

where to play

MASSACHUSETTS YOUTH SOCCER ASSOCIATION

This nonprofit organization promoting soccer for youths 19 and under has more than 100,000 affiliated players in towns throughout the state, including Boston and the suburbs. Call to find out about leagues and fees. *311 Great Rd., Littleton, 508/486–0516.*

SWIMMING

A number of hotels offer swimming pools for guests, but the best indoor pool in the city isn't at a posh spa or a private health club—it's at the **Greater Boston YMCA** (*see* Fitness Centers &

Health Clubs, *below*). The 22.9-meter (25-yard) heated pool with three wide lap lanes is open to anyone for $10 a visit, less for Y members.

MDC PUBLIC POOLS

The MDC operates outdoor pools in **Brighton** (two), **Cambridge** (two), **Somerville** (two), **Boston, Roxbury, Hyde Park, West Roxbury,** and the suburbs of Everett, Waltham, Watertown, Stoneham, Malden, and Chelsea. They're open all week from 11 AM to 7 PM, late June to early September. For exact locations and fees, call 617/727–9547.

1 *g-5*
CITY BEACHES

You may wonder why anyone would swim in a pool when the ocean is so close. Its seafaring history notwithstanding, Boston isn't exactly known for its beaches. Though the harbor is certainly swimmable—it's dramatically cleaner than it was even five years ago—it's still a working harbor more hospitable to boats than to people, and what few neighborhood beaches exist are tucked away in spots far from downtown. That doesn't mean, however, that you shouldn't take a dip. The Boston Harbor cleanup has led to spruced-up beaches, improved facilities, and an all-out campaign to lure people back to the seaside.

Castle Island Beach, City Point Beach, and the **M Street Beach** are all off Day Boulevard in South Boston; **Malibu Beach** and **Savin Hill Beach** are off Morrissey Boulevard in Dorchester. Lifeguards are on duty daily from 10 AM to 6 PM from late June to early September, though beaches may be closed in bad weather or in case of pollution.

HARBOR ISLAND BEACHES

Ferries from Long Wharf travel several times a day to the largest Harbor island, Georges Island. From there, free water taxis will shuttle you to Gallops, Lovells, Grape, Bumpkin, and Peddocks islands. Only **Lovells Island** has a swimming beach. Lifeguards are on duty daily from 10 AM to 6 PM from late June to early September, weather permitting.

REVERE BEACH

This beach in a working-class suburb just north of the city draws the buff, the bronzed, and the big-haired for its stretch of sand, distant panoramic view of downtown Boston, and deliciously greasy clam shack. Best of all, the Blue line stops a block from the surf. *T stop: Revere Beach.*

TENNIS

where to watch

1 *b-5*
LONGWOOD CRICKET CLUB

Despite the name, no cricket is played here—but the U.S. Pro Tennis Championships are held here for a week each July. Tickets go fast, so call well in advance. *564 Hammond St., Brookline, 617/731–2900, tickets 617/731–4500. T stop: Chestnut Hill.*

where to play

MDC

The MDC operates tennis courts at **Tenean Beach** in Dorchester, **Constitution Beach** in East Boston, **Dale Street** (lighted), the **Truman Parkway,** and **Reservation Pond** in Hyde Park, **River Street** in Mattapan, **Commercial Street** in the North End, **Dilboy Field** and **Foss Park** in Somerville, **Marine Park** (lighted) in South Boston, and **Charlesbank Park** (lighted) and **Southwest Corridor Park** (lighted) in the West End. Unlighted MDC courts are open from dawn to dusk; lighted courts close at 11 PM.

PARKS AND RECREATION DEPARTMENT

The city maintains 103 tennis courts which are open dawn to dusk on a first-come, first-served basis. For locations and hours, call 617/727–9547.

1 *e-7*
SPORTSMEN'S TENNIS CLUB

This facility has seven outdoor courts and three indoor courts, and offers a summer tennis camp for kids under 18. *950 Blue Hill Ave., Dorchester, 617/288–9092. Daily 7 AM–2 AM.*

WRESTLING

6 *d-2*
FLEETCENTER

When pro wrestling comes to town—not that often—matches take place at the FleetCenter. For information, call 617/624–1050.

YOGA

1 *a-3*

INTERFACE

This center for holistic adult education usually offers at least one day and one evening class per term, taught by local yoga instructors; call for a catalog. *218 Walnut St., Newtonville, 617/964–9360.*

6 *c-4*

THE YOGA STUDIO

Founded in 1980, this Beacon Hill yoga school is the oldest in Boston devoted exclusively to hatha yoga. Founder Barbara Benagh was dubbed a *Boston* magazine "Best of Boston" for her teaching in 1995 and leads workshops nationwide. The small, friendly classes run on a term basis, but students are welcome to drop in at any time to take a single class. New students are encouraged to attend a free trial class. *74 Joy St., 617/523–7138. T stop: Government Center, Charles/MGH, or Bowdoin.*

fitness centers & health clubs

With dozens of health clubs to choose from, you can base your choice on atmosphere, price, available equipment, classes offered—even location. Most clubs will offer a free tour on request, and many will allow prospective members one or two complimentary workouts. If you're just visiting, ask about reciprocal arrangements that let members of other clubs work out at reduced rates.

1 *g-4*

BOSTON ATHLETIC CLUB

The lofts and industry of South Boston's waterfront are home to this comprehensive club, which operates a shuttle van to and from South Station to save members the rather long walk from the T. The offerings are many: seven indoor tennis courts; an indoor pool; racquetball, handball, and squash instruction; spinning, step, walking, and water aerobics; fitness equipment; basketball and volleyball; personal trainers; yoga; karate; on-staff nutritionists, massage therapists, physical therapists, and chiropractor; even special social programs to bring members together. *653 Summer St., 617/269–4300 or 888/278–4312. T stop: South Station.*

4 *e-4*

BOSTON SPORTS CLUB

Well-heeled and well-toned young professionals flock to this fitness center, which was known as The Squash Club until it affiliated in July 1997 with a downtown club. Free weights, state-of-the-art fitness machines, eight squash courts, full-court basketball, personal trainers, even a sports café—but the biggest draw here seems to be the funk aerobics instructor, who has a fervent, faithful following of members who trust him to sculpt them into shape. Limited parking is available. *15 Gorham St., 617/731–4177. T stop: Long Avenue on B line.*

8 *b-6*

GREATER BOSTON YMCA

The best swimming in the city isn't at a posh spa or a private health club—it's here at the Y, which has a 25-yard heated indoor pool. It also has a fully equipped gym, an indoor track, a three-court gymnasium, and brand new fitness equipment. Nonmembers can work out for $10 a visit, members of other Massachusetts YMCAs have access for $5 a visit, and YMCA members from out of state can present their membership cards for up to two weeks of unlimited free usage. *316 Huntington Ave., 617/536–7800. T stop: Northeastern on E line.*

3 *c-1*

HEALTHWORKS

You won't find a pick-up scene or macho displays at this small local chain of women-only fitness centers. You will find plenty of aerobics, yoga, boxing, fitness machines, and fully equipped locker rooms for women who appreciate feeling welcome whatever their age, shape, or size. All locations also have nutritionists and personal trainers on staff as well as on-site child care. The downtown Boston center has the newest equipment; the Brookline location, currently being renovated, draws kudos for its instructors; the Cambridge club has the most parking. *441 Stuart St., 617/859–7700. T stop: Copley or Back Bay.*

4 *g-4*

920 Commonwealth Ave., Brookline, 617/731–3030. T stop: St. Paul St. on B line.

8 d-4

Porter Sq. Shopping Center, Cambridge, 617/497–4454. T stop: Porter Sq.

8 f-4

METROPOLITAN HEALTH CLUB

This funky yet no-nonsense fitness center where the Back Bay meets the South End has a huge gay male clientele, but women and straight men will also feel comfortable with the fully equipped weight room and full schedule of aerobics. You don't have to be devoted to the Body Beautiful to work out here; you will, however, likely notice that many of the patrons are merely further chiseling already superb physiques. *209 Columbus Ave., 617/536–3006. T stop: Copley or Back Bay.*

3 c-1

THE NO FRILLS AEROBIC FACTORY

The name says it all: no juice bars, no pro shop, just 60-plus aerobics, dance, and conditioning classes a week. There are special kids' and teens' classes, free weights, and cardiovascular equipment as well as kung fu, tai chi, and kick boxing, but what this health club is best at (and best known for) is funk and hip-hop aerobics classes that are somehow almost as much fun as an evening of club-hopping. *624 Somerville Ave., Somerville, 617/625–2700. T stop: Porter Sq.*

chapter 7

HOTELS

You'll have no trouble finding lodgings in Boston if your taste runs to giant hotels with lobby cocktail bars, spacious rooms, and plush bathrobes hanging on doorhooks. The Marriots, Sheratons, and Hiltons of the world have found here a large and enthusiastic market for anonymous luxury among the business travelers who bustle in and out of town. And then there are the two super-deluxe rivals overlooking the Public Garden: The Four Seasons, with room service for pets and a Presidential Suite spacious enough for state dinners, is a favored stop among visiting celebrities, while the Ritz-Carlton, with its white-gloved elevator operators, private butlers, and working fireplaces, remains the place to stay for society dowagers and others of discreet wealth.

But if the idea of spending more than $200 a night for either new-fangled extravagance or old-fashioned elegance jars your perception of Boston as the heart of Yankee thrift, fret not. The frugal visitor will find numerous places to stay and still have enough money for a budget-busting, bargain-hunting Filene's Basement binge. Yes, there are motels within the city; there are also smaller, older hotels and inns, less posh than their larger kin but no less comfortable and welcoming. If you don't mind morning chit-chat with other guests, you'll find dozens of small bed-and-breakfast inns scattered from hip Cambridge to gaslit Beacon Hill. And many of the large luxury hotels offer special weekend rates designed to fill the rooms vacated when their business clients head home on Friday afternoon—ask around and you may even land a package deal with perks like free parking, breakfast, or cocktails.

While it's usually possible to find a room in almost any neighborhood at almost any time, there are two exceptions worth noting: First, the giant business-oriented hotels in the Back Bay fill up rapidly whenever the Hynes Convention Center is hosting a large event. Second, it's nearly impossible to find a room anywhere in greater Boston during May or early June, when more than five dozen local colleges hold their commencement ceremonies. If you're planning to visit during graduation season, book your room well in advance—or risk being banished to the distant suburbs at bedtime.

price categories & credit cards

When considering prices, keep in mind that room rates generally don't include service charges, parking (which can cost $20 or more per night), or the room tax, presently 9.7%, which is added when you pay up.

The following prices are regular weekday rates for a standard double room. The number of rooms available at this rate may be limited.

Very Expensive	over $220
Expensive	$160–$220
Moderate	$110–$160
Inexpensive	under $110

Below, hotels are grouped by price category; the Bed & Breakfast listing is ordered alphabetically, with price categories listed in the service information. For hostels, actual bed rates are provided.

All hotels, hostels, and B&Bs listed take major credit cards (American Express, Discover, Diner's Club, MasterCard, and Visa) unless otherwise specified.

parking

In the rare instances where hotels offer free parking, we note it. Otherwise, many hotels and other accommodations offer parking facilities at a fee—either at a hotel garage or, more usually, validated parking services at a nearby garage. Hotels providing valet service to shepherd your car to and from the garage are noted.

LUXURY LODGING

6 g-5

BOSTON HARBOR HOTEL AT ROWES WHARF

A luxurious part of the Rowes Wharf mixed-use complex of offices and pricey condos, the Boston Harbor Hotel does everything on a grand scale, starting with the dramatic entrance—an 80-foot archway topped with a rotunda. Almost every room has an impressive view of either the ocean or the city, and there's no stinting on amenities: terry robes, hair dryers, twice-daily maid service, nightly turn-down services, shoeshine services (just leave them outside the door!), 24-hour room service, and a lavish health club/spa with a 60-foot lap pool, sauna, Jacuzzi, facials, massages, and herbal wraps. The Rowes Wharf restaurant offers a spectacular, if expensive, Sunday brunch, which draws Bostonians and visitors alike. The Boston Harbor Hotel is within walking distance of Faneuil Hall, the North End, the New England Aquarium, the Financial District, *and* the Big Dig. Relax: the construction work going on just outside the front door is invisible and unheard from within the hotel's walls. *70 Rowes Wharf, Financial District, 617/439–7000 or 800/752–7077, fax 617/330–9450. 230 rooms, 26 suites. Restaurant, bar, outdoor café, beauty salon, health club/spa, concierge, business services, pet-walking services, parking. T stop: South Station.*

8 e-3

THE COPLEY PLAZA

Built in 1912, the Copley Plaza was taken over in 1996 by the Fairmont hotel group and is undergoing major renovations to all rooms, slated to be completed in 1998. Any work done here can only burnish the opulence of this stately landmark; the public spaces recall an era long gone, with gilded ceilings, mosaic floors, marble pillars, and crystal chandeliers and even the guest rooms themselves have custom furniture from Italy and elegant marble bathrooms. (Some things never change—the local debs still make their debuts here.) One of the restaurants has been spruced up and renamed the Oak Room to match its twin in New York's Plaza Hotel; the other, the Copley Room, has also been given a face-lift, and afternoon tea is still served in the palm-bedecked lobby daily from 3 to 5 PM. Yet despite the imposing Victorian surroundings, the atmosphere is nothing less than gracious and welcoming, thanks to the helpful multilingual staff. *138 St. James Ave., Back Bay, 617/267–5300 or 800/826–7539, fax 617/247–6681. 379 rooms, 60 suites. 2 restaurants, 2 bars, 2 non-smoking floors, 24-hour room service, barbershop, beauty salon, complimentary privileges at nearby health club, parking. Children under 18 free in parents' room. T stop: Copley.*

8 f-2

FOUR SEASONS HOTEL

The only hotel in Boston other than the Ritz-Carlton to overlook the Public Garden is also (to the discreet chagrin of the Ritz) the only five-star hotel in the city. Beautifully situated overlooking the Public Garden (once only the Ritz could boast that fact), its antiques-filled public spaces have an old-world elegance. In guest rooms, it specializes in the sort of personal service demanded by celebrities: huge rooms with king-size beds, stocked minibars, HBO, terry bathrobes, hair dryers, and that rarest of amenities, windows that actually open. There's also valet service, twice-daily maid service, same-day laundry, 24-hour concierge and room service, and computerized check-in, as well as a fully equipped health club with whirlpool, sauna, and a heated 51-foot swimming pool overlooking the Garden. The Four Seasons is home to Aujourd'hui, one of the city's most acclaimed restaurants, which, despite its French name, serves American food. The Bristol Lounge serves high tea—every bit as good as tea at the Ritz—daily at 3 PM. *200 Boylston St., Back Bay, 617/338–4400 or 800/268–6282, fax 617/423–0154. 288 rooms. Restaurant, lounge, 24-hour room service, health club/spa, laundry service, 24-hour concierge, valet parking. T stop: Arlington.*

6 f-5

LE MERIDIEN BOSTON

Once the Federal Reserve Building, this 1922 landmark in the center of the Financial District still exudes an almost intimidating aura of money and power—everyone seems to be stiffly suit-clad even on weekends, and Julien, one of the city's best French nouvelle cuisine restaurants, is jacket-and-tie land. But Le Meridien has a hidden light side: The informal Café Fleuri hosts an all-chocolate buffet each Saturday afternoon! The airy, soundproof guest rooms have a small sitting area with a writing desk and two phone lines as well as a minibar, remote-control TV with free cable and in-room movies, hair dryers, and terry bathrobes. Some guest rooms are bilevel loft suites with skylights. *250 Franklin St. at Post Office Sq., Financial District, 617/451–1900 or 800/543–4300, fax 617/423–2844. 326 rooms, 22 suites. 2 restaurants, 2 lounges, no-smoking floor, 24-hr room service, health club, laundry/valet service, concierge, parking. T stop: State St. or South Station.*

6 f-4
THE REGAL BOSTONIAN

What a perfect place for a hotel, right in the Quincy Market district, adjacent to Government Center and the financial district, and just an underpass away from the old-world Italian North End. It's a small, privately owned luxury hotel, and it shows: lovely touches include fresh flowers in each guest room, small, private, flower-accented balconies, and French windows. The hotel is actually an intriguing blend of old and new: The Harkness Wing, built as a warehouse in 1824, has rooms with working fireplaces, exposed-beam ceilings, and brick walls, while the newer wing with its glass-and-steel atrium has rooms with Jacuzzis. Seasons, the hotel's four-star restaurant, sits atop the glass-enclosed roof overlooking Quincy Market. Since Quincy Market awakens at dawn, light sleepers may want to request a room facing away from the street to keep from being awakened at the same time. *Faneuil Hall Marketplace, Government Center, 617/523–3600 or 800/343–0922, fax 617/523–2454. 152 rooms, 16 suites. Restaurant, lounge, room service, valet parking. Children under 12 free in parents' room. T stop: Government Center.*

7 f-2
THE RITZ-CARLTON HOTEL

Although the four-star Ritz lost its "best of Boston" designation when the Four Seasons acquired its fifth star, many (rather well-off) visitors would never dream of staying anywhere else, thanks to its unmatched location, dignified elegance, and fierce devotion to the comfort and privacy of its guests. All rooms have refrigerators, bathroom phones, and in-room safes; the coveted suites in the older section have parlors with wood-burning fireplaces and the best views of the Public Garden. Among the other amenities: 24-hour room service

with serving pantries on each floor staffed by individual floor waiters, same-day laundry and cleaning services, complimentary shoeshine, twice-daily maid service, nightly turn-down, and complimentary weekday-morning limo service. There's even a new Chanel boutique on the ground floor, naturally bearing the address of "No. 5" Arlington Street. The extra-pricey rooms on the top three floors include butler service and admission to the Ritz-Carlton Club, with complimentary food and drinks, newspapers, and adult and children's games. And for the child with everything, how about a night in the Junior Presidential Suite? In addition to all the parents' amenities, kids get their own scaled-down kids' bedroom with furniture and bath fixtures in proportions to suit the smaller set, all for a most adult-size $600. *15 Arlington St., Back Bay, 617/536–5700 or 800/241–3333, fax 617/536–9340. 237 rooms, 48 suites. 2 restaurants, 2 lounges, 24-hour room service, barbershop, beauty salon, health club/sauna, baby-sitting, laundry service, concierge, parking. T stop: Arlington.*

8 d-4
WESTIN COPLEY PLACE

The 36-story Westin, one of the tallest hotels in the city, is one of the two hotel-anchors of the upscale Copley Place shopping mall and connected to it by a skybridge. The rooms are spacious and furnished in Queen Anne style; those on the Charles River side have superb views. Non-smoking rooms are available, and 40 rooms are specially designed to accommodate the physically challenged. The three restaurants include the elegant Turner Fisheries Bar and Restaurant with its oyster bar and live jazz every night at 8 PM. For relaxation, the fully equipped health club has a whirlpool, sauna, and hot tub. *Copley Pl., Back Bay, 617/262–9600 or 800/228–3000, fax 617/424–8957. 756 rooms, 48 suites. 3 restaurants, 24-hour room service, indoor pool, health club, hot tub, sauna, concierge, valet parking. T stop: Copley or Back Bay.*

EXPENSIVE LODGING

9 b-4
BACK BAY HILTON

Directly across from the Hynes Convention Center, this 25-story luxury hotel in the Back Bay is a short walk to Newbury Street, the Prudential Center, the Christian Science Church, and Berklee College of Music. The large rooms with panoramic views and contemporary decor are soundproofed and have bay windows that open; many rooms even have balconies. Fitness buffs will enjoy the enclosed year-round swimming pool, warm-weather outdoor sun deck, and full-service health club with Nautilus, sauna, and a trained staff. Nonsmoking floors are available. Boodle's, the restaurant, is a grill serving real meat-and-potatoes meals, and the Rendezvous lounge is popular with locals as well as visitors. Ask about discount coupons at the Sony Cheri, a first-run movie theater next door. *40 Dalton St., Back Bay, 617/236–1100 or 800/874–0663, fax 617/267-8893. 330 rooms, 1 suite. 2 restaurants, lounge, 24-hour room service, health club/sauna, parking. Children of all ages free in parents' room. T stop: Hynes Convention Center/ICA.*

8 f-3
BOSTON PARK PLAZA HOTEL & TOWERS

When a new management team took over here in early 1997, it promptly began extensive renovations to the rooms and public areas. However, the Park Plaza, which began life as the flagship of the Statler chain in 1927, still retains its decorative plaster moldings and other old-fashioned touches—some of the cozy rooms, which tend to be smaller than those in newer hotels, even have two (!) bathrooms. It's in a stellar location, one block from the Public Garden and a short walk to Beacon Hill, the theater district, Newbury Street, and public transportation—and for shoppers, it's a credit-card's throw away from Boylston and Newbury streets. A branch of the rightfully famous Legal Sea Foods is on the ground floor, as is a lobby bar with live piano music. The employees are infinitely patient and utterly friendly despite constant distraction. Sightseeing tours all pick up and return here; there's also free indoor parking and a direct airport shuttle as well as several airlines offices on the premises. The top floors are known as Plaza Towers, a hotel-within-a-hotel of 84 rooms, with more luxurious amenities at correspondingly higher rates. If you're traveling with children, ask about the "Cub Club" package including a fully soundproofed room with two bathrooms, dis-

count coupons for local attractions and baby-sitting, and a daily story hour. *64 Arlington St. at Park Plaza, Back Bay, 617/426–2000 or 800/225–2008, fax 617/426–5545. 966 rooms, 10 suites. 2 restaurants, bar, room service, beauty salon, drugstore, health club, dry cleaning, laundry service, concierge, foreign currency exchange, travel services, valet parking. T stop: Arlington.*

3 f-6
CAMBRIDGE CENTER MARRIOTT

This modern 26-story hotel in Kendall Square—the high-tech heart of Cambridge—is just steps from MIT and the Red Line, which can whisk you straight to downtown or out to Harvard Square. Large rooms have either two double or one king-size bed and a TV with free HBO. The gym has exercise machines, a sauna, lockers, stationary bikes, an indoor pool with whirlpool, and a sundeck in season. For a bit more money, the concierge level on the top floors features these additional amenities: complimentary newspapers and continental breakfast, private lounge, and honor bar. The restaurant is satisfactory, but with a branch of legendary Legal Sea Foods half a block away, you might never eat in the hotel. *2 Cambridge Center, Cambridge, 617/494–6600 or 800/228–9290, fax 617/494–0036. 425 rooms, 10 suites. Restaurant, bar, indoor pool, sauna, gym, concierge, valet parking. Children under 18 free in parents' room. T stop: Kendall Sq.*

7 a-3
CHARLES HOTEL

You can't stay much closer to the center of Harvard Square than at this first-class hotel adjacent to the Kennedy School of Government. The interior is contemporary, yet homey, with antiques and work by local artists. Rooms boast honor bars, terry robes for guest use, hair dryers, quilted down comforters on every bed, and Bose radios instead of standard-issue alarm clocks; suites have fireplaces. There's also a health spa and salon for fitness, swimming, sauna, steam room, whirlpool, and European hair, skin, and beauty treatments; full concierge services; and 24-hour room service—and if you haven't read any good books lately, "Room Service Books" provides prompt delivery of phone orders. Both restaurants are excellent, and the Regattabar is one of the area's hottest spots for jazz. *1 Ben-*

nett St., Cambridge, 617/864–1200 or 800/882–1818, fax 617/864–5715. 296 rooms, 44 suites. 2 restaurants, bar, pool, health club/spa, parking. T stop: Harvard.

8 *c-5*

COLONNADE HOTEL

Conveniently located across from the Hynes Convention Center and next to Copley Place, this small, relatively non-hectic and modern hotel has more personality than some of the larger business-oriented high rises on the other side of Huntington Avenue. All rooms have minibars, cable TV with remote control, bathrobes, and hair dryers. There's concierge service and twice-daily maid service as well as a barbershop and beauty salon. In the summer, the rooftop swimming pool is open, with live entertainment in the evenings; otherwise, work out in the fitness room with Universal equipment. Complete executive services include multilingual translation and foreign currency exchange. *120 Huntington Ave., South End, 617/424–7000 or 800/962–3030, fax 617/424–1717. 285 rooms, 10 suites. Restaurant, bar, 24-hour room service, exercise room, barbershop/beauty salon, baby-sitting, concierge, parking. Children under 12 free in parents' room. No pets. T stop: Prudential.*

3 *c-6*

DOUBLETREE GUEST SUITES

Part of a chain of all-suite hotels, each unit in this 15-story building features a living room with sofa bed and refrigerator, bedroom with king-size bed, and full bath with telephone. There are five two-level penthouse suites. The renowned Scullers Jazz Club is one of the best places in town to see both local and national jazz performers. There's also an indoor swimming pool, whirlpool, sauna, and game room. This hotel is located next to the Massachusetts Turnpike, making it more convenient to Cambridge than city-center Boston. It's far from the subway, but a courtesy van will take you around Boston and Cambridge at no extra charge. *400 Soldiers Field Rd., Allston, 617/783–0090 or 800/222–8733, fax 617/783–0897. 305 suites, 5 bilevel penthouses. Restaurant, indoor pool, sauna, game room, free parking. Children under 18 free in parents' room. No pets.*

8 *a-4*

ELIOT HOTEL

Once a modest semi-residential hotel suitable for travelers on a budget, the Eliot has gone upscale, emerging from comprehensive renovation as a luxurious all-suite hotel with kitchenettes, Italian marble bathrooms, two cable-equipped televisions in every room, and a tastefully European pastel-hue decor. The marble lobby, with its vast chandelier, has also been spruced up. Alas, the legendary Eliot Lounge where Marathoners once slaked their thirst is now gone but has been replaced by Clio's, an airy new restaurant garnering rave reviews for its serene ambiance and outstanding American cuisine. Fortunately, the breakfast room still serves big breakfasts at a small price. The Eliot is located next to the Harvard Club, steps from Newbury Street and a short walk to Kenmore Square. *370 Commonwealth Ave., Back Bay, 617/267–1607 or 800/443–5468, fax 617/536–9114. 91 suites. Restaurant, parking. Children under 12 free in parents' room. No pets. T stop: Hynes Convention Center/ICA.*

3 *d-8*

HYATT REGENCY CAMBRIDGE

Dubbed the "pyramid on the Charles," this ziggurat-shape luxury hotel is beautifully situated on the river two miles from downtown Boston. The 14-story atrium on the Charles has a glass elevator and the "Great Window," a 100-foot-high glass wall for spectacular views of Boston, topped with a revolving rooftop lounge and Italian restaurant. All rooms overlook the Charles or the atrium; some even have private balconies. Fifteen rooms on the third floor are wheelchair-accessible; the seventh floor is for nonsmokers; Regency Level on the tenth floor offers special amenities at a premium. There's also a comprehensive health and fitness facility, with a glass-enclosed junior-Olympic-size pool and open sundeck in season, and a well-equipped outdoor children's playground. Unfortunately, although the hotel is directly across the river from Boston University, and near both MIT and Harvard, it's nowhere near public transportation. *575 Memorial Dr., Cambridge, 617/492–1234 or 800/228–9000, fax 617/491–6906. 500 rooms. 2 restaurants, bar, indoor pool, health club, baby-sitting, playground, concierge, parking. Children under 18 free in parents' room.*

7 *b-3*

THE INN AT HARVARD

The newest hotel in the Harvard Square area is run by Doubletree Hotels for the university and caters to a largely academic crowd (although tourists and business travelers are welcome). It's an unobtrusive four-story brick building with modern, neutral-hue rooms decorated in cherrywood, brass, and fabrics in geometric patterns. In both the rooms and the common areas, 17th- and 18th-century artworks on loan from Harvard's Fogg Art Museum hang side-by-side with contemporary paintings. All guest rooms have large windows overlooking either the Yard or the Square; many even have small balconies. Six rooms also overlook the hotel's quietly striking glass atrium. In addition to being just outside the walls of Harvard Yard, the hotel is an easy walk from the furniture stores, specialty shops, and ethnic eateries that abound on the stretch of Massachusetts Avenue between Harvard and Central squares. *1201 Massachusetts Ave., Cambridge, 617/491–2222 or 800/222–8733, fax 617/491–6520. 113 rooms. Dry cleaning, laundry service, business services, valet parking. No pets. T stop: Harvard Sq.*

8 *d-4*

MARRIOTT AT COPLEY PLACE

There are three impressive ways to enter this "megahotel," the second largest in the city: through a four-story greenhouse atrium complete with waterfall; via a glass skybridge from the Prudential Center and Hynes Auditorium complex; or directly from the upscale Copley Plaza shopping mall. The attractive rooms, with Queen Anne–style furnishings, have individual climate control, cable TV with free HBO, mini-refrigerators, and views of the Charles. The 28th floor, dubbed the Concierge Level, has special amenities and a private lounge. Four entire floors are set aside for nonsmokers, and 30 rooms are specially designed to be wheelchair-accessible. *110 Huntington Ave., Back Bay, 617/236–5800 or 800/228–9290, fax 617/236–5885. 1,139 rooms, 77 suites. 3 restaurants, 2 lounges, 24-hour room service, valet service, indoor pool, barbershop, beauty salon, health club, sauna, whirlpool, recreation room, business center, valet parking. No pets. T stop: Copley or Back Bay.*

6 *h-4*

MARRIOTT LONG WHARF

A vast brick ship moored at the wharf with its prow pointing into the harbor, this hotel is convenient to the Aquarium, Faneuil Hall, and the North End, and it abuts romantic Christopher Columbus Park, where a tiny rose garden with a fountain honors Rose Kennedy, the Kennedy family matriarch. Rooms here feature king-size or double beds, individual climate control, in-room movies, and direct-dial phones. Most rooms have at least some view of the harbor; all open onto a dramatic five-story atrium. The best views are found on the top-floor Concierge Level, slightly higher priced to include cocktail hour, a business center, and a free Continental breakfast. Other amenities include an indoor pool with poolside service, an outdoor sundeck, a fully equipped health club with whirlpool and sauna, and a game room. The Marriott Long Wharf also offers some of the best weekend packages in town. *296 State St., North End, 617/227–0800 or 800/228–9290, fax 617/227–2867. 402 rooms, 12 suites. Restaurant, bar, indoor pool, health club/sauna, parking. Children under 18 free in parents' room. No pets. T stop: Aquarium.*

6 *e-5*

OMNI PARKER HOUSE

Although this particular building went up in 1927, the Parker House is the oldest continuously operating hotel in America. It opened in 1855 and has sheltered the likes of author Charles Dickens and actress Sarah Bernhardt; John Wilkes Booth, in town to visit his famous actor brother Edwin, practiced on the downstairs firing range eight days before assassinating Abraham Lincoln. Appropriately, this historic hotel is located opposite old City Hall, near Government Center, and right on the historic Freedom Trail. Even though the smallish rooms have all the modern amenities, they still seem quaint. The Parker House is known for three things in particular: political press conferences—particularly of the Republican variety—and fresh Parker House rolls and Boston cream pie, both of which were invented here. (The rolls and cream-filled cake are still served in the dining room, as is a bountiful Sunday brunch.) Renovation work underway at press time is gradually updating the plumbing and electrical systems and replacing worn carpeting and wallpaper, while restoring the lobby and rooms to their former beauty. *60 School St., Downtown Crossing, 617/227–8600 or 800/843–6664, fax 617/742–5729. 482 rooms, 70 suites. 2 restaurants, 2 bars, room service, barbershop, beauty salon, baby-sitting, concierge, parking. Children under 16 free in parents' room. No pets. T stop: Park St. or Government Center.*

2 *e-1*

ROYAL SONESTA HOTEL

Overlooking the Charles River, with wonderful views of Beacon Hill and the skyscrapers of the Financial District, this hotel has one of the most scenic locations in the city. The inside is also lovely, with an impressive collection of modern art scattered throughout. Many of the rooms were completely renovated in 1996; all have color TV, air-conditioning, and minibars. For dining, there's the excellent Davio's Restaurant & Café and the Charles Bar as well as room service till 1 AM on weekdays and 2 AM on weekends. Then, work off the calories in a health club including exercise equipment, sauna, whirlpool, tanning beds, spa services, and an enclosed heated swimming pool with retractable roof. The ninth and tenth floors of the West Tower are the exclusive Royal Club concierge level with extra amenities. The hotel is close to the Museum of Science, adjacent to the Cambridgeside Galleria shopping mall, and across the street from Lotus, the software company; a courtesy van goes to MIT, Kendall Square, Massachusetts General Hospital, Quincy Market, and the Prudential Center daily from 7 AM to 10 PM. For family groups, the hotel offers superb packages including boat rides, ice cream, and free bicycle rentals. *5 Cambridge Pkwy., Cambridge, 617/491–3600 or 800/766–3782, fax 617/661–5956. 400 rooms, 28 suites. 2 restaurants, room service, indoor pool, health club, spa, baby-sitting, parking. Children under 18 free in parents' room. No pets. T stop: Lechmere.*

8 *b-4*

SHERATON BOSTON HOTEL & TOWERS

Wherever you are in the Back Bay, you can't miss the twin 29-story towers of New England's largest hotel, connected directly to the Hynes Convention Center and the Prudential Center. Rooms are decorated in hushed pastels, with mahogany furniture and wide windows displaying panoramic city views—ask for a room facing the Christian Science Center or the Charles River. The top three floors, known as the Towers, are more luxurious (with butler service and a VIP lounge) and about 20% more expensive. Non-smoking and wheelchair-accessible rooms are available. The hotel also boasts the city's largest indoor/outdoor swimming pool, with poolside service; health club facilities with Universal equipment and whirlpool; 24-hour room service; and concierge and valet service. This hotel is immensely popular with conventioneers for its size and for its proximity to both the convention center and other Back Bay attractions. *39 Dalton St., Back Bay, 617/236–2020 or 800/325–3535, fax 617/236–1702. 1,191 rooms. 2 restaurants, 2 lounges, indoor/outdoor pool, health club, hot tub, baby-sitting, concierge, business services, parking. Children under 17 free in parents' room. T stop: Hynes Convention Center/ICA.*

6 *d-6*

SWISSÔTEL

This luxuriously European 22-story hotel has a handsome mahogany lobby with Waterford crystal chandeliers—even in the elevators—and one of Boston's most regal ballrooms. It's the sort of place where housekeepers turn down your bedcovers and leave "sweet dreams" chocolates on the pillows. Rooms are appointed with Chippendale reproductions, televisions with free HBO and Showtime, fully stocked minibars, and phones in the bathrooms; some are equipped for those with special needs, and one entire floor is designated non-smoking. There's also a charming café, concierge service, and a health club with a large indoor heated swimming pool and sun terrace. Unfortunately, the hotel is attached to the failed Lafayette Place mixed-use complex (plans are underway to redevelop it once more) and is on the edge of the former Combat Zone, a neighborhood that can be slightly dicey at night, but there's still no reason to avoid the plush atmosphere and otherwise excellent location one block from Downtown Crossing. *One Ave. de Lafayette, Downtown Crossing, 617/451–2600 or 800/621–9200, fax 617/451–2198. 500 rooms, 23 suites. Café, bar, 24-hour room service, indoor pool, health club, concierge, business services, parking. T stop: Downtown Crossing.*

MODERATE LODGING

8 *d-4*

COPLEY SQUARE HOTEL

Built in 1891, the Copley Square is one of the city's oldest hotels and a true value. It is informal and busy, but it's comfortable, well priced, and extremely popular with tour groups, budget-minded families, and European travelers who appreciate its old-world style, quirky turn-of-the-century charm, winding corridors, and convenient location adjacent to the Public Library and the Prudential Center. No room is exactly like another, but since a recent refurbishing, all have voice mail, modems, air-conditioning, big bay windows that open, safes, hair dryers, and automatic coffee makers (with coffee and filters, of course) in addition to all the ordinary amenities. Non-smoking rooms are available. The quietest rooms are on the top floor overlooking the courtyard. Café Budapest, which serves Hungarian food, is a popular romantic spot with low lighting, soft music, and plush decor. There's also a coffee shop and a sports bar. *47 Huntington Ave., Back Bay, 617/536–9000 or 800/225–7062, fax 617/267–3547. 143 rooms, 12 suites. 2 restaurants, 2 bars, coffee shop, parking. Children under 17 free in parents' room. No pets. T stop: Copley.*

7 *a-3*

HARVARD SQUARE HOTEL

Formerly the Harvard Manor House, this four-story motel was totally refurbished in 1996 and now features new wallpaper, furniture, and carpeting in addition to air-conditioning and color TV. It's still one of the least expensive options for staying in Cambridge, and the location can't be beat—it's half a block from the center of the Square. It sits atop a parking garage. *110 Mount Auburn St., Cambridge, 617/864–5200 or 800/458–5886, fax 617/864–2409. 73 rooms. Café, parking. Children under 16 free in parents' room. No pets. T stop: Harvard Sq.*

4 *g-5*

HOLIDAY INN BROOKLINE

Located in a residential neighborhood 10 minutes from downtown Boston, this one-time motor lodge grown into a sleek hotel has a lush garden atrium, an indoor swimming pool, and even a putting green. Rooms have remote-control TV with in-room movies, individual climate control, and king-size beds. Non-smoking and wheelchair-accessible rooms are available. There's free parking in an underground garage, and the Green line stops just across the street for a 20-minute ride to downtown. *1200 Beacon St., Brookline, 617/277–1200 or 800/465–4329, fax 617/743–6991. 225 rooms. Restaurant, bar, pool, barbershop, beauty salon, free parking. Children under 17 free in parents' room. No pets. T stop: St. Paul St. (C line).*

2 *b-5*

HOWARD JOHNSON'S FENWAY

Baseball fans won't be able to resist staying here—it's literally next door to Fenway Park, within earshot of the roaring crowd. It's also near the Isabella Stewart Gardner Museum, the Museum of Fine Arts, and the dance clubs of Lansdowne Street, and it's a short T ride to downtown. The rooms are clean and comfortable. There's also room service till midnight (beverages only), and during the summer months, an outdoor swimming pool with lifeguard. Best of all, parking is free. *1271 Boylston St., the Fens, 617/267–8300 or 800/654–2000, fax 617/267–2763. 94 rooms. Restaurant, lounge, room service, outdoor pool, free parking. Children under 18 free in parents' room. T stop: Kenmore.*

2 *b-4*

HOWARD JOHNSON'S KENMORE SQUARE

Half a block from Kenmore Square and a five-minute stroll from Fenway Park and the clubs of Lansdowne Street, this hotel is popular with baseball fans and parents visiting offspring who attend Boston University. The soundproof rooms are modern, with color TV and air-conditioning. Non-smoking rooms are available. There's also a swimming pool, a rooftop disco, and free parking. One note of caution: since the hotel is actually on the BU campus, students and their friends often stay there and may still be up partying at hours when you might prefer to be sleeping. *575 Commonwealth Ave., Kenmore Square, 617/267–3100 or 800/654–2000, fax 617/424–1045. 170 rooms. Restaurant, lounge, indoor pool, baby-sitting, free parking. Children under 18 free in parents' room. T stop: Kenmore.*

8 *d-3*

LENOX HOTEL

The Lenox, built in 1900, has managed to transform itself from a comfortable but unexceptional spot in the center of the Back Bay into a charming and handsomely traditional first-class choice—all while remaining moderately priced. All rooms are soundproof, have cable TV and AM/FM radio, individually controlled heat and air-conditioning, and bath amenities and sewing kits. The decor varies from New England colonial to French provincial to Oriental. A recent $20-million renovation uncovered period details, particularly in the corner rooms, many of which have working fireplaces. The fireplace in the extremely gracious blue and gold lobby, too, is set ablaze in winter. The Samuel Adams Brew House, a brewpub, and Anago Bistro, a popular eatery newly transplanted from Cambridge, add the finishing touch to the metamorphosis. The Boston Public Library is on one side, Lord & Taylor is on the other, and Newbury Street is half a block away. *710 Boylston St., Back Bay, 617/536–5300 or 800/225–7676, fax 617/266–7905. 212 rooms. 2 restaurants, room service, baby-sitting, valet parking. Children under 17 free in parents' room. No pets. T stop: Copley.*

8 *c-5*

MIDTOWN HOTEL

This aging motel-style hotel holds its own against its large, expensive neighbors by offering comfortable rooms at reasonable rates in a location convenient to the Prudential Center, Symphony Hall, and the Christian Science Center. Tour groups love it. Amenities include free parking, valet service, 24-hour laundry service, a multilingual staff, and an attractive outdoor pool with lifeguard in season. Ask about larger rooms for families. *220 Huntington Ave., Back Bay/South End, 617/262–1000 or 800/343–1177, fax 617/262–8739. 159 rooms. Restaurant, pool, barbershop, beauty salon, free parking. Children under 18 free in parents' room. No pets. T stop: Prudential.*

3 *b-3*

SHERATON COMMANDER HOTEL

This sedate brick hotel, built in 1926, named in honor of Commander-in-Chief George Washington, overlooks Cambridge Common and is just a block from Harvard Yard, and a short stroll from the many unusual shops on Massachusetts Avenue. Rooms are decorated in Colonial style; many even have four-poster beds and rocking chairs. All have color TV and air-conditioning, and some have kitchenettes. Other amenities include a multilingual staff, a non-smoking floor, wheelchair-accessible rooms, and business services. Cambridge Common is a venue for wonderful free concerts in the summer; if you aren't a music fan or plan to go to bed early, ask for a room on the other side of the hotel. Otherwise, open your windows and enjoy. *16 Garden St., Cambridge, 617/547–4800 or 800/325–3535, fax 617/868–8322. 176 rooms, 20 suites. Restaurant, gym, concierge, business services, free parking. Children under 17 free in parents' room. No pets. T stop: Harvard Sq.*

8 *h-3*

TREMONT HOUSE

The 15-story Tremont House, in the center of the Theater District, is a popular home-away-from-home for the casts of current shows. The lobby here is quite grand, with a 16-foot-high crystal chandelier (a replica of the original), high ceilings, and liberal use of marble and gold leaf. Built in 1925 as the national headquarters for the Benevolent Protective Order of the Elks and transformed into a hotel in the 1950s, the building retains some hints of its past—look for the original Elks Club brass doorknobs in the guest rooms! All rooms have color TV with movie channels and individual climate control. There are two non-smoking floors. The Roxy, Boston's largest dance club (*see* Chapter 6), is on the premises. *275 Tremont St., Theater District, 617/426–1400 or 800/331–9998, fax 617/338–7881. 281 rooms, 34 suites. Room service, dinner theater, laundry service, concierge, valet parking. No pets. T stop: Boylston.*

BUDGET LODGING

8 *b-3*

BEACON GUESTHOUSES

These simply furnished studio apartments with kitchenettes and private baths are an excellent choice for a long-term visit; they're surprisingly inexpensive given their location, a short jaunt away from some of the city's most pricey boutiques. Rent by the night or by the week. *248 Newbury St., Back Bay, 617/266–7142 or 617/266–1771, fax 617/266–7276. 20 rooms in summer, 10 rooms* in winter. No pets. MC, V only. T stop: Auditorium.

4 *c-6*

BEST WESTERN TERRACE MOTOR LODGE

Incongruously located in a residential neighborhood between Boston University and Boston College, almost on the Brookline line, this motel is inexpensive, clean, recently refurbished, and less than a block from the T. Some rooms have kitchenettes; there's a supermarket 2 blocks away. Two great pluses: free Continental breakfast and free parking. *1650 Commonwealth Ave., Allston/Brighton, 617/566–6260 or 800/ 242–8377, fax 617/731–3543. 73 rooms. Free parking. Children under 18 free in parents' room. No pets. T stop: Sutherland Rd. (B line).*

8 *f-4*

CHANDLER INN

This cozy little hotel with economical rates and a friendly staff is one of the best bargains in the city. Located at the end of one of the South End's prettiest streets, it's an easy walk to the Back Bay or any of Tremont Street's trendy restaurants. Rooms are small but comfortable, with private baths and air-conditioning. The restaurant is only open for Saturday and Sunday brunch. Like much of this diverse part of town, the Chandler Inn is gay-friendly; the bar is a popular neighborhood hangout year-round, and it's wall-to-wall during Gay Pride Week. *26 Chandler St., South End, 617/482–3450, fax 617/542–3428. 56 rooms. Restaurant, bar. T stop: Back Bay or Arlington.*

 b-4

HOTEL BUCKMINSTER

Once a residential hotel, the Buckminster has been transformed into an economical and tastefully decorated spot with spacious rooms decorated in Chippendale-style antiques. The hotel is European-style, with maids but no bellhops, and serves breakfast by room service only. Though there's no restaurant in the hotel, the ground floor of the building houses a branch of the Pizzeria Uno chain as well as an excellent sushi bar, and Kenmore Square itself offers a wide range of cuisines. The Buckminster is two blocks from the nightlife of Lansdowne Street and the grassy outfield of Fenway Park. *645 Beacon St., Kenmore Square, 617/236–7050 or 800/727–2825,* fax 617/236–0068. 120 rooms. Room service (breakfast only). T stop: Kenmore.

6 *b-3*

JOHN JEFFRIES HOUSE

This turn-of-the-century house across from Massachusetts General Hospital has been renovated into an elegant inn with a Federal-style double parlor and guest rooms decorated in French Country. Triple-glazed windows block virtually all noise from busy Charles Circle. Most rooms have kitchenettes, many have views of the Charles River, and two of the five floors are non-smoking. Located at the foot of Beacon Hill, it's an easy walk to public transportation and most of downtown. *14 Embankment Rd., Beacon Hill, 617/367–1866, fax 617/742–0313. 46 rooms and suites ($$) with baths. Free Continental breakfast, 24-hour coffee service. No pets. T stop: Charles/MGH.*

 g-7

SUSSE CHALET MOTOR LODGE

This pair of clean, reliable, low-frill chain motels just off Interstate 93 in Dorchester is 10 minutes by car (traffic permitting) from downtown Boston. *800 and 900 Morrissey Blvd., Dorchester, 617/287–9100 or 617/287–9200, fax 617/265–9287 or 617/282–2365. 176 and 106 rooms, respectively. 2 restaurants, bar, pool, coin laundry, free parking. No pets.*

HOSTELS

For information on Boston-area hostels and membership information, write to the **Greater Boston Council of American Youth Hostels,** *1020B Commonwealth Ave., Boston, MA 02215,* or call *617/731– 5430.*

8 *f-3*

BERKELEY YWCA

This YWCA facility on the edge of the South End has single rooms ($42), doubles ($64), and triples ($75) for women only; nonmembers pay a $2 surcharge. The desk is staffed around the clock for guests' security. A dining room serves inexpensive meals. Guests have access to a local gym and indoor pool. It's an easy walk to the Back Bay and less than a block to the T. For long stays, you must apply at least three weeks in advance. *40 Berkeley St., South End, 617/ 482–8850, fax 617/482–9692. 200 rooms with shared baths. Lounge, coin laundry.*

No children or pets. MC, V only. T stop: Back Bay.

 8 *a-4*

BOSTON INTERNATIONAL HOSTEL

Run by American Youth Hostels, this *very* low-cost option near the Museum of Fine Arts is ideal for travelers on a budget who don't mind sharing space with strangers. Guests sleep three to five people to a dormitory with shared bath and must provide their own sheets or sleep sack (no sleeping bags allowed). The maximum stay is three nights in summer and two weeks the rest of the year. During peak season, AYH membership is required; you can apply on the spot. Member or not, it's best to make reservations. Arrive before midnight (2 AM on weekends), at which hour the doors are locked. Rates are $18 a night for members, $21 a night for non-members. *12 Hemenway St., the Fens, 617/536–9455, fax 617/424–6558. Capacity 205. Lounge, shared kitchenette. No pets. MC, V only. T stop: Hynes Convention Center/ICA.*

8 *b-6*

GREATER BOSTON YMCA

This coed facility near the Museum of Fine Arts and Symphony Hall rents single rooms ($38), doubles ($56), and triples ($76) with in-room TVs, free breakfasts, and access to the outstanding fitness facilities. A refurbishing effort begun in 1995 is lightening up the somewhat gloomy rooms. Important: As of 1997, the Y rents rooms only between June and September; the rest of the year, the rooms are given over to students. You *must* write in advance to reserve a room, especially if you plan to bring children. *316 Huntington Ave., the Fens, 617/536–7800. 180 rooms, most share baths. Cafeteria, pool, sauna, health club, track, coin laundry. No pets. MC, V only. T stop: Symphony.*

HOTELS NEAR THE AIRPORT

1 *h-3*

HARBORSIDE HYATT CONFERENCE CENTER AND HOTEL

The city's newest luxury hotel, which resembles a giant glass lighthouse, is perfectly situated on a point of land separating Boston Harbor from the Atlantic Ocean. The best rooms have either a sweeping view of the Boston skyline or a panoramic sea vista. It's easy to get anywhere from here; the Hyatt operates its own shuttle to all Logan Airport terminals and the Airport T stop, and guests get a discount on the water shuttle which runs between the airport and downtown. *101 Harborside Dr., East Boston, 617/568–1234 or 800/233–1234, fax 617/567–8856. 270 rooms, 11 suites. Restaurant, lounge, pool, health club/sauna, business services, parking. No pets. T stop: Airport. Very Expensive.*

1 *h-3*

LOGAN AIRPORT HILTON

It's not within walking distance of any tourist activities, but this Hilton is very convenient indeed for early morning departures or late-night arrivals. The only hotel actually within the boundaries of the airport, it operates a free around-the-clock shuttle service to all terminals and the T. The modern, air-conditioned rooms are soundproofed to keep out airport noise. In season, you can order drinks and food at the outdoor swimming pool with lifeguard. And naturally, given the location, the staff is multilingual. *75 Service Rd., Logan International Airport, East Boston, 617/569–9300 or 800/722–5004, fax 617/567–3725. 542 rooms. Restaurant, bar, pool, exercise room, baby-sitting, airport shuttle, parking. Children under 18 free in parents' room. T stop: Airport. Expensive.*

BED & BREAKFASTS

3 *b-2*

A CAMBRIDGE HOUSE BED & BREAKFAST

Listed on the National Register of Historic Places, this beautifully restored 1892 Greek Revival house four blocks from Harvard Square is a gracious haven of polished wood and Oriental carpets, with an imposing mahogany fireplace often used in winter. A well-tended lawn keeps busy Massachusetts Avenue at bay. Rooms are cozy and filled with antiques; the best one, called "the suite," has a working fireplace and a four-poster canopy bed. Smoking is forbidden throughout. There's also a reservations service for other area host homes. Harvard Square is a long walk away, but a bus stops just outside for easy access. *2218 Massachusetts Ave.,*

Cambridge, 617/491–6300 or 800/232–9989, fax 617/868–2848. 16 rooms (4 share baths). Full breakfast, non-smoking, free parking. No pets. MC, V. T stop: Harvard Sq. Expensive.

6 a-5
BEACON HILL BED AND BREAKFAST

Staying at this six-story Victorian row-house on Beacon Hill will give you a tiny taste of the elegant Brahmin lifestyle for far less than you'd pay to stay in a posh hotel. In front, it overlooks a narrow cobblestone street with gaslights. From the rear, bay windows look out on the Charles River Esplanade. The three rooms are huge, with built-in book-cases, couches, and Victorian antiques. Don't bring a car; there's nowhere to park in this neighborhood, and you can walk everywhere from here anyway. If, that is, you can walk at all after the full breakfasts. *27 Brimmer St., Beacon Hill, 617/523–7376. 3 rooms. Full breakfast, non-smoking. No pets. No credit cards. T stop: Park St. or Charles. Expensive.*

4 h-5
BEACON INNS

These two guest houses in the "street-car suburb" of Brookline, owned by the same family, are convenient to several local colleges and to the T, which stops just outside. 1087 Beacon Street is a Victorian brick town house with period detailing and large rooms; 1750 Beacon Street is less showy but still clean and spacious. *1087 Beacon St., Brookline, 617/566–0088 or 800/726–0088, fax 617/397–9267. 11 rooms (3 share baths). Continental breakfast, parking. AE, MC, V. T stop: 1087: Hawes St. (C line). Moderate.*

4 c-7
1750 Beacon St., Brookline, 617/566-0088 or 800/726–0088, fax 617/397–9267. 13 rooms (7 share baths). Continental breakfast, parking. AE, MC, V. T stop: Dean Rd. (C line). Moderate.

4 h-5
BEACON STREET GUEST HOUSE

This homey Victorian town house in Brookline is on the Federal Historic Register. Rooms are furnished with antiques; most have (nonworking) fireplaces and private baths. The Green line stops right outside the door for a 15-minute ride to the center of downtown. *1047 Beacon Street, Brookline, 617/232–0292*

or 800/872–7211, fax 617/734–5815. 14 rooms (3 share baths). Morning coffee and tea, parking. AE, MC, V. T stop: St. Mary's St. (C line) Inexpensive.. $

BED & BREAKFAST AGENCY OF BOSTON

This agency lists 120 homes in some of the city's most-visited neighborhoods. *47 Commercial Wharf, 617/720–3540 or 800/248–9262, fax 617/523–5761.*

BED & BREAKFAST ASSOCIATES BAY COLONY LTD.

This agency has more than 150 listings of homes and rooms in Boston, Cambridge, the North and South shores, and Cape Cod and the islands. *P.O. Box 57166, Babson Park Branch, Boston 02157, 617/449–5302 or 800/347–5088, fax 617/449–5958.*

4 g-6
THE BERTRAM INN

This Victorian/Tudor-style house built in 1907 on a quiet residential street in Brookline still has its original leaded windows, oak floors, front porch, stone fireplaces, and wide front staircase with landing. Most of the antiques-furnished rooms have private baths and air-conditioning; all have color TV. In addition to a buffet-style breakfast, the inn serves afternoon tea and cookies daily. The inn is a short walk to both the T and the bustling Coolidge Corner shopping district. *92 Sewall Ave., Brookline, 617/566–2234 or 800/295–3822. 12 rooms. Breakfast, non-smoking, air-conditioning, free parking. T stop: St. Paul St. (C line). Moderate.*

4 f-6
BROOKLINE MANOR

Owned by the same people who own the Beacon Street Guest House, this brick house is on a residential street in Brookline's charming Coolidge Corner. The T is only a block away for easy access to the rest of the city. *32 Centre St., Brookline, 617/232–0003 or 800/201–9676, fax 617/734–5815. 40 rooms (25 shared baths). Morning coffee and tea, parking. AE, MC, V. T stop: Coolidge Corner (C line). Inexpensive.*

8 f-5
CLARENDON SQUARE B&B

Built in 1885, this South End rowhouse was thoroughly rehabbed in 1994 and now boasts light-filled rooms, a sundeck on the roof, and a working fireplace in the living room. All guest rooms have private baths—one with a silver-leaf vaulted ceiling! The best (and most expensive) room is a suite with a kitchen and its own private entrance. Note that the minimum stay is three nights; longer stays are discounted. Children "of well-behaved parents" are welcome. As with most South End establishments, the Clarendon Square is gay-friendly. *81 Warren Ave., South End, 617/536–2229. 3 rooms. Continental breakfast, non-smoking, air-conditioning. No pets. T stop: Arlington. Moderate.*

8 *f-4*

82 CHANDLER STREET

A welcoming redbrick rowhouse built in 1863, this South End B&B is spacious, sunny, and gay-friendly. The rooms, decorated in bright primary colors, are non-smoking and have pedestal sinks, Oriental rugs, and a tidy kitchenette with refrigerator and microwave oven. The best room, on the top floor, has a working fireplace, a bathroom skylight, and wide bay windows encompassing an expansive view of downtown. It's a short walk to Back Bay station, where you can catch the T or Amtrak. *82 Chandler St., South End, 617/482–0408. 5 rooms. Full breakfast, air-conditioning. No pets. No credit cards. T stop: Back Bay or Copley. Moderate.*

HOST HOMES OF BOSTON

This agency has listings for about 40 rooms in Boston, Cambridge, Brookline, Newton, and around Route 128. There is a two-night minimum stay. You must indicate whether children are in your party. Smoking and pets are not permitted in most homes. Write or call for a Host Home Directory. *Box 117, Waban Branch, Boston, 02168, 617/244–1308, fax 617/244–5156.*

7 *c-2*

IRVING HOUSE

This friendly, affordable B&B is large, but still feels more like a house than a hotel. It's on a quiet residential street just three blocks from Harvard. All the rooms have air-conditioning and telephones, most have private baths, and some have kitchenettes. Rates include a Continental breakfast. Children 6 and under stay free; those under 15 stay at a discount. There's even limited free off-street parking, a real coup in car-clotted Cambridge. *24 Irving St., Cambridge, 617/547–4600, fax 617/576–2814. 40 rooms. Continental breakfast, non-smoking, limited free parking. No pets. T stop: Harvard Sq. Inexpensive–Moderate.*

NEW ENGLAND BED AND BREAKFAST, INC.

This agency lists 20 homes in Boston and Cambridge, all within walking distance of public transportation. Rates include Continental breakfast. *1045 Centre St., Newton, 02159, 617/244–2112.*

8 *b-3*

NEWBURY GUEST HOUSE

Originally built in 1882 as a private residence, this elegant brick-and-brownstone building with a carved oak staircase has been restored as a charming family-run inn with Victorian-style decor. Well-managed by a father-and-son team, it's always full and immensely popular for its ideal location in the center of stylish Newbury Street. The Continental buffet breakfast is served in the cozy lounge or, in fine weather, on the outdoor patio. At $10 for 24 hours, the limited parking is a steal. *261 Newbury St., Back Bay, 617/437–7666, fax 617/262–4243. 32 rooms. Full breakfast, parking. No pets. T stop: Copley. Moderate.*

chapter 8

HELP!

resources for residents

educational resources

With more than 50 two-year and four-year colleges in the greater Boston area, learning is most definitely in the air. But some of the most intriguing classes in town have nothing to do with degrees or certificates. Adult education here goes far beyond high school equivalency tutoring—it runs the gamut from personal growth to home repair. Kids, too, can sign up for lessons beyond what they get during the school day.

ACTING SCHOOLS

8 *h-2*

ACTORS WORKSHOP

This non-profit organization offers days, evening, and weekend classes in theater, television, and film acting, with full-time and part-time certificate programs as well as special offerings for kids. *40 Boylston St., Theater District, 617/423–7313. T stop: Boylston.*

ADULT-EDUCATION PROGRAMS

In addition to the following, Boston's leading colleges and universities (*see below*) also offer courses.

8 *f-2*

BOSTON CENTER FOR ADULT EDUCATION

The extravagant Baylies Mansion, built on the most prestigious block of Commonwealth Avenue in 1904 for a wealthy merchant family, now houses one of the area's largest adult education programs. In addition to the usual cooking, art, music, and business courses, the BCAE often brings in big names like novelist Kurt Vonnegut and Boston Pops maestro Keith Lockhart. Even if you don't have time for a class, stop in to admire the opulent mirrored ballroom. Call for a current course catalog. *5 Commonwealth Ave., Back Bay, 617/267–4430. T stop: Arlington.*

3 *b-4*

CAMBRIDGE CENTER FOR ADULT EDUCATION

Where else can you learn to speak Chinese or build your own computer in a building listed in the National Register of Historic Places? The CCAE holds its courses in two such spots: Brattle House, built in 1727, and Blacksmith House, former home of that "Village Blacksmith" immortalized by Longfellow. Watch for periodic Wednesday evening panel discussions on "The Writer's Life: Working and Living as a Writer in Boston," cosponsored by the National Writers Union—they regularly draw standing-room-only crowds. Call for a current catalog. *42 Brattle St., Cambridge, 617/547–6789. T stop: Harvard Sq.*

1 *a-3*

INTERFACE

If you're intrigued by spirituality, psychology, healing, and the world's cultures, you'll find like-minded folk at Interface. This center for "holistic education" has been offering classes exploring the limits of human potential since 1975 and frequently hosts well-known speakers like biologist/psychologist Dr. Joan Borysenko and radical theologian Matthew Fox. Call for a current catalog. *218 Walnut St., Newtonville, 617/964–9360.*

ART SCHOOLS

8 *a-6*

MASSACHUSETTS COLLEGE OF ART

This is a state college well-known for its degree programs in all areas of the fine arts. *621 Huntington Ave., the Fens, 617/232–1555. T stop: Northeastern (E line).*

8 *a-7*

SCHOOL OF THE MUSEUM OF FINE ARTS

Affiliated with Tufts University, the Museum School offers courses both to aspiring professional artists and to motivated dabblers. *230 the Fenway, the Fens, 617/267–6100. T stop: Museum on E line.*

CHILDREN'S PROGRAMS

1 b-5

BOSTON CHILDREN'S THEATRE SCHOOL

This school offers classes for kids grades K–12 in all of the theater arts including drama, dance, and music. Three terms per year start in September, January, and March, and last seven weeks each. Classes are held Monday to Friday after school and on Saturday. Scholarships are available. *652 Hammond St., Chestnut Hill, 617/277–3277.*

4 h-5

BROOKLINE ARTS CENTER

Arts and crafts classes in pottery, painting, jewelry making, and lots more are open to children age 2 and older. Classes meet once a week for nine weeks; summer sessions are shorter. Scholarships are available. *86 Monmouth St., Brookline, 617/566–5715.*

8 e-5

COMMUNITY MUSIC CENTER

This private, nonprofit music center in the South End offers private and group lessons in all areas of music to kids age 4 and up. The "Music Is Fun" program for ages 4–7 is an introduction to music through movement, dance, singing, and simple instruments. *34 Warren Ave., South End, 617/482–7494. T stop: Back Bay or Copley.*

1 e-7

MO VAUGHN YOUTH DEVELOPMENT PROGRAMS

The Red Sox slugger lends his name and support to this after-school program which encompasses activities, tutorials, and homework help. Call the office for information. *895 Blue Hill Ave., Dorchester, 617/436–7448.*

COLLEGES & UNIVERSITIES

1 a-5

BOSTON COLLEGE

This is the local bastion of the most potent force in Catholic education: the Society of Jesus, or Jesuits. Founded in 1863, with more than 14,000 total enrollment, Boston College has long been a springboard to professional and social advancement for the scions of the Boston area's Irish families. Particularly noted is the B.C. Law School—who better to teach law than the rhetorically precise, legalistic, and debate-loving Jesuits? Note, however, than only 3% of the entire faculty are members of the clergy. Even B.C. undergraduates take philosophy along with their theology and other required courses, as much for the sake of argument as evaluation. Boston College sits on Chestnut Hill, at the point where Newton, Brookline, and the Brighton section of Boston come together. *140 Commonwealth Ave., Newton, 617/552–8000.*

4 h-4

BOSTON UNIVERSITY

Busy Kenmore Square is the gate to Boston University, founded in 1839, with more than 28,000 total enrollment. B.U.'s real estate lies between Commonwealth Avenue and the Charles River; as you approach the B.U. Bridge on Storrow Drive, you can identify the campus by its Deco-Gothic towers and the high-rise Mugar Library. Along with Northeastern, B.U. is the most urban of the Hub's big universities. It also has the most faces: to some, it is radio station WBUR, the National Public Radio affiliate and voice of B.U. School of Public Communications; to others it's the medical and dental schools, based at University Hospital, or the strong programs in engineering and public health. As if to exemplify the school's eclectic character, the Mugar Library contains the papers of Martin Luther King, Bette Davis, Alistair Cooke, and Heinrich Böll. *771 Commonwealth Ave., Kenmore Square, 617/353–2000.*

4 h-4

BRANDEIS UNIVERSITY

Tucked into a quiet corner of suburban Waltham, some ten miles west of Boston, Brandeis was founded in 1948, has about 3,200 total enrollment, and attracts some of the most brilliant students in the nation. It is the only Jewish-sponsored, nonsectarian college or university in the United States, and by far one of the newest and smallest institutions to be officially accredited as a research university. Offering a rigorous approach to the liberal arts, a Brandeis education has a cultural rather than religious inclination; other denominations are well represented in the student body. The university was named for liberal U.S. Supreme Court Justice Louis Brandeis (1856–1941), and its liberal ideas are reflected in the social activism of many of its students. *415 South St., Waltham, 617/736–2000.*

7 *a-1*

HARVARD UNIVERSITY

Founded in 1636, with more than 16,000 combined graduate and undergraduate enrollment, Harvard is different things to different people—the *ne plus ultra* of the Ivy League, a colossus riding roughshod over a small neighborhood section of Boston, a guarantee of better-than-equal footing in the competition of profes- sional ascendancy. But certain things can be quantified: only 16% of applicants are accepted; of these, 70% enroll. The fac- ulty's credentials are so impeccable that the university doesn't bother with the alphabet soup of degrees in its catalogue listings. And—last but not least—Har- vard boasts the largest endowment of any college or university in the United States. For all its monolithic presence, Harvard is a composite entity. Spread over the blocks surrounding Harvard Square are Harvard and Radcliffe Col- leges, the Law School, and the Kennedy School of Government. Here is the Widener Library, with its nine million vol- umes the largest university library in the world; here also are the Fogg Museum and the classic campus buildings such as Massachusetts Hall, Memorial Chapel, and Sever Hall, along with not-so-tradi- tional Carpenter Center, designed by Le Corbusier. Across the river is the Harvard School of Business, while on Huntington Avenue out past the Museum of Fine Arts is the Medical School. Pressure, competition, and excellence are the watchwords at Harvard. It isn't enough to go to the Law School; you've got to get onto the Law Review if you *really* want the big firms to stand up and take notice. Even the irreverent is grandly institution- alized here—the Harvard Lampoon is probably the nation's most august insti- tution dedicated to making fun of things, including institutions. All in all, forget about those recent magazine surveys that say *Yale* is now at the top of the heap—Harvard will always be No. 1. (*See also* Chapter 2.) *45 Quincy St., Cambridge, 617/495-1000.*

3 *g-6*

MASSACHUSETTS INSTITUTE OF TECHNOLOGY

This august place of learning—founded in 1861, with about 10,000 total enroll- ment—betrays its preoccupations in its architecture: the low, tawny buildings along the Charles look like pure reason frozen in stone, domed temples to the empirical method. The students who work behind those walls have top-flight academic records, who go out into the world providing the brainpower for today's high-technology enterprises. The phrase "they're working on it at MIT" has entered the language as an all-pur- pose announcement of the next round of gee-whiz technology. If they aren't working on it at MIT, chances are they aren't anywhere else either. It's likely that no other single institution has done as much to make Route 128 into the high-tech capital of the eastern United States. Keep in mind that the stereotype of the MIT student—calculator in a hol- ster at the ready, brow furrowed in con- sternation over some abstruse equation, oblivious to humanistic concerns—is just that. (*See also* Chapter 2.) *77 Massa- chusetts Ave., Cambridge, 617/253–1000.*

2 *g-6*

NORTHEASTERN UNIVERSITY

On your way out to the Museum of Fine Arts via Huntington Avenue, you will pass Northeestern, founded in 1898, and with a total enrollment of about 25,000. It is one of the largest coopera- tive universities in the world. Classroom work is often augmented with field-ser- vice assignments, particularly in socially critical areas like air pollution, rehabilita- tion programs, and law enforcement. There is a big engineering school, and most of its component colleges address the problem of how to get things done—in nursing, computers, business administration, pharmacy, criminal jus- tice, and so on. There is even a law school, yet another in what stands behind only Washington and New York as a city of lawyers. *360 Huntington Ave., The Fens, 617/373–2000.*

1 *d-1*

TUFTS UNIVERSITY

Up in Medford, three towns north of Boston, Tufts—opened 1852, with about 7,000 total enrollment—sits on a quiet, 150-acre hilltop looking a lot like the set for a thirties movie about campus life. But Tufts is right up to date, and it reaches well beyond Medford. There is a vigorous and locally influential environ- mental studies program, a nutrition institute, the Fletcher School of Law and

Diplomacy, and a venerable veterinary medicine school. In addition to its prestigious medical and dental schools—based at the New England Medical Center in downtown Boston—the university is also strong in liberal arts. *Medford, 617/628–5000.*

other institutions

6 *d-5*

EMERSON COLLEGE
100 Beacon St., Beacon Hill, 617/824–8500.

7 *g-1*

LESLIE COLLEGE
29 Everett St., Cambridge, 617/868–9600.

2 *a-6*

SIMMONS COLLEGE
300 The Fenway, The Fens, 617/521–2000.

6 *a-6*

SUFFOLK UNIVERSITY
8 Ashburton Place, Beacon Hill, 617/521–2000.

1 *g-6*

UNIVERSITY OF MASSACHUSETTS–BOSTON
100 Morrissey Blvd., South Boston, 617/287-5000.

WELLESLEY COLLEGE
106 Central St., Wellesley, 617/283–1000.

LANGUAGE SCHOOLS

2 *b-4*

BOSTON LANGUAGE INSTITUTE
This school claims to teach languages "from Arabic to Zulu." It has a large English as a Second Language faculty, too. *636 Beacon St., 617/262–3500. T stop: Kenmore.*

MUSIC SCHOOLS

If you're looking for individual lessons, many faculty members and some advanced students at local music schools are happy to oblige. In particular, check the classified ads in the weekly *Boston Phoenix.*

8 *a-4*

BERKLEE COLLEGE OF MUSIC
Internationally known for its jazz program, Berklee attracts serious students of all forms of music as well as those who aspire to manage musicians. *1140 Boylston St., Back Bay, 617/266–1400. T stop: Hynes Convention Center/ICA.*

3 *b-3*

LONGY SCHOOL OF MUSIC
Primarily devoted to classical music, Longy is well-known for its chamber music program, which sponsors free performances almost every week. *1 Follen St., Cambridge, 617/876–0956. T stop: Harvard Sq.*

8 *a-4*

NEW ENGLAND CONSERVATORY OF MUSIC
The New England Conservatory is known for its opera program as well as its other classical music training. *290 Huntington Ave., Back Bay, 617/262–1120. T stop: Hynes Convention Center/ICA.*

resources

If you can't find what you need in this section, or if you aren't sure what you need, call the information and referral line of the United Way at 617/624–8000, the Massachusetts Citizen Information Service at 617/727–7030, or the Federal Information Center at 800/688–9889.

AIDS ASSISTANCE & ADVICE

8 *e-4*

AIDS ACTION COMMITTEE OF MASSACHUSETTS
The city's oldest and largest organization dealing with AIDS provides advice and services, supports other groups helping people with AIDS, and sponsors the annual Boston AIDS Walk. *131 Clarendon St., 617/437–6200. Hot line: 617/536–7733 or 800/235–2331. T stop: Back Bay or Copley.*

ALCOHOLISM COUNSELING

ALCOHOLICS ANONYMOUS
Contact the Boston service office for a list of local meetings. *617/426–9444.*

RATIONAL RECOVERY
This alternative to AA is based on cognitive therapy. Call for a meetings list. *617/891–7574.*

BABY-SITTING SERVICES

3 *e-5*

CHILD-CARE RESOURCE CENTER
An information and referral center about preschool child-care programs, private and public day-care centers, nursery schools, and summer camps. *130 Bishop Richard Allen Dr., Cambridge, 617/547–9861. T stop: Central Sq.*

4 *c-6*

PARENTS IN A PINCH
Professional, screened, and trained sitters provide long- and short-term child care at home or in your hotel. *45 Bartlett Crescent, Brookline, 617/739–5437.*

THE TAB
This community newspaper, which often has two pages or more of "child care needed" ads, is widely considered *the* place to advertise for nannies, live-in child care, and baby-sitters. Ads run in all 17 editions, which cover the city and close suburbs. *TAB Community Newspapers, 254 Second Ave., Needham, 617/433–8200.*

CATERING

8 *e-8*

EAST MEETS WEST
This perennial favorite based in the South End serves up delicious, healthy food ranging from broiled lobster to blueberry pie. *560 Harrison Ave., 617/426–3344 or 617/426–3806.*

1 *d-1*

JULES
From bar mitzvahs to business meetings, this Somerville caterer provides food, party planning, decorations—even flowers—to suit any budget and any size group. The *Improper Bostonian* dubbed it a favorite in 1997. *508 Medford St., Somerville, 617/628–5977.*

CHILD CRISIS SERVICES

CHILD AT RISK HOT LINE
This hot line for reporting potential abuse operates 24 hours a day. *800/792–5200.*

PARENTAL STRESS LINE
A hot line for parents on the verge of a nervous breakdown. *800/632–8188.*

COAST GUARD

General information, 617/223–8600. Search and rescue emergencies, 617/565–9200.

CONSUMER-PROTECTION INFORMATION

8 *f-3*

BETTER BUSINESS BUREAU
Check out businesses here before giving them your money, and file complaints if necessary. *20 Park Plaza, 617/426–9000.*

6 *d-3*

MASSACHUSETTS ATTORNEY GENERAL'S OFFICE
Report suspected fraud to the consumer complaint section. *200 Portland St., 617/727–8400.*

CRIME-VICTIM ASSISTANCE

8 *f-4*

VICTIM/WITNESS ASSISTANCE
Boston Police Dept., 154 Berkeley St., 617/343–4400.

DOCTOR & DENTIST REFERRALS

MASSACHUSETTS DENTAL SOCIETY
508/651–7511 or 800/342–8747.

MASSACHUSETTS MEDICAL SOCIETY
800/322–2303.

DRUG-ABUSE COUNSELING

MASSACHUSETTS DEPARTMENT OF PUBLIC HEALTH
Call for referrals to local treatment programs. *617/624–5111.*

NARCOTICS ANONYMOUS
Call the Boston area service office for a list of meetings. *617/884–7709.*

EMERGENCIES

Dial 911 for police, fire, ambulance.

MASSACHUSETTS GENERAL HOSPITAL (MGH)
55 Fruit St. (bordered by Blossom, Parkman, Fruit, and Charles Sts.), Old West End. 617/726–2000.

DOCTOR PHYSICIAN REFERRAL SERVICE
Weekdays 8:30–5. *617/726–5800.*

DENTAL EMERGENCY
508/651–3521.

POISON CONTROL
617/232–2120.

See also Traveler's Aid *below.*

FAMILY PLANNING

4 *h-5*

PLANNED PARENTHOOD LEAGUE OF MASSACHUSETTS
Two local clinics provide family planning counseling, pregnancy testing, birth control, abortion, and gynecological care. *1031 Beacon St., Brookline, 617/738–1370 or 800/682–9218.*

4 *c-7*
1842 Beacon St., Brookline, 617/731–2525.

GAY & LESBIAN CONCERNS

GAY AND LESBIAN HELP LINE
617/267–9001.

PFLAG—PARENTS AND FRIENDS OF LESBIANS AND GAYS
617/547–2440.

HOUSECLEANING HELP

1 *c-1*

MCMAID
Selected "Best of Boston" by *Boston* magazine, they serve the city and suburbs. *2464 Massachusetts Ave., Cambridge, 617/354–7788.*

LANDLORD/ TENANT SERVICES

BOSTON MAYOR'S OFFICE OF CONSUMER AFFAIRS AND LICENSING
Call for information and referrals. *City Hall, 617/635–4165.*

LEGAL SERVICES

LAWYER REFERRALS
Boston Bar Association, 617/742–0625.

6 *e-3*
GREATER BOSTON LEGAL SERVICES
This organization provides free or inexpensive legal services to people with low incomes. *197 Friend St., 617/357–5757.*

LOST & FOUND

LOST ANIMALS
Blanket the neighborhood where you lost your pet with flyers including a description, your phone number, and a photo if possible. Take out ads in local papers. Call local animal shelters with a detailed description of your pet.

8 *f-4*
ANIMAL RESCUE LEAGUE OF BOSTON
This shelter in the South End has a lost-and-found program and will help you track down your missing pet. *10 Chandler St., South End, 617/426–9170. T stop: Arlington or Back Bay.*

5 *h-2*

MASSACHUSETTS SOCIETY FOR THE PREVENTION OF CRUELTY TO ANIMALS

Many lost pets end up in Jamaica Plain at the largest animal shelter in the city. *350 South Huntington Ave., Jamaica Plain, 617/522–5055.*

lost credit cards

Contact the bank that issued your credit card as soon as you realize your card is missing. It's a good idea to keep a list of your credit card numbers and the telephone numbers of their issuers; when you're traveling, pack the list separately from the cards themselves.

For refunds for lost or stolen American Express Traveler's Checks, call 800/221–7282.

on transportation

AIRPORT

Contact the airline on which you traveled (*see* Travel and Vacation Information, *below*), or call the Massachusetts State Police, 617/567–2233.

INTERCITY BUS

Intercity bus service operates out of the new bus terminal at South Station, adjacent to the train station.

South Station: *617/345–7456.*

Greyhound: *617/292–4700.*

Peter Pan/Trailways: *800/237–8747, Ext 246.*

MBTA

Each subway line has its own lost and found department, as do the buses and the commuter rail. If you aren't sure where you lost something, try them all.

Blue Line: *617/222–5533.*

Green Line: *617/222–5221.*

Red Line: *617/222–5317.*

Orange Line: *617/222–5403.*

Buses: *617/222–5607.*

Commuter Rail: *617/222–3600.*

TAXI

By law, anything left in a taxi must be turned in to the police station closest to where you were dropped off. To report a loss, call the Boston Police Department, at 617/343–4200.

TRAIN

Back Bay Station: *617/345–7958.*

North Station: *617/222–3600.*

Route 128 Station: *617/345–7920.*

South Station: *617/345–7456.*

MENTAL-HEALTH INFORMATION & REFERRAL

MASSACHUSETTS DEPARTMENT OF MENTAL HEALTH

617/727–5500.

ON-LINE SERVICES

The national on-line services have multiple dial-ups in the Boston area, and numerous Internet access providers are also a local phone call away. Here are some well-reputed providers and the numbers to call to speak to a human being for more information:

Mindspring: *800/719–4332.*

Netcom: *800/638–2661.*

ShoreNet: *617/477–2000.*

TIAC: *617/932–2000.*

The World: *617/739–0202.*

To find a local modem dial-up for CompuServe, call 800/848–9990.

To find a local modem dial-up for America Online, call 800/827–6364.

PETS

adoptions

B *f-4*

ANIMAL RESCUE LEAGUE OF BOSTON

The adoption center is open daily. This organization also offers veterinary services and educational programs and maintains a pet cemetery. *10 Chandler St., 617/426–9170. T stop: Arlington.*

`5` *h-2*

MASSACHUSETTS SOCIETY FOR THE PREVENTION OF CRUELTY TO ANIMALS

The MSPCA operates an adoption center for cats, dogs, and (occasionally) other small animals. *350 South Huntington Ave., 617/522–5055.*

NORTHEAST ANIMAL SHELTER

This no-kill shelter about an hour north of Boston includes free spaying/neutering and free shots in its adoption fee. No animal brought here will ever be euthanized simply to make room for another. Cats and dogs, and the occasional rabbit or ferret, may stay for as long as it takes to find them new homes. *204 Highland Ave., Salem, 508/745–9888.*

grooming

THE BARKING LOT

Make an appointment by phone and this mobile pet-grooming van, a traveling landmark for 10 years, will arrive at your doorstep to wash, dry, trim, and pamper cats and dogs who can't or won't travel. *Cambridge, 617/868–8172.*

training

HAPPY DOG TRAINING

From April through October, Happy Dog offers five-week basic and intermediate obedience classes at reduced rates at the Jackson Mann Community Center in Brighton and various sites in the suburbs (private in-home training is also available). On Wednesdays and Thursdays from 3 to 9 PM, call for free answers to your questions about dog training and behavior. *63 Colborne Rd., 617/789–DOGS (789–3647).*

veterinarian referrals

`5` *h-2*

ANGELL MEMORIAL ANIMAL HOSPITAL

Affiliated with the Massachusetts Society for the Prevention of Cruelty to Animals, Angell Memorial is also a full-service veterinary hospital treating every animal, from hamsters to horses. *350 South Huntington Ave., 617/522–7282.*

PHARMACIES OPEN 24 HOURS

`1` *d-1*

CVS

Porter Sq., Cambridge, 617/876–5519.

`3` *g-3*

OSCO DRUG

14 McGrath Hwy., Somerville, 617/628–2870.

`1` *f-8*

WALGREENS

757 Gallivan Blvd., Dorchester, 617/282–5246.

PHONE COMPANY

The local telephone company was NYNEX until recently. Since its summer 1997 merger with another Baby Bell, it's now Bell Atlantic.

TO CONNECT RESIDENTIAL SERVICE

In East Boston and Somerville: *800/870–9999.*

In Boston Central, Brighton, Brookline, Cambridge, Charlestown, Dorchester, Hyde Park, Jamaica Plain, Mattapan, Readville, Roslindale, Roxbury, South Boston, and West Roxbury: *800/980–9999.*

FOR REPAIRS

617/555–1611.

TO ACCESS LONG DISTANCE SERVICES

Use these numbers to avoid hotel surcharges.

AT&T: *800/874–4000.*

MCI: *800/444–4444.*

Sprint: *800/793–1153.*

POSTAL SERVICES

For information about services and local post offices, call the main Boston postal station, located behind South Station. *25 Dorchester Ave., 617/654–5001 during business hours, 617/654–5223 after business hours.*

Postage stamps are available at all branch post offices, some stores that sell postcards, and (for a surcharge) many ATMs.

For ZIP code information, call 617/654–7567.

RAPE CRISIS

These hot lines will help you cope, direct you to legal and health resources, and arrange for an advocate to support you if you decide to need to pursue legal action.

Cambridge, 617/492–7273.

Boston, 617/442–6300.

SENIOR-CITIZEN SERVICES

6 *d-5*

MASSACHUSETTS DEPARTMENT OF ELDER AFFAIRS
Call for information and referrals about services and issues of interest to those 65 and older. *1 Ashburton Pl., 617/727–7750.*

SENIOR SOURCE
this hot line makes referrals to various home-care services: companions, meal preparation, housekeeping, transportation, home repair, even in-home salon services. *617/278–6280 or 800/318–0220*

SUICIDE-PREVENTION COUNSELING

SAMARITANS
This hot line staffed by volunteers is open around the clock. *617/247–0220.*

TELEVISION/CABLE COMPANIES

Outside the immediate metro area, check pages 4 and 5 of the *Boston Sunday Globe's* "TV Week" to determine which cable company serves your area.

BOSTON
Cablevision of Boston, 617/787–6616.

BROOKLINE
Cablevision of Brookline, 617/731–1343.

CAMBRIDGE
Cable TV Dept., 617/349–4296.

SOMERVILLE
Time Warner Cable, 617/397–8400.

TRAVELER'S AID

6 *f-7*
TRAVELER'S AID SOCIETY OF BOSTON
Weekdays 8:30–7. This nonprofit social service agency provides counseling, emergency financial aid, and travel assistance to travelers in crisis. There is also a branch in Terminal E at the Logan International Airport, 617/567–5385. *17 East St., 617/542–7286. South Station Information Booth, 617/737–2880.*

UTILITIES

These utility companies serve most of the metropolitan area. If you aren't in their service area, they will direct you to the appropriate provider. At press time, the electricity-generating industry was in the process of being deregulated, promising to present many more choices and a good bit more confusion.

Boston Gas (cooking and heating gas): *617/523–1010.*

Boston Edison (electricity): *617/375–6661.*

Boston Water & Sewer (water connections): *617/330–9084.*

ZONING & PLANNING

If you're building an addition to your home, need to know where underground pipes run, have a question about where to open a business, or want to lobby for a stoplight on your street, here's where to call.

BOSTON
Inspectional Services Dept., Planning and Zoning, 617/635–5312.

BROOKLINE
Planning/Community Development, 617/730–2130.

CAMBRIDGE
City Hall, 617/349–4000.

SOMERVILLE
City Hall, 617/625–6600.

travel & vacation information

AIRLINES

Most large airlines and many small ones fly in and out of Logan International Airport. However, Boston isn't on every airline's itinerary, schedules change constantly, and airlines frequently change names or go out of business. Check with your travel agent or call airlines directly with any questions.

AER LINGUS
800/223–6537.

AEROLINEAS ARGENTINAS
800/333–0276.

AEROMEXICO
800/237–6639.

AIR ATLANTIC CANADIAN AIRLINES
800/426–7000.

AIR CANADA
800/776–3000.

AIR TRAN
800/825–8538.

ALITALIA
800/223–5730.

AMERICA WEST
800/235–9292.

AMERICAN AIRLINES/AMERICAN EAGLE
800/433–7300.

AVIANCA AIRLINES
800/284–2622.

BRITISH AIRWAYS
800/247–9297.

CAPE AIR
800/352–0714.

CHINA AIRLINES
800/227–5118.

CONTINENTAL AIRLINES
800/523–3273.

DELTA AIR LINES
800/221–1212.

DELTA EXPRESS
800/345–3400.

FINNAIR
800/950–5000.

IBERIA AIR LINES OF SPAIN
800/772–4642.

ICELANDAIR
800/223–5500.

JAPAN AIRLINES
800/525–3663.

KLM ROYAL DUTCH AIRLINES
800/374–7747.

KOREAN AIR LINES
800/438–5000.

LUFTHANSA
800/645–3880.

MIDWAY AIRLINES
800/446–4392.

MIDWEST EXPRESS AIRLINES
800/414–5219.

NORTHWEST AIRLINES
Domestic: 800/225–2525; International: 800/447–4747.

OLYMPIC AIRWAYS
617/451–0500.

PHILIPPINE AIRLINES
800/435–9725.

QANTAS AIRWAYS
800/227–4500.

SABENA BELGIAN WORLD AIRLINES
800/955–2000.

SCANDINAVIAN AIRLINES
800/221–2350.

SINGAPORE AIRLINES
800/742–3333.

SOUTHWEST AIRLINES
800/435–9792.

SWISSAIR
800/221–4750.

TAP AIR PORTUGAL
800/221–7370.

THAI AIRWAYS INTERNATIONAL
800/426–5204.

TRANS WORLD AIRLINES (TWA)
800/221–2000.

USAIRWAYS/ USAIRWAYS EXPRESS
800/428–4322.

UNITED AIRLINES
800/241–6522.

VIRGIN ATLANTIC AIRWAYS
800/862-8621.

AIRPORT

information booths
Terminals A and C at Logan International Airport (*see* Transportation *in* Chapter 1). *No phone. Daily 7:30 AM–8 PM.*

Terminal E Information Booth and language assistance. *Oct.–June, daily 10–8; July–Sept., daily 7:30 AM–11 PM.*

Interpreter booth in customs. *Winter, daily noon–8; summer, daily 11–11.*

financial
BANKBOSTON
Full-service bank, Terminal E. *Weekdays 9–3; Sat. 11:30–3.*

Deposits, withdrawals, payments, Terminal D. *Tues, Thurs., and Fri. noon–3.*

Also ATMs located throughout the airport.

currency exchange
BANKBOSTON
Terminals C and E. *617/569–1172.*

fax
MUTUAL OF OMAHA BUSINESS CENTER
Terminal C, *617/569–4635. Weekdays 6 AM–10 PM, Sat. 8 AM–10 PM, Sun. 10–10.*

duty-free shops
Terminal A. *Daily 6 AM–8 PM.*

Terminal B. *Daily 6 AM–8 PM.*

Terminal C. *Daily 6 AM–10 PM* (or last departing international flight).

Terminal E. *Daily 6 AM–10 PM* (or last departing international flight).

medical
The MASSPORT emergency hot line operates 24 hours a day and will send emergency medical personnel to your aid wherever you are within the airport. *617/567–2020.*

hotel reservations
Terminals C and E, lower levels, have reservation counters in the baggage claim areas; other terminals have direct telephones near the baggage carousels.

rental lockers
Terminals B, C, and E.

CAR RENTAL

AVIS
For domestic reservations and information about local rental locations, call 800/331–1212.

BUDGET RENT-A-CAR
For locations in metropolitan Boston, call 617/497–1800. For out-of-town reservations and information, call 800/527–0700.

HERTZ
For reservations and information about local rental locations, call 800/654–3131.

6 *f-7*
THRIFTY RENT-A-CAR
125 Summer St., 617/330–5011.

3 *h-1*
264 Monsignor O'Brien Hwy., Somerville, 617/629–5323.

EMBASSIES & CONSULATES
The keys to the international community, embassies and consulates are the places to call for information about visas, inoculations, green cards, doing business in another country, and local cultural events.

8 *f-3*
AUSTRALIA
20 Park Plaza, 617/542–8655.

6 *e-5*
AUSTRIA
15 School St., 617/227–3131.

BELGIUM
300 Commercial St., Malden, 617/397–8566.

8 *f-3*
BRAZIL
20 Park Plaza, 617/542–4000.

8 *d-4*
CANADA
3 Copley Pl., 617/262–3760.

8 *d-3*
CAPE VERDE
535 Boylston St., 617/353–0014.

6 *f-5*
CHILE
79 Milk St., 617/426–1678.

8 *d-3*
COLOMBIA
535 Boylston St., 617/536–6222.

COSTA RICA
52 Mulberry, Springfield, 413/781–5400.

8 *f-3*
DENMARK
20 Park Plaza, 617/266–8418.

8 *f-3*
DOMINICAN REPUBLIC
20 Park Plaza, 617/482–8121.

6 *d-5*
ECUADOR
One Beacon St., 617/573–5876.

8 *f-3*
FRANCE
31 St. James Ave., 617/542–7374.

8 *d-4*
GERMANY
3 Copley Pl., 617/536–4414.

6 *f-7*
GREAT BRITAIN
600 Atlantic Ave., 617/248–9555.

8 *f-1*
GREECE
86 Beacon St., 617/523–0100.

8 *c-3*
HAITI
545 Boylston St., 617/266–3660.

2 *e-1*
HUNGARY
75 Cambridge Parkway, Cambridge, 617/621–0886.

8 *d-3*
IRELAND
535 Boylston St., 617/267–9330.

8 *f-3*
ISRAEL
20 Park Plaza, 617/542–0041.

8 *e-3*
ITALY
100 Boylston St., 617/542–0483.

6 *f-7*
JAPAN
600 Atlantic Ave., 617/973–9772.

8 *f-3*
MEXICO
20 Park Plaza, 617/426–4942.

8 *f-3*
NETHERLANDS
6 St. James Ave., 617/542–8452.

6 *f-5*
NORWAY
286 Congress St., 617/423–2515.

8 *d-2*
PAKISTAN
393 Commonwealth Ave., 617/267–5555.

6 *f-7*
PERU
745 Atlantic Ave., 617/338–1144.

6 *g-5*
POLAND
31 Milk St., 617/357–1980.

8 *b-4*
PORTUGAL
899 Boylston St., 617/536–8740.

6 *f-7*
REPUBLIC OF KOREA
1 Financial Center, 617/348–3660.

8 *c-3*
SPAIN
545 Boylston St., 617/536–2506.

6 *f-5*
SWEDEN
286 Congress St., 617/350–0111.

8 *f-3*
SWITZERLAND
20 Park Plaza, 617/357–1617.

8 *e-3*
THAILAND
420 Boylston St., 617/536–6552.

8 *c-3*
VENEZUELA
545 Boylston St., 617/266–9368.

INOCULATIONS & VACCINATIONS

To find out what specific inoculations you need for the countries you plan to visit, contact that country's consulate (*see above*), or call the Boston Quarantine Station at Logan International Airport, 617/567–6543.

EAST BOSTON LOGAN HEALTH SERVICES

All inoculations are given. *Logan International Airport, Terminal D, 2nd floor, 617/ 569–8652.*

7 *a-3*
HARVARD UNIVERSITY HEALTH SERVICES

All inoculations are available here; appointments are required. *75 Mount Auburn St., Cambridge, 617/496–9019.*

8 *g-4*
NEW ENGLAND MEDICAL CENTER

All inoculations are given, by appointment only. *260 Tremont St., 617/956– 7002.*

PASSPORTS

6 *d-3*
UNITED STATES PASSPORT OFFICE

Apply at least six weeks before your planned departure. Be sure to call first to find out exactly what documents you'll need to bring with your application; you will definitely need two forms of valid identification and two identical photos. Some renewals can be done through the mail. *10 Causeway St., 617/ 565–6998. T stop: North Station.*

PASSPORT PHOTOGRAPHS

Many photo-developing and camera shops can provide the necessary two identical photos, as long as they fit the required specifications. Call the passport office (*see above*) for details.

6 *d-3*
PASSPORT PHOTO SERVICE

Conveniently located across the hall from the U.S. Passport Office, this shop provides color and black-and-white photos while you wait. *10 Causeway St., 617/ 523–4524. T stop: North Station.*

ROUTING SERVICES FOR U.S. TRIPS

AAA SOUTHERN NEW ENGLAND

Members can get free maps, guidebooks, and the famous AAA "Trip Tiks," which are detailed directions including tolls and detours. Membership also includes emergency road service— invaluable if your car breaks down or won't start. Call for more information. *1050 Hingham St., Rockland, 800/222– 8252 or 617/871–5880.*

TOURIST OFFICES

See Sightseeing Information *in* Chapter 2.

U.S. CUSTOMS

General information. *617/565–6147.*

VISA INFORMATION & TRAVEL ADVISORIES

U.S. Immigration & Naturalization Service. *617/565–3879.*

DIRECTORIES

alphabetical listing of resources & topics

restaurants by neighborhood

shops by neighborhood

resources & topics

restaurants by neighborhood

KENMORE SQUARE

Atlas Bar and Grill (American casual), 114

Audubon Circle (American casual), 114

Cask 'n Flagon (American casual), 115

NORTH END

Artú (Italian), 133

Caffé Paradiso (cafés and pubs), 119

Daily Catch (fish and seafood), 127

Five North Square (Italian), 134

Giacomo's (Italian), 134–135

Mamma Maria (Italian), 135

Oasis Cafe (American), 113

Pizzeria Regina (Italian), 135–136

Pomodoro (Italian), 136

Trattoria a Scalinatella (Italian), 136–137

Trattoria il Panino (Italian), 137

SOMERVILLE

Bertucci's Pizza (Italian), 133

Dali Restaurant (Spanish), 143

Eat (American), 112

Elephant Walk (Vietnamese and Southeast Asian), 145

Gargoyles on the Square (contemporary), 123

Redbones (Soul/Southern), 143

The Rosebud Diner (American), 113

SOUTH BOSTON

Farragut House (American casual), 116

Bob the Chef's Restaurant (Soul/Southern), 142–143

Charlie's Sandwich Shoppe (breakfast/lunch), 118

Claremont Café (Mediterranean), 139

The Delux Cafe & Lounge (American casual), 115

Franklin Café (contemporary), 123

Giacomo's (Italian), 134–135

Hamersley's Bistro (French), 130

Icarus (contemporary), 123

Jae's Cafe and Grill (Korean), 138

La Bettola (Italian), 135

Mistral (French), 131

Tremont 647 (contemporary), 125

SYMPHONY

Pizzeria Uno Restaurant & Bar (Italian), 136

THEATER DISTRICT/BACK BAY

Pignoli (Italian), 135

Red Herring (wine and tapas bars), 146

THEATER DISTRICT

Galleria Italiana (Italian), 134

Jae's Cafe and Grill (Korean), 138

WATERFRONT

Anthony's Pier 4 (fish and seafood), 126

Barking Crab (fish and seafood), 126

Boston Sail Loft (fish and seafood), 126–127

The Chart House (steak), 143

Daily Catch (fish and seafood), 127

Jimmy's Harborside Restaurant (fish and seafood), 127

No-name Restaurant (fish and seafood), 128

Rowes Wharf Restaurant (rooms with a view), 142

shops by neighborhood

ALLSTON

Brookline Liquor Mart (wine & spirits), 189

City Sports (sporting goods & clothing, sports apparel), 185

Eastern Mountain Sports (sporting goods & clothing, camping), 185–186

Herrell's (food, ice cream), 174

Legal Seafood Marketplace (food, fish & seafood), 173

ARLINGTON

Art Beat (hobbies), 176

BACK BAY

Alan Bilzerian (clothing for men/general, classic), 166

Allston Beat (clothing for women/general, contemporary), 161

American Animated Classics (fun & funky), 175

The Andover Shop (clothing for men/general, classic), 166

Ann Taylor (clothing for women/general, classic), 160

Arche (clothing for women/specialty, shoes & boots), 165

Army Barracks, Inc. (clothing for men/general, resale/vintage/surplus), 168

Autrefois Antiques (antiques), 151

Avanti (beauty, hair), 154

Avenue Victor Hugo (books, antiquarian), 158

The Back Bay Framery (framing), 175

Back Bay Wines & Spirits (wine & spirits), 189

Bally of Switzerland (clothing for men/general, shoes & boots; clothing for women/specialty, shoes & boots), 165, 168

Banana Republic (clothing for women/general, contemporary), 161–162

Beadworks (jewelry, costume jewelry), 181–182

Bellezza Home and Garden (home furnishings, china, glassware, porcelain, & pottery), 177

Ben & Jerry's (food, ice cream), 174

Benetton (clothing for women/general, contemporary), 162

Betsey Johnson (clothing for women/general, contemporary), 162

CITY NOTES

CITY NOTES

CITY NOTES

CITY NOTES

CITY NOTES

Fodor's Travel Publications has guidebooks to fit the
needs of all kinds of travelers from families to adventure
seekers, from nature enthusiasts to urban weekenders.
With the range of coverage and the quality of information, it
is easy to understand why smart travelers go with **Fodor's**.

At bookstores everywhere.
http://fodors.previewtravel.com/